Evolutionary Origins
of Morality

Published in the UK by Imprint Academic
PO Box 1, Thorverton EX5 5YX, UK

Published in the USA by Imprint Academic
Philosophy Documentation Center, Bowling Green State University,
Bowling Green, OH 43403-0189, USA

ISBN 0 907845 07 X (paperback)

First reprint: 2002

ISSN 1355 8250 (*Journal of Consciousness Studies*, **7**, No.1–2, 2000)

British Library Cataloguing in Publication Data
A catalogue record for this book is available from the British Library
Library of Congress Card Number : 99–068338

Cover illustration from an etching by Rembrandt
Cover photo by Frans B.M. de Waal
*Begging and food sharing between unrelated group members, including adults, oc-
curs not only in humans but also in other primate species. In the cover photograph
the chimpanzee Mai of the Yerkes Regional Primate Research Center Field Station,
with her new baby in her arms, shares not only with her daughter but also with an unrelated male youngster, thus showing possible stages on the way from maternal care
to food sharing in response to begging by adult chimpanzees and the giving of alms
to beggars etched by Rembrandt.*

Evolutionary Origins of Morality

Cross-Disciplinary Perspectives

edited by
Leonard D. Katz

IMPRINT ACADEMIC

Contents

2. How, When and Why Did the Unique Aspects of Human Morality Arise?

continued

3. Are We Really Altruists?

4. Can Fairness Evolve?

Leonard D. Katz

Toward Good and Evil
Evolutionary Approaches to Aspects of Human Morality

Moral Origins and Adaptation

People are curious about how things began and especially about the origins of things they deem important. Besides satisfying such curiosity, accounts of origin may acquire broader theoretical or practical interest when they go beyond narrating historical accident to impart insight into more enduring forces, tendencies or sources from which the phenomena of interest more generally proceed. Accounts of evolutionary adaptation do this when they explain how and why a complex adaptation first arose over time or how and why it has been conserved since then, in terms of selection on heritable variation. Thus the eye was shaped and conserved over evolutionary time on account of its usefulness for sight and if we want to explain why its lens is transparent but its pupil black we shall tell how transmitting light to the retina but preventing scatter behind it both help us see. In such cases evolutionary accounts of origin may provide much of what early Greek thinkers sought in an *arche*, or origin — a unified understanding of something's original formation, source of continuing existence, and underlying principle (Huffman, 1993, pp. 78–92; McKirahan, 1998).

We should not expect to find so single and unified an account of human morality as of the eye or visual system because both the goals concerned and the means to these are likely much more varied. Our eye contributes to our survival and fitness mainly through the single function of sight; a long history of adaptation under uniform constraints of optics and physiological possibility have led to a fairly uniform result. To the extent that human morality is the result of specific adaptations for human social life, which has long varied between groups, times and environments, we may expect their contributions to our capacity for this social life to be more various and facultatively variable. We may wonder with Darwin how exactly to divide the credit for morality between natural selection, culture and learning, but suspect like him that, especially at the later stages of the evolution of morality, culture and learning, both individual and social, had the larger roles (1871, pp. 80–81, 166, 394, 404). Still, as Noam Chomsky says, 'it certainly seems reasonable to speculate that the moral and ethical system acquired by the child owes much to some innate human faculty' and is 'rooted in our nature' (Chomsky, 1988, p. 153). Minimally, morality has roots in our

Journal of Consciousness Studies, **7**, No. 1–2, 2000, pp. ix–xvi mammalian social nature, which goes back to the mother–child bond (Cicero, *De Finibus Bonorum et Malorum*, sects. 62–3, reporting Stoic views; Darwin, 1871, pp. 80–1; Midgley, 1991, p. 8) and this may be as deeply rooted on both sides as anything in our evolved psychology is.

It is, however, much less likely that morality is the product of only one or very few informationally encapsulated specialist mental modules than that language is. Moral considerations are typically accessible to consciousness and deliberation, as the intermediate products of syntactic and phonological processing are not. And moral competence involves the appropriate use of diverse kinds of information to govern the deployment, restraint and balancing of different motives and emotions, such as compassion and indignation, in situationally sensitive and open-ended ways. Even where the perception of moral demands of diverse kinds may be psychologically mandatory and clear, their weighting against each other and against other reasons may be painfully problematic rather than automatic. Consonantly, whereas language seems to depend on discrete brain systems vulnerable to local lesions that may leave other functions largely unimpaired, the brain damage that most specifically impairs moral competence and development seems to impair cognitive–affective connections — minimally, the cognitive conditioning of fear and anxiety and the situation-sensitive generalization of behavioural restraint built on these — more generally (cf. Damasio *et al.,* 1990; Damasio, 1994; Anderson *et al.*, 1999). And studies of amoral criminally-inclined 'psychopaths' or 'sociopaths' (who may sometimes be so disposed more by psychological adaptation to opportunity-poor or socialization-poor environments than by originally abnormal temperament based in physiology) seem compatible with this view (see Wilson, 1993, pp. 105–8; Lykken, 1995; Mealy, 1995; Black, 1999, Ch. 6). These considerations suggest that morality may be the outcome of interactions between various systems that support and regulate social and affective learning and responding more generally and others that do much else besides, rather than of any single or of very few dedicated strictly modular faculties (cf. Darwin, 1871; Midgley, 1991; Flack and de Waal, Principal Paper and Response, and Railton, below).

Morality, however, may be a product of natural selection without having been itself selected as a functional adaptation (Flack and de Waal, Response, p. 74), by being an outcome of tendencies and capacities that were. Individual learning may organize moral competence from these, by adaptation to a human environment shaped by social learning and cultural evolution — as these 'adaptive processes, operating at different levels and timescales' (Brian Skyrms, Response, p. 335), interact. The integration of inherited quasi-modular capacities with human 'representational, inferential, epistemic, and communicative capacities' (Peter Railton, below, p. 58) may be largely self-organizing, as elsewhere in cognitive development it seems to be (Carey, forthcoming). But moral development may also adaptively respond to the demands of life stages, from early obedience, through dealings with peers, to nurturing, as Dennis Krebs suggests (below, p. 320).

The four principal papers presented here, with interdisciplinary commentary discussion and their authors' responses, represent contemporary approaches to an evolutionary understanding of morality — of the origins from which, and the paths by which, aspects or components of human morality evolved and converged. Their authors come out of no single discipline or school, but represent rather a convergence of largely independent work in primate ethology, anthropology, evolutionary biology, and dynamic systems modelling on related problems, conjectures and tentative conclusions. In inviting contributions I deliberately made no attempt to define morality more sharply than common language and understanding have left it, including our ordinary responses to right and wrong, but not all of the very diverse thinking about this and other practical concerns — and about what we should make of all these — that ethics encompasses. This was not because of any lack of past definitions of morality, but because the history of controversy over these makes it advisable not to prejudge the question pending our inquiry's results. From these we may see some outlines of plausible answers begin to emerge, only a brief sketch of some of which I can attempt here, sampling the hypotheses, scientific support, critical discussion of this, and refinement of positions in authors' responses.

Toward a Natural Prehistory of Morality and Politics

In our first principal paper, Jessica Flack and Frans de Waal describe aspects of the social behaviour and inferred psychology of monkeys and apes, the living animals most closely related to us, in which they find 'building blocks' for the later evolution of human morality. Following Darwin, they, like Christopher Boehm in his following contributions, seek psychological traits we share with our closest relatives and presumably also with our common ancestor, from which, given the course of human cognitive evolution, and the need to adjust individual and shared interests in a social life, morality would naturally emerge. They find in the simple rules, expectations, order, and sense of social regularity implicit in the social interactions of group-living primates 'elements of rudimentary moral systems' arising out of the interaction of sympathetic, cooperative and competitive sentiments and the interpenetration of cognitive judgement and emotion, in ways that prefigure human morality and that can be used as clues to its evolution and dynamics. But as they make clear in responding to Kummer, Railton and others (p. 68, below), it is in the sentiments and capacities underlying the social behaviours they discuss, rather than in the behaviours themselves, that they find the raw material for the evolution of human morality.

The following commentary and controversy lines up partly along generational lines, in keeping with the generation-long progressive relaxation of norms against ascribing cognitive and conscious states to nonhuman animals in behavioural science. Human developmental psychologist Jerome Kagan, the firmest sceptic, asserts that 'animals have no conscious intentions' and feel no guilt for past failures to live up to internalized standards, which they lack. Two veteran primatologists voice lesser degrees of scepticism about the cognitive and moral capacities of apes. Irwin Bernstein doubts that questions about animal intention and awareness of norms are experimentally tractable and apparently believes that less cognitive explanations of behaviour should therefore be preferred. Flack and de Waal in their Response oppose to such 'cognitive parsimony' a 'principle of evolutionary parsimony', a heuristic assumption of similarity between closely related species (such as humans and chimpanzees) for the guidance of hypothesis formation and research (pp. 72–3, below), which would tell also against Bernard Thierry's suggestion that if 'elements of rudimentary moral systems' are attributed to chimpanzees they might as well be attributed to the less cognitively sophisticated macaque monkeys with which he works, on the sole ground of similar behaviour. Hans Kummer also resists some of the cognitive and motivational interpretation for which de Waal especially is known, emphasizing that moral judgement is at the core of morality. But he also suggests relevant experiments, as does the younger experimentalist Josep Call, for investigating non-human primates' understanding of intention and of social norms.

Flack and de Waal's discussion of calculated reciprocity, conflict resolution and community concern, especially among chimpanzees, leads naturally to our second principal paper, in which cultural anthropologist Christopher Boehm leads us down a path moral evolution may have taken starting from the ancestor we had in common with chimpanzees and bonobos, which presumably like these descendants had inherited tendencies to dominate others but also to dislike being dominated. Boehm hypothesizes that an ancestral regime of despotic social dominance and fearful submission led in the human line to successful collective action to intentionally suppress tyrants and bullies in nomadic bands — like Chomsky, seeing opposition to such 'forms of oppression, hierarchy, domination and authority' as characteristic of morality (Chomsky, 1988, p. 154). The distributed consciously exercised social control thus established was then used for other ends besides, constituting 'morality as a sense of right and wrong that is born out of group-wide systems of conflict management based on shared values' that 'constrains individual behaviour through a system of approval and disapproval' — as Flack and de Waal express their agreement with this aspect of Boehm's view in their Response (p. 69, below). While people are thus able through human culture, cognition and language to collectively suppress social dominance hierarchy in a way not possible for chimpanzees and bonobos and to more effectively avoid and manage intragroup conflict, in so doing they draw on a potential for concerted collective action that is occasionally observed at work in chimpanzees and that is presumably based in capacities inherited from a common ancestor.

Bruce Knauft, a cultural anthropologist who has long been developing theories related to Boehm's, stresses, as does the primatologist Bernard Thierry, the difference language makes in enabling the sharing of explicit norms, but argues that symbolic communication had been coevolving with brain enlargement even during our *Homo erectus* past. This permitted the symbolically mediated internalization of socially prescribed norms as part of a larger suite of features including 'constraints on sexual behaviour, a rudimentary division of labour, the gendering of morality, socialized control over junior males [especially with regard to their access to mates], increased group size, [and] increased home range' — as well as 'the reduction of bullying behaviour, and a reverse dominance hierarchy that enforces egalitarianism among fully adult males' posited by Boehm (p. 138, below). Ethnographer Robert Dentan also remarks the generally unequal status of women and younger males and observes that the moral order established by the local arbiters of this may not serve equally the interests of all members of even simple societies. Donald Black advocates a 'pure sociology' that dispenses with all psychology, individual or collective, and seeks to explain the social control aspects of morality in terms of social structure and relations alone. Boehm in his Response defends his psychological explanation of the arising of egalitarian morality in small, autonomous groups (in which all people lived in Paleolithic times and some still do today) as the product of deliberate collective action and the permanent threat of the same, with reference to the ethnographic evidence. And evolutionary psychologist Dennis Krebs discusses the need for cooperators to curb cheating and free-riding, and to curb dominance as a means to this end, and the mixed motives that lead people to use morality to restrain each other even as they seek to evade the same restraints themselves. His genetic individual selectionist approach, which draws especially on the work of R.D. Alexander, contrasts with those presented in the remaining two principal papers.

How Kindness and Fairness Can Evolve and Survive

Elliott Sober and David Sloan Wilson's book, *Unto Others: The Evolution and Psychology of Unselfish Behavior* (1998), which is summarized and commented on next, and Brian Skyrms' paper, which draws in part on his book, *Evolution of the Social Contract* (1996), operate mainly at a more theoretical level. Their concern is more with showing how individually unselfish adaptations are possible in principle, given reasonable but idealized assumptions, than with any specific adaptation or historical scenario. Wilson, an evolutionary biologist, and Sober, a philosopher of biology, argue for functional adaptations on the level of groups, of which the group-benefitting and self-denying behaviour of humans following groupish moralities are presumptive examples. Skyrms shows the advantages of computational modelling using evolutionary rather than classical game theory for producing explanatory theories in the social and behavioural sciences. One class of the adaptive dynamical models Skyrms discusses, those based on correlated evolutionary game theory, model the evolutionary biology used in Part One of *Unto Others* to show how individually self-denying behaviour can evolve and survive in a Darwinian world.

The consciously Darwinian plots of some Thomas Hardy novels bring out the problem these address almost as starkly as does game theory. In *The Trumpet Major* and again in *The Woodlanders*, Hardy presents loyal, conscientious, self-sacrificing heroes whose virtue's reward is the loss of love and life. Nature may not craft plots as telling as Hardy's, but she is just as unremitting and has much more time. Any heritable trait or strategy that advances the propagation of competitors more than it does its own (net of the cost to itself) incurs a fitness disadvantage relative to otherwise similar ones that benefit from the sacrifices of the first without reciprocating, and will thus inexorably tend to be selected out in favour of these others over time. It seems that nice traits and nice guys finish last. But where, then, could what we take to be our own sometimes altruistic behaviour, and the motives and attitudes that seem to be sometimes behind this and to let us join Hardy in identifying with these heroes, have come from? Or are we just fooling ourselves, the better to fool others, when we see ourselves in this light, as Krebs' commentary on Boehm may suggest?

Hardy's trumpet major gives up on the woman he loves in his brother's favour. Since brothers tend to share heritable traits (although not all the hero's estimable ones in this case), such evolutionary sacrifice is less than it at first appears, and may even be selected for in harsh environments when it is the best one can likely do. So much has long been uncontroversial in evolutionary biology. David Wilson's work has emphasized that what is essential here is not kinship but that the benefits conferred by self-denial are not spread randomly through the population (as early models tended to assume) but rather biased toward those that have the altruistic trait. His group selection approach catches what is general in this: a trait that is locally disadvantageous may evolve by conferring sufficient benefits sufficiently concentrated within 'trait groups' in which it is sufficiently overrepresented with respect to the total (or meta)population for its frequency in the metapopulation to grow or remain stable even as its share in each of the disproportionately productive trait groups declines. The nonrandomness of the interactions relevant to the trait's fitness is expressed mathematically by a correlation coefficient, as also in Skyrms' correlated evolutionary game theory models of the same phenomena. As Stevens' commentary on *Unto Others* makes clear, such group selection appears to be at work in actual biological cases, even where cognition and preference play no role.

In the human case, people's spending their time and good deeds with those of their kind is frequently and easily done. For example, altruists may be drawn by their altruism to meet as volunteers at the fire house and rescue squad, and in consequence end up befriending each other and helping each other far more than they help random others. Even random differences in group composition and the effects of geography may yield correlation enough, and kinship also plays its role. So the kind being kind more to their kin and other associates of their kind may explain how selection can make and keep a species somewhat kind, by the kind benefitting from the kindness of others who are kind more than unkind others do. As Sober and Wilson explain, this is made easier in human groups by the culturally-mediated enforcement of social norms, which may be less costly to the individual and hence more able to evolve than the primary practice unenforced would be. The cost of enforcement may be small and such joint institutions easily established — especially if the moral institution of social control described by Boehm is already in place. And variation in social norms, helped along by cultural drift and social conformity, would reinforce the phenotypic homogeneity within, and heterogeneity between, groups that group selection requires.

Boehm observes that human culture has thus created a niche in which group selection for genes, as well as for heritable cultural traits, could occur. The evolutionary biologists Kevin Laland, John Odling-Smee and Marc Feldman, however, remain skeptical that genetic group selection has actually been important in nature, although they accept the importance of cultural group selection in explaining human unselfish behaviour. Amotz Zahavi goes further, suggesting that the theoretical possibilities for group selection, which none of these biologists contest, notwithstanding, individual-level selectionist explanations of altruistic behaviour will be more important in every case, as in his examples. Herbert Gintis discusses evidence from computer simulations and from experimental economics on the emergence of equality and fairness and their enforcement, while Alex Rosenberg suggests that enforcement of norms would have been too much against the enforcers' own interests to function in simple human societies such as those in which we evolved, and concludes that the question requires a wider range of evidence and modelling results of the kinds discussed by Brian Skyrms and his commentators. Among the results of interest that Skyrms discusses is a bargaining game in which equality and fairness fall out automatically from the adaptive dynamics, whereas concerns for these, observed in everyday human life and in experiments, such as some discussed by Gary Bolton, are paradoxical for theories based on the exclusively selfish rational choice commonly assumed in social science (pp. 276–8, below). Skyrms suggests that our evolved ends may differ from those of Darwinian fitness (p. 282, below). And Dennis Krebs seeks to build on correlated evolutionary game theory not a group selection theory, such as Sober and Wilson's, but one of overlapping circles of indirect reciprocity in which people's individual interests in their reputations, because of the rewards of cooperation dependent on these, keep them somewhat honest — but perhaps only as honest as their individually-selected genetically-based adaptations (generalized by the limitations of their cognitive and affective discriminations) make them.

Love, Strife and Community Design

One face of our nature directs a compassionate gaze upon the good of others; a second more particularly regards moral relations between persons and characterizes their attitudes and actions toward each other as right and wrong. While it may nod in moral approval, its stare of righteous anger and the enduring internalized fear this inspires are more forceful in morality's most urgent tasks of deterring and avoiding harm. But without the first concern, for well-being, providing guidance, the moral machinery of social control and self-control would seem to lack any rational point. It is thus fitting that our authors address our capacities for both perspectives and their interactions with strategic self-interest. As Boehm especially reminds us, morality consists in large part in the intentional use of social control for a common good. In keeping with this, Sober and Wilson, after presenting their account of how altruistic behaviour may evolve, proceed in Part II of *Unto Others* to argue for an evolved plurality within human motivation, including some readiness to take another's good as an ultimate end. They argue that this would evolve because it would be more efficient and reliable in, for example, caring for one's children to have ultimate desires directly for their welfare than to have only desires about one's own pleasant and painful feelings.

The attraction that pleasure and the affections rooted in it have for us may lead us to care ultimately about more distal objects such as another's good as easily as about our own (Schlick, 1939 [1930], II.8, pp. 47–51). Empedocles, the first natural selection theorist (Aristotle, *Physics* II.8:198b24–32; Furley, 1987, pp. 94–8), even identified pleasure with Love, the cause of friendly thoughts and conjoint action, which brings together animals from their parts, people into couples and communities, and all things 'out of many into one' — in opposition to Strife, which separates them (Fragments 17 and 20; Furley, 1987, pp. 83–6). But Nature, as we now know, regards ultimately only fitness and not our happiness (Darwin, 1871, p. 298), and does not scruple to use hate, fear, punishment and even war alongside affection in ordering social groups and selecting among them, just as she uses pain as well as pleasure to get us to feed, water and protect our bodies and also in forging our social bonds.

But evolutionary competition for genetic and cultural propagation need not be violent, as relations between human groups under some conditions often are. Dennis Krebs (p. 320, below) asks how this will play out in our increasingly interconnected world, as does Robert Axelrod elsewhere, discussing suggestive agent-based modelling results about the conditions under which multiple large internally homogeneous groups arise (1997, Ch. 7). Perhaps we may look toward such bottom-up modelling for guidance in designing a world of overlapping and open communities supporting individual freedom and intergroup intercourse rather than between-group polarization. The failed top-down utopian plans of the last century have given social design a bad name. But, as Boehm and Knauft remind us, we have been living in intentional communities since humanity began. Our inherited social nature and needs leave us no choice, and the cognitive capacities that coevolved with these may enable us to continue to learn to navigate together, between the emotional isolation of individual

selfishness and total absorption in group chauvinism, neither of which wholly satis-
fies our evolved nature — perhaps toward values that this complex nature enables us
to judge are better.

Acknowledgments

I thank Christopher Boehm, Noam Chomsky and William Harms for their helpful comments,
the authors for their instruction, and Daniel Dennett and the students in his Tufts University
seminar of Fall 1999 for theirs.

References

Anderson, S.W., Bechara, A., Damasio, H., Tranel, D. and Damasio, A. R. (1999), 'Impairment of
    social and moral behavior related to early damage in human prefrontal cortex', *Nature Neurosci-
    ence*, **2** (11), pp. 1032–7.
Axelrod, Robert (1997), *The Complexity of Cooperation: Agent-Based Models of Competition and
    Collaboration* (Princeton: Princeton University Press).
Black, Donald W. with Larson, C. Lindon (1999), *Bad Boys, Bad Men: Confronting Antisocial Per-
    sonality Disorder* (New York and Oxford: Oxford University Press).
Carey, Susan (forthcoming), *The Origin of Concepts: Evolution vs. Culture* (Cambridge, MA: MIT
    Press).
Chomsky, Noam (1988), *Language and Problems of Knowledge: The Managua Lectures*
    (Cambrdge, MA: MIT Press).
Damasio, Antonio R. (1994), *Descartes' Error: Emotion, Reason, and the Human Brain* (New
    York: Putnam).
Damasio, A. R., Tranel, D. and Damasio, H. (1990), 'Individuals with sociopathic behavior caused
    by frontal damage fail to respond to autonomically social stimuli', *Behavioural Brain Research*,
    41, pp. 81–94.
Darwin, Charles (1871), *The Descent of Man, and Selection in Relation to Sex* (London: Murray
    [reprinted, Princeton: Princeton University Press, 1981]).
Furley, David (1987), *The Greek Cosmologists*, Vol. 1, *The Formation of the Atomic Theory and Its
    Eleatic Critics* (Cambridge and New York: Cambridge University Press).
Huffman, Carl A. (1993), *Philolaus of Croton: Pythagorean and Presocratic* (Cambridge: Cam-
    bridge University Press).
Lykken, David T. (1995), *The Antisocial Personalities* (Hillsdale, NJ: Erlbaum).
McKirahan, Richard (1998), *Arche*, in *Routledge Encyclopedia of Philosophy*, Vol. 1, ed. Edward
    Craig (London and New York: Routledge).
Mealy, Linda and Commentators (1995), 'The sociobiology of sociopathy: An integrated evolution-
    ary model', *Behavioral and Brain Sciences*, **18**, pp. 523–99.
Midgley, Mary (1991), 'The Origins of Ethics,' in *A Companion to Ethics*, ed. Peter Singer (Oxford:
    Blackwell).
Schlick, Moritz (1939, 1962 [1930]), *Problems of Ethics*, trans. David Rynin (New York:
    Prentice-Hall; reprint, New York: Dover Publications, 1962 [Fragen der Ethik (Vienna:
    J. Springer Verlag)]).
Skyrms, Brian (1996), *Evolution of the Social Contract* (Cambridge and New York: Cambridge
    University Press).
Sober, Elliott and Wilson, David Sloan (1998), *Unto Others: The Evolution and Psychology of
    Unselfish Behavior* (Cambridge, MA: Harvard University Press).
Wilson, James Q. (1993), *The Moral Sense* (New York: Free Press).

Online Resources Related to Section 4

Our fourth section presents a selective review of aspects of some relevant mathematical theories and
computational modelling results. Skyrms (1996) overlaps in coverage with his principal paper for
this section. William Harms' online simulators to go with Skyrms' book may be found at:
<http://eame.ethics.ubc.ca/Skyrms/index.htm>. Axelrod's (1997) Appendix B has exercises and
advice for starting out in agent-based modelling, an approach to modelling evolution different from
the adaptive dynamic modelling discussed by Skyrms, but on which, for example, Harms' own
results reported in his commentary are based. This Appendix has an associated Web page:
<http://pscs.physics.lsa.umich.edu/Software/CC/CCAB.html> with links to online resources.

Jessica C. Flack and Frans B.M. de Waal

'Any Animal Whatever'

Darwinian Building Blocks of Morality in Monkeys and Apes

To what degree has biology influenced and shaped the development of moral systems? One way to determine the extent to which human moral systems might be the product of natural selection is to explore behaviour in other species that is analogous and perhaps homologous to our own. Many non-human primates, for example, have similar methods to humans for resolving, managing, and preventing conflicts of interests within their groups. Such methods, which include reciprocity and food sharing, reconciliation, consolation, conflict intervention, and mediation, are the very building blocks of moral systems in that they are based on and facilitate cohesion among individuals and reflect a concerted effort by community members to find shared solutions to social conflict. Furthermore, these methods of resource distribution and conflict resolution often require or make use of capacities for empathy, sympathy, and sometimes even community concern. Non-human primates in societies in which such mechanisms are present may not be exactly moral beings, but they do show signs of a sense of social regularity that — just like the norms and rules underlying human moral conduct — promotes a mutually satisfactory modus vivendi.

Introduction

Any animal whatever, endowed with well-marked social instincts, the parental and filial affections being here included, would inevitably acquire a moral sense or conscience, as soon as its intellectual powers had become as well developed, or nearly as well developed, as in man.

Charles Darwin, *The Descent of Man* (1982 [1871], pp. 71–2)

Thomas Huxley, in his famous lecture, *Evolution and Ethics* (Huxley, 1894), advanced a view of human nature that has since dominated debate about the origins of morality. Huxley believed that human nature is essentially evil — a product of a nasty and unsympathetic natural world. Morality, he argued, is a human invention explicitly devised to control and combat selfish and competitive tendencies generated by the evolutionary process. By depicting morality in this way, Huxley was advocating that the search for morality's origins be de-coupled from evolution and conducted outside of biology.

Journal of Consciousness Studies, **7**, No. 1–2, 2000, pp. 1–29

Proponents of Huxley's dualistic view of nature and morality abound today. Among them is the evolutionary biologist, Richard Dawkins, who in 1976 (p. 3) wrote

> Be warned that if you wish, as I do, to build a society in which individuals cooperate generously and unselfishly towards a common good, you can expect little help from biological nature. Let us try to teach generosity and altruism, because we are born selfish.

Another well-known evolutionary biologist, George C. Williams (1988, p. 438), also reaffirmed, with minor variation, Huxley's position when he stated, 'I account for morality as an accidental capability produced, in its boundless stupidity, by a biological process that is normally opposed to the expression of such a capability'. And recently, the philosopher Daniel Dennett (1995, p. 481), although admitting that it is conceivable that perhaps the great apes, whales, and dolphins possess some of the requisite social cognition on which morality depends, wrote

> My pessimistic hunch is that the main reason we have not ruled out dolphins and whales as moralists of the deep is that they are so hard to study in the wild. Most of the evidence about chimpanzees — some of it self-censored by researchers for years — is that they are true denizens of Hobbes' state of nature, much more nasty and brutish than any would like to believe.

But if, as Dawkins suggests, the origins of morality — of the human sense of right and wrong used by society to promote pro-social behaviour — are not biological, then what is the source of strength that enabled humanity to escape from its own nature and implement moral systems? And from where did the desire to do so come? If, as Williams suggests, morality is an accidental product of natural selection, then why has such a 'costly' mistake not been corrected or eliminated by the very process that inadvertently created it? Our inability to answer these questions about the origins and consequences of moral systems is an indication that perhaps we need to broaden the scope of our search. After all, the degree to which the tendency to develop and enforce moral systems is universal across cultures (Midgley, 1991; Silberbauer, 1991), suggests that moral systems, contrary to Huxley's beliefs, do have biological origins and are an integral part of human nature.

Morality indeed may be an invention of sorts, but one that in all likelihood arose during the course of evolution and was only refined in its expression and content by various cultures. If, as we believe, morality arose from biological origins, then we should expect at a minimum that elements of it are present in other social species. And indeed, the evidence we will present in this paper suggests that chimpanzees and other social animals are not the 'true denizens of Hobbes' state of nature' they are surmised to be by Dennett. It may well be that chimpanzees are not moral creatures, but this does not mean that they do not have elements of moral systems in their societies. If we are to understand how our moral systems evolved, we must be open to the idea that the sets of rules that govern how non-human animals behave in their social groups provide clues to how morality arose during the course of evolution. These simple rules, which emerge out of these animals' social interactions, create an element of order that makes living together a possibility, and in a liberal sense, reflect elements of rudimentary moral systems. The order that these sets of rules create is vital to maintaining the stability of social systems and probably is the reason why human morality (whether or not an evolutionary accident) has not been eliminated by natural selection (Kummer, 1979). Garret Hardin (1983, p. 412) captured the essence of this argument in a statement about the importance of justice — 'The first goal of justice is to create a *modus vivendi* so that life can go on, not only in the next few minutes, but also indefinitely into the future.'

Had Huxley acknowledged that the origins of morality lay in biology but argued against searching within biology for the *specifics* of our moral systems, his case might have been more persuasive today. Such an argument would have at least fit the contemporary framework for addressing questions about why we are the way we are, which in the case of morality has been explored intensely (Nitecki and Nitecki, 1993, and contributions therein). Indeed, the only pertinent question seems to us: *To what degree* has biology influenced and shaped the development of moral systems? One way to determine the extent to which human morality might be the product of natural selection is to explore behaviour in other species that is analogous (similar traits that arose by convergent evolution due to the presence of similar selection pressures or evolutionary conditions), and perhaps homologous (traits that evolved in a common ancestor and that remain present in related species due to common phylogenetic descent) to our own.

Many non-human primates, for example, seem to have similar methods to humans for resolving, managing, and preventing conflicts of interests within their groups. Such methods, which include reciprocity and food sharing, reconciliation, consolation, conflict intervention, and mediation, are the very building blocks of moral systems in that their existence indicates, as Mary Midgley (1991, p. 12) wrote, 'a willingness and a capacity to look for shared solutions' to conflicts (see also Boehm, 2000). Furthermore, unlike strict dominance hierarchies, which may be an alternative to moral systems for organizing society, advanced methods of resource distribution and conflict resolution seem to require or make use of traits such as the capacity for empathy, sympathy, and sometimes even community concern. Conflict resolution that reflects concern for and possibly understanding of a predicament in which a fellow group member finds himself or herself provides for society the raw material out of which moral systems can be constructed.

Non-human primates in such societies may not be exactly moral beings, but they do show indications of a sense of social regularity that parallels the rules and regulations of human moral conduct (de Waal, 1996a; 1996b, chapter 3). In addition to conflict resolution, other key components or 'prerequisites' of morality recognizable in social animals are reciprocity, empathy, sympathy, and community concern. These components, which also include a sense of justice, and perhaps even the internalization of social norms, are fundamental to moral systems because they help generate connections among individuals within human and animal societies despite the conflicts of interests that inevitably arise. By generating or reinforcing connections among individuals, these mechanisms facilitate co-operative social interaction because they require individuals to make 'commitments' to behave in ways that later may prove contrary to independent individual interests (used throughout this paper in reference to those interests that are truly independent as well as in reference to those interests for which pursuit requires engaging in competition) that when pursued can jeopardize collective or shared interests (Frank, 1988; 1992).

Although many philosophers and biologists are sceptical that evolution can produce components of moral systems such as the capacity for sympathy and empathy or even the capacity for non-kin based co-operation that require the suspension of short term, independent interests, there also exists a tradition going back to Petr Kropotkin (1902) and, more recently, Robert Trivers (1971), in which the view has been that animals assist each other precisely because by doing so they achieve long term, collective benefits of greater value than the short term benefits derived from straightforward competition. Kropotkin specifically adhered to a view in which organisms struggle not necessarily against each other, but collectively against their environments. He strongly objected to Huxley's (1888) depiction of life as a 'continuous free fight'. Although some of Kropotkin's rationale was seriously flawed, the basic tenet of his ideas was on the mark. Almost seventy years later, in an article entitled 'The Evolution of Reciprocal Altruism', Trivers refined the concepts Kropotkin advanced and explained how co-operation and, more importantly, a system of reciprocity (called 'reciprocal altruism' by Trivers) could have evolved. Unlike simultaneous co-operation or mutualism, reciprocal altruism involves exchanged acts that, while beneficial to the recipient, are costly to the performer. This cost, which is generated because there is a time lag between giving and receiving, is eliminated as soon as a favour of equal value is returned to the performer (see Axelrod and Hamilton, 1981; Rothstein and Pierotti, 1988; Taylor and McGuire, 1988).

According to Richard Alexander (1987), reciprocity is essential to the development of moral systems. Systems of indirect reciprocity — a type of reciprocity that is dependent on status and reputation because performers of beneficent acts receive compensation for those acts from third parties rather than necessarily from the original receiver — require memory, consistency across time, and most importantly, a sense of social regularity or consensual sense of right and wrong (Alexander, 1987, p. 95). It is not yet clear whether systems of indirect reciprocity exist in non-human primate social groups, but certainly there is evidence from studies on food-sharing, grooming, and conflict intervention that suggest the existence of reciprocal systems and, at least among chimpanzees, a sense of social regularity (e.g. Cheney and Seyfarth, 1986; de Waal, 1991; 1996a; 1996b, chapter 3; 1997a; 1997b; Silk, 1992).

Food Sharing, Reciprocal Exchange, and Behavioural Expectations in Primates

Food sharing is known in chimpanzees (Nissen and Crawford, 1932; Kortlandt, 1962; Goodall, 1963; Nishida, 1970; Teleki, 1973; Boesch and Boesch, 1989; de Waal, 1989b; 1997a; Kuroda *et al.*, 1996), bonobos (Kano, 1980; Kuroda, 1984; Hohmann and Fruth, 1993; de Waal, 1992b), siamangs (Fox, 1984), orangutans (Edwards and Snowdon, 1980), and capuchin monkeys (Perry and Rose, 1994; Fragaszy, Feurerstein, and Mitra, 1997; de Waal, 1997b; Rose 1997). It is an alternative method to social dominance and direct competition by which adult members of a social group distribute resources among themselves. Most food sharing requires fine-tuned communication about intentions and desires in order to facilitate inter-individual food transfers. The food transfers typically observed are passive, involving selective relinquishment of plant and animal matter more frequently than active giving (de Waal, 1989b). Three non-exclusive hypotheses have been forwarded to explain the proximate reasons why one individual would voluntarily allow another to take food.

Richard Wrangham (1975) suggested that food possessors share with other group members in order to deter harassment and reduce the possibility that, as possessors,

they will become the recipients of aggression. This idea, known as the 'sharing-
-under-pressure' hypothesis, resembles Nicholas Blurton-Jones' (1987) 'tolerated-
-theft' model, according to which it is more common for possessors to let food be
taken from them than for them to actually give it away. Blurton-Jones reasoned that
possessors tolerate theft in order to avoid potentially risky fights.

The 'sharing-to-enhance-status hypothesis' has been used by Adriaan Kortlandt
(1972) and James Moore (1984) to explain male chimpanzee food sharing and the displays that frequently accompany the treatment of objects in the environment such as
captured prey. Both the act of sharing and the displays — for example, branch shak-
ing — draw attention to the food possessor in a way that may raise his or her status in
the group. Illustrative examples of this strategy can be found in Toshisada Nishida *et
al.*'s (1992) description of a chimpanzee alpha male in the wild who kept his position
through 'bribery' (i.e. selective food distribution to potential allies), and in de Waal's
(1982) account of a male contender for the alpha position in a zoo colony, who
appeared to gain in popularity by acquiring and distributing food to the group to
which the apes normally had no access.

A similar hypothesis was developed for human food distribution by Kristen
Hawkes (1990), an anthropologist, who suggested that men who provide food to
many individuals are 'showing off'. Showing off in this manner, according to
Hawkes, signals hunting prowess and generosity, two characteristics that may be
attractive to potential mates or potential political allies.

A third hypothesis — the reciprocity hypothesis — proposes that food sharing is
part of a system of mutual obligations that can involve material exchange, the
exchange of social favours such as grooming and agonistic support, or some combination of the two. For example, de Waal (1982) found that subordinate adult male
chimpanzees groom dominant males in return for an undisturbed mating session.
Suehisa Kuroda (1984) and de Waal (1987) found indications that adult male bonobos
exchange food with adolescent females in return for sex. The reciprocity hypothesis
thus differs significantly from the sharing-under-pressure hypothesis because it
addresses possessors and 'beggars' as potential long-term co-operators rather than
merely as present competitors who use sharing to appease one another. It differs from
the 'sharing-to-enhance-status' hypothesis because it emphasizes the co-operative
nature of the relationship between possessors and beggars and, consequently, emphasizes how sharing benefits both the possessor and the beggar rather than just the possessor. One advantage of the 'sharing-to-enhance-status' hypothesis is, however, that
it provides a testable proximate account of what social factors might motivate possessors to initially share with beggars, in that it suggests that possessors share because by
doing so they increase their social status in the group. In fact, the 'sharing-to-
-enhance-status' hypothesis, although a partial explanation of sharing, is useful if
considered in conjunction with the reciprocity hypothesis because it provides a proximate motivational explanation for why possessors allow some of their food to be
taken by others. Consequently, this hypothesis is not necessarily in conflict with the
reciprocity hypothesis, and may be an extension of it. Furthermore, the 'sharing-to-
-enhance-status' hypothesis, like the reciprocity hypothesis, involves the exchange of
favours between individuals using apparently equivalent, although unequal, curren-
cies: For example, a form of reciprocal exchange may emerge if A shares food with B,

which makes A more popular with B resulting — as suggested by Hawkes — in agonistic support or matings.

De Waal (1989b; 1997a; 1997b) examined whether food itself is exchanged reciprocally over time or is shared in return for some social favour by investigating the food sharing tendencies of brown capuchin monkeys and chimpanzees. Results of the capuchin study indicated that female brown capuchins share food reciprocally. The methodology used in this study differed substantially from the chimpanzee study described next. The primary difference was that the capuchin's food sharing tendencies were examined in a dyadic context rather than in the presence of the entire group as in the chimpanzee study. As shown in Figure 1, adult capuchins were separated into pairs and placed into a test chamber divided into two sections by a mesh partition. One capuchin was allowed continuous access to a bucket of attractive food. The individual with access to the food was free to monopolize all of it or could move close to the mesh and share actively or passively by allowing his counterpart access to pieces he had dropped. The situation was then reversed so that the second individual had access to the attractive food (which was of a new type) and the first did not. The rate of transfer between pairs of adult female capuchins was found to be reciprocal while the rate of transfer between pairs of adult males was not. Males, however, were less discriminating than females in terms of with whom they shared, and more generous in the amount of food they shared. Although this study examined food-sharing in capuchins in an artificial environment created by the experimenters, the results were not anomalous — food sharing among unrelated adults has been observed both among capuchins in a colony at the Yerkes Regional Primate Centre as well as among wild capuchins (Perry and Rose, 1994; Rose, 1997).

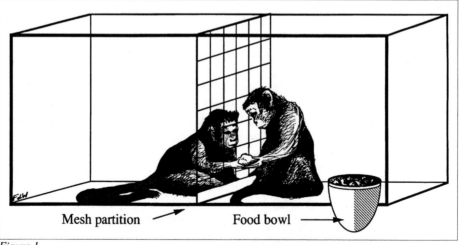

Mesh partition ⟶   Food bowl ⟶

Figure 1

Schematic drawing of the pair-test setup. One subject at a time receives food from a bowl attached to the outside of the chamber. A mesh partition divides the test chamber, preventing direct access to the food by the other subject. In a rare instance of active sharing, a male (right) hands a piece of food to a female who reaches through the mesh to accept it. Both subjects visually monitor the transfer. This drawing (by the second author) was made from an actual video still. From de Waal (1997b).

In order to study how chimpanzees share food in a social context, a situation was created in which a monopolizable food source was available to individuals in the social group. To accomplish this, a captive group of chimpanzees at the Field Station of the Yerkes Regional Primate Research Centre was provided with branches and leaves that were tightly bundled together so that the possibility existed for some group members to keep all of the food for themselves. Based on an analysis of nearly 7,000 recorded interactions over food, de Waal found that food exchanges between nine adult group members were quite balanced per dyad so that, on average, individuals A and B shared the same amount with each other. If individual A, however, shared a particular day with individual B, this did not necessarily result in B being more likely to share with A the following day. Grooming, on the other hand, did affect the likelihood to share when sharing and grooming occurred on the same day. For example, A was less likely to share with B if A had also groomed B the same day, but A was more likely to share with B if it had been B who had groomed A earlier that day. Other data indicating that food possessors actively resisted approaches by individuals who had not previously groomed them bolstered this result. Lastly, individuals who were reluctant to share their food had a greater chance of encountering aggression when they themselves approached a food possessor.

Although the chimpanzee food-sharing study confirmed one part of the prediction of Wrangham's and Blurton-Jones' hypotheses that there should be a negative correlation between rate of food distribution and frequency of received aggression, de Waal (1989b; 1996b, pp. 152–3) considers his results inconsistent with the tolerated theft model. He found that most aggression is directed not against the possessors of food, as the tolerated theft model predicts, but against beggars for food. In fact, even the lowest-ranking adult possessors are able to hold on to food unchallenged due to the 'respect of possession' first noted, with astonishment, by Goodall (1971, chapter 16), who wondered why the alpha male of her community failed to claim food possessed by others, and actually had to beg for it (Goodall, however, noted that the apparent respect for possession she observed among chimpanzees only applied to animal matter and not to bananas or other kinds of vegetable matter. This led her to suggest another somewhat different, although not mutually exclusive, explanation that focused more on the motivational state of the possessor and the corresponding response to this by the beggars). Respect of possession exists also in other primates, and was experimentally investigated by Sigg and Falett (1985), Kummer and Cords (1991), and discussed by Kummer (1991).

In fact, in de Waal's (1989) study the observed negative correlation between an individual's food distribution rate and the probability of aggression received concerned this individual as an *approacher* rather than as food possessor. This suggests either that food distributors respond to stingy individuals by sharing less with them than with others *or* that individuals, who for whatever reason, are more likely to be aggressively rebuffed when approaching food possessors, in turn become more reluctant themselves when they possess food to share with others.

Thus, the food sharing data are most in line with the reciprocity hypothesis. It is conceivable, though, that receipt of a favour (whether it be a service such as grooming or an object, such as food) positively influences an individual's social attitude so that this individual is willing to share indiscriminately with everyone else in its group (Hemelrijk, 1994). This so-called 'good mood' hypothesis, however, is not supported by the data (de Waal, 1997a), which show that if A receives grooming from B, A is only more likely to share with B but not with others in the group. The exchange between grooming and food is, therefore, partner-specific.

These studies on capuchins and chimpanzees address whether reciprocity is calculated or a by-product of frequent association and symmetrical relationships (de Waal and Luttrell, 1988; de Waal, 1997a). Calculated reciprocity is based on the capacity to keep mental note of favours given and received. It is a more sophisticated and cognitively complex (and consequently less easily accepted) form of reciprocity than symmetry-based reciprocity, which occurs when individuals preferentially direct favours to close associates. Since association is a symmetrical relationship characteristic (if A associates often with B, B does so often with A), the distribution of favours automatically becomes reciprocal (for a more in-depth discussion of what constitutes symmetry-based reciprocity, see de Waal, 1996b, p. 157). Although important, such symmetry-based reciprocity is not as cognitively demanding as calculated reciprocity, which was shown above to occur in chimpanzees and possibly female capuchins.

Calculated reciprocity — unlike symmetry-based reciprocity — raises interesting questions about the nature of expectations. The possibility that chimpanzees withhold favours from ungenerous individuals during future interactions, and are less resistant to the approaches of individuals who previously groomed them (de Waal, 1997a) suggests they have expectations about how they themselves and others should behave in certain contexts.

Other evidence to suggest that some primates have expectations about how others should behave comes from studies of patterns of conflict intervention. Chimpanzees and some species of macaques exhibit what appears to be calculated reciprocity in beneficial interventions, or the interference by a third party in an ongoing conflict in support of one of the two conflict opponents (de Waal and Luttrell, 1988; Silk, 1992). Thus, if A intervenes in favour of B, B is more likely to intervene in favour of A. In de Waal's and Luttrell's study, chimpanzees, but not macaques, also exhibited reciprocity in harmful interventions, suggesting the existence of a so-called 'revenge system'. In other words, in the chimpanzee group under study there existed a significant correlation between interventions given and received so that if A intervened against B, B was more likely to intervene against A in the future. This retaliatory pattern was not found in stumptail and rhesus macaque groups. Silk (1992), however, found evidence for a revenge system among males in bonnet macaque society in that the males in her study group appeared to monitor both the amount of aggression that they received from and directed at other males. Although Silk's data and numerous anecdotes suggest that macaques do have the capacity to engage in revenge, it is likely that revenge of this sort is not commonplace due to the greater risks in a macaque society (compared to a chimpanzee society) associated with directing aggression at dominants.

Revenge of another sort — indirect revenge — does, on the other hand, appear to be relatively common in at least one macaque species. Indirect revenge occurs when recipients of aggression redirect their aggression at the uninvolved juvenile or younger kin of their opponents. In this way, these often low ranking macaques are still able to 'punish' their attackers but are able to do so without much cost to themselves (Aureli, Cozzolino, Cordischi and Scucchi, 1992). For example, Aureli and colleagues found that Japanese macaque recipients of aggression were significantly more likely to attack the kin of their former opponents within one hour after the original conflict had occurred than if no conflict had occurred at all. One could argue, as the authors pointed out, that it is possible that this increase in aggression towards an opponent's kin after a conflict may be due to a general rather than selective aggressive tendency that is triggered by fighting and thus does not reflect a revenge system. Additional analyses revealed, however, that this hypothesis is not supported by the data — the relative probability that the original recipient of aggression would attack, following the conflict, the kin of a former opponent was significantly higher than the probability that the original recipient of aggression would attack following the conflict any group member subordinate to it. The existence of this form of revenge in macaque society suggests that a macaque's capacity to be vindictive is constrained by its rank in society rather than by its cognitive abilities.

These examples of retributive behaviour indicate that some form of calculated reciprocity is present in primate social systems. This kind of reciprocity and the kinds of responses seen by chimpanzees in the food-sharing study exemplify how and why prescriptive rules, rules that are generated when members of a group learn to recognize the contingencies between their own behaviour and the behaviour of others, are formed. The existence of such rules and, more significantly, of a set of expectations, essentially reflects a sense of social regularity, and may be a precursor to the human sense of justice (de Waal, 1991; Gruter, 1992; see also Hall, 1964; Nishida, 1994).

Trivers (1971) daringly labelled negative reactions to perceived violations of the social code, *moralistic aggression*. He emphasized that individuals who respond aggressively to perceived violations of the social code help reinforce systems of reciprocity by increasing the cost of not co-operating and, even more importantly, by increasing the cost of cheating, or failing to return a favour. When one individual cheats another, that individual exploits a relationship that is based on the benefits the partners previously obtained by co-operating. By doing so, the cheater benefits himself or herself at the partner's expense and destabilizes the system of reciprocity. Moralistic aggression, which often manifests itself as protest by subordinate individuals or punishment by dominant individuals, helps deter cheating. Consequently, it contributes to the creation of order, an element essential to the maintenance of the stability or integrity of social systems (de Waal, 1996a; Hardin, 1983). If unchecked, however, moralistic aggression can also lead to a spiral of spiteful retaliation that confers advantage on neither the original defector nor the moralistic aggressor, as is the case when those seeking retributive justice exacerbate conflicts to such a degree that feuds develop (Boehm, 1986; de Waal, 1996b, chapter 4).

Conclusion: Monkeys and apes appear capable of holding received services in mind, selectively repaying those individuals who performed the favours. They seem to hold negative acts in mind as well, leading to retribution and revenge. To what degree these reciprocity mechanisms are cognitively mediated is currently under investigation, but at least for chimpanzees there is evidence for a role of memory and expectation.

Conflict Resolution

Conflicts are inevitable in social groups. They may be generated by disagreement over social expectations or simply by competition over access to resources. Regardless of what triggers conflicts, group-living individuals need mechanisms for negotiating resolutions to them and for repairing the damage to their relationships that results once conflicts of interests have escalated to the point of aggression. One of the simplest ways that conflicts are regulated and resolved is through the establishment of clear-cut dominance relations (see Carpenter, 1942; Mendoza and Barchas, 1983; Bernstein, 1981; Bernstein and Ehardt, 1985; de Waal, 1996b; for a review, see Preuschoft and van Schaik, in press).

Primates in hierarchical social systems typically have many methods by which they communicate who is dominant and who is subordinate. Subordinate rhesus macaques, for example, bare their teeth in a ritualized expression and often present their hindquarters to an approaching dominant group member. Such displays signal to the dominant individual that the subordinate recognizes the type of relationship they share, which consequently eliminates any question of ambiguity or need for aggression and promotes harmony and stability at the group level (de Waal, 1986). Interestingly, it appears that the bared-teeth expression is a *formal* dominance signal in despotic species, such as the rhesus macaque, in that it is almost exclusively displayed by subordinate individuals (de Waal and Luttrell, 1985; Preuschoft, 1999). In more egalitarian and tolerant macaque species, such as Tonkean macaques, power asymmetries between individuals are less evident than in despotic species, like rhesus macaques. Coinciding with this difference in power is a difference in use of the bared-teeth expression, which in Tonkean macaques is neither ritualized nor formal but common to both subordinate and dominant individuals (Thierry, Demaria, Preuschoft and Desportes, 1989).

Strict dominance relationships are often an effective means by which conflicts can be negotiated. When conflicts persist despite dominance relationships, or in primate species where dominance relations are relaxed or almost absent, there must be alternative ways to work out problems and repair relationships (this does not, however, imply that the development of egalitarian social systems led to the development of conflict management devices or vice versa, only that generally the two go together). One of the most important of these post-conflict behaviours is *reconciliation*. Reconciliation, which is defined as a friendly reunion between former opponents not long after a confrontation, is illustrated in the following description of an agonistic interaction between two chimpanzees and the post-conflict behaviour that followed (de Waal, 1989c, p. 41):

> . . . Nikkie, the leader of the group, has slapped Hennie during a passing charge. Hennie, a young adult female of nine years, sits apart for a while feeling with her hand the spot on the back of the neck where Nikkie hit her. Then she seems to forget about the incident; she lies down in the grass, staring into the distance. More than fifteen minutes later, Hennie slowly gets up and walks straight to a group that includes Nikkie and the oldest female, Mama. Hennie approaches Nikkie with a series of soft pant grunts. Then she stretches out her arm to offer Nikkie the back of her hand for a kiss. Nikkie's hand-kiss consists of taking Hennie's whole hand rather unceremoniously into his mouth. This contact is followed by a mouth-to-mouth kiss.

Reconciliation enables the immediate, negative consequences of aggression to be counteracted and reduces the tension-related behaviour of recipients of aggression (de Waal and van Roosmalen, 1979; Aureli and van Schaik, 1991; de Waal and Aureli, 1996; Aureli, 1997). Perhaps more importantly, though, reconciliation enables former opponents to restore their relationship (Kappeler and van Schaik,

1992) and indeed one can increase the rate of reconciliation by experimentally enhancing the value of the relationship, e.g. by making the food-intake of two individuals dependent on their co-operation (Cords and Thurnheer, 1993). This form of post-conflict behaviour has been demonstrated in many primate species, each of which has its own typical 'peacemaking' gestures, calls, facial expressions and rituals, including, for example, kissing and embracing (see de Waal and Yoshihara, 1983; Cords, 1988; de Waal and Ren, 1988; York and Rowell, 1988; Aureli, van Schaik and van Hooff, 1989; Judge, 1991; Ren *et al*, 1991; Kappeler, 1993). We label friendly post-conflict behaviour 'reconciliation' if we can demonstrate empirically that the former opponents are selectively attracted so that they tend to come together in this manner more than usual and more with each other than with individuals who had nothing to do with the fight. In order to determine the percentage of conflicts followed by reconciliation for individuals of a particular species, we compare the post-conflict period (PC) to a matched-control period (MC). We use the matched-control period because it enables us to determine whether the affiliation that takes place during the post-conflict period is triggered by the conflict, or if it is simply due to chance (for a detailed discussion of the PC/MC method, see Veenema, Das and Aureli, 1994). As seen in Figure 2, former stumptail macaque opponents affiliate considerably more in post-conflict periods than they do in the matched-control periods.

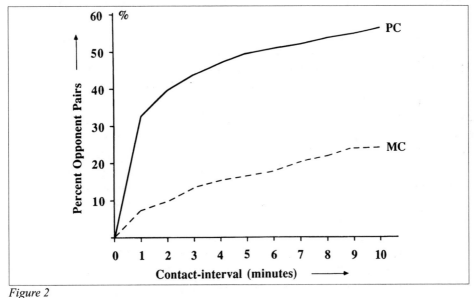

Figure 2

Cumulative percentage of pairs of opponents making their first nonagonistic body contact within a certain time interval. PC = post conflict observation, MC = matched control observation, N = number of pairs. From de Waal and Ren (1988).

Although reconciliation has been observed in most primate species and appears to be a universal method of repairing disturbed relationships, the degree to which it is used differs across primate species in a pattern that may reflect the level of integration and cohesion in a primate society. For example, analysis of post-conflict/matched-control (PC/MC) data from 670 pairs of former stumptail macaque opponents with PC/MC data from 573 pairs of former rhesus macaque opponents, revealed that stumptail monkeys reconciled on average significantly more often (i.e. 51.6 per cent) than rhesus monkeys (i.e. 21.1 per cent) (de Waal and Ren, 1988). In general, individuals in despotic species reconcile less frequently after conflicts than individuals in more tolerant and egalitarian species, most likely because the strict dominance hierarchies that are present in despotic species constrain the development of strong symmetrical relationships among group members (de Waal, 1989a).

Another way primates regulate and resolve conflicts of interests between group members is through conflict intervention. Although many studies have shown that interventions are related to coalition building and alliance formation, some interventions may have other functions as well (e.g. Reinhardt, Dodsworth and Scanlan, 1986; Bernstein and Ehardt, 1986; Boehm, 1994; Petit and Thierry, 1994; for reviews see Harcourt and de Waal, 1992). In some species, interventions by the highest ranking members of the social group end fights or at least reduce the severity of aggression that occurs during fights. The alpha male chimpanzee often plays such a role in fights involving females and/or juveniles in his group (de Waal, 1982). For example, if two juveniles are playing and a fight erupts, the alpha male just has to approach the area of the conflict to stop the fight. By doing so, he directly reduces the levels of aggression within the group, and also prevents the fight from escalating further by ending it before the juveniles' mothers intervene and possibly begin fighting themselves. Another example of this type of intervention in chimpanzees is given by the following excerpt from *Chimpanzee Politics* (1982, p. 124):

> On one occasion, a quarrel between Mama and Spin got out of hand and ended in biting and fighting. Numerous apes rushed up to the two warring females and joined in the fray. A huge knot of fighting, screaming apes rolled around in the sand, until Luit leapt in and literally beat them apart. He did not choose sides in the conflict, like the others; instead anyone who continued to fight received a blow from him.

This pattern of behaviour, often referred to as the 'control role' has been described in other species of primates as well, (e.g. Bernstein, 1964; Tokuda and Jensen, 1969; Reinhardt *et al.,* 1986), and is a type of arbitration. The most interesting types of interventions that fall under the control role heading are those that are impartial. Individuals who intervene without choosing sides seem to do so in order to restore peace rather than simply aid friends or family (de Waal and van Hooff, 1981; de Waal, 1982; Goodall, 1986). The ability to put one's own preferences aside in this manner is another indication that a rudimentary form of justice may exist in the social systems of non-human primates (Boehm, 1992; de Waal, 1996a; 1996b). On the other hand, one might argue that although such interventions ultimately may have the effect of restoring the peace and reducing overall levels of aggression in the group, it is possible that the intervener's intentions were simpler, and that he or she was motivated only by the desire to terminate an aversive stimulus — the noisy conflict — and not by any group-oriented motivation. Evidence from chimpanzees and macaques suggests, however, that this explanation for impartial interventions may be inadequate. Such interventions may indeed be motivated in part by a desire to terminate an aversive stimulus but, if that were the only motivation, we might expect the interventions to be severe and partial, and in favour of the individual with whom the intervener shares the best relationship. Furthermore, agonistic interventions, in particular, can trigger agonistic and nonagonistic involvement by other individuals and intense screaming by the target or targets of the intervention (Gouzoules, Gouzoules and

Marler, 1984). Thus, interventions often temporarily exacerbate the aversive stimuli that supposedly the intervener sought to suppress.

Another type of intervention that falls under the control role is the protective intervention. Interventions in this group include those that occur on behalf of recipients of aggression. When expressed in this form, the control role can be viewed as a way that lower ranking or weaker (either physically *or* socially) individuals are protected from higher ranking, stronger (either physically *or* socially) group members.

A particularly salient example of the power of control animals to protect recipients of aggression in some primate societies that demonstrates not only the degree to which a control animal can influence the outcome of a conflict, but also that other individuals in the group recognize this capacity in certain individuals, comes from an experiment in which the composition of a pigtail macaque group was manipulated (Flack and de Waal, unpublished data). During this experiment, the three highest-ranking male pigtail macaques were removed for the day once per week and confined to their indoor housing. We studied the patterns of conflict intervention and aggression that occurred in the group when the males were present and when the males were absent. During removal periods, although confined to their indoor housing, the males had vocal and very restricted visual access to the group in that they were separated from the group by only a two foot long tunnel (to the indoor housing), divided in the middle by a metal door that did not completely seal off the indoor area from the outdoor area.

Three very low-ranking females typically received moderate levels of aggression from other group members when the males were present, but the males often intervened in these conflicts and, when this occurred, the aggression that had been directed at the females usually subsided. During the period when the males were removed, the intensity and frequency of aggression directed at these low ranking females increased substantially, and severe biting (biting for more than five seconds in duration), in particular, was more common. Several times, the aggression directed at these females became so severe that the investigator was forced to intervene.

Over the course of the study period, however, the females discovered a way to deal with the increase in severe aggression that they received when the high-ranking males were absent. This began when one female started running into the tunnel that separated the indoor housing from the outdoor housing. Once in the tunnel, the female solicited support from the males locked inside. The males, who could hear the conflict, were always waiting at the door. The female being attacked would scream, bare her teeth, and stick her arm though a small space in the door as her attackers were rushing forward. Each time this occurred, one of the males confined to the indoor housing would emit a threat bark, and the female would scream, clearly distressed by both her attackers and the threat, but not move from her position. Her attackers, however, would jump back and cease their abusive behaviour. The female would then lie prone in the tunnel for the next fifteen minutes or so, and each time her attackers attempted to bite her, a male inside would emit a threat bark and the attack would cease. The other two females, too, learned that when they were severely attacked they could appeal to the confined high-ranking males in this way, and as the study period progressed, this behaviour increased in frequency. Notably, no individuals ever escaped from aggression by running into the tunnel when the males were present in the group, presumably because doing so prohibited escape and thus was very dangerous.

Interestingly, among chimpanzees, the individual who plays this control role need not be the alpha male of the group. The control animal may be any group member who the community permits — in the sense that none of the individuals in the social group protests the control animal's involvement in the conflict nor prohibits the particular control animal from 'playing' his or her role (de Waal, 1996b, chapter 3). Pascale Sicotte (1995) described a similar mechanism for resolving conflicts in bi-male groups of mountain gorillas in which females and infants sometimes interposed themselves between two fighting silverbacks. These interpositions, which occurred in 10–25 per cent of conflicts between silverbacks, involved more than just passive or chance interference in the agonistic dyad by a third party. Sicotte only included as interpositions those third party interventions in which a previously uninvolved individual interacted nonagonistically with at least one of the two males engaged in conflict, and in which the course of the initial agonistic interaction between the males was modified because one of the opponents directed its attention towards the third party. Notably, in one of the two groups Sicotte studied, he found that interpositions significantly increased the time between the end of the fight in which it occurred, and the start of the next fight.

One other important method of conflict resolution that has been identified in primate groups is mediation. Mediation occurs when a third party to a conflict becomes the bridge between two former opponents who cannot seem to bring themselves to reconcile without external help. It is characterized in the following example (de Waal and van Roosmalen, 1979, p. 62).

> Especially after serious conflicts between two adult males, the two opponents sometimes were brought together by an adult female. The female approached one of the males, kissed or touched him or presented towards him and then slowly walked towards the other male. If the male followed, he did so very close behind her (often inspecting her genitals) and without looking at the other male. On a few occasions the female looked behind at her follower, and sometimes returned to a male that stayed behind to pull at his arm to make him follow. When the female sat down close to the other male, both males started to groom her and they simply continued when she went off.

In the above example of mediation, a female, who apparently is trying to reunite two former opponents in her social group, seems to show community concern in that she apparently cares about resolving a conflict in which she had no part and, more importantly, about restoring a disturbed relationship that is not her own. Although such examples are rare in primates, and perhaps unlikely in any but apes, a very similar pattern of behaviour to that illustrated by the example above was observed in stumptail macaques (Flack, personal observation), suggesting that individuals in several species may have a sense of community concern that comes from having a stake in the quality of life within the group as a whole.

De Waal (1996b, p. 31) explained the evolution of community concern as follows:

> Inasmuch as every member benefits from a unified, cooperative group, one expects them to care about the society they live in, and to make an effort to improve and strengthen it similar to the way the spider repairs her web, and the beaver maintains the integrity of his dam. Continued infighting, particularly at the top of the hierarchy, may damage everyone's interests, hence the settlement of conflict is not just a matter of the parties involved,

it concerns the community as a whole. This is not to say that animals make sacrifices for their community, but rather that each and every individual has a stake in the quality of the social environment on which its survival depends. In trying to improve this quality for their own purposes, they help many of their group mates at the same time. A good example is arbitration and mediation in disputes; standard practice in human society — courts of law serve this function — but recognizable in other primates as well.

Two other patterns of behaviour in monkeys and apes illustrative of community concern are triadic reconciliation — the involvement of third parties in the reconciliation process — and the group-wide celebration that often follows the reconciliation of dramatic conflicts of chimpanzees (de Waal, 1992b; 1996b, chapter 4). These patterns of behaviour suggest that monkeys and apes devote time and energy to making sure their social group remains peaceful, perhaps because group members recognize the value that a harmonious coexistence can have to achieving shared interests. In this sense, community concern can be extremely beneficial to individuals within social groups — even if it requires subordinating independent interests (non-shared), at least on occasion, to community interests — so long as many common goals are shared among group members. This kind of community concern, however, does not require that monkeys and apes worry about how the community, as an abstract entity, is doing. It only requires that the individual works toward creating a community atmosphere that reflects his or her own best interests. Consequently, the evolution of community concern in individuals may not necessarily require group selection. Its evolution can most likely be explained using selection at the level of the individual (although it is possible that individual selection may perhaps provide only a partial explanation for the evolution of such behaviours — for more discussion of this matter, see Wilson and Sober, 1994, and this issue), particularly if we consider the other behaviours that probably co-evolved with community concern in order to mitigate the risks and reduce the short-term costs to individuals generated by investing in the community.

Punishment, for example, or the imposition of a cost or penalty by one individual (usually who has some authority or power over the other individual) on another for its behaviour (Bean, 1981), and perhaps indirect reciprocity and social norms, help offset the cost of placing community (shared) interests above individual (independent) interests. Punishment and indirect reciprocity facilitate the evolution of investment in community interests because they help deter cheating (as discussed earlier) and reinforce community-oriented behaviours by making it possible for reciprocity to become generalized — so that if one individual performs a favour for another, that favour may be returned by a third party (for discussion of punishment, see Boyd and Richerson, 1992; Clutton-Brock and Parker, 1995; for discussion of indirect reciprocity, see Alexander, 1987; Boyd and Richerson, 1989). As Axelrod (1986) discussed, an especially powerful mechanism by which cheating can be deterred emerges when punishment against defectors becomes linked with negative indirect reciprocity, or punishment of nonpunishers. This *metanorm,* as Axelrod calls it, makes the 'norm' against defection self-policing. Whether this occurs in non-human primates, however, remains to be empirically demonstrated.

There is, however, evidence from a recent study of play signalling patterns in juvenile chimpanzees that suggests primates may modify their behaviour in anticipation of punishment (Jeannotte, 1996). Lisa Jeannotte found that older play partners were significantly more likely to emit play signals, such as 'play face', during play bouts that occurred in proximity to adults, particularly those adults who were mothers of younger play partners and who were themselves young, than was the case when these adults were absent. These results suggest that an older juvenile play partner may increase its play signalling in the presence of a young mother to make clear that its interaction with the younger play partner is benign and does not warrant intervention or punishment.

Another mechanism that might enable the evolution of community concern is docility, or the receptivity to social influence that is common to social primates and that is useful for acquiring valuable information without the need for direct experience or evaluation (Simon, 1990). Thus, if certain values, like community concern, are fostered in a particular social environment, then an individual, simply due to its docile disposition, may adopt and become committed to those values even though at times those values or sentiments may encourage a course of action that is counter to an individual's independent (non-shared) interests. In this way, community concern evolves as a by-product of selection for docility (for a related argument about a similar mechanism, the 'conformist transmission', by which community concern might evolve, see Boyd and Richerson, 1985; 1992; Henrich and Boyd, 1998; see also Cronk, 1994 for a Marxian argument about how docility may actually make it possible in some moral systems for certain individuals to justify and perpetuate inequalities of power and access to resources).

Although at present, direct evidence for punishment, docility, and especially indirect reciprocity is scant or fragmented in the primate literature, such behavioural mechanisms by which collective action is facilitated do probably exist to varying degrees. The existence of these mechanisms, which are likely complementary rather than alternative methods that act in concert to produce stability in social systems (Henrich and Boyd, 1998), is indirectly supported by the presence of learned adjustment, succourant behaviour, empathy, and sympathy in non-human primates.

Conclusion: Despite inevitable conflicts of interests, a certain degree of stability must be maintained in primate societies so that individuals can realize their collective interests and make worthwhile their investments in sociality. Dominance relationships provide one simple way to regulate and order societies. Social systems with more level dominance relationships require additional mechanisms, however, such as reconciliation; consolation; impartial, protective, and pacifying interventions; and perhaps community concern. All of these mechanisms are present to varying degrees in monkeys and apes.

Empathy, Sympathy and Consolation

Although food-sharing, social reciprocity in general, and the different forms of conflict resolution seen in primates need not require a capacity for sympathy and empathy, it is likely that both are involved to some degree in all of these behaviours, and to a high degree in at least the more sophisticated forms of conflict intervention such as mediation. In order to help others, as the female in the mediation example was doing, individuals need to be concerned about and be able to understand others' needs and emotions.

Learned adjustment, which is common in primates, is a precursor to such behaviour in that it demonstrates the ability of monkeys and apes to change their behaviour as they become familiar with the limitations of those with whom they interact without requiring that these individuals understand why they should adjust their behaviour. Juvenile chimpanzees, for example, commonly restrict the degree of force they use in wrestling matches while playing with younger juveniles and infants (Hayaki, 1985). Monkeys and apes also adjust their behaviour in the presence of disabled group members (e.g. Fedigan and Fedigan, 1977; de Waal, 1996b, chapter 2; de Waal, Uno, Luttrell, Meisner and Jeannotte, 1996c). The adjustment may include increased social tolerance towards individuals who behave abnormally or intervention on behalf of disabled individuals who seem unaware of when they are involved in a dangerous predicament. Although the examples discussed above are most parsimoniously explained using learned adjustment, the possibility that cognitive empathy — the ability to comprehend the needs and emotions of other individuals — may provide a more accurate explanation for some of these behaviours needs to be explored in future studies.

An especially important area that needs investigation is how learned adjustment and cognitive empathy relate to the internalization of social norms. One study that begins to address this question is Jeannotte's previously mentioned study (1996) of play-signalling in juvenile chimpanzees in relation to social context and environment. Results of this study indicate that an older juvenile is not significantly more likely to play roughly when the age difference between it and its partner is small as opposed to large. Although this result seems to contradict findings from previous research that suggested that juvenile chimpanzees restrict the intensity of play when interacting with younger play partners, it does not necessarily do so. Jeannotte found that there was a strong correlation between the play intensity of one partner with that of the other. One likely explanation for this 'matching' is that it may be a consequence of restraint on the part of the older partner and escalation on the part of the younger partner (Hayaki, 1985).

Succourant behaviour, which includes care-giving and providing relief to distressed individuals who are not kin, is also an example of a category of behaviours that seem to require attachment to and concern for others and, in some cases, an understanding of other's needs and emotions (Scott, 1971). Succourant tendencies develop in primates early in life; even infants respond to tension generated by aggression by mounting one another or by mounting kin or even the individuals involved in the agonism. Although these infants probably are not helping to reduce tensions between the individuals involved in the agonism by responding in this way, they may be comforting themselves. This simple need to comfort oneself after or during a fight in which the infant itself was not involved suggests that the infant perceives distress in others and reacts vicariously to it by becoming distressed itself. This 'emotional contagion' (Hatfield, Cacioppo and Rapson, 1993) may be the mechanism underlying the development of succourance and suggests that primates do have the ability to empathize.

Non-human primates may be able to empathize with one another in that other group member's feelings and actions emotionally affect them, but are non-human primates also concerned about individuals who appear distressed? In other words, do they sympathize with or just react to individuals in their group who are distressed?

There is evidence suggesting that some primates do have concern for fellow group members; it comes from studies of consolation, or the appeasement of distressed individuals through affiliative gestures such as grooming and embracing by third parties following a fight (de Waal and van Roosmalen, 1979). The predominant and immediate effect of consolation — the alleviation of distress (de Waal and Aureli, 1996), is illustrated by the following example observed by Jane Goodall (1986, p. 361):

> An adult male challenged by another male often runs screaming to a third and establishes contact with him. Often both will then scream, embrace, mount or groom each other while looking toward the original aggressor. This . . . is how a victim tries to enlist the help of an ally. There are occasions, however, when it seems that the primary goal is to establish reassurance contact — as when fourteen-year-old Figan, after being attacked by a rival, went to hold hands with his mother.

In the above example, however, the recipient of aggression is *seeking* consolation. This type of consolation occurs in several primate species but may not require that the third party sympathizes with the recipient who approaches for reassurance (for other examples see Lindburg, 1973; de Waal and Yoshihara, 1983; Verbeek and de Waal, 1997). *Active* consolation, on the other hand, occurs when a third party approaches and affiliates with a recipient of aggression following a fight. Such action may require that the third party not only recognize the distress of the recipient of aggression but also be concerned enough about that individual to approach and appease it. Sometimes, for example, a juvenile chimpanzee will approach and embrace an adult male who has just lost a confrontation with his rival (de Waal, 1982).

There exist systematic data to support the conclusion that chimpanzees have the capacity to engage in active consolation (de Waal and Aureli, 1996). An analysis of 1,321 agonistic incidents among a captive group of seventeen chimpanzees housed in a large compound at the Field Station of the Yerkes Regional Primate Research Center revealed that significantly more affiliative contacts initiated by bystanders occurred immediately (within several minutes) after a conflict than after longer time intervals or in control periods not preceded by conflict. Furthermore, significantly more affiliative contacts initiated by bystanders occurred following serious incidents than mild incidents (this is particularly important because, if consolation occurs to alleviate distress, and if an individual's level of distress is proportional to the aggression intensity of the conflict in which it participated, then consolation should occur more frequently following serious aggressive incidents). And finally, bystanders initiated significantly more affiliative contact with the recipients of aggression than with the aggressors themselves.

In contrast to these findings for chimpanzees, researchers have been unable to quantitatively demonstrate active consolation in four macaque species (Aureli, 1992; Aureli and van Schaik, 1991; Judge, 1991; Aureli, Veenema, van Panthaleon van Eck and van Hoof, 1993; Aureli, Das, Verleur and van Hooff, 1994; Castles and Whiten, 1998; for a review, see de Waal and Aureli, 1996). This suggests that consolation may be limited to the great apes, possibly because it requires more sophisticated cognition than present in monkeys. Alternatively, it may be limited to apes because within their social systems, such behaviour is more advantageous and perhaps less costly than in monkey social systems in which approaching recipients of aggression, and areas of conflicts generally, can be dangerous due to the frequency with which aggression is redirected to bystanders in many monkey societies (de Waal and Aureli, 1996).

Conclusion: Moral sentiments such as sympathy, empathy, and community concern, engender a bond between individuals, the formation of which facilitates and is facilitated by co-operation. This bond is enabled by an individual's capacity to be sensitive to the emotions of others. Monkeys and apes are capable of learned adjustment, and have succourant tendencies, in that they comfort and console one another when distressed. But are they capable of genuine concern for others based on perspective-taking? There is some evidence to suggest that apes, like humans, are capable of cognitive empathy but its existence in monkeys remains questionable.

Implications of Primate Research for Understanding Human Morality

In the opening pages of a *Theory of Justice* (1971, p. 4), John Rawls elegantly states the central problem that plagues those human (and animal) societies in which implicit or explicit rules of conduct exist to make co-operation possible:

> . . . although a society is a co-operative venture for mutual advantage, it is typically marked by a conflict as well as by an identity of interests. There is an identity of interests since social cooperation makes possible a better life for all than any would have if each were to live solely by his own efforts. There is a conflict of interests since persons are not indifferent as to how the greater benefits of their collaboration are distributed, for in order to pursue their ends they each prefer a larger to a lesser share.

This problem, as identified above by Rawls, has in practice no true solutions. Furthermore, the research on the natural history and social behaviour of our non-human primate relatives illustrates how both our capacity and tendency to pursue our independent interests and our capacity and tendency to pursue shared interests are natural and important, at least from a biological point of view (see de Waal, 1992a). This suggests that morality was not *devised* to subjugate the independent interests of individuals. Rather, a moral system *emerged* out of the interaction of the two sets of interests, thus providing a way to express both. This conclusion should not be mistaken as justification for using natural selection as a model for what we ought to do or *not* do. What we ought to do and how we decide this is a separate question from why and how moral systems arose.

It is particularly important that in our pursuit of the origins and purpose of moral systems we resist the temptation to let our moral views frame, and thus obscure, how in the end we describe and explain the moral standards embodied in implicit social contracts. Even more importantly, we need to be careful not to hold up as moral systems only those that in our view wholly subjugate the independent interests of individuals in favour of those interests that are shared, simply because we value that these systems suppress conflict and deliver consensus. Doing so precludes from consideration those systems that from an operational standpoint are moral systems, but that may not fit perfectly our moral views of what is right, of worth, or of value.

Humans, nonetheless, may be the only truly moral creatures. Although one could argue that several elements of human morality are present in non-human primates — particularly in apes — there is no evidence at this time to suggest that non-human primates have moral systems that mirror the complexity of our own. In some species, individuals, by interacting every day, may create a kind of social contract that governs which types of behaviour are acceptable and tolerable and which are punishable —

yet these individuals have no way to conceptualize such decisions or abstract them from their context, let alone debate them amongst themselves. Consensus is only obvious in the absence of protest and prohibition.

Consensus achieved in this tacit manner, however, is not uncommon in our own species. This observation, in conjunction with the above research that suggests that an actual social contract of sorts arises out of interactions between group members in primate societies, makes plausible the idea that human morality is best understood as having arisen out of an implicit agreement among group members that enabled individuals to profit from the benefits of co-operative sociality.

Acknowledging that morality may have a social function and stressing that it may have emerged from such a social contract does not require that we accept this kind of 'actual' social contract as the medium through which we decide what is moral. Nor does it suggest that we revert to some form of Social Darwinism, an approach to deciding what we ought to do that was based not only on a misconceived, red-in-tooth-and-claw representation of natural selection, but worse, also on the idea that this interpretation of 'nature's way' should be used to guide (and justify) our own behaviour. Although we need to recognize that the social contract does in fact often represent the process by which we come to agree (as a group) what is acceptable, we also need to recognize that this is probably the case because the social contract is useful from an evolutionary perspective because it enables individuals in groups to reach consensus with minimal, if any, need for explicit co-ordination. Certainly, from a social perspective, one of the major limitations of any actual social contract is that such contracts do not necessarily produce the most 'moral' solutions to problems. The outcome such contracts produce is no more than a reflection of compromise, and of the behaviour that as a group we practice.

Another important observation about human behaviour made by David Hume (1739), Adam Smith (1759), and Edward Westermarck (1912) is that human morality is powerfully influenced by emotional responses and is not always governed by the abstract, intellectual rules upon which we have supposedly agreed. The primate research implicitly suggests that this emphasis on the role of emotions is both insightful and accurate — in primate groups individuals are motivated to respond to others based on the emotional reactions they have to one another's behaviour. That sympathy, based on empathy, seems to direct the emotional responses of some primates to others may reflect their ability to differentiate between self and other and, more significantly, to care for one another. Yet, the idea that emotion may be fundamental to morality contradicts what many philosophers — most significantly Immanuel Kant (1785) — have argued: That the human sense of right and wrong is more a consequence of rational processes than of emotional reactions. It would be quite erroneous, however, to equate moral emotions with a lack of rationality and judgement. The emotions discussed by Hume, Smith and Westermarck are actually very complex, involving retribution, reciprocity and perspective taking. The latter, as is now increasingly apparent from research into so-called Theory-of-Mind, involves complex mental abilities (for a review of Theory-of-Mind in non-human primates, see Heyes and Commentaries, 1998).

Darwin (1871; 1872), who was familiar with the thinking of Hume and Smith, advocated a perspective on human morality in line with these ideas in that he saw human nature as neither good nor bad but neutral. He recognized that moral systems enable individuals to reconcile what Hume saw as two sides to human nature — the dark, competitive side, which is dominated by greed and competition, and the 'sentimental,' co-operative side, which is marked by social instincts and compassion. To Darwin, this dualism in human nature arose from the evolution of two strategies (the individual and social) that together provided a method by which individuals can obtain limited resources. Thus, Darwin recognized that moral systems not only govern the expression and use of these strategies but also reflect their interaction.

Opposition to this more integrated view by some contemporary evolutionary biologists, such as Richard Dawkins and George Williams (see Introduction), leads us to propose that their views on morality be classified not as Darwinian but Huxleyan. For example, Dawkins recently reconciled human moral ideals with his interpretation of evolution by saying that we are entitled to throw out Darwinism ('in our political and social life we are entitled to throw out Darwinism, to say we don't want to live in a Darwinian world', *Human Ethology Bulletin,* March 1997). Because Darwin himself perceived absolutely no contradiction or dualism between the evolutionary process and human moral tendencies (e.g. de Waal, 1996b; Uchii, 1996), such views represent a considerable narrowing of what Darwin deemed possible.

The Kantian view of morality as an invention of reason supplemented with a sense of duty remained pervasive despite Darwin's insights. Perhaps primate research that suggests that morality is a consequence of our emotional needs and responses as well as of our ability to rationally evaluate alternatives is strong enough to warrant making room for a more integrated perspective of morality that acknowledges its biological basis and emotional component as well as the role of cognition. Perhaps Hume and Kant were both correct.

The foundations of morality may be built on our emotional reactions to one another but morality itself is no doubt also tempered and sometimes modified by two additional factors. First, morality may be modified by our ability to evaluate the situation generating these emotional reactions. Second, it may be tempered by our understanding of the consequences that our responses to the behaviour that elicited the emotional reaction have for ourselves and others. A problem, however, remains even after we acknowledge that what generates in each of us an understanding of what is good or virtuous is a combination of two factors: 1) the emotional reaction and intuition of each individual that jump-start the moral process, with 2) the cognitive-rational evaluations that enable the individual to determine what is right. The problem that remains despite this integration is how to translate the resultant conception in the individual of what is good to action at the community level. In human societies, as in animal societies, this is often achieved by some manifestation of the social contract. But as mentioned earlier, 'actual' social contracts, as rough compromises between competing agents, often with unequal powers and needs, may be unsatisfactory from a normative standpoint because they do not fully respect worth, value or rights.

Conclusion

Sympathy-related traits such as attachment, succourance, emotional contagion and learned adjustment in combination with a system of reciprocity and punishment, the ability to internalize social rules and the capacity to work out conflicts and repair relationships damaged by aggression, are found to some degree in many primate species, and are fundamental to the development of moral systems (Table 1).

All of these elements of moral systems are tools social animals — including humans — use to make living together a possibility. These capacities help keep in check the inevitable competition among group members due to conflicting interests. More importantly, however, sympathy-related traits and the capacity to work out con-

Table 1

It is hard to imagine human morality without the following tendencies and capacities also found in other species. These tendencies deserve to be called the four ingredients of morality:

Sympathy Related
Attachment, succourance, and emotional contagion.
Learned adjustment to and special treatment of the disabled and injured.
Ability to trade places mentally with others: cognitive empathy.*

Norm Related
Prescriptive social rules.
Internalization of rules and anticipation of punishment.*
A sense of social regularity and expectation about how one ought to be treated.*

Reciprocity
A concept of giving, trading, and revenge.
Moralistic aggression against violators of reciprocity rules.

Getting Along
Peacemaking and avoidance of conflict.
Community concern and maintenance of good relationships.*
Accommodation of conflicting interests through negotiation.

*It is particularly in these areas — empathy, internalization of rules, sense of justice, and community concern — that humans seem to have gone considerably further than most other animals.

flicts and repair relationships help promote cohesion, co-operation and social bonding, characteristics of a social group that may, from an evolutionary perspective, make group living a functionally effective strategy and, therefore, an attractive strategy in which individuals should invest resources. As the anthropologist Ruth Benedict wrote in 1934 (p. 251):

> One of the most misleading misconceptions due to this nineteenth-century dualism was the idea that what was subtracted from society was added to the individual and what was subtracted from the individual was added to society. . . . In reality, society and the individual are not antagonists. His culture provides the raw material of which the individual makes his life. If it is meagre, the individual suffers; if it is rich, the individual has the chance to rise to his opportunity.

At the end of this paper, in which we have discussed the possible evolutionary building blocks of human moral systems, it is essential to also point out the limitations of biological approaches to human morality. After all, we have in the past seen attempts to derive moral rules directly from nature, resulting in a dubious genre of literature going back to Ernest Seton's (1907) *The Natural History of the Ten Commandments*. Other biblical titles have followed, principally in the German language, spelling out how moral principles contribute to survival (e.g. Wickler, 1971). Much of this literature assumed that the world was waiting for biologists to point out what is Normal and Natural, hence worth being adopted as ideal. Attempts to derive ethical norms from nature, however, are highly questionable.

Our position is quite different. While human morality does need to take human nature into account by either fortifying certain natural tendencies — such as sympathy, reciprocity, loyalty to the group and family, and so on — or by countering other tendencies — such as within-group violence and cheating — it is in the end the society that decides, over a period of many generations, on the contents of its moral system. There is a parallel here with language ability: The capacity to develop and learn a very complex communication system such as language is naturally present in humans, but it is filled in by the environment resulting in numerous different languages. In the same way, we are born with a moral capacity, and a strong tendency to absorb the moral values of our social environment, but we are not born with a moral code in place. The filling in is done by the social environment often dictated by the demands of the physical environment (de Waal, 1996b).

Interestingly, moral development in human children hints at the same emphasis on conflict resolution and reciprocity (principles of 'fairness') as emphasized above for non-human primates. Instead of the traditional, Piagetian view of morality imposed upon the child by the all-knowing adults, increasingly it is thought that children develop moral rules in social interaction with each other, particularly during the resolution of conflict (e.g. Killen and Nucci, 1995; Killen and de Waal, in press).

At the same time that our moral systems rely on basic mental capacities and social tendencies that we share with other co-operative primates, such as chimpanzees, we also bring unique features to the table, such as a greater degree of rule internalization, a greater ability to adopt the perspective of others, and of course the unique capacity to debate issues amongst ourselves, and transmit them verbally, including their rationale. To communicate intentions and feelings is one thing, to clarify what is good, and why, and what is bad, and why, quite something else. Animals are no moral philosophers.

But, while there is no denying that we are creatures of intellect, it is also clear that we are born with powerful inclinations and emotions that bias our thinking and behaviour. It is in this area that many of the continuities with other animals lie. A chimpanzee stroking and patting a victim of attack or sharing her food with a hungry companion shows attitudes that are hard to distinguish from those of a person taking a crying child in the arms, or doing volunteer work in a soup kitchen. To dismiss such evidence as a product of subjective interpretation by 'romantically inspired naturalists' (e.g.: Williams, 1989, p.190) or to classify all animal behaviour as based on instinct and human behaviour as proof of moral decency is misleading (see Kummer, 1979). First of all, it is uneconomic in that it assumes different processes for similar behaviour in closely related species. Second, it ignores the growing body of evidence for mental complexity in the chimpanzee, including the possibility of empathy.

One wonders if, on the basis of external behaviour alone, an extraterrestrial observer charged with finding the only moral animal on earth would automatically end up pointing at *Homo sapiens*. We think it unlikely that human behaviour in all its variety, including the occasional horror, will necessarily strike the observer as the most moral. This raises of course the question how and whether morality sets us apart from the rest of the animal kingdom. The continuities are, in fact, quite striking, and need to weigh heavily in any debate about the evolution of morality. We do hesitate to call the members of any species other than our own 'moral beings', but we also believe that many of the tendencies and cognitive abilities underlying human morality antedate our species' appearance on this planet.

Acknowledgements

The authors thank Rudolf Makkreel and, especially, Leonard Katz for very helpful comments and suggestions. The first author thanks Meredith Small, Adam Arcadie, and Richard Baer, Jr. for patient and stimulating discussion about the evolution of morality.

References

Alexander, R.D. (1987), *The Biology of Moral Systems* (New York: Aldine de Gruyter).

Aureli, F. (1992), 'Post-conflict behaviour among wild long-tailed macaques (*Macaca- fascicularis*)', *Behavioural Ecology and Sociobiology*, **31**, pp. 329–37.

Aureli, F. (1997), 'Post-conflict anxiety in non-human primates: The mediating role of emotion in conflict resolution', *Aggressive behaviour*, **23**, pp. 315–28.

Aureli, F., Cozzolino, R., Cordischi, C., and Scucchi, S. (1992), 'Kin-oriented redirection among Japanese macaques — an expression of a revenge system?', *Animal Behaviour*, **44**, pp. 283–291.

Aureli, F., Das, M., Verleur, D., and van Hooff, J. (1994), 'Postconflict social interactions among Barbary macaques (*Macaca sylvanus*)', *International Journal of Primatology*, **15**, pp. 471–85.

Aureli, F., and van Hooff, J. (1993), 'Functional-aspects of redirected aggression in macaques', *Aggressive behaviour*, **19**, pp. 50–1.

Aureli, F., van Panthaleon van Eck, C. J., and Veenema, H. C. (1995), 'Long-tailed macaques avoid conflicts during short-term crowding', *Aggressive behaviour*, **21**, pp. 113–22.

Aureli, F., and van Schaik, C.P. (1991), 'Post-conflict behaviour in long-tailed macaques (*Macaca fascicularis*).2. Coping with the uncertainty', *Ethology*, **89**, pp. 101–14.

Aureli, F., van Schaik, C.P., and van Hooff, J. (1989), 'Functional-aspects of reconciliation among captive long-tailed macaques *(Macaca fascicularis)*', *American Journal of Primatology*, **19**, pp. 39–51.

Aureli, F., Veenema, H.C., van Panthaleon van Eck, C.J., and van Hooff, J. (1993), 'Reconciliation, consolation, and redirection in Japanese macaques (*Macaca fuscata*)', *Behaviour*, **124**, pp. 1–21.

Axelrod, R. (1986), 'An evolutionary approach to norms', *American Political Science Review*, **80**, pp. 1095–111.

Axelrod, R. and Hamilton, W.D. (1981), 'The evolution of co-operation', *Science*, **211**, pp. 1390–96.

Bean, P. (1981), *Punishment: A Philosophical and Criminological Inquiry* (Oxford: Rutherford).

Benedict, R. (1989 [1934]), *Patterns of Culture* (Boston: Houghton Mifflin Company).

Bernstein, I.S. (1964), 'Group social patterns as influenced by the removal and later reintroduction of the dominant male rhesus', *Psychological Reports*, **14**, pp. 3–10.

Bernstein, I.S. (1981), 'Dominance: The baby and the bathwater', *Behavioural and Brain Sciences*, **4**, pp. 419–58.

Bernstein, I.S., Ehardt, C. (1986), 'The influence of kinship and socialization on aggressive behaviour in rhesus monkeys (*Macaca fascicularis*)', *Animal Behaviour*, **34**, pp. 739–47,

Bernstein, I.S. and Ehardt, C.L. (1985), 'Intragroup agonistic behaviour in rhesus monkeys', *International Journal of Primatology*, **6**, pp. 209–26.

Blurton-Jones, N.G. (1987), 'Tolerated theft, suggestions about the ecology and evolution of sharing, hoarding, and scrounging', *Social Science Information*, **26**, pp. 31–54.

Boehm, C. (1986), 'Capital punishment in tribal Montenegro: Implications for law, biology, and Theory of Social Control', *Ethology and Sociobiology*, **7**, pp. 305–20.

Boehm, C. (1992), 'Segmentary warfare and the management of conflict: Comparison of east African chimpanzees and patrilineal-patrilocal humans', in *Coalitions and Alliances in Humans and Other Animals*, ed. A. H. Harcourt and F. B. M. de Waal, (Oxford: Oxford University Press), pp. 137–73.

Boehm, C. (1994), 'Pacifying interventions at Arnhem zoo and Gombe', in *Chimpanzee Cultures*, ed. R.W. Wrangham, W.C. McGrew, F.B.M. de Waal, and P.G. Heltne (Cambridge, MA: Harvard University Press), pp. 211–26.

Boehm, C. (2000), 'Conflict and the evolution of social control', *Journal of Consciousness Studies*, **7** (1–2), pp. 79–101.

Boesch, C. and Boesch, H. (1989), 'Hunting behaviour in wild chimpanzees in the Tai National Park', *American Journal of Physical Anthropology*, **78**, pp. 547–73.

Boyd, R. and Richerson, P.J. (1985), *Culture and the Evolutionary Process* (Chicago: University of Chicago).

Boyd, R. and Richerson, P.J. (1989), 'The evolution of indirect reciprocity', *Social Networks*, **11**, pp. 213–36.

Boyd, R. and Richerson, P.J. (1992), 'Punishment allows the evolution of cooperation (or anything else) in sizable groups', *Ethology and Sociobiology*, **13**, pp. 171–95.

Carpenter, C.R. (1942) 'Sexual behaviour of free-ranging rhesus monkeys, *Macaca mulatta*, 1: Specimens, procedures, and behavioural characteristics of oestrus', *Journal of Comparative Psychology*, **33**, pp. 113–42.

Castles, D.L., and Whiten, A. (1998), 'Post-conflict behaviour of wild olive baboons. I. Reconciliation, redirection and consolation', *Ethology*, **104**, pp. 126–47.

Cheney, D., Seyfarth, R. (1986), 'The Recognition of social alliances in vervet monkeys', *Animal Behaviour*, **34**, pp. 350–70.

Clutton-Brock, T.H. and. Parker, G.A. (1995), 'Punishment in animal societies', *Nature*, **373**, pp. 209–15.

Cords, M. (1988), 'Reconciliation of aggressive conflicts by immature long-tailed macaques', *Animal Behaviour*, **36**, pp. 1124–35.

Cords, M. and Thurnheer, S. (1993), 'Reconciling with valuable partners by long-tailed macaques', *Ethology*, **93**, pp. 315–25.

Cronk, L. (1994), 'Evolutionary theories of morality and the manipulative use of signals', *Zygon*, **29**, pp. 81–101.

Darwin, C. (1965 [1872]), *The Expression of Emotion in Man and Animals* (Chicago: University of Chicago Press).

Darwin, C. (1982 [1871]), *The Descent of Man, and Selection in Relation to Sex* (Princeton: Princeton University Press).

Dawkins, R. (1976), *The Selfish Gene* (Oxford: Oxford University Press).

Dawkins, R. (1997), 'Interview', *Human Ethology Bulletin*, **12**, (1).

Dennett, D.C. (1995), *Darwin's Dangerous Idea: Evolution and the Meaning of Life* (New York: Simon and Schuster).

Edwards, S. and Snowdon, C. (1980), 'Social behaviour of captive, group-living orang-utans', *International Journal of Primatology*, **1**, pp. 39–62.

Fedigan, L.M. and Fedigan, L. (1977), 'The social development of a handicapped infant in a free-living troop of Japanese monkeys', in *Primate Bio-social Development: Biological, Social and Ecological Determinants*, ed. S. Chevalier-Skolnikoff and R.E. Poirier, (New York: Garland), pp. 205–22.

Fox, G. (1984), 'Food transfer in gibbons', in *The Lesser Apes*, ed. H. Preuschoft, D.J. Chivers, W.Y. Brockelman, and N. Creel, (Edinburgh: Edinburg University Press), pp. 32–32.

Fragaszy, D.M., Feurerstein, J.M., and Mitra, D. (1997a), 'Transfers of food from adult infants in tuffed capuchins (*Cebus apella*)', *Journal of Comparative Psychology*, **111**, pp. 194–200.

Frank, R.H. (1988), *Passions Within Reason: The Strategic Role of the Emotions* (New York: Norton).

Frank, R. (1992), 'Emotion and the costs of altruism', in *The Sense of Justice: Biological Foundations of Law*, ed. R.D. Masters and M. Gruter, (Newbury, Calif.: Sage Publications), pp. 46–67.

Goodall, J. (1963), 'My Life Among Wild Chimpanzees', *National Geographic*, **124**, pp. 272–308.

Goodall, J. (1971), *In the Shadow of Man* (Boston: Houghton Mifflin).

Goodall, J. (1986), *The Chimpanzees of Gombe: Patterns of Behaviour* (Cambridge, Mass.: Belknap Press, Harvard University Press).

Gouzoules, S., Gouzoules, H., and Marler, P. (1984), 'Rhesus monkey (*Macaca mulatta*) screams: representational signaling in the recruitment of agonistic aid?' *Animal Behaviour*, **32**, pp. 182–93.

Gruter, M. (1992), 'An ethological perspective on law and biology',in *The Sense of Justice: Biological Foundations of Law*, ed. R.D. Masters and. M. Gruter, (Newbury Park, Calif.: Sage Publications), pp. 95–105.

Hall, K.R.L. (1964), 'Aggression in monkey and ape societies', in *The Natural History of Aggression*, ed. J. Carthy and F. Ebling, (London: Academic Press), pp. 51–64.

Harcourt, A.H. and de Waal, F.B.M. (eds.) (1992), *Coalitions and Alliances in Humans and Other Animals* (Oxford: Oxford University Press).

Hardin, G. (1983), 'Is violence natural?', *Zygon*, **18**, pp. 405–13.

Hatfield, E., Cacioppo, J.T., and Rapson, R.L. (1993), 'Emotional contagion', *Current Directions in Psychological Science*, **2**, pp. 96–9.

Hawkes, K. (1990), 'Showing off: Tests of an hypothesis about men's foraging goals', *Ethology and Sociobiology*, **12**, pp. 29–54.

Hayaki, H. (1985), 'Social play of juvenile and adolescent chimps in the Mahale Mountains National Park, Tanzania', *Primates*, **26**, pp. 343–60.

Hemelrijk, C.K. (1994), 'Support for being groomed in longtailed macaques, *Macaca fasicularis*', *Animal Behaviour*, **48**, pp. 479–81.

Henrich, J., and Boyd, R. (1998), 'The evolution of conformist transmission and the emergence of between-group differences', *Evolution and Human Behaviour*, **19**, (4) pp. 215–41.

Heyes, C.M. and Commentators (1998), 'Theory of mind in non-human primates', *Behavioural and Brain Sciences*, **21**, pp. 101–48.

Hobbes, T. (1991 [1651]), *Leviathan* (Cambridge: Cambridge University Press).

Hohmann, G. and Fruth, B. (1993), 'Field observations on meat sharing among bonobos (*Pan paniscus*)', *Folia Primatologica*, **60**, pp. 225–9.

Hume, D. (1978 [1739]), *A Treatise of Human Nature* (Oxford: Oxford University Press).

Huxley, T.H. (1888), 'Struggle for existence and its bearing upon man', *Nineteenth Century*, Feb, 1888.

Huxley, T.H. (1989 [1894]), *Evolution and Ethics* (Princeton: Princeton University Press).

Jeannotte, L.A. (1996), *Play-signaling in juvenile chimpanzees in relationship to play intensity and social environment*, Unpublished Master's Thesis (Atlanta, Ga: Emory University).

Judge, P.G. (1991), 'Dyadic and triadic reconciliation in pigtail macaques (*Macaca nemestrina)*', *American Journal of Primatology*, **23**, pp. 225–37.

Kano, T. (1980), 'Social behaviour of wild pygmy chimpanzees (*Pan paniscus*) of Wamba: A preliminary report', *Journal of Human Evolution*, **9**, pp. 243–60.

Kant, I. (1947 [1785]), 'Groundwork for the metaphysics of morals', *The Moral Law*, (London: Hutchinson).

Kappeler, P.M. (1993), 'Reconciliation and post-conflict behaviour in ringtailed lemurs, *Lemur catta*, and redfronted lemurs, *Eulemur fulvus rufus*', *Animal Behaviour*, **45**, pp. 901–15.

Kappeler, P.M., and van Schaik, C.P. (1992), 'Methodological and evolutionary aspects of reconciliation among primates', *Ethology*, **92**, pp. 51–69.

Killen, M. and Nucci, L.P. (1995), 'Morality, autonomy and social conflict', in *Morality in Everyday Life: Developmental Perspectives*, ed. M. Killen and D. Hart, (Cambridge: Cambridge University Press), pp. 52–86.

Killen, M. and de Waal, F.B.M. (in press), 'The evolution and development of morality', in *Natural Conflict Resolution*, ed. F. Aureli and F.B.M. de Waal, (Berkeley: University of California Press).

Kortlandt, J. (1962) 'Chimpanzees in the wild', *Scientific American*, **206**, pp. 128–39.

Kortlandt, J. (1972) *New Perspectives on Ape and Human Evolution*, (Amsterdam: Stichting voor Psychobiologie).

Kropotkin, P. (1972 [1902]) *Mutual Aid: A Factor of Evolution*, (New York: New York University Press).

Kummer, H. (1980), 'Analogs of morality among non-human primates', in *Morality as a Biological Phenomenon*, ed. G.S. Stent, (Berkeley and Los Angeles: University of California Press), pp. 31–49.

Kummer, H. (1991), 'Evolutionary transformations of possessive behaviour', *Journal of Social Behaviour and Personality*, **6**, pp. 75–83.

Kummer, H. and M. Cords (1991), 'Cues of ownership in long-tailed macaques, *Macaca fascicularis*', *Animal Behaviour*, **42**, pp. 529–49.

Kuroda, S. (1984), 'Interaction over food among pygmy chimpanzees', in The *Pygmy Chimpanzee,* ed. R. Susman, (New York: Plenum), pp. 301–24.

Kuroda, S., Suzuki, S., and Nishihara, T. (1996), 'Preliminary report on predatory behaviour and meat sharing in tschego chimpanzees (*Pan troglodytes troglodytes*) in the Ndoki Forest, northern Congo', *Primates*, **37**, pp. 253–59.

Lindburg, D.G. (1973) 'Grooming as a social regulator of social interactions in rhesus monkeys', in *Behavioural Regulators of Behaviour in Primates*, ed. C. Carpenter, (Lewisburg: Bucknell University Press), pp. 85–105.

Mendoza, S.P. and Barchas, P.R. (1983), 'Behavioural processes leading to linear hierarchies following group formation in rhesus monkeys', *Journal of Human Evolution*, **12**, pp. 185–92.

Midgley, M. (1991), 'The origin of ethics', in *A Companion Guide to Ethics*, ed. P. Singer, (Oxford: Blackwell Reference), pp. 1–13.

Moore, J. (1984), 'The evolution of reciprocal sharing', *Ethology and Sociobiology*, **5**, pp. 5–14.

Nishida, T. (1970), 'Social behavior and relationship among chimpanzees of the Mahale Mountains', *Primates*, **11**, pp. 47–87.

Nishida, T. (1994), 'Review of recent findings on Mahale chimpanzees', in Chimpanzee Cultures, ed. R. Wrangham, W.C. McGrew, F.B.M. de Waal and P.G. Heltne (Cambridge, MA: Harvard University Press).

Nishida, T., and Turner, L.A. (1996), 'Food transfer between mother and infant chimpanzees of the Mahale Mountains National Park, Tanzania', *International Journal of Primatology*, **17**, pp. 947–68.

Nishida, T., Hasegawa, T., Hayaki, H., Takahata, Y., Uehara, S. (1992), 'Meat-sharing as a coalition strategy by an alpha male chimpanzee?', in *Topics in Primatology, Vo.l. 1, Human Origins*, ed. T. Nishida, W.C. McGrew, P. Maler, F.B.M. de Waal, (Tokyo: University of Tokyo Press) pp. 159–74.

Nissen, H.W. and Crawford, M.P. (1932), 'A preliminary study of food sharing behaviour in young chimpanzees', *Journal of Comparative Psychology*, **22**, pp. 383–419.

Nitecki, M.H., Nitecki, D.V. (1993), *Evolutionary Ethics* (Albany, NY: State University of New York Press).

Perry, S. (1997), 'Male-female social relationships in wild white-faced capuchins (*Cebus capucinus*)', *Behaviour*, **134**, pp. 477–510.

Perry, S. and Rose, L. (1994), 'Begging and food transfer of coati meat by white-faced capuchin monkeys *Cebus capucinus*', *Primates*, **35**, pp. 409–15.

Petit, O., and Thierry, B. (1994), 'Aggressive and peaceful interventions in conflicts in Tonkean macaques', *Animal Behaviour*, **48**, pp. 1427–36.

Preuschoft, S. (1999), 'Are primates behaviourists? Formal dominance, cognition, and free-floating rationales', *Journal of Comparative Psychology*, **113**, pp. 91–5.

Preuschoft, S. and van Schaik, C.P. (in press), 'Dominance and communication: Conflict management in various social settings', in *Natural Conflict Resolution*, ed. F. Aureli and F.B.M. de Waal, (Berkley, Calif.: University of California Press).

Rawls, J. (1971), *A Theory of Justice* (Oxford: Oxford University Press).

Reinhardt, V., Dodsworth, R. and Scanlan, J. (1986), 'Altruistic interference shown by the alpha female of a captive group of rhesus monkeys', *Folia primatologica*, **46**, pp. 44–50.

Ren, R., Yan, K., Su, Y. Gi, H. Liang, B., Bao, W. and de Waal, F.B.M. (1991), 'The reconciliation behavior of golden monkeys (*Rhinopithecus roxellanae*) in small groups', *Primates*, **32**, pp. 321–7.

Rose, L.M. (1997), 'Vertebrate predation and food-sharing in Cebus and Pan', *International Journal of Primatology*, **18**, pp. 727–65.

Rothstein, S. I. and Pierotti., R. (1988), 'Distinctions among reciprocal altruism, kin selection, and cooperation and a model for the initial evolution of beneficent behaviour', *Ethology and Sociobiology*, **9**, pp. 189–209.

Scott, J.P. (1971), *Internalization of Social Norms: A Sociological Theory of Moral Commitment* (Englewood Cliffs, NJ: Prentice-Hall).

Seton, E.T. (1907), *The Natural History of the Ten Commandments* (New York: Scribners).

Sicotte, P. (1995), 'Interpositions in conflicts between males in bimale groups of mountain gorillas', *Folia primatologica*, **65**, pp. 14–24.

Sigg, H. and J. Falett (1985), 'Experiments on respect of possession and property in hamadryas baboons (*Papio hamadryas*)', *Animal Behaviour*, **33**, pp. 978–84.

Silberbauer, G. (1991), 'Ethics in small scale societies', in *A Companion Guide to Ethics*, ed. P. Singer, (Oxford: Blackwell Reference), pp. 14–29.

Silk, J.B. (1992), 'The patterning of intervention among male bonnet macaques: Reciprocity, revenge and loyalty', *Current Anthropology*, **31**, pp. 318–24.

Simon, H.A. (1990), 'A mechanism for social selection and successful altruism', *Science*, **250**, pp. 1665–8.

Smith, A. (1937 [1759]), *A Theory of Moral Sentiments* (New York: Modern Library).

Taylor, C.E. and McGuire, M.T. (1988), 'Reciprocal altruism: Fifteen years later', *Ethology and Sociobiology*, **9**, pp. 67–72.

Teleki, G. (1973), 'Group response to the accidental death of a chimpanzee in Gombe National Park, Tanzania', *Folia primatologica*, **20**, pp. 81–94.

Thierry, B., Demaria, C., Preuschoft, S., and Desportes, C. (1989), 'Structural convergence between the silent bared-teeth display and the relaxed open-mouth display in the Tonkean macaque (*Macaca tonkeana*)', *Folia primatologica*, **52**, pp. 178–84.

Tokuda, K. and Jensen, G. (1969), 'The leader's role in controlling aggressive behaviour in a monkey group', *Primates*, **9**, pp. 319–22.

Trivers, R. (1971), 'The evolution of reciprocal altruism', *Quarterly Review of Biology*, **46**, pp. 35–57.

Uchii, S. (1996), 'Darwin and the evolution of morality', Paper presented at the Nineteeth Century Biology, International Fellows Conference, Centre for Philosophy of Science, University of Pittsburg, Published on internet: www.bun.kyoto-u.ac.jp/~suchii/D.onM.html

Veenema, H.C., Das, M., and Aureli, F. (1994), 'Methodological improvements for the study of reconciliation', *Behavioural Processes*, **31**, pp. 29–37.

Verbeek, P. and de Waal, F.B.M. (1997), 'Postconflict behaviour of captive capuchins in the presence and absence of attractive food', *International Journal of Primatology*, **18**, pp. 703–25.

de Waal, F.B.M. (1982), *Chimpanzee Politics: Power and Sex Among Apes* (London: Jonathon Cape).

de Waal, F.B.M. (1986), 'Integration of dominance and social bonding in primates', *Quarterly Review of Biology*, **61**, pp. 459–79.

de Waal, F.B.M. (1987), 'Tension regulation and nonreproductive functions of sex among captive bonobos *(Pan paniscus)*', *National Geographic Research*, **3**, pp. 318–35.

de Waal, F.B.M. (1989a), 'Dominance "style" and primate social organization' , in *Comparative Socioecology: The Behavioural Ecology of Humans and Other Mammals*, ed. V. Standen and. R.A. Foley (Oxford: Blackwell), pp. 243–64.

de Waal, F.B.M. (1989b), 'Food sharing and reciprocal obligations among chimpanzees', *Journal of Human Evolution*, **18**, pp. 433–59.

de Waal, F.B.M. (1989c), *Peacemaking Among the Primates* (Cambridge, MA: Harvard University Press).

de Waal, F.B.M. (1991), 'The chimpanzee's sense of social regularity and its relation to the human sense of justice', *American Behavioural Scientist*, **34**, pp. 335–49.

de Waal, F.B.M. (1992a), 'Aggression as a well-integrated part of primate social relationships: Critical comments on the Seville Statement on Violence' , in *Aggression and Peacefulness in Humans and Other Primates*, ed. J. Silverberg and J.P. Gray (New York: Oxford University Press), pp. 37–56.

de Waal, F.B.M. (1992b), 'Appeasement, celebration, and food sharing in the two *Pan* species', in *Topics in Primatology, Vol 1 Human Origins* , ed. T. Nishida, W.C. McGrew, P. Marler, F.B.M. de Waal, (Tokyo: Univeristy of Tokyo Press), pp. 37–50.

de Waal, F.B.M. (1993), 'Reconcilation among the primates: A review of empirical evidence and unresolved issues', in *Primate Social Conflict*, ed. W.A. Mason and S.P. Mendoza, (Albany: State University Press), pp. 111–44.

de Waal, F.B.M. (1996a), 'Conflict as Negotiation', in *Great Ape Societies*, ed. W.C. McGrew, L.F. Marchant, and T. Nishid, (Cambridge: Cambridge University Press), pp. 159–72.

de Waal, F.B.M. (1996b), *Good Natured: The Origins of Right and Wrong in Primates and Other Animals* (Cambridge, MA: Harvard University Press).

de Waal, F.B.M. (1997a), 'The chimpanzee's service economy: Food for grooming', *Evolution and Human Behaviour*, **18**, pp. 375–86.

de Waal, F.B.M. (1997b), 'Food transfers through mesh in brown capuchins', *Journal of Comparative Psychology,* **111**, pp. 370–78.

de Waal, F.B.M. and Aureli, F. (1996), 'Reconciliation, consolation, and a possible cognitive difference between macaques and chimpanzees',in *Reaching into Thought: The Minds of the Great Apes,* ed. A.E. Russon, K.A. Bard, and S.T. Parker, (Cambridge: Cambridge University Press), pp. 80–110.

de Waal, F.B.M. and Johanowicz, D.L. (1993), 'Modification of reconciliation behaviour through social experience: An experiment with two macaque species', *Child Development,* **64**, pp. 897–908.

de Waal, F.B.M. and Luttrell, L.M. (1989), 'Toward a comparative socioecology of the genus *Macaca*: Intergroup comparisons of rhesus and stumptail monkeys', *American Journal of Primatology,* **10**, pp. 83–109.

de Waal, F.B.M. and Luttrell, L.M. (1988), 'Mechanisms of social reciprocity in three primate species: Symmetrical relationship characteristics or cognition', *Ethology and Sociobiology,* **9**, pp. 101–18.

de Waal, F.B.M. and Luttrell, L M. (1985), 'The formal hierarchy of rhesus monkeys: An investigation of the bared-teeth display', *American Journal of Primatology,* **9**, pp. 73–85.

de Waal, F.B.M. and Ren, M.R. (1988), 'Comparison of the reconcilation behaviour of stumptail and rhesus macaques', *Ethology,* **78**, pp. 129–42.

de Waal, F.B.M., Uno, H., Luttrell, L.M., Meisner, L.F., and Jeannotte, L.A. (1996), 'Behavioural retardation in a macaque with autosomal trisomy and aging mother', *American Journal on Mental Retardation,* **100**, pp. 378–90.

de Waal, F.B.M.and van Hooff, J.A.R.A.M. (1981), 'Side-directed communication and agonistic interactions in chimpanzees', Behaviour, 77, pp. 164–98.

de Waal, F.B.M. and van Roosmalen, A. (1979), 'Reconciliation and consolation among chimpanzees', *Behavioural Ecology and Sociobiology,* **5**, pp. 55–66.

de Waal, F.B.M. and Yoshihara, D. (1983), 'Reconciliation and re-directed affection in rhesus monkeys', *Behaviour,* **85**, pp. 224–41.

Westermarck, E. (1912), *The Origin and Development of the Moral Ideas* (London: Macmillan).

Wickler, W. (1981 [1971]), *Die Biologie der Zehn Gebote: Warum die Natur für uns Kein Vorbid ist* (Munich: Piper).

Williams, G.C. (1988), 'Reply to comments on "Huxley's evolution and ethics in a sociobiological perspective" ', *Zygon,* **23**, pp. 383–407.

Williams, G.C. (1989), 'A sociobiological expansion of "Evolution and Ethics" ', *Evolution and Ethics,* (Princeton: Princeton University Press), pp. 179–214.

Wilson, D.S. and Sober, E. (1994), 'Reintroducing group selection to the human behavioural sciences', *Behaviour and Brain Sciences,* **17**, pp. 585–654.

Wrangham, R. (1975), *The Behavioural Ecology of Chimpanzees in Gombe National Park, Tanzania.* Unpublished Doctoral Dissertation, (Cambridge: Cambridge University).

Wrangham, R.W. (1979), 'On the evolution of ape social systems', *Social Science Information,* **18**, pp. 335–68.

York, A.D. and Rowell, T.E. (1988), 'Reconciliation following aggression in patas monkeys (*Erythrocebus patas*)', *Animal Behaviour,* **36**, pp. 502–9.

Commentary Discussion of Flack and de Waal's Paper

THE LAW OF PARSIMONY PREVAILS
Missing Premises Allow Any Conclusion

I.S. Bernstein

Flack and de Waal (2000) present evidence for behaviour in non-human primates that functions to share food, terminate fights and reconcile opponents. Consolation and punishment are also suggested. These functions are assumed to be the motivation for the behaviour. Animals indeed have expectations about signal meaning and the likely immediate consequences of their behaviour. This does not mean they understand genetic fitness, peacekeeping or justice, even if these functions are achieved. Instrumental aggression is used to achieve a goal, not to punish wrong doers. More elaborate motivation would indeed require empathy, sympathy, community solutions and morality. Although more parsimonious explanations for the behaviour described are rejected as not necessarily being true, less parsimonious explanations are not necessarily true either, no matter how appealing.

In 1880, L.W. Lauder meticulously amassed evidence of the influence of mind on disease in animals. He concluded that, based on their behaviour, animals understood good and evil and recognized criminal behaviour in themselves and others. They responded with shame for their own transgressions and with outrage as they punished the crimes of others.

Despite Tinbergen's (1974) careful separation of the four *why* questions in the study of behaviour, we still struggle with the temptation to equate motivation, an unobservable proximal cause, with function. Since natural selection favours individuals that act in ways that achieve particular functional consequences, individuals are said to engage in these activities in order to achieve the consequences. This can erroneously be construed to be the motivation for their behaviour. It is true that a mother that cares for her young may improve her genetic fitness. Mothers do respond to the cries of their young, but not because of a desire to improve their own genetic fitness and not because they know that the infant is distressed and want to alleviate its suffering. Proximal causes and function are often quite distinct.

To the frustration of those of us who study animal behaviour, motivation is a private internal state. Extreme behaviourists tried to equate it with hours of deprivation; extreme cognitivists took a subjective anthropomorphic, or egomorphic, stance. Whereas physiologically inclined investigators search for organic measures of motivation, the rest of us struggle in the area between the extremes. Even when language is available, it is extraordinarily difficult to learn what the motivation of another truly is; we only know what they say it is.

The study of morality must begin by defining terms and then indicating what measures would be required to demonstrate that the terms properly applied to a situation or subject. How shall we define and measure: sympathy, community concern and concerted efforts by community members to find shared solutions to social conflicts?

Socially living animals must coordinate their activities. Members of a social group would not long be social if each travelled where and when it pleased with no concern for the whereabouts of others. Social facilitation (docility?) means group members coordinate travel, feeding, drinking, resting and social interactions lest they be forced to leave the group to seek food, water or resting sites when they individually desire to do so. Socially living animals respond jointly to environmental challenges including predators, other groups and even disturbances within their own group. As de Waal (1989) has previously written, social living provides opportunities for conflicts, competition and agonistic encounters, but social mechanisms exist to counter the disruptive effects of conflicts within the group. Neither social facilitation nor peacemaking skills necessarily require a knowledge of group norms, empathy or 'mind-reading'. All social animals must coordinate activities and counteract the effects of competition and conflicts with group members.

Flack and de Waal indicate that many primates show behaviour that functions reciprocally, results in sharing of resources, reconciles antagonists and consoles victims. They believe that to achieve these functions, primates must be capable of empathy, sympathy and community concern. They argue that reciprocity is evidence of a sense of justice and, perhaps, even an internalization of social norms which, I agree, would be fundamental to moral systems. Proof of the existence of these traits and abilities is an entirely different matter. Alexander is cited as stating that reciprocity requires a consensual sense of right and wrong, but I see no reason to invoke this to explain why two individuals groom one another, seek each other out and enlist and aid one another in response to challenges from the physical and social environment. Members of a matriline often do all of these things but neither because of a sense of justice nor a knowledge of genetic relatedness. Socially living primates form social attachments to group members in general and certain individuals in particular. Individual bonds are readily demonstrated. When infants are separated from their mothers, they vocalize loudly, become hyperactive, show disturbance behaviour and physiological responses associated with stress. Separation of adult squirrel monkey females, heterosexual pairs of titi monkeys and indeed unrelated cage-mates of a variety of species produces similar responses. Socially living primates establish and maintain social bonds with others and use these relationships to solve environmental problems. Kummer (1971) stated that primates have few ecological specializations other than the way that they behave in groups.

Finding food is fundamental to survival; any sign of food sharing may, therefore, seem altruistic. Of course we may expect parents to feed their young, as many birds do, but non-human primates rarely actively food share. In the case of the capuchins described: male capuchins tolerated theft better than females, good friends were better tolerated, good friends groomed one another and animals did not readily share with individuals that they were likely to fight with. This tells us that feeding animals sometimes seek the proximity of a favoured partner and tolerate theft of the food they carry with them. This is not the same as *fine tuned communication about intentions and desires*. What measures do we have of status (in what sense?) being enhanced or of *popularity* being improved by food sharing? Where is the testable proximate account of motivation we were promised? None of the data presented require mental notes or elaborate bookkeeping of favours given and received. None of this even approaches the much more extensive and even active food sharing seen in social carnivores, yet few have suggested that social carnivores do mental bookkeeping, or are moral creatures.

Animals may be described as having expectations. A signal by one animal may reliably indicate what it is likely to do next. Animals also learn about the consequences of their own behaviour. If they do behaviour A, they expect consequence X and, if they do behaviour B, they expect consequence Y. The consequence may be due to the behaviour of a social partner in response to their behaviour, or a consequence of their action on the physical environment, such as moving a block of wood to uncover a food well. This has nothing to do with how the other animal, or the block of wood, *should* behave in a moral sense.

When the usual consequences to a behaviour do not follow, an individual may be elated or frustrated. When frustrated, aggression can be used as an instrumental act to achieve a goal. If a subordinate, who usually defers to an approach, brazenly remains and feeds, aggression against the subordinate can be used to displace it and obtain the food. This is not *moralistic aggression* and, if the aggression only occurs until the subordinate yields, it is not *punishment* for what has already occurred but rather aggression to achieve a goal.

Reconciliation and control role behaviour are functionally defined. We have to guess at the actors' motivations. A control animal might be trying to restore peace, or might be displaying a rudimentary sense of justice. On the other hand it may be responding to any aggressive signal as one potentially directed to itself. An infant may respond with distress to aggressive signals for fear of its own safety rather than empathizing with the plight of the victim or expressing community concern. Infants are terribly egocentric and any aggressive signal might lead to distressed caregivers and possible personal discomfort. This *killjoy* explanation is hardly congruent with recognition of the value of harmonious coexistence to achieve shared interests.

Is there evidence of punishment of non-punishers as a causal chain? Flack and de Waal admit that the evidence is scant or *fragmented* (read anecdotal?). They claim data to support the existence of sympathy but seem rather to rely on their belief that more accurate explanations need not be more parsimonious. When animals play, the vigour of their behaviour is often matched to the opponent regardless of absolute size or strength. Does this demonstrate social norms? While it may *seem* that the goal of some behaviour is to reassure, we need evidence that this is indeed the motivation as well as the functional consequence. Consolation, we are told, has only been demonstrated in great apes (chimpanzees) but in the very next paragraph Flack and de Waal conclude that it is present in monkeys as well (pp. 18–19, above).

Of course it is possible that animals have a sense of justice and morality. No one ever proved that Lauder was wrong in 1880. In science, however, one must present evidence that a certain relationship is true and that no plausible alternative is possible. Lauder failed to convince us that his interpretation was the only reasonable explanation for the evidence he presented. Flack and de Waal may well be correct that the basis of human morality may be found in the behaviour of those animals most similar to ourselves. Evolutionary theory and biological continuity support such a position. Surely if morality has a biological basis, its rudiments must be present in the behaviour of non-human primates. Demonstrating the existence of these rudiments is quite another matter.

It may be difficult, or even impossible, to conclusively demonstrate a sense of morality in an animal without language. Group norms, beliefs and values perhaps can only be accessed using questionnaires and language. If this is so, morality in animals may lie outside of the realm of measurement techniques available to science and we can happily debate the merits of believing that animals are or are not moral.

References

Flack J. and de Waal, F.B.M. (2000), '"Any Animal Whatever": Darwinian building blocks of morality in monkeys and apes,' *Journal of Consciousness Studies*, **7** (1–2), pp. 1–29.
Kummer, H. (1971), *Primate Societies: Group techniques of ecological adaptation* (Chicago: Aldine-Atherton).
Lauder, W. (1880), 'Mind in the lower animals', *Health and Disease, Volume II, Mind in Disease* (New York: D. Appleton and Company), p. 571.
Tinbergen, N. (1974), *The Study of Instinct* (New York: Oxford University Press).
de Waal, F.B.M. (1989), *Peacemaking Among Primates* (Cambridge, MA: Harvard University Press).

INTENDING AND PERCEIVING
Two Forgotten Components of Social Norms

Josep Call

Flack and de Waal (2000) argue that reciprocity, revenge, and moralistic aggression are important components of the social norms that exist in some non-human primates. These and other phenomena (i.e., empathy) are seen as the evolutionary building blocks of human morality. Although focussing on these phenomena is a good starting point for studying the question of morality in non-human animals, they only provide a partial answer. Two other issues deserve careful attention: perception of intentions, and the distinction between using and perceiving social norms. First, perception of intention is particularly important because it modulates whether retribution (either positive or negative) is justified. There is some preliminary evidence that may indicate that some primates are sensitive to the behavioural intentions of others. Second, the evidence regarding use of social norms does not necessarily imply that individuals also perceive them (i.e., explicitly know that there are rules that govern their social exchanges). This distinction seems particularly important in any comparative analysis of morality that includes humans. Currently, it is unclear whether non-human animals are capable of perceiving social norms. Future studies should devote more attention to these issues and some possible ways to investigate them are indicated.

If I invite you for coffee and, while I am handing you a cup, I look into your eyes and very slowly pour the coffee onto your lap, you will probably think that I am a malicious person. On the other hand, if when I am handing you a cup, an earthquake hits the city and, despite my best efforts, I cannot help but spill the coffee on your lap, you will probably not think I am a bad person. Note that the end result in both cases is the same: hot coffee on your lap, but the interpretation that we make of them is very different. While my actions are clearly blameworthy in the first case, I should not be blamed for the spillage in the second case. The critical difference between them lies in my intention, or better still, on your perception of the intention behind my actions. As Flack and de Waal (2000) point out in their well-articulated paper, reciprocity and revenge are a part of the system of social norms that exist in some non-human primates. Moreover, some non-human primates even seem to engage in things like moralistic aggression directed toward those who violate certain social norms. In this commentary, I argue that, although reciprocity, revenge, and moralistic aggression are good starting points for studying morality in non-human animals, they are only part of the story. I would like to call attention to two other topics that constitute important components of social norms and morality in humans: perception of intentions and the distinction between using and perceiving social norms. I am hoping that this commentary will help stimulate research in these two largely neglected areas.

Perception of motive and intention is at the core of what humans consider right or wrong. Our laws, social norms, and even our games are grounded on them. For example, the difference between murder and manslaughter resides in the intention to kill. Similarly, whether a defender is punished with a penalty kick for handling the ball inside the box in a football match is based on whether he or she did so with the intention of intercepting the ball's trajectory. There are many more examples that highlight the importance of the perception of intention and motive in the way we judge others' actions.

One issue that makes understanding of motive particularly important for the question of morality is that it may modulate whether retribution (either positive or negative) is justified. For instance, pouring coffee on you because you wrecked my car and are unwilling to pay for the repairs may be seen not as a malicious act but simply as revenge and reciprocity. Translating this into a non-human primate scenario, primate mothers may react differentially to actions directed towards their offspring depending on the perception of motive by the perpetrator (see Savage-Rumbaugh and McDonald, 1988, for two suggestive anecdotes).

Flack and de Waal's omission of intention and motives in their review of non-human morality is partly understandable due to the very few studies that have tackled this issue in non-human animals (see Tomasello and Call, 1997, for a review). To complicate things further, the meagre evidence that is currently available is mixed. While some studies support understanding of intentions in chimpanzees (Premack and Woodruff, 1978; Povinelli, 1991; Call and Tomasello, 1998), others have failed to provide any positive results (Povinelli et al., 1998) or have not ruled out alternative explanations (Savage-Rumbaugh et al., 1978; Tomasello and Call, 1997). This mixed bag of results, however, should not discourage researchers from looking carefully into this issue. In a recent study, Call and Tomasello (1998) found that orang-utans, chimpanzees, and two-year-old children were able to distinguish the intentional from the accidental actions of a human experimenter. In this study, subjects witnessed a human indicating the location of food in one of three boxes by placing a marker on top of the baited box. In each trial, subjects observed the human experimenter both deliberately placing the marker on a box (intentional action) to indicate the correct food location and accidentally (i.e., due to clumsiness) dropping the marker onto an incorrect box (accidental action), in counterbalanced order. Thus, in any given trial the experimenter's actions resulted in two marked boxes (one intentionally and one accidentally) and subjects had to decide which box they wanted to select. If subjects understood something about the intentions of the experimenter, they should disregard the accidental marking, and select the box that was intentionally indicated by the experimenter. All three species preferred the box that was intentionally marked. Although these results are suggestive of an understanding of intention, we should remain cautious at this point until more evidence accumulates. It is very likely that subjects in this study did not have a full-fledged (i.e., human adult-like) understanding of intention, but at least it points to the possibility that apes, like young children, have some level of understanding of intention. One possibility is that both young children and apes understand intention at a behavioural level, not at a mental level. That is, they are capable of perceiving intention in the actions of others (Searle, 1983), but do not necessarily understand intention as a mental construct (see Call and Tomasello, 1998, for a more detailed discussion). Future studies will be needed to provide a more solid answer to the question of understanding of intention in non-human animals, and of the levels of intention to which different species are sensitive.

A second issue that I would like to address in this paper is the distinction between using social norms and perceiving them (i.e., explicitly knowing that there are rules that govern social exchanges). Flack and de Waal (2000) have presented some evidence suggesting that non-human primates possess and use social norms. This is supported, for instance, by the ability of chimpanzees to engage in reciprocity and the ability of male bonnet macaques to use revenge. Further support for their position is provided by episodes of moralistic aggression in chimpanzees following the violation of norms governing food sharing. However, I argue that this evidence for the use of social norms does not necessarily imply that individuals also perceive and understand those norms. Several studies have shown that there is a dissociation between use and comprehension in some domains such as tool use and gestural communication both for monkeys and apes (Visalberghi and Limongelli, 1996; Hess et al., 1993; Limongelli et al., 1995; Call and Tomasello, 1994). These studies show that although primates are proficient users of tools or gestures, they do not seem to fully comprehend why or how those behaviours work. In others words, being able to carry out some procedure, for instance, using a tool of the right shape to obtain a reward, does not necessarily translate into an understanding of why only tools of a certain shape are appropriate for solving a particular task. Similarly, it may be argued that using social norms does not necessarily translate into perceiving and understanding those norms. The distinction between using and perceiving social norms is, in my opinion, particularly important if at some point we want to compare and/or contrast the non-human and the human systems of morality. In human adults, moral systems are based on our ability to agree upon a set of shared rules and values. However, to be able to so agree, individuals first have to realize that there is something to be shared with others. In this way, a first step in the construction of explicitly shared social rules is based on the perception that such social rules exist. Currently, there is no conclusive evidence indicating that non-human animals are capable of fully perceiving social norms. It is true that some studies have suggested that primates have a sophisticated knowledge of their social environment, particularly in regard to their perception of third party relationships. For instance, Cheney and Seyfarth's (1980, see also Cheney and Seyfarth, 1990) playback experiments revealed that vervet monkeys look at the mother whose infant is screaming, thus suggesting that individuals perceive that that particular mother has some special relationship with that particular infant. Similarly, Dasser (1988) found that longtail macaques are able to discriminate pictures of mother–infant pairs from unrelated adult–infant pairs. Furthermore, it is also known from the extensive literature on conditional discrimination and reversal learning that primates are capable of acquiring rules to respond to sets of stimuli (see Tomasello and Call, 1997, for a review). On some occasions, these rules are based on perceiving relationships (e.g., same–different) between pairs of stimuli (Premack, 1983; Burdyn and Thomas, 1984), not mere perceptual similarity between a single pair of stimuli. However, these abilities of perceiving social relationships and creating rules still fall short of supporting the perception of social rules in non-human primates.

In the end, to resolve the issue of whether non-human primates, or other animals for that matter, perceive the social rules that govern their behaviour, it will be necessary to directly investigate this issue. Perhaps one way to begin this research program would be to study how bystanders react to aggressive incidents between third parties depending on the context in which these aggressive incidents took place. For instance, imagine two hypothetical scenarios based on de Waal's (1989) study on food sharing in captive chimpanzees. In the first scenario, a subadult female is eating a big piece of cabbage and repeatedly refuses an adult female's numerous requests for food despite the adult's obvious signals of distress (e.g., fear grimace). On a later occasion, the subadult is empty-handed and approaches the adult who is eating a piece of cabbage. After the subadult begs insistently for several minutes without much success, the adult bites the subadult's hand. The subadult screams and attempts to recruit other group members to join her against the aggressor. In the second scenario, the subadult is eating a big piece of cabbage and, upon request, she willingly shares it with the adult. On a later occasion, the subadult is empty-handed and approaches the adult who is eating a piece of cabbage. After the subadult begs insistently for several minutes, the adult bites the subadult who screams and tries to recruit other chimpanzees against her aggressor. If a bystander witnessed both scenarios and ignored the subadult's cry for help in the first case but rushed to her aid in the second, one possible interpretation is that the bystander was able to perceive that a social rule involving food sharing had been breached. That is, the bystander knows that sharing food should be paid back on later occasions, and that failure to pay back results in deserved punishment. Although other interpretations of the bystander's behaviour are certainly possible (e.g., that bystanders are less likely to react in situations in which one of the contenders has shown distress), it is still necessary to find out whether chimpanzees (and other primates) are capable of making such subtle distinctions. If indeed they are capable of making those distinctions, future studies will have to investigate the different alternative explanations for the bystander's reactions. In this commentary I have highlighted two additional components that I think are important for investigating the question of morality in animals from a comparative perspective: perception of intentions and the distinction between using and perceiving social norms. Flack and de Waal (2000) have pointed out other important components of moral systems such as reciprocity and moralistic aggression. Future studies should attempt to integrate both sets of components to obtain a more balanced picture of the differences and similarities between the moral systems in human and non-human animals.

References

Burdyn, L.E. and Thomas, R.K. (1984), 'Conditional discrimination with conceptual simultaneous and successive cues in the squirrel monkey (Saimiri sciureus)', *Journal of Comparative Psychology,* **98**, pp. 405–13.

Call, J. and Tomasello, M. (1994), 'Production and comprehension of referential pointing by orang-utans (Pongo pygmaeus)', *Journal of Comparative Psychology,* **108**, pp. 307–17.

Call, J. and Tomasello, M. (1998), 'Distinguishing intentional from accidental actions in orang-utans (Pongo pygmaeus), chimpanzees (Pan troglodytes), and human children (Homo sapiens)', *Journal of Comparative Psychology,* **112**, pp. 192–206.

Cheney, D.L. and Seyfarth, R.M. (1980), 'Vocal recognition in free-ranging vervet monkeys' *Animal Behaviour,* **28**, pp. 362–67.

Cheney, D.L. and Seyfarth, R.M. (1990), *How Monkeys See the World* (Chicago, IL: The University of Chicago Press).

Dasser, V. (1988), 'Mapping social concepts in monkeys', in *Machiavellian Intelligence. Social Expertise and the Evolution of Intellect in Monkeys, Apes, and Humans* , ed. R.W. Byrne and A. Whiten (New York: Oxford University Press).

Flack J. and de Waal, F.B.M. (2000), '"Any Animal Whatever": Darwinian building blocks of morality in monkeys and apes,' *Journal of Consciousness Studies*, 7 (1–2), pp. 1–29.

Hess, J., Novak, M.A. and Povinelli, D.J. (1993), 'Natural pointing in a rhesus monkey, but no evidence of empathy', *Animal Behaviour*, 46, pp. 1023–5.

Limongelli, L., Boysen, S.T. and Visalberghi, E. (1995), 'Comprehension of cause-effect relations in a tool-using task by chimpanzees (Pan troglodytes)', *Journal of Comparative Psychology*, 109, pp. 18–26.

Povinelli, D.J. (1991), *Social Intelligence in Monkeys and Apes*. Unpublished doctoral dissertation, Yale University, New Haven, CT, USA.

Povinelli, D.J., Perilloux, H.K., Reaux, J.E. and Bierschwale, D.T. (1998), 'Young and juvenile chimpanzees' (Pan troglodytes) reactions to intentional versus accidental and inadvertent actions', *Behavioural Processes*, 42, pp. 205–18.

Premack, D. (1983), 'The codes of man and beasts', *The behavioural and Brain Sciences*, 6, pp. 125–67.

Premack, D. and Woodruff, G. (1978), 'Does the chimpanzee have a theory of mind?' *The behavioural and Brain Sciences*, 4, pp. 515–26.

Savage-Rumbaugh S. and McDonald, K. (1988), 'Deception and social manipulation in symbol-using apes', in *Machiavellian Intelligence. Social Expertise and the Evolution of Intellect in Monkeys, Apes, and Humans* , ed. R.W. Byrne and A. Whiten, (New York: Oxford University Press).

Searle, J. (1983), *Intentionality* (Cambridge: Cambridge University Press).

Tomasello, M. and Call, J. (1997), *Primate Cognition* (New York: Oxford University Press).

Visalberghi, E. and Limongelli, L. (1996), 'Acting and understanding: Tool use revisited through the minds of capuchin monkeys', in *Reaching into Thought: The Minds of the Great Apes*, ed. A.E. Russon, K.A. Bard and S.T. Parker, (Cambridge: Cambridge University Press).

de Waal, F.B.M. (1989), 'Food sharing and reciprocal obligations among chimpanzees', *Journal of Human Evolution*, 18, pp. 433–59.

BUILDING BLOCKS OF LEGAL BEHAVIOUR
The Evolution of Law

Margaret Gruter and Monika Gruter Morhenn

Flack and de Waal's exploration of basic building blocks of moral systems among non-human primates indicates that human legal systems and legal behaviour are not purely the product of the environment. An examination of some of the ways in which capacities for reciprocity, retributive behaviours, moralistic aggression, dispute resolution, sympathy, and empathy play roles in contemporary law and legal behaviour shows that these capacities are both ubiquitous and facilitative of legal systems. No attempt is made to reduce all legal systems or legal behaviour to these building block predispositions. However, the creation of legal systems and the willingness and ability to make and abide by laws emerged from certain human predispositions — the 'basic building blocks'.

'The law can ask no better justification than the deepest instincts of man.'

Oliver Wendell Holmes

Flack and de Waal's paper 'Any Animal Whatever: Darwinian Building Blocks of Morality in Monkeys and Apes' (2000) is a welcome contribution to the growing literature on the evolution of law. Flack and de Waal's documentation of behaviours among non-human primates provides great insight into the understanding that legal systems and legal behaviour among humans emerged from certain basic building block behaviours. 'Legal behaviour' as used herein refers to an individual's willingness and ability to adapt his or her behaviour to the law.[1] As the authors explain, capacities for reciprocity, revenge, retaliation, moralistic aggression, dispute resolution, sympathy, and empathy form the raw materials of social regularity and moral systems among non-human primates; for it is these basic building blocks that enable non-human primates to resolve and prevent conflicts within their groups (where primates are able to achieve long term benefits of greater value than the benefits derived from straightforward competition (Trivers, 1971)). By exploring the behaviour in non-human primates which is similar to that of humans, we may conclude that humans have predispositions for this behaviour.

Flack and de Waal show that there are basic behavioural building blocks which exist because of the need for primates to resolve and prevent conflicts within their groups, dispelling long-postulated theories maintaining that the origins of legal systems have no basis in human nature and are, instead, purely 'man-made', or environmentally influenced. Indeed, in the last century, the prevailing view among social scientists as well as many legal theorists has been that legal behaviour and social norms are entirely learned. While the all-nurture view of the origins of human legal behaviour should invoke scepticism given the virtually universal existence of legal systems and legal behaviour across cultures, some observers and even biologists still maintain that legal systems and legal behaviour are purely human inventions. (e.g. Dawkins, 1976; 1997). Flack and de Waal's demonstration of the existence of basic building blocks of legal behaviour gives welcome insight to the otherwise troubling question of why humans create legal systems and engage in legal behaviour.

The remainder of this comment focuses on how the 'essential building blocks' of moral systems among non-human primates play ubiquitous roles in human legal behaviour even in today's world of often exhaustingly complex laws. Two principles deserve emphasis from the outset. First, behaviour is central to law; for the degree to which any law can be effective depends on the willingness and ability of individuals to adapt their behaviour to the law. Second, it should be emphasized that in no way should this be interpreted to be deterministic.[2]

First, the role of calculated reciprocity. As Flack and de Waal point out, a system of calculated reciprocity requires that participants possess capacities for memory, a sense of consistency across time, and a sense of regularity or expectation (see also Alexander, 1987). De Waal has demonstrated the capacity for calculated reciprocity, as opposed to symmetry based reciprocity, in chimpanzees and capuchin monkeys. (de Waal and Luttrell, 1988; de Waal, 1997). This indication — that certain non-human primates have expectations about how they and others should behave — appears to be at the very root of law: law codifies expectations about how members of a group should behave. Expectations are thus inherent in the law.[3]

---

[1] For a more detailed discussion of legal behaviour see Gruter (1992); Hoebel (1972).

[2] For a more detailed discussion of the illogical 'Naturalistic Fallacy' committed when an observer mistakenly concludes that because natural selection endows humans with a particular predisposition, society should permit it, see Elliott (1997); Jones (1994).

[3] The existence of a system of expectations is different, however, from a determination of what specific expectations an individual might have, or which a group might select. A relevant analysis in this context appears in Gruter (1992), discussing the capacity or mechanism for the 'sense of justice'. See also Gruter (1991).

For example, that calculated reciprocity serves as a ground stone of contract law seems unmistakable. Indeed, contracts are a chief method by which humans make explicit statements about their expectations about their and others' behaviour. This is true of the broadest of contracts — the social contract — and the most particularized contracts, such as technology licensing agreements. Intuitively, there must be mechanisms by which to enforce the expectations enunciated in and agreed to in contracts.

Unsurprisingly, we see retributive mechanisms among non-human primates (Flack and de Waal, 2000). Revenge and retaliation behaviour undergirds the system of calculated reciprocity, and provides further evidence that primates indeed have expectations concerning their and others' behaviour. So too, humans have developed highly specified systems of retribution to enforce our expectations of one another.

While complicated contracts such as technology licensing agreements — you can use X if you pay me Y — are obviously far more complex than the systems of calculated reciprocity among certain non-human primates, the predisposition to have and enforce certain expectations about behaviour is significant to legal theory nonetheless. One might say that natural selection has given us the raw material from which to build laws. At the same time, however, the law must also cope with other innate tendencies, such as, *inter alia*, deception and self-deception. In this way, the complexity of law as we presently know it is both facilitated by and also necessitated by our innate predispositions.[4] Add to this pot-pourri the enormous influence of a constantly changing environment, education and culture and it is easy to see how humans have come to create laws which are highly complex and not always effective.[5]

Moralistic aggression (i.e., negative reaction to perceived violations of the social code (Trivers, 1971)) also serves to enforce individuals' expectations about how others should behave. As explained by Trivers (1971), moralistic aggression helps to enforce systems of reciprocity by increasing the cost of 'cheating' or disregarding others' expectations. This, in turn, deters cheating and contributes to a system of order (de Waal, 1996; Hardin, 1983).

One need not look hard to find examples of moralistic aggression in humans. The research discussed above indicates that, contrary to the all-nurture perspective, moralistic aggression is in part based on our own innate predispositions.[6] Further, it is evident that moralistic aggression sometimes contributes to the creation and maintenance of order in human social systems. In many instances, the law permits and/or regulates moralistic aggression against perceived defections from the social code. For example, the law often requires civil and/or criminal fines, and even imprisonment of individuals whose behaviour conflicts with that which is expected of them. One particularly clear example of moralistic aggression which has been, so to speak, codified by American law appears in the practice of debarring and/or civilly fining

---

[4] Some have observed that law may be thought of as an 'evolutionary prosthesis' by which law enables humans to overcome the 'shortcomings of biology in adapting us to live in our current environment . . .' (Elliott, 1997). Given Flack and de Waal's exploration of the behavioural building blocks of moral systems, and the prevalent role of these building blocks in contemporary legal behaviour, one might say that law is both an evolutionary prosthesis *as well as* an evolutionary outcome.

[5] For a rich discussion of the roles of deception and self-deception in the law, see Gruter and Masters (1998) and Rodgers (1992); see also Trivers (1985) for a discussion of the effectiveness of self-deception.

[6] For a discussion of the manifestation of moralistic aggression in humans, see Frank (1988).

professional service providers who violate the codes governing their professions. The purpose of such laws is to increase the cost of failing to abide by a professional code and thus to prevent cheating or exploitative behaviour from destabilizing relationships of expected reciprocity and order within the profession.

We also can see that when moralistic aggression goes too far, i.e., when negative reactions to perceived violations of a social code are rampant and/or violent, moralistic aggression can destabilize systems of social order. For example, one may characterize various violent hate crime groups' persistent use and threat of violence in response to perceived violations of their social codes as examples of moralistic aggression destabilizing social order.

Flack and de Waal's discussion of conflict resolution mechanisms among non-human primates, another basic building block, provides additional insight into law-related behaviour among humans. As the authors explain, group-living individuals require mechanisms for coping with inevitable conflict. Among monkeys and apes, behaviours including reconciliation, intervention, and mediation are used to prevent conflicts, repair relationships damaged by conflict and to resolve ongoing conflicts within a group.[7]

Our legal system's approaches to and theories of dispute resolution are replete with methods bearing semblance to those which are seen among non-human primates, as documented by Flack and de Waal (e.g. the use of impartial interventions; and the power of 'control animals' among pigtail macaques removed from their groups). This suggests that capacities for dispute resolution are innate.

Yet perhaps even more significant is the scarcity of certain dispute resolution mechanisms in present day legal theories concerning dispute resolution, most notably that of reconciliation. Described by Flack and de Waal as a post-conflict behaviour consisting of a friendly reunion between former opponents *not long after a confrontation*, reconciliation enables former opponents to restore their relationship by counteracting the immediate, negative consequences of aggression and reducing the tension-related behaviour of recipients of aggression. (Flack and de Waal, 2000, pp. 10–12 and the host of sources cited therein). Since restoration of relationships is a frequent goal of dispute resolution, such as in the case of dispute resolution between parties involved in ongoing contractual relationships, current methods may well stand to benefit by facilitating reconciliation *soon after* a confrontation between confronting parties.[8]

Another basic building block of legal behaviour lies in the capacities for sympathy and empathy. Flack and de Waal's exploration of behaviours such as succourance, reassurance, consolation, and conflict intervention indicates a capacity for sympathy and empathy among non-human primates, especially the great apes.[9] These tendencies, in turn, facilitate cooperation and conflict resolution within a group.

---

[7] In addition to Flack and de Waal (2000), see authors cited therein at pp. 11–15.

[8] While reconciliation is known to occur in contemporary dispute resolution procedures, it often occurs by chance rather than by design, and perhaps more importantly, it occurs too late (e.g. years after a dispute arises, rather than within hours or days).

[9] See also the research cited in Flack and de Waal (2000), pp. 14–16. For a discussion of these behaviours as ubiquitous among humans, see Eibl-Eibesfeldt (1989).

The roles of sympathy and empathy are prevalent in the law. Indeed, they appear to be prerequisites to the very tendency in humans to have laws: for if an individual agrees to obey laws which are against his or her individual self-interest (e.g. pick almost any income tax, welfare benefit, or political asylum law, to name but a few), but which are for the benefit of the group, then sympathy and empathy for others must play roles to some degree.[10] Why do lawmakers, at the behest of their constituencies, create laws which allocate great resources to others with whom they are unlikely ever to come in contact? Likewise, why do lawmakers and courts attempt to regulate 'private conduct' such as spousal abuse? It would be overly cynical to assert that such pursuits are not in part influenced by sympathy and empathy. Capacities for sympathy and empathy are also central to law in that bystanders' reactions to a given scenario are of critical importance in legal systems. For example, it is commonplace that litigators will spend thousands of dollars researching and selecting a jury whose members are most likely to sympathize and/or empathize with a particular client.

The insight that sympathy and empathy have roots in human nature comports with the universality of these tendencies across cultures, and dispels jurisprudential theories which contend that laws which promote benefits to a group are purely environmentally created and are in *constant* struggle against individuals' independent interests. (e.g. critical legal theory).

To conclude, the purpose of this comment has been to highlight the implications of Flack and de Waal's paper for legal theory. Specifically, their exploration of basic building blocks of moral systems suggests that human legal systems and legal behaviour are not purely the product of the environment. By examining some of the ways in which innate human capacities for reciprocity, retributive behaviours, moralistic aggression, dispute resolution, sympathy, and empathy play roles in contemporary law and legal behaviour, one can see that these capacities are both ubiquitous and facilitative of legal systems. However, no attempt is made or should be made to reduce all legal systems or legal behaviour to these building block behaviours. To the contrary, numerous other human predispositions and environmental circumstances influence our ability and willingness to create, obey, or disregard laws, often contributing to the development of highly complex legal systems. These factors notwithstanding, however, the creation of legal systems and the willingness and ability to make and abide by laws emerged from innate human predispositions.

References

Alexander, R. (1987), *The Biology of Moral Systems* (New York: Aldine de Gruyter).

Dawkins, R. (1976), *The Selfish Gene* (Oxford: Oxford University Press).

Dawkins, R. (1997), 'Interview', *Human Ethology Bulletin*, **12** (1).

Eibl-Eibesfeldt, I. (1989) *Human Ethology* (New York: de Gruyter).

Elliott, E. Donald (1997), *Law and Biology: The New Synthesis*.

Flack J. and de Waal, F.B.M. (2000), '"Any Animal Whatever": Darwinian building blocks of morality in monkeys and apes,' *Journal of Consciousness Studies*, **7** (1–2), pp. 1–29.

Frank, R. (1988), *Passions Within Reason: The Strategic Role of the Emotions* (New York: W.W. Norton).

Gruter, M. (1991) *Law and the Mind: Biological Origins of Human behaviour* (Newbury Park, CA: Sage Publications).

[10] While it is true that benefits to a group are often also beneficial to the individual, especially in the long term (Trivers, 1971), this does not negate the existence of sympathy and empathy as demonstrated by Flack and de Waal in behaviours such as succourance, consolation, and reassurance.

Gruter, M. (1992), 'An ethological perspective on law and biology', in *The Sense of Justice: Biological Foundations of Law*, ed. R. D. Masters and M. Gruter (Newbury Park, CA: Sage Publications).

Gruter, M. and Masters, R.D. (1998) 'Compassion, common sense, and deception: Social skills and the evolution of law' *Festschrift fuer Wolfgang Fikentscher* (Tuebingen: J.C.B. Mohr Verlag), pp. 91–113.

Hardin, G. (1983), 'Is Violence Natural?' *Zygon*, **18**, pp. 405–13.

Hoebel E.A. (1972) *The Law of Primitive Man* (New York: Atheneum).

Holmes, Oliver Wendell (1897), 'The Path of the Law', *10 Harvard L. Rev.*, pp. 476–77.

Jones, Owen D. (1994), 'Law and evolutionary biology: Obstacles and opportunities', *J. Contemp. Health Law & Policy*, **10**.

Rodgers, W. (1992) 'Intuition, altruism, and spite: Justice as justification', in *The Sense of Justice: Biological Foundations of Law*, ed. R.D. Masters and M. Gruter (Newbury Park, CA: Sage Publications).

Trivers, R. (1971), 'The Evolution of Reciprocal Altruism', *Quarterly Review of Biology*, **46**, pp. 35–57.

Trivers, R. (1985) *Social Evolution* (Menlo Park, CA: The Benjamin/Cummings Publishing Co).

de Waal, F.B.M. (1996), 'Conflict as negotiation', in *Great Ape Societies*, ed. W.C. McGrew, L.F. Marchant and T. Nishida (Cambridge: Cambridge University Press).

de Waal, F.B.M. (1997), 'The Chimpanzee's service economy: Food for grooming', *Evolution and Human behaviour*, **18**, pp. 375–86.

de Waal, F.B.M. and Luttrell, L. M. (1988), 'Mechanisms of social reciprocity in three primate species: Symmetrical relationship characteristics or cognition', *Ethology and Sociobiology*, **9**, pp. 101–18.

MORALITY BASED ON COGNITION IN PRIMATES

Sandra Güth and Werner Güth

Traditional evolutionary biology views animal behaviour as based on instincts that leave no room for deliberated morality. In their informative essay, Jessica Flack and Frans de Waal (2000) provide convincing evidence that monkeys and, even more so, apes often cognitively perceive the physical and emotional needs of others and that they try to help others, e.g. by consolation or sharing food. We mainly discuss aspects neglected by Flack and de Waal, such as how (im)morality can be clearly defined and whether it evolves genetically or culturally.

I: Introduction

When early researchers of primate behaviour observed prosocial patterns of behaviour in monkeys and apes and claimed similar reasons as for human cooperation, they were accused of anthropomorphism. The opposite mistake is, however, also possible, namely to claim cognitively deliberated morality only for humans in spite of all obvious similarities and of the — in evolutionary time — recent separation into distinct species.

Jessica Flack and Frans de Waal (2000) review and discuss competing hypotheses and the available evidence on how monkeys and apes consciously perceive others' physical and emotional needs and try to help them by food sharing, engaging in mutually beneficial reciprocity, active conflict resolution or consolation. As in experimental psychology and in experimental economics, they can discriminate between hypotheses by investigating carefully collected field evidence or by ingeniously designed experiments. It is interesting that Flack and de Waal in their discussion of morality in animals refer to philosophical concepts such as a fictitious social contract, whereas the philosopher Brian Skyrms (2000) relies on evolution when trying to explain human cooperation.

After investigating the notion of morality, our discussion focusses on whether morality has genetically evolved or is phenotypically learnt. To explore the details of these processes is, in our view, more important than to convince 'romantically inspired naturalists' or 'religiously inspired humanists'.

II: On (Im)morality

How can one prove that primates reveal basic aspects of morality? A first important step would be to provide a clear definition of morality. Flack and de Waal (2000) do not specify in full generality what morality is. Instead they review reliable aspects of primate behaviour such as food sharing or consolation which can be expected to pass undisputedly as evidence for morality. For Flack and de Waal's purpose of contradicting the hypothesis that only humans can be moral, this may suffice. In view of the arguments supplied by Flack and de Waal, the existence of features of moral behaviour in non-human primates seems to be beyond doubt.

But it remains to understand the origins and evolution of morality. Progress in this direction as well as an account of the differences between human and non-human morality require a precise definition of morality. Before such a definition can be offered, basic questions have to be answered: Can behaviour only be 'moral' if it is voluntary? Or can fear of punishment enforce morality? How are local conventions and rituals related to morality? Social norms, e.g. the (im)morality of promiscuous sexual intercourse, differ substantially across societies.

More generally, Flack and de Waal (2000) largely neglect immorality, an aspect where primates also seem to resemble humans. A rather drastic example would be 'Passion' and 'Pom', a chimpanzee mother and daughter who, according to Goodall (1971), were cannibals. Like prosocial behaviour also, 'immoral behaviour' seems to be well deliberated.

III: Genetic *versus* Cultural Evolution

All higher developed species, for example all primate species, live in complex environments due to variations in climatic, geographical, or social conditions. To imagine that all their behaviour is based on instinct would require a much too complex genotype. The escape route of evolution apparently has been the development of costly brains allowing cognition and deliberated choices. In monkeys and apes this is demonstrated by their distinctive reactions to unnatural living conditions, e.g. to being raised in human families or to living in a zoo environment (Kummer, 1995).

In our view, a costly brain allows deliberated choices in general problem solving including social interaction. More specifically, deliberated morality, which has to be distinguished from prosocial attitudes based on instinct, requires a cognitive representation of one's social environment and an awareness of behavioural alternatives as well as of their likely consequences. If one confronts many structurally different social challenges in addition to purely technical problems such as using tools, e.g. in nut cracking or ant eating, it can be an evolutionarily stable strategy to develop a costly brain.

Flack and de Waal (2000) report how monkeys and apes perceive the physical and emotional needs of others in their group and thus claim basic aspects of morality for non-human primates. The authors are, however, rather vague about the specific processes by which morality evolves. Especially the question of what is due to genetical evolution (e.g. in the sense of developing a complex and costly brain) and what is due to cultural evolution is hardly discussed. Evidence for cultural evolution could be found in local habits in the same species. Terminology such as 'born with powerful inclinations and emotions' (Flack and de Waal, 2000) that bias thinking and behaviour suggest a genetic disposition for morality. If, however, moral norms are not obeyed if one does not fear punishment (like 'Passion and Pom' when killing and eating the child of a handicapped mother in the same group), the hypothesis of genetically determined or intrinsic morality (Frey, 1997) is clearly wrong.

Cultural evolution in monkey and ape societies has been detected earlier. Potato washing in a group of Japanese monkeys (*Macaca fuscata*, Kawai, 1965) and nut cracking among West African chimpanzees are perhaps the most popular examples. But, as far as we know, the reported evidence of cultural evolution is always concerned with 'practical matters', usually food gathering, not with social norms. Are there local differences, for example, in the treatment of fighting group members by individuals who are not involved in the conflict? Or does the catalogue of 'misbehaviour' which leads to sanctions within the group vary over subpopulations of the same species? Observations of such rudimentary predecessors of legal systems would clearly indicate that the degree of morality in a society is not genetically determined, but established by means of culturally evolved enforcement systems.

On the other hand, morality certainly requires many genetically determined abilities. One cannot expect cognitive empathy from an alligator or peacemaking from a fly. But it is not at all obvious whether the role of genetical evolution in the development of morality is limited to providing a multi-functional brain which can serve both purposes, to internalize social norms and to injure others most effectively. Flack and de Waal seem to favour the hypothesis that more than the mere capacity of thinking is genetically predetermined. An insuppressible food cry inducing food sharing (Goodall, 1971) suggests that prosocial primate behaviour is not entirely based on deliberate choices. Which elements of morality evolved genetically, and which culturally, could be detected by observing individuals who are brought up outside their natural environment. To what extent do solitarily raised apes meet the social standards of their species? Such individuals can hardly ever be integrated into zoo or wild populations. It could be very informative to learn whether 'immoral' behaviour or violations of rules unrelated to morality cause these failures.

IV: Final Remarks

To avoid the anthropomorphism of 'romantically inspired naturalists' and the naive defence of *Homo sapiens* as the only species capable of cognitively deliberated morality, Flack and de Waal discuss specific hypotheses which are then evaluated in the light of the available evidence. In the case of food sharing, for instance, one distinguishes sharing under pressure or tolerated theft, reciprocal sharing, and sharing to enhance status. Some of these can be rejected for certain species. Based on such findings, the authors conclude that, like humans, monkeys and apes have powerful inclinations and emotions that bias their thinking and behaviour. So one should not assume 'different processes for similar behaviour in closely related species' and claim cognitively deliberated morality only for humans (Flack and de Waal, 2000). We fully agree.

One wonders why primatologists continuously have to defend themselves when claiming morality as the reason for the prosocial behaviour of our close relatives in the animal kingdom. Why do not those who claim that only humans show deliberated empathy accept the burden of proof? Of course, chimpanzees do not know how to travel to the moon nor do they engage in philosophical disputes or mathematical studies. But their cognitive and emotional capabilities are apparently rudimentary versions of their human analogues as suggested by the interpretation that human superiority has resulted from small steps in evolutionary adjustment over an evolutionarily short time span. According to most of our religions, mankind has been created instead of having evolved. Thus we seem to be used to the idea of considering ourselves as unique and qualitatively superior. Flack and de Waal implicitly have accepted the obligation to prove that animals can be deliberately moral. The null hypothesis, which they challenge, is the uniqueness of deliberated morality in humans.

In view of the evidence, which they report, this null hypothesis can hardly be maintained. Of course, 'religiously inspired humanists' will still favour other explanations and doubt the (interpretation of the) evidence, reviewed by Flack and de Waal (2000). In our view, future research should be directed to how clearly defined morality can evolve and be maintained in animal societies.

References

Flack, J.C. and de Waal, F.B.M. (2000), ' "Any animal whatever": Darwinian building blocks of morality in monkeys and apes', *Journal of Consciousness Studies*, **7** (1–2), pp. 1–29.

Frey, B. S. (1997), *Not Just For the Money* (Cheltenham: Edward Elgar Publishing).

Goodall, J. (1971), *In the Shadow of Man* (Boston, MA: Houghton Mifflin).

Kawai, M. (1965), 'New acquired precultural behaviour of the natural troop of Japanese monkeys on Koshima islet', *Primates*, **6**, pp. 1–30.

Kummer, H. (1995), *In Quest of the Sacred Baboon: A Scientist's Journey* (Princeton: Princeton University Press).

Skyrms, B. (2000), 'Game theory, rationality and evolution of the social contract', *Journal of Consciousness Studies*, **7** (1–2), pp. 269–84.

HUMAN MORALITY IS DISTINCTIVE

Jerome Kagan

The behaviours Flack and de Waal describe as origins of human morality lack the most essential features of the human ethical competence; namely, application of the concepts good and bad to events, the capacities for guilt and empathy for another's state, and the ability to suppress actions that would compromise the self's virtue. These serious differences between apes and humans challenge the suggestion that primate behaviour lies on a continuum with human morality.

Flack and de Waal (2000) make two related claims: acts like food sharing and grooming that maintain the harmony of a group of apes are proper referents for morality and for this reason it is reasonable to suggest that the behaviour of infra-human primates represents an appropriate origin for human morality. This argument is vulnerable on several counts.

First, when the term moral is applied to humans, it usually refers to thoughts and emotional states, especially awareness of the concepts of good and bad, a capacity for the emotions of guilt and empathy, and the ability to suppress actions that might hurt another (Moore, 1903; Garth, 1978; Kagan, 1984). Food sharing and grooming are not the usual referents for human morality; in part, because they can be the product of instrumental learning.

Humans share food with a hungry stranger because of an empathy for the need of the latter. The human action is not the product of a set of contingencies that taught the person that he or she might be attacked if they did not share. The differences between apes and humans in the origins of food sharing render the two behaviours distinctive. Thus, a potential error in the Flack–de Waal argument is the assumption of similar biological origins for behaviours that appear, on the surface, to resemble each other. Bees, bats, and birds fly, but for different reasons.

Human morality is defined by intention, not by behaviour. But because biologists are unable to know the intentions of animals, they classify behaviours that benefit another as altruistic. However, if an adult put an old television set in the garbage and a passer-by took the set home for personal use, the former did not commit an altruistic act, even though the passer-by benefited. Even an action that did not benefit another could be altruistic. An adult who jumps in a cold lake to save a child and drowns both of them has committed a morally praiseworthy, altruistic act because the intention was benevolent.

Humans are motivated by two different goal states; attainment of a conscious feeling of pleasure that originates in changes in sensory modalities, as well as a desire for consonance between a representation of an ideal state and a particular action, feeling, or thought. There is no good evidence that apes possess the latter motive (Koehler, 1925; Yerkes, 1925). The first signs of morality appear in children early in the second year when they look warily at a parent after violating a sanctioned act, like spilling food on the floor (Kagan, 1984). This sensitivity to facial and sensory signals issued by adults probably has an origin in similar primate behaviours. But, by age three, children show an ability to empathize with the distress of another, set themselves ideal goals to attain, and by five or six years of age, are capable of guilt. There is no evidence that these latter three competences are possible in apes.

It is appropriate, therefore, to ask why there has been so much writing during the last decade on a moral sense in apes (Alexander, 1987; Ridley, 1996). I suspect it is because our community is troubled over what it perceives as excessive self-interest and a rash of violent aggression. The community wishes to understand these troubling events and looks to biological scientists for an answer that might reduce their uncertainty. Biologists help by telling citizens that apes have a moral sense and, therefore, there is a natural foundation in humans to be cooperative, fair, and kind. These scientists also tell citizens that self-interest is natural because it can be observed in all animals. Both messages, which are therapeutic, represent a modern form of preformationism that seems to serve the same function it did in the seventeenth century; modern citizens do not understand why humans have become so narcissistic and it is helpful to be told that this attitude is a natural, evolutionary derivative of our primate ancestry.

Evolutionary biologists freely borrow popular terms invented initially to describe human behaviour and apply them to animals (Wilson, 1975). But I suspect they would be peeved if students of human behaviour called a rhesus female unfaithful because she copulated with four males in an hour. A husband who throws a knife at his wife is called aggressive. But a six-month-old infant who throws a knife at a parent is not regarded as aggressive because we recognize that an intention to hurt is absent. Because animals have no conscious intentions, it is misleading, and theoretically regressive, to describe the animal behaviour with words that have intentionality as a primary feature. Otherwise, the hypersexed rhesus female is a tart.

The emotion of guilt, which is central to human morality, can not occur in any primate other than humans because guilt requires the agent to know that a voluntary act has hurt another and the behaviour could have been suppressed. Guilt requires the ability to infer the state of another, to reflect on a past action, to compare the products of that reflection with an acquired standard, to realize that a particular action that violated a standard could have been inhibited, and, finally, to evaluate the self's virtue as a consequence of that violation. Guilt is not a possible state for chimpanzees. Indeed, these animals are unable to make much simpler inferences; for example, they do not assume that a blindfolded adult can not see their actions (Povinelli and Eddy, 1996).

The human moral sense was necessary for a species with a frontal lobe that permits the individual to harbour resentment, envy, jealousy, and hostility for a long time after the emotion of acute anger has passed. Perhaps that is why it was adaptive for the first sign of a moral sense to emerge by the second birthday, long before reproductive maturity. It is possible that the early appreciation of right and wrong was necessary to control the resentment an older sibling might hold toward a younger one. Every four-year-old has the opportunity, motive, and strength to hurt the new child in the family, but the frequency of such seriously violent acts is so tiny, each occurrence becomes a screaming headline in the local newspaper. The human moral sense, like a spider's web, is a unique product of evolution that has been maintained because it ensures our survival.

References

Alexander, R.D. (1987), *The Biology of Moral Systems* (New York: De Gruyter).
Flack, J.C. and de Waal, F.B.M. (2000), ' "Any animal whatever": Darwinian building blocks of morality in monkeys and apes', *Journal of Consciousness Studies*, **7** (1–2), pp. 1–29.
Garth, A. (1978), *Reason and Morality* (Chicago: University of Chicago Press).
Kagan, J. (1984), *The Nature of the Child* (New York: Basic Books).
Köhler, W. (1925), *The Mentality of Apes* (New York: Harcourt Brace & World).
Moore, G.E. (1903), *Principia Ethica* (Cambridge: Cambridge University Press).
Povinelli, D.J. & Eddy, T.J. (1996), 'What young chimpanzees know about seeing', *Monographs of the Society for Research in Child Development*, **61**, pp. 1–151.
Ridley, M. (1996), *The Origins of Virtue* (New York: Viking; Harmondsworth, Middlesex: Penguin).
Tomasello, M., Call, J. and Gluckman, A. (1997), 'Comprehension of novel communicative signs by apes and humans in children', *Child Development*, **68**, pp. 1067–80.
Wilson, E.O. (1975), *Sociobiology* (Cambridge, MA: Harvard University Press).
Yerkes, R.M. (1925), *Almost Human* (London: Jonathan Cape).

WAYS BEYOND APPEARANCES

Hans Kummer

While I admire the reviewed discoveries on the social techniques by which monkeys and apes cope with the conflicts within their communities, I am worried about some of the high-level interpretations given by the authors. In my view the processes reviewed are not 'building blocks of morality' but objects of human moral judgements. Their interpretation as 'shared solutions' is not supported by a demonstrated ability of non-human primates to identify their own acts with those of the other group members. There is no evidence of a 'concerted effort by community members to find shared solutions' rather than individual learning of these solutions. The postulate of a 'community concern' implies a concept of community which is not supported by evidence.

Applying terms coined for humans to other species is useful only if one eventually justifies it by appropriate experimentation. Possible methods are suggested.

Flack and de Waal (2000) present a fascinating review of social techniques by which monkeys and apes cope with the danger that the ever present conflicts in their groups get out of hand and cause lasting damage to the component relationships. My own research was not on morality, but on mechanisms that build and perpetuate groups and on related cognition. I have been invited to comment because 20 years ago I wrote an article on 'Analogs of morality among nonhuman primates' (Kummer, 1978). At that time the processes reviewed by Flack and de Waal were mostly undiscovered. In the paper I focussed on core topics of the Ten Commandments: killing, sexual infidelity, false information and stealing. With regard to stealing, I reviewed the inhibition of hamadryas baboon males from taking over females of weaker males by force (Kummer *et al.*, 1974) as a possible analogue of morality. Apart from the inhibition a new behaviour appeared in these experiments. As soon as the conflict over the female was settled, the winning male initiated intense and repeated friendly contacts with the loser. We interpreted this as an attempt 'to establish or re-establish a positive relationship after a confrontation'. I was disappointed that the phenomenon went unnoticed. When de Waal and Yoshihara later (1983) discovered such post-conflict affiliations in rhesus monkeys and named them 'reconciliation' the same phenomenon attracted wide attention. At my time, such a term could have endangered the reputation of a biologist. That 'reconciliation' does in fact restore mutual tolerance among the former contestants, as the term implies, was experimentally demonstrated only in 1992 by Cords. Frans de Waal introduced terms like consolation, celebration and obligation. He and I have always disagreed about interpretative terms for scientific reasons and aside from their public appeal. The following critique addresses the even higher level of Flack and de Waal's present interpretations.

Our articles also differ with regard to the contents of morality. I had searched the literature for processes that *prevented* disruptive interactions including reward and sanction. The harvest was meagre. De Waal, however, set about discovering processes that mitigate or *alleviate* the consequences of disruptive interactions. This search was much more successful. These mitigating interactions, together with reciprocal exchange and empathy form the core of Flack and de Waal's impressive review. They see them as 'building blocks of morality' and interpret them as 'concerted efforts by community members to find shared solutions to social conflict' (p. 1, above).

My first comment concerns the term 'building blocks' The anthropologist Walter Goldschmidt (personal communication) once defined culture as 'the symbolic re-interpretation of biological imperatives' — we would prefer to speak of biological tendencies or solutions. If one agrees that morality is a cultural universal it is not the interactional pattern itself that belongs to morality, but the judgement to which humans subject it. Thus Flack and de Waal do not describe building blocks but objects of morality, kinds of social behaviour to which humans apply 'generally accepted value judgements, or norms' (Bischof, 1978).

The objects of morality are biological in origin. They resemble each other across species, including humans, because similar problems resulted in similar evolutionary solutions, the more so the more closely related the species are. Where they differ between monkeys, apes and humans, it is mostly because the species differ in their cognitive equipment, not because of the presence or absence of a moral sense. For example, reciprocal altruism is apparently absent in lower vertebrates because they are incapable of estimating, comparing and remembering the costs and values of mutual altruistic acts over time. Monkeys seem to lack empathy because they do not internally represent the mental states of others, as experiments have shown (Cheney and Seyfarth, 1990, pp. 220–2; Povinelli et al., 1991).

The findings reviewed by the authors show which social problems monkeys and apes face and which cognitive levels they reached in their solutions, but the question central to the evolutionary origin of morality is not how the objects of moral judgements evolved, but the capacity of moral judgement itself. Flack and de Waal focus on interactions that control social conflicts, which are the objects of human jurisdiction, but if we shift our attention to other kinds of interactions the inadequacy of the building block metaphor becomes more obvious. Monogamy, for example, is judged morally in our culture. But we would not consider monogamy in birds or crustaceans as a 'building block of morality'. It is a biological solution which humans happened to make an object of moral norms.

My second difficulty concerns the term 'shared solutions'. I take this to mean that group members not merely do the same thing in the same situation, which is common to all species, but that member A knows that she and all other members will behave in the same way. Thus she must be able to compare her actions with the actions of others. One piece of evidence that an individual is indeed able to equate her own and the others' behaviour is true imitation, but monkeys have not been shown to imitate (e.g. Visalberghi and Fragaszy, 1990; Zuberbühler et al., 1996), and in one study even chimpanzees convincingly imitated only when raised by humans (Tomasello and Call, 1994). The meaning of 'shared' thus remains obscure to me.

I have a similar problem with the term 'community concern'. De Waal and Roosmalen (1979) observed how female chimpanzees, in a few cases, led one male toward another male with whom he had just fought and thus induced them to be reconciled. Her behaviour strongly suggests that she knows and provokes the beneficial effects of reconciliation among the males involved. Flack and de Waal see such episodes as illustrations of a 'community concern', which implies that members are aware of and motivated to improve the state of the entire community. They write, however, that the term 'does not require that monkeys and apes worry about how the community, as an abstract entity, is doing', but only 'that the individual works toward creating a community atmosphere that reflect his or her own best interests' (p. 15). Apart from the fact that a given community is not an abstract entity, I find these statements contra- dictive as to whether members do or do not represent their community and therefore can be concerned about it. Whether nonhuman primates have a concept of 'community' can be investigated. In one of our most difficult experiments, Verena Dasser (1988) showed that macaques have a concept of mother–child relationships as opposed to other relationships. She trained individual macaques to select colour slides of one mother and her child from the colony with two psychological methods. When confronted with slides of other colony members for the first time, the subjects selected all the mother–child relationships with 90% correctness and ignored other kin relationships. They did so even if the child was adult and older than the subjects themselves. If the term 'community concern' is here to stay, I would be happy to eventually see the respective experiments done. I am worried about the application of terms coined for humans to monkeys and apes unless one is determined to justify them empirically.

As it stands Flack and de Waal's interpretation of observed conflict regulations as a 'concerted effort by community members to find shared solutions' seems unclear in its meaning and unnecessary in the light of the evidence. There is no indication that members communicate about and jointly search for solutions rather than learning them individually in the course of their own interactions. A concerted effort would be convincingly supported by a concerted stand of all adult members against violators of rules, or even expulsion of violators from the group. I am not aware of any such observation in nonhuman primates. The infant-killing female chimpanzee in the Gombe community continued this activity for years. The inhibition of male hamadryas baboons from interacting with and appropriating females of weaker male members was not enforced by uninvolved band males, but was later found to be a function of female preference for one of the males involved (Bachmann and Kummer, 1980).

What evidence could begin to show whether monkeys and apes share a body of rules furthering group harmony? David and Ann Premack (e.g. 1983) trained chimpanzees in a 'language' using plastic shapes in order to map the chimps' concepts of the physical world. The method could be used to explore whether chimps have social concepts of aggression or conflict and connect these with concepts of good or of objectionable behaviour.

The possible concepts of monkeys could be investigated with the methods used by Dasser. Do they have categories corresponding to our terms group member versus stranger? Do they place reconciliations in the same category regardless of the individuals shown, demonstrating that this solution is indeed generalized and in some sense shared? Do they prefer to view video clips of a reconciliation among their group members to the preceding conflict, or at least of peaceful group activity to aggression?

In the absence of such data, Flack and de Waal are rightly cautious. Terms like 'appears' and 'suggests' abound in their interpretations. The way beyond appearances is difficult. In addition to further collections of conflict-resolving interactions, it demands an in-depth search for the mental operations that make up human morality from early childhood to adulthood, their operationalization, and an attempt at conclusive experimentation on monkeys and apes. Otherwise, the demanding interpretations of Flack and de Waal remain speculative. The work reported in their article is a rich inductive basis for such progress.

References

Bachmann, Christian and Kummer, Hans (1980), 'Male assessment of female choice in hamadryas baboons', *Behavioral Ecology and Sociobiology*, **1**, pp. 315–21.

Bischof, Norbert (1978), 'On the phylogeny of human morality', in *Morality as a Biological Phenomenon*, ed. G. S. Stent (Berlin: produced for Dahlem Konferenzen by Abakon Verlagsgesellschaft; rev. ed. 1980).

Cheney, Dorothy L. and Seyfarth, Robert M. (1990), *How Monkeys See the World* (Chicago and London: University of Chicago Press).

Cords, Marina (1992), 'Post-conflict reunions and reconciliation in long-tailed macaques', *Animal Behaviour*, **44**, pp. 57–61.

Dasser, Verena (1988), 'A social concept in Java monkeys', *Animal Behaviour*, **36**, pp. 225–30.

Flack, Jessica and de Waal, Frans (2000), ' "Any animal whatever": Darwinian building blocks of morality in monkeys and apes', *Journal of Consciousness Studies*, **7** (1–2), pp. 1–29.

Kummer, Hans (1978), 'Analogs of human morality among nonhuman primates', in *Morality as a Biological Phenomenon*, ed. Gunther. S. Stent (Berlin: produced for Dahlem Konferenzen by Abakon Verlagsgesellschaft; rev. ed., Berkeley, Los Angeles, London: University of California Press, 1980).

Kummer, Hans, Götz, Walter and Angst, Wafter (1974), 'Triadic differentiation: An inhibitory process protecting pair bonds in baboons', *Behaviour*, **49**, pp. 62–87.

Povinelli, D.J., Nelson, A. and Novak, M.A. (1991), 'Do rhesus monkeys (Macaca mulatta) attribute knowledge and ignorance to others?', *Journal of Comparative Psychology*, **105**, pp. 318–25.

Premack, David and Premack, Ann (1983), *The Mind of an Ape* (New York and London: W.W. Norton).

Tomasello, M. and Call, J. (1994), 'Social cognition of monkeys and apes', *Yearbook of Physical Anthropology*, **37**, pp. 273–305.

Visalberghi, Elisabetta and Fragaszy, Dorothy M. (1990), 'Do monkeys ape?', in *Language and Intelligence in Monkeys and Apes: Comparative and developmental perspectives*, ed. S.D. Parker and K.R. Gibson (Cambridge: Cambridge University Press).

de Waal, Frans and van Roosmalen, A. (1979), 'Reconciliation and consolation among chimpazees', *Behavioral Ecology and Sociobiology*, **5**, pp. 55–66.

de Waal, Frans and Yoshihara, D. (1983), 'Reconciliation and redirected affection in rhesus monkeys', *Behaviour*, **85**, pp. 224–41.

Zuberbühler, Klaus, Gygax, Lorenz, Harley, Nerida and Kummer, Hans (1996), 'Stimulus enhancement and spread of a spontaneous tool use in a colony of long-tailed macaques', *Primates*, **37**, pp.1–12.

MORALITY AND THE ELEPHANT
Prosocial Behaviour, Normativity and Fluctuating Allegiances

Jim Moore

Human morality is composed of three elements: prosocial behaviour, a normative imperative, and the tendency to adjust the boundaries of the social network to which these apply in a flexible, self-interested fashion. A credible case for human uniqueness can be made for the last element only. Because defining social boundaries can be done rationally (though rational thought is not required), the intersection of this tactical approach with the psychological bases (i.e., emotions) underlying the first two elements can help resolve the conflict between emotion and Kant cited by Flack and de Waal. They make a solid case for prosociality, though their discussion of reciprocal sharing has some problems. The perspectives of Boehm and of Sober and Wilson are needed to understand our boundary-adjusting (though Sober and Wilson needlessly cloud the issue by over-extending group selection). A satisfying theory of morality's evolution should integrate, not distinguish amongst, the three elements.

My daughter and I are reading *Ivanhoe* — a tale of a very moral world, in which men brag of making Saracen widows, anti-Semitism is right and proper, killing for honour is not a necessary evil but a career choice, and the 'Queen of Love and Beauty' presides over a sporting event at Ashby in which the mortality rate is about four per cent. This is a very different morality than that to which I am accustomed. What is morality; what are morals? Is it immoral to dump a wastebasket full of trash into the street? The answer probably depends on whether one is in rural India or downtown Singapore. If one were to take a small dog to the beach at Santa Cruz and slaughter and barbecue it, would one be acting immorally or simply unwisely?

Flack and de Waal cite a nice analogy with language: we are born with the capacity to develop a moral sense, but what that is composed of is learned. They do not adhere to this analogy, though, for they conclude by talking about which earth species an alien observer would consider 'the most moral'; a bit like asking whether English is 'more language' than Hawaiian because it has more phonemes.[11] According to Flack

---

[11] One *could* operationalize the term 'morality' appropriately, but that has not been done. A useful starting point for such an effort would be Altmann's discussion of what it means to ask which sex is 'more aggressive'(1974).

and de Waal, morality is based on 'the human sense of right and wrong used by society to promote pro-social behaviour'. This is evidently close to the sense of Sober and Wilson (1998, pp. 237–40), in which morality is close to (but not isomorphic with) altruism. For them, causing harm to a third party, or great harm to many targets (e.g., the actions of many Nazi camp guards) would be examples of morally wrong behaviour.[12] Of course, causing harm is not necessarily immoral — cf. moralistic aggression. Or *is* moralistic aggression immoral? How do you feel about the death penalty, and is it morally salient whether the executioner feels (moral) outrage while carrying out his job? Ah — his *job*, as an arm of the State: this brings us to Boehm's usage of morality as the outcome of shared values determining what is right and wrong, and those shared values being imposed by the group (aka society) against deviants (Boehm, this volume). This last is closer to my dictionary's definition of moral: 'Conforming to a standard of what is good and right; virtuous' (*Webster's New Collegiate Dictionary*, 1951). Morality seems to be more about conforming than about the standard to which one conforms; Wilfred of Ivanhoe is moral, even if his behaviour is not always pro-social.

I belabour the point not with any hope of defining good and evil, but because I think we will need to be very careful about the definition of 'morality' before we can understand the evolution of the phenomenon, and none of these three articles give much rigorous and consistent attention to distinguishing morality from being nice according to UN-sanctioned principles of behaviour. The authors make (varyingly) strong arguments that we can search for evolutionary antecedents of both phenomena among non-humans, but I think it quite likely that the underlying psychological mechanisms are distinct, or at least arose via distinct pathways. Flack and de Waal make an important contribution to this problem with their separation of tendencies and capacities into 'the four ingredients of morality' (p. 22). We need to be careful to avoid thinking we understand a trait because we've named it ('docility' comes immediately to mind), and similarly be cautious of slipping from conceptually distinct putative traits to discrete mental modules (see Elman *et al.*, 1996 for an alternative approach).

Flack and de Waal distinguish three hypotheses to account for food sharing and reciprocal exchange; to the degree that mine (Moore, 1984) can be identified with one or another of these three, my original discussion must have been confusing and I thank them for the opportunity to try again. I believe that not only are these three hypotheses non-exclusive, but all three are *required* to explain the evolution of reciprocal sharing in our species.

'Sharing to enhance status' (or 'showing off'; the category into which my paper is placed) is inadequate to explain the origin of sharing behaviour because it does not (itself) address the problem of how the behaviour began: a flash of insight ('Gee, I bet everyone will defer to me if I give away part of this monkey') seems implausible. Status had to be enhanced by sharing before sharing could be engaged in to enhance status.

'Sharing under pressure' (or 'tolerated theft') readily can explain sharing by appeal to simple self-interest: to quote Calvin and Hobbes, one is merely to 'give before it hurts'. It doesn't go anywhere, though: one is left with a nasty, brutish system of

---

[12] Note that this involves an implicit moral metric that should be made explicit when we try to sort out evolutionary antecedents, since, as Flack and de Waal point out, sometimes causing 'harm to a target' is an inevitable component of social life; see footnote 11.

extortion by the powerful, not a system of reciprocity such as we observe in humans (yes, the irony is deliberate and, I believe, important).

Reciprocity (no quotes needed here?) describes well what humans, chimpanzees and capuchins actually do, but is vague about the process by which the behaviour evolved. (Technically of course all these hypotheses are vague about the actual process — we have not found 'reciprocity genes' and any adaptationist story needs to keep that in mind.) A full accounting for a trait should include a plausible scenario for how it came to arise from an ancestor in which it was absent. As I read it, the scenario offered here for reciprocity is that increased cognitive complexity made possible calculated reciprocity based upon expectations concerning the behaviour of others plus a sense of fair play, a sense that one should not only 'keep mental note of favours given and received' but should act on those notes . . . well, reciprocally. I am not sure that this circularity is inevitable, and invite Flack and de Waal to put together an explicit model based on desire for predictability plus emergent properties of theory of mind (TOM).

In my 1984 paper, I tried to offer an *evolutionary* account — i.e., a diachronic model — for the evolution of reciprocal altruism by way of (first) sharing under pressure, which fostered (via developmental psychology) sharing to enhance status, which established conditions favouring calculated reciprocal sharing, thus providing the basis for the evolution of the capacity for generalized reciprocity. It is worth noting that such a model incorporates non-reciprocity (e.g. extortion) as part of the same integrated system, rather than a psychologically unrelated simple selfishness.

Now that I've established (I hope) what I was trying to say, the question remains, was I correct? I'm not sure. If, as Kummer (1978) argues, predictability is a necessary feature of complex sociality, and if TOM arises inevitably from cognitive complexity, then I believe Flack and de Waal's reciprocity model predicts widespread reciprocity amongst cognitively complex social animals. In contrast, the model I proposed situates the evolution of reciprocal altruism (exclusive of close kin and mates) in a narrower set of antecedent conditions that apply to chimpanzees, humans, probably some dolphins, and not too many other organisms. I am not sure yet whether capuchins decide the case in favour of Flack and de Waal or not, but they are problematic for my hypothesis; on the other hand, the recent conclusion of Pusey and Packer (1997) that there are no solid examples of reciprocal altruism among non-humans (not even baboons?) somewhat supports my view. We shall see.

In the meantime, a minor quibble: contra de Waal, I do not believe that the tolerated theft model predicts that most aggression among food-holding chimpanzees be directed against the possessors of the food. The model simply predicts that possessors be at high enough risk of attack that they cannot eat in peace; it is a logical error to assume that 'beggar should attack holder' implies 'holder should not attack beggar'. Indeed, it is central to the tolerated theft model that the possessor may be ambivalent about sharing, and thus inclined to try mild aggression to discourage any but the most persistent beggars. The important thing to remember is that the respect for possession noted by Flack and de Waal is neither absolute nor invariable (Moore, 1984; e.g., Kummer and Cords, 1991).

So, what of morality? I believe there are three more-or-less distinct elements to the trait these authors are discussing (as the proverbial elephant has trunk, legs and tail).

1. Prosocial behaviour, which can arise for various reasons (kin selection, tactical sharing, mutualism; perhaps group selection in a few taxa). Flack and de Waal focus here and have established a valuable framework from which to work.

2. A sense of normativity and the importance of predictability, as outlined by Kummer (1978). In a sense, evolution has committed the naturalistic fallacy: what is, ought to be. This is a powerful element of morality that is not necessarily prosocial. It remains to be seen whether this 'trait' has been favoured by natural selection (cf. Kummer) or derives epiphenomenally from Hebbian learning processes in complex brains (see Elman *et al.*, 1996).

3. A higher-level, cognitively based propensity to adjust the social context in which elements 1 and 2 operate, according to tactical expediency (i.e., politically).

Unlike the first two elements, which as Flack and de Waal show seem fairly widespread among non-humans, this flexibility may be unique to ourselves. It makes possible the extension of the moral community to apes (e.g., Cavalieri and Singer, 1993) as well as its withdrawal from humans (e.g., Hochschild, 1998). This is where Boehm and much of Sober and Wilson have made real contributions. See Moore (1994) for a discussion of how their work when combined can suggest a scenario for the origin of the genus *Homo*, and Alexander (1989) for an extremely valuable discussion of the role of intergroup processes in the evolution of the human psyche.

References

Alexander, Richard D. (1989), 'Evolution of the human psyche', in *The Human Revolution*, ed. P. Mellars and C. Stringer (Princeton: Princeton University Press).

Altmann, Jeanne (1974), 'Observational study of behaviour: Sampling methods', *Behaviour*, **49**, pp. 227–67.

Cavalieri, Paola and Singer, Peter (1993), *The Great Ape Project: Equality Beyond Humanity* (New York: St. Martin's Press).

Elman, Jeffrey L., Bates, Elizabeth A., Johnson, Mark H., Karmiloff-Smith, Annette, Parisi, Domenico and Plunkett, Kim (1996), *Rethinking Innateness: A Connectionist Perspective on Development* (Cambridge: MIT Press).

Hochschild, Adam (1998), *King Leopold's Ghost : a story of greed, terror, and heroism in Colonial Africa* (Boston: Houghton Mifflin).

Kummer, Hans (1978). 'On the value of social relationships to non-human primates: A heuristic scheme', *Social Science Information*, **17**, pp. 687–705.

Kummer, Hans and Cords, Marina (1991), 'Cues of ownership in long-tailed macaques, *Macaca fascicularis*', *Animal Behaviour*, **42**, pp. 529–49.

Moore, Jim (1984), 'The evolution of reciprocal sharing', *Ethology and Sociobiology*, **5**, pp. 5–14.

Moore, Jim (1994), 'Hominids, coalitions and weapons; not vehicles', *Behavioral and Brain Sciences*, **17**, p. 632.

Pusey, Anne E. and Packer, Craig (1997), 'The ecology of relationships', in *Behavioural Ecology: an Evolutionary Approach (4th Edition)*, ed. J.R. Krebs and N.B. Davies (Oxford: Blackwell Scientific).

Sober, Elliott and Wilson, David S. (1998), *Unto Others: The Evolution and Psychology of Unselfish Behaviour* (Cambridge: Harvard University Press).

DARWINIAN BUILDING BLOCKS

Peter Railton

Although the 'naturalistic fallacy' and the is/ought distinction have often been invoked as definitive grounds for rejecting any attempt to bring evolutionary thought to bear on ethics, they are better interpreted as warnings than as absolute barriers. Our moral concepts themselves — e.g. the principle that 'ought implies can' — require us to ask whether human psychology is capable of impartial empathetic thought and motivation characteristic of normative systems that could count as *moral. As the essay by Flack and de Waal shows, evolutionary theory and evidence can help us answer the question whether the psychological 'building blocks' needed for morality are indeed likely to be present in a given species, including Homo sapiens. It is important, however, not to think that a positive answer to this question commits us to attributing identifiable moral **concepts** to actual members.*

I

The distrust with which attempts to bring evolutionary thought to bear on morality have come to be viewed is, in truth, well earned. It therefore is unsurprising that a principled basis for rejecting any such project has been sought. Yet the *genetic fallacy*, the *'is'/'ought' gap*, and the *naturalistic fallacy* are perhaps better seen as warnings than as outright barriers, reminding us of ways in which the project can fail, and indeed often has failed. But they should not warn us off the project altogether, since the need to ask how morality fits with our best empirical understanding of ourselves and our place in nature and history arises from within normative moral thought itself.

For example: Suppose we accept the familiar point that normative moral thought is concerned with how things *ought to be*, rather than how they *are* or *came to be*. Still, it is a central principle of normative thought that *'ought implies can'*. If humans are to fall under the scope of any moral — or epistemic, or rational — *ought*, then their psychological and social repertoire must contain the wherewithal to be *guided* in some appropriate sense by this *ought*. Otherwise, as Kant would say, the *ought* can be no more than a delusion.

To investigate the human psychological and social repertoire, with the aim of discovering whether we do indeed have it in us to be appropriately guided by moral — or epistemic, or rational — norms, it might be useful to ask how *Homo sapiens* came onto the scene. I say only 'might be useful', because reflections on the bearing of evolution on human psychology and sociology have too often been essentially speculative and removed from serious evidential control.

Though the situation in evolutionary thought has been improving, still we seem to run at least as great a risk of naturalizing existing psychological and sociological preconceptions by reading them back into evolutionary biology as we do of having our psychological and sociological misconceptions corrected. Assessments of animal evidence, such as that discussed by Jessica Flack and Frans de Waal (2000),[13] possess a similar mixture of peril and promise. Anthropocentric projection — whether intended to the credit or derogation of actual animals — continually threatens to undermine the enterprise.

II

The preconceptions that have so coloured this discussion go beyond the psychological and sociological. Some are normative — epistemic as well as moral. A commonly encountered view holds that the theory of natural selection can be used to *debunk* human moral pretence. Humans flatter themselves that they are capable of the sort of impartial benevolence essential to morality, the argument goes, but natural selection would have long since culled out any such motivational tendencies. A capacity for 'moral illusion' might have been selected for, as a way of disguising from the self and

---

[13] All parenthetic page references in the text are to this principal paper.

others the opportunistic motivations underneath actual behaviour. As scientifically minded individuals, however, we have to face the facts and draw the conclusion Kant so feared.

However, this seemingly hard-headed argument is really more of a threat to itself than to morality. For it presupposes a normative premise that it tends by its own reasoning to undercut. Why is it 'facing facts' to force moralists to confront theories of natural selection? — Because these theories are epistemically well-confirmed. Who confirmed them, and how? — Humans did, by using scientific methods. But this assumes that humans are psychologically and socially equipped to carry out scientific inquiry, to produce and test hypotheses in ways that yield impartial epistemic justification, despite the fact that our perceptual, cognitive, linguistic, and deliberative capacities all have been shaped by a process of natural selection in which opportunism — not impartiality, warrant, or truth — rules. Why, then, isn't human epistemic pretense illusory? The hard-headed argument hammers itself into the same ground into which it had previously pounded morality.

Surely, it will be protested, this is too quick. We must look at the case in more detail, to see how opportunistic evolutionary 'interests' might have been served by capacities capable of sustaining relatively impartial and objective processes of inquiry, thus leaving *Homo sapiens* equipped for science. I agree, and ask only that we look with equal care into the moral case.

III

It would be a foolish vanity on my part to think I could do better than others at separating the sheep from the goats. But it does seem to me that Flack and de Waal have found a happy way of posing what may be the key question. For they ask whether human evolutionary history, opportunistic as it might have been, would likely have equipped us with the wherewithal — the 'building blocks', as they put it — to engage in genuinely moral thought and agency. Moreover, they have found a way of looking for evidence that might help us answer it: attend carefully to the behaviour of such relevant species as monkeys and apes — species to whom we are more or less closely related and who have experienced evolutionary conditions similar to those of our ancestors. If non-human primate behaviour suggests the presence of various 'building blocks', this is evidence for thinking that natural selection could be hospitable to the emergence of morality. They report observations of monkey and ape behaviour suggesting capacities for: regularity in resource distribution and conflict resolution, empathy and sympathy, reciprocity, moderation of aggression, revenge, reconciliation, ritualized expression, hierarchy and shared social expectations, mediation, consolation, acquiescence, succourance, and conflict intervention. Clearly, these are among the building blocks of moral life.

A critic will be quick to point out that they are also among the building blocks for patterns of social organization that are non-moral or even immoral. So what is being claimed? We may need to fix meanings a bit.

We should, I think, distinguish between a *modus vivendi* by means of which individuals can live together in a stable arrangement that provides some mutual benefits and reduces certain kinds of costly conflict, and social practices or individual behaviours that are distinctively *moral* in character. Moral life involves many relations of reciprocity or mutual interest, but it involves as well norms and motivations that embody a capacity for some measure of impartiality, fairness, and generalized benevolence. Flack and de Waal are aware of the need to find building blocks that would permit social groups of humans or primates to go beyond a mere *modus vivendi*, and so they seek to discern among monkeys and apes patterns of behaviour they characterize as involving 'expectations about how they themselves and others should behave' (p. 8), 'rules and, more significantly, a set of expectations [that] essentially reflects a sense of social regularity, and may be a precursor to the human sense of justice' (p. 9), an 'ability to put one's own preferences aside . . . another indication that a rudimentary form of justice may exist in the social systems of non-human primates' (p. 12), and 'a sense of community' (p. 14).

Such purported observations will strike many as wishful over-interpretation on Flack and de Waal's part. Now it would ill behove me to have an opinion, having myself neither confidence in *a priori* philosophical arguments on this subject nor first-hand experience of the social life of non-human primates. But I will risk a friendly suggestion. Flack and de Waal could place themselves on a firmer footing — while still accomplishing virtually as much toward answering their central question — if they conceived their inquiry into building blocks somewhat more broadly. I fear that the dynamic of the debate with debunkers of morality sometimes lures those who know better into unfortunate ways of defending their position. Flack and de Waal summarize their inquiry thus:

> To what degree has biology influenced and shaped the development of moral systems? One way to determine the extent to which human moral systems might be the product of natural selection is to explore behaviour in other species that is analogous and perhaps homologous to our own. Many non-human primates, for example, have similar methods to humans for resolving, managing, and preventing conflicts of interests within their groups. Such methods . . . reflect a concerted effort by community members to find shared solutions to social conflict (p. 1).

Contrast this way of framing the issue with Darwin's own in *The Descent of Man*, quoted by Flack and de Waal immediately after the remarks excerpted above:

> Any animal whatever, endowed with well-marked social instincts, the parental and filial affections being here included, would inevitably acquire a moral sense of conscience, as soon as its intellectual powers had become as well developed, or nearly as well developed, as in man (cited, p. 1).

Darwin believes he sees in animals building blocks of morality, but does not think this requires him to look for anything like a 'rudimentary sense of justice', 'sense of community', or 'concerted effort by community members to find shared solutions'. It is enough if we have inherited from our prelinguistic animal forebears perceptual, cognitive, and motivational capacities which, once joined to our representational, inferential, epistemic, and communicative capacities, make attainable something like a moral point of view. We need not also find a 'proto-form' of the moral point of view in animals, or even have a clear idea of what that might mean.

Consider once again the epistemic parallel. The debunker typically assumes that we are capable of genuine scientific knowledge and epistemic justification. He assumes, then, that our inherited perceptual, cognitive, and motivational capacities are such that, once the explosive development of human representational, inferential, and communicative capacities takes place, a community of inquirers can arise that regulates itself by scientific norms possessing genuine epistemic authority. He need not additionally assume that non-human primates possess some proto-form of 'a scientific point of view', or could be understood as 'making a concerted effort to develop credible methods to settle their epistemic disputes'. It is enough, then, if our inheritance — sensory systems that provide reasonably accurate and sophisticated information about various features of our bodies and environment, memory systems that can retain information in some selectively organized representation, cognitive systems that can make comparisons of similarity and difference and form revisable expectations based on patterns of memory and experience, motives that include curiosity, behavioural dispositions that include exploration and trial-and-error, linguistic capacity, etc. — permits scientific practices to emerge, function, and take hold (thanks to their manifest benefits) within human communities. Any debunker who proclaims that morality could not emerge if natural selection did not *itself* do the work of implanting within us a sense of justice, fairness, impartiality, etc. is welcome to explain how epistemology could have emerged since natural selection did not (I presume) *itself* do the work of implanting within us a devotion to truth for truth's own sake or a commitment to impartial norms of epistemic assessment. Neither human morality nor human scientific practice is comfortably described as 'the product of natural selection'.

IV

I have urged that Flack and de Waal conceive their project more broadly. Many of the key building blocks of morality are not themselves moral. Language, memory, perception, causal inference, learned adjustment, acquiescence, deliberation, choice, self-control, etc. all are essential to morality without themselves being 'dedicated' to moral tasks. Moreover, many of these capacities involve some of the same features that are thought to make morality problematic, thereby enabling us to investigate relevant issues without the entanglements that always seem to accompany discussions of morality. For language, just as much as morality, involves acquiescence in impersonal norms of use, representational accuracy, sincerity, information-sharing, etc. And memory and causal inference, just as much as morality, involve a capacity for attributing authority to representations of states of affairs in ways that are not indexed to personal gain or kin advantage. And empathy — understood as a capacity to simulate the internal states of others (even when one has no particular sympathy or concord with them) by modelling them using one's own cognitive and motivational repertoire — is important not only to impartial benevolence, but also to language learning and communication, social accommodation, escaping or attacking an enemy, courting a mate, hunting a prey, or deceiving one's audience.

Flack and de Waal do an impressive job of bringing together observations of animal conduct that would support the idea that descendants of non-human primates would likely possess many of the building blocks of morality. Their observations do much to undermine the idea that all motivation is traceable to self-interest (whether the 'self' is personal or 'genetic') and thus to block the corollary (drawn by Hobbes) that mutually beneficial social arrangements can only be stable under a real or delusory regime of external incentives or threats. Nothing they turn up suggests that capacities for relatively impersonal motivation or representation would be entirely absent wherever natural selection has done its job. And of course we find in daily moral *and epistemic* life many examples supporting the idea that more or less impersonal motivation and representation can be found among *Homo sapiens*. All this enables us to see more clearly how evolutionary history might furnish us with many of the blocks needed to build morality (or science), without having to do the final or near-final assembly itself.[14]

Reference

Flack, Jessica and de Waal, Frans (2000), ' "Any animal whatever": Darwinian building blocks of morality in monkeys and apes', *Journal of Consciousness Studies*, **7** (1–2), pp. 1–29.

BUILDING ELEMENTS OF MORALITY ARE NOT ELEMENTS OF MORALITY

B. Thierry

Do monkeys and apes display 'elements of rudimentary moral systems'? If these elements correspond to individual abilities, it could be misleading to label them moral. The prosocial abilities of non-human primates may just constitute the foundations necessary to the emergence of morality in human beings, yet their Darwinian significance should be explained on their own, without reference to their possible functions in human beings. On the other hand, if moral elements refer to parts of moral systems, this implies the development of shared norms through cultural evolution. In this respect, the absence of communication about mental representations forbids the directional transmission of learned social rules in non-human primates.

A main contribution of behavioural primatology in the last decades was the demonstration that the social relations of non-human primates cannot be reduced to mere force and struggle (de Waal, 1986; 1996). Monkeys and apes experience cooperation and exchange, protection and control of aggression, reconciliation and negotiation. Reviewing these findings, Flack and de Waal conclude that these behavioural elements likely constituted the foundations necessary to the development of morality in human beings. I fully agree with such a statement, therefore I will not further comment on it.

A second message of the authors is that 'elements of rudimentary moral systems' may be found in non-human primates. This raises several questions. First of all, can some animals have morality? A clear statement expressing the authors' stance is lacking in the target paper as in de Waal's previous work (1996). Flack and de Waal contend that non-human primates have no 'moral systems that mirror the complexity of our own' and that 'animals are no moral philosophers'. But this falls short of the question.

It would not be enough to answer that animals display some elements of a multiple-layered phenomenon. Most of us were taught that the roots of our brain may be found in the cerebral ganglions of earthworms; this does not mean, however, that something like the essence of the brain should be found in earthworms. If we find in animals some behaviours that could be components of the moral systems of humans, this does not imply that animals are moral (cf. Kummer, 1978). The view developed

---

[14] Conversations over the years with Robert Axelrod, Allan Gibbard, Randy Nesse, and Richard Nisbett have much influenced my thinking about evolution and morality, though they might be appalled to read the results.

by Flack and de Waal is fruitful as long as it looks for the building components necessary to the emergence of morality. But since such components are not sufficient by
themselves to produce morality, it would be unproductive to label them moral elements. Said succinctly, building elements of morality are not elements of morality.
The point will be clearer if we pay attention to the fact that 'moral elements' may be
understood alternatively as individual abilities or as parts of moral systems. This is
not mere semantics. According to the meaning retained, the mechanisms of evolution
envisioned are not the same.

If we consider individual abilities, it is relevant to look for their evolutionary origins. As argued by Flack and de Waal, we may investigate whether non-human primates display such capacities as empathy, sharing or reciprocity. However, by calling
them Darwinian blocks of morality, we are at risk of the retrospect fallacy; that means
ascribing to a character observed in animals a function fulfilled in human beings only.
For instance, experimental studies of possession in monkeys have shown that object
and food are more likely to be taken away if they are valuable or difficult to transport
and escape with (Thierry *et al.*, 1989; Kummer and Cords, 1991). The occurrence or
absence of takeovers may therefore be accounted for by tactical factors without relying on respect of possession. Likewise, when a third individual intervenes in an ongoing conflict in a seemingly impartial manner, the impartiality of his motives is not
granted (Petit and Thierry, in press). Even the evidence regarding calculated reciprocity in chimpanzees is still questioned (Hemelrijk, 1996). This does not detract from
the evolutionary significance of abilities that enhance exchanges and lower conflicts
of interest. The use of features that were not initially designed for their current function is a chief mechanism of biological evolution (Gould and Vrba, 1982). A number
of cognitive skills and motivational dispositions contribute to social control and
bonding. They may have constituted a source of raw material for the subsequent
development of morality through the hominization process.

According to a second meaning, moral elements are parts of moral systems. As
generally recognized, moral systems rest on collectively shared norms (Durkheim,
1930). They are not just phenomena emerging from interactions between individuals
gifted with given biological abilities; they include socially transmitted components.
Since we are on the side of cultural evolution, homology between human moral systems and the social phenotypes observed in non-human primates is not warranted. In
chimpanzees, adolescent subjects know how they should approach an adult male and
in which context they have to avoid him; they would otherwise expose themselves to
punishment. When individuals prevent some gestures that might induce an aggression from their mates, it may be said that they follow a prescriptive rule (de Waal,
1996). We know that chimpanzees may obey learned rules. Flack and de Waal
hypothesize that such rules can be internalized by individuals. Would that mean that
some cultural drift could occur and give way to enduring sets of acquired rules? As a
mind experiment, let us consider an influencing male who would be especially intolerant. An outcome of his way of behaving might be that all young community members learn strict rules of submission. After reaching maturity, the latter could similarly
behave in an intolerant way and transmit the rule to the next generation. However, in
the absence of a norm explicitly recognized by the whole community, the rule can be
objectivized only through individual sanction. As a consequence, any individual variation in tolerance levels will be liable to bring the community back to the modal

behaviour of the species. As a matter of fact, no evidence of drift in the social relationships and organizations of chimpanzee has been reported. Whereas dozens of variations in behaviour patterns differentiate chimpanzee communities (Whiten *et al.*, 1999), their social relationships and organizations are reportedly similar everywhere in Africa. There are no mechanisms that allow the establishment of social norms and the setting up of cultural drift in apes (Thierry, 1994; 1997).

The hominization process did not occur in a vacuum. To unravel the origins and specificities of human societies, it is critical to understand how sophisticated social rules stem from the prosocial abilities of non-human primates. To this aim, Flack and de Waal deserve credit for defining the right research agenda. Nonetheless, in fulfilling this program, we have to avoid the pitfalls of a neo-social Darwinism. Moral systems cannot develop outside the context of cultural evolution. Consequently, their emergence in human beings should not be reduced to the laws of biological evolution. As for monkeys and apes, they cannot communicate about collective frames of reference. Being unable to share representations, they live in a fundamentally amoral world. We may save the concept of morality when accounting for their behaviours.

References

Durkheim, E. (1930), *De la Division du Travail Social* (Paris: Presses Universitaires de France).

Gould, S.J. and Vrba, E.S. (1982), 'Exaptation — a missing term in the science of form', *Palaeobiology*, **8**, pp. 4–15.

Hemelrijk, C. (1996), 'Reciprocation in apes: From complex cognition to self-structuring', in , *Great Ape Societies*, ed. W.C. McGrew, L.F. Marchant and T. Nishida (Cambridge: Cambridge University Press).

Kummer, H. (1978), 'Analogs of morality among non-human primates', in *Morality as a Biological Phenomenon*, ed. G.S. Stent (Berlin: Dahlem Konferenzen).

Kummer, H. and Cords, M. (1991), 'Cues of ownership in long-tailed macaques, *Macaca fascicularis*', *Animal Behaviour*, **42**, pp. 529–49.

Petit, O. and Thierry, B. (in press), 'Do impartial interventions occur in monkeys and apes?', in *Natural Conflict Resolution*, ed. F. Aureli and F.B.M. de Waal (Berkeley: University of California Press).

Thierry, B. (1994), 'Social transmission, tradition and culture in primates: from the epiphenomenon to the phenomenon', *Techniques et Culture*, **23/24**, pp. 91–119.

Thierry, B. (1997), 'De la relation entre le développement des facultés d'attribution et les prémices de l'évolution culturelle chez les primates', in *Les Neurosciences et la Philosophie de l'Action*, ed. J.L. Petit (Paris, Vrin).

Thierry, B., Wunderlich, D. and Gueth, C. (1989), 'Possession and transfer of objects in a group of brown capucins (*Cebus apella*)', *Behaviour*, **110**, pp. 294–305.

de Waal, F.B.M. (1986), 'The integration of dominance and social bonding in primates', *Quarterly Review of Biology*, **61**, pp. 459–79.

de Waal, F.B.M. (1996), *Good Natured: The Origins of Right and Wrong in Humans and Other Animals* (Cambridge, MA: Harvard University Press).

Whiten, A., Goodall, J., McGrew, W.C., Nishida, T., Reynolds, V., Sugiyama, Y., Tutin, C.E.G., Wrangham, R.W. and Boesch, C. (1999), 'Cultures in chimpanzees', *Nature*, **399**, pp. 682–5.

HUMAN AND OTHER NATURES

John Troyer

While I agree with the main theses put forward by Flack and de Waal, I am sceptical about whether we learn much about human morality by looking at the behaviour of other primates or our own evolutionary history. I am especially doubtful about attempts to use such data as a base for conclusions about 'human nature'. More direct methods of studying human nature indicate that our genotype is compatible with a very wide range of behaviours, including all those required by even the most

demanding ethical theories. Unfortunately, the same is true of all the behaviours for-
bidden by even the least demanding ethical theories. The important question, it seems
to me, is whether we can identify the developmental and environmental factors that
bring out our best.

I agree with almost all the main theses put forward by Flack and de Waal (2000),
among them the following:

1. Moral practices arose during the course of evolution (p. 2).
2. Many human moral practices almost certainly developed as adaptive strategies
    for dealing with problems arising from social situations that are, in Rawls' words,
    'typically marked by a conflict as well as by an identity of interests' (p. 19).
3. Practices akin to some human moral practices can be found in other animals, per-
    haps especially in other primates (p. 3, *et passim*).
4. There is no evolutionary reason to think that humans, or chimpanzees, or any
    other organisms, will 'by nature' be base or selfish or brutish or 'true denizens of
    Hobbes' state of nature' (p. 2).
5. An extraterrestrial observer, judging 'on the basis of external behaviour alone',
    would be unlikely to judge *Homo sapiens* the 'most moral' animal on the planet
    (p. 24).

But my agreement with these theses (and others) is accompanied by a considerable
scepticism about whether we learn anything much about morality by looking at the
behaviour of other primates or by reflecting on what we know about the evolution of
Homo sapiens. This scepticism seems, at times, to be shared by Flack and de Waal —
for example, when they write that 'Humans . . . may be the only truly moral creatures'
(p. 19), warn that 'Attempts to derive ethical norms from nature . . . are highly questionable' (p. 23), and conclude that 'What we ought to do and how we decide this is a
separate question from how and why moral systems arose' (p. 19). At other points in
the article, however, they appear more sanguine than I am about the prospects for
using knowledge of 'human nature' to inform our moral thinking (see, for example,
p. 23, where they write that 'human morality does need to take human nature into
account'). And indeed one of the main tenets of their paper is that the behaviour of
other primates indicates that 'human nature' may not be so foul as Huxley and others
have claimed.

While I agree with Flack and de Waal that neither fact nor theory supports the view
that 'human nature is essentially evil', I am doubtful that either knowledge of our
evolutionary history or the study of other species can add much to what we learn
about human nature from more direct investigation — the sort of investigation undertaken by anthropologists, historians, psychologists, etc. What this direct investigation
shows is that human nature is compatible with a very wide range of behaviour; people
can live together as peacefully and cooperatively as the Old Order Amish, but they
can also engage in internecine wars, torture innocent children, and practice 'ethnic
cleansing'. If it made sense to talk about the behaviour of 'average people in average
circumstances', perhaps we could get some measure of how virtuous (or vicious)
humans are 'by nature', but I doubt that it does make sense. And even if we had a measure of how well average people can be expected to behave in average circumstances,
it wouldn't tell us how well they could be expected to behave in slightly altered

circumstances. After all, what's given biologically is the genotype, and (as everyone knows) identical genotypes may yield very different phenotypes in different environments. The difference between queen bees and workers is produced not by genes but diet, and genetically identical hydrangeas will bear blue flowers in acid-soils and pink flowers in alkaline. In cases where a phenotype is ubiquitous in a species it may seem that it must have a particularly tight link to the genotype, but this is not true. If all hydrangeas grew in acid soil, having blue flowers would be a ubiquitous phenotype; but the first hydrangea planted in alkaline soil would not, to be able to produce pink flowers, have to overcome some innate tendency to produce blue flowers.

But while everyone knows this, it is tempting to write as if what we are given biologically is a disposition to behave in certain ways, rather than a disposition to behave in certain ways *given a particular developmental environment*. This way of writing, when combined with the (until recently) quite reasonable assumption that we can't do much about our genotypes, leads quite naturally to the mistaken conclusion that our basic behavioural patterns are settled by 'human nature', and that we'd best design our social practices to fit these 'natural tendencies'. Thus Trivers and DeVore, in a brochure describing their film 'Sociobiology: Doing What Comes Naturally', write that:

> . . . it's time we started viewing ourselves as having biological, genetic and natural components to our behaviour, . . . we should start setting up a physical and social world which matches these tendencies. (Caplan, 1978, p. 321.)

This (mistaken) way of thinking will lead to quite different conclusions about how our physical and social world should be fashioned, depending on where you look to determine our 'natural' behavioural tendencies. If you look to food-sharing and grooming behaviour in chimpanzees, you may find yourself agreeing with Kropotkin that cooperative anarchistic communities are the way to go. If you instead stumble on apes that are killing and eating their conspecifics, you may find yourself agreeing with Hobbes that only a strong state and a large police force can keep us from annihilating one another. If you look at human history — which seems to me a more reasonable area to investigate — you find that people behave very differently at different times and places. Perhaps it's the confusion produced by this variability that leads people to look to other primates, or to inquire into our evolutionary history, to decide what constitutes 'real' human nature. But the problem is not that it's hard to find our 'true biological nature', but that our biology does not, in general, impose narrow limits on our behaviour.

Of course biology does, like physics, put constraints on our behaviour. We can't travel faster than the speed of light (in any environment) or fly by flapping our arms (except in space stations) and perhaps we can't behave in ways demanded by some systems of ethics in any currently accessible environments. If so, such systems are mistaken, given that 'ought' implies 'can'. Some philosophers, and I think some biologists, have thought that *any* system of ethics that requires an individual to sacrifice self-interest runs afoul of 'human nature', which is 'selfish' in a way that prohibits all such sacrifices. And some philosophers have thought that *all* systems of ethics require such sacrifices. If so, then biology would show that all systems of ethics are mistaken.

I think the belief that evolutionary theory shows people are inherently selfish, in conjunction with the belief that morality often requires sacrifice, accounts for much of the worry, on the part of Huxley and others, that people are by nature evil and that biology and morality are inevitably at odds. One response to this is to show that good behaviour often makes good selfish sense. Cooperation often pays, favours are often returned, non-violent methods of resolving conflict often work to everyone's advantage, etc. As the evidence compiled by Flack and de Waal demonstrates, other primates have cottoned on to this — or at least behave as if they had — and there seems no reason why we couldn't have as well. And indeed some of us have. Of course reciprocal altruism isn't *really* altruism at all, but there seems to be no reason to suspect evolution would outlaw true altruism (i.e. behaviour in which an agent sacrifices her own interests to benefit others). J.B.S. Haldane is alleged to have said that he would give up his life for three siblings or nine first cousins, and even if he didn't say it, its import has been elegantly established by Hamilton and other exponents of kin selection. And of course even Darwin was well aware of the fact that if some parental sacrifices increase the probability that the number of progeny will be maximized, a tendency to make such sacrifices will be adaptive.

However *some* ethical theories, for example Classical Utilitarianism, demand sacrifice *whenever* it maximizes total net utility, irrespective of who the beneficiaries of the sacrifice are. Indeed, as Bentham emphasized, the beneficiaries need not be *Homo sapiens* — any sentient being's pains and pleasures are, he claimed, as morally significant as our own. It's hard (though not impossible) to imagine circumstances in which a tendency to perform such utilitarian sacrifices would be adaptive, but this does not entail that human nature prohibits such sacrifices. And indeed we know that people sometimes *do* make sacrifices for other animals on utilitarian grounds; indeed they sometimes make sacrifices for reasons that make even less sense from an evolutionary point of view. People choose to be burned to death rather than conceal their religious beliefs, opt for death rather than dishonour, and carry out suicide attacks against those they dislike. They also kill their children (and themselves), practice celibacy, risk their lives to save endangered species or to be the first (or fifty-first) person to climb Mount Everest, and make preparations for nuclear war. What Mr. Squeers (in Dickens's *Nicholas Nickleby*) says about nature in general is perhaps especially true of human nature: 'She's a rum 'un is Natur' . . . . Natur' is more easier conceived than described'.

Human nature is such 'a rum 'un', I contend, that trying to mould our social practices to 'fit' it is like trying to tailor a swimming suit for an amoeba. No swimming suit will fit the amoeba, but the amoeba will fit into a wide range of suits. Of course people are not amoebas; but while we are much less protean than they with respect to shape, we are much more so when it comes to behaviour. If we could design social institutions that seemed reasonable to all, it's hard to see that anything in our genes would keep us from adopting them. Of course we *might* discover that something in our genotype *does* prevent our behaving reasonably in *every* accessible environment. But if we learn this much about the genotype we may also learn how to alter it. I have claimed that history shows few features of human behaviour are 'in our genes'; it also suggests that we are close to a time when not even our genes will be 'in our genes'.

References

Caplan, Arthur L. (ed. 1978), *The Sociobiology Debate* (New York: Harper and Row).
Flack, J.C. and de Waal, F.B.M. (2000), ' "Any animal whatever": Darwinian building blocks of morality in monkeys and apes', *Journal of Consciousness Studies*, **7** (1–2), pp. 1–29.

Jessica C. Flack and Frans B.M. de Waal

Being Nice Is Not a Building Block of Morality

Response to Commentary Discussion

[T]he question to be answered is not what emotions may prompt people to pronounce moral judgments — there are certainly many different emotions that may do that — but whether there are any specific emotions that have led to the formation of the concepts of right and wrong, good and bad, and all other moral concepts.

Edward Westermarck (1932, p. 62)

Behaviour *versus* Building Blocks

Ever since Aristotle, moral philosophers, including David Hume, Adam Smith, and Edward Westermarck, have argued that there are two distinct layers to human morality: (1) moral emotions or sentiments and (2) the capacity for moral judgment and reasoning. We tend to focus on this first layer when we compare humans with other animals because it is closer to direct behavioural expression, hence easier to measure. Investigating the extent to which primates are capable of moral judgement and reasoning is a much more challenging task, and as **Call** discusses, the lack of data in this area constrains what conclusions can be drawn. This explains why we have been reluctant to claim that any animals other than ourselves are moral beings even though some of our commentators seem to think we did.

Regardless of this limitation, moral sentiments are a necessary starting point for investigations of the origins of morality. These sentiments are the very building blocks of morality in that they reflect the tendencies and capacities (for example, the capacities for empathy and perspective taking) without which human morality as we know it would be unthinkable. The moral sentiments, and their underlying capacities, however, are not necessarily *objects* of morality. For example, we would, with Westermarck (1912), classify the tendency for retribution as a prerequisite for a rule-based, just society — hence as a critical building block of morality — whereas we may, at the same time, morally disapprove of many of its expressions. Furthermore, and as **Railton** points out, many important building blocks of morality, such as deliberation and learned adjustment, are 'all essential to morality without themselves being "dedicated" to moral tasks'.

Distinguishing between the behaviours that we judge and the capacities that make these behaviours and judgments possible seems to be a major source of confusion for

Journal of Consciousness Studies, **7**, No. 1–2, 2000, pp. 67–77

some of our commentators, such as **Kummer** and **Troyer** — and **Kagan**, who suggests that if we allow the use of anthropomorphic terms when describing animal behaviour, we may legitimately conclude that a 'hypersexed female rhesus monkey is a tart'. This confusion is not new, going back to Seton (1907) and several ethologists (for example, Wickler, 1981; Kummer, 1978, critically reviewed by Vogel, 1985) who have tried to determine natural analogues to the Ten Commandments. Even if such analogues exist, they tell us very little — as **Kummer** correctly points out with his example of monogamy in birds — about the origins of morality. Consequently, we need to sharply distinguish the moral evaluation of animal behaviour — which is indeed a naive and rather useless enterprise — from the search for moral abilities and tendencies in animals other than ourselves.

Recently, the important distinction between behaviour and capacity in the discussion of morality was emphasized by Arnhart (1998), who argues that biologically-based desires and cognitive capacities form the basis for the emergence of morality. He stresses that these natural capacities can not be realized except through social learning and moral habituation, thus distinguishing them from the social instincts. Furthermore, he argues that although the specific content of this learning is structured by the natural repertoire of desires and capacities, it is variable according to the social and physical circumstances of the society in question. Anyone who understands this argument quickly realizes that although, for example, the capacity for cognitive empathy often contributes to the production of behaviour that we judge moral (for example, sharing food), it also at times contributes to the production of behaviour that we judge immoral (for example, deception). The capacity itself is not subject to moral evaluation. It is also important to recognize, as Arnhart points out, that it is not correct to characterize these kinds of capacities as innate. Humans and other animals may indeed be predisposed to developing certain capacities but these capacities develop through learning and experience. Thus, we must resist the temptation to conclude, as do **Gruter and Gruter**, that a particular capacity, which is part of the human repertoire, is innate because it is also present in the repertoire of our primate relatives. We agree with **Güth and Güth,** and also **Thierry**, that such an assumption likely underestimates the complexity and frailty of the pathway from predisposition to behavioural expression.

It should by now be clear that instead of arguing that food-sharing is a building block of morality, our intention was to emphasize the capacities thought to *underlie* human food-sharing (for example, high levels of tolerance, sensitivity to others' needs, reciprocity), and to argue that the existence of food-sharing in some non-human primates suggests that they, too, are likely endowed with these capacities. It is these capacities that are the building blocks of morality, not the behaviour resulting from them. Food-sharing, and its counterpart, the punishment of stingy individuals, are important for other reasons as well. They suggest something that monogamy in birds cannot. The observation of these behaviours in non-human primates, although not directly evidence for the biological origins of morality, suggests that there may be room in their societies for an implicit system of conflict management that is based on shared values and expectations. It does not matter what these values are — only that they exist. We thus agree with **Railton** that we must be able to identify more than just a *modus vivendi* in primate societies if we are to suggest that within these societies there are building blocks of moral systems.

Let us therefore try to define what morality is, as requested by **Troyer, Bernstein** and **Moore**. This is not an easy task — nor is it a task to be taken lightly — as many definitions, conceptions, and versions of morality exist. In an effort not to detract from the significance of this variability, we prefer a broad characterization over a definition of morality and moral systems, one that should obviously be devoid of moral prescription. We understand morality as a sense of right and wrong that is born out of group-wide systems of conflict management based on shared values. This characterization of morality and moral systems is close to Boehm's (this issue), for whom morality is the product of shared values imposed on the individual by the group, and to Alexander's (1987), for whom moral systems are systems of indirect reciprocity. Moral systems thus provide a set of rules and incentives to resolve competition and conflicts within the group in the service of the 'greater good', that is, the benefits (to individuals) derived from resource distribution and collective action. Morality, by this definition, is closely related to prosocial behaviour.

Only superficial consideration combined with preconceptions about the 'morality' of prosocial behaviour could lead, however, to the conclusion that the definitions discussed here do little to distinguish morality from being nice, as **Moore** suggests. If prosocial behaviour is any behaviour that facilitates long-term, ultimately positive, iterated interaction between and among individuals, as we define it (for an alternative conception, see Batson, 1998), then punishment of wrongdoers can be as prosocial as reconciliation and forgiveness. All moral behaviour is necessarily prosocial *on some level of analysis*; but by no means is all prosocial behaviour moral. In addition to producing moral outcomes, prosocial behaviour can produce immoral, and more importantly, amoral outcomes. For example, a day camp counsellor who remains friendly and tolerant with a child that is causing a lot of trouble for other children in the group may be called prosocial at one level even though he is failing to instill moral values. An even more poignant example of a prosocial behaviour pattern that may be evaluated as immoral (albeit sympathetically), is the reconciliation that often follows physical or verbal assault in abusive relationships. Prosocial behaviour that may produce an amoral outcome includes engaging in mutualism, which involves no obligation, and thus cannot be subject to shared values or expectations. To sum up, building blocks of morality are *not* behaviours that are 'good' and 'nice', but rather mental and social *capacities* that permit the construction of societies in which shared values constrain individual behaviour through a system of approval and disapproval. Animals, including chimpanzees, have not evolved moral systems anywhere near the level of ours, but they do show some of the behavioural capacities that are built into our moral systems.

Support for the Project

We were pleased to see so much support for the basic premises of our project. None of the commentators tries to place morality fully outside the evolutionary realm as Huxley (1894) and his followers have done. This indicates that we are all on the same Darwinian line. Even **Kagan**, who otherwise is a critic, concludes at the end of his commentary that the human moral sense is an evolutionary product that is maintained because it is adaptive. He doesn't say, however, how and why morality is adaptive. We of course argue that as soon as one ponders this question, it becomes clear that some of the tendencies involved must predate the arrival of our species. **Railton** recognizes the likelihood of this conclusion in his thoughtful and highly constructive commentary in that he agrees that the studies of primate behaviour 'enable us to see more clearly how evolutionary history might furnish us with many of the blocks needed to build morality without having to do the final or near-final assembly itself'. It is, however, the last component of this statement that reflects particularly important insight about how an emergent phenomenon like morality might result from evolutionary processes. Implicit in **Railton's** statement is the idea that natural selection shaped the building blocks of morality from raw materials, while some other process or mechanism (perhaps self-organization) made possible the transition from building blocks to a full-blown phenomenon (see below for more discussion on this).

Despite reservations that our approach may reflect an attempt to reduce the emergence of moral systems to the laws of biological evolution, **Thierry**, like **Kagan**, acknowledges a place for biology in the study of moral systems. He agrees that those motivational dispositions and cognitive abilities that contribute to the formation and maintenance of social relationships may also provide the raw material from which morality develops. He is unwilling, however, to extend the concept of morality in any sense beyond the human domain. To support this conclusion, **Thierry** suggests that morality is a product of the interaction of cultural and biological evolution. This process, he argues, does not occur in any animal societies for if it did, there would be evidence of cultural drift (or selection) and also for the social transmission of behaviour. **Thierry** is right to point out that (1) morality is a product of feedback between the social (perhaps cultural) and individual (perhaps biological) levels and that, (2) thus far the evidence for cultural drift and social transmission of behaviour in animal societies is sparse. As discussed earlier, we agree with Arnhart (1998), **Güth and Güth**, and **Troyer** that the developmental pathway between predisposition and behavioural expression is complex, influenced by learning, and mediated by the social environment. Research is sorely needed in this area, but contrary to what **Thierry** suggests, there is substantial variation among social systems in some animal societies, such as those of chimpanzees (de Waal, 1994).

Thierry makes another important contribution to the project through his observation that in our attempt to understand the degree to which moral systems have been influenced by our biological heritage, we in some sense appropriate from ideas about human morality the building blocks we seek in other animals (retrospect fallacy). In theory, the retrospect fallacy can be avoided if we use a top-down approach to outline (1) how a moral system should, from an evolutionary point of view, operate and function and, (2) what criteria are essential for the emergence of such a system. In practice, however, it is impossible to avoid entirely the retrospect fallacy because in order to study moral systems, we must have some idea of what they are, and this is necessarily influenced by our own experience with them (especially when we believe we have no other standard for comparison). **Moore** also identifies this problem when he writes, 'We need to be careful to avoid thinking we understand a trait because we've named it . . . and similarly be cautious of slipping from conceptually distinct punitive traits to discrete mental modules.'

In a manner quite different from that of the other commentators, **Gruter and Gruter** demonstrate agreement with our project's thesis in that they extend the approach to the study of legal systems. They suggest that some of the same building blocks of morality (for example, capacities underlying moralistic aggression, sympathy, reciprocity, etc.) that are present in our non-human primate relatives, are also the building blocks of legal systems. In addition to bringing into our project a perspective from another field, **Gruter and Gruter's** commentary touches on an important problem. How is it that we distinguish within a *biological point of view* a moral system from a legal system? Furthermore, assuming that the two systems can be distinguished within a biological point of view, how is it that two different systems emerge from the same building blocks? Perhaps the major difference is that in moral systems, norms must be internalized, whereas in legal systems, individuals simply need to recognize the rules and the costs that may accrue from breaking them. Furthermore, because norms are not necessarily internalized in legal systems, third party monitoring of behaviour becomes a more important mechanism of control. In this sense, legal systems must be more public than moral systems, in that they require stated, explicit agreement among individuals. Until one considers this last point, it may seem that a legal system would be more likely than a moral system to emerge in animal societies.

Two Different Principles of Parsimony

Kagan, Kummer, and **Bernstein** chide us for postulating similarities between humans and other primates that may not exist. At the same time they are perfectly willing to take the converse risk of denying similarities that are very well possible. **Kagan** even postulates unproven differences, such as when he assumes that chimpanzees share food only under pressure. This position is not borne out by the facts. For example, sharing through a mesh partition occurs even though the risk of aggression has been eliminated, the most generous sharers are often the most dominant individuals who have little to fear, and respect for possession is found in a variety of primates (de Waal, 1996, pp. 152–3). Furthermore, to support his view, **Kagan** capriciously claims that a chimpanzee will not jump into a cold lake to save another. It is unclear what we can learn from such highly specific comparisons, especially with a species that doesn't swim, but it may help to quote Goodall (1990, p. 213) on this issue:

> In some zoos, chimpanzees are kept on man-made islands, surrounded by water-filled moats . . . . Chimpanzees cannot swim and, unless they are rescued, will drown if they fall into deep water. Despite this, individuals have sometimes made heroic efforts to save companions from drowning — and were sometimes successful. One adult male lost his life as he tried to rescue a small infant whose incompetent mother had allowed it to fall into the water.

Both **Kummer** and **Kagan** mention negative test results as if such results carry much weight, whereas we all know that failure to demonstrate a presence is not the same as a demonstration of an absence. The ongoing debate about theory-of-mind in monkeys and apes is far from closed. Even as we write this reply, some researchers are obtaining positive results — which *are* interpretable. **Call's** commentary, in which he rightly speaks of a 'mixed bag' of results, provides a more careful phrasing of the possibilities as currently perceived by people in this field.

The bias betrayed in all of this, and in **Bernstein's** implicit call for parsimony, is that the burden of proof is placed on those who postulate fundamental mental and emotional similarities between humans and apes, rather than those who prefer to err on the other side. Is it really likely that similar behaviour in closely related species is differently motivated and organized? If a person embraces a victim of attack, we assume empathy and perspective-taking to underlie her behaviour. On what grounds would we conclude otherwise when a chimpanzee embraces a victim of attack? To propose a different explanation in the case of these animals seems uneconomic, and from an evolutionary perspective, thoroughly puzzling because identical actions under functionally similar circumstances are unlikely to be produced through entirely different emotional and cognitive channels. Hence we join **Güth and Güth** in asking why those who claim that only humans have empathy feel no need to support their position.

Our willingness to err on the side of similarity rather than difference also implies that we don't shy away from what **Kummer** calls 'interpretative' terminology, or what we would rather call 'heuristic' terminology. We certainly don't assume that by choosing certain words we are relieved of our obligation to substantiate our hypothesis or its alternatives. When **Kummer** explains that as early as 1974 he suggested some form of relationship-repair after fights, which was unfortunately ignored in the literature, he hits precisely on the great advantage and stimulating power of an explicit, testable albeit speculative formulation of underlying processes.

Kummer was not the only one to have suggested relationship-repair before de Waal and van Roosmalen (1979) created a new field of enquiry by introducing the term reconciliation to the primatological literature. A recent review by de Waal (in press) documents several other such suggestions all the way back to Köhler (1925). However tantalizing these early one-line suggestions were, they did not demand the same attention as an explicit functional label accompanied by clear-cut predictions and systematic observational data. Cord's (1992) study tested in an elegant experiment a prediction derived from the 'reconciliation' label, namely that the process should restore baseline tolerance between former opponents. Conducted in Kummer's own laboratory, this study was clearly inspired by precisely the 'reconciliation' label and its corresponding implications.

Both **Kummer** and **Bernstein** seem to advocate a largely descriptive primatology in which the observer does not dwell beyond the immediately observable. Perception without expectation and interpretation is, however, an illusion. Commonly accepted terms, such as 'threat', 'courtship', 'play', and 'dominance', are heavily infused with intentionality and functional significance. Both commentators themselves have introduced to the primate literature or made extensive use of terms that make assumptions about underlying processes, such as 'respect for possession' (Kummer, 1978), 'control role' (Bernstein and Sharpe, 1966), and 'socialization' (for example, Bernstein and Ehardt, 1985). We have nothing against these terms for the same reason as that mentioned above — they help us organize reality in a testable way – but we do object to criticism that we use overly demanding interpretations by scientists who don't mind speaking of 'marriage' in baboons (Kummer, 1996).

The disagreement between **Kummer, Kagan**, and **Bernstein**, on the one hand, and us, on the other, seems to boil down to a difference in *assumptions* rather than a difference in the agreed-upon practice of empirical science. While we agree that similarities are as hard to demonstrate as differences, and that we need to keep working in this area, we adhere to the principle of evolutionary parsimony, and so urge scientists to avoid postulating differences between closely related species unless compelled by available evidence (de Waal, 1991; 1997). The primary point is that social complexity and intelligence in monkeys, apes, and humans varies along a continuum and thus is distinguished by degree and not categorically. Depending on one's perspective, this may seem an elevation of the cognitive abilities of monkeys and apes to the human level, or by the same token it may seem a demotion of the cognitive abilities of humans to a lower level. Neither view of human and animal behaviour is much in line with our cultural heritage of human–animal dualism, but there is no point in trying to develop models of how and why we became cultural, political, and moral beings while maintaining a pre-Darwinian perspective.

Needless to say, the evolutionary parsimony principle has as long and distinguished a history as the cognitive parsimony principle advocated by behaviourists, and echoed by **Kagan**, **Kummer**, and **Bernstein**. It was most clearly expressed well before Darwin in the touchstone of David Hume (1739, p. 226):

> 'Tis from the resemblance of the external actions of animals to those we ourselves perform, that we judge their internal likewise to resemble ours; and the same principle of reasoning, carry'd one step farther, will make us conclude that since our internal actions resemble each other, the causes, from which they are deriv'd, must also be resembling. When any hypothesis, therefore, is advanc'd to explain a mental operation, which is common to men and beasts, we must apply the same hypothesis to both.

Empirical Difficulties and Evolutionary Issues

Railton suggests that we conceive our inquiry into the building blocks of morality more broadly so as to avoid having to resort to unfortunate arguments, such as ascribing to our primate relatives a rudimentary sense of justice, to defend our position. **Railton** views such characterizations as an attempt by us to find in primates a 'proto-form' of the moral point of view, which he thinks may represent 'wishful over-interpretation'. At the same time he clearly agrees with us that one needs to look behind the behaviour at the capacities that produce it, writing that ' . . . perceptual, cognitive, and motivational capacities which, once joined to our representational, inferential, epistemic, and communicative capacities, *make attainable* something like a moral point of view' [emphasis added]. Thus, **Railton** asks us to build a house out of pine while forbidding us from using wood in its construction in that he wants these capacities to be studied but is unwilling to allow them to be studied in the only way they are presently accessible: By looking at their products.

It is unfortunate that these perceptual, cognitive, and motivational capacities cannot be studied by themselves. The only way we can tackle them is through behavioural experimentation and observation. In this sense we are in the same boat as Darwin, who also didn't stop at behaviour *per se* when he surmised that 'parental and filial affections' (what we would now called attachment and bonding) are essential ingredients of morality. Darwin faced the same dilemma that moral capacities are only accessible to the human observer by studying their products. As **Bernstein** points out, this confronts us with some serious empirical difficulties. We differ from **Bernstein**, however, in that we see these difficulties as a challenge rather than an obstacle. The explicit description of behaviour that appears to reflect a rudimentary sense of justice, for example, may stimulate further research. **Call** creatively suggests ways to tackle these issues because he recognizes that the potential gains from resolving methodological problems warrant the pursuit.

Some of **Railton's** motivation for suggesting that we conceive of our project more broadly appears to stem from concerns about whether it is accurate to describe morality and moral systems as products (although not solely) of natural selection. But something that is a product of selection need not also be, nor have ever been, an object of selection either directly or indirectly. Natural selection did not necessarily, as **Railton** worries we are suggesting, 'do itself the work of implanting within us a sense of justice, fairness, impartiality, etc. . . .' Morality and moral systems, like social systems in general, are emergent in that they arise out of the interactions of smaller parts yet are not necessarily reducible to those parts. Morality has few, if any, universal rules precisely because the specifics are not biologically dictated: It is an open-ended system that at the same time rests on species-typical tendencies and capacities.

Future Research

There are two distinct research agendas the pursuit of which are bound to help us better understand how moral systems and morality evolved. The goal of one agenda should, as we see it, be to study how a moral system emerges from its component parts. The goal of the other agenda should be to replicate and extend the work that has been reviewed here, attending in particular to some questions about expectations, social rules, and transgressions, which have rarely been addressed. We have reviewed in this paper those studies that thus far have generated data relevant to the study of moral systems, and we have tentatively concluded — with support from several commentators — that some elements of moral systems are present in the societies of other animals. There remain, however, several research areas that demand attention. The most notable of these areas have been identified or addressed by commentators including **Call, Kummer, Thierry,** and **Bernstein. Bernstein**, for example, points to the importance of distinguishing motivation from function, a particularly precarious task when we study how conflicts among individuals in society are managed and negotiated. It is easy to forget that morality is just one mechanism by which this end may be achieved. Legal systems may have similar effects to moral systems in this regard, and although they are in many respects similar, how social stability is generated through the legal system may be quite different from how it is done through the moral system. For example, legal systems may be entirely contractual whereas moral systems have a more significant affective component.

Bernstein emphasizes that empirically assessing motivation is an extremely tricky issue, although an essential one to be addressed before we can expect to reach any conclusion about whether our moral sense is (or is not) unique. When a subordinate macaque takes a piece of fruit that is in proximity to a dominant individual, and then is attacked by the dominant, we need to ask if the motivation for the dominant animal's response arose out of frustration over losing the food, thus prompting a desire to get back the food, or whether the response arose from frustration that a *subordinate* dared to take a piece of fruit that was essentially in the dominant animal's possession, thus prompting the desire to 'teach' the subordinate a lesson about violating rules. It is possible that the dominant animal's attack may have been motivated by both desires (note that it can easily serve both functions without being motivated by both desires), for example, if the intensity of aggression of the attack was higher than that which was required to simply retrieve the fruit. An empirically clearer example of punishment might be if the dominant attacked the subordinate, retrieved the food, ate or stored the food, and then, unprovoked, directed aggression at the subordinate again. Empirically demonstrating either case, however, is not easy because doing so requires the use of multiple controls to eliminate confounds and special attention to context and sequence of events.

Call discusses in his constructive commentary some of the finer theoretical and methodological issues that need to be distinguished in the study of social rules and norms, concepts that reflect the basis of human morality. He points out that social rules or norms may in animals rest on the capacity to use and perceive norms without full understanding or perception of intention, which he suggests is at the 'core of what humans consider right or wrong'. This suggests several complementary lines of inquiry: First, *do* animals use social rules because they perceive and are influenced by them, and if so, what are these rules, and what are the constraints on their application? Furthermore, how can prescriptive social rules be empirically distinguished from descriptive rules or inter-individual behavioural constancy? And how are social rules initially negotiated and socially transmitted? The last line of inquiry involves questions such as: Can animals perceive the intentions of others, and do they modify their response to a behaviour that deviates from their understanding of the actor's intentions?

Call suggests studying bystander reaction to social interactions as a promising method by which to extract some of this information. This is an approach on which we are currently working. In one set of studies on macaques, which will eventually be extended to chimpanzees, we are investigating the context and factors of dyadic and polyadic conflict that are associated with third-party interference in general, taking into account the type of intervention that occurs, the cost to the intervener, how the conflict changes after the intervention occurs, and most importantly, to whom in the original conflict the agonistic and non-agonistic components of the intervention were directed. This last aspect of our investigation is particularly important because after we have determined how an individual typically intervenes, we may ask in what contexts does this intervention pattern deviate. For example, let's say we observe that a particular male almost always intervenes on behalf of a favourite female when she is involved in a conflict with another female. This situation provides us with the opportunity to compare those interventions in which the male intervenes in favour of this favourite female (the base-line pattern) with those interventions in which the male sided with the female for whom he has no preference, asking if there is something about these particular conflicts that may have motivated the male to deviate from his regular pattern (for an example of this behaviour in chimpanzees, see de Waal, 1982, p. 171).

In addition to the more traditional observational and experimental studies that shed light on questions about the origins of moral systems, there are some recently developed experimental approaches that are promising. **Kummer** refers in his commentary to Dasser's (1988) work in which she demonstrated that macaques have a concept of the mother–child relationship using a paradigm in which the macaques are presented with slides in which different social relationships are recognizable. **Kummer** suggests that this paradigm may be useful for demonstrating empirically that non-human primates are capable of something such as community concern. Recent technological advances and methodological improvements by our team have made it possible to conduct similar experiments with both static and dynamic images presented on computer screens (for example, Parr and de Waal, 1999; Parr *et al.*, 2000). This may make it possible to 'ask' monkeys and apes 'questions' about their evaluation of or preferences for particular social situations, or to systematically study expectations by manipulating the outcome of a presented social interaction. These methodologies are especially important in light of recent results by Anderson *et al.* (1999) that suggest that one cause of defective social and moral reasoning in humans may be damage to the prefrontal cortex early in life that disrupts systems in the brain that may 'hold covert, emotionally related knowledge of social situations'.

Finally, in line with our claim that the building blocks of morality are not to be confused with 'nice' behaviour, we should also look at the other side of the coin. De Waal (1996) already pointed out that cruelty engages the same perspective-taking abilities as sympathy (i.e. in order to be intentionally cruel, one needs to understand the effects of one's behaviour on the other), and a recent study lends empirical support to *psychopathy* as a useful construct in the evaluation of chimpanzee personality (Lilienfeld *et al.*, in press). Hence, an evolutionary perspective on morality automatically leads us to consider in other animals immoral as well as moral tendencies. Ironically, morality and immorality make use of the same capacities.

Conclusion

The study of the biological basis of morality and moral systems is a blossoming field. Despite occasional methodological and theoretical disagreement, it is apparent to us that it is worthwhile to consider the origins, development, and operation of moral systems from an evolutionary perspective. At the very least, such consideration will continue to produce a lively debate that will stimulate and shape future research on the topic. The studies reviewed throughout this paper suggest that one of the most promising methods available for addressing the questions that arise from the topic has been and will continue to be the detailed comparison between humans and other social animals with respect to expressions of empathy, reciprocity, social rules, and conflict resolution.

Acknowledgements

We thank the commentators for their stimulating responses to our paper and Leonard Katz for his suggestions. We also thank Harold Gouzoules, Jason Davis, Sarah Brosnan, David Brown, and Sutton Edlich for helpful discussion of the topic.

References

Alexander, R.D. (1987), *The Biology of Moral Systems* (New York: Aldine de Gruyter).
Anderson, S.W., Bechara, A., Damasio, H., Tranel, D. and Damasio, A. (1999), 'Impairment of social and moral behavior related to early damage in human prefrontal cortex', *Nature Neuroscience*, **2** (11), pp. 1032–7.
Arnhart, L. (1998), *Darwinian Natural Right: The Biological Ethics of Human Nature* (Albany, NY: State University of New York Press).
Batson, C.D. (1998), 'Altruism and prosocial behavior', in *The Handbook of Social Psychology, Vol. 2 (4th ed.)*, ed. D.T. Gilbert, S.T. Fiske *et al.* (Boston: McGraw-Hill).
Bernstein, I.S. and Ehardt, C.L. (1985), 'Age–sex differences in the expression of agonistic behaviour in rhesus monkeys (*Macaca mulatta*) Groups', *Journal of Comparative Psychology*, **99** (2), pp. 115–32.
Bernstein, I.S. and Sharpe, I.G. (1966), 'Social Roles in a rhesus monkey group', *Behaviour*, **26**, pp. 91–104.

Cords, M. (1992), 'Post-conflict reunions and reconciliation in long-tailed macaques', *Animal Behaviour*, **44** (1), pp. 57–63.

Dasser, V. (1988), 'A social concept in Java monkeys', *Animal Behaviour*, **36**, pp. 225–30.

Goodall, J. (1990), *Through a Window: My Thirty Years with the Chimpanzees of Gombe* (Boston: Houghton Mifflin Company).

Hume, D. (1978 [1739]), *A Treatise of Human Nature* (Oxford: Oxford University Press).

Huxley, T. (1894 [1989]), *Evolution and Ethics* (Princeton: Princeton University Press).

Kohler, W. (1925), T*he Mentality of Apes* (New York: Vintage).

Kummer, H. (1978), 'Analogues of human morality among non-human primates', in *Morality as a Biological Phenomenon*, ed. G.S. Stent (Berlin: Abakon Verlagsgesellschaft).

Kummer, H. (1996), *In Quest of the Sacred Baboon: A Scientist's Journey* (Princeton: Princeton University Press).

Lilienfeld, S.O., Gershon, J., Duke, M., Marino, L., and de Waal, F.B.M. (1999), 'A preliminary investigation of the construct of psychopathic personality (psychopathy) in chimpanzees (*Pan troglodytes*)', *Journal of Comparative Psychology*, **113**, pp. 365–75.

Parr, L.A., Winslow, J.T., Hopkins, W.D., and de Waal, F.B.M. (2000), 'Recognizing facial cues in chimpanzees (*Pan troglodytes*) and rhesus monkeys (*Macaca mulatta*)', *Journal of Comparative Psychology* (in press).

Parr, L.A., and de Waal, F.B.M. (1999), 'Visual kin recognition in chimpanzees' *Nature*, **399**, pp. 647–8.

Seton, E.T. (1907), *The Natural History of the Ten Commandments* (New York: Scribners).

Vogel, C. (1985), 'Evolution und Moral', in *Zeugen des Wissens*, ed. H. Maier-Leibnitz (Mainz: Hase & Koehler).

de Waal, F.B.M. (1982), *Chimpanzee: Power and Sex Among Apes* (London: Jonathon Cape).

de Waal, F.B.M. (1991), 'Complementary methods and convergent evidence in the study of primate social cognition', *Behaviour*, **118**, pp. 297–320.

de Waal, F.B.M. (1994), 'The Chimpanzee's adaptive potential: A comparison of social life under captive and wild conditions', in *Chimpanzee Cultures*, ed. R.W. Wrangham, W.C. McGrew, F.B.M. de Waal and P. Heltne (Cambridge, MA: Harvard University Press).

de Waal, F.B.M. (1996), *Good Natured: The Origins of Right and Wrong in Primates and Other Animals* (Cambridge, MA: Harvard University Press).

de Waal, F.B.M. (1997), 'Are we in anthropodenial?', *Discover*, **6** (97), pp. 50–3.

de Waal, F.B.M. (In press), 'The first kiss: Foundations of conflict resolution research in animals', in *Natural Conflict Resolution*, ed. F. Aureli and F.B.M. de Waal (Berkeley: University of California Press).

de Waal, F.B.M. and van Roosmalen, A. (1979), 'Reconciliation and consolation among chimpanzees', *Behavioral Ecology and Sociobiology*, **5**, pp. 55–66.

Westermarck, E. (1912 [1906]), *The Origin and Development of Moral Ideas (Vol. 1)* (London: Macmillan).

Westermarck, E. (1932), *Ethical Relativity* (New York: Harcourt, Brace and Company).

Wickler, W. (1971 [1981]), *Die Biologie der Zehn Gebote: Warum die Natur uns kein Vorbild ist* (Munich: Piper).

Christopher Boehm

Conflict and the Evolution of Social Control

With an interest in origins, it is proposed that conflict within the group can be taken as a natural focus for exploring the evolutionary development of human moral communities. Morality today involves social control but also the management of conflicts within the group. It is hypothesized that early manifestations of morality involved the identification and collective suppression of behaviours likely to cause such conflict. By triangulation the mutual ancestor of humans and the two Pan *species lived in pronounced social dominance hierarchies, and made largely individualized efforts to damp conflict within the group, exhibiting consolation, reconciliation, and active pacifying intervention behaviour. It is particularly the active interventions that can be linked with social control as we know it. It is proposed that when this process became collectivized, and when language permitted the definition and tracking of proscribed behaviour, full-blown morality was on its way. Because early humans lived in egalitarian bands, a likely candidate for the first behaviour to be labelled as morally deviant is not the incest taboo but bullying behaviour, of the type that egalitarian humans today universally proscribe and suppress.*

Morality as Politics

All humans live in moral communities of the type discussed by Durkheim (1933), in which public opinion decisively shapes the behaviour of individuals. Shared values define specific rights and wrongs of behaviour, and the group decides which individuals are deviant and sanctions them accordingly. These are constants of human social life, and on this basis a moral community engages actively in social control. It has been chiefly sociologists (see Black, 1998) who have taken responsibility for explanations in this area, and their theories are regularly couched in terms of social forces that result in 'deviance and social control'. Substantial insights have derived from this approach — which has been borrowed heavily by anthropologists (e.g., Selby, 1974).

A number of attempts have been made to explain moral origins. Unfortunately, scholars have been slow to recognize protomoral behaviours in other species (e.g., Stent, 1981), and not a great deal has been accomplished specifically with respect to origins since the work of Darwin (1859; 1865; 1871) and Westermarck (1894). This is

Journal of Consciousness Studies, **7**, No. 1–2, 2000, pp. 79–101

the case even though the relation of certain aspects of moral behaviour to natural selection has been explored by a number of social biologists (e.g., Wilson, 1978; Fox, 1983; Alexander, 1987; Wright, 1994; Ridley, 1996) and others (e.g., Campbell, 1965; 1972; Wilson, 1993; Wilson and Sober, 1994; Sober and Wilson, 1998). Here, in explaining the evolutionary development of moral behaviour, the analysis will be more 'political' than 'sociological'. Indeed, I shall suggest that moral systems are driven very heavily by considerations of power (Weber, 1947; see also Black, 1998). In effect, a large, *ad hoc*, community-wide political coalition serves as watchdog over individual behaviours that could lead to victimization of others, or to conflict within the group (see Boehm, 1982, 1999b). This macro-coalition is prepared to use coercive force, if it must, to protect individual group members from predatory exploitation or other harm, and to protect the entire group from disruption and stress brought on by disputes.

Social control is about the power of deviants to harm or distress others, but it is also about the power of a vigilant, assertive group that is bent upon manipulating or eliminating its deviants. In even the smallest band or tribe, the price of deviance can be assassination: capital punishment is one of the sanctions used against those who become seriously out of line (e.g., Boehm, 1985; 1993). This universal pattern of group vigilance is based on behavioural dispositions that are quite ancient, for in effect moral communities amount to political coalitions and power coalitions are found in many of the higher primates. In fact, they also are found in other social mammals (see Harcourt and de Waal, 1992), and coalitions sometimes grow very large as entire communities defend themselves against external predators, sometimes unite against neighbouring groups, and, rarely but significantly, sometimes turn against individuals in the same group.

There is far more to morality than a group's momentarily uniting against a deviant individual: morality involves common agreement as to which behaviours are unacceptable, and it also involves a group's overall conception of a satisfactory quality of social and political life. There also has to be a precise exchange of information among group members as they carefully track the behaviours of other individuals, and a capacity to manipulate deviants strategically in order to satisfy this pattern. Thus, some major further developments had to take place, and in their definitive form they probably arrived in the Late Palaeolithic, as modern humans emerged (Boehm, 1999b).

If we could hypothesize what other pre-adaptations existed, and how those developments evolved, we would be on the road to an evolutionary explanation of moral behaviour. A first task, however, is to determine what the overall social life of Late Palaeolithic foragers was like. Fortunately, there are some important shreds of direct archaeological evidence (see Mithen, 1990; Tattersall, 1993). Anatomically Modern Humans foraged as nomads as they hunted and gathered in smallish bands, and it seems likely that bands were composed of at least thirty persons (Dunbar, 1996) and therefore were larger than nuclear families. There is no evidence of humans being sedentary 100,000 years ago, or even 25,000 years ago, so presumably their bands moved around within familiar home ranges. However, radical changes of climate (see Potts, 1996) led them periodically to undertake migrations (see Tattersall, 1993) that eventually led to major geographic radiations of this species. These people sometimes seem to have cared for the injured, and they sometimes buried their dead — an act also performed by Neanderthals. However, aside from group size there is little evidence that can be related directly to social control.

This very minimal social portrait fits with extant foragers who remain nomadic, and the similarities of band size, local migration pattern, and subsistence strategy at least provide an anchor for analysis-by-triangulation. We may now consider central behavioural tendencies of extant bands, and ask whether they might be projected back into the Late Palaeolithic. Such bands are highly variable in their social organization and subsistence pattern (Ember, 1978; Kelly, 1995), but so long as they remain mobile — rather than sedentary — they are remarkably uniform in their social, moral, and political makeup. Band size fits nicely with the range suggested by Dunbar, while bands are composed of some related and some unrelated families (Kelly, 1995). Families tend to move back and forth from band to band (see Palmer *et al.*, 1998), but in spite of this the members of a band co-operate intensively, particularly in sharing their large-game meat (Kelly, 1995). Bands invariably are moralistic, for they practice sanctioning according to established values that assist in identifying deviants. The lists of deviant behaviour are remarkably uniform from one continent to another, and these mobile bands are uniformly egalitarian (see Cashdan, 1980; Gardner, 1991) with respect to relations among adult males. By this I mean that they suppress undue competition, and head off attempts of individuals to exert domination or control; as a result, they tolerate very little leadership (see Furer-Haimendorf, 1967). It is very likely that all of these features of extant bands pertain to the Late Palaeolithic (see Mithen, 1990; Boehm, 1999b).

There is another avenue for drawing some *general* inferences about that earlier epoch. Cladistic analysis (e.g., Wrangham, 1987) enables us to compare the two *Pan* species with our own, and see which social and political features all three share. The assumption is that any feature shared by all three is likely to have been present in the ancestor shared by *Homo* and *Pan,* who lived five million years ago by molecular reckoning. In the area of social and political behaviour, our beginning list of shared features is impressive (see Boehm, 1999b). All three species forage for a living and live in territorially-oriented communities that are subject to internal fission and fusion. All three are prone to status rivalry and competition based on flexible innate dispositions to dominate and submit, and all three work in political coalitions that often are dyadic but can become triadic or larger. Therefore, all three experience conflict. All three also engage in deliberate conflict resolution. These basic socio-political factors pertain to the Mutual Ancestor of *Pan* and *Homo*, and to any intermediate lineage that connects directly with one of the three extant species. They will figure very importantly in the analysis of moral communities and their origins, and I shall provide greater detail as we proceed.

To outline the key factors that helped to shape the evolutionary transition from pro-tomorality to full morality as we know it, I shall be drawing together a number of hypotheses developed previously (Boehm, 1982; 1989; 1993; 1997a; 1997b; 1999a; 1999b; 1999c). I shall not be considering highly refined theories of ethics developed by philosophers and others, for my aim is to identify what I would call the basics of morality: the antisocial predatory behaviours of individual group members that result in exploitation or conflict, and the group's response to such behaviour. The group responses involve the operation of large, cohesive political coalitions, and these assertive moral communities are best known for their capacity to punish (see Black,

1976; 1998). To this end, they engage in identification of deviants through gossiping and they actively apply social sanctions to manipulate or eliminate such individuals. Such acts are accompanied by anger, and sometimes by fear. However, because their overall orientation is heavily prosocial (Boehm, 1999c; see also Hinde and Groebel, 1991), they also praise individuals who are worthy and — this is important — they try to manage conflicts that arise within the group with the aim of restoring social harmony.

Morality is based heavily on social pressure, punishment, and other kinds of direct social manipulation by which the hostilely aroused majority use their power over individuals in a band. To understand such use of power in nomadic bands, one must focus on the fact that extant hunter-gatherers are politically egalitarian (Boehm, 1993), and that Late Palaeolithic bands surely assumed a similar political form (Boehm, 1999b). This means that members of Late Palaeolithic band communities formed broad coalitions of subordinates which severely limited the potential of any male (or female) to attain ascendancy over other adults in the band. In focusing on egalitarian politics, I set aside the question of domination behaviour within families, which is evident both in apes and in humans, including those who subscribe to egalitarianism. It is the group that interests us here, and I shall focus just on the behaviour of adults.

This suppression of dominance behaviour among family heads enabled the local group, as a large political coalition, to control the actions of all its members. These included individuals endowed with great physical strength or aggressiveness, those chosen to lead, those who produced strongly as hunters, and shamans connected with unusual supernatural powers. It did so as a local moral community that held commonly established views about which behaviours were likely to threaten members individually, or spoil the group's quality of life. It was prepared to deal with antisocial deviants, and, as with extant foragers who make their livings as nomads, a major focus was on the proscription of bullying behaviour at the level of band politics. But moral pressures were also focused on other problems that I shall list presently, problems of antisociality that are regularly experienced by hunter-gatherers today.

Ultimately, the moral sanctioning I am speaking of would appear to stem heavily from individual self interest (see Alexander, 1987), for many types of socially-defined deviance (for example, rape, theft, deception, adultery, and murder) are predatory behaviours that directly threaten such interests. But I emphasize that social control cannot be reduced entirely to individual interests; indeed, collective interests appear to be very important in guiding both moral sanctioning and the management of conflict (see Boehm, 1997b; 1999b; see also Sober and Wilson, 1998).

A wholly individualistic response to predatory antisocial behaviour would be self-help (e.g., Black, 1998), by which an aggrieved individual and possibly his close relatives retaliate against an aggressor independently of any reaction from the larger group. Among hunter-gatherers, this is likely to happen after a homicide. Also 'individualistic' is a response by which the members of a band act together because they sense a direct threat to themselves as individuals: they may band together in immediate (and sometimes desperate) self-defence. They also may try to control a certain type of behaviour pre-emptively because it could end up victimizing them personally in the future.

It also makes sense to view moral communities as groups of people who have common concerns that go well beyond such individual interests. Hunter-gatherers are concerned with the overall quality of socio-political life they share, and they realize that if the entire group works together, it can improve the quality of that life. In short, they have social ideals (Boehm, 1999b; see also Nader, 1990), and they are able to speak about what is good or bad for the group. In this context, they identify any serious dyadic conflict as the entire group's social problem, no matter who is involved individually, because life is disrupted for the entire group. Usually, they see this as a problem that must be resolved, or 'managed', collectively.

Both individualistic and collectivistic methodologies (see Sober and Wilson, 1998) can be useful in explaining social control, and they may also be appropriate for considering how natural selection has helped to produce this type of behaviour. In this analysis, I shall try to find a balance between 'methodological individualism' (a habit that seems to be entrenched in evolutionary biology) and the kind of 'methodological collectivism' that has characterized many social analyses by sociologists and anthropologists, some worthy and some unduly biased.

When humans act as moral communities, in many respects they can be very astute as non-literate social engineers. In matters of deviance and social conflict, they understand intuitively both the immediate social and political dynamics of their own groups, and the ultimate effects of conflict. Often, as they all but unanimously manipulate individual behaviour in desired directions, they consciously understand the social strategies they engage in (e.g. Boehm, 1993). Often the strategies are directed squarely at the deviant, who they try to control, reform, or eliminate from the group. But sometimes they seem to be more interested in dealing with the conflict in its own right: they focus just on resolving the dispute — rather than on addressing the individual deviance involved — and this type of behaviour cannot easily be reduced to individual interests alone.

To the degree that extant humans are evolved to take a special interest in their group's overall welfare, an interest that probably goes beyond selfishness or nepotism (see Boehm, 1997b), it may be necessary to invoke group selection arguments to explain such evolution (see Eibl-Eibesfeldt, 1982; Wilson and Sober, 1994; Boehm, 1997a; 1999b; Sober and Wilson, 1998). It is beyond the scope of the paper to consider this controversial and complicated issue, but a more complete treatment of the evolution of moral behaviour would have to explore it; I have done so elsewhere (Boehm, 1997a; 1997b; 1999a; 1999b; 1999c), and the problem is further addressed by Sober and Wilson (2000) in this volume.

Conflict as a Stimulus for Moral Behaviour

All human groups experience competition and conflict, and one major type of within-group conflict is *political,* in the sense that humans are innately disposed to vie for power and position (Masters, 1989). This is something we share with many species, including chickens: when their innate tendencies to status rivalry are expressed at the dyadic level, the result is a highly predictable social hierarchy (Schjelderup-Ebbe, 1922). This applies to humans after the Neolithic, for our larger societies exhibit a social order that an ethologist would call despotic (see Vehrencamp, 1983). There is substantial social competition with a limited number of positions at the top (Fried, 1967) and leaders have either substantial legitimate authority or coercive force at their disposal (Service, 1975). However, an older type of human society is the politically-equalized group I have described above. Vehrencamp (1983) would designate this ethologically as an egalitarian society, for the expression of tendencies to dominance and submission is not pronounced. This is because individual rank is not a major factor in reproductive success, and because leaders are not very dominant.

Normally, in discussions of ethological despotism or egalitarianism, the characterizations are specific to a species. But it would appear that humans, with their noteworthy cultural flexibility, are all over the map. When people live in chiefdoms, primitive kingdoms, or nation states, political life can be ethologically defined as despotic. When they live in mobile bands, small tribes, or tribal confederations, their political life is ethologically egalitarian. People in the latter type of society also are called 'egalitarian' by cultural anthropologists like Service (1962) and Fried (1967), whereas the contrastive *cultural* term is 'hierarchical'. The fact that human groups reach both of these extremes, and land at various intermediate points as well, raises an important question. As a species, are we innately given to ethological egalitarianism, to ethological despotism, or to neither?

To resolve this question, we must consider the fact that innately egalitarian primates like squirrel monkeys (see Boinski, 1994) lack any very strong genetic preparations to dominate or submit. In this they are very different from chickens, or chimpanzees. Because the original humans were egalitarian for scores of millennia, we must ask if our species might be innately egalitarian — but that under Post-Palaeolithic conditions we somehow managed to 'hierarchize' ourselves on a cultural basis. These important questions were raised by Knauft (1991), and subsequently (Boehm, 1993) I made the case that humans can remain egalitarian only if they consciously suppress innate tendencies that otherwise would make for a pronounced social dominance hierarchy. In effect, it is necessary for a large power-coalition (the rank and file of a band) to dominate the group's would-be 'bullies' if egalitarianism is to prevail — otherwise, the group will become hierarchical with marked status differences and strong leadership.

On this basis, it can be argued that humans are innately disposed to despotism in Vehrencamp's ethological sense of the word. My point is that humans are not just naturally egalitarian: if we wish to keep social hierarchy at a low level, we must act as intentional groups that vigilantly curtail alpha-type behaviours. This curtailment is accomplished through the cultural agency of social sanctioning (Boehm, 1993), so political egalitarianism is the product of morality.

In this connection, I think that as moral communities began to form, the first type of behaviour to be dubbed 'deviant' could have been alpha-male type behaviour (Boehm, 1997a). There were two good reasons to suppress such behaviour. One was based on innate political dispositions: in a despotic species given to strong status rivalry there is a natural propensity for adults to behave dominantly. This results in a dislike of being dominated oneself, and it makes for subordinate rebellion against superiors (Boehm, 1999b). If resentful subordinates manage to collectivize and institutionalize their rebellion, you have a human type of politically egalitarian society, in which there is a major tension between the group and its more rivalrous individuals. The other reason was economic. Anatomically Modern Humans obtained an important part of their diet from large-game hunting, and this provided a practical reason to outlaw alpha males (see Erdal & Whiten, 1994; 1996). In prehistoric bands that depended significantly on meat, the need for equalized distribution of food was great. People needed to reduce variation in their intake of rarely or sporadically acquired high-quality foods, notably large-game meat, and as brains grew larger humans gained enough actuarial acumen to set up uncentralized systems for *equalized* food redistribution, and also other kinds of co-operative security nets (see Boehm, 1999c). The basic idea was to average out risks of individuals and families (Smith and Boyd, 1990; see also Cashdan, 1990) by collectivizing the products of hunting, and outlawing alpha domination behaviour was critical to satisfying these aims. This eliminated bullies who would seek a lion's share, and thereby disrupt such a delicately-equalized system of give and take (see Boehm, 1999c).

Extant hunter-gatherers uniformly insist on egalitarianism — at least until they settle in one place. If they do sedentarize, either as hunters or horticulturists, they often continue to be suspicious of authority — and politically egalitarian (e.g., Gould, 1982). But as people lose their obsession with staying equalized, they develop a substantial degree of hierarchy that is consistent with what anthropologists describe as 'chiefdoms' (see Service, 1975). In terms of culture change, hierarchy can assert itself quickly because of the innate political dispositions discussed above, and because, as they govern larger groups, strong, responsible leaders (the good ones) provide obvious benefits to all. This is so even though they also gain personal economic privileges and social status never seen in bands or tribes.

For human prehistory, this raises an important question. How did an innately despotic species manage to become phenotypically egalitarian in the first place? I have suggested, already, that the moral community might have developed originally as a collective means of eliminating the political, social, and economic problems that go with alpha domination (Boehm, 1982; 1999b). However, an alternative hypothesis would be that the moral community first developed for some other reason, but was put to use in the service of political egalitarianism once the subordinates realized they had collective power sufficient to eliminate the alpha role (see Boehm, 1997a). Either way, there developed a full-blown egalitarian moral community that was in firm command of its own social life.

Here, I shall be developing a more general hypothesis that helps to account for either of these possibilities. Today, typical behaviours that are reasonably well-controlled by the egalitarian band would seem to be: bullying behaviours; cheating or shirking in the context of co-operative efforts; serious degrees of deception or theft; and 'sexual crimes' like adultery, incest, and rape. If we examine this list of negatively sanctioned actions, these also are the behaviours that account for many of the serious conflicts in bands. Assuming that moral sanctioning is intentional, and this seems indisputable, this means that humans are singling out competitive or predatory behaviours that are likely to cause conflict, and, by suppressing them, they are, in effect, damping conflicts pre-emptively (Boehm, 1982). On this basis, a formal hypothesis is possible. Moral communities arose out of group efforts to reduce levels of internecine conflict, as well as to avoid undue competition, domination, and victimization.

The striking anomaly for this hypothesis is murder. Hunter-gatherer homicide is quite frequent, and it usually takes place because of problems with male competition over women (Knauft, 1991). While wholeheartedly condemned, internecine killing is not well controlled by the group; it is coped with more on a personal, self-help basis, and through avoidance (see Knauft, 1991; Kelly, 1995). Adultery is a major cause of serious disputes, and, while in general it is condemned, adultery seems to be insusceptible of definitive control. For one thing, its genetic basis is firmly grounded in sexual selection, and the motives would appear to be powerful. For another, it involves careful collusion between the offenders so it is difficult to detect adultery in a definitive way — even in a gossiping hunter-gatherer band that engages in constant social surveillance. Thus, this major cause of homicide is difficult to detect, and therefore difficult to suppress. In other areas of deviance, hunter-gatherers do quite nicely with their deliberate and often pre-emptive approach to social control.

By contrast, among chimpanzees and bonobos we have seen that routine competition over food (and mating) is patterned by a self-organizing despotic social system that is based upon a social dominance hierarchy: the dominant individual (or the dominant dyadic-coalition) usually wins, so conflict is moderate. By establishing and maintaining a politically egalitarian order, human foragers obviously have rid themselves of this type of hierarchical system. In freeing themselves from domination by powerful individuals, they have lost the functional benefits of a typical primate linear dominance hierarchy — notably, a self-organizing social hierarchy with an alpha individual in the control role. In the absence of any authoritative central leadership on the part of strong, responsible individuals, they handle their social problems as well as they can. They do so on a collective and *deliberate* basis, through social control, and their main problem seems to be homicide involving male sexual competition.

I am suggesting that egalitarian societies are 'intentional communities' (Boehm, 1993), societies whose members have a certain type of social order in mind. As individuals they have decided to give up on climbing to the alpha level, and have settled, instead, for personal autonomy without either dominance or submission. They must work together *collectively* to accomplish this, and this same type of intentionality is applied to other spheres. It sometimes becomes quite reflective, for hunter-gatherers seem always to emphasize social harmony in philosophizing about their own social life. This normative emphasis is something that anthropologists have noted about non-literate people in general (see Sober and Wilson, 1998), and it is aimed at improving the quality of social life. Foragers' standard lists of deviant behaviour are lists of behaviours that are likely to cause conflict within the group, and degrade the overall quality of social life — for everyone.

I must make a special point, here, about hunter-gatherer disputes and how they are handled once pre-emptive sanctioning has failed and conflict becomes conspicuous and troubling. People do not necessarily become moralistic in dealing with the conflict. For one thing, squabbles and serious disputes often develop without any moral rules being broken. Two individuals, driven by self-interest, may simply hold differing interpretations of a situation — or a clash of personalities may be involved. Such conflicts tend to be taken simply as social problems that require 'management' by the group and its best peacemakers, rather than as instances of deviance that require sanctioning. However, even if the conflict clearly was initiated by some kind of deviant aggression, the group may choose to treat the problem neutrally from a moral perspective. Once a conflict has become heated, often the obvious and pressing social problem is to restore order, rather than identify and punish a deviant. This is common in egalitarian societies, be they bands or tribes, and it stems from the fact that the best way to manage a conflict — even if its provenance involves moral malfeasance by one party — is to split the differences. This reduces the chance that the same problem will arise in the future, with the dissatisfied party as instigator (e.g., Boehm, 1986).

At stake is the band's ability to live together in a not too stressful way, and to co-operate in ways that may be critical to health and survival. Having set aside hierarchical living except for within the family, hunter-gatherers have used their very large brains *collectively*, to diagnose and actively treat a wide variety of social problems at the band level. The pre-emptive side of conflict resolution involves suppressing deviant behaviours that lead to conflict. This helps to account for the peaceful, co-operative side of band life. When foragers do see conflicts developing, they are quite good at heading them off — so long as they do not reach the homicidal level (see Knauft, 1991). It is this corporate, highly deliberate, and basically *pre-emptive* approach to the avoidance of conflict that distinguishes human moral communities from largely self-organizing communities of other highly social animals, which actively control conflicts only when they become active. This will be discussed further.

Is Aversiveness to Conflict Innate?

Egalitarian moral communities work in a variety of ways, using praise and persuasion as well as negative social pressure, ostracism, and coercion. But one reason that 'social pressure' works so well is that deviants know the community can take things further, by seriously distancing them socially or by ejecting them from the group, occasionally by administering beatings, and, apparently everywhere if rarely, by putting them to death. Thus, the negative side of social sanctioning is ultimately *political*.

The implications of political power are pervasive in social control. First, problems of deviance often involve relations of power and domination, and second, social control is based on the group's power over individuals who are abusing power or are acting in some other predatory or otherwise antisocial capacity. Because the standard proscription-list of aggressive, self-interested behaviours is also a list of behaviours that cause conflict within the group, one must ask if there might be some innate aversion to conflict that helps to 'motivate' sanctioning strategies. An alternative hypothesis would be that the active social force is provided by the intelligence of non-literate humans, as social engineers who have rationally discerned the costs of conflict and therefore have invented ways to manipulate their own social environments in an anticipatory fashion.

The obvious intentionality of social control suggests that the latter hypothesis holds, but are these two hypotheses contradictory? I believe that human nature may be shaping human intentions rather decisively in this case. A specific prehistoric hypothesis would be that Anatomically Modern Humans were innately aversive to social conflict in their immediate social environments, that is, within their bands, and that precursors for such an aversion should be identifiable in the ape ancestral to both of *Homo* and *Pan*.

To explore this important question, we must return to the type of cladistic analysis that was employed earlier. Humans living in bands consistently try to mediate conflicts between individuals, with varying success depending on the nature of the conflict. Non-human primates seem to manage aggression in a variety of ways (Cords, 1997), which involve reconciliation, consolation, and active intervention by third-parties. With chimpanzees, high-ranking individuals and particularly the alpha males act in a control role (see Erhardt and Bernstein, 1994; Boehm, 1994) to stop fights, often before they escalate very far. Bonobos are generally less prone to ago-nism but they, too, intervene in conflicts (Parish, personal communication). This means that our Mutual Ancestor was likely to have intervened in conflicts, but what was the motivation?

It is difficult to discuss motives for an animal species five million years ago, but it helps to have worked with the very rich long-term data set at the Gombe Stream Research Centre, which spans decades. I also have spent more than a year watching and videotaping members of the same wild chimpanzee group, with an interest in dis-putes and conflict interventions. It might seem far-fetched to suggest that chimpan-zees actually have the intention to pacify a conflict when they engage in an intervention, but when a highly intelligent animal utilizes a wide variety of tactics to accomplish the same strategic end, the manipulative behaviour would appear to be deliberate (see Boehm, 1992; 1994).

Tactics I observed at Gombe did vary widely. Usually, a male or female dominant chimpanzee would display at the (subordinate) adult protagonists and scatter them, or a male would charge right between them with the same effect. But I also have watched the Gombe alpha male successively herding two females in opposite directions to stop a serious fight up in a tree, and once I saw a high-ranking male pry apart two ado-lescent males after his charging at them had no effect. (Also, at Gombe, a subordinate female was also seen once to remove a stone from a male's hand when he was about to display at another group member.) In all of these cases, the dispute was ameliorated. In captivity, the same variegated tactical patterns prevail, but the prying-apart and removal-of-object behaviours are common, rather than rare (de Waal, 1982). The argument for intentionality is further supported by the fact that a dominant animal try-ing to control a fight often will sit down for a time between the protagonists after hav-ing separated them (see Goodall, 1986; Boehm, 1994), rather than immediately returning to feeding, resting, mating, grooming, or whatever the prior activity may have been. The fact that he has just decisively intimidated them makes this an effec-tive means of forestalling further conflict.

In sum, these behaviours add up to a strategy of deliberate pacification that is pres-ent in a variety of chimpanzee environments. But what are the *specific* motives involved? It makes sense that chimpanzees could be protecting kin or coalition part-ners from injury, but in that case one would expect them to intervene on a partisan basis, directing their effort at one protagonist rather than both, and for them to inter-vene only when fights involved kin or partners. What is distinctive, with most of the intervention strategies I have described, is that they appear to be *impartial* — rather than partial. Interventions only occur in a fraction of the total disputes observed at Gombe, so one still might posit that high-ranking animals acting in the impartial con-trol role were intervening mainly to afford protection to kin or allies. However, in the long-term database there was no such trend (Boehm, 1994).

If protection is at issue motivationally, it is afforded to both parties — and I should point out that victims sometimes wound aggressors (see Goodall, 1986). With protection being provided randomly to other group members, these impartial inter-ventions in adult disputes would appear to be 'altruistic' in the genetic sense of the word (see Boehm, 1981) — whatever the immediate motives. Some degree of a chim-panzee version of empathy does seem possible, however, insofar as the control indi-vidual himself has experienced the stress of being attacked, or of getting into a bad fight.

Another innately-prepared motivation could be operating. It is possible that these controlling third parties are reacting to the intensely-agonistic behaviours of others as an environmental irritant, and simply wish to remove this perturbation as a selfish act. This explanation alone could account for interventions that are impartial and pacify-ing. One might also argue that interventions are simply a means of reinforcing one's high status. All of these motivations are possible, and there may be others, as well. But one thing is clear. *Pacifying interventions* surely are motivated differently from those that stem from a desire to assist a relative or well-bonded coalition partner in winning a contest. Indeed, such interventions are quite different tactically, for the bluff or attack is directed at just one individual, not both of them. Partisan interven-tions tend to escalate, rather than damp, the original conflict.

Because the conflict itself seems to be a major focus, I suggest that chimpanzees are innately aversive to conflict. If one compares the two *Pan* species (see Boehm, 1999b), evidence for generalized conflict aversiveness is far more evident in the one that actually exhibits more conflict, *Pan troglodytes*. Although bonobos do interfere sometimes in conflicts to pacify them, with chimpanzees this is a regular and promi-nent pattern, both in the wild and in captivity.

Active power-intervention is not the only tool that these apes have for reducing the effects of conflict. De Waal's (1982; 1989;1996) work with a variety of primates dem-onstrates that reconciliation behaviour can be prominent, and functionally important at the level of social life. With *Pan troglodytes* and *Pan paniscus*, reconciliation is often dyadic. But after altercations there are also instances in which third parties assist in the reconciliation process that calms down the protagonists and consoles the victims in particular (de Waal, 1989; 1996). Humans, too, 'make up' after many of their within-group fights (e.g., Turnbull, 1961), and sometimes tribal people who feud intensively devise elaborate rituals that involve asking for and granting forgive-ness (e.g., Boehm, 1986).

Knauft (1991) has emphasized that hunter-gatherers who are nomadic are rela-tively adept at heading off or resolving lesser conflicts, but at the same time are quite ineffective in dealing with heated conflicts that are likely to involve homicide. This impotency stems from the lack of a strong control role. Indeed, a would-be mediator, whose authority is guaranteed to be little in a band that insists upon egalitarianism, may himself be a casualty of a serious conflict with which he attempts to interfere (e.g. Lee, 1979). With respect to resolving conflicts *before* they become hot, extant hunter-gatherers have devised a variety of rituals that serve to ameliorate tensions within the band. These include not only talking things over, but also many different types of verbal or physical duelling which have the function of discharging social ten-sions before homicide occurs (see Hoebel, 1954). As with chimpanzees, a number of manipulative tactics are being directed at precisely the same end. My suggestion, then, is that conflict management has an innate basis, but it also is a form of intelligent problem solving.

Scholars tend to treat ethics, social control, and conflict management as separate spheres. However, I view them as being closely related (Boehm, 1982; 1999b). We have seen that one good reason to crack down on socially-defined deviants is that many are predators who potentially or directly threaten other group members as individual victims. This personal sense of being threatened motivates people to unite as a moral community. However, another reason is that deviants create disturbing conflicts that degrade the immediate quality of social life and impair group functions. Thus, even if one is not being singled out as a victim, one's social environment will be disturbed, and a useful web of co-operation that everyone profits from can be seriously disrupted. Both are good reasons to crack down on deviant behaviour pre-emptively, rather than permitting it to lead to active conflict. However, once a conflict becomes a threat to group welfare, and creates a high degree of social stress, it is significant that moral considerations may be set aside as the resolution of the conflict takes precedence over the dislike of the group for deviants. The conclusion for humans is that aversion to conflict has an innate basis, and that this helps to draw people together as moral communities that are interested in addressing social problems.

How close was the Mutual Ancestor to humans? We have seen that pacifying interventions can be both impartial and effective, in both wild and captive chimpanzees whose conflict interventions are well studied. These interventions tend to be individual, rather than collective. But the potential for collective interventions is there: at Gombe there have been rare instances of several males simultaneously intervening in a control role (Boehm, 1994), and in captivity a large coalition of females did the same (de Waal, 1996). This potential can be taken as a pre-adaptation that made humans more likely to invent the moral community as we know it.

In addition, we must consider the fact that humans take a highly pre-emptive approach to social problem-solving. The Pan species have no conspicuous behaviour that suggests any systematic suppression of deviant behaviour by an entire group. However, with respect to pre-emptiveness it may be significant that most of the chimpanzee third-party interventions I have witnessed take place before the conflict becomes very developed.

Pre-adaptations for Moral Behaviour

Let us focus, now, on the entire range of pre-adaptations for moral life. First, there are the basics of group size and social composition, and the adaptations to physical and political environments with which they evolved. This ancestral ape lived in multifamily foraging communities that were subject to fusion and fission: this is a pattern clearly shared by chimpanzees, bonobos, and human hunter-gatherers. These groups were at least moderately 'territorial' (Wrangham and Peterson, 1996; see also Boehm, 1999b), and they may have approached a chimpanzee degree of territoriality, with patrolling by large coalitions of males and lethal attacks on individual neighbours. I suggest this because humans also engage in perimeter defence (Cashdan, 1983; see also Dyson-Hudson and Smith, 1978) — but bonobos are not fully studied in this respect (see Stanford, 1998). At present, we know that the adult male bonobos sometimes behave as hostile large-coalitions when two groups meet (Wrangham and Peterson, 1996) — but so far they have not been seen to engage in lethal behaviour.

All three species do unite against neighbouring groups, then, and it seems likely that all three unite to mob predators that threaten them and possibly to hunt larger game (Boehm, 1999b). There also are solid data that document small male or female coalitions in all three species, so in ancestral communities small coalitions of males or females surely worked together in vying for political status within the group. In doing so, they mitigated (but came far from neutralizing) the social dominance hierarchy that saw high-ranking individuals (male or female) decisively dominating those of lower rank (see Boehm, 1999b). If we put together all the large and small coalition behaviours of all three species, it seems likely that the Mutual Ancestor at least had the potential to form large coalitions *within* its communities, and to direct political force at individuals who aroused the ire of the rest of the group.

What about morality as I have discussed it? Goodall (1982) has characterized the social life of extant chimpanzees as involving 'order without law'. Her point is that the linear dominance hierarchies of chimpanzees mediate and pattern the natural competitiveness of individuals, and keep conflict within tolerable limits. Chimpanzee social life may be noisy and agonistic, and sometimes it is troubled by pronounced dominance instabilities as the alpha role changes hands, but basically it is orderly and stable. She emphasizes that the overall system is self-organizing: chimpanzees are not partially 'creating' their societies as humans do — by gearing deliberate social control to the betterment of individual and group life. Hence, 'order without law', which means order without morality.

Essentially Goodall is correct, but she may not be entirely correct. Recently, de Waal (1996) has considered the possibilities of proto-moral behaviour in both apes and monkeys, and has made a persuasive case for moral-like behaviours in certain restricted areas (see also Flack and de Waal, 2000). Some of his insights relate to sympathy that extends beyond the confines of parental nurturance or kinship, a response well documented in the wild by Goodall (1986) in her discussion of chimpanzee altruism (see also Eibl-Eibesfeldt, 1989). But other insights relate more directly to the raw materials of morality — taken as social control of commonly disapproved antisocial behaviour by a concerned local community.

Captive chimpanzee colonies are particularly interesting in this respect. Spatial constriction and easy availability of food provide advantages of power to the adult females: they now have time to devote to 'politics' because their lives are no longer devoted to largely solitary foraging, and in captivity these females form much larger coalitions than the males. In the sizeable groups at Arnhem Zoo in Holland and at Yerkes Regional Primate Research Centre in Atlanta, captive female allies have been able to control certain behaviours of males who are individually dominant over them, and do so in ways that are striking. They usually manage to play 'kingmaker', and they always seem to control which male will be involved with peacemaking; that is, if they fail to get their choice of alpha male they may at least divest him of his control role (that of peacemaker) and permit his rival to perform those valuable services for them (see de Waal, 1982). The females do this on a manipulative basis that appears to be intentional, and the process is similar to social control in that a large, well-unified, rank-and-file political coalition is successfully manipulating key behaviours of individuals that are threatening to other individuals.

Such behaviour is routine in large captive groups, and it can lead to rare behaviours that become startlingly similar to human social control. At Yerkes, it is recorded that the alpha male was chasing a sexual rival with the intention to do him damage, and the females reacted by collectively issuing hostile waa-barks, directed at the alpha. As the intensity and unanimity of the calls built, this signalled an impending attack by all of them — and the alpha male desisted (see de Waal, 1996). It was the size and cohesiveness of the female coalition that made the difference in controlling his behaviour, for in the wild the strongly defiant individual waa-barks of a few disapproving females will be ignored by high-ranking males that are engaged in making attacks.

Large-coalition political behaviour is not unknown in the wild. At Gombe, males regularly form large coalitions to go on patrol or cope with predators (see Nishida, 1979; Goodall, 1986; Byrne and Byrne, 1988; Boehm, 1992), but when they compete for power within the group normally they operate dyadically, as pairs of close allies. However, after over thirty years of field observation the following male behaviour was observed at Gombe (Goodall, 1992). The alpha male had been defeated in a fight with a rival, and then he tried to make a comeback. Uncharacteristically, the males of the group threatened him *collectively*, and forced him to leave the group. He remained socially peripheralized until he was willing to return in a submissive role. Similar episodes, involving smaller coalitions that nonetheless surpass the dyadic level, have been recorded at Mahale, the one other long-term African field site at which social data are well-recorded and well-published (e.g. Uehara, Hiraiwa-Hasegawa, Hosaka, and Hamai, 1994; Nishida, Hosaka, Nakamura and Hamai, 1995).

In these rare wild episodes and well-routinized captive ones, it would appear that among members of large coalitions there is some kind of consensus that develops — as to what kind of behaviour they are taking issue with, what their political objectives are, and whether they are in a position to exert control. I do not believe I am engaging in a fantasy about 'intentions at work'. Chimpanzees have the waa vocalization that is closely associated with hostile defiance (Goodall, 1986; see also Boehm, 1999b), and when they hear the waa-barks of others they can decide individually whether to join in. The overall pattern would appear to involve something like 'public opinion' (see de Waal, 1996), and in its dynamics this political process can be likened to social control because the same macro-coalition that arrives at a consensus may decide to intervene physically. Although male bonobos do appear to stick together politically when they encounter groups of strangers, as with chimpanzees, within the community the females operate in small coalitions of two or more all the time, whereas the males do not join in small coalitions. For this reason, the females are in a position to engage in status rivalry with males — essentially on an equalized basis (see Kano, 1992; Wrangham and Peterson, 1996).

With chimpanzees, the collective reactions by large male or female coalitions are, respectively, of great interest in terms of protomorality. But with humans an important difference is that both males *and* females unite into one very large, community-wide political coalition, which manipulates or eliminates deviants. It does so on the basis of explicitly shared opinions about what is deviant, this in the context of long-term social objectives that are formally articulated. Another difference is that humans are constantly engaged in a vigilant search for deviance: this is accomplished quite systematically, by gossiping, and even predatory behaviour that takes place one-on-one becomes known to the entire group (see Boehm, 1999b). Another difference stems from the egalitarian nature of human bands. Ethologically speaking, with an egalitarian as opposed to a despotic social order, it is far easier for the human group to unite against its higher-ranking deviants because they already have been placed in a relatively weak political position. Chimpanzees, being despotic, put down their leaders only partially, or episodically, and they always have strong leaders. Humans, as egalitarians, are in a position to do so continuously, routinely, and decisively.

The formation of major coalitions that deliberately suppress unwanted individual behaviours is basic to human morality. Chimpanzees have the potential to form male or female coalitions on a large scale, and bonobo female coalitions at least rise above the dyadic level as females unite to hold their own politically against the more physically powerful males. This means that such a potential was likely to be present in the Mutual Ancestor of *Pan* and *Homo*, and that therefore a major political pre-adaptation was already in place when human communities moved toward practising social control as we know it today.

The Full Blown Moral Community

By the later Late Palaeolithic, when Anatomically Modern Humans were becoming widely established, it is likely that the fully developed human moral community also was well established in the form we discover in extant hunting groups (see Boehm, 1999a; 1999b). People lived in similarly egalitarian bands, and their routinized curtailment of excessive individual assertiveness placed them in a position to exert effective social control when other types of deviance arose. They manipulated group members in their own selfish interest, to protect themselves from the types of social deviance discussed earlier. However, because they had an eye to group dynamics and to maintaining a good quality of social life in the group, they also worked to reduce disruptive conflicts that did not arise out of moral deviancy. These might arise simply through differences of personality or an individual's state of emotional irritation, and sometimes they arose because someone mentally ill was out of control. Because of an innate aversiveness to conflict, and because people were able to calculate the damage rationally and in advance, such conflicts were 'managed' as much as possible in the direction of resolution.

My best hypothesis is as follows. A signal and fundamental accomplishment of early moral communities was to define domination behaviours as morally deviant, and then to back this up with sanctioning by the entire group. Because dominance tendencies operating at the community level are strongly innate (see Tiger and Fox, 1971; Masters, 1989), they are difficult to control. A vigilant egalitarian response became universal in the Late Palaeolithic, and the result was an egalitarian political order, one in which the band's main political actors — possibly just the adult males — enjoyed an essential political parity. Parity applied when it came to personal autonomy in the band, and also in the making of group decisions (see Knauft, 1991; Boehm, 1996). There were, of course, definite differences of prestige, rank, and status (see Flanagan, 1989); but tendencies of individuals to carry such differences too far were held in check, and the definition of 'too far' was quite restrictive.

In suppressing deviant behaviours likely to damage individuals and breed conflict within the group, a noteworthy failure that I have mentioned in passing came in the realm of sexual competition among males for females: it would appear that our species is motivated so strongly in this area that even our inquisitive and manipulative moral communities cannot control this aspect of social life very well. They do understand its implications, in terms of disruptive conflict and as a leading cause of homicide, but their efforts are less than totally effective. What hunter-gatherers do know, in addition to the fact that male sexual competition is likely to cause conflict and homicide beyond their control, is that once a homicide takes place usually the killer will remove himself from the band — either permanently, or until tempers cool. Thus, in a sense this kind of dire conflict 'takes care of itself': a homicide within the band is intensely disruptive, but the conflict will quickly cease unless a feud ensues.

By contrast, other types of conflict were coped with quite efficiently much of the time. Indeed, mobile hunter-gatherer communities are regularly commended by anthropologists with respect to how well people seem to get along (see Knauft, 1991), and most of the commendation is valid even though certain groups seem to be unusually conflict-prone when it comes to sharing their large-game meat (e.g., Holmberg 1950; Blurton-Jones, 1984; Peterson, 1993).

I have chosen the Late Palaeolithic as the epoch during which this type of egalitarian moral community was likely to have reached its full development. In theory, such development was possible before the advent of Anatomically Moderns. We have seen that important pre-adaptations were in place five million years ago: the capacity to form coalitions larger than dyadic ones; the individual preference to dominate with a concomitant dislike of being subordinated that leads to egalitarianism (Boehm, 1999b), and the tendency to actively control conflicts within the group. But there was another pre-adaptation that probably was critical to the appearance of the fully modern moral community. This was the development of rapid-fire, phonemically-based communication (Lieberman, 1998) that was referential and involved displacement (Hockett, 1963) — displacement involves the planning of future activities, or the description of events that took place elsewhere. Abstract communication, mostly verbal, permitted the articulation and refinement of group values having to do with morality, and it also facilitated the kind of highly specific gossiping (with displacement) that is universal in human groups (Boehm, 1999b). Gossiping serves as a means of building social networks (see Dunbar, 1996); but, perhaps more importantly, it also enables group members to arrive privately and safely at a negative consensus about dangerous deviants. Language also makes it possible for groups to conspire, and ambush even the most fearsome dominator to execute him. Language probably was important to the establishment of egalitarian political orders. It definitely was critical to the invention of moral communities as we know them.

Both language ability and the capacity to devise and enforce moral codes are good candidates for gradual evolution at the genetic level, with genetic evolution interacting with cultural patterns. The advent of full linguistic communication (as we know it) is thought to have arrived, at latest, with Anatomically Modern Humans something over 100,000 years ago (Lieberman, 1998; see also Marshak, 1992), and it would be difficult to argue that such an acumen arrived more recently. However, let us consider what was happening with communication five million years ago. It is clear that today chimpanzees and bonobos have many and subtle ways of communication (e.g., Goodall, 1986; de Waal, 1996) even though apparently they have no meaningless building-blocks like phonemes, and even though their communication system does not facilitate displacement.

Thus, the Mutual Ancestor was likely to have had a rather strong communication capacity — but language as we know it was absent. So was the capacity to develop anything like a modern moral community, which not only names and discusses different types of deviance but is capable of discussing the immediate and longer-term social future of the group. One selection pressure that might have acted on language evolution in its later phases could have been human tendencies to form moral communities that were egalitarian. I have in mind the attempts of subordinates to control more aggressive group members. This can be a risky enterprise, but it is one by which the allied subordinates individually gain reproductive success at the expense of their political superiors. Effective communication is important to their work as a large political coalition, for this enables them to track individual behaviours that may be deviant, including predatory acts that are perpetrated away from the group. If necessary, it also enables them to chart a precise course of action before the deviant is confronted by the group — as with assassination of a dominator too powerful to control otherwise (see Boehm, 1999b).

A final detailed summary is in order. As they began to form moral communities, the pre-adaptive ingredients available to prehistoric humans included the capacity to form very large coalitions within the group, an increasingly potent communication capacity, and, of course, a developed capacity to transmit cultural traditions over generations — something we share with *Pan* (see McGrew, 1992). In the Late Palaeolithic, a full-blown moral community took the following form. It was nomadic and smallish, it was composed of related and unrelated families, and it was politically egalitarian: while males may have dominated their female partners within the family, group life was equalized with respect to relations among the heads of households and with respect to making decisions as a group. People had a high degree of what I have called 'actuarial intelligence' (Boehm, 1999c), which helped them to set up cooperative systems of sharing and to calculate the damage that uncontrolled conflict might do to the group. While active conflicts were 'managed' as much as possible, as with Pan, the group also was able to *anticipate* conflict on a long-range basis and to manipulate the behaviours that were likely to produce it. These were basics of moral life. In addition, these people surely were capable of moral philosophizing — just as more gifted non-literate egalitarian individuals are today (see Radin, 1927). This enabled people to fine-tune their moral systems.

Conclusions

In explaining the evolutionary origins of morality, I have focused on what I deem to be fundamental aspects of moral behaviour: the group's culturally-transmitted definitions of deviance, group sanctions that manipulate or eliminate deviant behaviour, and a deep concern with social harmony as an ideal that is largely realized. The analysis has been decidedly political, and I justify this on three bases. One is that much of deviance involves force: included are murder, rape, non-consensual incest, and bullying behaviour in general. Another is that the group must have strong counter-force at its disposal in order to control such deviance. Third, it is particularly the *political* aspects of morality that lend themselves to the kind of three-species cladistic triangulation I have relied upon, in looking for pre-adaptations.

Morality surely did not emerge on an all-at-once basis. As de Waal (1996) has shown, protomoral behaviours are identifiable in extant non-human primates. The stronger the case for protomorality, the better the support for the idea that the moral community arrived in stages, and not as a saltation that definitively set aside humans from all other species. With *Pan troglodytes* the best instances of protomoral behaviour are found with captive female chimpanzees. At two different sites, they live in large groups and form permanent large coalitions that routinely target and decisively manipulate *certain* bullying behaviours of males (see de Waal, 1982; 1996). Because this routinization of sanctioning resembles the regularized ways in which humans in moral communities manipulate deviance, I place this behaviour of female chimpanzees ahead of the rare rebellions of adult males in the wild. It is female chimpanzees, at Arnhem Zoo and Yerkes, who have advanced the furthest in collectively exploiting their political potential to *routinely* suppress and manipulate behaviours they do not approve of.

I have emphasized heading off and managing conflicts as an important, overarching aim of humans acting as moral communities. All three species exhibit an active concern for social harmony, intervening in disputes. This concern also manifests itself in reconciliation and consolation behaviours that are dyadic, or triadic. But in both of the Pan species, the response is to manage conflicts as they actually develop — if often early in their development — but not to systematically suppress the behaviours that predictably lead to conflict, as humans do very systematically.

In *Pan,* there also are some altruistic behaviours (see de Waal, 1989, 1996; Goodall, 1986) that might be deemed relevant to morality. Altruism is intimately involved with human moral codes, particularly as groups call on their members to set aside self-interest and co-operate (Campbell, 1972; see also Boehm, 1999c). That is a positive approach to managing conflict. But here the focus has been on conflict and its management through social pressure or force — as a basic *political* dynamic that underlies every moral system in its fundamental workings.

My conclusion is that morality is essentially a political phenomenon as well as a social one, and that this political aspect lends itself rather nicely to evolutionary analysis. There is more to morality than politics, of course, and there is far more to deviance and social control than an innate aversiveness to conflict within the group. But in concentrating on these political basics I have been able to single out features of extant moral behaviour that not only are universal among humans living in bands, but can be linked to the behavioural repertoires of the two *Pan* species. The more widespread a human behaviour is, the greater the probability that it is receiving help from human nature (see Kluckhohn, 1953; Brown, 1991). The general conflict-management features I have worked with are universal not only among mobile hunter-gatherers, but among all humans wherever they live autonomously in local groups. They also are highly probable in the ancestral ape I have modelled by triangulation, which makes innate propensities to conflict resolution quite likely for humans.

We may never create a perfect approximation of how morality evolved, as an adaptively useful form of cultural problem-solving by which entire groups routinely shape their socio-political life on the basis of clearly designated goals. We may never know which behaviours were first defined, moralistically, as sins that the entire group must react to. But if we look to our ancestral precursor, five million years ago, in all probability there existed some limited 'social control' of certain individual group members by the rest of the group. This involved subordinate rebelliousness which led to manipulation of powerful individuals at the top of the hierarchy, but basically the groups remained ethologically despotic — with a prominent role for alpha individuals.

The hypothesis is that the first behaviour to be decisively outlawed and controlled by a human group may well have been the expression of dominance — dominance of the type that occurs all the time in chimpanzee and bonobo groups in the wild, and which occurs rather predictably in our own post-Neolithic societies whenever scale increases dramatically. I favour this theory for several reasons. For one thing, dominance and submission seem to be firmly established in our nature (Tiger, 1969; Tiger and Fox, 1971; Masters, 1989; Wrangham and Peterson, 1996). For another, we, like other primates, prefer usually to dominate rather than to be dominated (see Boehm, 1999b). Thus, we tend to become rebellious in a subordinate role. It is institutionalized subordinate rebellion that leads to an egalitarian polity, in which individuals agree implicitly to eschew domination so that they may remain autonomous and uncontrolled. And it is the same united rank and file who crack down on deviance in a wide variety of other forms.

Anthropologists interested in moral origins have tended to focus upon incest, as a universal taboo that is negatively sanctioned everywhere (e.g. Westermarck, 1894; Fox, 1983; Durham, 1991). In many instances incest is likely to create conflict, and therefore within the above evolutionary framework it would be a perfectly logical candidate for the first 'sin'. However, I think the better candidate is alpha-type bullying behavior, which requires a powerful coalition of the entire band if it is to be declared deviant and outlawed.

Whatever the evolutionary Original Sin may be, I offer the above analysis as a starting point for the explanation of moral origins. We remain an ethologically despotic species, one in which competitive dispositions to dominance remain strong in spite of scores of millennia under egalitarianism, and our economic, social, sexual, and political rivalries make for a group life that is prone to conflict. Morality is the human invention that addresses such problems, and it is based very heavily upon ancestral dispositions. These were the raw materials, out of which moral communities were forged.

The evolution of moral communities could have been very gradual, with bands slowly improving their capacity to cope with the aggressive deviants in their midst. The ability to fit into such a community could have become increasingly useful to individual fitness, for strong social sanctioning can be extremely punishing reproductively. However, if the first behaviour to be routinely and systematically sanctioned by the group was bullying behaviour, the human moral community might have arrived rather quickly. I engage in this final speculation because a group's taking over power from an alpha-male despot is something of an all-or-nothing enterprise, and something that was behaviourally in reach for our ancestors as they began to acquire language. In effect, I am saying that once humans had acquired a sophisticated system of communication, they were ready to start acting as a community-wide coalition with a political goal of living without domination. The rest was up to culture.

Once a prehistoric hunting band institutionalized a successful and decisive rebellion, and did away with the alpha-male role *permanently*, at least a proto-moral community came into existence — as a cultural entity. It is easy to see how this institution would have spread, for its advantages were perceptually obvious. Members of bands dominated by alpha despots would have visited with egalitarian groups, and they

would have seen entire bands routinely keeping down their strongest individuals —
with the rank and file enjoying personal autonomy previously inconceivable. This
could have served as a stimulus to rapid cultural diffusion — but here I am moving
from careful triangulation to speculation.

This paper has been based on many speculative assumptions, but hopefully the triangulation has been systematic. Hypotheses about an evolutionary Original Sin need
not dilute the basic analysis. Five million years ago, an ancestral ape was in a position
to engage in protomoral behaviours as it dealt with its dislike of alpha bullying, and as
it coped with its distaste for internecine conflict. 100,000 years ago, humans, aided by
much larger brains and by an advanced form of communication, created communities
that could hold down not only domination behaviours by alpha individuals, but any
other behaviour they identified as being directly or potentially deleterious to members of the group — or deleterious to the group's functioning as they saw it. This is a
specific hypothesis that can be tested against other formulations about moral origins.

Acknowledgments
I thank Leonard Katz for helpful comments and suggestions. I also thank the National Endow-
ment for Humanities and the Harry Frank Guggenheim Foundation and the L.S.B. Leakey
Foundation for fellowships and grants that supported research relevant to this paper.

References

Alexander, Richard D. (1987), *The Biology of Moral Systems* (New York: Aldine de Gruyter).
Black, Donald (1976), *The Behaviour of Law* (New York: Academic Press).
Black, Donald (1998), *The Social Structure of Right and Wrong. Revised Edition*; originally pub-
lished 1993 (London: Academic Press).
Blurton-Jones, Nicholas G. (1984), 'A selfish origin for human food sharing: Tolerated theft' *Ethol-
ogy and Sociobiology* **4**, pp. 145–7.
Boehm, Christopher (1981), 'Parasitic selection and group selection: A study of conflict interfer-
ence in Rhesus and Japanese Macaque Monkeys' in *Primate Behaviour and Sociobiology*, ed. A.
B. Chiarelli and R. S. Corruccini (Berlin: Springer-Verlag), pp. 160–82.
Boehm, Christopher (1982), 'The evolutionary development of morality as an effect of dominance
behaviour and conflict interference', *Journal of Social and Biological Sciences*, **5**, pp. 413–22.
Boehm, Christopher (1985), 'Execution within the clan as an extreme form of ostracism', *Social
Science Information*, **24**, pp. 309–21.
Boehm, Christopher (1986), *Blood Revenge: The Enactment and Management of Conflict in Monte-
negro and Other Tribal Societies* (Philadelphia: University of Pennsylvania Press).
Boehm, Christopher (1989), 'Ambivalence and compromise in human nature', *American Anthro-
pologist*, **91**. pp. 921–39.
Boehm, Christopher (1992), 'Segmentary "warfare" and the management of conflict: Comparison
of East African chimpanzees and patrilineal-patrilocal humans' in *Coalitions and Alliances in
Humans and Other Animals*, ed. A. H. Harcourt and F. B. M. de Waal (Oxford: Oxford University
Press), pp. 137–73.
Boehm, Christopher (1993), 'Egalitarian society and reverse dominance hierarchy', *Current
Anthropology*, **34**, pp. 227–54.
Boehm, Christopher (1994), 'Pacifying interventions at Arnhem Zoo and Gombe', in *Chimpanzee
Cultures*, ed. Richard W. Wrangham, W. C. McGrew, Frans B. M. de Waal, and Paul G. Heltne,
(Cambridge, MA: Harvard University Press), pp. 211–26.
Boehm, Christopher (1997a), 'Egalitarian behaviour and the evolution of political intelligence', in
Machiavellian Intelligence II, ed. D. Byrne and A. Whiten, (Cambridge: Cambridge University
Press), pp. 341–64.
Boehm, Christopher (1997b), 'Impact of the human egalitarian syndrome on Darwinian selection
mechanics', *American Naturalist*, **150**, pp. 100–21.

Boehm, Christopher (1999a) 'Forager hierarchies, innate dispositions, and the behavioral reconstruction of pre-history ', in *Hierarchies in Action: Cui Bono?*, ed. Michael W. Diehl (Center for Archaeological Investigations, Occasional Paper number 27. Carbondale, IL: SIU Press).

Boehm, Christopher (1999b), *Hierarchy in the Forest* (Cambridge: Harvard University Press).

Boehm, Christopher (1999c), 'The natural selection of altruistic traits', *Human Nature* [details forthcoming].

Boinski, Sue (1994), 'Affiliation patterns among male Costa Rican squirrel monkeys,' *Behaviour*, **130**, pp. 191–209.

Brown, Donald (1991), *Human Universals* (New York: McGraw-Hill).

Byrne, R.W., and Byrne, J.M. (1988), 'Leopard killers of Mahale', *Natural History*, **97**, pp. 22–6.

Campbell, Donald T. (1965), 'Ethnocentric and Other Altruistic Motives', in, *Nebraska Symposium on Motivation*, ed. David Levine, (Lincoln: University of Nebraska Press), pp. 283–311.

Campbell, Donald T. (1972), 'On the genetics of altruism and the counter-hedonic component of human culture', *Journal of Social Issues*, **28**, pp. 21–37.

Cashdan, Elizabeth, ed. (1990), *Risk and Uncertainty in Tribal and Peasant Economies* (Boulder: Westview).

Cashdan, Elizabeth A. (1980), 'Egalitarianism among hunters and gatherers', *American Anthropologist* **82**, pp. ll6–20.

Cashdan, Elizabeth A. (1983), 'Territoriality among human foragers: Ecological models and an application to four bushman groups', *Current Anthropology*, **24**, pp. 47–66.

Cords, Marina (1997), 'Friendships, alliances, reciprocity and repair', in *Machiavellian Intelligence II*, ed. D. Byrne and A. Whiten, (Cambridge: Cambridge University Press), pp. 24–49.

Darwin, Charles (1859), *On the Origin of Species*, Facsimile ed. 1964, (Cambridge, MA: Harvard University Press).

Darwin, Charles (1865), *The Expression of the Emotions in Man and Animals* [1972] (Chicago: University of Chicago Press).

Darwin, Charles (1871), *The Descent of Man and Selection in Relation to Sex* (New York: D. Appleton).

Dunbar, Robin (1996), *Grooming, Gossip and the Evolution of Language* (London: Faber and Faber).

Durham, William H. (1991), *Coevolution: Genés, Culture, and Human Diversity* (Stanford, CA: Stanford University Press).

Durkheim, E. (1933), *The Division of Labor in Society* (New York: Free Press).

Dyson-Hudson, Rada and Smith, Eric A. (1978), 'Human territoriality: An ecological reassessment', *American Anthropologist* **80**, pp. 21–41.

Eibl-Eibesfeldt, Irenus (1982), 'Warfare, man's indoctrinability and group selection', *Zoologische Tierpsychologie* **60**, pp. 177–98.

Eibl-Eibesfeldt, Irenus (1989), *Human Ethology* (New York: Aldine de Gruyter).

Ember, Carol (1978), 'Myths about hunter-gatherers', *Ethnology* **17**, pp. 439–48.

Erdal, David and Whiten, Andrew (1994), 'On human egalitarianism: An evolutionary product of machiavellian status escalation?', *Current Anthropology* **35**, pp. 175–84.

Erdal, David and Whiten, Andrew (1996), 'Egalitarianism and Machiavellian intelligence in human evolution', in *Modelling the Early Human Mind*, ed. P. Mellars and K. Gibson (Cambridge: MacDonald Institute for Archeological Research), pp. 139–50.

Erhardt, Carolyn and Bernstein, Irwin S. (1994), 'Conflict intervention behaviour by adult male macaques: Structural and functional aspects', in *Coalitions and Alliances in Humans and Other Animals*, ed. A. H. Harcourt and F. B. M. de Waal, (Oxford: Oxford University Press), pp. 83–112.

Flack Jessica and de Waal, Frans (2000), '"Any Animal Whatever": Darwinian building blocks of morality in monkeys and apes,' *Journal of Consciousness Studies*, **7** (1–2), pp. 1–29.

Flanagan, James G. (1989), 'Hierarchy in simple "egalitarian" societies', *Annual Review of Anthropology*, **18**, pp. 245–66.

Fox, Robin (1983), *The Red Lamp of Incest: An Inquiry into the Origins of Mind and Society* (Notre Dame, Ind: University of Notre Dame Press).

Fried, Morton H. (1967), *The Evolution of Political Society: An Essay in Political Anthropology* (New York: Random House).

von Furer-Haimendorf, Christoph (1967), *Morals and Merit: A Study of Values and Social Controls in South Asian Societies* (Chicago: University of Chicago Press).

Gardner, Peter (1991), 'Foragers' pursuit of individual autonomy', *Current Anthropology* **32**, pp. 543–58.

Goodall, Jane (1982), 'Order without law' *Journal of Social and Biological Structures*, **5**, pp. 349–52.

Goodall, Jane (1986), *The Chimpanzees of Gombe* (Cambridge, MA: Harvard University Press).

Goodall, Jane. (1992), 'Unusual violence in the overthrow of an alpha male chimpanzee at Gombe', in *Topics in Primatology, Volume 1*, ed. Nishida, W.C. McGrew, P. Marler, M. Pickford, and F.B.M. de Waal, (Tokyo: University of Tokyo Press), pp. 131–42.

Gould, Richard A. (1982), 'To have and have not: The ecology of sharing among hunter-gatherers', in *Resource Managers: North American and Australian Hunter-Gatherers*, ed. N.M. Williams and E. S. Hunn, (Boulder, Colo.: Westview), pp. 69–81.

Harcourt, Alexander H. and de Waal, Frans B.M., eds. *1992 Coalitions and Alliances in Humans and Other Animals* (Oxford: Oxford University Press).

Hinde, Robert A., and Groebel, Jo, eds. (1991), *Cooperation and Prosocial Behavior* (Cambridge: Cambridge University Press).

Hockett, C.F. (1963) 'The problem of universals in language', in *Universals of Language*, ed. J.H. Greenberg (Cambridge: MIT Press).

Hoebel, E. Adamson (1954), *The Law of Primitive Man: A Study in Comparative Legal Dynamics* (Cambridge, MA: Harvard University Press).

Holmberg, Allen (1950), *Nomads of the Long Bow: The Siriono of Eastern Bolivia* (Washington: Smithsonian Institution Press).

Kano, T. (1992), *The Last Ape: Pygmy Chimpanzee Behavior and Ecology* (Stanford:Stanford University Press).

Kelly, Robert L. (1995), *The Foraging Spectrum: Diversity in Hunter-Gatherer Lifeways* (Washington: Smithsonian Institution Press).

Kluckhohn, Clyde (1953), 'Universal categories of culture, in *Anthropology Today*, ed. A.L. Kroeber, (Chicago: University of Chicago Press), pp. 507–23.

Knauft, Bruce B. (1991), 'Violence and sociality in human evolution', *Current Anthropology*, **32**, pp. 391–428.

Lee, Richard B. (1979), *The !Kung San: Men, Women, and Work in a Foraging Society* (Cambridge: Cambridge University Press).

Lieberman, Philip (1998), *Eve Spoke: Human Lanaguage and Human Evolution* (New York: Norton).

McGrew, William C. (1992), *Chimpanzee Material Culture: Implications for Human Evolution* (Cambridge: Cambridge University Press).

Marshak, Alexander (1992), 'The origin of language: An anthropological approach', in *Language Origin: A Multidisciplinary Approach*, ed. J. Wind, E. G. Pulleyblank, E. de Grolier, and B. H. Bichakjian, *et al.*, (Dordrecht: Kluwer), pp. 421–48.

Masters, Roger D. (1989), *The Nature of Politics* (New Haven: Yale University Press).

Mithen, Steven J. (1990), *Thoughtful Foragers: A Study of Prehistoric Decision Making* (Cambridge: Cambridge University Press).

Nader, Laura (1990), *Harmony Ideology: Justice and Control in a Zapotec Mountain Village* (Stanford: Stanford University Press).

Nishida, Toshisada (1979), 'The social structure of chimpanzees of the Mahale mountains', in *The Great Apes*, ed. D.A. Hamburg and E.R. McCown, (Menlo Park, CA: Benjamin/Cummings), pp. 73–122.

Nishida, T., Hosaka, K., Nakamura, M., and Hamai, M. (1995), 'A within-group gang attack on a young adult male chimpanzee: Ostracism of an ill-mannered member', *Primates*, **36**, pp. 207–11.

Nishida, Toshisada, and Kazuhiko Hosaka (1996), 'Coalition strategies among adult male chimpanzees of the Mahale mountains, Tanzania', in *Great Ape Societies*, ed. W. C. McGrew, L. F. Marchant, and T. Nishida, (Cambridge: Cambridge University Press), pp. 114–34.

Palmer, Craig T., Fredrickson, B. Eric, and Tilley, Christopher F. (1998), 'Categories and gatherings: Group selection and the mythology of cultural anthropology', *Ethology and Sociobiology*, **18**, pp. 291–308.

Parish, Amy (1998), Personal Communication.

Peterson, Nicolas (1993), 'Demand sharing: reciprocity and the pressure for generosity among foragers', *American Anthropologist*, **95**, pp. 860–74.

Potts, Richard (1996), *Humanity's Descent: The Consequences of Ecological Instability* (New York: Avon).

Radin, Paul (1927), *Primitive Man as Philosopher* (New York: Appleton).

Ridley, Matt (1996), *The Origins of Virtue: Human Instincts and the Evolution of Cooperation* (New York: Penguin).

Schjelderup-Ebbe, T. (1922), 'Beitrage zur Socialpsychologie des Haushuhns', *Zeitschrift Psychologie*, **88**, pp. 225–52.

Selby, Henry A. (1974), *Zapotec Deviance: The Convergence of Folk and Modern Sociology* (Austin, TX: University of Texas Press).

Service, Elman R. (1962), *Primitive Social Organization: An Evolutionary Perspective* (New York: Random House).

Service, Elman R. (1975), *Origin of the State and Civilization: The Process of Cultural Evolution* (New York: Norton).

Smith, Eric Alden, and Boyd, Robert (1990), 'Risk and reciprocity: Hunter-gatherer socioecology and the problem of collective action', in *Risk and Uncertainty in Tribal and Peasant Economies*, ed. Elizabeth A. Cashdan, (Boulder, CO: Westview), pp. 167–92.

Sober, Eliott, and Wilson, David S. (1998), *Unto Others: The Evolution and Psychology of Unselfish Behavior* (Cambridge, MA: Harvard University Press).

Sober, Eliott, and Wilson, David S. (2000), 'Unto others: The evolution and psychology of unselfish behavior,' *Journal of Consciousness Studies*, **7** (1–2), pp. 185–206.

Stanford, Craig B. (1998), 'The social behavior of chimpanzees and Bonobos: Empirical evidence and shifting assumptions', *Current Anthropology*, **14**, pp. 399–420.

Stent, Gunther S. (ed. 1980 [1978]), *Morality as a Biological Phenomenon: The Presuppositions of Sociobiological Research* (Berkeley: University of California Press).

Tattersall, Ian (1993), *The Human Odyssey : Four Million Years of Human Evolution* (New York: MacMillan).

Tiger, Lionel (1969), *Men in Groups* (Random House, New York).

Tiger, Lionel, and Fox, Robin (1971), *The Imperial Animal* (New York: Delta).

Turnbull, Colin M. (1961), *The Forest People: A Study of the Pygmies of the Congo* (New York: Simon and Schuster).

Uehara, Shigeo, Hiraiwa-Hasegawa, Mariko, Hosaka, Kazuhiko, and Hamai, Miya (1994), 'The fate of defeated alpha male chimpanzees in relation to their social networks', *Primates*, **35**, pp. 49–55.

Vehrencamp, Sandra. L. (1983), 'A model for the evolution of despotic versus egalitarian societies', *Animal Behavior*, **31**, pp. 667–82.

de Waal, Frans (1982), *Chimpanzee Politics: Power and Sex among Apes* (New York: Harper and Row).

de Waal, Frans (1989), *Peacemaking Among Primates* (Cambridge, MA: Harvard University Press).

de Waal, Frans (1996), *Good Natured: The Origins of Right and Wrong in Humans and Other Animals* (Cambridge, MA: Harvard University Press).

Weber, Max (1947), *The Theory of Social and Economic Organization*, ed. Talcott Parsons. (New York: Free Press).

Westermarck, Edward (1894), *The History of Human Marriage* (New York: MacMillan).

Wilson, David S. and Sober, Elliot (1994), 'Reintroducing group selection to the human behavioural sciences', *Behavioral and Brain Sciences*, **17**, pp. 585–654.

Wilson, Edward O. (1978), *On Human Nature* (Cambridge, MA: Harvard University Press).

Wilson James Q. (1993), *The Moral Sense* (New York: Free Press).

Wrangham, Richard (1987), 'African apes: the significance of African apes for reconstructing social evolution', in *The Evolution of Human Behavior: Primate Models*, ed. W.G. Kinzey (Albany, NY: SUNY Press).

Wrangham, Richard, and Peterson, Dale (1996), *Demonic Males: Apes and the Origins of Human Violence* (Boston: Houghton-Mifflin).

Wright, Robert (1994), *The Moral Animal: Why We are the Way We Are: The New Science of Evolutionary Psychology* (New York: Vintage).

Commentary Discussion of Christopher Boehm's Paper

MORALITY AS ADAPTIVE PROBLEM-SOLVING FOR CONFLICTS OF POWER

Christoph Antweiler

Boehm's paper is a piece of speculation, but of careful and empirically founded speculation, which is stimulating methodologically and empirically. Being a cultural anthropologist, I will confine my comments mainly to the parts of Boehm's argument concerned with social control mechanisms using moral pressure.

Boehm argues in the first section that the social makeup of human bands throughout the world — so long as they remain mobile — is remarkably uniform. This holds at least for their moral and political backup. Especially relevant are their quite similar sanctions against deviant behaviour. But Boehm's argument that human societies have consciously to suppress tendencies of inequality could be strengthened further. Especially relevant here are recent studies of human foragers focussed specifically on levelling mechanisms related to the sharing of meat (Bird-David, 1990; 1992; Blige Bird and Bird, 1997; Burch, 1992; Cashdan, 1989; Ingold, 1993; Minnegal, 1997; Silberbauer, 1995). Sharing is understood here as the procurement of goods consumed by others; respectively the reciprocal resource transfer through pooling and redistribution of individual harvests. One key issue that arises from the ethnographic observation is that even in quite egalitarian societies there are regularly cases of egoistic behaviour. Such behaviour seems to have an innate basis and a multitude of such measures has been documented in recent ethnographic studies and compared through many cases (Kent, 1995; especially Wiessner, 1996). The conclusion strengthens Boehm's argument that human egalitarian societies actively have to maintain their egalitarian structure through specific measures. They need specific levelling mechanisms to counter bullying and other egoistic behaviour.

The studies mentioned and the recent debate on levelling mechanisms in forager meat sharing point to an even more complex array of measures for levelling power than Boehm illustrates. These studies are specifically relevant for Boehm's assumption of deliberate conflict resolution. He writes 'All three [species (the two *Pan* species and *Homo*)] also engage in deliberate conflict resolution' (Boehm, 2000, p. 81). The question regarding the two *Pan* species is whether their measures for conflict resolution are really conscious and deliberate. In the accompanying figure I have tried to show how complex levelling mechanisms around the sharing of meat may be in humans (see figure 1; cf. Antweiler, 1998). We have to assume complex processes with interrelated cognitive operations and far-reaching effects on the behaviour of other individuals as well as of entire groups. Woodburn aptly calls that a 'politics of sharing' (1998).

Journal of Consciousness Studies, **7**, No. 1–2, 2000, pp. 103–48

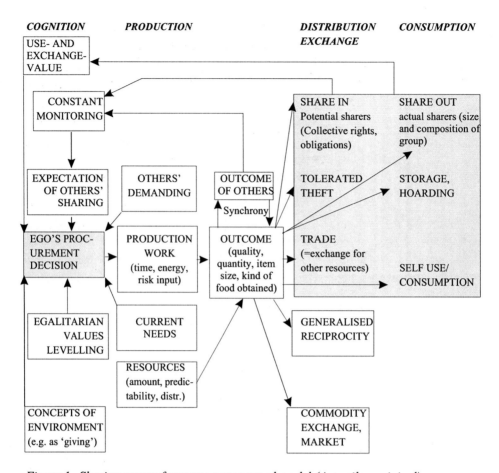

Figure 1. Sharing among foragers: a processual model (Antweiler, original).

Furthermore, Boehm assumes common concerns beyond individual interests, but whole societies or groups have no aims. Methodological individualism would require that we show the material situation as well as the cognitive operations on the level of the acting individual and their interaction. Thus it would be necessary to show empirically which of the actors are conscious of their aims, aware of the effects of others' behaviour and anticipating long-term consequences. In which situations and to what degree? And to what degree do they have common concerns, and are most individuals conscious of group interests and the overall quality of sociopolitical life? These questions are already hard to answer about human actors. To this date most studies about human foragers concerning sharing remain on the level of behaviour. That's why I think that more empirical studies of human foragers are needed not only on behaviour and possibly shared norms or values but also on individuals' cognitions related to social control in egalitarian human societies.

These open questions regarding deliberate measures of conflict-resolution are even harder to resolve empirically in the non-human sphere. There we can only observe and not ask the individuals. Cladistic arguments and triangulation, as Boehm uses them, are methodologically important as methods for inference and explanation, especially as regards the non-human sphere and protohuman issues.

References

Antweiler, Christoph (1998), 'Sharing as a normative principle. A review of its practice and the limits of food sharing among foragers', Paper, Symposium on Morality, Zentrum für Interdisziplinäre Forschung (ZIF), Bielefeld, Germany.

Bird-David, Nurit (1990), 'The giving environment: Another perspective on the economic system of gatherer-hunters', *Current Anthropology*, **31**, pp. 2189–96.

Bird-David, Nurit (1992), 'Beyond the original affluent society', *Current Anthropology*, **33** (1), pp. 25–47.

Blige Bird, Rebecca L. and Bird, Douglas W. (1997), 'Delayed reciprocity and tolerated theft. The behavioural ecology of food-sharing strategies', *Current Anthropology*, **38** (1), pp. 49–78.

Boehm, Christopher (2000), 'Conflict and the evolution of social control', *Journal of Consciousness Studies*, **7** (1–2), pp. 79–101.

Burch, Ernest S. (1992), 'Comment' (in Bird-David 1992), *Current Anthropology* **33** (1), p. 37.

Cashdan, Elizabeth (1989), 'Hunters and gatherers', in *Economic Anthropology*, ed. Stuart Plattner (Stanford: Stanford University Press).

Ingold, Tim (1993), 'Globes and spheres: the topology of environmentailsm', in *Environmentalism: The Perspective from Anthropology*, ed. Kay Milton (London: Routledge).

Kent, Susan (ed. 1995), *Cultural Diversity among Twentieth-Century Foragers. An African Perspective* (Cambridge: Cambridge University Press)

Minnegal, Monica (1997), 'Consumption and production. Sharing and the social construction of use-value', *Current Anthropology*, **38** (1), pp. 25–48.

Silberbauer, J.G. (1995), in Kent (1995).

Wiessner, Polly (1996), 'Leveling the hunter: Constraints on the satus quest in forager societies', in *Food and the Status Quest: An Interdisciplinary Perspective*, ed. Polly Wiessner and Wulf Schiefenhövel (Providence and Oxford: Berghahn Books).

Woodburn, James (1998), 'Sharing is not a form of exchange: an analysis of property-sharing in immediate-return hunter-gatherer societies', in *Property Relations*, ed. Chris M. Hann (Cambridge: CUP).

LOGIC AND HUMAN MORALITY
An Attractive If Untestable Scenario

I.S. Bernstein

Boehm reasons that human morality began when several heads of households formed a coalition to limit the despotic bullying of an alpha male. The logic is clear and the argument is persuasive. The premises require that: (1) dominant individuals behave like chimpanzees, bullying their subordinates, (2) early humans somehow developed one-male units from a chimpanzee like society and, (3) the power of a despot is limited by group consensus and political activities. Not all alpha males behave like chimpanzees; most primate societies show little evidence of bullying. One-male units are formed by some monkeys but there is little evidence of such tendencies in chimpanzees and bonobos. Hamadryas males do not compete with familiar males for females or possessions regardless of their dominance relationships, but this inhibition is not based on group consensus or coalitions repressing alpha males. Boehm's argument is, nonetheless, possible and plausible but cannot be empirically tested.

Boehm's paper is essentially an exercise of logic. Premises are induced based on observations of human hunter-gatherers, bonobos and chimpanzees. Based on these premises, Boehm deduces what the last common ancestor must have been like and hypothesizes a sequence of events which would have led to the development of morality; a community consensus of what behaviour is unacceptable enforced by political means. This set of hypotheses cannot be subjected to empirical test; there is no way to recreate the situation or visit the past. Instead, the hypotheses are tested for logical consistency and their ability to satisfactorily account for what we know about living forms. The account produced is possible, the logic makes it plausible, and the rigour of reasoning makes it attractive. Deductions are, however, dependent on the premises that they are based on.

It is assumed that the last common ancestor displayed chimpanzee-like male social dominance. Dominance is viewed as despotic with alpha males bullying other group members. Early human heads of household are hypothesized to have banded together to limit the power of the alpha male and establish a more egalitarian society such as seen in modern hunter-gatherers. Since larger human societies that become sedentary establish chiefdoms and status differentials, it is assumed that dominance striving is innate and must be actively suppressed for humans to form egalitarian societies.

Dominance, however, is defined by the immediate submissive behaviour of subordinates to the aggressive displays of dominant individuals. Dominant individuals may use aggression as an instrumental act to claim priority of access to resources or to 'bully' subordinates, but this is not part of the definition of alpha animals. Alpha animals may or may not use their status to claim resources and rarely bully other group members simply because they can. Primates are, first of all, social and dependent on the social group for meeting environmental challenges. Individuals that harass and bully group members and deprive them of essential resources drive subordinates from the group. In order to maintain a social group, mechanisms must exist to insure that all have access to essential resources. Dominance may serve primarily to regulate turn taking when resources are clumped but abundant; only in rare cases is power used to abuse and bully group members.

Chimpanzee males are indeed prone to vigorous, boisterous displays which often involve physical contact with subordinates. The alpha male in many other primate societies is less rambunctious. Often the outstanding behaviour of an alpha male is loud calling and intervention in any disturbance. As Boehm states, group members are aversive to conflict within their own group. They depend on the group to act jointly, and internal fighting is counter productive. The alpha animal is no exception. Intervention in a fight does not require empathy. The alpha may simply regard any aggressive expression, other than his own or in support of his own, as a challenge. The alpha can intervene on behalf of the victim or aggressor and even against an innocent third party. As long as the alpha's aggression supercedes all other aggression in the group and disrupts ongoing fighting, this intervention will function to reduce intragroup fighting (Bernstein, 1964; 1966a; 1966b). It need not be 'fair' to function.

It troubles me that the crucial step from chimpanzee dominance to egalitarian hunter-gatherer societies is the coalition formed by heads of household. Whereas chimpanzee and bonobo females often do band together to curtail male aggression, as Boehm describes, there are no 'households' or one-male units within chimpanzee or bonobo societies. One-male units are found in societies of hamadryas baboons, geladas, possibly drills and mandrills and maybe some Rhinopithecus groups. Among the hamadryas, Kummer (1968; 1978) indicates that dominance relations among familiar males are limited by respect for possession. Males will not attack a familiar male over females or resources in the immediate possession of the other. In fact, few primates will demand food from the mouth of another or try to take something in another's hand by force. Theoretically an alpha should be able to do so, but subordination is not passivity, and any subordinate can be provoked into resistance. Reaching into another's mouth for food places vulnerable fingers dangerously close to teeth. Trying to get something in another's hand will only provoke flight and not necessarily release of the object. Consistent use of these tactics will eventually drive others as far from you as possible, even out of the group. Kummer talks of 'respect for possession' as an evolved mechanism which allows for multiple one-male units to band together without dominance penalties. These bands can use the few available nocturnal refuges together and act jointly against other bands or predators. The advantages favour toleration of group members, even though it is still possible to see consistent dominance relationships among one-male unit leaders. Is respect for possession a sign of moral behaviour? There does not seem to be any group consensus or political means of enforcement operating.

The crucial question that remains unanswered is how did humans form 'households' from a bonobo or chimpanzee social structure? Many primates form coalitions and intervene in agonistic episodes. Savannah baboon males may use coalitions to compete against more dominant individuals. Coalitions may allow an individual to dominate another that it could not best alone. In fact the social inheritance of rank in some macaques describes just such a process wherein maturing females, with matrilineal aid, achieve dominance over all individuals that their families outrank regardless of individual fighting ability. None of this requires empathy, group consensus or morality. Boehm, however, does suggest that the banding together of heads of households to curtail the power of a despotic alpha may have been the first human moral system. The suggestion is intriguing, the argument is persuasive and the logic is superb.

There are a few niggling doubts remaining. The formation of households is crucial. The development of bullying despotic males is less troublesome given the nature of chimpanzee alpha males. Coalitions are demonstrable in chimpanzees and bonobos. Female coalitions are more prominent perhaps only because there are generally more females in the group. When Boehm states that this is a hypothesis that can be tested against other formulations about moral origins, surely he means 'tested' by logic and the goodness of fit to existing data. I know of no way to use empirical means to sort among the alternatives or falsify these hypotheses. I do not know how to deduce specific hypotheses of yet unobserved, but testable events, that will crucially discriminate among the hypotheses. 'Test' here must mean logical testing and not empirical scientific testing.

References

Bernstein, I.S. (1964), 'Role of the dominant male rhesus in response to external challenges to the group', *Journal Comp. Physiol. Psycholo.*, **57**, pp. 404–6.

Bernstein, I.S. (1966a), 'Analysis of a key role in a capuchin (*Cebus albifrons*) group', *Tulane Studies in Zoology*, **13**, pp. 49–54.

Bernstein, I.S. (1966b), 'An investigation of the organization of pigtail monkey groups through the use of challenges', *Primates*, **7**, pp. 471–80.

Kummer, H. (1968), *Social organization of hamadryas baboons* (University of Chicago Press), p. 189.

Kummer, H. (1978), 'Analogs of morality among nonhuman primates', in *Morality as a Biological Phenomenon* ed. G.S. Stent (Berkeley, CA: University of California Press).

ON THE ORIGIN OF MORALITY

Donald Black

Christopher Boehm proposes that morality began when a society of hunter-gatherers punished a member for violating its rules. He claims social control of this kind is universal, and that apes have related tendencies. Emile Durkheim had a similar conception of social control in the simplest and earliest societies. But both are wrong: Hunter-gatherers rarely, if ever, handle conflict in a law-like and penal fashion, and the society as a whole rarely if ever is the agent of social control. Individuals typically handle their own conflicts, and avoidance is more common than punishment. Pure sociology predicts and explains the handling of conflict with its location and direction in social space — its social structure. The nature of morality depends, for example, on the social distance and degree of inequality between the parties, whether humans or nonhumans. Morality varies from case to case. It is relative rather than universal. Boehm therefore describes the origin of something that has never existed. All that is universal are the principles of structural relativity.

The origin of anything is always interesting. But if something very old has continued until the present — the universe, life, or the human species, for example — its origin is especially interesting. Something that has not continued (such as crucifixion or the drawing and quartering of criminals) may be historically interesting, but its disappearance diminishes the scientific attention it might otherwise receive. Since the subject matter of the natural sciences (such as physics, astronomy, and biology) typically has a long history that continues into the present, while the subject matter of the social sciences (such as anthropology, history, and sociology) often does not, natural scientists understandably devote more attention to the origins of various phenomena than do social scientists. Even so, social scientists occasionally claim that something in modern life has a very long history, and that it is possible to investigate how it began. They may even claim that something is universal across societies — the incest taboo, for instance — and then seek to explain how or why it came into being (see, for example, Durkheim, 1897; Murdock, 1949, chapter 9).

Anthropologist Christopher Boehm suggests that morality is universal in human life — a constant — and seeks to explain its origin among hunter-gatherers many thousands of years ago. Boehm regards morality as a process by which society as a whole endorses rules of proper conduct and punishes any of its members who violate those rules: 'Shared values define specific rights and wrongs of behaviour, and the group decides which individuals are deviant and sanctions them accordingly. These are constants of human social life, and on this basis a moral community engages actively in social control' (Boehm, 2000, p. 79). Such a view of morality is not unusual. It commonly appears in introductory sociology and anthropology classes as well as law school lectures, political speeches, and religious sermons.

Boehm assumes that the anthropological literature on the simplest societies known to exist — hunter-gatherers — provides the best indirect evidence about the nature of morality in its earliest days. He likewise assumes that because apes are biologically similar to humans, the behaviour of apes — especially the ability of chimpanzees to form 'coalitions on a large scale' — provides further evidence about the ancestry of 'social control as we know it today' (Boehm, 2000, p. 93; see also his 1982). He thus proposes that morality began when something was 'declared deviant and outlawed' by 'a coalition of the entire band' of hunter-gatherers (p. 97). Here I leave aside the substance of morality (such as the prohibition of murder or adultery) and focus only on its procedures: the handling of right and wrong.[1] Morality

---

[1] Boehm proposes that the first prohibited conduct was 'bullying behaviour' — the domination of one person by another — a violation of the egalitarian nature of hunter-gatherer society (2000, pp. 82, 85, 95–7; see also 1993). In the following pages, I do not discuss whether or why hunter-gatherers define bullying behaviour as deviant. Instead, I focus on Boehm's conception of *how* hunter-gatherers handle bullying behaviour and other conduct they define as deviant. I am primarily concerned with how the

in this sense is synonymous with the sociological concept of social control: any process that defines and responds to deviant behaviour (Black, 1984b, p. 21, note 1).[2]

Professor Boehm invokes the scholarly authority of classical sociologist Emile Durkheim who a century ago characterized social control in the simplest and earliest societies as a crude version of criminal justice: 'In primitive societies, . . . law is wholly penal', and 'it is the assembly of the people which renders justice' (1893, p. 76).[3] Punishment enforces standards of right and wrong shared by all — the 'collective conscience' (idem, chapter 2). Although 'restitutive law' (or civil law requiring compensation) increasingly displaces penal law as societies develop a division of labour, penal law continues into modern times (idem, p. 90). It is universal.

Boehm's conception of morality is similar to Durkheim's conception of penal law. Like Durkheim, his image of social control in the simplest and earliest societies is legalistic and penal: Rules explicitly define what is prohibited and punished by the group. Like Durkheim, he also regards social control as a characteristic of entire societies. Unfortunately, however, Durkheim was wrong: He overlegalized and oversocietalized the nature of social control.

The Overlegalization of Simple Societies

Durkheim was wrong to believe that the simplest and earliest societies rely heavily on penal law — prohibitions enforced by public punishments. Anthropological observations of hunter-gatherers across the world reveal that they typically have no explicit conception of law-like rules of conduct, and, when asked by an anthropologist to list such rules, find it difficult or impossible to do so (see Black, 1989, pp. 92–3; 1993a, pp. 145–6).[4] Punishment by the group as a whole is rare if not totally absent as well. Such societies are stateless — without chiefs or other authorities of a political nature — and the handling of most if not all conflict is radically decentralized among the

---

simplest hunter-gatherers — those who have, for example, the smallest, most egalitarian, and most intimate bands — handle right and wrong. For a discussion of differences between the simplest and the more complex hunter-gatherers, see Knauft (1991).

[2] My concept or social control is in turn synonymous with alternatives such as 'conflict management' and 'dispute settlement' (see Black, 1984b, p. 22, note 7). This concept entails no assumptions or implications about the impact of social control, such as whether or how it influences the conduct of anyone subjected to it or aware of its application (see idem, pp. 3–5).

[3] Because Durkheim speaks of 'penal law' as the punishment of rule violations by the group as a whole, his conception of 'law' does not require the existence of a state or state-like structure (compare, for example, Black, 1976, p. 2).

[4] Scholars sometimes distinguish between a morality of rules and a morality of ideals. The former explicitly prohibits particular conduct on pain of punishment or other deprivation, while the latter recognizes proper, desirable, or admirable conduct with rewards or other expressions of appreciation. Legal philosopher Lon Fuller thus speaks of a 'morality of duty' and a 'morality of aspiration' (1964, pp. 5–6), and moral philosopher William Frankena speaks of a 'morality of principles' and a 'morality of traits of character' (1963, pp. 53–4). Many simple societies largely or totally lack an explicit morality of rules and operate instead with a morality of ideals. Consider, for example, the Piaroa of Venezuela, who practice simple horticulture as well as hunting, fishing, and gathering:

> The Piaroa are as allergic to a notion of social 'rule' as to the idea of 'the right of command'. While there are proper ways of doing things, it is up to the individual to *choose* or *not to choose* to do them. . . . The notion of giving up one's rights to a 'whole community' or of submitting to a decision forthcoming from the community or a portion of it would be a strange and abhorrent idea to them (Overing, 1989, p. 89; italics in original).

adversaries and their partisans (see Knauft, 1991, p. 395). They do not even have third parties such as judges or arbitrators who intervene authoritatively in the conflicts of their fellows.[5] The only such third party among the Mbuti (once known as Pygmies) of Zaire, for example, is the so-called 'camp clown', who dampens conflicts by drawing attention to himself and making everyone laugh (Turnbull, 1965, pp. 182–3). In other societies, onlookers may simply beg the adversaries to stop, step between them, or pull them apart when they quarrel and threaten to fight — a common practice, for instance, among the Kiowa Indians of the North American Plains (Richardson, 1940, p. 19).[6] But most adversaries handle their own problems with no help from anyone (see, e.g., Lee, 1979, pp. 370–3; Woodburn, 1979, pp. 252–3). In short, hunter-gatherers have little or no penal law in Durkheim's sense.[7] And if morality requires enforcement by the group as a whole — Boehm's usage — they have little or no morality.

Hunter-gatherers normally handle major conflicts by reducing or terminating contact — a form of social control known as 'avoidance' (see Baumgartner, 1988, chapter 3; Black, 1990, pp. 79–82). Thus, among the Chenchu of southern India: 'There is no institutionalized system of arbitration and no provision for any coercive action in more serious cases such as the abduction of a wife. Under these circumstances it is usual for one of the parties to leave the group, and the rivals will then avoid each other.' (von Fürer-Haimendorf, 1967, p. 20; see also pp. 21–3). Or the Hadza of northern Tanzania: 'The Hadza have no procedures for arbitration. They have to solve their disputes for themselves almost always without any intervention by third parties. In fact, most disputes are resolved by self-segregation and attract hardly any attention: Units are highly unstable with individuals constantly joining and breaking away, and it is so easy to move away that one of the parties to the dispute is likely to decide to do so very soon, often even without acknowledging that the dispute exists' (Woodburn, 1979, p. 252). Or the Netsilik Eskimos of the Arctic: 'Whenever a situation came up in which an individual disliked somebody or a group of people in the band, he often pitched his tent or built his igloo at the opposite extremity of the camp or moved to another settlement altogether. This is common practice even today' (Balikci, 1970, p. 192).

Although hunter-gatherers sometimes use violence as a form of social control (especially in adultery cases and in response to other violence), it is typically inflicted by the aggrieved party alone rather than the band as a whole.[8] Among Eskimos, for example, a male relative of the victim traditionally takes vengeance against a killer, though occasionally a small group will decide that a repeat killer or other dangerous person should be assassinated — often by a relative of the offender (Balikci, 1970,

---

[5] The authoritativeness of third-party intervention is a matter of degree and pertains to the use of rules, decisiveness, force and punishment (see Black, 1993a, pp. 145–9; see also the typology of third parties in Black and Baumgartner, 1983).

[6] I mention the Kiowa only because an anthropologist discusses their efforts to dampen conflict in the manner above. Even so, partly because of their individual ownership of horses, Plains Indians such as the Kiowa and Cheyenne are less egalitarian than the simplest hunter-gatherers. Their involvement in buffalo hunting also entails patterns of organization uncommon among the simplest hunter-gatherers (see, for example, Richardson, 1940; Llewellyn and Hoebel, 1941).

[7] Although hunter-gatherers have no government by the whole society on a permanent basis, they may have a temporary chief or other officials during collective undertakings such as communal hunts or warfare with foreigners (for examples and references, see Black, 1976, pp. 87–91).

[8] Violence in all societies is usually a form of social control, whether or not it is also defined as deviant — even a crime — in its own right (see Black, 1984a, ; 1998, pp. 14–16).

pp. 189–93; see also Hoebel, 1954, pp. 87–90). A violent conflict among some hunter-gatherers may escalate briefly into a larger fracas involving the close associates of the adversaries (see, for example, Lee, 1979, chapter 13), but rarely if ever does it (or anything else) result in collective action by what Durkheim calls 'an assembly of the people' (1893, p. 76). In a number of societies, even individual violence is rare if not completely absent.[9] The Chewong of Malaysia (shifting horticulturalists as well as hunter-gatherers) apparently have neither violent deviants nor violent agents of social control, and claim they cannot remember a single case of collective or individual violence resulting in a personal injury within their tribe. Asked what would happen if a killing were to occur, they replied that the killer 'would be so ashamed' he or she 'would leave the region altogether never to return' (Howell, 1989, p. 55; see also, for example, Overing, 1989, pp. 79–80). Certainly all hunter-gatherers have conflicts of a moral nature, but Durkheim was drastically wrong to say that the handling of these matters resembles modern criminal law, with its many rules and public punishments. He thus overlegalized social control in the simplest and earliest societies.

Durkheim was wrong not only to think the simplest societies have a great deal of penal law, but also to think penal law evolves before restitutive law — the compensation of injuries. While the simplest societies have virtually no penal *or* restitutive law, restitutive law precedes and predominates over penal law when societies first evolve to higher levels of complexity (see Black, 1987, pp. 51, 62, note 6). In Europe, for example, the law of the Germanic tribes (who were agriculturists) was overwhelmingly restitutive (see, for example, Drew, 1973; 1991),[10] and as late as the early Middle Ages even homicide required only compensation to the victim's family (see, for example, Pollock and Maitland, 1898, Volume 1, pp. 46–53). Durkheim's view of legal evolution was backwards.[11]

But Durkheim's errors are not surprising: Because anthropology had hardly been born when he was writing, he had little information about the reality of social control in the simplest societies. Instead he had to rely almost entirely on descriptions of social control in ancient civilizations such as early Greece, Rome, Egypt, Palestine, India, and China (see generally Durkheim, 1893).[12] He knew that such societies have highly penal systems of law, including punishments as severe as any in human history, and possibly reasoned that if ancient civilizations have so much penal law,

---

[9] For an overview emphasizing that the simplest hunter-gatherers have less violence than more complex hunter-gatherers and other tribal societies, see Knauft (1991).

[10] 'In general, little distinction was made between suits of a civil or criminal nature — or, it more accurately might be said that all offences were treated as if they were civil offences. . . . The barbarian codes set out in minute detail what "compensation" (or composition) would have to be paid by the offending party or his family' (Drew, 1973, p. 8).

[11] In a later work (1900, pp. 32–7), Durkheim partially corrects himself by proposing a direct association between the centralization of the state and the development of penal law.

[12] Durkheim's references to tribal societies in his 1893 book on legal evolution are limited to studies of Germanic tribes (that apparently did not describe the compensatory nature of their law) and American Indian tribes (mainly Iroquois), both of which were more complex than pure hunter-gatherers. It is also possible that he had some knowledge of the hunter-gathering Australian Aborigines later featured in his work on religion (1912). If so, however, his conception of hunter-gatherers would have been distorted by peculiarities of the Aborigines, such as their highly patriarchal families and their abundance of sacred taboos, sometimes enforced in a collective and penal style that included capital punishment (see, for example, Meggitt, 1962, pp. 251–62; see also Woodburn, 1979, pp. 258–60).

earlier and simpler societies would have even more. But he was wrong: We now know that penal law occurs in a curvilinear pattern across time and social evolution, with the least in the earliest and simplest societies on the one hand, and in the latest and most complex societies on the other. The most penal law occurs between those extremes, in ancient civilizations and similarly hierarchical societies such as the medieval and Renaissance monarchies of Europe and the various kingdoms of pre-colonial Africa. Durkheim's portrait of the handling of right and wrong in the earliest and simplest societies was understandable, then, but wrong. Boehm's portrait of morality mirrors Durkheim's and is equally wrong.

The Oversocietalization of Social Control

Boehm's conception also mirrors another feature of Durkheim's work: He regards social control as a characteristic of societies as a whole. Both claim that each hunter-gatherer society handles conflicts according to conceptions of right and wrong shared by all and applicable to all. Their image resembles that found in modern ideology about the rule of law and equality before the law: Society applies its rules universally. But the society is the wrong unit of analysis, and social control is not universal.

Society as a whole tells us little about law or morality. Everyone in a society may agree that certain forms of human behaviour (such as murder, rape, and theft) are wrong, but how people actually define and handle these offences varies from one case to another. Different societies have different possibilities, but in no society do all cases of the same kind have the same fate. Consider, for example, a killing: One results in a single act of blood vengeance, another in feuding or warfare, mediation or arbitration, execution by the killer's group or government, imprisonment for various lengths of time, various amounts of compensation to the victim's family, labelling of the killer as mentally ill or otherwise abnormal, voluntary exile or banishment, sorcery against the killer, a ceremony to appease the gods, an apology, approbation of the killer as an enemy of evil, or almost nothing at all — to mention only some of the possibilities. Why does this variation occur?

The handling of each case depends on who kills whom and who else, if anyone, participates as a third party. For example, the outcome depends on the relational distance between the killer and the victim: Is the killer close to the victim, such as a member of the same family, or are they members of different families in the same community, mere acquaintances from different communities, or complete strangers? The outcome also depends on the social status of each: Are they equal or unequal? Equally high or equally low? If not, who is higher? Is the killer, say, an aristocrat or master while the victim is a peasant or slave, or vice versa? The outcome depends on their cultural location: Are they culturally similar or not? Is one a member of a cultural minority? And it depends on the support each attracts: Who are their partisans, if any, and what is the relationship between the partisans of each? Is either represented by a group? A state? It depends on who handles the case as well: Who intervenes to find a solution? Is a trial held? If so, who participates? All these elements and more — the relational distance between everyone involved, the social status of each, the cultural distance between them, their organization — together constitute the social structure of a killing and predict and explain how it will be handled, including whether it is defined as misconduct in the first place.

We know, for example, that across the world and across history the severity of social control increases with the relational distance between the killer and victim (see, for example, Middleton, 1965, pp. 51–2; Peters, 1967, pp. 263–75; Koch, 1974, chapter 3; Lundsgaarde, 1977). We also know that an upward killing (of a social superior) attracts more social control than a lateral or downward killing (of an equal or inferior) (see, for example, Gough, 1960, p. 48; van der Sprenkel, 1962, p. 27; Hallpike, 1977, pp. 148–54, 191; Bowers and Pierce, 1980). The greater the differences in their social location and direction, the greater the differences in how killings are handled. The same applies to all clashes of right and wrong in all societies: What happens depends on who participates.[13]

The foregoing is an application of pure sociology, a radically new theoretical paradigm that predicts and explains the behaviour of social life with its multidimensional location and direction in social space (see, for example, Black, 1976; 1995; 1998). Pure sociology eliminates psychology (subjectivity of any kind), teleology (the explanation of social life as a means to an end), and even people from social science.[14] Yet the formulations of pure sociology are readily testable, simple, and extremely general — applicable, as we shall see, even beyond the human species. A considerable body of theory (illustrated below) thus specifies how the handling of conflict varies with its location and direction in social space. The social structure of each case — its geometry — predicts and explains what happens.[15]

The structural relativity of right and wrong implies that morality is not a characteristic of society as a whole.[16] Nor is it universal. It obeys sociological principles from one case to another. For example, the penal style of social control — in which the group punishes a wrongdoer — is more likely and more severe in downward and distant cases, especially where the aggrieved party is at once socially superior and relationally and culturally distant from the alleged wrongdoer (Black, 1976, pp. 29–30, 47–48; 1993a).[17] The penal style is also more likely and more severe when the third party who handles the case is a superior who is socially distant from the adversaries. The more inequality and social distance between all three parties — the larger the area of the conflict triangle — the more penal and moralistic the handling of the conflict is likely to be (see Black, 1993a, pp. 144–9; 1995, pp. 834–7, especially note 41).

---

[13] When I say above that society as a whole tells us little about law or morality, I refer to the society as a unit in itself and not to the particular conflicts we may infer it contains. Information about the social structure of a society's typical conflicts allows us, in principal, to predict and explain its typical patterns of social control.

[14] Although I sometimes speak of the behaviour of people in the text for ease of communication, the theoretical formulations of pure sociology speak only of the social phenomena whose behaviour is addressed — such as the behaviour of law or the behaviour of art (see, for example, Black, 1976; 1995, pp. 858–61).

[15] For other works on social control applying the paradigm of pure sociology, see, for example, Baumgartner (1978; 1988; 1992), Cooney (1997; 1998), Horwitz (1990), Morrill (1992; 1995), Morrill et al., (1997), Senechal de la Roche (1996; 1997a), Tucker (1999a; 1999b), and Tucker and Ross (1999).

[16] I speak of the 'structural relativity of right and wrong' and the 'structural relativity of morality' in Black (1998, pp. 23–6) — first published in 1993 (see also Black, 1989, pp. 8, 90, 94).

[17] Moralism — the tendency to treat people as enemies — is a direct function of social remoteness and superiority (Black, 1993a, p. 144). This formulation applies to the behaviour of adversaries on their own as well as the behaviour of third parties who intervene in a conflict. It implies, for example, that (when the grievance is the same) downward and more distant violence is greater than lateral, upward, and closer violence.

Now we can understand why the ancient civilizations discussed earlier have so much penal law: It is because they have so much inequality and social distance between their members. A conflict across such great expanses in social space, particularly when the complainant or victim is socially superior and relationally and culturally distant from the alleged wrongdoer, is vastly more likely to be handled in a penal and otherwise moralistic fashion than a similar case between close equals. In fact, ancient civilizations have so much inequality and social distance in some conflicts (such as those between masters and slaves of different ethnicities or between the monarchy and its foreign subjects) that their penal law and moralism reach historic levels, including diverse forms of agonizing torture, mutilation (such as the amputation of limbs, facial features, and testicles), and aggravated modes of capital punishment (such as death by burning, boiling, slicing, crushing, and being thrown to wild beasts).

Because the simplest hunter-gatherers have little or no inequality or social distance within each band, they have no such practices. They have no law on a permanent basis, and little or no penal or moralistic behaviour such as punishment by the group as a whole.[18] As noted earlier, they do not even have adjudication, arbitration, or other modes of authoritative intervention. They lack the raw materials for penal law and moralism: They are too equal, intimate, and homogeneous. Only when they capture foreign invaders do they collectively humiliate, torture, mutilate, and kill particular individuals. Some North American Indians, for example, rarely if ever executed their own members, but they occasionally roasted their captives alive (see, for example, Knowles, 1940, pp. 188–9, 192–3).

The handling of right and wrong is everywhere relative rather than universal, variable rather than constant, situational rather than global. It does not originate in society as a whole, and it is not a characteristic of society as a whole. Durkheim therefore oversocietalizes the handling of right and wrong, and so does Boehm.[19]

The Morality of Apes

Pure sociology applies to all social life — nonhuman as well as human. The same principles of structural relativity predict and explain differences in the handling of conflict within a single species, between members of a species in the wild and those in captivity, and between species, including differences between humans and nonhumans. Morality everywhere varies with its social structure. Consider, for example, the nonhumans studied by Boehm in his search for the origin of morality: chimpanzees.

Just as the severity of violence increases with the social distance between humans (for example, Black, 1990, pp. 75–9; 1993a, pp. 148–54; Senechal de la Roche, 1996,

---

[18] Collective violence against a single member — a lynching — occurs occasionally in some simple societies: normally when an individual becomes marginal and isolated from other members who, in turn, form a solidary group of partisans against him (Senechal de la Roche, 1997b). Even so, such violence rarely if ever reaches the level found in ancient civilizations and other social settings where the degree of inequality and social distance is greater.

[19] Both Durkheim and Boehm also reason psychologically and teleologically about the behaviour of individuals and the nature of social control — elements of their work I disregard for these purposes. I would only note that while a focus on society as a whole oversocietalizes social control, a focus on the individual (such as individual feelings, perceptions, or intentions) overpersonalizes social control (see Black, 1995, pp. 852–8). A focus on either the society or the individual overlooks the social structure of the conflict.

pp. 106–12), for instance, so it increases with the social distance between chimpanzees.[20] Wild chimpanzees are more violent toward members of other chimpanzee communities than members of their own community.[21] A group may attack, mutilate, and kill a chimpanzee stranger, whereas violence of this degree is less common among captive chimpanzees who have no contact with chimpanzee strangers and who otherwise have little social distance within their closed community (see, for example, Goodall, 1986, pp. 313, 331, chapter 7; de Waal, 1982, p. 82; 1989, pp. 61–78; Boehm, 1992, pp. 153–5).[22] Both wild and captive chimpanzees are sometimes violent within their own community, but they limit the injuries inflicted: Biting is 'rare' within wild bands, for example (Goodall, 1968, p. 376), and captives almost always bite only 'extremities, usually a finger or a foot, and less frequently a shoulder or the head' (de Waal, 1982, p. 112; but see 1989, pp. 61–78). Captive male chimpanzees are more distant among themselves than captive females, and accordingly captive males are more violent among themselves than captive females among themselves (de Waal, 1989, pp. 52–3, 56–7). And because wild male chimpanzees are typically more distant from each other than are male humans in the simplest societies, the former are more violent than the latter (see Knauft, 1991).[23] All chimpanzees are likewise more dangerous to humans with whom they are unacquainted (see, for example, de Waal, 1982, pp. 20, 28–9, 82; Goodall, 1986, p. 282).

Chimpanzees sometimes intervene in the conflicts of their fellows, usually by taking sides with one party but also impartially in some instances (see, for example, de Waal, 1982, pp. 42–5, 196–7; Boehm, 1992, pp. 144–9). Again, social distance has the same relevance as in human conflicts: Chimpanzees take the side of a friend or relative against a more distant adversary (see, for example, de Waal, 1982, p. 196; Goodall, 1986, p. 319; de Waal, 1992, pp. 237–41; see also Black, 1993b).[24] Social inequality is relevant as well:[25] Like humans, chimpanzees of higher status

[20] My theory predicts and explains variation in the handling of conflict only when the nature of the conflict is constant. Intimate humans may be extremely violent toward each other — as violent as distant humans — but this occurs primarily when they have conflicts peculiar to intimates, such as conflicts about sexual infidelity or the end of a close relationship. If the conduct is the same, however, such as a theft or insult, the likelihood of violence increases with the social distance between the parties.

[21] Like human violence, most chimpanzee violence is moralistic, such as a response to trespassing or theft, the enforcement of a hierarchy, an element of a fight, or a mode of intervention in a conflict (but see, for example, Goodall, 1968, pp. 190–2; 1986, pp. 282–5).

[22] The social distance between chimpanzees is measureable with such observables as the time they spend together in close proximity, the activities they share, and the amount and nature of communication and physical contact between them (see, for example, de Waal, 1992, p. 237). Close male chimpanzees groom each other, for instance, and very close males may even synchronize their body movements as they walk side by side (idem, pp. 235, 237).

[23] Wild male chimpanzees are more violent than humans only when they are compared to the simplest hunter-gatherers, and not to relatively complex hunter-gatherers and other societies of a tribal nature (Knauft, 1991).

[24] Partisanship is a joint function of the social closeness and superiority of one side and the social remoteness and inferiority of the other (Black, 1993b, p. 127). Chimpanzees equidistant from the adversaries should be more impartial (Black, 1993b, pp. 134–5). If the closeness of the parties is constant, chimpanzees should be more likely to take the side of a superior against an inferior than the side of an inferior against a superior. For patterns of partisanship in other primates, especially monkeys, see Ehardt and Bernstein (1992).

[25] Inequality among chimpanzees is known by the presence of 'dominance' in a chimpanzee relationship. A dominant chimpanzee receives a 'submissive greeting' from a subordinate. Such a greeting

are more likely to intervene in conflicts and to do so more authoritatively (see Black and Baumgartner, 1983, p. 122; Black, 1993a, pp. 144–9).[26] For example, male chimpanzees — socially superior to females — intervene more often and use more authoritative methods, including coercion and violence (for example, de Waal, 1982, p. 196; 1989, p. 59). Females normally intervene in a warmer and less direct fashion, such as by kissing a male and leading him to his adversary or by taking a stick or rock out of an angry male's hand (de Waal, 1982, pp. 37–8, 114–5; 1996, p. 32).[27] But 'dominant' chimpanzees of both sexes are more likely to intervene in conflicts and to do so forcefully, and the highest ranking males are the most likely and most forceful of all (Boehm, 1992, pp. 144–9; de Waal, 1996, pp. 128–32, 241, note 36). Notice, moreover, that chimpanzees of higher status handle right and wrong more authoritatively than any of the simplest hunter-gatherers, who rarely if ever intervene in conflicts coercively and punitively. Such chimpanzees are more like legal officials.[28] And my theory explains why: Hunter-gatherers are more intimate and egalitarian than chimpanzees.

Conclusion

The principles of pure sociology predict and explain variation in the handling of right and wrong, including the style and amount of social control a conflict will attract (see especially Black, 1976; 1998). Morality varies with the social structure of each case: the social distance it spans, its social elevation, its direction in social space, and so on. Only a small minority (if any) of a society's conflicts have a penal structure, for example, and only these attract punishment. Similarly, only some (if any) of an individual's conflicts have a penal structure, and no one is punitive all the time (see Black, 1995, pp. 852–8). Social structures have morality, not societies or individuals.

Like biology, pure sociology applies to both humans and nonhumans.[29] But pure sociology is a new science that predicts and explains the social life of various species entirely without regard to biological considerations.[30] The morality of chimpanzees

---

normally involves a sequence of short, panting grunts (known as 'pant-grunting' or 'rapid-ohoh') in a lowered posture, often accompanied by a series of deep bows (known as 'bobbing'). Other forms of deference include extending a hand or kissing the feet, neck or chest of the dominant individual (de Waal, 1982, pp, 86–90).

[26] Recall that authoritativeness also varies with social distance, including relational and cultural distance: It is a direct function of the third party's social distance from the adversaries (Black and Baumgartner, 1983, p, 123; Black 1993a, pp. 144–9).

[27] Human children may similarly intervene in the conflicts of their parents.

[28] Goodall speaks of social control among chimpanzees as 'order without law' (1982). But the same conception applies equally if not more appropriately to social control among humans in many situations, post-tribal as well as tribal. A recent book on social control among cattle ranchers in modern California even employs the title, *Order without Law* (Ellickson, 1991).

[29] Social science normally includes assumptions, assertions, or implications about human psychology and teleology that do not readily extend to nonhumans. An exception is the branch of psychology known variously as behaviourism, learning theory, or reinforcement theory — which has demonstrated that individual nonhumans as well as humans maximize conduct for which they are rewarded. Sociology, however, almost never reaches beyond the human species (but see Caplow, 1968, chapter 4).

[30] Pure sociology contrasts especially sharply with sociobiology, a branch of biology that addresses the social life of animals, including humans, as a genetically-based adaptation to the environment (see, for

thus obeys the same principles as the morality of humans, and these principles are sociological rather than biological. Chimpanzee morality varies with the social structure of each case, and this morality is no more universal than the morality of humans. It is relative, variable, situational.

Universal morality is a myth.[31] Morality is universal only when the social structure of conflict is universal. And it never is.[32] A search for the origin of universal morality is therefore a search for the origin of something that has never existed.

Yet morality still had a beginning. What, then, was the origin of human morality? It began with conflicts over right and wrong, conflicts surely present from the beginning of human life. Morality is a characteristic of the human species.[33] But it is not uniquely human: Morality began before humans — in any and all species with conflicts over right and wrong.[34] And it was always variable. All that is universal are the principles that predict and explain its behaviour.

Acknowledgements

For comments on earlier drafts, I thank M.P. Baumgartner, Albert Bergesen, Theodore Caplow, Randall Collins, Ellis Godard, Marcus Mahmood, Teelyn Mauney, Alexandra Scott, Roberta Senechal de la Roche, Christopher Stevens, and James Tucker.

References

Balikci, Asen (1970), *The Netsilik Eskimo* (Garden City: Natural History Press).
Baumgartner, M.P. (1978), 'Law and social status in colonial New Haven, 1639–1665', in *Research in Law and Sociology: An Annual Compilation of Research*, **I**, ed. Rita J. Simon, (Greenwich: JAI Press).
Baumgartner, M.P. (1988), *The Moral Order of a Suburb* (New York: Oxford University Press).
Baumgartner, M.P. (1992), 'War and peace in early childhood', in Tucker (1992).
Black, Donald (1976), *The Behavior of Law* (New York: Academic Press).
Black, Donald (1984a), 'Crime as social control', in Black (1998).
Black, Donald (1984b), 'Social control as dependent variable', in Black (1998).
Black, Donald (1987), 'Compensation and the social structure of misfortune', in Black (1998).
Black, Donald (1989), *Sociological Justice* (New York: Oxford University Press).
Black, Donald (1990), 'The elementary forms of conflict management', in Black (1998).
Black, Donald (1993a), 'Making enemies', in Black (1998).
Black, Donald (1993b), 'Taking sides', in Black (1998).
Black, Donald (1995), 'The epistemology of pure sociology', *Law & Social Inquiry*, **20**, pp. 829–70.
Black, Donald (1998), *The Social Structure of Right and Wrong* (San Diego: Academic Press, revised edition; first edition, 1993).

example, Wilson, 1975). For an overview of the biology of social life and its relevance to morality, see de Waal (1996, chapter 1).

[31] Again, here and elsewhere I refer only to universal modes of handling conflict — not to the conduct that causes conflict in the first place.

[32] It would nevertheless be possible to reduce or obscure social differences across cases of conflict. For instance, we could 'desocialize' a court of law by providing it with little or no information about the social characteristics of its cases, such as the social distance or inequality between the parties involved (Black, 1989, chapter 4; see also chapter 3).

[33] Some might argue that social order requires morality. But what is social order? Empirically speaking, it is present as long as a species, human or otherwise, does not exterminate itself. The mere evolution of a species implies that it has social order, and it has social order as long as it reproduces. If morality is necessary for social order, it begins with the species as well. The quality of social order or morality is another matter — one that requires value judgments beyond the competence of science.

[34] Pure sociology disregards how humans and nonhumans might experience their own conduct and instead examines their social life alone. Nonhumans handle conflicts over right and wrong whenever they have clashes about matters such as access to territory, food, or sexual partners. Such is their morality — and it is readily observable without knowledge of their subjectivity.

Black, Donald, and Baumgartner, M.P. (1983), 'Toward a theory of the third party', in Black (1998).

Boehm, Christopher (1982), 'The evolutionary development of morality as an effect of dominance behavior and conflict interference', *Journal of Social and Biological Structures*, **5**, pp. 413–21.

Boehm, Christopher (1992), 'Segmentary "warfare" and the management of conflict: comparison of East African chimpanzees and patrilineal-patrilocal humans', in Harcourt and de Waal (1992).

Boehm, Christopher (1993), 'Egalitarian behaviour and reverse dominance hierarchy,' *Current Anthropology*, **34**, pp. 227–53.

Boehm, Christopher (2000), 'Conflict and the evolution of social control', *Journal of Consciousness Studies*, **7** (1–2), pp. 79–101.

Bowers, William J., and Pierce, Glenn L. (1980), 'Arbitrariness and discrimination under post-*Furman* capital statutes', *Crime and Delinquency*, **26**, pp. 563–635.

Caplow, Theodore (1968), *Two against One: Coalitions in Triads* (Englewood Cliffs: Prentice-Hall).

Cooney, Mark (1997), 'The decline of elite homicide', *Criminology*, **35**, pp. 381–407.

Cooney, Mark (1998), *Warriors and Peacemakers: How Third Parties Shape Violence* (New York: New York University Press).

Drew, Katherine Fischer (ed. 1973), *The Lombard Laws* (Philadelphia: University of Pennsylvania Press).

Drew, Katherine Fischer (ed. 1991), *The Laws of the Salian Franks* (Philadelphia: University of Pennsylvania Press).

Durkheim, Emile (1893), *The Division of Labor in Society* (New York: Free Press, 1964).

Durkheim, Emile (1897), *Incest: The Nature and Origin of the Taboo* (New York: Lyle Stuart, 1963).

Durkheim, Emile (1900), 'Two laws of penal evolution', *University of Cincinnati Law Review*, **38** (1969), pp. 32–60.

Durkheim, Emile (1912), *The Elementary Forms of Religious Life* (New York: Free Press, 1995).

Ehardt, Carolyn L., and Bernstein, Irwin S. (1992), 'Conflict intervention behaviour by adult male macaques: structural and functional aspects', in Harcourt and de Waal (1992).

Ellickson, Robert C. (1991), *Order without Law: How Neighbors Settle Disputes* (Cambridge: Harvard University Press).

Frankena, William K. (1963), *Ethics* (Englewood Cliffs: Prentice-Hall).

Fuller, Lon L. (1964), *The Morality of Law* (New Haven: Yale University Press).

Goodall, Jane (1968), 'The behaviour of free-living chimpanzees in the Gombe Stream Reserve', *Animal Behaviour Monographs*, **1**, pp. 161–311 (published as Jane van Lawick-Goodall).

Goodall, Jane (1982), 'Order without law', *Journal of Social and Biological Structures*, **5**, pp. 353–60.

Goodall, Jane (1986), *The Chimpanzees of Gombe: Patterns of Behavior* (Cambridge: Harvard University Press).

Gough, E. Kathleen (1960), 'Caste in a Tanjore village', in *Aspects of Caste in South India, Ceylon and North-West Pakistan*, ed. E.R. Leach (Cambridge: Cambridge University Press.

Hallpike, C.R. (1977), *Bloodshed and Vengeance in the Papuan Mountains: The Generation of Conflict in Tauade Society* (Oxford: Oxford University Press).

Harcourt, Alexander H., and de Waal, Frans B.M. (ed. 1992), *Coalitions and Alliances in Humans and Other Animals* (Oxford: Oxford University Press).

Hoebel, E. Adamson (1954), *The Law of Primitive Man: A Study in Comparative Legal Dynamics* (Cambridge: Harvard University Press).

Horwitz, Allan V. (1990), *The Logic of Social Control* (New York: Plenum Press).

Howell, Signe (1989), '"To be angry is not to be human, but to be fearful is": Chewong concepts of human nature', in Howell and Willis (1989).

Howell, Signe, and Willis, Roy (ed. 1989), *Societies at Peace: Anthropological Perspectives* (London: Routledge).

Knauft, Bruce M. (1991), 'Violence and sociality in human evolution', *Current Anthropology*, **32**, pp. 391–428.

Knowles, Nathaniel (1940), 'The torture of captives by the Indians of eastern North America', *Proceedings of the American Philosophical Society*, **82**, pp. 151–225.

Koch, Klaus-Friedrich (1974), *War and Peace in Jalémó: The Management of Conflict in Highland New Guinea* (Cambridge: Harvard University Press).

Lee, Richard Borshay (1979), *The !Kung San: Men, Women and Work in a Foraging Society* (Cambridge: Cambridge University Press).

Llewellyn, Karl N., and Hoebel, E. Adamson (1941), *The Cheyenne Way: Conflict and Case Law in Primitive Jurisprudence* (Norman: University of Oklahoma Press).

Lundsgaarde, Henry P. (1977), *Murder in Space City: A Cultural Analysis of Houston Homicide Patterns* (New York: Oxford University Press).

Meggitt, M.J. (1962), *Desert People: A Study of the Walbiri Aborigines of Central Australia* (Sydney: Angus and Robertson).

Middleton, John (1965), *The Lugbara of Uganda* (New York: Holt, Rinehart and Winston).

Morrill, Calvin (1992), 'Vengeance among executives', in Tucker (1992).

Morrill, Calvin (1995), *The Executive Way: Conflict Management in Corporations* (Chicago: University of Chicago Press).

Morrill, Calvin, Snyderman, Ellen, and Dawson, Edwin J. (1997), 'It's not what you do, but who you are: informal social control, social status, and normative seriousness in organizations', *Sociological Forum*, **12**, pp. 519–43.

Murdock, George Peter (1949), *Social Structure* (New York: Free Press).

Overing, Joanna (1989), 'Styles of manhood: an Amazonian contrast in tranquillity and violence', in Howell and Willis (1989).

Peters, E.L. (1967), 'Some structural aspects of the feud among the camel-herding Bedouin of Cyrenaica', *Africa*, **37**, pp. 261–82.

Pollock, Frederick, and Maitland, Frederic William (1898), *The History of English Law: Before the Time of Edward I* (Cambridge: Cambridge University Press, 1968, second edition; first edition, 1895). Two volumes.

Richardson, Jane (1940), *Law and Social Status among the Kiowa Indians* (Seattle: University of Washington Press).

Senechal de la Roche, Roberta (1996), 'Collective violence as social control', *Sociological Forum*, **11**, pp. 97–128.

Senechal de la Roche, Roberta (1997a), 'The sociogenesis of lynching', in *Under Sentence of Death: Lynching in the South*, ed. W. Fitzhugh Brundage (Chapel Hill: University of North Carolina Press).

Senechal de la Roche, Roberta (1997b), 'Why is collective violence collective?', paper presented at the annual meeting of the American Society of Criminology, San Diego, California, November 22.

Tucker, James (ed. 1992), *Virginia Review of Sociology*, **1**: *Law and Conflict Management* (Greenwich: JAI Press).

Tucker, James (1999a), *The Therapeutic Corporation* (New York: Oxford University Press).

Tucker James (1999b), 'Therapy, organization, and the state: a Blackian perspective', in *Counseling and the Therapeutic State*, ed. James J. Chriss (New York: Aldine de Gruyter).

Tucker, James, and Ross, Susan (1999), 'Corporal punishment and Black's theory of social control', in *Corporal Punishment in Theoretical Perspective*, ed. Michael J. Donnelly and Murray A. Strauss (New Haven: Yale University Press).

Turnbull, Colin M. (1965), *Wayward Servants: The Two Worlds of the African Pygmies* (Garden City: Natural History Press).

van der Sprenkel, Sybille (1962), *Legal Institutions in Manchu China: A Sociological Analysis* (New York: Humanities Press, 1966).

von Fürer-Haimendorf, Christoph (1967), *Morals and Merit: A Study of Values and Social Controls in South Asian Societies* (Chicago: University of Chicago Press).

Wilson, Edward O. (1975), *Sociobiology: The New Synthesis* (Cambridge: Harvard University Press).

de Waal, Frans (1982), *Chimpanzee Politics: Power and Sex among Apes* (New York: Harper & Row).

de Waal, Frans (1989), *Peacemaking among Primates* (Cambridge: Harvard University Press).

de Waal, Frans (1992), 'Coalitions as part of reciprocal relations in the Arnhem chimpanzee colony', in Harcourt and de Waal (1992).

de Waal, Frans (1996), *Good Natured: The Origins of Right and Wrong in Humans and Other Animals* (Cambridge: Harvard University Press).

Woodburn, James (1979), 'Minimal politics: the political organization of the Hadza of north Tanzania', in *Politics in Leadership: A Comparative Perspective*, ed. William A. Shack and Perry S. Cohen (Oxford: Oxford University Press).

BOEHM'S GOLDEN AGE
Equality and Consciousness In Early Human Society

Alan Carling

Boehm's interesting hypothesis concerning the origins of human morality within egalitarian hunter-gatherer society relies on a one-sided view of the genetic inheritance of proto-humans, and on an over-optimistic view of the egalitarian effects of evolving human consciousness. The four papers as a whole would benefit from a richer conception of evolved human nature, involving the interaction of normative, affective, and rational elements.

Equality, Hierarchy and the Human Inheritance

Boehm (2000) wrestles in his contribution with two discrepant observations. The first is that human hunter-gatherers are 'uniformly egalitarian' in their social organisation; the second is that humans share with the two extant *Pan* species (and therefore the presumed ancestor of all three species) a proneness to 'status rivalry and competition based on flexible innate dispositions to dominate and submit' (p. 81). The discrepancy raises the question: 'how did an innately despotic species manage to become phenotypically egalitarian?' (p. 85). Boehm's answer is that the potential lower orders in hunter-gatherer society band together to impose control over the bullying behaviour of potential alpha males: 'it is institutionalized subordinate rebellion that leads to an egalitarian polity, in which individuals agree implicitly to eschew domination so that they may remain autonomous and uncontrolled' (p. 97). Anti-harassment policy is thus the Ur-case of moral control: a cultural device invented by the weak to keep the strong in line, as Nietzsche also reckoned morality. But with the development of agriculture, these egalitarian controls were lost, and mankind embarked on a dismal history of hierarchy and class division.

This is a bold and at times speculative hypothesis, as Boehm concedes. Part of its charm for this commentator lies in its resonance with a classical Marxist sequence, in which an egalitarian age of primitive communism gives way to concentrations of wealth in permanent human settlements, coupled with the inevitable exploitations of class society. But I am nevertheless concerned about the logic of Boehm's argument. His case is 'that humans can remain egalitarian only if they consciously suppress innate tendencies that otherwise would make for a pronounced social dominance hierarchy' (p. 84). This looks as if human morality is being invoked as the antidote for ancestral primate biology, in the Huxley/Dawkins line of contrast between nature and nurture rightly criticized by Flack and de Waal (2000). Just to compound the problem, morality, having been invoked for the Golden Age of hunter-gatherer egalitarianism, must presumably be uninvoked for the subsequent age of hierarchical class societies, in which the ape-like principle of social dominance rears its head once again, and the fit between society and biology is apparently restored.

Part of Boehm's problem arises from his overemphasis in programmatic statements on the contrast between hunter-gatherer egalitarianism on the one hand and the *Pan* species' social hierarchy on the other. First, even on his account, the hunter-gatherers are not uniformly egalitarian or entirely moralized: family relations are characterized by dominance, and murder allegedly evades direct social control.[35] Second, he neglects the evidence given in his own study, and also that presented copiously by Flack and de Waal, for pro-social behaviour in primates and apes, such as conflict resolution and 'reciprocity, empathy, sympathy and community concern' (Flack and de Waal, 2000, p. 3).[36] In fact, the genetically-given raw material for human sociality seems to include not just social dominance (which would then have

---

[35] Boehm (p. 94) says that in cases of hunter-gatherer homicide, the murderer will make themselves scarce, so that 'this kind of dire conflict "takes care of itself" ', but adds 'unless a feud ensues', in which case it presumably doesn't take care of itself.

[36] For Boehm's sense of the strength of the *Pan–Homo* contrast cf.: 'Chimpanzees, being despotic, put down their leaders only partially, or episodically, and they always have strong leaders. Humans, as egalitarians, are in a position to do so continuously, routinely and decisively.' (p. 93)

to be overcome by the apparently extraneous development of a 'civilizing' moral impulse) but social dominance plus the elements of proto-morality just listed. Proto-humans thus entered the most recent lap of their evolutionary journey with some combination of both hierarchical and egalitarian instincts (i.e., at some yet-to-be-determined point on a spectrum that makes each species either more hierarchical or more egalitarian in its fundamental disposition).

The Impact of Consciousness

What difference did the evolution of consciousness make to this proto-human instinctive complex? Boehm argues that consciousness inevitably pushed humans in the egalitarian direction:

> Abstract communication, mostly verbal, permitted the articulation and refinement of group values having to do with morality, and it also facilitated the kind of highly specific gossiping (with displacement) that is universal in human groups . . . [gossiping] enables group members to arrive privately and safely at a negative consensus about dangerous deviants. Language also makes it possible for groups to conspire, and ambush even the most fearsome dominator to execute him . . . . It definitely was critical to the invention of moral communities as we know them (p. 94).

The obvious retort is that gossip also helps the powerful to identify dangerous deviants who may threaten their position, thereby enabling them to nip the revolution in the bud. There is also such a thing as verbal bullying; language can be used in deceitful and manipulative ways, and used to maintain hierarchy as easily as to pull it down. I am not at all persuaded that language shows an inherent bias to the good.

Part of the difficulty here is with terminology, and especially the use of 'morality' to designate Boehm's principal focus of interest. Contrast 'ideology', 'norms' and 'morality' as alternative descriptors. 'Morality' carries a powerful message that the action thus described really is the correct action to take, as well as that required by a specific moral community. Thus, the statement 'it is moral to smother half the girl children' seems repugnant and perverse, even if it correctly describes the accepted social practice of a putative group of girl-smotherers. 'Ideology' is equally loaded, but in the negative direction, since it suggests that the relevant belief system is either false (in the contrast of 'ideology' with 'science') or that it serves merely as a cover for other undisclosed (and probably less idealistic) interests. So 'norms' seems the most appropriate (since the most neutral) term, with some norms being moral (or indeed immoral), and some being ideological. In this spirit, we would expect the norms that establish themselves in particular communities sometimes to normalize egalitarian practices, and sometimes to normalize hierarchical ones.

What appears to be universal in this area — applying *throughout* human history, and not just in a presumed Golden Age — is the fact that norms can be transmitted culturally (thus serving to reproduce communities), but also that they can be debated, negotiated, and amended, as part of the ongoing cultural practice of the community. It is then an open question — or, rather, the subject matter for a theory of history — whether the social norms operative in a particular society are operating more at the egalitarian or more at the hierarchical end of the spectrum. The issue is further complicated by the fact that societies of any degree of complexity will exhibit admixtures of egalitarian and hierarchical organization in their several parts or institutions. Thus, the platoon of an Army in the field may resemble in its operations the egalitarian conduct of a hunter-gatherer band, despite remaining embedded within a (ferociously) hierarchical formal institution, and a similar point might apply to a research team in a university.

Alternatively, there might be election by equal votes to an unequal position of high office, and it is not clear in any case that social inequality among humans is reducible to ape-like relations of interpersonal dominance — the capitalist is content to rip-off the consumer without also requiring ritualized displays of submission. For all these reasons, and classical Marxism notwithstanding, it is not obvious that history is adequately characterized by movements along a single dimension between the poles of equality and hierarchy. And in the respects in which hunter-gatherers are more egalitarian than other human groups, the reason is probably best sought in their specific history and external circumstances, not in any generalized effect of a recently evolved normative consciousness.

Human Nature and Human Society

The question underlying all four target papers is the fundamental one of human science: what is human nature; how did it come about, and how does it constrain the possible forms of human social organization? Despite the strides made in these papers, I am left wondering whether the conception of human nature is yet rich enough to sustain this intellectual project. Clearly, instrumental reason of the classic economistic type is insufficient — this is the plausible import of Skyrms's contribution to this volume, and also Sober and Wilson's.[37] But what else must be added to economic rationality? The normative dimension is one answer that emerges strongly here, so that the ego must be joined by the super-ego. But what about the id? It is surprising that the emotions are left out of the equation by Boehm and Frank/de Waal, especially given Darwin's original lead on the issue.

Recent work suggests that however and why ever the higher cognitive faculties evolved, their corresponding brain circuitry interacts with the affect program modules, which are presumably shared more or less by other primate species (Griffiths, 1997). And the interaction goes both ways: the emotions became conceptualizable (raising the possibility of conscious control of primitive affective responses à la Boehm on morality), but the concepts also became emotionalized, so that the conscious domain became a new field of operation for the emotions. For example, a person might exhibit the classical physical symptoms of surprise, or disgust, or anger at the perceived violation of a social norm, or happiness at the evidence of social approval from the group. And both the norms and the emotions can in turn be rationalized, both in the sense of being explained and/or modified in the light of reason, and in the sense of creating a conceptual field in which strategic calculations can come into play.[38]

The way forward for the evolution programme in the study of human development would seem to lie in a greater attention to the interactions among affect, reason and social norms in the evolved human psyche. And there is the small matter of a theory of history, to make good the understanding of cultural evolution.

---

[37] See Carling (1997) for a discussion of this point in relation to Skyrms, and the interview with Sober (1999) in relation to the Sober/Wilson project on altruism.

[38] It can be seen from this perspective that the evolutionary psychology programme suffers from a one-sidedness converse to that of standard economic theory: the one concentrates exclusively on instrumental reason, the other reduces all mental functioning to the operation of affect-like modular routines.

References

Boehm, Christopher (2000), 'Conflict and the evolution of social control', *Journal of Consciousness Studies*, **7** (1–2), pp. 79–101.

Carling, Alan (1997) 'Rational vervet: Social evolution and the origins of human norms and institutions', *Imprints*, **2** (2), pp. 157–73.

Flack J. and de Waal, F.B.M. (2000), '"Any Animal Whatever": Darwinian building blocks of morality in monkeys and apes,' *Journal of Consciousness Studies*, **7** (1–2), pp. 1–29.

Griffiths, Paul E. (1997) *What Emotions Really Are* (Chicago: University of Chicago Press).

Sober, Elliott (1999) 'Altruism, biology and society: An interview with Elliott Sober', *Imprints*, **3** (3), pp. 197–213.

PUZZLING QUESTIONS, NOT BEYOND ALL CONJECTURE
Boehm's 'Evolutionary Origins of Morality'

Robert Knox Dentan

Christopher Boehm's always intriguing and stimulating work in biological anthropology in some ways revives the interest in reconstructing origins which preoccupied cultural anthropology in the last half of the nineteenth century. This essay falls into a difficulty the earlier studies encountered, a tendency to metaphysical speculation leading to assertions which do not readily lend themselves to the confirmation or disconfirmation procedures that allow scientific advance. More seriously, the notion of 'common good' is also less precise and nuanced than any theory of morality and its origins requires.

Introduction

Christopher Boehm has never feared big questions. Moreover, in pursuing his studies, he deploys a wide range of skills, from cladistics to comparative ethnology. His vision of what anthropology is about harks back to the comparative empiricist tradition of the 1930s and 1940s and to the late nineteenth century concern with 'large questions' like the origins of marriage or of war. In this essay I restate what I understand to be Boehm's theory in sociocentric terms which I think would relieve it of some unnecessary baggage and thus allow it to avoid discussing 'human nature', which seems to me a red herring.

Restatement

The restatement runs like this. Most vertebrate behaviour, especially among primates, reflects the 'Premack principle', named after the libertarian psychologist David Premack: other things being equal, organisms will choose to reward themselves over being rewarded by caretaking organisms. Among the foragers Boehm discusses, and egalitarian swiddeners like the Sengoi Semai, this tendency manifests itself as a stress on individual autonomy (e.g., Gardner, 1991). The presumption in evolutionary biology would be that, for most organisms, following the Premack principle enhances comprehensive fitness; that is, over the long term, autonomous organisms leave more fertile offspring than dependent ones. But outside the laboratories in which Premack did most of his work, 'other things' are rarely 'equal'. Primates tend to follow a 'K reproductive strategy' adapted to an environment nearing its carrying capacity (K). In contrast with 'r reproductive strategy,' which entails maximizing the number of offspring, a K reproductive strategy produces a limited number of offspring but maximizes their chances of survival. (Humans are a little 'less K' than the other anthropoids with which Boehm compares them). Group life lets adults in general protect and care for children. Among common baboons, for example, which as terrestrial band-living primates are in some social ways more akin to humans than the genetically closer chimpanzees are, the spatial distribution of a troop, with infants and youngsters in the protected centre, is a vivid visual reflection of this function of band organization. Moreover, cooperation enhances subsistence activities: 'many hands make light work'. Lone baboons have a hard time surviving, let alone reproducing. So group life, as Boehm argues, has significant survival value. Morality, he suggests, emerges from people's realization of the long-term benefits of group membership.

> A new commandment gave I unto you, that ye love one another. Yes, this it was that saved me. Aside from higher considerations, charity often operates as a vastly wise and prudent principle — a great safeguard to its possessor. Men have committed murder for jealousy's sake, and anger's sake, and spiritual pride's sake; but no man, that ever I heard of, ever committed a diabolical murder for sweet charity's sake. Mere self-interest, then, if no better motive can be enlisted, should, especially with high-tempered men, prompt all beings to charity and philanthropy (Melville, 1974 [1853], p. 924).

Semai, the usually non-violent egalitarian swiddeners with whom I have worked, talk about their affairs as Boehm's reconstruction suggests they should. I had a conversation with a Semai shaman, Nudy's-Father, and an elder, Puk's-Grandfather in 1991:

> *Nudy's-Father:* Let me give one answer to your question [about why Semai traditionally commit so little violence]. When someone does something wrong, like stealing, we don't beat them up badly or kill them. We bring them to judgement under our laws. We are one family, one people. Maybe we fine them, but only a little. And we bawl them out, urge them to change their ways, not to set a bad example for the kids. We don't want to kill/beat people. We would be ashamed. And, number two, we would be like the beasts that kill/harm people.
> *Puk's-Grandfather:* Right. What we think is, if we beat/kill them, we lose out, we lose a friend. So, we withdraw and suffer in private [kra'di'] . We feel bad. But we need help in clearing swiddens, in feeding ourselves. We realize, if we kill/harm our friends, we lose out.

This sort of quasi-capitalist cost/benefit analysis plays an important part in Darwinian evolutionary theory. Under the influence of social scientists at the University of Chicago, it has spread to studies of the intra-group egoistic self-seeking and violence against which, Boehm argues, morality is a partial protection (e.g., Gelles, 1973; Gelles and Straus, 1988, pp. 17–36). Thus sociological, evolutionary and capitalist theory converge in Boehm's analysis with the theories voiced ironically by Melville and, as partial explanation of intragroup non-violence, by Semai intellectuals. But the benefits of group life are not randomly distributed. Age and sex segment all human societies, and different segments receive different benefits. Again, a look at the spatial distribution of a baboon troop exemplifies one way this unevenness occurs. When the troop is in motion, the young males lead the way. As the vanguard, they are most exposed to predation, the most expendable members of the troop, from the point of view of the troop's survival; but from the point of view of the individual young male, maximizing his own comprehensive fitness, his individual survival is of primary importance. There are a number of evolutionary reasons for and consequences of the expendability of young males among terrestrial primates, but the only point here is that a reflective and self-interested young man might feel less bound to the group and its values than another member would. Perhaps as a result, in most human societies, young men are the most violent cohort, especially when questions of sex are involved. That is, the evolutionary argument that, in the long run, all group members benefit by subordinating their individual interests to those of the group, is not in the short run always so obvious. In such cases, individuals called upon to sacrifice for the greater good may feel anger. 'Anger', the emotion or tension that results from a challenge over some resource to which an interested individual feels a claim (Blanchard and Blanchard, 1984), threatens the social cohesion of the group. Thus conflict necessarily attends group life. The simplest solution to conflict, if space and subsistence resources are available and abundant, is for dissatisfied individuals and groups to fission off, sometimes to fuse with another group. This fission–fusion pattern seems associated with low rates of intragroup violence (Dentan, 1992). Patterns of fission vary according to social segmentation by age and sex (e.g., Cords and Rowell, 1986), reflecting the differential distribution of benefits and power in the community, as discussed below. There are many other ways to reduce conflict. Critics used to mock the British social anthropologists of the 1950s for seemingly asserting that any and all social institutions functioned to 'promote social cohesion'; but doubtless many institutions do that. Intervention by parties not directly involved is a common primate pattern, not necessarily to resolve the dispute but to reduce attendant tensions. Boehm concentrates on the sense that group survival is more important than individual fitness and authoritative intervention by dominant individuals. Since submission to dominance violates the Premack principle, Boehm argues that submission to group authority '[resul]ts in part from the conscious and rational appreciation of the benefits of group living, the whole praxis constituting "morality" '.

Advantages of the Restatement

1. Simplicity

Other things being equal, the theory which involves the fewest assumptions is best, says Occam's Razor. Restating Boehm's theory in sociocentric terms allows theorists to ignore intrinsically suspect observations like whether violence is a human 'universal' and to avoid drawing intrinsically undemonstrable conclusions about whether violence 'inheres' in whatever 'human nature' may be. The restated theory argues that most, perhaps but undemonstrably all, human societies at some times experience intragroup violence; most, perhaps but undemonstrably all, most of the time are free of such violence. Since both non-violence and violence are 'universals' in this paradoxical usage, variation in violence is the proper focus of investigation, not its presumptive 'universality'. The focus on universality leads to postulating entities whose existence is not currently demonstrable: 'human nature' and so on. Any review of debates about 'human nature' in this context reveals their remarkable sterility and contamination by politico-religious bias (Blanchard *et al.*, 1999; Dentan and Otterbein, 1996; Robarchek and Dentan, 1987; cf. Horton, 1970). Biologists and anthropologists, for evolutionary reasons, study diversity; physicists and chemists study homogeneity.

2. Empirical falsifiability

Restating Boehm's theory in terms of variables rather than innate tendencies facilitates empirical research and falsifiability, the basis of scientific 'truth claims'. Even true 'universals' do not require postulating 'inherent tendencies'. Otterbein's classic study of the 'universality' of capital punishment (1986) has not led anyone to postulate an inherent tendency toward capital punishment in the human genome. It is perhaps the vagueness of general terms like 'capital punishment' or 'fission' (see above), let alone 'inherent tendency', 'dominance', and 'violence' or 'aggression' (see, e.g., Blanchard *et al.*, 1999) and so on that conveys the impression that the phenomena to which the terms refer are homogeneous and unvarying.

3. Precision

The question of why humans submit to social control is complex and has generated a wide range of theories. Boehm suggests, drawing on Otterbein (1986), that people abandon deviance not only out of recognition of a common good but also out of fear of punishment even unto death. But Otterbein himself resists such explanations, on the grounds suggested in part two of this critique (Dentan and Otterbein, 1996). In fact the social bases of obedience and deviance are more polymorphous, and conformity to the 'common good' more ambivalent and ambiguous than Boehm could possibly deal with in so short an essay. The 'reason' which leads people to 'recognize' the benefits of group life is also a biological product, motivated by parochial and transient cultural tendencies and current individual impulses. Moore (1978) and Gramsci (1971) suggest that 'reasonable' ideas about overall group benefits work to preserve not only social cohesion but also social privilege. Calne (1999), Lakoff and Johnson (1998), Freud (1948) and Dentan (1994; 1997) argue that 'reason' serves more often to rationalize, justify and obfuscate pre-existing individual or social tendencies than to give rise to them. Scott (1985) suggests that most people feign adherence to such 'reasonability' while actively seeking to subvert the social order. Boehm's study is as much about hypocrisy as about morality, as he might agree. This observation gives rise to a final one. If, as Boehm and I agree, social segmentation occurs in even the most homogeneous societies, then it is unlikely that the arbiters of morality or definers of the social good are in any particular society completely representative of that society. The vague idea that group cohesion enhances collective fitness can serve as a rationalization for enhancing the benefits of one segment of society at an exorbitant cost to the fitness of others. The most disturbing part of Boehm's reconstruction is his dismissal of 'family affairs' and thus of children (and to some extent women) from the data he analyzes. In band level societies childcare is rarely a 'family affair' (e.g., Dentan, 1978; 1998a; 1999). If it were, the benefits of group living for a K reproductive strategy would be drastically reduced. Moreover, any analysis which excludes children from the beneficiaries whose individual welfare needs to be taken into account is distorted. Infanticide is often demonstrably good for the fitness of the non-infantile members of the group, but never for the infant. Similarly, although in a few societies, mostly rainforest foragers, gender equality seems predominant (e.g., Endicott and Endicott, MS), usually men run things, with the partial exclusion of 'family affairs'. The Semai elders quoted above describe a system in which they deserve respect; but at that moment a youngish woman was treating it with cheerful contempt: their common good was not hers (Dentan, 1998b). In short, I think that the commonality of the 'common good' needs more demonstration than Boehm could give it in this restricted space. In conclusion, Christopher Boehm always makes a reader think. I hope that he can develop his ideas at greater length, so that he can deal more with human variability (and less with 'human nature') than in this brief essay.

References

Blanchard, D. Caroline, and Blanchard, Robert J. (1984), 'Affect and aggression: An animal model applied to human behaviour', in *Advances in the Study of Aggression Vol. 1*, ed. R.J. Blanchard and D.C. Blanchard (London and New York: Academic).

Blanchard, D. Caroline, Hebert, Mark and Blanchard, Robert J. (1999), 'Continuity vs. political correctness: Animal models and human aggression', *The HFG Review* [special issue on the Biology of Aggression] 3 (1), pp. 3–12.

Calne, Donald B. (1999), *Within Reason: Rationality and Human Behaviour* (New York: Pantheon).

Cords, Marina, and Rowell, T.E. (1986), 'Group fission in blue monkeys of the Kakemega Forest, Kenya', *Folia Primatologica*, **46**, pp. 70–82.

Dentan, Robert Knox (1978), 'Notes on childhood in a non-violent context: the Semai case', in *Learning Nonaggression*, ed. Ashley Montagu (London: Oxford).

Dentan, Robert Knox (1992), 'The rise, maintenance and destruction of peaceable polity', in *Aggression and Peacefulness in Humans and Other Primates*, ed. J. Silverberg and J.P. Gray (New York: Oxford).

Dentan, Robert Knox (1997), 'The persistence of received truth: How the Malaysian ruling class constructs Orang Asli', in *Indigenous Peoples and the State: Politics, Land, and Ethnicity in the Malaysian Peninsula and Borneo*, ed. Robert Winzeler. Monograph 46/Yale University Southeast Asia Studies. (New Haven: Yale University Southeast Asia Studies).

Dentan, Robert Knox (1998a), 'Update on Semai kids,' http://www.noogenesis.com/malama/bood.html.

Dentan, Robert Knox (1998b), 'Semai Freedom' http://www.noogenesis.com/malama/bood.html.

Dentan, Robert Knox (1999), 'Enduring scars: Cautionary tales among the Semai', in *Traditional Storytelling Today: An International Sourcebook*, ed. Margaret Read MacDonald (London and Chicago: Fitzroy–Dearborn (Garland)).

Dentan, Robert Knox, and Otterbein, Keith (1996), 'Sterile quarrels', *In These Times* (11 November).

Dentan, Robert Knox (1994), 'Surrendered men: Peaceable enclaves in the postEnlightenment west', in *The Anthropology of Peace and Nonviolence,* ed. L.E. Sponsel and T. Gregor (Boulder, CO: Lynne Rienner).

Endicott, Karen L. and Endicott, Kirk M. (M.S.), *The Batek: Sexually Egalitarian Foragers of Peninsular Malaysia.*

Freud, Anna (1948), *The Ego and the Mechanisms of Defence* (London: Hogarth).

Gardner, Peter M. (1991), 'Foragers' pursuit of individual autonomy', *Current Anthropology,* **32**, pp. 543–58.

Gelles, Richard J. (1973), 'Child abuse as psychopathology: A sociological critique and reformulation', *American Journal of Orthopsychiatry*, **43**, pp. 611–21.

Gelles, Richard J. and Straus, Murray A. (1988), *Intimate Violence* (New York: Simon and Schuster).

Gramsci, Antonio (1971), *Selections from the Prison Notebooks*, ed. and tr. Q. Hoare and G.N. Smith (London: Lawrence and Wishart).

Horton, John (1970), 'Order and conflict theories of social problems as competing ideologies', in *The Sociology of Sociology: Analysis and Criticism of the Thought, Research and Ethical Folkways of Sociology and Its Practitioners*, ed. L.T. Reynolds and J.M. Reynolds (New York: David McKay Co.).

Lakoff, George, and Johnson, Mark (1998), *Philosophy in the Flesh: The Embodied Mind and Its Challenge to Western Thought* (New York: Basic Books).

Melville, Herman (1974 [1853]), 'Bartleby the Scrivener', in *The American Tradition in Literature*, ed. S. Bradley, R.C. Beatty, G. Hudson Long and G. Perkins, vol. I. (New York: Grosset and Dunlap).

Moore, Barrington, Jr. (1978), *Injustice: The Social Bases of Obedience and Revolt* (New York: Prentice-Hall).

Otterbein, Keith (1986), *The Ultimate Coercive Sanction* (New Haven: Human Relations Area Files).

Robarchek, Clayton A. and Dentan, Robert Knox (1987), '"Blood drunkenness" and the bloodthirsty Semai: Unmaking another anthropological myth', *American Anthropologist, 89*, pp. 356–65.

Scott, James C. (1985), *Weapons of the Weak: Everyday Forms of Peasant Resistance* (New Haven, CT: Yale University Press).

WHICH CULTURE TRAITS ARE PRIMITIVE?

Peter M. Gardner

Since early in this century, a number of cultural anthropologists and archaeologists have been theorizing that some of the very culture traits Boehm regards as 'primitive' are, in fact, partial products of the difficult circumstances of the last few thousand years. For instance, the mobility and egalitarianism of some foragers may have been amplified by their culture contact experiences. Boehm must consider these theories if he hopes to identify foragers whose cultures may be representative of the past.

Boehm's attempt to delineate the evolution of social control should be applauded. As a cultural anthropologist, however, I suggest that we examine his paper in relation to, not just ethnographic, but also comparative literature. Although Boehm sounds as if he is on safe ground when he claims that mobile, egalitarian foragers are representative of the past, some of his colleagues have argued that this is not necessarily the case. Their stance bears careful scrutiny.

Let me begin by revisiting history. Forty years ago, with 'The social life of monkeys, apes, and primitive man', M.D. Sahlins drew plaudits for his attempt to make inferences about 'general trends in primate social organization' from review of field data on infrahuman primates and 'ethnographic accounts of simple hunters and gatherers' (Sahlins, 1959a; 1959b, p. 187). It was a fitting paper for the Darwin Centennial year. I mention it for two reasons: (1) the method and logic of Boehm's piece are broadly similar to Sahlins' triangulation exercise, and (2) Boehm, like Sahlins, gives little attention to selecting a sample of recent foragers which best reflects the cultural patterns of the past. Surely there should be acknowledgement that the latter subject has been a perennial concern of archaeologists as well as cultural anthropologists. Witness, for instance, the debate between H. Parker and the Seligmanns about the culture contact of the Veddas and about the extent to which their way of life is aboriginally primitive (Parker, 1909; Seligmann and Seligmann, 1911).

How problematic is this? Sahlins included in his sample some of the very enclaved foragers whose displacement and disruption, harassment, depleted resources, and marketing arrangements have long been theorized to contribute to fluid or flexible social groups, mobility and aloofness, egalitarianism, and emphasis on the individual or the nuclear family. The theoretical literature on this is a continuing one (Seligmann and Seligmann, 1911; Kroeber, 1928; 1945; Jenness, 1932; Steward, 1936; Miller and Dollard, 1941; Gillin, 1942; Leacock, 1954; Bose, 1956; Hickerson, 1960; James, 1961; Service, 1962; Gardner, 1966; 1985; 1991; Deetz, 1968; Fox, 1969; Bender, 1978; Testart, 1988; Foley, 1988; Sandbukt, 1988; Dentan, 1988; and so on). What is worse, it should already be apparent that precisely the same traits were regarded by Sahlins as primitive and by the dissenting theorists as products of culture contact. By my count, three well-formulated theories offer recent and situational explanations for the extreme egalitarianism of many foragers; five theories do this for their flexibility; and three do it for their individualism (Gardner, 1991).

To his credit, Sahlins did note the economic symbiosis of Philippine pygmies, Congo pygmies, and Bushmen with their respective neighbours and he remarked on its social impact; he also mentioned Leacock's work on outside influences on the social structure of the Naskapi (Sahlins, 1959b, pp. 190–1). Yet these four cultures, plus the Semang, constituted some forty-two per cent of his twelve-culture sample as he went on to speak of the mobility, family-level organization, flexibility, cooperative food sharing, and lack of ranking hierarchies which characterize foragers in general (1959b, pp. 191, 195–6, 197, 199).

Boehm needs to walk with extreme care if he wishes to retread this ground. His precise argument is fun and it is not actually the same as Sahlins', yet can Boehm really afford to include in his set of cultures the same enclaved foragers as his predecessor when triangulating on the past? If some of the foragers which Boehm thinks exemplify the traits of the Palaeolithic are even partially shaped by Holocene circumstances, his main argument loses considerable strength. This is a fascinating and important problem, and one which I think Boehm will be able to deal with in the long run. For now, I hold that the sampling problem still stands in his way.

References

Bender, Barbara (1978), 'Gatherer-hunter to farmer; a social perspective', *World Archaeology*, **10**, pp. 204–22.

Bose, Nirmal Kumar (1956), 'Some observations on nomadic castes of India', *Man in India*, **36**, pp. 1–6.

Deetz, James (1968), 'Hunters in archaeological perspective', in *Man the Hunter*, ed. R.B. Lee and I. DeVore (Chicago: Aldine).

Dentan, Robert K. (1988), 'Band-level Eden: A mystifying chimera', *Cultural Anthropology*, **3**, pp. 276–84.

Foley, Robert (1988), 'Hominids, humans, and hunter-gatherers: An evolutionary perspective', in *Hunters and Gatherers Vol. I, History, Evolution and Social Change*, ed. T. Ingold, D. Riches, and J. Woodburn (Oxford: Berg).

Fox, Richard (1969), '"Professional primitives": Hunters and gatherers of nuclear South Asia', *Man in India*, **49**, pp. 139–60.

Gardner, Peter M. (1966), 'Symmetric respect and memorate knowledge: The structure and ecology of individualistic culture', *Southwestern Journal of Anthropology*, **20**, pp. 389–415.

Gardner, Peter M. (1985), 'Bicultural oscillation as a long-term adaptation to cultural frontiers', *Human Ecology*, **13**, pp. 411–32.

Gardner, Peter M. (1991), 'Foragers' pursuit of individual autonomy', *Current Anthropology* **32**, pp. 543–72.

Gillin, John (1942), 'Acquired drives in culture contact', *American Anthropologist*, **44**, pp. 545–54.

Hickerson, Harold (1960), 'The Feast of the Dead among the seventeenth-century Algonkians of the upper Great Lakes', *American Anthropologist*, **62**, pp. 81–107.

James, B. J. (1961), 'Social-psychological dimensions of Ojibwa acculturation', *American Anthropologist*, **63**, pp. 721–46.

Jenness, Diamond (1932), *The Indians of Canada* 2 ed. (Ottawa: National Museums of Canada, Bulletin 65).

Kroeber, Alfred L.(1928), *Peoples of the Philippines* rev. ed. (NY: American Museum of Natural History).

Kroeber, Alfred L. (1945), 'The ancient *oikoumene* as a historic culture aggregate: The Huxley Memorial Lecture for 1945', *Journal of the Royal Anthropological Institute*, **75**, pp. 9–20.

Leacock, Eleanor (1954), *The Montagnais 'Hunting Territory' and the Fur Trade* (Washington: American Anthropological Association, Memoir 78).

Miller, Neal E. and Dollard, John (1941), *Social Learning and Imitation* (New Haven: Yale University Press).

Parker, H. (1909), *Ancient Ceylon: An account of the aborigines and a part of the early civilisation* (London: Luzac).

Sahlins, M.D. (1959a), 'The social life of monkeys, apes and primitive men', *Human Biology*, **31**, pp. 54–73.

Sahlins, M.D. (1959b), 'The social life of monkeys, apes and primitive men', in *Readings in Anthropology, Volume II, Readings in Cultural Anthropology*, ed. M.H. Fried (New York: Thomas Y. Crowell).

Sandbukt, Øyvind (1988), 'Tributary tradition and relations of affinity and gender among the Sumatran Kubu', in *Hunters and Gatherers, Vol. I, History, Evolution and Social Change*, ed. T. Ingold, D. Riches, and J. Woodburn (Oxford: Berg).

Seligmann, Carl G. and Seligmann, Brenda Z. (1911), *The Veddas* (Cambridge: Cambridge Univ. Press).

Service, Elman R. (1962), *Primitive Social Organization: An Evolutionary Perspective* (New York: Random House).

Steward, Julian H. (1936), 'The economic and social basis of primitive bands' in *Essays in Anthropology presented to A. L. Kroeber*, ed. R. H. Lowie (Berkeley: University of California Press), pp. 331–50.

Testart, Alain (1988), 'Some major problems in the social anthropology of hunter- gatherers', *Current Anthropology*, **29**, pp. 1–31.

SYMBOLS, SEX, AND SOCIALITY
IN THE EVOLUTION OF HUMAN MORALITY

Bruce M. Knauft

Boehm's model conceptualizes a common ancestor to humans, chimpanzees, and bonobos at several million years B.P., followed by a model of prehistoric foragers at 25,000-50,000 B.P. based on ethnographic data from twentieth-century hunters and gatherers. By putting processes of complex communication into the picture, we can refine Boehm's model considerably by filling in significant scenarios for humans beginning at perhaps 2 million years ago. These include a suite of features that include constraints on sexual behaviour, a rudimentary division of labour, the gendering of morality, socialized control over junior males, increased group size, increased home range size, the reduction of bullying behaviour, and a reverse dominance hierarchy that promotes egalitarianism among fully adult males. Boehm's model emphasizes the last two of these, but it is consistent with the others as well. Cultural or proto-cultural elaboration of beliefs and associated practices is the symbolic dimension of morality and is an important component of human evolution. Boehm's model is extremely important for outlining socio-political mechanisms and concomitants in the formation of adult male egalitarian groups, and, in the process, identifying a key element in the evolution of human morality.

Christopher Boehm's recent work, refracted in the present article, marks a major development in our understanding of the origins of human morality. Though his specifics sometimes bear refinement or larger context, as will be discussed, his argument gains in directness and power what it lacks in larger connection — while still being largely consistent with existing evidence. This is a signal contribution. Of particular significance here are the social mechanisms Boehm adduces — such as coalitions of increasing size — that make the enforcement of social control a gradual and yet tidal process that grows incrementally from the so-called proto-morality of great apes (and our own common ancestor) to the development of morality among anatomically modern humans. A further contribution is Boehm's articulation of social control issues and the evolution of morality to the distinctive features of competitive egalitarianism that characterize simple human foraging societies. Finally, the political and moral overthrow of would-be despots in his analysis links rather than divorces the study of egalitarianism in our species history to more contemporary political developments and processes.[39]

My present comments complement and probe an overall argument by Boehm that is in many ways quite masterful. My remarks come under the headings of morality versus politics, human diversity, great ape diversity, the role of language, the role of women, and the role of sex.

---

[39] This said, there is also a danger of implicitly retro-jecting modern state–society notions of democratic social contract onto pre-state societies where this dynamic was much less formally or institutionally conceptualized.

Morality *versus* Politics

Boehm's article links morality to politics but is ultimately more about the latter than the former. His argument emphasizes behavioural control and the use of socially coercive force by subordinates to dissuade would-be superiors from being too despotic. This extremely important argument, concerning what Boehm (1993) has elsewhere called a 'reverse dominance hierarchy', helps explain exactly how it is that competitive and rivalrous tendencies are negotiated and 'dampened' in the egalitarianism that is so pronounced among adult men in simple human societies. This behavioural emphasis on social action makes his argument concrete as well as allowing greater triangulation with great ape species for purposes of hypothesizing evolutionary trajectories, as he notes. However, 'morality', in a strict sense, is a symbolic or ideological construction, particularly one that is internalized. As such, it begs processes of subjective awareness and self-monitoring as reinforced by culturally derived values. These values are given explicit social and cultural force, regardless of whether or not they resonate with so-called 'innate' aversion to conflict (as Boehm calls it).

The internalization of moral rules in accordance with culturally prescribed norms is a distinctive feature of human morality largely lacking in non-human primates. Likewise, the psychic tensions and mental ambivalence that pits self-interested desires against the internalization of moral precepts is both particularly human and in recursive relationship with the kinds of social control and responsive action that Boehm calls to our attention. Morality entails the evolution of a whole set of subjective processes that provide the complement to what Boehm describes in more behavioural and political terms. This is not to argue that social rules of morality are ever totally internalized; cheating and the indulgence of counter-normative desires are common in all human societies. What remains unique and distinctive in humans, however, is that self-interested impulses are dampened by internalized symbolic processes and reinforced through public assertions of moral rules — as well as by behavioural constraints and counteractions taken by coalitions or groups against individuals. This is important to the more behavioural argument that Boehm develops because internalization lessens, over time, the need for direct constraint by group force against individuals. More importantly, it makes efficacious the iconic or symbolic show of force as well as myriad ways through which social groups call attention to rules and morality and enforce a sense of individual guilt or self-monitoring. Without symbolic internalization as a complement to external behavioural constraint, the maintenance of moral egalitarianism as a political system would be difficult to maintain in evolutionary terms.

Human Diversity

In recent decades, the study of human evolution has been increasingly relinquished by cultural anthropologists and left to the province of primatologists and bio-behavioural evolutionists. One of the resulting difficulties, ironically, is that recent models that triangulate human social evolution are often more attuned to the adaptations of non-human primates to relatively narrow ecological niches than to the great diversity of human social adaptations to different conditions. To some extent, Boehm supplies an important corrective. By emphasizing that humans retain a propensity for conflict while also intensifying a socially encoded need to avoid conflict, Boehm's argument affords human evolution dynamism in both the expression of self-interested dominance and its control through collective constraint. The latter was more pronounced in simple human societies, while despotism has been more pervasive in rank and archaic state societies (chiefdomships and pre-industrial states) in which status competition has led to formal stratification in the context of food production, sedentism, and unequal access to wealth and property.

This said, Boehm still tends to collapse the range of variation *within* simple hunter-gatherer or foraging societies. While it is useful for heuristic purposes and for simplicity to consider simple humans as a single type, this ultimately leads to a kind of 'ideal-type' analysis that risks logical integration at the expense of empirical responsiveness — full openness of the model to empirical testing and alteration on the basis of new results. Because I believe that Boehm's theory (and my own, which it in some ways parallels [Knauft, 1987; 1989; 1991; 1994a–c; 1996]) merits empirical testing and refinement, it is important to stress the most important ranges of empirical variation for his argument.

First, many if not most foraging societies are highly seasonal or have significant periods of both social aggregation and social dispersion. Depending on the concentration of resources in the ecozone as a whole, foraging societies also exhibit great diversity in their overall level of social aggregation versus atomization. Particularly distinctive features of human foraging groups relative to non-human species are, first, that they tend to have quite large home ranges and, second, that they tend to have a sexual division of labour. These two features are enormously adaptive and prime reasons in an eco-demographic sense that *Homo* was able to migrate so successfully over so much of the globe between two million and 50,000 years ago.

As Rodseth *et al.* (1991) have noted, complex symbolic communication is particularly important here: language allows a sense of social collectivity and the reinforcing of social ties in the absence of continuous spatial proximity (see also Dunbar, 1993; Aiello and Dunbar, 1993). Referential communication and the ability to quickly restore social ties through verbal reinforcement allows human groups to maintain themselves as 'groups' despite the fact that they are separated for significant time and cover great distances. Not only does language (or proto-language, in *Homo erectus*) allow the sharing of key information about the changing availability of dispersed and patchy food resources, it also serves as a social glue or 'verbal grooming', as Ian Dunbar (1996) might call it, that keeps the social relationships of a large group intact.

Of course, language or its symbolic equivalent is also easily used to enforce a sense of internalized morality despite the splitting up or individuation of the group to maximally exploit dispersed local resources. These same forces operate on longer time scale, seasonally, so that group members maintain prosocial disposition to each other upon reunification despite significant periods of internal separation.

The range of variation in forager dispersion should relate to variations in morality as discussed by Boehm and can provide a window on potentially testable hypotheses. In particular, there should be a significant range of variation between more dispersed and less dispersed foragers in their need for ideological and behavioural enforcement of collective morality. That is, all foragers are not created equal, even when it comes to the need for egalitarianism and morality. One would expect much less need to reinforce collective morality among isolated groups of semi-desert Shoshone Indians in small groups, or dispersed Eskimo families engaged in summer caribou hunting, than in the large-scale collective hunting of big game that was characteristic of many late Pleistocene populations in peri-arctic Eurasia. In short, it is not simple societies *per se* that place a premium on morality, but rather the ecological and socio-demographic conditions that make it maximally advantageous to maintain large groups and their cooperation and division of labour despite diurnal and/or weekly or monthly dispersion.

Awareness of these patterns helps attune Boehm's hypothesis to the kinds of variation that archeologists are most adept in plumbing in the study of prehistoric foragers, including seasonal and yearly resource exploitation and habitation patterns. As such, the selective pressures for maintaining large home ranges and increasing group size could potentially be tied in more empirically refined ways to Boehm's argument and, in the process, to a more nuanced model of moral evolution over time and space.

Primate Diversity

Boehm is almost unique among anthropologists in having done significant field research among both human and primate populations on issues of conflict and aggression (e.g., Boehm, 1981; 1984; 1994). This said, his primary work among apes has been with *Pan troglodytes* (common chimpanzees) and this emphasis informs his argument. In particular, the complementary species of chimpanzees — *Pan paniscus* (pygmy chimpanzees, or bonobos) — is somewhat short-changed in his account. In some ways, Boehm's model risks the same shortcomings as that of Wrangham (1987, Manson and Wrangham, 1991) who also studied common chimpanzees in the wild. In both cases, there is a tendency in the final analysis to assume that patterns prominent among common chimpanzees can be taken as largely synonymous with that of a common ancestor between apes and humans — so long as the model is consistent with at least part of the range of variation found among humans (and remember that humans are and have been diverse!).

The model weakens when chimpanzee patterns are counter-indicated by findings from bonobos, and it is here that Boehm's primatological argument must be considered more cautiously. As shown by de Waal (1997), bonobos are at least as much of a female-dominant as a male-dominant species. The characteristics of territoriality and stalk-and-attack interactions that characterize common chimpanzees are highly muted if not absent among bonobos. Moreover, dispersed human foragers also exhibit a striking *lack* of territoriality, in contrast to what Boehm seems to suggest. This is consistent with ecological conditions in which resources are dispersed and patchy: it is expensive in time and energy to defend such resources and more advantageous for groups to disperse and shift flexibly over the landscape.

Human foragers are overwhelmingly permissive in allowing neighbouring groups to forage on their land. (Indeed, the notion of land 'ownership' is itself typically foreign.) Over time, members shift easily between bands. Among contemporary foragers, this process is intensified by relations of formalized friendship, trading partnerships, namesake relations, and kinship between adjacent groups. In prehistoric terms, the ability of members from different bands to share information and strategies with respect to shifting resources — that is, through language or proto-language — is, as emphasized by Kurland and Beckerman (1985), a crucial adaptive advantage. This is the inter-group corollary of the human ability to mediate social relations and maintain relatively peaceful coexistence *within* groups that commonly range between twenty-five and fifty individuals. Revealingly, warfare between bands of simple human foragers is rare to nonexistent — a point which is corroborated in an intriguing sequence of time-stratified rock paintings of prehistoric human conflict in northern Australia (Knauft, 1994c; Tacon and Chippendale, 1994).[40]

The range of variation shown by bonobos and simple human foragers with respect to both domination and territoriality calls into question Boehm's assertion that they as well as common chimpanzees are territorial and, as stated most starkly in his article's abstract, that they share 'pronounced social dominance hierarchies'. This is not to argue against Boehm's larger notion that combatting rivalry and undercutting dominance have been key in human social and moral evolution. But it does caution us that the range of variation on this score could have already been great at two or four or six million years ago; it does not mark an implicitly unilineal transition from chimpanzee-style dominance and territoriality in a common ancestor of apes and humans to a modern form of morality and egalitarianism among ostensibly homogeneous human foragers by 25,000 BP.

The Role of Language

Linguistic evolution arises as a key issue at this juncture. Boehm appears to be 'conservative' in applying his scenario of developed human morality principally to the last 25,000 to 50,000 years. In so doing, he attempts to skirt the issue of whether language was a relatively early or a relatively late development in human evolution. However, I think this narrower view short-circuits the longer term implications of moral evolution. Other aspects of human social evolution emerge that are consistent with the early rise of social coalitions for the purpose of counter-dominance and the inculcation of collective morality.

Whether language that was fully grammatical and morphemic arose early or late in human evolution should not distract us from general agreement on a broader issue, namely, that extremely complex proto-language (if not full language) was a major feature of our genus' evolution prior to the relatively late emergence of anatomically modern humans (see Deacon, 1997; Bickerton, 1990; 1995; Pinker, 1994; cf. Lieberman, 1984; 1998). Linguistic communication and symbolism were in all likelihood quite important in human evolution since the emergence of *Homo erectus* close to two million years ago. This fact throws into a much richer context the complex co-evolution between neural and symbolic-cum-moral development, which on Boehm's analysis might emerge in fully developed form only for the final one or two per cent of the evolution of *Homo* (contrast Deacon, 1997).

Features of symbolic internalization raised earlier in my comments become particularly relevant here. The co-evolution of brain enlargement and symbolization introduces the significance of morality as a long-standing dimension of human evolution and perhaps itself a contributing factor to the emergence of anatomically modern *Homo sapiens*. Though Boehm skirts this implication, I think it is important to raise it.

---

[40] Raymond C. Kelly (forthcoming) is on the cusp of publishing a powerful cross-cultural argument concerning the absence of war in what he calls 'unsegmented' human societies.

Correspondingly in ecological terms, the ability of linguistic communication to mediate social relations, internalize rules, and dampen social conflict and reduce despotism is crucial not just to morality but to the socio-demographic expansion of home ranges and that cooperative exploitation of dispersed and patchy resources that allowed *Homo* to be so spectacularly adaptive as a single radiating species. In this respect, I think Boehm's model is consistent with a bolder and more revolutionary argument that considers the suite of human cultural socialization, complex symbolic communication, and morality as key features of human evolution since the emergence of *Homo erectus* perhaps two million years ago.

The Role of Women

When it comes to gender, Boehm's argument stays implicitly patriarchal. This is because a politically-inclined definition of morality emphasizes the force of physical constraint, which is usually more pronounced among males in mammalian species with even a slight degree of sexual dimorphism. This emphasis is also reinforced by Boehm's ultimate tendency to favour chimpanzee models in assessing the features of a common ancestor between humans and great apes, since, as we have noted, bonobos do not have pronounced male dominance hierarchies and might even be considered matri-centric. These biases notwithstanding, Boehm is highly insightful in noting the significance of female coalitions in captive great ape species, and he uses this information as an implicit 'bridge condition' between the propensities of a presumed common ancestor and palaeolithic human foragers.

To expand on this insight, it bears emphasis that models of human social and political and symbolic evolution need to take the role of females and their relation to both males and other females much more seriously than has usually been the case. This enlarged perspective goes hand-in-hand with exploring the early significance of symbolic communication in the spread and development of *Homo erectus* and the evolution of *Homo sapiens*. If some have argued that men are stronger or more dominant in physical force, few could think of making the same gendered argument with respect to the development or evolution of language. Primary in many senses of the word is child socialization, whereby language and the social rules it enforces are transmitted by males but more often by mothers and other women to children of both sexes in their earliest years. This use of language obviously inculcates the symbolization of norms and the internalization of social rules at a young age, so they become part of ontogenic as well as phylogenetic evolution. As such, the development of cognitive maturation goes hand-in-hand with rule-internalization in humans — and at the same time that self-interested desires also acquire words and meanings for the developing child. Given that the socio-moral context of infant and early childhood socializing is often matri-centric and not uncommonly isolated from male social interaction, especially in larger groups, gendered inflections of linguistic and moral socialization could be significant even if one declines the possibility that women are as much the verbal moralizers for children as men implicitly are for the physical constraint of bullying behaviour and despotism.

Adult women's relations with both men and other women are also crucial in moral evolution. If extant ethnographic knowledge about the gendering of sexual morality is any guide, there is likely to have been at least as much if not more emphasis on female than male sexual propriety in human evolution. This can be read as consistent not just with the threat caused by uncertain paternity (the mother knows it is her child, but the husband may not be sure it is his), but the fact that males have higher overall reproductive variance and a higher risk of biogenetic non-propagation — a trait humans share with other mammals. That control of female sexual morality is often important — and that it is in humans so importantly enforced by other women — puts the evolution of morality as a whole in a somewhat different context. Especially when, from a neo-Darwinian perspective, biogenetic success is granted to be an important evolutionary force, even if it must compete with cultural imperatives for more altruistic behaviour. The ways that females may circumvent moral rules, and the ways they can exert major influence in mate choice, are also important to the evolution of morality. The dampening of bullying and despotism, often associated with men, finds an important complement in the ways morality is used by and for women with respect to sexual propriety and other forms of morality, including through the verbal force of shaming, ridicule, and gossip.

The Role of Sex

The role of sexuality in human evolution is considered by Boehm, but he tends to consider the moral control of sexual behaviour more of a qualified evolutionary failure than as a success — especially when contrasted to the moral ability to control bullying and despotic behaviour. Though this can easily be a question of viewing the glass as 'half empty' rather than 'half full', large implications arise when we attend more specifically to the unique change brought about by even partial control of human sexual behaviour through the inculcation of moral norms.

It can be granted, indeed emphasized, that moral constraints on sexuality have been incomplete and often contravened by sexual cheating. From a pre-human point of view, however, any constraint on sexual behaviour that derives from the imperatives of group-selective altruism is itself revolutionary. It runs against the tide of individual reproductive success — the primary tenet of Darwinian evolution — and makes cultural evolution indeed unique (contrast Foley, 1987).

The revolutionary nature of socio-sexual morality as even a partial constraint on sexual behaviour is fully consistent with distinctive features of human evolution at least since the expansion of *Homo erectus*: large social groups and yet high paternal investment in the provisioning of offspring, increasingly complex social relations, increased symbolic communication, and a sexual division of labour that maximizes adaptive exploitation of dispersed and patchy food resources across large and environmentally diverse home ranges. From a pre-human point of view, the biggest problem with this distinctive socio-ecological adaptation is that males are provisioning children of females who may be off with other members of the group for significant periods of time. As the work of Rodseth *et al.* (1991) highlight, the question of how social bonds and mating commitments can be maintained despite breaks in social proximity is key to explaining the distinctive social characteristics of human evolution. One of the answers, of course, is language. Robin Dunbar (1996) has explored this hypothesis, though more in terms of courtship and enticement-to-mating than in terms of morality and the maintenance of socio-sexual bonds over time.

What is really revolutionary from the point of view of morality and social rules is the enforcement of mating relationships through normative social rules and collective punishments. These strictures and their moral precepts have ultimately evolved into what we now call marriage. Of course, there is no reason to ascribe marital relations to *Homo erectus*. But any rule-governed or moral constraint on sexual behaviour that legitimates certain mating relations and prohibits others — that is, any form of proto-marriage — is itself revolutionary. Symbolically enforced constraint on sexual behaviour pits the interests of the cooperative group against the self-interest of each individual in maximizing his or her reproductive success. In terms of human evolution, this constraint on sexuality is crucial for survival since — as I have elsewhere noted (Knauft, 1991; 1994, pp. 48–50), and as Boehm also notes — sexual conflict is one of the most deep-seated and difficult threats to living in large, gregarious, and mixed-sex social groups. The whole adaptive regime of dispersing labour and resource exploitation across expansive or diverse ecological regimes is at stake. Against the great advantage this adaptation affords *vis-a-vis* other species is the stark fact that conflicts over sexual access can be explosive and disintegrate the social group. To say that this problem is never fully solved — which, I agree, is it not — should not prevent us from realizing that some moral and symbolically mediated constraint on sexual activity is crucial to make human group-living not just possible but maximally viable.

This sexual constraint may fall heavily on women, as noted before, but it is quite likely to fall as well on junior males. In this sense, the divide between married and unmarried men — or, more accurately, between males who have legitimate access to mates and those who do not — creates a major fault line of inequality and political asymmetry that cross-cuts what otherwise seems like egalitarianism, at least among men. In this respect, morality is not just an 'equalizer' among men, as Boehm suggests, but an equalizer among adult or senior men that also facilitates life-stage domination of their juniors — as anthropologists such have Jane Collier (Collier and Rosaldo, 1981; Collier, 1988) have convincingly shown.

In this regard, Boehm's argument about the relative unimportance of the incest taboo in human social evolution needs to be considered in larger perspective. As Lévi-Strauss (1963) so brilliantly showed, the incest taboo is merely the semiotic kernel of sexual exchange, that is, a symbol of the moral imperative to allow one's kinswomen to enter into legitimate sexual unions with others in order for the male kin of these women to themselves receive wives. We need not restrict ourselves to Lévi-Strauss' patricentric bias; men can be considered exchanged between women as well as the reverse. The larger point is that there is an ethic of equitable sharing in the realm of sexual resources that is the clear counterpart of food sharing within the group. Indeed, the two are almost intrinsically linked, since in almost all decentralized human societies, the sharing of food between in-laws is the greatest and more strongly enforced dimension of resource allocation to non-kin: food is shared with those who provided one's sexual partner.

None of this is possible without some legitimacy to sexual unions in the form of strong moral precepts that distinguish between proper and improper sexual relationships, and which promote the continuity of legitimate mating relationships over time. That these norms may be contravened, and indeed, that their contravention can result in lethal violence, serves to underscore their importance. In a cultural environment,

this also underscores what might be termed an arms race that pits the moral imperatives to control sexuality for the benefit of group interests against the self-interested
imperative to maximize one's sexual and reproductive output. It is perhaps for this
reason that humans are, at once, so sexually preoccupied as well as so morally concerned about sexuality, including in the simplest foraging societies.[41]

In short, sexual control and its relation to both the internalization of morals and
group survival are key features of human social evolution that complement but are in
no sense secondary to the social control of bullies or despots that Boehm focuses on.

Conclusions

Boehm's model conceptualizes a common ancestor to humans, chimpanzees, and
bonobos at several million years BP, followed by a model of prehistoric foragers at
25,000–50,000 BP based on ethnographic data from twentieth-century hunters and
gatherers. These ends of the human evolutionary continuum are mediated by social
processes such as egalitarian coalitions against bullies or despots that are reasoned to
have intensified over the intervening period. By putting processes of complex communication into the picture, however, we can refine Boehm's model considerably by
filling in significant scenarios for humans beginning at perhaps two million years
ago. These include a suite of features that include constraints on sexual behaviour, a
rudimentary division of labour, the gendering of morality, socialized control over
junior males, increased group size, increased home range size, the reduction of bullying behaviour, and a reverse dominance hierarchy that enforces egalitarianism among
fully adult males. Boehm's model emphasizes the last two of these, but it is consistent
with the others as well. It should be emphasized, however, that all of these features are
likely to have been highly variable depending on ecozone and socio-demographic
factors. As Potts (1998, p. 94; cf. 1996) states for hominid evolution generally, 'Early
bipedality, stone transport, diversification of artifact contexts, encephalization, and
enhanced cognitive and social functioning all may reflect adaptation to environmental novelty and highly varying selective contexts'. Chimpanzees and bonobos themselves exhibit significant variations depending on sub-species and environment. And
everything we know about humans suggests that such ranges of variation are explo-
sively increased in the evolution of *Homo*. Cultural or proto-cultural elaboration of
beliefs and associated practices is the symbolic dimension of this process and an
important component of human evolution. Boehm's model is extremely important for
outlining socio-political mechanisms and concomitants in the formation of adult
male egalitarian groups, and, in the bargain, identifying a key element in the evolution of human morality.

References

Aiello, Leslie C. and Dunbar, Robin, I. (1993), 'Neocortex size, group size, and evolution of language',
    Current Anthropology, **34**, pp. 184–93.
Bickerton, Derek (1990), *Language and Species* (Chicago: University of Chicago Press).
Bickerton, Derek (1995), *Language and Human Behavior* (Seattle: University of Washington Press).
Boehm, Christopher (1981), 'Parasitic selection and group selection: A study of conflict interference in
    rhesus and Japanese macaque monkeys', in *Primate Behavior and Sociobiology*, ed. A.B. Chiarelli and
    R.S. Corruccini (Berlin: Springer).

---

[41] One might contrast this with bonobos, who are hyper-sexual, but unselfconsciously so.

Boehm, Christopher (1984), *Blood Revenge: The Anthropology of Feuding in Montenegro and Other Nonliterate States* (Lawrence, KA: University of Kansas Press).

Boehm, Christopher (1993), 'Egalitarian behavior and reverse dominance hierarchy', *Current Anthropology*, **34**, pp. 227–54.

Boehm, Christopher (1994), 'Pacifying interventions at Arnhem Zoo and Gombe', in *Chimpanzee Cultures*, ed. R.W. Wrangham, W.C. McGrew, F.B.M. de Waal and P.G. Heltnes (Cambridge, MA: Harvard University Press).

Collier, Jane F. (1988), *Marriage and Inequality in Classless Societies* (Stanford, CA: Stanford University Press)

Collier, Jane F. and Rosaldo, Michelle Z. (1981), 'Politics and gender in simple societies', in *Sexual Meanings: The Cultural Construction of Gender and Sexuality*, ed. S.B. Ortner and H. Whitehead (New York: Cambridge University Press).

Deacon, Terrence W. (1997), *The Symbolic Species: The Co-evolution of Language and the Brain* (New York: Norton)

Dunbar, Robin I. (1993), 'Coevolution of neocortex size, group size, and language in humans', *Behavioral and Brain Sciences*, 16, pp. 681–94.

Dunbar, Robin I. (1996), *Grooming, Gossip, and the Evolution of Language* (London: Faber & Faber).

Foley, Robert (1987), *Another Unique Species: Patterns in Human Evolutionary Ecology* (New York: Longman).

Kelly, Raymond C. (forthcoming), *Warless Societies and the Evolution of War* (Ann Arbor: Unoversity of Michigan Press).

Knauft, Bruce M. (1987), 'Reconsidering violence in simple human societies: Homicide among the Gebusi of New Guinea', *Current Anthropology*, **28**, pp. 457–500.

Knauft, Bruce M. (1989), 'Sociality versus self-interest in human evolution', *Behavioral and Brain Sciences*, **12**, pp. 712–13.

Knauft, Bruce M. (1991), 'Violence and sociality in human evolution', *Current Anthropology*, **32**, pp. 391–428.

Knauft, Bruce M. (1994a), 'Culture and cooperation in human evolution', in *The Anthropology of Peace and Non-violence*, ed. L. Sponsel and T. Gregor (Boulder, CO: Lynne Rienner).

Knauft, Bruce M. (1994b), 'On human egalitarianism', *Current Anthropology*, **35**, 181–2.

Knauft, Bruce M. (1994c), 'Commentary on Taçon and Chippindale, "Australia's ancient warriors"', *Cambridge Archaeological Journal*, **4**, pp. 228–31.

Knauft, Bruce M. (1996), 'The human evolution of cooperative interest', in *A Natural History of Peace*, ed. T. Gregor (Nashville, TN: Vanderbilt University Press).

Kurland, Jefrey A. And Beckerman, Stephen J. (1985), 'Optimal foraging and hominid evolution: Labor and reciprocity', *American Anthropologist*, **87**, pp. 73–93.

Lévi-Strauss, Claude (1963), *The Elementary Structures of Kinship* (Boston, MA: Beacon).

Lieberman, Philip (1984), *The Biology and Evolution of Language* (Cambridge, MA: Harvard University Press).

Lieberman, Philip (1998), *Eve Spoke: Human Language and Human Evolution* (New York: Norton).

Manson, Joseph H. and Wrangham, Richard W. (1991), 'Intergroup aggression in chimpanzees and humans', *Current Anthropology*, **32**, pp. 188–91.

Pinker, Steven (1994), *The Language Instinct* (New York: W. Morrow).

Potts, Richard (1996), *Humanity's Descent: The Consequences of Ecological Instability* (New York: Avon).

Potts, Richard (1998), 'Environmental hypotheses of hominim evolution', *Yearbook of Physical Anthropology*, **41**, pp. 93–136.

Rodseth, Lars, Wrangham, Richard W., Harrigan, Alisa and Smuts, Barbara B. (1991), 'The human community as a primate society', *Current Anthropology*, **32**, pp. 221–55.

Taçon, Paul S. and Chippindale, Christopher (1994), 'Australia's ancient warriors: Changing depictions of fighting in the rock art of Arnhem Land, NT', *Cambridge Archaeological Journal*, **4**, pp. 211–48.

de Waal, Frans B.M. (1997), Bonobo: The Forgotten Ape (Berkeley, CA: University of California Press).

Wrangham, Richard W. (1987), 'The significance of African apes for reconstructing human social evolution', in *The Evolution of Human Behavior: Primate Models*, ed. W.G. Kinzey (Albany, NY: SUNY Press).

AS MORAL AS WE NEED TO BE

Dennis Krebs

In response to the idea that morality originated when subordinate members of groups banded together to constrain more dominant members, I argue that a more general function of morality is to uphold systems of cooperative exchange ever threatened by the temptation to contribute less than one's share and to take more than one's share. Humans inherit biologically-evolved dispositions to behave morally, that is to say to uphold systems of cooperation, and to behave immorally, that is to say to exploit the systems of cooperation from which they benefit. We are as moral as we need to be to reap the benefits of cooperation.

The anthropologist Christopher Boehm theorizes that morality originated when coalitions of subordinate primates suppressed the innate despotic behaviour of dominant members of ancestral groups, which fostered social harmony and gave rise to egalitarian moral norms. Boehm focuses on the prohibitive side of morality, particularly the suppression of bullying and excessive selfishness, and the conflicts such behaviours cause within groups. The main question I address in this commentary is, how close can we get to dispositions to uphold the egalitarian moral norms that characterize contemporary societies by way of the mechanisms of biological evolution? To answer this question, I need to say a few words about the mechanisms of biological evolution and my conception of morality.

I have been persuaded by Dawkins (1989), Trivers (1985), Williams (1966) and other evolutionary biologists that the most appropriate units of natural selection are genes, which are propagated by individuals. Although group selection is a theoretical possibility, the conditions necessary for selection at the group level to outpace selection at the individual or genetic level are rarely met. With respect to criteria for moral behaviour, I invoke prescriptiveness and universalizability. Universalizability implies behaving in ways that uphold the rights and duties of everyone involved in a moral decision in an unbiased way. In this sense, morality tends to be egalitarian with respect to opportunity.

The, or at least a, central problem of morality arises because dispositions that have evolved through natural selection are dispositions that helped our ancestors maximize their genetic gains, but, on most people's definition, behaving morally entails a willingness to foster the interests of others and to forgo opportunities to foster one's interests. Natural selection and sociality seem incompatible. How can individuals bent on maximizing their gains coexist? In Boehm's terms, shouldn't everyone be evolved to be as dominant and despotic as possible? It isn't possible for everyone to obtain more than his or her share, so isn't conflict inevitable? Faced with suppression by and exploitation from dominant members of groups, it makes evolutionary sense to form a coalition with other subordinates, which, as Boehm documents, is exactly what some primates do. But note that the upshot of such coalition formation entails, in the first instance, substituting a dominant gang for a dominant individual. Yes, the coalition curtails the selfishness of dominant individuals, and in this sense the coalition's behaviour may qualify as moral, but if the coalition then keeps the resources it obtains for itself, it undoes the moralizing effect of its behaviour. And what is to stop the more powerful individuals in the coalition from taking the lion's share of the resources?

How can we get from dominant coalitions to egalitarian groups? Boehm suggests primates may inherit an aversion to conflict and, by implication, an attraction to social harmony, and that this innate disposition may motivate them to take measures to curtail conflicts among members of their groups. This idea is helpful in the sense that it suggests a kind of payoff to those performing a policing function that does not entail, directly at least, a disproportionate share of resources. But innate dispositions evolve because they foster the inclusive fitness of the ancestors of those who inherit them. What genetic benefits might an aversion to conflict and the disposition to curtail it have reaped? Citing evidence that some conflict-reducing interventions in primates are impartial and not directly rewarded — that is to say they are directed at breaking up fights rather than helping allies or obtaining resources — Boehm suggests these interventions may stem from empathy, be motivated to reduce an 'environmental irritant', or constitute a means of 'reinforcing status' (Boehm, 2000, p. 89). To flesh out these suggestions, Boehm would have to explore the adaptive value of each of these dispositions and motives in ancestral environments. If the capacity for empathy has evolved (see Hebb, 1972; Hoffman, 1981), why don't we see more evidence of empathic behaviours in primates (Krebs, 1972; 1987)? What genetic benefits accrued to ancestors who found conflicts irritating? Why would dominant individuals or coalitions reinforce their status by breaking up fights instead of in more self-interested ways? Even if there were good answers to these questions, we would still have a long way to go to get to community control of within-group conflict for the common interest.

Boehm asks the question, 'are we innately given to ethological egalitarianism, to ethological despotism, or to neither'? His answer is that we are innately despotic, 'and can remain egalitarian only if [we] consciously suppress innate tendencies that otherwise would make for a pronounced social dominance hierarchy'. 'If we wish to keep social hierarchy at a low level, we must act as intentional groups that vigilantly curtail alpha-type behaviours. This curtailment is accomplished through the cultural agency of social sanctioning . . .' (p. 84). Fair enough, but where do dispositions to consciously suppress innate tendencies come from? How did we acquire dispositions to form intentional groups? How did cultural sanctions originate? Have these processes somehow become uncoupled from biological evolution, as Dawkins (1989) has suggested? Perhaps, but whatever autonomy mental structures may have obtained, they all evolved biologically.

I feel unwilling to give up on biological routes to human morality (Krebs, 1998). I'm not sure they can take us the distance, but I believe they can get us a little closer than Boehm implies. Turning to Boehm's question, my answer is that we are innately given to both egalitarianism and despotism. All of us inherit despotic and egalitarian dispositions, as well as the higher order strategy of activating the disposition that paid off best genetically for our ancestors in various environmental conditions. I believe this duality is reflected in the structure of our social relations, with individuals dominating when they are able to, submitting when they must, and curtailing dominance in others when it is in their interest. The onus, then, is on me to explain how dispositions to uphold egalitarianism could evolve biologically, which, in my way of thinking, entails explaining how such dispositions could have enhanced the inclusive fitness of our ancestors.

I begin with the adaptive benefits of coalition-formation. By the same token as a coalition of two is usually more powerful than the most dominant individual in a group, a coalition of three is usually more powerful than a coalition of two, and so on. So, I hypothesize, there was an adaptive advantage among our ancestors of forming increasingly large coalitions. Individuals form coalitions when they share interests and need one another to advance their interests. The reason why individuals band together in groups is because they benefit from group living. Mutual defence against predators and large game hunting are important examples. Inasmuch as all members of a group benefit from the presence of the other members of the group, it is in their interest to preserve the group. So too with coalitions. The underlying principle is this: inasmuch as the probability of me propagating my genes is increased when I form a cooperative relationship with you, dispositions to form such relationships should evolve. Chimpanzees form relatively small groups when they go out on patrol and engage in mutual defence. Humans form much larger groups. Biologists such as Alexander (1987) have suggested that dispositions to form large cooperative groups were selected in the human species because large cooperative groups were necessary to combat other large cooperative groups of hominids, giving rise to a kind of arms race.

Given a group whose existence is threatened by hostile environmental forces such as other groups, it is in the genetic interest of every member of the group to cooperate enough to preserve the group on which he or she is dependent. This is not group selection in its usual form because it does not necessarily involve dispositions to sacrifice one's own interests for the sake of one's group. It involves mutuality and indirect reciprocity, with members working together and helping one another in order to advance their individual genetic interests. On this line of thought, the optimal size of a group would be defined as the smallest number necessary to optimize benefits. Environmental factors such as threats from out-groups create the conditions necessary for the formation of cooperative in-groups. It makes sense in these terms for members of groups to invest energy in fostering the welfare of their fellows and cultivating enough harmony for the group to perform its function optimally, so each of them can reap the benefits.

I believe the benefits of cooperation contain the key that will unlock the door to an explanation of the evolution of morality. As demonstrated in game theory research (e.g., Axelrod, 1984), in certain conditions every single member of a group can obtain more for himself or herself by cooperating than by behaving selfishly. Particularly important is the mechanism of indirect reciprocity — helping one member of a group in return for help from another member of the group — , which Alexander (1987) believes has mediated the evolution of human morality. As demonstrated recently by game theorists such as Nowak and Sigmund (1998), indirect reciprocity is a winning strategy in groups able to identify and discriminate against cheaters. Cooperation captures the essence of most people's conceptions of morality. If everyone cooperated, there would be no conflict within groups and everyone would come out ahead — the egalitarian moral ideal.

But there are at least four catches to this good-news principle. First, conditions must be conducive to cooperation, which means that individuals must be able to obtain more for themselves by cooperating than by not cooperating. Dominance hierarchies are not conducive to egalitarian cooperation because it is not in the interest of dominant individuals to give subordinates an equal share when they, the more dominant, are able to obtain more for themselves. I agree with Boehm that constraining the selfishness of dominant members of groups is an important aspect of morality.

Second, cooperative systems must contain antidotes to cheating, which may come in the despotic forms described by Boehm and other forms aimed at maximizing one's gains at the expense of others and exploiting systems of cooperation. One of the greatest evolutionary ironies is that although unabated cheating eventually produces a social system in which everyone gets less than he or she would by cooperating (because there are no cooperators left to exploit), cheating will evolve if it pays off better than cooperation on an individual basis. For moral systems based in indirect reciprocity to evolve, individuals must acquire the ability to identify cheaters and the wherewithal to discriminate against them. This, I believe, is why individuals value their reputations, experience moral indignation, possess a sense of justice, and are disposed to gossip about those they believe are not doing their share.

Third, people should be evolved to form cooperative coalitions with the smallest number of others necessary to maximize their individual benefits, and to compete against other coalitions when it is to their benefit, thereby confining their morality to relations with members of their in-groups. Finally, people should be evolved to show nepotistic biases favouring kin because, in assisting relatives, people are, in effect, assisting replicas of their genes carried by their relatives.

I believe that the logic of evolution outlines a picture that captures well the human condition. We are evolved to behave morally, that is to say to cooperate, when it is in our genetic interests, but we also are evolved to behave immorally when it is not. We are evolved to cooperate with in-group members when we need them to advance our interests — or more exactly in circumstances in which they advanced the interests of our ancestors — and also to fudge, when we are able to, in favour of ourselves and our relatives. We are motivated to preach and impose morality — to exhort and force others to do their duties — and to punish transgressions, but we also are tempted to cheat when we believe we can get away with it. We are evolved to uphold egalitarianism because it is in our interest to curtail the dominance of others. However, we also are evolved to behave dominantly when it pays off for us and for our kin. Our social systems rest on a tenuous and dynamic equilibrium in which everyone holds everyone else in check. We are moral, but only as moral as we need to be.

References

Alexander, R.D. (1987), *The Biology of Moral Systems* (New York: Aldine de Gruyter).

Axelrod, R. (1984), *The Evolution of Cooperation* (New York: Basic Books).

Boehm, C. (2000), 'Conflict and the evolution of social control', *Journal of Consciousness Studies*, **7** (1–2), pp. 79–101.

Dawkins, R. (1989), *The Selfish Gene* (Oxford: Oxford University Press).

Hebb, D.O. (1972), 'Comment on altruism: The comparative evidence', *Psychological Bulletin*, **76**, pp. 409–10.

Hoffman, M. (1981), 'Is altruism part of human nature?', *Journal of Personality and Social Psychology*, **40**, pp. 121–37.

Krebs, D. (1972), 'Infrahuman altruism', *Psychological Bulletin*, **76**, pp. 411–14.

Krebs, D.L. (1987), 'The challenge of altruism in biology and psychology', in *Sociobiology and psychology: Ideas, issues and applications*, ed. C. Crawford, M. Smith and D. Krebs (Hillsdale, NJ: Erlbaum).

Krebs, D.L. (1998), 'The evolution of moral behaviour', in *Handbook of Evolutionary Psychology: Ideas, Issues, and Applications*, ed. C. Crawford and D. L. Krebs (Hillsdale, NJ: Erlbaum).

Nowak, M.A. and Sigmund, K. (1998), 'Evolution of indirect reciprocity by image scoring', *Nature*, **393**, pp. 573–7.

Trivers, R. (1985), *Social evolution* (Menlo Park, CA: Benjamin Cummings).

Williams, G. (1966), *Adaptation and natural selection* (Princeton, NJ: Princeton).

GROUP SANCTIONS WITHOUT SOCIAL NORMS?

B. Thierry

High propensities to form coalitions and to negotiate and prevent conflict escalation may be found in monkeys as in great apes. However, there is no evidence that non-human primate communities intend to suppress individual power that grows too strong. Qualifying as protomoral those abilities needed to keep low the dominance gradient is not useful. When communication about social norms appeared in some hominids, it would not have been limited to sanctions against domination.

When I am in the midst of my study-group of Tonkean macaques (*Macaca tonkeana*), what I gaze upon is a never-ending succession of socially controlled actions. Quarrels stemming from conflicting interests are frequent but wounds are exceptional. Threatened individuals often protest and retaliate against their adversaries, keeping low the dominance gradient between conspecifics. Exchanges of graded threats and appeasements allow opponents to avoid escalation, a majority of quarrels is followed by conciliatory contacts (Thierry, 1986; Demaria and Thierry, 1992). In case of competition over incentives, dominant individuals sometimes refrain from taking them over if subordinates have priority of access (Bélisle, unpublished results). The balance of power is finely tuned and achieving a control role in conflicts may be risky in Tonkean macaques. When intervening in a quarrel between immatures, even the highest-ranking male in the group may face the lunge of an angry mother. Help is most often provided to relatives but sometimes to an unrelated group member even against a kin-related one. Some interventions are not aggressive but peaceful; third parties stop disputes by appeasing one of the opponents. For an observer, the interveners' behaviour looks impartial; they may protect a partner without endangering their relationship with its opponent (Petit and Thierry, 1994, in press). To initiate affiliative interactions, Tonkean macaques use a silent bared-teeth display that looks like a smile (Thierry *et al.*, 1989). They also regularly engage in 'collective arousals', those instances of general excitement in which group members exchange many friendly contacts and appeasement signals as in chimpanzee 'celebrations' (de Waal, 1992).

The propensities of Tonkean macaques to form coalitions, negotiate and prevent conflict escalation, remind one of those reported for chimpanzees. Yet social processes are not supported by the same cognitive abilities in macaques and chimpanzees. Whereas it is believed that great apes are capable of ascribing intentions to others, we know that monkeys have no 'theory of mind'. Experiments have shown that macaques cannot attribute beliefs, knowledge or ignorance to conspecifics: a mother does not understand that she should warn her offspring about a danger that he cannot perceive and of which she was informed; an individual does not discriminate between a human being's knowing where a reward is hidden or being unaware of its location; two partners are unable to cooperate in a task requiring that each understand the other's goal (Cheney and Seyfarth, 1990; Tomasello and Call, 1997). If we resort to concepts like 'politics', 'morality' or 'intentional social harmony' to account for chimpanzee performances, should we apply them to the behaviours observed in Tonkean macaques as well? I would answer that we do not need these concepts either for monkeys or for apes. I understand Boehm's concern. Like Flack and de Waal

(2000), he rightly advocates the view that morality did not develop from scratch in human beings but that the sophisticated abilities for cooperation and control of aggression in non-human primates paved the way for the emergence of moral behaviours. However, it its unhelpful to name the above features 'protomoral'. Like protolife, protoculture or protolanguage, protomorality is a fuzzy concept that cannot be defined in a satisfactory way.

Boehm puts forward his argument in two forms. In its sharper formulation, morality is held to originate from collective efforts to suppress individual aggression and domination. This argument amounts to first reducing morality to its penalty dimension, then searching for cases of collective physical constraint in animals. However, if group members intend to repress exaggerated domination or serious violation of social harmony, on what scale could the degree of deviance be measured? In non-human primates, coalitions respond to immediate circumstances. Bullying behaviours may be punished but we have no evidence for anything like group sanctions. In chimpanzees, several reports describe instances of cannibalism by adult males of infants from their own community (Hiraiwa-Hasegawa, 1992), yet the males responsible were never sanctioned or expelled from the community. In the chimpanzees of Gombe, an adult female and her daughter seized, killed and ate the infants of group members for some years (Goodall, 1977). Commenting on these events, Kummer (1978, p. 44) notes,

> The mothers of the victims fought back, learned to avoid the two dangerous females, and were on occasion defended by adult males; but the killers simply tried again, and in the end they were usually successful. In consequence only two infants have survived in the last three years. Nevertheless, the community has taken no decisive action against its destructive members.

If we turn to human societies, we find that there are many more prohibited actions among hunter-gatherers than those directly related to domination behaviours. Anthropologists testify that 'crimes' as diverse as transgressions of kinship and exchange rules, or violations of territorial, ritual and religious taboos may lead to heavy punishment. Besides, the composition of bands of hunter-gatherers is quite flexible (Woodburn, 1982). Their egalitarian way of life is related to the lower costs of leaving and group splitting than in other forms of social organization. Individuals have a high degree of autonomy; they are not bound together by the necessity of maintaining property (Lee and DeVore, 1968). Therefore, for hunter-gatherers, it is easier to deal with conflicting interests and any kind of domination by leaving the group rather than by forming coalitions.

Collective physical constraint alone is insufficient for the emergence of morality in human beings. Therefore, Boehm reintroduces the existence of social norms in a second formulation of his argument. The advent of language would have favoured the collective prohibition of domination through the establishment of shared values. However, cultural evolution is not a mere prolongation of biological evolution. Individual mental representations are reshaped as soon as they are named. When definitions of deviance came to be collectively built and transmitted by social inheritance, there is no reason why they should have been limited to the reduction of individual power. If some hominids started to communicate about shared representations, they were early able to construct sets of shared norms accompanied by sanctions for deviance — that is, genuine moral systems as defined by Durkheim (1930).

References

Cheney, D.L. and Seyfarth, R.M. (1990), *How Monkeys see the World* (Chicago: Univ. of Chicago Press).

Demaria, C. and Thierry, B. (1992), 'The ability to reconcile in Tonkean and rhesus macaques', Abstracts of the 14th Congress of International Primatological Society (Strasbourg), p. 101.

Flack J. and de Waal, F.B.M. (2000), '"Any Animal Whatever": Darwinian building blocks of morality in monkeys and apes,' *Journal of Consciousness Studies*, 7 (1–2), pp. 1–29.

Durkheim, E. (1930), *De la Division du Travail Social* (Paris: Presses Universitaires de France).

Goodall, J. (1977), 'Infant killing and cannibalism in free-living chimpanzees', *Folia Primatologica*, 28, pp. 259–82.

Hiraiwa-Hasegawa, M. (1992), 'Cannibalism among non-human primates', in *Cannibalism: Ecology and Evolution Among Diverse Taxa*, ed. M. Elgar (Oxford: Oxford University Press).

Kummer, H. (1978), 'Analogs of morality among nonhuman primates', in *Morality as a Biological Phenomenon*, ed. G.S. Stent (Berlin: Dahlem Konferenzen).

Lee, R.B. and DeVore, I. (eds.) (1968), *Man the Hunter* (New York: Aldine).

Petit, O. and Thierry, B. (1994). 'Aggressive and peaceful interventions in conflicts in Tonkean macaques', *Animal Behaviour*, 48, pp. 1427–36.

Petit, O. and Thierry, B. (in press), 'Do impartial interventions occur in monkeys and apes?', in *Natural Conflict Resolution*, ed. F. Aureli and F.B.M. de Waal (Berkeley: University of California Press).

Thierry, B. (1986), 'A comparative study of aggression and response to aggression in three species of macaque', in *Primate Ontogeny, Cognition, and Social Behaviour*, ed. J.G. Else and P.C. Lee (Cambridge: Cambridge University Press).

Thierry, B., Demaria, C., Preuschoft, S. and Desportes, C. (1989), 'Structural convergence between silent bared-teeth display and relaxed open-mouth display in the Tonkean macaque (*Macaca tonkeana*)', *Folia Primatologica*, 52, pp. 178–84.

Tomasello, M. and Call, J. (1997). *Primate Cognition* (Oxford: Oxford University Press).

de Waal, F.B.M. (1992), 'Appeasement, celebration, and food sharing in the two *Pan* species', in *Topics in Primatology, Vol. 1*, ed. T. Nishida, W.C. McGrew, P. Marler, M. Pickford and F.B.M. de Waal (Tokyo: Tokyo University Press).

Woodburn, J.A. (1982), 'Egalitarian societies', *Man*, 17, pp. 431–51.

THE INTERNAL TRIANGLE

Lionel Tiger

While it is obviously interesting, it is not necessary as Boehm does to relate the analysis of morality to lives of primates other than humans. Exposition of human prehistory and history offer ample basis for comparative work. Especially, the transition from hunting/gathering/foraging to agriculture/pastoralism appears to have generated urgent moralistic behaviour. In an interesting historical curiosity, Max Weber himself perceived the basis of morality, or legitimacy, in biosocial processes.

This is a skilful and interesting paper, my brief comment on which will, however, have to begin with a tonally irritated observation that in my book, *The Manufacture Of Evil: Ethics, Evolution, And The Industrial System* (1987/1989), I confronted early a number of the issues which Boehm does. Hence my remark may seem unduly solipsistic, however I trust it will be clear this style has been driven by an interest in the subject and the paper rather than a risible episode of self-regard.

Boehm chooses to compare the evolution of morality in other primates, especially the Pan species, in order to identify the 'Mutual Ancestor' whose stirrings of the sense of equity predispose us all to act in moral rather than solely individualistic ways. Perhaps he is right to do so. Fox and I did just this too when we sought to identify elements of a behavioural grammar — a biogrammar — which would unite elements of human social behaviour with that of other primates just as from Darwin on in *The Expression* (1998), it seemed plausible to seem elements of communication such as facial gestures in common cross-species. However, those who write of the environment of evolutionary adaptiveness also assume that humans are products of the arrangement in which we spent the overwhelming number of genetically formative evolutionary years — so many years that it may be unnecessary to go to the other primates to explore our modern behaviour. Interesting and valuable no doubt, but necessary, no.

For the purposes of an historic account which includes a prehistoric and hence genotypic approach to the matter, let's leave the other apes out of this to see where we get. There seems little question that we spent our formative species years as opportunistic foragers committed to cooperative food-gathering and food-sharing. This occurred in relatively small groups in which members knew each other, or much about each other, and the concept and reality of 'the impersonal' did not exist. Even the ancient Greeks had no word for 'person'. Boehm is surely correct in stressing that in small groups without supervening external systems of dominance, inegalitarian or bossy behaviour is generically irritating and generally understood to be so. Therefore, when at a small buffet dinner I chastised John McEnroe whom I had met neither before or since for cutting in front of me at the curried shrimp line, he rapidly apologized — a gesture popular among onlookers who presumably shared the view that his remarkable athletic skill and planetary reputation did not enable him to violate the envelope of civility on which small group conduct depends. Otherwise, it is simply too dangerous.

Early humans were relatively good at operating the small groups in which we spent so much evolutionary time — we can kind of assume that because we did it for so long in a host of ecologies. Not that there were no chimp-like conflicts at the borders or the 'primitive wars' so troubling to the Rousseauists still among us. But we could manage. However, as Boehm notes and I stated in *Manufacture*, agriculture and pastoralism presented another kettle of fish. Suddenly the mathematics changed. One ear of corn could generate ten dozen plants, two sheep could in near-time produce sixteen, etc., and thus was created the opportunity to leverage sharply the impulses to inegalitarian behaviour which already existed and which were presumably inextricably linked to patterns of sexual selection always roiling in any human system. (About which, by the way, Boehm could make more of.)

Voila! A new human problem. How did we solve the problem of migrating from the Palaeolithic system and scale to the agricultural and pastoral? By producing the major moral structures which continue to support the regnant legal and ethical systems still governing the planet. Christianity, Buddhism, Hinduism, Islam later, all were the products of small farmers and shepherds trying to make do. 'The Lord Is My Shepherd' is a clue to the world of the producers of the Bible. That is to say, to deal with the crisis of the suddenly-escalated possibility of that irritating inequality, a series of fiercely demanding rules were created and codified, using the improbable weapon of God and the wholly inventive notions of heaven and hell as punitive devices. Obviously language was important here as Boehm stresses, especially when it could be written down in special books which claimed magical power. And so rules were formulated to deal with the real new problems: don't covet your neighbour's animals, don't cuckold him, don't kill anybody, provide social security for your old folks, like that.

Again, as I stress in *Manufacture,* once we moved to the industrial system, we continued to use, or tried to, the old pastoral and small-farmer morality. What we had was a triangle. A hunting-gathering ape skilled at small-scale cooperative life had to cope with a novel and brilliantly coercive system of vast and intricate impersonality. All they had to work with were the ethical precepts of small farmers and shepherds who lived thousands of years ago. Obviously, this is an immense challenge which the repertoire of the human species struggles with, often in bewildered and belligerent confusion. The fact is, the industrial system has failed to produce an ethical system calibrated to its special nature and also congenial to the human biogrammar. Marxism was one effort (recall Marx's interest in Darwin) but it failed because it presupposed too much efficacy in human rationality. Utilitarianism is a more plausible ongoing effort but it has failed to generate the redolent systems of symbols such as churches, Five-Year-Plans, and perfect Utopian futures which have been part of the more popular schemes. It is not much fun, and it is difficult to define obvious enemies — as the Bible-thumpers can or the early Marxists.

So, paradoxically, we can discern evidence of hominid morality in precisely the fact that is necessary for scholars to examine whether or not humans are moral. If we assume that morality is for working purposes cognate to an acknowledgment that being in a group is better than being alone, then there is no alternative to the notion that a species as gregarious as ours would have had to generate a compromise between individual desires and social needs and allergies which we can call morality. Boehm recalls once such important effort — Max Weber's concern with political legitimacy (1947). It is worth noting here that in discussing his three categories of legitimacy; traditional, rational–legal, and charismatic, Weber noted that the latter is intrinsically unstable and will tend to become one of the other two. He also makes the prescient comment about the nature of charisma almost entirely ignored by sociologists allergic to biology and the sociological explanations which may flow from it, that

> In the later field of phenomena (charisma and traditional action) lie the seeds of certain types of psychic 'contagion' . . . . These types of action are very closely related to phenomena which are understandable either only in biological terms or are subject to interpretation in terms of subjective motives only in fragments, and with an almost imperceptible transition to the biological.

In other words, here we have one of the outstanding core figures of classical sociology indicating a strong link between formal patterns of political legitimacy and 'biological terms and "the biological"'. These are presumably words which, in the lexicon available to Weber at the time would refer to primordial-like processes supposedly on the culture side of the nature–culture divide represented to this day by the distinction in universities between natural and social sciences. This was a distinction in fact influentially and rather destructively supported by Emile Durkheim to whom Boehm refers and, interestingly, whose dissertation director was the biologist Alfred Espinas. Weber's insight is robust support for the ongoing importance of Boehm's endeavour

References

Darwin, Charles, (1998), *The Expression of the Emotions in Man and Animals*, Third Edition, ed. Paul Ekman (New York & Oxford, Oxford University Press).

Tiger, Lionel, (1987/ 1989), *The Manufacture of Evil: Ethics, Evolution, and the Industrial System* (New York: Harper & Row; London & New York: Marion Boyars).

Tiger, Lionel and Fox, Robin (1971; 1998), *The Imperial Animal* (New York: Holt Rinehart and Winston; London and New York: Transaction).

Weber, Max (1947), *The Theory of Social and Economic Organization* (Glencoe, IL: The Free Press).

Christopher Boehm

The Origin of Morality as Social Control

Response to Commentary Discussion

In answering these widely ranging commentaries, I concentrate on the origins of morality and further elaborate the Common Ancestral cladistic model used in my principal paper. I also advocate, strongly, the inclusion of human nature as an important variable for anthropological analysis. In addition, I argue for a methodologically collectivistic, psychologically-oriented approach to the evolutionary explanation of moral behaviour, taking the sometimes well-unified moral community as the primary unit of analysis. It is emphasized that the first behaviour to be morally sanctioned in human groups was likely to have been bullying behaviour, and that once human groups had established an effective methodology of social control, other behaviours such as free-riding began to be sanctioned. With their interest in reducing conflict levels, eventually moral communities were able to create institutions like the human family.

It is gratifying that hypotheses advocated in the principal paper stimulated extensive commentary. The ideas were first presented in skeletal form several decades ago (Boehm, 1982; 1984). More recently, I have developed them further (Boehm, 1993; 1996; 1999a; 1999b; 1999c), but the principal presentation was streamlined because of space limitations. In responding to the commentaries, I shall draw from these other publications as I also discuss some new issues. In the principal paper, I concentrated on ancestral preadaptations and on how moral communities work among extant hunting bands, without discussing in great detail the transition from a non-moral Common Ancestor to Anatomically Modern Humans as a moral species. With respect to this transition, Bruce **Knauft** has asked searching questions that go well beyond the scope I allowed myself, and he provides some very interesting hypotheses that I have not considered in the publications mentioned above.

The second act of streamlining was to keep the focus on relations of power, concentrating on the social control of deviants and on manipulative interventions that reduce conflict. In effect, I set aside a kinder, gentler side of moral life, which has been explored at the level of precursors by Frans de Waal (1996; see also Flack and de Waal, 2000): these include primate tendencies to offer reassurance or help with reconciliation after conflicts, and they suggest some capacity to identify with others in times of trouble. On the positive side, I did treat conflict aversiveness as an important force, and elsewhere (Boehm, 1999c) I have considered the possibility that genetic altruism could be contributing to human social cooperation.

In the principal paper, the focus was on power relations because I consider such relations to be basic — and because space was limited. They are basic because a cooperative moral order of the hunter-gatherer type could be difficult to maintain unless group members were exerting some really firm control over social predators. In bands, social control always is needed, and this involves applications of group power against deviants. The aim is either to reform them or else to eliminate them from the band. Morality is many other things, as well, but at its base it is social control. I believe the most essential precursors of human life in moral communities can be identified in this sphere.

Group sanctioning surely was fundamental to human moral life in the Upper Palaeolithic, and it is important today. If you live long enough in any small human group, social predators will appear: exploiters like bullies, cheats, thieves, or individuals who ignore the local code of sexual conduct. It is group opinion that defines such deviance, and the fact that the rank and file are individually capable of moral outrage underlies sanctioning as a group activity. Whenever strongly negative feelings spread to the entire group, there is the basis for assertive coalitional behaviour that effectively manipulates the deviant in question — or eliminates him. This behaviour is intentional, so in spite of **Black**'s vehement structuralist strictures, a full and adequate explanation of social control must include a liberal dose of psychology, including group psychology.

In the principal paper I, suggested that such group dynamics obtain today in all human societies and that our Common Ancestor as of five million years ago was preadapted for such behaviour. Given the entire suite of ancestral behaviours I identified, the earliest type of deviance to be sanctioned by groups in the human line may well have been bullying behaviour — of the type exhibited by high ranking chimpanzees, bonobos, or humans when groups (as political coalitions) feel a group member is exerting too much power. No other behaviour of the Common Ancestor is suggestive of any of the more important and widespread moral proscriptions that we see in bands today, whereas every band — in fact, every human society of any type — has its limits when the abuse of power is at issue (Boehm, 1999b).

With respect to **Knauft**'s commentary, I admit to being conservative in two ways. One was in working just with 'power' aspects of moral behaviour that were readily identifiable in ancestral precursor form; the other was in taking a very restrained position with respect to when full blown morality might have originated. I did this so that my hypotheses might be considered open mindedly by all scholars who work with Palaeolithic data, knowing that a few are willing to grant humans a fully cultural status only quite recently, with the arrival of lunar calendars and cave paintings. My basic position in the principal paper was that fully modern moral behaviour arose, at latest, with Anatomically Modern Humans about 100,000 years ago. I see this not as a definitive position, but as a conservative place to start.

As a theoretician who takes on very large questions, Knauft (1987; 1991) has been far less conservative. He has argued that *Homo erectus* is a candidate for many of the social capacities we see more fully developed in ourselves, and intuitively I would agree that this seems possible. More specifically, elsewhere he has argued (Knauft,

1991) that human egalitarianism could go back two million years, and here he suggests that moral behaviour could be equally ancient. He also engages with the problem of how morality could have developed in stages, over the several million years it took for Anatomically Moderns to appear.

There is much food for thought in **Knauft**'s comments. Let us begin, though, with a small semantic point. Whereas **Knauft** refers to *Pan troglodytes* as 'common chimpanzees' to contrast them with *Pan paniscus* (bonobos), I simply use the term 'chimpanzees' for *Pan troglodytes*. With that clarified, **Knauft** believes that I have not only underemphasized *Pan paniscus* in creating an ancestral model, but in some important ways I have misinterpreted bonobo behaviour with respect to social dominance behaviour and territoriality. In effect, I have been 'chimpocentric'.

Knauft refers to the advantages and disadvantages that come with being a hybrid cultural anthropologist/primatologist who has come to know only a single species. I agree that it is useful to have studied in the field a primate that offers homological explanation possibilities for one's own species, for in evolutionary studies, homology means that similar functions derive from similar underlying mechanisms because of common (and relatively recent) origins. I can claim to know wild chimpanzees fairly well, for in addition to sixteen months' observation in the field, I also have worked for a decade with the extensive Gombe-based videotape archive we have at the University of Southern California. The disadvantage of knowing chimpanzees but not bonobos is obvious. Bonobos are far less well studied than chimpanzees, both longitudinally and in hours of field observation, and one is tempted to fill in the gaps, making some common sense adjustments, with data from chimpanzees.

Knauft suggests that bonobo social dominance hierarchies are less pronounced than I make them, but this really depends on what species they are compared with. In comparison with chimpanzees, with their flamboyant male obsessions about competing for rank, bonobos may seem to be rather quiescent with respect to competition and aggression. However, if one compares bonobos with squirrel monkeys (Boinski, 1994) or murquis (Strier, 1994), and thinks about Vehrencamp's (1983) ethological continuum between 'egalitarian' and 'despotic' species, bonobos with their high and low ranking males and females and their powerful female coalitions would have to be placed definitively on the despotic side of the continuum — even though they are not as despotic as chimpanzees. I say this because bonobos use their rank aggressively to compete in feeding, and they definitely compete for status.

With respect to competition for power, there is also an interesting difference between these species in the wild. Female chimpanzees basically operate on their own politically, whereas males form coalitions to get ahead. The result is that females are always dominated by males. With bonobos, it is the females who form political coalitions whereas the males do not, and the result is that females hold their own with males: males and females share not only high positions in the group, but also very low ones. Where bonobos are notably less competitive than chimpanzees is in mating (see Kano, 1992), but there may be special reasons of physiology that explain this (Wrangham and Peterson, 1996). In adding all of this up, I shall stay with my assessment that bonobos are quite despotic by primate standards, which means they are given to forming social dominance hierarchies and they act, individually, as competitive bullies.

Knauft also believes I was off base when I characterized the Common Ancestor as having territorial inclinations and inter-group conflict tendencies. He believes that bonobos stand in the way of this generalization because they exhibit little or no territorial behaviour as this is defined in chimpanzee terms, with hostile calling between groups and male patrols (Nishida, 1979; Goodall, 1979), occasional large excursions that encroach on resources (Goodall, 1986), and lethal attacks on strangers that are now documented at Gombe, Mahale, and Kibale. **Knauft**'s clear implication is that bonobos' lack of interest in defending resources is species specific, but there are several reasons to question this position.

One is that bonobo food sources permit quite large groups to forage (see Wrangham and Peterson, 1996), which suggests that scarcity conditions that might stimulate more active types of territorial behaviour are absent. Another is that neighbouring groups do sometimes emit hostile calls (Kano, 1992), and when they meet, there can be a curiously mixed reaction: the females cross the line to socialize, whereas the adult males hold back (see Wrangham and Peterson, 1996). More basically, bonobos live in discernible communities in which, like chimpanzees, the males basically stay in place whereas the females tend to transfer, and these communities show a noteworthy tendency to keep to separate home ranges (Kano, 1992).

Taken all together, these behaviours make bonobos stand in sharp contrast to gorillas (Boehm, 1992), whose silverbacks simply do not seem to be defensive about natural resources which appear to be plentiful. At the same time, I see also a distinct but muted similarity to the chimpanzee pattern. Another decade or two of bonobo field studies may enlighten us further (see Wrangham and Peterson, 1996), and given the incremental nature of our past insights into chimpanzee territoriality, this further information may well take bonobos still further in the direction of chimpanzees.

Knauft also raises the issue of ancestral inter-group conflict. My assumptions about the common ancestor, and about prehistoric human bands, may seem fairly Hawkish. There are many — not Bruce Knauft — who seem to associate such assumptions with personal acceptance of warfare in human life, so I must say a word about this. The century we are just ending has been incredibly bloody, and as a matter of practical politics I believe it better that anthropologists be thinking a bit pessimistically about our human behavioural potential, rather than trying to give it the benefit of the doubt. To the extent that policy makers responsible for world political order may occasionally listen to us, it is desirable that they fully realize what they are up against, rather than being lulled into complacency by messages that suggest our species is not actually prone to warfare. I believe that as scientists, and also as citizens of a troubled world, we must remain open-minded with respect to conflict potential in the Common Ancestor, with respect to lower-level warfare possibilities in the Upper Palaeolithic, and with respect to ourselves as animals that seem to be prone to intergroup violence.

Aside from criticisms I have tried to answer here, **Knauft** has provided some very important insights into possibilities for moral evolution if it was extremely gradual, which I certainly consider to be an open question. Like myself, he has taken into account the extreme variability of Upper Palaeolithic climatic conditions, and of variable human responses to them. However, our views involve some differences of emphasis. I would agree that prehistoric foragers sporadically had to face serious environmental scarcity, and that one likely response would have been that bands simply broke down into individual families and spread out. Extant models include not only the Shoshone, but certain groups in desert Australia (Gould, 1982). However, I have argued that there may be other responses to scarcity, as well, and that these involve conflict among bands (see also Boehm, 1999a; 1999c).

I also agree with **Knauft** that at many times, Upper Pleistocene nomads were able to function ecologically as compact bands (see Dunbar, 1996), which equitably shared their meat. Meat-sharing was a way of evening out protein and fat intake, and this was facilitated by finding a moral consensus in favour of cooperation. In extant foragers, there is support for such assumptions, for Kelly (1995) has discussed theories of variance reduction that apply to all extant foragers who remain nomadic. An egalitarian political order obviously facilitates equalized sharing of sporadically acquired large game (see Erdal and Whiten, 1996; Wiessner, 1996; Boehm, 1999b), and prehistorically a moral consensus not only supported this cooperative practice, but it prevented camp bullies and other free-riders from taking advantage of the cooperators.

If one wishes to set aside **Knauft**'s gradualist scenario for moral evolution and consider the possibility of morality arriving rather quickly through cultural invention, the elimination of camp bullies could have taken place as an act of political rebellion by the rank and file — assuming they were pre-adapted to do so in terms of language and cultural capacity (Boehm, 1999b). The resulting egalitarian order would have made possible equalization of access to meat, and, once this morally-based egalitarian syndrome was in place in one band, these interlocking customs might have spread readily. I say this because their advantages (getting rid of alpha domination and eating meat regularly) would have been perceptually obvious to the rank and file of any band. There is no doubt that Anatomically Modern Humans were prepared to do this, and possibly Neanderthals. As one goes backwards in time, relative brain size becomes smaller and so do the chances of a culturally-based political revolution that could be stabilized through social control.

There is no reason that this type of hypothesis cannot be incorporated into the long-term scenario that **Knauft** favours. Ephemeral subordinate rebellions were probable in the Common Ancestor, and it would appear that what was needed, for egalitarian moral communities to appear, was the ability to somehow institutionalize such rebellions. This capacity would have advanced as language ability and cultural capacity advanced, and it is likely that they advanced gradually because biological evolution was involved. Thus, in all probability some kind of gradual co-evolutionary process (see Durham, 1991) was involved in setting the stage for the advent of moral communities as we know them. There remains an important question: did morality simply have to await the development of language, or was proto-moral behaviour intimately involved with language evolution?

Let us return to **Knauft**'s reluctance to project into the Palaeolithic the extensive fighting between bands that we see in today's foraging nomads (Ember, 1978). In effect, he suggests that a small group of extant simple foragers — people who are nomadic, tend to have immediate return economic systems (Woodburn, 1982), and generally do not seem to fight as bands — should be the models for prehistoric reconstruction (see also Knauft, 1991). In 1991, these arguments were far more persuasive, for in light of the recently dynamic picture we have of the Upper Palaeolithic (Potts, 1996), analysis based on any particular forager 'type' may not work as effectively as a more polymorphous approach.

Kelly (1995) has shown extant bands to be highly variable socially and ecologically, often in ways that have little to do with the arrival of the Neolithic and the subsequent environmental marginalization discussed by Rodseth (1991). It makes sense that Upper Palaeolithic bands were still more variable in their social organization, ecological adaptation, and political relations with other bands, for extant patterns have been able to stabilize over the past 10,000 years in the absence of major glaciations.

Did this climatic variability sometimes promote inter-band conflict? Extant bands fight a lot (Ember, 1978), and they seem more likely to fight if they have a history of having to deal with some environmental unpredictability (Ember and Ember, 1992). They also seem more prone to fighting if hunting is predominantly their subsistence strategy (Knauft, 1991). These extant bands rather often engage in social boundary defence or perimeter defence (Cashdan, 1983), and this includes not only some of the simpler foragers, but the great majority of foragers who continue the Palaeolithic pattern of nomadism. Because outright fighting was quickly suppressed by colonial regimes (see Service, 1975), we may assume that a few hundred years ago there was a still greater degree of intergroup conflict.

On an immediate basis, the 'territorial' behaviours we know about seem to be a response to a combination of scarcity and economic defensibility of resources (Dyson-Hudson and Smith, 1978), but there is also a human tendency to retaliate for homicide (e.g., Balikci, 1970; Lee, 1979. see also Ember, 1978; Boehm, 1999c) that can make conflicts continue beyond a specific time of scarcity. My suggestion, both for extant and prehistoric foragers, is that the human potential for hostile competition over resources is likely to emerge whenever the appropriate environmental stimulation is present, and once such conflict becomes lethal, a continuing pattern of lethal exchange is not unlikely. We are probably speaking about raiding, here, rather than intensive warfare in which all the males of a group line up to fight — or make genocidal surprise attacks.

Eventually, new archaeological evidence may be able to disconfirm or support such hypotheses, but for the time being I think it unwise to set aside prehistoric group conflict just because a subsample of extant bands seems to be exempt. In this context of using the present to predict the past, I turn for a moment to **Gardner**'s brief and searching comment, which asks how we know that extant hunter-gatherers are at all similar to those who evolved our genes for us in the Upper Palaeolithic. To begin, I acknowledge that there are extant forager types we must avoid in modelling. Some are totally encapsulated and may be politically cowed; others, like the Mbuti, are engaged economically with post-Neolithic types, and others, like Plains Indians, hunt using domesticated horses. Others stay in villages year round and store their food, like the Kwakiutl. All of these hunter-gatherers should be heavily suspect. Others, like the various Kalahari foragers, have had protracted or substantial culture contact with non-foragers.

'Marginalization' is often proposed as a further and pervasive basis for disqualification (e.g., Rodseth, 1991), and at first blush this argument seems persuasive. It holds that after the Neolithic, hunter-gatherers were pushed into less productive environments by tribal farmers and others, and this introduced novel patterns with respect to both politics and ecology. However, if we look at certain Australian Aborigines and Inuit, people who at the time of study had no prior contact with Neolithic types, a number of these bands were living in highly marginal environments (e.g., Balikci, 1970; Gould, 1982) — even though the only people around them were other hunter-gatherers.

Now let us consider the Upper Palaeolithic. People surely were dislocated rather frequently as a result of radical climatic cycles lasting from a few thousand years to almost ten thousand years (see Potts, 1996), and in times of increasing scarcity, very likely some bands would have held on to deteriorating habitats as their home ranges had to expand, while others would have been forced into still more marginal environments. Thus, in important ways, today's marginalized foragers may not be such bad models, after all — if they are not also sedentary, or encapsulated, or somehow involved with domestication.

It is time to rethink other triangulation habits, as well. For example, the Inuit, with their excellent credentials with respect to social isolation, should not be set aside just because their environment is so different from the temperate savannas that have been widely posited for the Upper Palaeolithic and earlier, and because they therefore rely almost exclusively on hunting. I say this because, recurrently, prehistoric glaciations caused certain regions to cool to a degree that tundras and even Arctic conditions were likely, and such environments are friendly to hunting and unfriendly to the gathering of vegetable foodstuffs. Keep in mind that hunting tends to correlate with increased conflict between groups.

Add this all up, and it would seem that extant patterns of social boundary defence and perimeter defence can be extrapolated into prehistory — particularly at times when regional climatic changes led to protracted scarcity. Both the methodology and the conclusion may stir further criticism, but we need a bolder and more variegated approach to extrapolating extant patterns backwards in time. For starters, it makes sense that in the many regions affected by glaciation cycles, territorially based conflict prevailed cyclically.

Gardner also raises the hypothesis that political egalitarianism of extant hunter-gatherers could be due to post-Neolithic culture contact. This seems extremely doubtful, for all extant foragers who remain nomadic are distinctly and similarly politically egalitarian — even though their degrees of cultural contact vary extremely. It seems possible that meeting with external societies that emphasize authority could have reinforced ancient egalitarian tendencies, but surely this is not the origin of egalitarianism. Indeed, Knauft (1991) has projected egalitarianism back several million years.

I have argued that a significant potential was already there five million years ago, but I also have suggested that egalitarian moral orders could have arisen rather quickly, and possibly rather late. In this connection, a greater emphasis on acquisition of large game could have brought a perceptually obvious need to live in bands large enough to reduce variance in meat consumption, and bullying behaviours could have become seriously problematic because they interfered with this cooperation. Large game acquisition increases with later Homo erectus and becomes a way of life with Neanderthals and Anatomically Moderns, so a reasonably conservative date for the rise of egalitarianism would be a few hundred thousand years ago or, at latest, with the rise of Anatomically Modern humans (Boehm, 1999b).

In spite of some significant disagreements, **Knauft** and I agree that hunter-gatherer egalitarianism goes back for scores of millennia, and that it once was a cultural universal for nomads living in bands. With respect to evolutionary time depth, one argument in favour of **Knauf**t's position would be that moral behaviour and language are so intimately connected. From the standpoint of moral communities, an ability to communicate with displacement is critical because such communities must continuously track everyone's behaviour and group members are often dispersed (Boehm, 1999b). It seems certain that language evolved very gradually, for physiological changes were involved (see Lieberman, 1998). If moral behaviour and language co-evolved genetically, then morality could have arrived in very gradual increments. If language evolved on its own then morality could have arrived much more quickly, as a cultural development. These are issues for the future, and they are important ones.

With respect to **Knauf**t's comments about gender, in a just-published fuller explication of my hypothesis (Boehm, 1999b) I do discuss gender issues, and the political role of females in earlier moral communities is deemed to be robust. In extant bands, women generally are treated subordinately to some degree, particularly within the family. However, when it comes to a small band's exchanging information about deviance, arriving at moral opprobrium or outrage, and engaging in sanctions such as criticism, ridicule, or ostracism, the females seem to be full partners with the males. This point may be separate from the useful and stimulating gender arguments made by **Knauft**, but it is important because it can be tied to female power-coalition behaviours of wild bonobos and captive chimpanzees.

There is also the role of sexuality and sexual competition, as targets for moral sanctioning. Bonobo social uses of sexuality, along with their minimal sexual competition, make it difficult to develop an ancestral base line. However, I believe that my treatment of sexually-based conflict is consistent with ideas developed by **Knauft** (1991) in an influential Current Anthropology article. There, he identified competition for mates and sexual partners as a chief cause of forager homicide within the band. In terms of moral origins, this brings us to the interesting question of what behaviours first were identified by human or proto-human groups as being deviant, and whether homicide or excessive sexual competition were controlled early on.

The analysis in my principal paper suggests that the definitive elimination of bullying behaviour is the best candidate for the first moral proscription; I would argue the case strongly because there are such definite preadaptations in this direction. These include subordinate coalitions rising either to prevent certain alpha candidates from establishing themselves, or to whittle away at existing alpha power. This started a job that was finished by human egalitarians when they all but eliminated the alpha role by continuously and vigilantly suppressing their political upstarts.

By contrast, I see nothing at all specific in the Common Ancestral behavioural suite that would suggest a specific preadaptation for group suppression of sexual competition, as an obvious social problem that might have been targeted by the earliest moral communities. My hypothesis is that when morally judgmental coalitions first swung into action as communicative moral communities that shared values and tracked deviant behaviour, their initial aim was to suppress alpha domination. This enabled such communities to establish an effective methodology of social control, which then placed them in a position to manipulate or eliminate other types of troublesome deviance that became obvious to them.

Because the Common Ancestor was aversive to conflict (Boehm, 1999b), sexual competition (or any other behaviour leading to serious altercations) would have been an obvious target for further manipulative sanctioning. There are various ways of dealing with conflict. One is to smooth things over afterwards (de Waal, 1996), and another is to intervene in fights directly. Still another (Boehm, 1982), is to pre-empt behaviours that are likely to result in strife. If sexual competition among males was so targeted, this could have fostered the cultural development of familial institutions.

In this respect, human nature gave these groups something to work with preadaptively. Obviously the formation of social bonds was a basic aspect of ancestral sociality, and early moral communities could have reinforced bonding between sexual partners — at the same time that they suppressed promiscuous male sexual competition or harem-building by dominants. Several commentators have asked about the origins of the family, and this provides a possibility — but it requires that we think about entire bands as problem-solving entities.

I do very much agree with **Knauft** that there may be an arms race of sorts between sexual competition and social control. If one takes into account the varying forms of pair bonding that make possible what we call the human family, and also the quite variable attitudes and sanctions that are directed at the problem of adultery in bands, it is clear that this balance of power could be tenuous. But in spite of this, all human foragers have families that exhibit some degree of stability, and they all seem to support the family as an institution. How this institution arose is a story I cannot explore further here, but **Knauft**'s extensive and innovative commentary has given me — and all of us — some very serious food for thought.

Lionel **Tiger**'s comments also provide important food for evolutionary thought. In *The Manufacture of Evil* (Tiger, 1987), a book of enormous scope, he took note of the 1982 article in which I first laid out the arguments developed in the present paper. Without the benefit of Wrangham's (1987) type of cladistic primatological analysis, I had relied on a referential mutual ancestor model using just chimpanzees, and at the time I had not begun field research with that species. My weakly modelled ancestor had hierarchical and anti-hierarchical dispositions and a tendency to pacify conflicts, and such dispositions were hypothesized to have shaped the band-level approach to political organization and moral sanctioning. A similar argument in the principal paper has much better cladistic support.[1]

My interest in 1982 (as now) was in pre-adaptations, and how they might have played out deep in prehistory. Tiger's (1987) interest was, rather, in the transition from hunting to agriculture to large, impersonal societies (see also Tiger and Fox, 1971). His commentary suggests that one might simply leave the other hominoids out of the picture, to focus upon 'opportunistic foragers committed to cooperative food-gathering and food-sharing' and what happened after they began to domesticate

---

[1]   Cladistic analysis (see Foley, 1995) was briefly defined in the principal paper. There I used chimpanzees, bonobos, and humans to triangulate to their shared ancestor. We know from molecular evidence that it lived about five million years ago, and the cladistic argument is that if all three species share a behaviour today, the behaviour was also present in the Common Ancestor because it is extremely unlikely that all three would have independently evolved the same behaviour on a convergent basis. Elsewhere (Boehm, 1999b), I have added gorillas to the equation, to triangulate to a Common Ancestor as of seven million years ago. A four-species model is still more conservative, and I shall introduce it presently, though not in its entirety.

animals and plants. The premise is that in the Neolithic, humans became so productive by farming, and by raising animals, that impulses to inegalitarian behaviour could be sharply leveraged. This is nicely borne out by what appeared next: chiefdoms, a few of which turned into early civilizations (Service, 1975), and eventually an industrial system that also manufactured social and psychological problems. However, during this same more recent time sequence there is a second story that seems worth telling.

Although a number of Neolithic tribesmen went on to form strong chiefdoms, the great majority remained fiercely egalitarian. A few came to tolerate big men, but they denied them any real or hereditary power. Just a few, like the Iroquois, formed multi-tribal republics that involved large numbers of people living as egalitarians, with political systems that involved clever antiauthoritarian checks and balances. In creating quite sizable egalitarian societies, they invented what amounted to representative government by consensus — and the framers of the American Constitution modelled our own checks and balances on the Iroquois system (Weatherford, 1988) even though they moved from consensus to majority rule. Today, the resultant democracies occupy a sizable (minority) niche in the world political scene, so in an important sense Palaeolithic-style notions about political parity have continued in an unbroken line (Boehm, 1999b).

This means that the Neolithic transition had highly variable political effects, which I believe can be explained in terms of an ambivalent political nature (Boehm, 1989; 1999b): one path led to Scandinavian democracies and the other to Nazi Germany. In his book, Tiger treats what modern societies share in common as he takes a hunter-gatherer-derived human nature and evaluates its problematic fit with a radically changed social and economic environment. I would very much like to see his analysis applied, separately, to modern democracies and to modern totalitarian orders, with the latter taken as being far more divergent, politically, from our Upper Palaeolithic egalitarian heritage.

With respect to the fate of egalitarianism after the Neolithic, **Carling** errs in attributing to me the notion that the development of agriculture led to the loss of egalitarian suppression of bullies. Indeed, except in Oceania, two centuries ago most non-literate people living in small, locally autonomous groups with domestication of plants or animals (let us call them 'tribesmen') had remained egalitarian since the Neolithic — rather than following a more hierarchical route. **Carling** also criticizes me for suggesting that morality is an antidote to 'primate biology', linking my arguments to Huxley's and Dawkins'. Actually, my evolutionary mentor was Donald T. Campbell, who correctly saw morality as a 'counterhedonic' component of culture (Campbell, 1975).

Carling goes on to say that I have short-shrifted the positive or prosocial side of moral behaviour. While I deliberately set aside the conciliatory behaviours discussed by de Waal (1996), I should point out that a major section of the principal paper was entitled, 'Is Aversiveness to Conflict Innate?' and that my answer was yes, for the three hominoids I was dealing with. That would be half of my answer. The other half is to be found in an article that will be published all but simultaneously with the present volume, in which I suggest that once morally-supported egalitarianism was in place, some modest selection of altruistic genes became possible for humans (see Boehm, 1999c). If this (to many) heretical thesis is correct, such altruism provided a basis not only for group calls for altruism and cooperation (Campbell, 1972), but for at least an ambivalent individual responsiveness to such calls (Boehm, 1999b). Part of that argument is available in my response to Sober and Wilson in this volume (see also Boehm, 1997b).

Other criticisms by **Carling** involve misreadings of my arguments or terminology, or insistence that I bring in imprecise variables (for example, Freud's Id) that would simply muddy the analytical waters. I do deal with emotions like moral outrage and fear, but these are carefully linked to behaviours that can be described ethologically, and in some cases could also be tied to hard-wired facial expressions. Finally, **Carling** calls for greater attention to the 'interactions among affect, reason, and social norms in the evolved human psyche'. It seems to me that this is precisely what I have attempted, in a conservative way. I have suggested that morality be viewed from a political perspective, which involves dominantly angry groups controlling not only fearfully submissive deviants but also dominantly angry deviants who have to be taken by surprise and eliminated. I also have suggested that egalitarian moral communities amount to intentional societies because the members of such groups often are aware of political outcomes they are implementing, and do so deliberately. I also have discussed social rules and moral values, which amount to 'norms'. I am not certain what I could do to make **Carling** less unhappy, but I suspect that **Knauft**'s analyses might please him.

Let me return to **Tiger**'s commentary. He praises Max Weber as a true interdisciplinarian who was willing to consider 'biological' variables. The same can be said of a handful of recent political scientists (e.g., Somit, 1976; Corning, 1984; Masters, 1989; Arnhart, 1998). Weber's (1947) notions about political legitimacy combine the moral and the political in very important ways, and I have suggested that the origins of moral life were heavily involved with politics and coercive power — though not power that is personally 'centralized'. It is the band, as a whole, that was the political centre.

Tiger comments on the interesting and relevant subject of Marxism and its involvement with evolutionary issues. In working with the useful notion of a human 'biogrammar,' Tiger and Fox (1971, p. 33) long ago pointed to the failure of idealistically-conceived socialist states to wither away, bringing in the 'earlier primate passion for pre-eminence' as a disposition that inhibits Utopian plans. In *Hierarchy in the Forest*, I have undertaken a similar argument, but in lieu of a more generalized biogrammar metaphor, I have developed a highly detailed portrait of the Common Ancestor's political dispositions, this in conjunction with an 'ambivalence and compromise' approach (Boehm, 1999b; see also Bidney, 1947; Campbell, 1965; Masters, 1989; Boehm, 1989) that permits one to examine conflicting tendencies in human nature at a high level of specificity. My idea is that certain underlying contradictions, such as dispositions to dominate, submit, or resent being dominated, lead to patterned psychological ambivalences which structure decision behaviour and cultural patterns. It is useful to consider Marx and Engels in this light.

Unfortunately, the two men who created communism's political blueprint were not informed by primate field studies, nor by cladistic analyses that showed our precursors to be innately despotic. They believed in a 'good' human nature, a cooperative, egalitarian, and probably altruistic nature that would express itself freely — once the evils of capitalism were remedied. Hence, the state just naturally withers away. For me, this innocent assumption underlies what proved to be a fundamental and tragic flaw in Marxist social and political engineering (Boehm, 1999b). The assumption is understandable in historical context, for it was based on the few ethnographic models that were available to these two theoreticians, and Morgan's (1901) work on the egalitarian Iroquois figured prominently.

The fatal error was a failure to see that humans will predictably form hierarchies — top-heavy ones that are given to the development of despotism — unless the subordinates have enough political leverage to keep individual domination in check. The Iroquois understood this, and they set up their checks and balances accordingly (Morgan, 1901). The error was fatal because problems of uncontrolled central power helped to bring down communism. It also was fatal because dozens of millions of people were liquidated in the name of a political Utopia that was anthropologically misconceived, and major wars (verging on nuclear ones) were fought in the interest of creating this 'truer' type of democracy.

Marxists did not understand that if the proletariat is to dictate, it must have in its own hands the power to do so. Dictatorship by proxy led to the same kind of self-aggrandizement that we see in chimpanzee alpha males. By contrast, 'Power to the People' is very much in effect with hunters in a nomadic band, or with agriculturalists living in small egalitarian tribes. It also is true of the willfully democratic Iroquois Confederacy with its strategic checks and balances, and it also is true to an important degree with weaker tribal chiefdoms — but certainly not with tribal kingdoms, whose leaders have standing armies to intimidate the people. To a very significant degree it is true, as well, of political democracies of the type described by de Toqueville (1994).

Tiger (1979) has discussed evolutionary reasons that humans as a species are given to optimism, and I believe that Marx and Engels were excessively optimistic about human political nature. In a general context, Marxist optimism can be related to the philosophical influence of Jean Jacques Rousseau, as well as a failure to understand how vigilant the Iroquois were about staying egalitarian. But what if Marx and Engels had read Tiger and Fox (1971) — who said the Common Ancestor was given to status rivalry, with dominance and submission, competition for food, and formation of hierarchies with powerful individuals at the top? What if they had read my own hypotheses about dominance hierarchies being reversed only with great vigilance? Their reaction is difficult to predict, for today many resist such nasty insights in the face of much better information about human nature.

I am not suggesting that human nature is inflexible. It is the human tendency to develop anti-authoritarian feelings (Gardner, 1991) and engage in counter-dominant behaviour (Erdal and Whiten, 1994; 1996) that helps to explain today's democracies with their checks and balances. But the same political animal that aggressively acts to counter dominance can fearfully or willingly submit to authority in order to avoid attack and secure protection. It also can identify with a charismatic leader who behaves despotically. But while human nature obviously allows for behavioural flexibility, this plasticity is far from infinite. These three political courses pretty well define the directions modern political societies are likely to take — until the next cultural surprise comes along (see Boehm, 1999b).

Tiger's commentary, and his book, raise a number of very large questions that I shall not respond to here. However, I would emphasize that the evils of industrial society may be emerging somewhat differently, depending on which of these routes to political centralization is taken. All stem from a Common Ancestor that pre-adapted us for both democracy and totalitarianism, and these contradictions may be explained by a biogrammar framework or by a more specified ambivalence model, one that is tied to the detailed model of the Common Ancestor I have come up with on the basis of recent information from primatology. If we are to further explain the varieties of political and moral life, it is essential to further understand such contradictory dispositions, and how they may work together or against each other.

Antweiler, like **Bernstein**, sees my principal paper as being speculative but reasonably logical. He believes I could take the arguments further, but at the same time he has some problems with my mixing of methodologically individualistic approaches with methodologically collectivistic ones — a problem that appears to disturb **Black** as well. I shall address this matter when I respond to **Black**. Also at issue for **Antweiler** are the specific goals of foragers who engage in moral sanctioning, and he calls for further field study — something I would welcome. In the space available, I cannot comment on **Antweiler**'s diagram, but he also raises the problem of what is on the minds of primates.

This brings me to **Thierry**'s commentary, which covers a rather wide range of issues from the standpoint of primatology. An important question he raises, is whether non-human primates are capable of the kind of mental representation that is shared by humans when they come up with norms. I shall get to this presently. **Thierry**'s overall viewpoint may be affected by the species of macaque monkey that he studies, which does exhibit many behaviours that are similar to those of chimpanzees. At the same time, he acknowledges some major differences in social cognition between monkeys and apes. The problem is that he nevertheless proceeds to lump monkeys and apes together, as he argues that I should avoid considering protomorality in such species.

In the principal paper, I took on the difficult subject of protomorality only in passing, for others have discussed it and I was content to deal in precursors. Elsewhere, I have focussed on a behaviour that can emerge both in wild male chimpanzees primarily, and in captive females, when very large coalitions reject the behaviours of individuals who are intent on domination of some type. This seems a likely precursor for social control as we know it, and I support de Waal's characterization that the Yerkes females were making unanimous threats against Jimoh to stop his bullying behaviour as their hostile vocalizations became unanimous and Jimoh stopped what he was doing (see de Waal, 1996). Similar behaviours are recorded in the wild (Boehm, 1999b), and whether this is considered as a precursor to social control or a proto form of that behaviour would appear to be largely a matter of semantics.

Protomorality is a fuzzy term and one we should perhaps avoid, but it does assist in scholarly communication so long as we remain on the same page. The main thrust of my arguments would stand if this term were set aside, for the objective was to identify ancestral preadaptive behaviours that could have facilitated the eventual evolution of morality as we know it in the human line. Such behaviours need not be classified with respect to protomorality; the issue is simply whether an ancestral behaviour might have become useful to the evolutionary development of social control as physical and social environments changed, and biological evolution proceeded.

Chimpanzee cannibalism has been taken as a kind of a test case for the presence of something like 'norms' in another species. I avoided discussing this behaviour because I think such discussions are likely to remain inconclusive. **Thierry** is correct in relying on Kummer's interpretation that intragroup cannibalism is not responded to by chimpanzees in any special way, even though males may intervene to prevent one female from attacking another. In addition, Goodall (1982) has argued eloquently that social order among chimpanzees results from self-organizing forces involved with social dominance hierarchy, and not from anything like group identification of deviance as humans do this.

I would suggest that if chimpanzees do have the potential to agree that some type of behaviour is undesirable, and to do something about it as a large coalition, the problematic behaviour would not be cannibalism. It would be vigorous domination by alphas, when for some special reason this is widely and strongly resented by a large number of subordinates who happen to be assembled at one place. I emphasize that the chimpanzee group reactions described in the principal paper take place in the here and now, even though chimpanzees remember well their past political interactions. Even at Gombe, where the cannibalistic pattern was protracted, there was no such collective forum. The female predatory pair generally caught mothers with infants alone, so the males had little means of assessing the situation. This underlines the fact that some kind of language, with displacement in time and space, is essential to the development of a moral community of the human type. People have to be able to report the specifics of transgressions by deviants — particularly if the community is subject to constant fission and fusion, as nomadic bands are. And such reports, disseminated through gossip, involve sophisticated conceptualizations of right and wrong (Boehm, 1999b).

Thierry similarly suggests that individual mental representations lie at the base of group conceptualizations of deviance. As we experience morality today, there is little doubt that these are learned partly through socialization, partly by observing others, and partly through communication acts involving language — especially in gossiping. When a large chimpanzee group mobs a predator, or issues hostile vocalizations while on patrol, or threatens or attacks one alpha male candidate in order to support another, or collectively stops its alpha male from brutalizing a lower-ranking male as de Waal (1996) described for the captive group at Yerkes, we may assume some commonality of purpose. And even though it is a long way from such an immediate negative response to a set of shared moral values that consistently orients social control in a human group, and does so stably over generations, the pre-adaptive potential we see in the chimpanzee responses is suggestive.

Thierry seems to have misread my strong emphasis on the suppression of bullying behaviour in early human moral life, which was based on examining the Common Ancestral behavioural suite for pre-adaptations that might have led to specific types of moral proscription. He argues that because people in bands can avoid both conflicts and dominators by leaving the band, the suppression of bullies would not be particularly salient for such moral communities. However, there is a logical flaw here, for hunter-gatherers do not simply 'leave' their bands; they move from one band to another. A specific family can avoid a specific conflict by transferring, for some neighbouring band is likely to have enough resources to accommodate one more family. Such moves take place rather frequently, and are quite predictable after a homicide. However, if an entire band is being tyrannized there may not be a sufficient number of berths in the few nearby bands to accommodate ten or twenty families all at once. That may be why we have a number of reports of bands executing serious dominators (Boehm, 1993), rather than fleeing them.

I would agree that physical constraint, by itself, cannot explain the emergence of morality in human beings, and I assume that by morality, **Thierry** means the moral life as a whole, with its combination of proscriptions and prescriptions, punishments and rewards, ideals about altruism, cooperation, family life, indigenous moral philosophies, and so on. However, I would argue that social control based on threat of force (or actual force) is a prerequisite to this emergence. I say this because by themselves, prescriptions, rewards, exhortations to behave properly, and verbal attempts to foster peace, would not remove the problem of serious group-internal predators, some of whom may be sociopathic, or even psychotic. Unless this basic problem of predator-control is addressed, I do not see how the rest of moral behaviour could have developed. And even with the degree of moralistic assertiveness we see in extant bands when they become aroused, the social predators keep on coming.

Morality is a complicated package, and de Waal (1996) has presented a strong case for a peacemaking component which applies nicely to the Common Ancestor. I have suggested that our universally altruistic ideologies are another component, but this might be more difficult to relate to behaviours of apes. Another component is social control, which I have directly linked to ancestral potentialities. This type of collective behaviour, which is based on a whole complex of mental representations, can be either rehabilitative or punitive. To summarize, in my opinion it would be extremely difficult for peacemaking, or prescriptions in favour of cooperation, to do their work if serious acts of deviance were not being forcefully suppressed to prepare the way. That explains my emphasis on ancestral power coalitions that focus their disapproval on individuals.

I turn now to the comments of Irwin **Bernstein**, a laboratory primatologist who is well known not only for his identification of the control role and his work on status hierarchies (Bernstein, 1970; Erhardt and Bernstein, 1994), but more generally for his rigour as a scientist. **Bernstein** makes explicit a general methodology that I did not take space to describe, but can elaborate briefly. The moral origins analysis is based on interlocking triangulating hypotheses, and by the standards of laboratory science this work is speculative, indeed. My justification would be that questions of human origins are sufficiently compelling that scientific communities are willing to relax standards of falsifiability. (To phrase things more vernacularly, I can get away with pushing my evidence because the questions are so important.) Having said that, I would emphasize that parsimony principles definitely apply — an issue raised by **Dentan**. I have tried to keep things simple, and one way to do this was to look just at the pre-adaptations and then at the end product, and to concentrate on aspects of morality that had the most obvious precursors in a Common Ancestor.

I would agree with **Bernstein** that if one is to work with a scientifically flimsy explanatory structure, one must keep one's premises in order. One that **Bernstein** thinks is not in order is that primate alphas invariably dominate and bully. However, his assumption seems to be that we should employ strategic modelling (see Tooby and DeVore, 1987) and look at a wide range of primates, rather than focussing on hominoids that are closely related to humans on a molecular basis. I have preferred to go with a cladistic analysis limited to African based hominoids, so we are playing by different rules of triangulation. If I gave the impression that all primate alpha males behave just like chimpanzee or bonobo bullies, I did not mean to.

For me, the question was: Do the African-based hominoids I was dealing with have social dominance hierarchies, and are apes at the top in a position to despoil their inferiors in situations of feeding or sexual competition, or to otherwise control them in ways they are resistant to? I believe that a bullying style of dominance is exhibited by all three hominoids, even though the patterns vary: with humans and chimpanzees male applications of power can extend to homicide, whereas with bonobos it is both high-ranking males and females who bully the males and females below them, and serious physical conflict is less strongly expressed (see Kano, 1992; Wrangham and Peterson, 1996).

Because he is interested in the entire primate repertoire, **Bernstein** focusses upon the one-male group, specifically hamadryas baboons' harem structure (Kummer, 1971), which in its lack of male competitiveness is suggestive of human egalitarianism. **Bernstein** demonstrates that male–male dominance behaviours appear to be absent or muted, and following Kummer's interpretation, he points to prior possession of females as a context that emboldens subordinates, and pre-empts overt male competition. A further explanation might be that a male with a harem doesn't dare to compete for females straying from a different male's harem precisely because he is aware of the tendencies of his own females to stray: in effect, he could easily lose several of his own females in trying to gain one more. Both hypotheses suggest that dominance tendencies are present among the hamadryas, but are situationally neutralized. In other contexts, however, hamadryas males do behave as bullies. These baboon harem masters continuously chase and bite at their ever-straying females, to threaten them into staying with the harem, so there is plenty of male dominance over females.

Purely at the level of functional analogy, the hamadryas situation is rather similar to what happens in many human bands: dominance is largely neutralized among males, at the same time that males can be quite dominant over their females. However, the underlying mechanisms are far from homologous: the egalitarian-seeming lack of mate-competition of the hamadryas is the result of males fearing the attacks of other males or, possibly, fearing the loss of harem females. Human egalitarianism results from a large subordinate coalition's outlawing bullying behaviour as a matter of conscious policy.

In this context, **Bernstein** asks if hamadryas' respect for possession might be a sign of moral-type behaviour, and he answers his own question correctly in my view: there is no group consensus or means of enforcement by the entire group or by a large coalition, so there is no precursor to morality here. The baboon system is self-organizing, and judgmental coalitions are not involved. If I were including the hamadryas in my cladistic analysis, and there are very good reasons of molecular distance not to do so, I would rate them as fairly high on male dominance potential, even though male–male dominance behaviour is so heavily inhibited.

While we are speaking about potential, I emphasize that in the cladistic analysis I was dealing not only with observed natural behaviours, but with captive ones. Normally, wild behaviours are given priority in considering what is species specific, but my interest was in the behavioural potential of the Common Ancestor as this related to preadaptive possibilities for development of moral communities as environmental and social conditions changed. In this light, captive conditions are simply a rather extreme type of new environment, one that tweaks behavioural potential in directions we might otherwise not be aware of. It was particularly the behaviour of female captive chimpanzees that was of interest, but if the Common Ancestor is ratcheted back another two million years, gorillas figure importantly.

In fact, most of the behaviours I adduced as being shared by chimpanzees, bonobos, and humans are shared by gorillas as well (Boehm, 1999b). There is a closed group, and males stalk and kill other males (Wrangham, 1987). There is a social dominance hierarchy with alpha individuals ranking high above those who are low on the hierarchy. There is some defence of resources, if not necessarily of natural resources, for silverbacks defend their harems vigorously and sometimes lethally, while humans, bonobos, and chimpanzees all show signs of defensiveness about their natural resources. There is impartial conflict intervention, for silverback gorillas control female conflicts by means of pig-grunts, and there are coalitions, for blackback sons of silverbacks sometimes remain with the harem and assist their fathers in defending it. Furthermore, in captivity there was an episode in which several female gorillas who had been ruled by a smallish blackback rejected a silverback who was introduced and tried to take over. The females acted as a power coalition (de Waal, 1982), and the silverback had to be removed. This means that the potential for coalition formation is definitely present for both male and female gorillas (Boehm, 1999b), even though it is seldom exhibited under wild conditions. The fact that a female coalition became rebellious in captivity tells us that gorillas fit with the pattern of political pre-adaptation for egalitarianism.

These behaviours were all included in the three-species cladistic model in the principal paper, and they provided pre-adaptations important to the development of moral communities. With the addition of gorillas, the cladistic method becomes still more conservative, for it is all but unthinkable that a behaviour shared by four different hominoids would have been absent in their ancestor. I have brought in the gorilla data to bolster my response to **Bernstein**'s concern, about whether bullying behaviour can be assumed in our precursor. All four hominoids exhibit bullying domination tendencies — even though this may not be true of all primates that have alpha males.

Bernstein and **Knauft** are interested in the origins of the human family, and so am I. However, neither a four-species cladistic model nor a three-species one can specify anything homologous about ancestral 'family' arrangements. This is because the two Pan species have mother–offspring families, whereas gorillas and humans regularly include males in the equation. However, because the origin of the human family is such an important problem, let me speculate a little with the benefit of **Knauft**'s analysis.

Universal family institutions today are kept in place by moral rules and social control, and one might ask if precursors to such rules existed in the Common Ancestral behavioural suite. My answer is that no specific precursors are discernible. Indeed, the only ancestral behaviour that strikes me as presaging social control by groups is the work of coalitions to whittle away at alpha power. On this basis, the first moral proscriptions were against bullying behaviour, and were not directly relevant to the evolution of the human family.

However, once a social control methodology was in place, group members could have put it to new uses. As **Knauft** emphasized, and as I acknowledge in my book (Boehm, 1999b), both language and cultural capacity would have been important in bringing this about. As a more generalized capacity to solve social problems developed, any behaviour that seriously disrupted group life, and cooperative endeavours in particular, might have been sanctioned (see Boehm, 1982). Now, let us consider hunter-gatherer mating competition today.

The number one unsolved sociopolitical problem is homicide within the group (see Knauft, 1991), and most homicides are connected with mating competition. It seems likely that this problem has prevailed ever since human groups became egalitarian, which was likely to have turned such competition into more of a free-for-all. As moral communities, bands can try to head off these killings pre-emptively (Hoebel, 1954); but, because hunter-gatherers are so vehemently egalitarian, there is no authority figure to step into a hot conflict and stop it. One way to ameliorate this stubborn problem would be to create rules that would reduce mating competition.

As **Knauft** points out, the group-supported institution of marriage involved a revolutionary cultural curbing of very powerful human dispositions. Did humans modify a harem system that conceivably came down from a Common Ancestor, or did they improve upon a promiscuous system? Goodall (1986) also has pointed to chimpanzee consortships as possibly involving an evolutionary crossroad between promiscuous and pair-bonding systems. These may be unanswerable questions, but as people in bands began to focus their new methodology of social control on problems other than bullying, it is possible that they began to use moral persuasion and moral sanctions to reinforce whatever natural tendencies there were to form pair bonds. If this took place relatively late, when anatomically modern brains were available, I believe the benefits of stabilizing pair-bonding tendencies would have been perceptually obvious. Indeed, it is difficult to imagine the often reasonably harmonious, cooperative group life of extant bands, if all the males were continuously competing (as political equals) over breeding partners.

In a sense, with humans in bands, a hamadryas-like system of 'mutual respect' among male household heads was created — but it was based on very different mechanisms. With humans, the system is morally based, and it works far less smoothly than the hamadryas system because in bands we have frequent fights over women — in spite of moral codes that strongly try to uphold the family and (to varying degrees) disapprove of adultery. But our mating system does work, nonetheless.

To return to methodology, I agree with **Bernstein** that even though I am using the language of science, I cannot cope with the challenge of falsification. This type of test is simply out of the question for the more general hypotheses, but fortunately there is also the forum of relative plausibility. Such evaluation is useful, not only in selecting preliminary hypotheses in a laboratory setting where the eventual aim is to devise a falsifiable experiment, but also for creating human origins scenarios. Falsification is, in fact, possible with respect to supporting facts I use. Thus, I believe the Common Ancestor did have alpha bullies. This can be falsified by showing that today one of the four hominoids involved does not have bullies. My unfalsifiable hypothesis is that humans took subordinate limitation of alpha power to a new level when moral communities were formed. Perhaps the best evidence for this is that, in spite of egalitarian enculturation and political vigilance on the part of the rank and file, today's hunter-gatherers still have to use capital punishment occasionally to get rid of bullies.

Today, hunter-gatherer upstarts bent on domination sometimes manage to establish themselves in power positions, do so even though they know their groups share egalitarian feelings. When people in bands resort to execution of serious deviants, I have followed Durkheim (1933) in characterizing this as collective action. However, my thinking about 'groups' and collective responses in a moral community context has been called into question. Donald **Black** has written a lengthy and care-fully-documented critical commentary, with which I shall take serious issue. At the same time, I shall try to keep my own response from contributing to the kind of mentalist versus antimentalist or lumper versus splitter 'free-for-all' in which scholars argue polemically, and nothing really is resolved. In terms of the Endless Controversy remarks I made in opening my commentary on Sober and Wilson, **Black** and I could be at it for many years. But I shall seek, instead, a middle ground.

Black has deemed me just plain wrong in my conception of small moral communities and how they operate. I admire **Black**'s work, particularly his rigorous, ethologically oriented social–spatial approach to data analysis and his skilful use of ethnography, which is evident here. On that basis alone, I should be distressed to hear I am just plain wrong. However, I consider myself to be in excellent company, for my errors were mentioned in the same breath as those of Durkheim.

I believe that Durkheim was at least partly right, and very importantly right, about groups having social functions that involve emergent effects and, I would add, group intentions. There is little doubt that Durkheim idealized small scale moral systems with respect to their degree of collectiveness, over-emphasizing the unity of conscious and unconscious attitudes and motives among their members. Sorokin (1937) countered this excess by focussing on diversity within the group, while conflict theory, provided by Coser (1956), provided a further antidote. These antidotes were needed. I also agree that Durkheim over-characterized the negative side of social control as being punitive, or penal. Elsewhere (Boehm, 1999c), I have emphasized that there is an important, positive side to the morality of small groups, which prescribes rather than proscribes behaviour and sometimes provides tangible rewards (Boehm, 1999c). These become obvious with outright praise or awarding of special office, but more generally hunter-gatherers are highly aware of their personal reputations. They may be prone to take moral risks, but their behaviour tends to be heavily constrained by desire for a good social standing.

By my reading, much of hunter-gatherer social manipulation, which at first blush seems to be oriented to negative reinforcement, basically involves positive aims. Even when sanctioning becomes cruel, the intention often is rehabilitation of the deviant, and in such cases punitive behaviours are far from being mean-spirited, gratuitously 'expressive', or definitively rejective. To wit, deviants in bands are more frequently criticized, ridiculed, or ostracized, than beaten, ejected from the group, or executed (Boehm, 1993; 1999b). These first three sanctions are not meted out in the form of 'sentences'. Rather, they seem to be conditional: if a deviant gives up the deviant behaviour, then criticism, ridicule, or ostracism can soon be set aside (e.g., Turnbull, 1961; Briggs, 1970). In this light, Durkheim's 'penal' characterization must be taken with a large grain of salt; manipulation aimed at redemption is often the name of the sanctioning game.

What about emergent properties that **Black** denies? In my mind, there is little doubt that Durkheim was on to something significant when he characterized band or tribal groups as gossipy, morally vigilant, collectively prone to punish, and exhibiting a noteworthy capacity for agreement on moral issues. This was also my personal reaction when I lived for two years in an isolated, partly literate Serbian tribe in Southern Hercegovina, and I think my reactions would have been similar even if I had not read Durkheim (1933). However, my field impressions led me more to a middle ground. Serbs I studied did exhibit a notable capacity for agreement on abstract moral issues (Boehm, 1972; 1980), but their individual positions on concrete cases could vary wildly, and very expediently.

I never got to see the entire tribe (or even one of its half dozen small settlements) engaged in unanimous moralistic outrage that was acted upon assertively. Publicly uncovered ultimate transgressions were rare, and if the evidence was at all ambiguous, people tended to take sides, favouring clansmen or friends. However, one major transgression became circumstantially obvious, and over weeks it was discussed continuously until a consensus of guilty arrived. Because the honour of living persons is involved, I shall not go beyond this, but it was taken to be a case for the police so no local action resulted. There was also one well-remembered case earlier in this century that was acted upon by the small settlement in question, one the size of a band. This involved a man and a woman engaged in a close degree of incest, and all informants were emphatic that the local group properly ran them out of the tribe.

Black says that in small egalitarian societies individuals solve their own problems and groups seldom or never take action as groups. He is totally wrong about 'never' and errs seriously in drawing implications about 'seldom'. Although unanimous or nearly unanimous moral outrage may arise infrequently, members of bands or local tribal units understand their group's social and political dynamics well enough to predict this. If one's outraged group is on the verge of forming a solid coalition that will either engage in direct punishment or very aggressively insist upon reform, this is a major deterrent when one is attracted to some major type of deviance. For example, a flagrant instance of cheating on a hunter-gatherer meat-sharing system will meet with such outrage. Every socially conscious group member knows this.

Turnbull (1961) observed an instance of spontaneous and all but unanimous moralistic outrage among the Mbuti of Zaire. During a cooperative net hunt, one man surreptitiously moves his net forward in order to succeed better as a hunter. He is then discovered, and back in camp most of the group members become involved actively in accusing and sanctioning him. One man calls him no better than an animal, an insult that would be unlikely in the absence of strong group backing, and his allies make no move to defend him as he cries. A youth deliberately fails to offer him a seat, women and children subject him to verbal ridicule, and no one offers a word of support. A few hours later, things begin to return to normal. The culprit is not ejected from the group, nor is he likely to cheat again. Other bands behave similarly.

In this Mbuti case, I cannot be certain that the man's close relatives participated actively in these hostile actions, but the ethnographic description is rich and it is apparent that no one tries to defend him. I freely admit that examples of entire bands actively ganging up on and manipulating or punishing deviants are difficult to find. But the scarcity attests to the effectiveness of the small-group type of social control that Durkheim attempted to describe. To an individual contemplating an act of serious deviance, the spectre of an outraged group coming after him, with his own coalition partners actively joining in or at least standing aside, is terrifying.

Black is correct that moral affairs can be divisive, and this should be no surprise with a species that is given to conflict. Morality becomes just one more tool of political conflict within the group, and in this context it tends to be used expediently: rules that the entire group agrees upon in principle are applied opportunistically for political advantage. This expedient moralistic infighting obviously is not what I have in mind when I describe group sanctioning; entire bands can become morally outraged — and because deviants know this, it seldom happens.

Collective sanctioning by a moral community requires that the great majority of the local community be in agreement, and in my Montenegrin tribe, individuals who confided in me closely made it clear that they themselves discerned a moral community out there. This frightening, potentially very aggressive community of interest could indict them without trial, and then assign them a bad reputation or manipulate or punish them with no hope of appeal. When worried about their reputations, people seldom talked about the opinions of individuals or factions: it was always the selo (settlement) or pleme (tribe) they feared, as collective watchdogs. With respect to others who thought they were keeping their deviance a secret, a favourite saying was, 'selo zna . . .' 'The village knows . . .'. In this case, of course, the speaker is identifying with the watchdog community rather than feeling victimized by it.

In short, the indigenous actors, themselves, were 'collectivizing' their local communities both as they feared them and as they participated in them. In a sense, they were methodological collectivists, themselves. Collective interpretations applied to the scattered settlements of a few hundred, but also to the tribal community of 1,800 people. Both were seen as collective monitors that operated monolithically — even though people knew that moral opinion often was divided and could be distorted by expedient infighting. For the potential deviant, a highly investigative, judgmental, and potentially aggressive united moral community was a real spectre. In the mind of an innocent community member, there was a community-wide coalition available to help guard against predatory deviants. I am talking psychology here, and without it I think the full ethnographic understanding of moral communities would founder.

This microcosmic analysis leads to an important general point about egalitarian moral communities, and why they seldom are observed to unite and strongly assert themselves. For most citizens of a band or other small egalitarian local group, the very threat of such a reaction is sufficient to damp seriously deviant behaviours, or to ensure that people engage in them with a very low probability of discovery. The threat is kept alive by oral tradition accounts of prior discovered misdeeds, and people, being human, will miscalculate often enough to occasionally feed new anecdotes into this same oral tradition.

Let me summarize this important point about why unified group action is seldom reported — even though it is reported quite regularly. For most citizens of a band (or tribe), the very threat of provoking a concerted community reaction is enough to ensure that they either avoid serious acts of deviance or keep the probability of discovery very low. They can predict community reactions of outrage because in their oral tradition there are at least a few stories of serious deviance discovered. The result, overall, is a very significant degree of conformity, but also an occasional incidence of serious miscalculation or discovery due to bad luck. Discovery provokes a serious community reaction, and this, as seen above, feeds into the band's oral tradition. As a result, a little bit of drastic sanctioning by the entire group goes a long way with respect to deterrence.

In two years of field work, I may never have seen an entire group come down actively on a deviant, but I learned that a century earlier, before a centralized state was formed in Montenegro, tribes were meeting as assemblies of all the men to discuss any important matter that affected the tribe as a whole. These were mainly problems of alliancing, and of war and peace, and the intention was always to find a consensus (Boehm, 1983). I was told that assemblies would also try cases of treason: the penalty for such deviance was capital punishment (Boehm, 1986). This analogue to penal law may well have been stimulated by exposure to nearby state societies, but typical band or tribal consensus-seeking was used for the decision making.

Black's indictment of my overall approach is two-pronged. First, I would seem to be a methodological collectivist, apparently as bad as Durkheim (I cited Durkheim favourably in the first page of the principal paper), because I am imagining that bands are unanimous about moral sanctioning. Second, I am a mentalist who clutters up what could be a tidy, scientific structural analysis with 'psychology'. As made, the charges seem serious, for they are bolstered by ethnographic evidence. To refute them definitively, I shall devote some space to hunter-gatherer consensus seeking, which involves *conscious intentions* to create *group unity* in the face of a strongly divisive potential. Because this psychological process of consensus building can be applied to cases of social deviance, understanding the consensus process will be critical in answering both of **Black**'s charges.

When scholars criticize Durkheim's (1933) all but mystical fascination with the collective consciousness/conscience, many (like **Black**) are missing an important point. True, conflict is often handled by just the parties involved, but people in small groups can quickly arrive at strong and full agreement if an obvious problem seriously threatens everybody — be the problem ecological, political, or moral. This is not accomplished by taking a vote; in groups that are egalitarian, consensus-seeking is the normal mode of operation.

There is no reason to infuriate anti-methodological collectivists by calling this process a manifestation of something mysterious like a group mind at work. Anthropologists have sorted out the nuts and bolts of how groups arrive at consensus (see Boehm, 1983; 1996), and egalitarians sometimes must work very hard to set aside their differences. There is no mystery to this process. Divisiveness often exists, but usually — not always — the majority can persuade a minority to go along, in the name of unity of purpose and action.

This 'unity of purpose' is not just a theoretical construct set forth by a misguided psychologizing teleologist. Ethnographically it has psychological reality, for the people involved talk about achieving consensus as a desirable end, and actively try to facilitate it. This is apparent from the few rich descriptions we have of egalitarian decision meetings: the goal of finding unanimity by bringing minorities into line is mentioned explicitly (Boehm, 1983), and decision leaders, who act as catalysts, avoid taking positions until they know that a consensus is building (Boehm, 1996). Thus, if consensus in fact is achieved, collective action in this context is not merely collective — it is *purposefully* collective. To talk about intentions, you must engage with psychology, and **Black** thinks this does not fit with structural analysis. However, if you are studying humans in small bands, psychology can add a very important dimension to any type of explanation.

In studying band-level political process, there can be an important interplay between the structural approach emphasized by **Black**, and the psychological/collectivist approach discussed above. The latter becomes important when groups realize they share a problem and can best resolve it by acting together. The problem with monolithic applications of pure structuralism is that such approaches fail to account for these emergent aspects of behaviour. Often emergent effects can be observed, and measured, when an array of similar individual purposes is transformed into concerted action that is collective.

Methodological accessibility to group processes is facilitated when group members exhibit a conscious sense of solving a problem as a group, and understand the advantages of doing so. And obviously, a band's being purposefully united rather than divided has important behavioural consequences. For example, if it is able to reach a consensus, it may be able to defend itself against a serious military attack, or against a frightening deviant. By contrast, a cluster of independent individuals or divisive factions will be far more vulnerable.

The proclivity of hunter-gatherer bands to make important decisions by consensus is well documented, and this has been discussed in an evolutionary context (Knauft, 1991; Boehm, 1996). Bands (and also tribes, for they too are egalitarian) have patterned ways of trying to develop a consensus: in the face of an egalitarian refusal to allot any real authority to individuals, people gently help the process along. Most decisions are routine ones about migration strategies — but another kind of decision is what to do about a predatory deviant whose behaviour directly threatens everyone in the group, or seriously threatens shared moral sensibilities of the type that Durkheim recognized.

Before I go into further ethnographic detail about how bands (and tribes) seek a consensus, let us consider in the context of primate behaviour what De Waal (1996) calls social contagion. This is a special instance of what ethologists (see Goodall, 1986) refer to as social facilitation, and I believe that social psychologists are on the right track when they try to isolate for study emergent effects involved in, say, human mob behaviour. Under the right circumstances, people's reactions can become mutually and commonly reinforcing on an instantaneous basis, and I would challenge a methodological individualist who is actively caught in a street riot to think otherwise.

Some detailed ethological analysis is in order. Chimpanzees mostly act as individuals as they form fission–fusion groups to optimize individual foraging needs. However, when they go on patrol, their very body language bespeaks unity of purpose. They take turns in cautiously leading the group, scanning terrain, and scouting, and every member of the patrol suppresses his vocalizations. They collectively rush toward strangers if they believe them to be alone and vulnerable, and they engage in prolonged gang attacks when they catch one of these unfortunates (Goodall, 1986). Chimpanzees also startle all but instantly as groups, climbing trees so simultaneously that it is difficult to decide which one started it. In many other behaviours, one can see social facilitation at work (Goodall, 1986); this pertains to excitement over a good feeding site or to social reunions involving many individuals. It also can apply to meat possession, which sometimes leads all of the males to display simultaneously (Boehm, 1999b). Chimpanzees also spontaneously converge to mob predators like large pythons (Boehm, 1999b) or leopards (Byrne and Byrne, 1988).

There is nothing inevitable about these collective reactions. Like egalitarian humans, members of a chimpanzee community have no leader who can force them to follow a group strategy. They may take individualistic paths and flee a predator rather than mobbing it. Likewise, when a recidivist killer intimidates all the members of a human band, his victims may cope individually by behaving submissively and trying to keep their distance, or by individually leaving the group. However, if such a threat does not go away, and if there is no easy way to leave the group, people will talk very quietly about the intolerable tension and danger, and eventually, if a consensus has arrived, one of their number will step forward to assassinate the intimidator (Boehm, 1993). Less often, an entire band may execute the deviant with everyone participating (Lee, 1979).

Black seems to acknowledge collective action by bands only if it is decided upon by an 'assembly of the people', and indeed this is where consensus seeking becomes most obvious. This is particularly true of tribal societies — whose egalitarian orders are extremely similar to those of bands. They are larger than bands, and therefore it is more difficult to achieve a consensus without everyone's meeting. With the tense warfare decisions of tribesmen, it is fascinating to see how they overcome their own factionalism. The collectivism of their approach is tangible, for all the warriors assemble, they all have the right to speak, and debates can be prolonged as dissenting minorities are persuaded to change their minds for the good of the group. If I am a methodological collectivist for seeing things this way, so are the tribesmen, themselves (see Boehm, 1996). When one's subjects engage self-consciously in behaviours oriented to finding a single opinion and acting on it as a unified group, this gives special strength to anthropological theories that follow a Durkheimian bent.

Black was referring to bands when he claimed that their moral behaviour is seldom or never unified, so let us focus on how consensus seeking works for small groups of hunting nomads. Typical hunter-gatherers engage in a series of annual major migrations, staying together as multi-family units. They do so even though in many cases people could at least survive as members of individual families that went their own ways. The goals that drive this behaviour are to enjoy one another's company and to profit economically from cooperation, and sometimes, surely, to find collective security against enemies. Consensus-seeking is the methodology that enables them to make unanimous decisions that affect the common welfare, and the need to find unity obtains whether they assemble as a group to make a decision all at once, which they sometimes do, or gradually negotiate their decisions by interacting in smaller sub-groups (see Boehm, 1999b).

Silberbauer (1982) shows, for Kalahari foragers, that their consensual decisions are arrived at through a succession of discussions among sub-groups of the band which eventually lead to a sense of agreement and a common strategy for migration. The same gradual process, with constant bilateral negotiations taking place between family heads, is evident for tribal pastoral nomads who gradually move toward group agreement when it is necessary to move camp (Barth, 1961), so hunter-gatherers are not unique in this pattern. In both cases, the integrity of the group is at stake: individuals know that in some ways they might do better at subsistence by operating alone with their families or kin, but that way they lose the advantages of group life. These people know one another intimately, and they can tell when they have basically arrived at a consensus.

Keeping **Black**'s critique in mind, let us focus, now, on band-level consensus seeking strictly in the moral field. I emphasize that this standard methodology for egalitarian local groups applies to moral crises, as well as to ecological or political ones. One of the most stressful decisions a band can make is to physically eliminate a group member whose behaviour has become intolerable. A typical band approach is for the group to arrive very quietly at a consensus that supports elimination of the dangerous deviant, and for the executioner to be a kinsman of the intimidator so as to preclude his being killed in revenge (Boehm, 1993). The same applies to tribes.

Because **Black**'s indictment is stated in such absolute terms, I shall make the case in some detail that band-level capital punishment is a form of penal collective behaviour even when just a single individual performs the execution. Let us begin with the more obvious case of executions that actively involve an entire local group. Lee (1979) tells how the males of a Kalahari hunting band ganged up to kill a threatening deviant, and how, at the end, the outraged females came in to inflict their own wounds, making it unanimous. This demonstrates that foragers can, in fact, assemble in one place and follow a single course of action in the field of social control. In this case there was an assembly of the people, and they made their decision, and enacted it, all at once. **Black** says that basically this doesn't happen.

Lee's account is not unique, especially if we consider tribal groups that are equally egalitarian. Among the ethnohistorical Montenegrin Serbs I studied, there was an episode reminiscent of the famous short story by Shirley Jackson, *The Lottery*. At the instigation of an Orthodox priest, a young man and woman were 'buried beneath the accursed stone heap' because of sexual impropriety (Boehm, 1986). The entire village participated, and in this feuding society, the chances of retaliation were nullified because it was impossible to target a killer.

A few instances of unanimous band-level execution might not be enough to falsify **Black**'s contention. But what about the case in which an entire band delegates a member to act on its behalf? Let me offer some examples that I can document. In an Inuit band, a man manages to intimidate other group members, and begins to behave despotically (Boehm, 1993). A solution is to do away with him, but the only way to arrive at a consensus is through carefully concealed gossip. Once this takes place, there remains the practical problem of subsequent retaliation for his death. Two solutions are possible, one of which was illustrated above with the entire band attacking the deviant simultaneously. The alternative is to assign a kin-related executioner who knows he has the group's backing.

I submit that such executions are collective, even though the act is delegated. A group consensus not only makes this action collective, but makes it morally proper. If group members failed to agree about the need for capital punishment, but one person went ahead and did the deed on his own with only partial group backing, we would have a morally ambiguous situation and a divided group, and a collectivist interpretation would founder. However, when the band reaches a consensus and leaves the deviant looking like a porcupine bristling with arrows, or when a band reaches a consensus and someone is appointed executioner, a collectivist approach provides real explanatory power.

In making the case that delegated executioners are supported by a moral consensus, I must bring in some psychology. In effect, the group's agreeing on execution of a deviant involves a special rule for breaking rules, for generally homicide within a band is morally abhorred. Thus, the executioner has to feel that his action will be approved by at least the great majority of group members; otherwise, instead of being treated as a hero, he will be treated as a serious deviant. I submit that if one looks to psychological variables, and particularly to human intentions, a far richer and more accurate analysis of moral behaviour can be made than in a strictly structural one that fails to deal with group reactions as emergent effects.

Personally, I do not see **Black**'s structural type of analysis as being at odds with an approach that looks to hunter-gatherer group dynamics, including cognitive aspects of how groups arrive at common policies, and also emotions like fear, hostility, and moral outrage. I do agree that it is easier to mobilize a group when there is great social distance between the sanctioners and the sanctioned, and that such distance is found in stratified societies rather than egalitarian societies. However, the methodological 'purity' **Black** insists upon does not make sense to me. It is true that from a structural standpoint, social distance within a band is minimal rather than great: not only is the band politically egalitarian, which reduces social distance as **Black** defines it, but strong bonding among non-relatives and still stronger bonding among kinsmen reduces it further. But in addition to social distance, there is another type of distance (see Boehm, 1985) that might be called psychological or moral. In a band, the distance that promotes a consensual finding against a serious deviant is moral and psychological, not social as **Black** uses this term for structural purposes, and this means that psychology is crucial to an adequate analysis of social control in small-scale egalitarian societies.

For **Black**, an obviously devoted structuralist, the locus of morality is in social structure. For me, the locus of morality is in socially interacting judgmental individuals who key their sanctioning to group standards, and in processes by which they decide to exert social manipulation, be this negative or positive as discussed above. These processes are embedded in social structures of various types, but the key word here is 'moral community' (see Boehm, 1999b). Moral communities may remain structurally latent most of the time, but when individual moral stances become aligned, we have a moral consensus — and a structurally-identifiable group that is capable of making a serious deviant look like a porcupine. Such a consensus must be explained psychologically, and its social force can be formidable.

I realize that structural analysis offers a heady kind of neatness and purity that suggests great scientific potency, and sometimes leads its adherents to think they have discovered the one true method, and not just an approach that is humbly acknowledged to be useful and combinable with other approaches. Anthropologists have suffered recurrently from this scientific–potency illusion, for example, in following charismatic structuralists such as Radcliffe-Brown (1965) and Levi-Strauss (1953). Other explanations have gained a similar vogue, as when Malinowski's (1939) holistic/functionalist approach was lionized before it, like excessively optimistic versions of structuralism, was rejected or replaced. For some reason, scholars who eclectically study ongoing cultural *processes* and the patterns of behaviour they generate have failed to attract this type of following. Perhaps this is for the best.

The end of **Black**'s extensive commentary suggests that because morality can be reduced to structural relations, moral components exist in any species that engages in conflict. In a sense, this is a totally ethological approach — in the old-fashioned sense of ethology taken as the study of overt behaviour and such behaviour alone, with no concern for intentions or feelings. Fortunately, the majority of ethologists who deal with higher primates have abandoned this antiseptic approach: they now are more comfortable with explanations that deal not just in behaviours, but in intentions where this makes sense.

I believe that at least certain precursors of morality could be studied from such a stark ethological perspective, for one could describe a fair amount of the Common Ancestral behavioural suite I reconstructed in strictly behaviourist terms. However, to be powerful at the level of explanation, the study of morality must deal with feelings and intentions, with social dynamics, and with any emergent properties that emerge when entire groups become outraged, or moralistically concerned, and activate decisive sanctioning. Just the fact that individuals sense this judgmental collective presence, and modify their actions according to their predictions of group reactions, makes psychological analysis imperative.

Black's commentary has made me think a bit about what I am doing analytically. One of the most fascinating things about humans, as self-interested, conscious, and often disputatious beings, is the way they can arrive at a common way of viewing a shared problem, and agree as a group on how to solve it. Obviously, in taking interest in such processes I am breaking two of **Black**'s rules: one violation apparently involves something like methodological collectivism; the other involves a mentalistic, psychological approach. In the second context I would also be criticized by Marvin Harris, who is well known for his aggressive disdain of 'mentalistic' explanations (see Boehm, 1988). However, I believe that a highly mentalistic species deserves a mentalistic analysis — or else the job is only partly done.

Black's predilection for structural hegemony leads to some bizarre conclusions. For example, universal morality is a myth because the social structure of conflict is not uniform across societies. Personally, I believe that moral universals can, in fact, be identified — at varying degrees of specificity. They simply cross-cut the structural diversity **Black** emphasizes. For anthropologists who wish to prove something universal, the incest taboo has been a holy grail of sorts. However, I think I can propose better candidates for moral universality: one would be cheating in a context of group cooperation, for free-rider control would appear to be universal among hunter-gatherers (Boehm, 1999b) and, more generally, all human societies tend to be cooperative to some degree, and therefore leery of free-riders.

A major candidate I have emphasized would be the abuse of power (see Boehm, 1999b). Every human group has some kind of leadership role, and, even though local definitions of what degree of authority is politically legitimate may vary wildly, if a leader seriously oversteps what is locally acceptable, then his group will become morally outraged. This applies to an Inuit shaman who turns into an intimidator, and it also applied to Senator Joe McCarthy in a large democracy in which consensus is replaced by majority rule. It even applied to Hitler, when his military policies began to seriously fail, though in a police state assassination may be the only possible route.

It is true, as **Black** nicely demonstrates, that morality often is suborned to individual interests, and becomes an expedient tool in personal or factional disputes. Such behaviour is all too noticeable, and is continuously encountered by an ethnographer who is privy to gossip sessions. These opportunistic uses of morality tend to obscure the more basic types of moral behaviour that Durkheim and I are talking about, in which group members very sincerely seek a consensus so that they may act decisively against deviants who threaten their collective interests. Unfortunately, **Black** seems to have focussed just upon self help and the opportunistic infighting that involves expedient moral justifications and is readily susceptible to a non-collectivist type of analysis that serves the cause of structural explanation, or pure sociology. The alternative is to focus on relatively infrequent but functionally very important group actions that involve such infighting being set aside, but this requires that one collectivize and psychologize. I do this quite proudly, in the interest of explaining moral behaviour when bands do, in fact, bear down unanimously on deviants.

Within its limited sphere, I acknowledge that pure sociology is potent, and **Black** is a master at structural analysis. But there is more, far more, to moral behaviour than the structural dimensions that **Black** restricts himself to. One very interesting thing about the moral behaviour of bands is its divisive side effects, which **Black** describes effectively. But another is its main thrust, which is collective, and this is the part that **Black** denies on a 'seldom or never' basis. Although this main thrust most definitely involves consensus seeking by entire bands, there is no reason to bring in something as mysterious as a 'group mind'. Non-literate egalitarians know exactly what they are doing when they seek a consensus, and their aim is to achieve a unified program of action even if there exists some dissension. Sometimes public opinion is already unified, and they have no problem. Sometimes they must be adept at patching together their differences. Sometimes, the effort fails and the band remains divided, with no decision and no collective action. But in studying small-scale egalitarian societies, analysts must be willing to identify all three of these outcomes — not just the last one.

Let us turn to conflict intervention and consider the degree to which, in hunting bands, this behaviour can be viewed as individualistic or collective. **Black** is correct when he states that in bands authority is poorly developed and therefore individuals are not in a good position to intervene. When they do try, they may merely beg the disputants to desist, or, at their own peril and with modest chances of success, they may try to intervene physically. However, **Black** goes much too far in suggesting that entire groups seldom or never intervene actively in conflicts.

I believe that individuals who try to intervene impartially in active conflicts assume they will receive group support, just as executioners do. To intervene, there is no time to arrive at a band consensus, either through gossiping in subgroups or by meeting as an assembly. The conflict requires immediate intervention to damp escalation, for there is the spectre of homicide, and following it, great tension and loss of personnel if the killer chooses to flee. Usually the killer does flee to avoid retaliation, but in either event group members are concerned about the disruption of group life.

I have suggested that one of the striking things about the way these small moral communities handle conflict, is that frequently they seem to 'decriminalize' it: instead of seeking out a culprit, or holding the disputants morally liable for disturbing the peace, the intention of other group members seems to be to split the disputants' differences in a way that reduces the chances of further conflict. In this way, conflict resolution efforts can be morally neutral, and I suggest that this impartial strategy is understood intuitively by band members. In a sense, this morally neutral approach can be likened to what individual chimpanzees, gorillas, and bonobos do when they impartially apply force to stop fights.

We have been speaking of individual interventions with implicit group backing. Is moralistic conflict resolution ever actively collective? For *individual* deviants, we do have a number of unanimously collective executions on record (Boehm, 1993), along with other unambiguous instances of bands ganging up (e.g., Turnbull, 1961). Group efforts to manage dyadic conflicts seem to be more subtle. When Eskimos stage drum-song contests (see Hoebel, 1954), the two parties known to be at serious odds are persuaded to compose mutually vilifying songs. This persuasion is based on strong community agreement that the conflict should be ameliorated before it turns homicidal, and this amounts to a group tradition that depends on consensus.

In a drum song, poetically expressed strings of insults are publicly iterated with the entire band as audience. This community is used to making migration and other decisions by consensus, and it applies the same strategy to this public contest, which definitely involves an assembly of all the people. At the end of the contest, the 'group' formally judges one disputant to be the victor. Traditional rules of the game dictate that once the contest is over, the two parties will set the conflict aside. This actually seems to work, and I submit that such contests involve a popular assembly. We are not talking about moral culpability here, or about sanctioning. Indeed, these issues are sidestepped as the group judges the contestants on the basic of their poetic and theatrical abilities. But there is a unified moral community at work, nonetheless, and its objective is to control conflict or aggressive behaviour. This is also the object in most cases of sanctioning.

In dealing with **Black**'s commentary, I have matched his attention to ethnographic detail in suggesting that the explanation of social control and its role in the management of conflict must look beyond individual or factional interests to account for consensus seeking that leads to actively collectivized sanctioning. This includes executions, delegated group executions, and group or group-backed efforts to intervene in conflicts. Although a consensus can be readily reached without a public meeting, sometimes even tiny bands may assemble to solve problems related to social control or conflict management. In short, Durkheim had something very important to say — even though he overstated his case. His collectivistic type of interpretation holds for extant hunter-gatherers, and for their precursors in the Upper Palaeolithic.

Let me turn to **Krebs**' commentary, which raises issues about natural selection mechanisms. He suggests that morality involves a willingness to help others, as well as an ability to work in a dominant coalition that can crack down on bullies and other free riders, and he has problems with how the altruistic dispositions could have been selected. So do many other scholars interested in evolutionary biology, but I can supply some tentative answers. In responding to **Krebs** I must reiterate that even though I have emphasized the role of dominant collectivized power in moral behaviour, I do not think that morality can be reduced just to manipulative or coercive power of moral communities over deviants. There are also the important issues of cooperation and altruism, and how these behaviours are moralistically promoted on a conscious basis.

Elsewhere, I have suggested two evolutionary routes to helping behaviour that is not socially coerced or reducible to selfish goals of individuals. One is group selection, and for humans (and humans alone), I have summarized my hypothesis in my commentary on Sober and Wilson (see also Boehm, 1997b; 1999a; 1999b; 1999c). A second route would involve individually maladaptive side-effects of nepotism that benefit non-relatives (Boehm, 1981; 1999c; see also Simon, 1990). The idea is that human nepotistic aid is channelled through the proximate mechanism of social bondedness, and in small bands, even non-relatives tend to be strongly bonded.

Helping one's non-relatives unilaterally once in a while would constitute a modest drain on a 'nepotistic gene' that reaps enormous (and frequent) parental-investment rewards, and my thought is that perhaps natural selection simply isn't efficient enough to eliminate such giveaways. Keep in mind that everyone in a band is likely to be a strong nepotist, and that, furthermore, many of these unilateral helping behaviours directed at non-kin will be returned over time just because all nepotists are vulnerable to this same individually maladaptive side effect. In a sense, I am adding pleiotropic genetic effects (see Boehm, 1981; 1999c) to Alexander's (1987) biocultural analysis.

The kind of generalized reciprocity networks suggested by Alexander (1987) and discussed by **Krebs** make sense to me, but I feel that they do not fully explain what is happening ethnographically. Either group selection, or perhaps these individually maladaptive extensions of nepotism, could strongly enhance the explanation of cooperative and caretaking systems that are found among hunter-gatherers. Both hypotheses may require further work, but at least they do not require that one explain psychological manifestations of altruism in terms of a total absence of altruism as this is genetically defined. My intuitions tell me that there is likely to be some genetic basis for psychological altruism, and it is apparent that a large number of sociobiologists, including Alexander and many others, have rather arbitrarily called off the search for such mechanisms (see also the Sober and Wilson, 2000).

Let me follow up on these intuitions briefly. If one begins with common sense, rather than with selection mechanisms, there does seem to be a prominent 'nice' side to moral behaviour: on the group's part, there are calls for altruism and cooperation as part of the moral code (see Campbell, 1975). This is a human universal apparently, and I have some trouble imagining that an animal entirely devoid of genetically altruistic impulses would think up such a code in the first place. I also have trouble imagining that Alexander's genetically selfish/neptotistic animal would be as responsive to this type of prescription as humans seem to be. Common sense is always suspect, and scientists delight in developing explanations that defy it. However, above I proposed two selection scenarios that might help to validate such 'sensible' intuitions. Hopefully, a few scholars in biology, more sophisticated than I in modelling mechanisms of natural selection, may be persuaded to explore these matters further.

Krebs asks where the dispositions I identified in the Common Ancestor came from, originally, and I admit to being curious about this ultimate question. At the same time, I had my hands full trying to derive egalitarian behaviour from Common Ancestral precursors without worrying about how the Ancestor acquired them. I shall not try to answer his question here, but it would be a legitimate one for a knowledgeable primatologist like Irwin Bernstein, who is interested in strategic modelling.

I have no argument with **Krebs'** contention that out of innate selfishness, humans behave only as morally as they must, for even if my scenario for group selection in the Upper Palaeolithic were to hold, human nature would contain only a modest altruistic component. In my view, this would merely set us up for some ambivalence, and in effect the end of **Krebs'** commentary focusses on innately structured ambivalences as part of the human condition. My main problem is with **Krebs'** total reliance on Alexander's general reciprocity model. It is a good model, but I think that it may be possible to combine generalized reciprocity models with a somewhat different view of human nature, one that acknowledges the possibility of some modest degree of group-selected genetic altruism — or at least some spillovers of generous behaviour that is firmly based in nepotism. This proposal flies in the face of sociobiological orthodoxy, but I think a more open-minded approach to the question of altruistic behaviours having some genetic basis could make social cooperation far easier to explain.

With respect to **Dentan**'s comments, I am in strong agreement that much of social control among hunter-gatherers is rehabilitative, rather than seriously punitive or eliminative. In closely linking the principal paper's restricted analysis to Common Ancestral behaviours, and in concentrating on applications of power, I may have given the impression that punishment was predominantly on my mind. In that ancestor I emphasized both power moves by hostile coalitions and forceful individuals as conflict managers interested in peacemaking. Particularly in the second case, the efforts can be interpreted as being rehabilitative.

With respect to hunter-gatherers, let us return briefly to the Mbuti. They definitely behaved punitively toward their cheater, calling him an animal and subjecting him to ridicule. Yet they did not expel him from the group, and there was no question of execution — even though more serious cases of cheating can have such a result in other band societies. Basically, he was roundly chastised and then permitted to re-enter the group as someone who hopefully had learned his lesson (see Turnbull, 1961). This one case would suggest that punishment and rehabilitation are readily combined, and it can be generalized.

Dentan pays obeisance to simplicity principles in restating my theory from a sociocentric standpoint — a perspective that carefully leaves human nature out of the equation. My whole point was to include human nature in the equation: hence, the discussion of ancestral precursors. Human nature is not an easy variable to work with, and the fact is that many cultural anthropologists, especially those of Postmodernist persuasion, are strongly biassed against even considering it. However, if you are interested in moral origins, it is useful and probably necessary to consider human nature.

Dentan also suggests that variance in violence should be the focus, rather than its universality. I would disagree, for I think both are equally important. Again, the problem seems to be with human nature, which by way of definition prepares us to learn certain behaviours more readily than others. Whether the universal potential to fight as groups is expressed or remains latent depends on stimulation from the natural and political environments, and also on cultural habit. In answering **Knauft**, I have discussed this matter at some length. Here I will add that generally the human potential for conflict is offset by the human potential for peacemaking: the two are likely to have co-evolved. However, we seem to be far, far better at keeping the peace within our groups than *between* them.

We need to be equally concerned with diversity, and with patterns that appear to be widespread, or universal. With intergroup violence being as widespread as it is among extant hunter-gatherers, we need to think simultaneously about environmental stimulation (in the form of scarcity) and local traditions, but also about a human nature that makes people prone to seek lethal retaliation for prior homicides. It may well be this vindictive propensity that helps to keep many local traditions group-conflictive even after environmental stimulation has abated.

Like other animals, humans do exhibit behavioural *tendencies* that are, in biological jargon, 'species-specific.' Given our formidable behavioural flexibility, any behaviour that seems to be reasonably widespread should be of interest. If it is universal, or even very nearly so, it is of very special interest. Although I would agree that some universals proposed by anthropologists are so general as to be mere 'categories of behaviour,' I do believe I have been reasonably specific in looking to moral universals such as condemnation of cheating and abuse of power. I also would include moral outrage, also sanctions like criticism, ridicule, and ostracism, as probable universals or near-universals. Their predictable emergence, in various types of human groups and on different continents, demands evolutionary explanation.

I chose to treat **Dentan**'s commentary last because the issue of human nature is a controversial one for many anthropologists and philosophers. I would like to close by saying that I hope the question of moral origins, and related questions about psychological altruism and how it might be selected genetically, will help to awaken a fresh interest in human nature — a nature that is not that dissimilar from the nature of the Common Ancestor I have reconstructed and discussed in its political dimension. With respect to moral origins, I have tried to provide the beginning and end of an evolutionary story, and **Knauft** has supplied us with some provocative hypotheses about what happened in between, and when this might have occurred. In *Hierarchy in the Forest*, I have supplied a few of my own. It is to be hoped that others will join us in this endeavour, for it goes to the heart of what it is to be human.

References

Alexander, Richard D. (1987), T*he Biology of Moral Systems* (New York: Aldine de Gruyter).
Arnhart, Larry (1998), *Darwinian Natural Right: The Biological Ethics of Human Nature* (Albany: State University of New York Press).
Balikci, Asen (1970), *The Netsilik Eskimo* (Prospect Heights, IL: Waveland).
Barth, Fredrik (1961), *Nomads of South Persia: The Basseri Tribe of the Kamseh Confederacy* (Boston: Little Brown).
Bernstein, I.S. (1970), 'Primate status hierarchies', in *Primate Behavior: Developments in Field and Laboratory Research, Volume I*, ed. L.A. Rosenblum (New York: Academic Press).
Bidney, David (1947), 'Human nature and the cultural process', *American Anthropologist*, **49**, pp. 375–99.
Boehm, Christopher (1972), 'Montenegrin Ethical Values', PhD Dissertation, Harvard University.
Boehm, Christopher (1980), 'Exposing the moral self in Montenegro: The use of natural definitions in keeping ethnography descriptive', *American Ethnologist*, **7**, pp. 1–26.
Boehm, Christopher (1981), 'Parasitic selection and group selection: A study of conflict interference in Rhesus and Japanese Macaque monkeys', in *Primate Behavior and Sociobiology*, ed. A.B. Chiarelli and R.S. Corruccini (Berlin: Springer-Verlag.)
Boehm, Christopher (1982), 'The evolutionary development of morality as an effect of dominance behavior and conflict interference', *Journal of Social and Biological Sciences*, **5**, pp. 413–22.
Boehm, Christopher (1983), *Montenegrin Social Organization and Values* (New York: AMS Press).
Boehm, Christopher (1984), 'Can hierarchy and egalitarianism both be ascribed to the same causal forces?', *Politics and the Life Sciences*, **1**, pp. 34–7.
Boehm, Christopher (1985), 'Execution within the clan as an extreme form of ostracism', *Social Science Information*, **24**, pp. 309–21.
Boehm, Christopher (1986), *Blood Revenge: The Enactment and Management of Conflict in Montenegro and Other Tribal Societies* (Philadelphia: University of Pennsylvania Press).
Boehm, Christopher (1988), 'Review of, Death, Sex and Fertility: Population Regulation in Pre-industrial and Developing Societies, by Marvin Harris and Eric B. Ross' (New York: Columbia University Press), (1987), *Population and Environment*, **10**, pp. 135–8.

Boehm, Christopher (1989), 'Ambivalence and compromise in human nature', *American Anthropologist*, **91**, pp. 921–39.

Boehm, Christopher (1992), 'Segmentary warfare and the management of conflict: Comparison of East African chimpanzees and patrilineal–patrilocal humans', in eds., *Coalitions and Alliances in Humans and Other Animals*, ed. A.H. Harcourt and F.B.M. de Waal (Oxford: Oxford University Press).

Boehm, Christopher (1993), 'Egalitarian society and reverse dominance hierarchy', *Current Anthropology*, **34**, pp. 227–54.

Boehm, Christopher (1996), 'Emergency decisions, cultural selection mechanics and group selection', *Current Anthropology*, **37**, pp. 763–93.

Boehm, Christopher (1997a), 'Egalitarian behaviour and the evolution of political intelligence', in *Machiavellian Intelligence II*, ed. D. Byrne and A. Whiten (Cambridge: Cambridge University Press).

Boehm, Christopher (1997b), 'Impact of the human egalitarian syndrome on Darwinian selection mechanics', *American Naturalist*, **150**, pp. 100–21.

Boehm, Christopher (1999a), 'Forager hierarchies and their effect on human behavioral dispositions', in *Hierarchies in Action* [pages forthcoming], ed. Michael Dietz (Carbondale, IL: Southern Illinois University Press).

Boehm, Christopher (1999b), *Hierarchy in the Forest* (Cambridge: Harvard University Press).

Boehm, Christopher (1999c), 'The natural selection of altruistic traits', *Human Nature, Special Issue on Group Selection* Christopher Boehm, guest editor.

Boinski, Sue (1994), 'Affiliation patterns among male Costa Rican squirrel monkeys', *Behaviour*, **130**, pp. 191–209.

Briggs, Jean L. (1970), *Never in Anger* (Cambridge, MA: Harvard University Press).

Brown, Donald (1991), *Human Universals* (New York: McGraw-Hill).

Byrne, R.W., and Byrne, J.M. (1988), 'Leopard killers of Mahale', *Natural History*, **97**, pp. 22–6.

Campbell, Donald T. (1965), 'Ethnocentric and other altruistic motives', in *Nebraska Symposium on Motivation*, ed. David Levine (Lincoln: University of Nebraska Press).

Campbell, Donald T. (1972), 'On the genetics of altruism and the counter-hedonic component of human culture', *Journal of Social Issues*, **282**, pp. 1–37.

Campbell, Donald T. (1975), 'On the conflicts between biological and social evolution and between psychology and moral tradition', *American Psychologist*, **30**, pp. 1103–26.

Cashdan, Elizabeth A. (1983), 'Territoriality among human foragers: Ecological models and an application to four bushman groups', *Current Anthropology*, **24**, pp. 47–66.

Corning, Peter (1984), T*he Synergism Hypothesis: A Theory of Progressive Evolution* (New York: McGraw-Hill).

Coser, Louis (1956), *The Functions of Social Conflict* (New York: Free Press).

Dunbar, Robin (1996), *Grooming, Gossip and the Evolution of Language* (London: Faber and Faber).

Durham, William (1991), *Coevolution: Genes, Culture and Human Diversity* (Stanford, CA: Stanford University Press).

Durkheim, Emile (1933), *The Division of Labor in Society* (New York: Free Press).

Dyson-Hudson, Rada, and Smith, Eric A. (1978), 'Human territoriality: An ecological reassessment', *American Anthropologist*, **80**, pp. 21–41.

Ember, Carol (1978), 'Myths about hunter-gatherers', *Ethnology*, **17**, pp. 439–48.

Ember, Carol and Ember, Melvin (1992), 'Resource unpredictability, mistrust, and war: A cross-cultural study', *Journal of Conflict Resolution*, **36**, pp. 242–62.

Erdal, David, and Whiten, Andrew (1994), 'On human egalitarianism: An evolutionary product of Machiavellian status escalation?', *Current Anthropology*, **35**, pp. 175–84.

Erdal, David, and Whiten, Andrew (1996), 'Egalitarianism and Machiavellian intelligence in human evolution', in *Modelling the Early Human Mind*, ed. P. Mellars and K. Gibson (Cambridge: MacDonald Institute for Archeological Research).

Erhardt, Carolyn, and Irwin S. Bernstein, Irwin S. (1994), 'Conflict intervention behaviour by adult male macaques: Structural and functional aspects', in *Coalitions and Alliances in Humans and Other Animals*, ed. A.H. Harcourt and F.B.M. de Waal (Oxford: Oxford University Press).

Flack, Jessica C. and de Waal, Frans B.M. (2000), '"Any Animal Whatever": Darwinian building blocks of morality in monkeys and apes,' *Journal of Consciousness Studies*, **7** (1–2), pp. 1–29.

Foley, Robert (1995), *Humans Before Humanity* (Cambridge, MA: Blackwell).

Gardner, Peter (1991), 'Foragers' pursuit of individual autonomy', *Current Anthropology*, **32**, pp. 543–58.

Goodall, Jane (1979), 'Life and death at Gombe', *National Geographic*, **155**, pp. 592–622.

Goodall, Jane (1982), 'Order without law', *Journal of Social and Biological Structures*, **5**, pp. 349–52.

Goodall, Jane (1986), *The Chimpanzees of Gombe* (Cambridge, MA: Harvard University Press).

Gould, Richard A. (1982), 'To have and have not: The ecology of sharing among hunter-gatherers', in *Resource Managers: North American and Australian Hunter-Gatherers*, ed. N.M. Williams and E.S. Hunn (Boulder, CO: Westview).

Hoebel, E. Adamson (1954), *The Law of Primitive Man: A Study in Comparative Legal Dynamics* (Cambridge, MA: Harvard University Press).

Kano, T. (1992), *The Last Ape: Pygmy Chimpanzee Behaviour and Ecology* (Stanford: Stanford University Press).

Kelly, Robert L. (1995), *The Foraging Spectrum: Diversity in Hunter-Gatherer Lifeways* (Washington: Smithsonian Institution Press).

Knauft, Bruce B. (1987), 'Reconsidering violence in simple human societies: Homicide among the Gebusi of New Guinea', *Current Anthropology*, **28**, pp. 457–500.

Knauft, Bruce B. (1991), 'Violence and sociality in human evolution', *Current Anthropology*, **32**, pp. 391–428.

Kummer, Hans (1971), *Primate Societies: Group Techniques of Ecological Adaptation* (Chicago, IL: Aldine de Gruyter).

Lee, Richard B. (1979), *The !Kung San: Men, Women, and Work in a Foraging Society* (Cambridge: Cambridge University Press).

Levi-Strauss, Claude (1953), 'Social structure', in *Anthropology Today*, ed. A.L. Kroeber (Chicago: University of Chicago Press).

Lieberman, Philip (1998), *Eve Spoke: Human Language and Human Evolution* (New York: Norton).

Malinowski, Bronislaw (1939), 'The group and the individual in functional analysis', *American Journal of Sociology*, **44**, pp. 938–64.

Masters, Roger D. (1989), *The Nature of Politics* (New Haven: Yale University Press).

Morgan, Lewis H. (1901), *League of the Ho-De-No-Sau-Nee or Iroquois. Volume I* (New York: Burt Franklin).

Nishida, Toshisada (1979), 'The social structure of chimpanzees of the Mahale Mountains', in *The Great Apes*, ed. D.A. Hamburg and E.R. McCown (Menlo Park, CA: Benjamin/Cummings).

Potts, Richard (1996), *Humanity's Descent: The Consequences of Ecological Instability* (New York: Avon).

Radcliffe-Brown, A.R. (1965), *Structure and Function in Primitive Society* (New York: Free Press).

Rodseth, Lars (1991), 'Response to Bruce Knauft, 1991, Violence and Sociality in Human Evolution', *Current Anthropology*, **32**, pp. 391–428.

Service, Elman R. (1962), *Primitive Social Organization: An Evolutionary Perspective* (New York: Random House).

Service, Elman R. (1975), *Origin of the State and Civilization: The Process of Cultural Evolution* (New York: Norton).

Silberbauer, George (1982), 'Political process in G/Wi bands', in *Politics and History in Band Societies*, ed. E. Leacock and R. Lee (Cambridge: Cambridge University Press).

Simon, Herbert (1990), 'A mechanism for social selection and successful altruism', *Science*, **250**, pp. 1665–8.

Sober, Elliott and Wilson, David Sloan (2000), 'Summary of "Unto Others: The evolution and psychology of unselfish behaviour"', *Journal of Consciousness Studies*, **7** (1–2), pp. 185–206.

Somit, Albert, ed. (1976), *Biology and Politics* (The Hague: Mouton).

Sorokin, Ptirim A. (1937), *Social and Cultural Dynamics* (New York: American Book Company).

Strier, Karen B. (1994), 'Brotherhoods among Atelins: Kinship, affiliation, and competition', *Behavior*, **130**, pp. 151–67.

Tiger, Lionel (1979), *Optimism: The Biology of Hope* (New York: Simon and Schuster).

Tiger, Lionel (1987), *The Manufacture of Evil: Ethics, Evolution and the Industrial System* (New York: Harper and Row).

Tiger, Lionel, and Fox, Robin (1971), *The Imperial Animal* (New York: Delta).

De Tocqueville, Alexis (1994), *Democracy in America* (New York: Knopf).

Tooby, John, and DeVore, Irven (1987), 'The reconstruction of hominid behavioural evolution through strategic modelling', in *The Evolution of Human Behavior: Primate Models*, ed. W.G. Kinzey (Albany: SUNY Press).

Turnbull, Colin M. (1961), *The Forest People: A Study of the Pygmies of the Congo* (New York: Simon and Schuster).

Vehrencamp, Sandra. L. (1983), 'A model for the evolution of despotic versus egalitarian societies', *Animal Behavior*, **31**, pp. 667–82.

de Waal, Frans (1982), *Chimpanzee Politics: Power and Sex among Apes* (New York: Harper and Row).

de Waal, Frans (1996), *Good Natured: The Origins of Right and Wrong in Humans and Other Animals* (Cambridge, MS: Harvard University Press).

Weatherford, Jack M. (1988), *Indian Givers: How the Indians of the Americas Transformed the World* (New York: Crown).

Weber, Max (1947), *The Theory of Social and Economic Organization* Edited by Talcott Parsons. (New York: Free Press).

Westermarck, Edward (1894), *The History of Human Marriage* (New York: MacMillan).

Wiessner, Polly (1996), 'Leveling the hunter: Constraints on the status quest in foraging societies', in *Food and the Status Quest: An Interdisciplinary Perspective*, ed. P. Wiessner and W. Schiefenhove (Oxford: Berghahn).

Woodburn, James (1982), 'Egalitarian societies', *Man*, **17**, pp. 431–51.

Wrangham, Richard (1987), 'African apes: The significance of African apes for reconstructing social evolution', in *The Evolution of Human Behavior: Primate Models*, ed. W.G. Kinzey (Albany: SUNY Press).

Wrangham, Richard, and Peterson, Dale (1996), *Demonic Males: Apes and the Origins of Human Violence* (Boston: Houghton-Mifflin).

Elliott Sober and David Sloan Wilson

Summary of: 'Unto Others

The Evolution and Psychology of Unselfish Behavior'

The hypothesis of group selection fell victim to a seemingly devastating critique in 1960s evolutionary biology. In Unto Others *(1998), we argue to the contrary, that group selection is a conceptually coherent and empirically well documented cause of evolution. We suggest, in addition, that it has been especially important in human evolution. In the second part of* Unto Others, *we consider the issue of psychological egoism and altruism — do human beings have ultimate motives concerning the well-being of others? We argue that previous psychological and philosophical work on this question has been inconclusive. We propose an evolutionary argument for the claim that human beings have altruistic ultimate motives.*

I: Introduction

Part One of *Unto Others* (Sober & Wilson, 1998) addresses the biological question of whether evolutionary altruism exists in nature and, if so, how it should be explained. Part Two concerns the psychological question of whether any of our ultimate motives involves an irreducible concern for the welfare of others. Both questions are descriptive, not normative. And neither, on the surface, even mentions the topic of morality. How, then, do these evolutionary and psychological matters bear on issues about morality? And what relevance do these descriptive questions have for normative ethical questions? These are problems we'll postpone discussing until we have outlined the main points we develop in *Unto Others*.

A behaviour is said to be altruistic in the evolutionary sense of that term if it involves a fitness cost to the donor and confers a fitness benefit on the recipient. A mindless organism can be an evolutionary altruist. It is important to recognize that the costs and benefits that evolutionary altruism involves come in the currency of reproductive success. If we give you a package of contraceptives as a gift, this won't be evolutionarily altruistic if the gift fails to enhance your reproductive success. And parents who take care of their children are not evolutionarily altruistic if they rear more children to adulthood than do parents who neglect their children. Evolutionary altruism is not the same as helping.

The concept of psychological altruism is, in a sense, the mirror image of the evolutionary concept. Evolutionary altruism describes the fitness effects of a behaviour, not the thoughts or feelings, if any, that prompt individuals to produce those behaviours. In contrast, psychological altruism concerns the motives that cause a behavior, not its actual effects. If your treatment of others is prompted by your having an ultimate, noninstrumental concern for their welfare, this says nothing as to whether your actions will in fact be beneficial. Similarly, if you act only to benefit yourself, it is a further question what effect your actions will have on others. Psychological egoists who help because this makes them feel good may make the world a better place. And psychological altruists who are misguided, or whose efforts miscarry, can make the world worse.

Although the two concepts of altruism are distinct, they often are run together. People sometimes conclude that if genuine evolutionary altruism does not exist in nature, then it would be mere wishful thinking to hold that psychological altruism exists in human nature. The inference does not follow.

II: Evolutionary Altruism — Part One of *Unto Others*

1. The problem of evolutionary altruism and the critique of group selection in the 1960s

Evolutionary altruism poses a fundamental problem for the theory of natural selection. By definition, altruists have lower fitness than the selfish individuals with whom they interact. It therefore seems inevitable that natural selection should eliminate altruistic behaviour, just as it eliminates other traits that diminish an individual's fitness. Darwin saw this point, but he also thought that he saw genuinely altruistic characteristics in nature. The barbed stinger of a honey bee causes the bee to die when it stings an intruder to the nest. And numerous species of social insects include individual workers who are sterile. In both cases, the trait is good for the group though deleterious for the individuals who have it. In addition to these examples from nonhuman species, Darwin thought that human moralities exhibit striking examples of evolutionary altruism. In *The Descent of Man*, Darwin (1871) discusses the behaviour of courageous men who risk their lives to defend their tribes when a war occurs. Darwin hypothesized that these characteristics cannot be explained by the usual process of natural selection in which individuals compete with other individuals in the same group. This led him to advance the hypothesis of *group selection*. Barbed stingers, sterile castes, and human morality evolved because groups competed against other groups. Evolutionarily selfish traits evolve if selection occurs exclusively at the individual level. Group selection makes the evolution of altruism possible.

Although Darwin invoked the hypothesis of group selection only a few times, his successors were less abstemious. Group selection became an important hypothesis in the evolutionary biologist's toolkit during the heyday of the Modern Synthesis (c. 1930–1960). Biologists invoked individual selection to explain some traits, such as sharp teeth and immunity to disease; they invoked group selection to explain others, such as pecking order and the existence of genetic variation within species. Biologists simply used the concept that seemed appropriate. Discussion of putative group adaptations were not grounded in mathematical models of the group selection process, which hardly existed. Nor did naturalists usually feel the need to supply a mathematical model to support the claim that this or that phenotype evolved by individual selection.

All this changed in the 1960s when the hypothesis of group selection was vigorously criticized. It was attacked not just for making claims that are empirically false, but for being conceptually confused. The most influential of these critiques was George C. Williams' 1966 book, *Adaptation and Natural Selection*. Williams argued that traits don't evolve because they help groups; and even the idea that they evolve because they benefit individual organisms isn't quite right. Williams proposed that the right view is that traits evolve because they promote the replication of genes.

Williams' book, like much of the literature of that period, exhibits an ambivalent attitude towards the idea of group selection. Williams was consistently against the hypothesis; what he was ambivalent about was the grounds on which he thought the hypothesis should be rejected. Some of Williams' book deploys empirical arguments against group selection. For example, he argues that individual selection and group selection make different predictions about the sex ratio (the proportion of males and females) that should be found in a population; he claimed that the observations are squarely on the side of individual selection. But a substantial part of Williams' book advances somewhat *a priori* arguments against group selection. An example is his contention that the gene is the unit of selection because genes persist through many generations, whereas groups, organisms, and gene complexes are evanescent. Another example is his contention that group selection hypotheses are less parsimonious than hypotheses of individual selection, and so should be rejected on that basis.

The attack on group selection in the 1960s occurred at the same time that new mathematical models made it seem that the hypothesis of group selection was superfluous. W.D. Hamilton published an enormously influential paper in 1964, which begins with the claim that the classical notion of Darwinian fitness — an organism's prospects of reproductive success — can explain virtually none of the helping behaviour we see in nature. It can explain parental care, but when individuals help individuals who are not their offspring, a new concept of fitness is needed to explain why. This led Hamilton to introduce the mathematical concept of *inclusive fitness*. The point of this concept was to show how helping a relative and helping one's offspring can be brought under the same theoretical umbrella — both evolve because they enhance the donor's inclusive fitness. Many biologists concluded that helping behaviour directed at relatives is therefore an instance of selfishness, not altruism. Helping offspring and helping kin are both in one's genetic self-interest, because both allow copies of one's genes to make their way into the next generation. Behaviours that earlier seemed instances of altruism now seemed to be instances of genetic selfishness. The traits that Darwin invoked the hypothesis of group selection to explain apparently can be explained by 'kin selection' (the term that Maynard Smith, 1964, suggested for the process that Hamilton described), which was interpreted as an instance of individual selection. Group selection wasn't needed as a hypothesis; it was 'unparsimonious'.

Another mathematical development that pushed group selection further into the shadows was evolutionary game theory. Maynard Smith, one of the main architects of evolutionary game theory, wanted to provide a sane alternative to sloppy group selection thinking. Konrad Lorenz and others had suggested, for example, that animals restrain themselves in intraspecific combat because this is good for the species. Maynard Smith and Price (1973) developed their game of hawks versus doves to show how restraint in combat can result from purely individual selection. Each individual in the population competes with one other individual, chosen at random, to determine which will obtain some fitness benefit. Each plays either the hawk strategy of all-out fighting or the dove strategy of engaging in restrained and brief aggression. When a hawk fights a hawk, one of them gets the prize, but each stands a good chance of serious injury or death. When a hawk fights a dove, the hawk wins the prize and the dove beats a hasty retreat, thus avoiding serious injury. And when two doves fight, the battle is over quickly; there is a winner and a loser, but neither gets hurt. In this model, which trait does better depends on which trait is common and which is rare. If hawks are very common, a dove will do better than the average hawk — the average hawk gets injured a lot, but the dove does not. On the other hand, if doves are very common, a hawk will do better than the average dove. The evolutionary result is a polymorphism. Neither trait is driven to extinction; both are represented in the population. What Lorenz tried to explain by invoking the good of the species, Maynard Smith and Price proposed to explain purely in terms of individual advantage. Just as was true in the case of Hamilton's work on inclusive fitness, the hypothesis of group selection appeared superfluous. You don't *need* the hypothesis to explain what you observe. Altruism is only an appearance. Dovishness isn't present because it helps the group; the trait is maintained in the population because individual doves gain an advantage from not fighting to the death.

Another apparent nail in the coffin of group selection was Maynard Smith's (1964) 'haystack model' of group selection. Maynard Smith considered the hypothetical situation in which field mice live in haystacks. The process begins by fertilized females each finding their own haystacks. Each gives birth to a set of offspring who then reproduce among themselves, brothers and sisters mating with each other. After that, the haystack holds together for another generation, with first cousins mating with first cousins. Each haystack contains a group of mice founded by a single female that sticks together for some number of generations. At a certain point, all the mice come out of their haystacks, mate at random, and then individual fertilized females go off to found their own groups in new haystacks. Maynard Smith analyzed this process mathematically and concluded that altruism can't evolve by group selection. Group selection is an inherently weak force, unable to overcome the countervailing and stronger force of individual selection, which promotes the evolution of selfishness.

The net effect of the critique of group selection in the 1960s was that the existence of adaptations that evolve because they benefit the group was dismissed from serious consideration in biology. The lesson was that the hypothesis of group selection doesn't have to be considered as an empirical possibility when the question is raised as to why this or that trait evolved. You know *in advance* that group selection is not the explanation. Only those who cling to the illusion that nature is cuddly and hospitable could take the hypothesis of group adaptation seriously.

2. Conceptual arguments against group selection

In *Unto Others*, we argue that this seemingly devastating critique of group selection completely missed the mark. The purely conceptual arguments against group selection show nothing. And the more empirical arguments also are flawed.

Let us grant that genes — not organisms or groups of organisms — are the *units of replication*. By this we mean that they are the devices that insure heredity. Offspring resemble parents because genes are passed from the latter to the former. However, this establishes nothing about why the adaptations found in nature have evolved.

Presumably, even if the gene is the unit of replication, it still can be true that some genes evolve because they code for traits that benefit individuals — this is why sharp teeth and immunity from disease evolve. But the same point holds for groups: even if the gene is the unit of replication, it remains to be decided whether some genes evolve because they code for traits that benefit groups. The fact that genes are *replicators* is entirely irrelevant to the units of *selection* problem.

The idea that group selection should be rejected because it is unparsimonious also fails to pass muster. Here's an example of how the argument is deployed, in Williams (1966), in Dawkins (1976), and in many other places. Why do crows exhibit sentinel behaviour? Group selection was sometimes invoked to explain this as an instance of altruism. A crow that sights an approaching predator and issues a warning cry places itself at risk by attracting the predator's attention; in addition, the sentinel confers a benefit on the other crows in the group by alerting them to danger. Interpreted in this way, a group selection explanation may seem plausible. However, an alternative possibility is that the sentinel behaviour is not really altruistic at all. Perhaps the sentinel cry is difficult for the predator to locate, and maybe the cry sends the other crows in the group into a frenzy of activity, thus permitting the sentinel to beat a safe retreat. If the behaviour is selfish, no group selection explanation is needed. At this point, one might think that two empirical hypotheses have been presented and that observations are needed to test which is better supported. However, the style of parsimony argument advanced in the anti-group selection literature concludes without further ado that the group selection explanation should be rejected, just because an individual selection explanation has been *imagined*. Data aren't needed, because parsimony answers our question. In *Unto Others*, we argue that this is a spurious application of the principle of parsimony. Parsimony is a guide to how observations should be interpreted; it is not a substitute for performing observational tests.

There is another fallacy that has played a central role in the group selection debate. The fallacy involves defining 'individual selection' so that any trait that evolves because of selection is automatically said to be due to individual selection; the hypothesis that traits might evolve by group selection thus becomes a definitional impossibility. In *Unto Others*, we call this *the averaging fallacy*. To explain how the fallacy works, let's begin with the standard representation of fitness payoffs to altruistic (A) and selfish (S) individuals when they interact in groups of size two. The argument would not be different if we considered larger groups. When two individuals interact, the payoff to the row player depends on whether he is A or S and on whether the person he interacts with is A or S (b is the benefit to the recipient and c is the cost to the altruistic A-type's behaviour):

| | | the other player is | |
		A	S
fitness of a	A	$x + b - c$	$x - c$
player who is	S	$x + b$	x

What is the average fitness of A individuals? It will be an average — an altruist has a certain probability (*p*) of being paired with another altruist, and the complementary probability (*1-p*) of being paired with a selfish individual. Likewise, a selfish individual has a certain probability of being paired with an altruist (*q*) and the complementary probability (*1-q*) of being paired with another selfish individual. Thus, the fitnesses of the two traits are

$$w(A) = p(x+b-c) + (1-p)(x-c) = pb + x - c$$
$$w(S) = (q)(x+b) + (1-q)(x) = qb + x.$$

By definition, the trait with the higher average fitness will increase in frequency, if natural selection governs the evolutionary process. The criterion for which trait evolves is therefore:

(1) $w(A) > w(S)$ if and only if $p-q > c/b$.

The quantity (*p-q*), we emphasize, is the difference between two probabilities:

(*p-q*) = the probability that an altruist has of interacting with another altruist minus the probability that a selfish individual has of interacting with an altruist.

This difference represents the *correlation* of the two traits.

Two consequences of proposition (1) are worth noting:

(2)   When like interacts with like, $w(A) > w(S)$ if and only if $b > c$.

(3)   When individuals interact at random, $w(A) > w(S)$ if and only if $0 > c/b$.

Proposition (2) identifies the case most favourable for the evolution of A — as long as the benefit to the recipient is greater than the cost incurred by the donor, A will evolve. Proposition (3), on the other hand, describes a situation in which A cannot evolve, as long as *c* and *b* are both greater than zero.

This analysis of the evolutionary consequences of the payoffs stipulated for traits A and S is not controversial. The fallacy arises when it is proposed that the selfish trait is the trait that has the higher average fitness, and that individual selection is the process that causes selfishness, so defined, to evolve. The effect of this proposal is that A is said to be selfish in situation (2) if $b > c$, while S is labelled selfish in situation (3), if $b,c > 0$. Selfishness is equated with 'what evolves', and individual selection is, by definition, the selection process that makes selfishness evolve. This framework entails that altruism cannot evolve by natural selection and that group selection cannot exist. We reject this definitional framework because it fails to do justice to the biological problem that Darwin and his successors were addressing. The question of what types of adaptations are found in nature is *empirical*. If altruism and group adaptations do not exist, this must be demonstrated by observation. The real question cannot be settled by this semantic sleight of hand.

Our proposal is to define altruism and selfishness by the payoff matrix given above. What is true, by definition, is that altruists are less fit than selfish individuals *in the same group*. If *b* and *c* are both positive, then $x+b > x-c$. However, nothing follows from this as to whether altruists have lower fitness when one averages *across all groups*. This will be not be the case in the circumstance described in proposition (2), if $b > c$, but will be the case in the situation described in (3), if $b,c > 0$.

Given the payoffs described, groups vary in fitness; the average fitness in AA groups is *(x+b-c)*, the average fitness in AS groups is *(x + [b-c]/2)*, and the average fitness in SS groups is *x*. Group selection favours altruism; groups do better the more altruists they contain. Individual selection, on the other hand, favours selfishness. There is no individual selection within homogeneous groups; the only individual (i.e., within-group) selection that occurs is in groups that are AS. Within such groups, selfishness outcompetes altruism. Here group and individual selection are opposing forces; which force is stronger determines whether altruism increases or declines in frequency in the ensemble of groups. Just as Darwin conjectured, it takes group selection for altruism to evolve.

Our proposal — that altruism and selfishness should be defined by the payoff matrix described above, and that group selection involves selection among groups, whereas individual selection involves selection within groups — is not something we invented, but reflects a long-standing set of practices in biology. Fitness averaged across groups is a criterion for which trait evolves. However, if one additionally wants to know whether group selection is part of the process, one must decompose this average by making within-group and between-group fitness comparisons.

This perspective on what altruism and group selection mean undermines the pervasive opinion that kin selection and game-theoretic interactions are alternatives to group selection. It also allows us to re-evaluate Hamilton's claim that classical Darwinian fitness cannot explain the evolution of helping behaviour (other than that of parental care) and that the concept of inclusive fitness is needed. The inclusive fitness of altruism reflects the cost to the donor and the benefit to the recipient, the latter weighed by the coefficient of relatedness (r) that donor bears to recipient:

$$I(A) = x - c + br.$$

The inclusive fitness of a selfish individual is

$$I(S) = x.$$

Notice that I(A) does not reflect the possibility that the altruist in question may receive a donation from another altruist, and the same is true of I(S) — it fails to reflect the possibility that a selfish individual may receive a donation from an altruist. The reason for these omissions is that we are assuming that altruism is *rare*. In any event, from these two inclusive fitnesses, we obtain 'Hamilton's rule' for the evolution of altruism:

(4)   *r>c/b*.

We hope the reader notices a resemblance between propositions (1) and (4). The coefficient of relatedness is a way of expressing the correlation of interactors. Contrary to Hamilton (1964), the concept of inclusive fitness is *not* needed to describe the circumstances in which altruism will evolve.

The coefficient of relatedness '*r*' is relevant to the evolution of altruism because related individuals tend to resemble each other. What is crucial for the evolution of altruism is that altruists tend to interact with altruists. This can occur because relatives tend to interact with each other, or because unrelated individuals who resemble each other tend to interact. The natural conclusion to draw is that kin selection is a kind of group selection, in which the groups are composed of relatives. When an altruistic individual helps a related individual who is selfish, the donor still has a lower fitness than the recipient. The fact that they are related does not cancel this fundamental fact. *Within* a group of relatives, altruists are less fit than selfish individuals. It is only because of selection *among* groups that altruism can evolve. This, by the way, is the interpretation that Hamilton (1975) himself embraced about his own work, but his changed interpretation apparently has not been heard by many of his disciples.

Similar conclusions need to be drawn about game theory. Perhaps the most famous study in evolutionary game theory is the set of simulations carried out by Axelrod (1984). Axelrod had various game theorists suggest strategies that individuals might follow in repeated interactions. Individuals pair up at random and then behave altruistically or selfishly towards each other on each of several interactions. The payoffs that come from each interaction are the ones described before. However, the situation is more complex because there are many strategies that individuals might follow. Some strategies are *unconditional* — for example, an individual might act selfishly on every move (ALLS) or it might act altruistically on every move. In addition, there are many *conditional* strategies, according to which a player's action at one time depends on what has happened earlier in his interactions with the other player. Axelrod found that the strategy suggested by Anatol Rappaport of Tit-for-Tat (TFT) did better than many more selfish strategies. TFT is a strategy of *reciprocity*. A TFT player begins by acting altruistically and thereafter does whatever the other player did on the previous move. Two TFT players act altruistically towards each other on every move; if there are n moves in the game, each obtains a total score of $n(x-b+c)$. When TFT plays ALLS, the TFT player acts altruistically on the first move and then shifts to selfishness thereafter; if there are n interactions, TFT receives $(x-c) + (n-1)x = (nx-c)$ in its interaction with ALLS, who receives $(x+b) + (n-1)x$. Finally, if two ALLS players interact, each receives nx.

It is perfectly true, as a biographical matter, that Maynard Smith developed evolutionary game theory as an alternative to the hypothesis of group selection. However, the theory he described in fact involves group selection. If TFT competes with ALLS, there is group selection in which groups are formed at random and the groups are of size 2. Groups do better the more TFTers they contain. There is individual selection within mixed groups, in which TFT does worse than ALLS. TFT is able to evolve only because group selection favouring TFT overcomes the opposing force of individual (within-group) selection, which favours ALLS.

3. Empirical arguments against group selection

Williams (1966) proposed that sex ratio provides an empirical test of group selection. If sex ratio evolves by individual selection, then a roughly 1:1 ratio should be present. On the other hand, if sex ratio evolves by group selection, a female-biased sex ratio will evolve if this ratio helps the group to maximize its productivity. Williams then claims that the sex ratios found in nature are almost all close to even. He concludes that the case against group selection, with respect to this trait at least, is closed.

A year later, Hamilton (1967) reported that female-biased sex ratios are abundant. One might expect that the evolution community would have greeted Hamilton's report as providing powerful evidence in favour of group selection. This is exactly what did not occur. Although Hamilton described his own explanation of the evolution of 'extraordinary sex ratios' as involving group selection, this is not how most other biologists interpreted it. Williams' sound reasoning that individual selection should produce an even sex ratio traces back to a model first informally proposed by R.A. Fisher (1930). Fisher assumed that parents produce a generation of offspring; these offspring then mate with each other at random, thus producing the grandoffspring of the original parents. If the offspring generation is predominately male, then a parent does best by producing all daughters; if the offspring generation is predominately female, the parent does best by producing all sons. Selection favours parents who produce the minority sex, and the population evolves towards an even sex ratio as a result. Hamilton introduced a change in assumptions. He considered the example of parasitic wasps who lay their eggs in hosts. One or more fertilized females lays eggs in a host; the offspring of these original foundresses mate with each other, after which they disperse to find new hosts and the cycle starts anew. The important point about Hamilton's model is that offspring in different hosts don't mate with each other.

Williams observed, correctly, that the way for a group to maximize its productivity is for it to have the smallest number of males that is necessary to insure that all females are fertilized. Group selection therefore favours a female-biased sex ratio, and this in fact is what Hamilton's model explains. The wasps in a host form a group, and groups with a female-biased sex ratio are more productive than groups in which the sex ratio is even. This is how Hamilton (1967, footnote 43) interprets his model, but most of his readers apparently did not. Rather, they construed Hamilton's model as describing individual selection; the reason is that Hamilton analyzed his model by calculating what the 'unbeatable strategy' is — that is, the strategy whose fitness is greater than the alternatives. This is the sex ratio strategy that will evolve. To automatically equate the unbeatable strategy with 'what evolves by individual selection' is to commit the averaging fallacy. Instead of considering what goes on within hosts as an instance of individual selection and differences among hosts as reflecting the action of group selection, the mistake is to meld these two processes together to yield a single summary statistic, which reflects the fitnesses of strategies averaged across groups. There is nothing wrong with obtaining this average if one merely wishes to say what trait will evolve. However, if the goal, additionally, is to say whether group selection is in part responsible for the evolutionary outcome, one can't use a framework in which what evolves is automatically equated with pure individual selection.

The other empirical argument we mentioned before, which was thought to tell against the hypothesis of group selection, is Maynard Smith's (1964) haystack model. It is a little odd to call this argument 'empirical', since it did not involve the gathering of data. Rather, the argument was 'theoretical', based on the analysis of a hypothetical model. In any event, let's consider how Maynard Smith managed to reach the conclusion that group selection is a weak force, unequal to the task of overcoming the opposing force of individual selection. The answer is that Maynard Smith simply *stipulated* that the within-haystack, individual selection part of his process was as powerful as it could possibly be. He *assumes without argument* that altruism is driven to extinction in all haystacks in which it is mixed with selfishness; the only way that altruism can survive in a haystack is by being in a haystack that is 100 per cent altruistic. We do not dispute that, as a matter of definition, altruism must *decline* in frequency in all mixed haystacks. But the idea that it must *decline to zero* in all such haystacks is *not* a matter of definition. In effect, Maynard Smith explored a worse-case scenario for group selection. This tells us nothing as to whether altruism can evolve by group selection. Twenty years later, one of us (DSW) explored the question in a more general setting. The result is that altruism can evolve by group selection for a reasonable range of parameter values. The haystack model is not the stake through the heart of group selection that it was thought to be.

4. Multilevel selection theory is pluralistic

It is one thing to undermine fallacious arguments against group selection. It is something quite different to show that group selection has actually occurred and that it has been an important factor in the evolution of some traits. We attempt to do both in *Unto Others*. Sex ratio evolution is an especially well documented trait that has been influenced by group selection. But there are others — the evolution of reduced virulence in disease organisms, for example. Rather than discussing other examples, we want to make some general comments about the overall theory we are proposing.

First, our claim is not that *all* sex ratios in *all* populations are group adaptations. As Fisher argued, even sex ratios are plausibly regarded as individual adaptations. And as for the female-biased sex ratios found in nature, our claim is not that group selection was the *only* factor influencing their evolution. We do not claim that these groups have the smallest number of males consistent with all the females being fertilized. Rather, we claim that the biased sex ratios that evolve are *compromises* between the simultaneous and opposite influences of group and individual selection. Group selection rarely, if ever, occurs without individual selection occurring as well.

The more general point we want to emphasize is that hypotheses of group selection need to be evaluated on a trait-by-trait and a lineage-by-lineage basis. Group selection influenced sex ratio in some species, but not in others. And the fact that group selection did not influence sex ratio in human beings, for example, leaves open the question of whether group selection has been an important influence on other human traits. Unlike the monolithic theory of the selfish gene, which claims that *all* traits in *all* lineages evolved for the good of the genes, the theory we advocate, *multilevel selection theory,* is pluralistic. Different traits evolved because of different combinations of causes.

5. Group selection and human evolution

In *Unto Others*, we develop the conjecture that group selection was a strong force in human evolution. Group selection includes, but is not confined to, direct intergroup competition such as warfare. But, just as individual plants can compete with each other in virtue of the desert conditions in which they live (some being more drought-resistant than others), so groups can compete with each other without directly interacting (e.g., by some groups fostering co-operation more than others). In addition, cultural variation in addition to genetic variation can provide the mechanisms for phenotypic variation and heritability at the group level (see also Boyd and Richerson, 1985).

As noted earlier, the evolution of altruism depends on altruists interacting preferentially with each other. Kin selection is a powerful idea because interaction among kin is a pervasive pattern across many plant and animal groups. However, in many organisms, including especially human beings, individuals *choose* the individuals with whom they interact. If altruists seek out other altruists, this promotes the evolution of altruism. Although kin selection is a kind of group selection, there can be group selection that isn't kin selection; this, we suspect, is especially important in the case of human evolution. However, it isn't *uniquely* human — for example, even so-called lower vertebrates such as guppies can choose the social partners with which they interact.

An additional factor that helps altruism to evolve, which may be uniquely human, is the existence of cultural norms that impose social controls. Consider a very costly act, such as donating ten per cent of your food to the community. Since this act is very costly, a very strong degree of correlation among interactors will be needed to get it to evolve. However, suppose you live in a society in which individuals who make the donation are rewarded, and those who do not are punished. The act of donation has been transformed. It is no longer altruistic to make the donation, but selfish. Individuals in your group who donate do better than individuals who do not. However, it would be wrong to conclude from this that the existence of social controls make the hypothesis of group selection unnecessary. For where did the existence and enforcement of the social sanctions come from? Why do some individuals enforce the penalty for nondonation? This costs them something. A free-rider could enjoy the benefits without paying the costs of having a norm of donation enforced. Enforcing the requirement of donation is altruistic, even if donation is no longer altruistic. But notice that the cost of being an enforcer may be slight. It may not cost you anything like ten per cent of your food supply to help enforce the norm of donation. This means that the degree of correlation among interactors needed to get *this* altruistic behaviour to evolve is much less.

We believe that this argument may explain how altruistic behaviours were able to evolve in the genetically heterogeneous groups in which our ancestors lived. Human societies, both ancient and modern, are nowhere near as genetically uniform as bee hives and ant colonies. How, then, did co-operative behaviour manage to evolve in them? Human beings, we believe, did something that no other species was able to do. Social norms convert highly altruistic traits into traits that are selfish. And enforcing a social norm can involve a smaller cost than the required behaviour would have imposed if there were no norms. Social norms allow social organization to evolve by reducing its costs. Here again, it is important to recognize that culture allows a form of selection to occur whose elements may be found in the absence of culture. Bees 'police' the behaviour of other bees. What is uniquely human is the harnessing of socially shared values.

In addition to these rather 'theoretical' considerations, *Unto Others* also presents some observations that support the hypothesis that human beings are a group selected species. We randomly sampled twenty-five societies from the Human Relations Area File, an anthropological database, consulting what the files say about social norms. The actual contents of these norms vary enormously across our sample — for example, some societies encourage innovation in dress, while others demand uniformity. In spite of this diversity, cultural norms almost always require individuals to avoid conflict with each other and to behave benevolently towards fellow group members. Such constraints are rarely present with respect to outsiders, however. It also was striking how closely individuals can monitor the behaviour of group members in most traditional societies. Equally impressive is the emphasis on egalitarianism (among males — not, apparently, between males and females) found in many traditional societies; the norm was not that there should be complete equality, but that inequalities are permitted only when they enhance group functioning.

In addition to this survey data, we also describe a 'smoking gun' of cultural group selection — the conflict between the Nuer and Dinka tribes in East Africa. This conflict has been studied extensively by anthropologists for most of this century. The Nuer have gradually eroded the territory and resources of the Dinka, owing to the Nuer's superior group organization. The transformation was largely underwritten by people in Dinka villages defecting to the Nuers and being absorbed into their culture. We conjecture that this example has countless counterparts in the human past, and that the process of cultural group selection that it exemplifies has been an important influence on cultural change.

We think that Part I of *Unto Others* provides a solid foundation for the theory of group selection and that we have presented several well-documented cases of group selection in nonhuman species. Our discussion of human group selection is more tentative, but nonetheless we are prepared to claim that human beings have been strongly influenced by group selection processes.

III: Psychological Altruism — Part Two of *Unto Others*

Psychological egoism is a theory that claims that all of our ultimate desires are self-directed. Whenever we want others to do well (or badly), we have these other-directed desires only instrumentally; we care about what happens to others only because we think that the welfare of others has ramifications for ourselves. Egoism has exerted a powerful influence in the social sciences and has made large inroads in the thinking of ordinary people. In Part Two of *Unto Others*, we review the philosophical and psychological arguments that have been developed about egoism, both *pro* and *con*. We contend that these arguments are inconclusive. A new approach is needed; in Chapter 10, we present an evolutionary argument for thinking that some of our ultimate motives are altruistic.

It is easy to invent egoistic explanations for even the most harrowing acts of self-sacrifice. The soldier in a foxhole who throws himself on a grenade to save the lives of his comrades is a fixture in the literature on egoism. How could this act be a product of self-interest, if the soldier knows that it will end his life? The egoist may answer that the soldier realizes in an instant that he would rather die than suffer the guilt feelings that would haunt him if he saved himself and allowed his friends to perish. The soldier prefers to die and have no sensations at all rather than live and suffer the torments of the damned. This reply may sound *forced*, but this does not show that it must be *false*. And the fact that an egoistic explanation can be *invented* is no sure sign that egoism is *true*.

1. Clarifying egoism

When egoism claims that all our ultimate desires are self-directed, what do 'ultimate' and 'self-directed' mean?

There are some things that we want for their own sakes; other things we want only because we think they will get us something else. The crucial relation that we need to define is this:

> *S* wants *m* solely as a means to acquiring *e* if and only if *S* wants *m*, *S* wants *e*, and
> *S* wants *m* only because she believes that obtaining *m* will help her obtain *e*.

An ultimate desire is a desire that someone has for reasons that go beyond its ability to contribute instrumentally to the attainment of something else. Consider pain. The most obvious reason that people want to avoid pain is simply that they dislike experiencing it. Avoiding pain is one of our ultimate goals. However, many people realize that being in pain reduces their ability to concentrate, so they may sometimes take an aspirin in part because they want to remove a source of distraction. This shows that the things we want as ends in themselves we also may want for instrumental reasons.

When psychological egoism seeks to explain why one person helped another, it isn't enough to show that *one* of the reasons for helping was self-benefit; this is quite consistent with there being another, purely altruistic, reason that the individual had for helping. Symmetrically, to refute egoism, one need not cite examples of helping in which *only* other-directed motives play a role. If people sometimes help for both egoistic and altruistic ultimate reasons, then psychological egoism is false.

Egoism and altruism both require the distinction between self-directed and other-directed desires, which should be understood in terms of a desire's propositional content. If Adam wants the apple, this is elliptical for saying that Adam wants it to be the case that *he has the apple*. This desire is purely self-directed, since its propositional content mentions Adam, but no other agent. In contrast, when Eve wants *Adam to have the apple*, this desire is purely other-directed; its propositional content mentions another person, Adam, but not Eve herself. Egoism claims that all of our ultimate desires are self-directed; altruism, that some are other-directed.

A special version of egoism is psychological hedonism. The hedonist says that the only ultimate desires that people have are attaining pleasure and avoiding pain. Hedonism is sometimes criticized for holding that pleasure is a single type of sensation — that the pleasure we get from the taste of a peach and the pleasure we get from seeing those we love prosper somehow boil down to the same thing (Lafollette, 1988). However, this criticism does not apply to hedonism as we have described it. The salient fact about hedonism is its claim that people are *motivational solipsists*; the only things they care about ultimately are states of their own consciousness. Although hedonists must be egoists, the reverse isn't true. For example, if people desire their own survival as an end in itself, they may be egoists, but they are not hedonists.

Some desires are neither purely self-directed nor purely other-directed. If Phyllis wants to be famous, this means that she wants others to know who she is. This desire's propositional content involves a relation between self and others. If Phyllis seeks fame solely because she thinks this will be pleasurable or profitable, then she may be an egoist. But what if she wants to be famous as an end in itself? There is no reason to cram this possibility into either egoism or altruism. So let us recognize *relationism* as a possibility distinct from both. Construed in this way, egoism avoids the difficulty of having to explain why the theory is compatible with the existence of some relational ultimate desires, but not with others (Kavka, 1986).

With egoism characterized as suggested, it obviously is not entailed by the truism that people act on the basis of their own desires, nor by the truism that they seek to have their desires satisfied. The fact that Joe acts on the basis of Joe's desires, not on the basis of Jim's, tells us *whose* desires are doing the work; it says nothing about whether the ultimate desires in Joe's head are *purely self-directed*. And the fact that

Joe wants his desires to be satisfied means merely that he wants their propositional contents to come true (Stampe, 1994). If Joe wants it to rain tomorrow, then his desire is satisfied if it rains, whether or not he notices the weather. To want one's desires satisfied is not the same as wanting the feeling of satisfaction that sometimes accompanies a satisfied desire.

Egoism is sometimes criticized for attributing too much calculation to spontaneous acts of helping. People who help in emergency situations often report doing so 'without thinking' (Clark and Word, 1974). However, it is hard to take such reports literally when the acts involve a precise series of complicated actions that are well-suited to an apparent end. A lifeguard who rescues a struggling swimmer is properly viewed as having a goal and as selecting actions that advance that goal. The fact that she engaged in no ponderous and self-conscious calculation does not show that no means/end reasoning occurred. In any case, actions that really do occur without the mediation of beliefs and desires fall outside the scope of both egoism and altruism.

A related criticism is that egoism assumes that people are more rational than they really are. However, recall that egoism is simply a claim about the ultimate desires that people have. As such, it says nothing about how people decide what to do on the basis of their beliefs and desires. The assumption of rationality is no more a part of psychological egoism than it is part of *motivational pluralism* — the view that people have both egoistic and altruistic ultimate desires.

2. Psychological arguments

It may strike some readers that deciding between egoism and motivational pluralism is easy. Individuals can merely gaze within their own minds and determine by introspection what their ultimate motives are. The problem with this easy solution is that there is no independent reason to think that the testimony of introspection is to be trusted in this instance. Introspection is misleading or incomplete in what it tells us about other facets of the mind; there is no reason to think that the mind is an open book with respect to the issue of ultimate motives.

In *Unto Others*, we devote most of Chapter 8 to the literature in social psychology that seeks to test egoism and motivational pluralism experimentally. The most systematic attempt in this regard is the work of Batson and co-workers, summarized in Batson (1991). Batson tests a hypothesis he calls the *empathy-altruism hypothesis* against a variety of egoistic explanations. The empathy-altruism hypothesis asserts that empathy causes people to have altruistic ultimate desires. We argue that Batson's experiments succeed in refuting some simple forms of egoism, but that the perennial problem of refuting egoism remains — when one version of egoism is refuted by a set of observations, another can be invented that fits the data. We also argue that even if Batson's experiments show that empathy causes helping, they don't settle whether empathy brings about this result by triggering an altruistic ultimate motive. We don't conclude from this that experimental social psychology will never be able to answer the question of whether psychological egoism is true. Our negative conclusion is more modest — empirical attempts to decide between egoism and motivational pluralism have not yet succeeded.

3. A bevy of philosophical arguments

Egoism has come under fire in philosophy from a number of angles. In Chapter 9 of *Unto Others*, we review these arguments and conclude that none of them succeeds. Here, briefly, is a sampling of the arguments we consider, and our replies:

— Egoism has been said to be *untestable*, and thus not a genuine scientific theory at all. We reply that if egoism is untestable, so is motivational pluralism. If it is true that when one egoistic explanation is discredited, another can be invented in its stead, then the same can be said of pluralism. The reason that egoism and pluralism have this sort of flexibility is that both make claims about the *kinds* of explanations that human behaviour has; they do not provide a detailed explanation of any particular behaviour. Egoism and pluralism are *isms*, which are notorious for the fact that they are not crisply falsifiable by a single set of observations.

— Joseph Butler (1692–1752) is widely regarded as having refuted psychological hedonism (Broad, 1965; Feinberg, 1984; Nagel, 1970). His argument can be outlined as follows:

1. People sometimes experience pleasure.

2. When people experience pleasure, this is because they had a desire for some external thing, and that desire was satisfied.

∴ Hedonism is false.

We think the second premise is false. It is overstated; although some pleasures are the result of a desire's being satisfied, others are not (Broad, 1965, p. 66). One can enjoy the smell of violets without having formed the desire to smell a flower, or something sweet. Since desires are propositional attitudes, forming a desire is a cognitive achievement. Pleasure and pain, on the other hand, are sometimes cognitively mediated, but sometimes they are not. This defect in the argument can be repaired; Butler does not need to say that desire satisfaction is the one and only road to pleasure. The main defect in the argument occurs in the transition from premises to conclusion. Consider the causal chain from a *desire* (the desire for food, say), to an *action* (eating), to a *result* — pleasure. Because the pleasure traces back to an antecedently existing desire, it will be false that the resulting pleasure caused the desire (on the assumption that cause must precede effect). However, this does not settle how two *desires* — the *desire for food* and the *desire for pleasure* — are related. Hedonism says that people desire food *because* they want pleasure (and think that food will bring them pleasure). Butler's argument concludes that this causal claim is false, but for no good reason. The crucial mistake in the argument comes from confusing two quite different items — the *pleasure* that results from a desire's being satisfied and the *desire for pleasure*. Even if the occurrence of pleasure presupposed that the agent desired something besides pleasure, nothing follows about the relationship between the *desire for pleasure* and the desire for something else (Sober, 1992; Stewart, 1992). Hedonism does not deny that people desire external things; rather, the theory tries to explain why that is so.

— We also consider the argument against egoism that Nozick (1974) presents by his example of an 'experience machine', the claim that hedonism is a paradoxical and irrational motivational theory, and the claim that egoism has the burden of proof. We conclude that none of these attacks on egoism is decisive.

There is one philosophical argument that attempts to support egoism, not refute it. This is the claim that egoism is preferable to pluralism because the former theory is more parsimonious. Egoism posits one type of ultimate desire whereas pluralism says there are two. We have two criticisms. First, this parsimony argument measures a theory's parsimony by counting the kinds of ultimate desires it postulates. The opposite conclusion would be obtained if one counted *causal beliefs*. The pluralist says that people want others to do well and that they also want to do well themselves. The egoist says that a person wants others to do well only because he or she *believes* that this will promote self-interest. Pluralism does not include this belief attribution. Our second objection is that parsimony is a reasonable tie-breaker when all other considerations are equal; it remains to be seen whether egoism and pluralism are equally plausible on all other grounds. In Chapter 10, we propose an argument to the effect that pluralism has greater evolutionary plausibility.

4. An evolutionary approach

Psychological motives are *proximate mechanisms* in the sense of that term used in evolutionary biology. When a sunflower turns towards the sun, there must be some mechanism inside the sunflower that causes it to do so. Hence, if phototropism evolved, a proximate mechanism that causes that behaviour also must have evolved. Similarly, if certain forms of helping behaviour in human beings are evolutionary adaptations, then the motives that cause those behaviours in individual human beings also must have evolved. Perhaps a general perspective on the evolution of proximate mechanisms can throw light on whether egoism or motivational pluralism was more likely to have evolved.

Pursuing this evolutionary approach does not presuppose that every detail of human behaviour, or every act of helping, can be explained completely by the hypothesis of evolution by natural selection. In Chapter 10, we consider a single fact about human behaviour, and our claim is that selection is relevant to explaining it. The phenomenon of interest is that human parents take care of their children; the average amount of parental care provided by human beings is strikingly greater than that provided by parents in many other species. We will assume that natural selection is at least part of the explanation of why parental care evolved in our lineage. This is not to deny that human parents vary; some take better care of their children than others, and some even abuse and kill their offspring. Another striking fact about individual variation is that mothers, on average, expend more time and effort on parental care than fathers. Perhaps there are evolutionary explanations for these individual differences as well; the question we want to address here, however, makes no assumption as to whether this is true.

In Chapter 10, we describe some general principles that govern how one might predict the proximate mechanism that will evolve to cause a particular behaviour. We develop these ideas by considering the example of a marine bacterium whose problem is to avoid environments in which there is oxygen. The organism has evolved a particular behaviour — it tends to swim away from greater oxygen concentrations and towards areas in which there is less. What proximate mechanism might have evolved that allows the organism to do this?

First, let's survey the range of possible design solutions that we need to consider. The most obvious solution is for the organism to have an oxygen detector. We call this the *direct solution* to the design problem; the organism needs to avoid oxygen and it solves that problem by detecting the very property that matters.

It isn't hard to imagine other solutions to the design problem that are less direct. Suppose that areas near the pond's surface contain more oxygen and areas deeper in the pond contain less. If so, the organism could use an up/down detector to make the requisite discrimination. This design solution is *indirect*; the organism needs to distinguish high oxygen from low and accomplishes this by detecting another property that happens to be correlated with the target. In general, there may be many indirect design solutions that the organism could exploit; there are as many indirect solutions as there are correlations between oxygen level and other properties found in the environment. Finally, we may add to our list the idea that there can be *pluralistic* solutions to a design problem. In addition to the monistic solution of having an oxygen detector and the monistic solution of having an up/down detector, an organism might deploy both.

Given this multitude of possibilities, how might one predict which of them will evolve? Three principles are relevant — *availability*, *reliability*, and *efficiency*.

Natural selection acts only on the range of variation that exists ancestrally. An oxygen detector might be a good thing for the organism to have, but if that device was never present as an ancestral variant, natural selection cannot cause it to evolve. So the first sort of information we'd like to have concerns which proximate mechanisms were *available* ancestrally.

Let's suppose for the sake of argument that both an oxygen detector and an up/down detector are available ancestrally. Which of them is more likely to evolve? Here we need to address the issue of *reliability*. Which device does the more reliable job of indicating where oxygen is? Without further information, not much can be said. An oxygen detector may have any degree of reliability, and the same is true of an up/down detector. There is no *a priori* reason why the direct strategy should be more or less reliable than the indirect strategy. However, there is a special circumstance in which they will differ. It is illustrated by the following diagram:

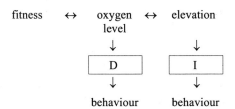

The double arrows indicate correlation; avoiding oxygen is correlated with fitness, and elevation is correlated with oxygen level. In the diagram, there is no arrow from elevation to fitness except the one that passes through oxygen level. This means that elevation is correlated with fitness *only because* elevation is correlated with oxygen, and oxygen is correlated with fitness. There is no *a priori* reason why this should be true. For example, if there were more predators at the bottom of ponds than at the top, then elevation would have two sorts of relevance for fitness. However, if oxygen level 'screens off' fitness from elevation in the way indicated, we can state the following principle about the reliability of the direct device D and the indirect device I:

(D/I) If oxygen level and elevation are less than perfectly correlated, and if D detects
       oxygen level at least as well as I detects elevation, then D will be more reliable
       than I.

This is the Direct/Indirect Asymmetry Principle. Direct solutions to a design problem
aren't always more reliable, but they are more reliable in this circumstance.

A second principle about reliability also can be extracted from this diagram. Just as
scientists do a better job of discriminating between hypotheses if they have more evidence rather than less, so it will be true that the marine bacterium we are considering
will make more reliable discriminations about where to swim if it has two sources of
information rather than just one:

(TBO) If oxygen level and elevation are less than perfectly correlated, and if D and I
       are each reliable, though fallible, detectors of oxygen concentration, then D
       and I working together will be more reliable than either of them working alone.

This is the Two-is-Better-than-One Principle. It requires an assumption — that the
two devices do not interfere with each other when both are present in an organism.

The D/I Asymmetry and the TBO Principle pertain to the issue of reliability. Let us
now turn to the third consideration that is relevant to predicting which proximate
mechanism will evolve, namely *efficiency*. Even if an oxygen detector and an elevation detector are both available, and even if the oxygen detector is more reliable, it
doesn't follow that natural selection will favour the oxygen detector. It may be that an
oxygen detector requires more energy to build and maintain than an elevation detector. Organisms run on energy no less than automobiles do. Efficiency is relevant to a
trait's overall fitness just as much as its reliability is.

With these three considerations in hand, let's return to the problem of predicting
which motivational mechanism for providing parental care is likely to have evolved
in the lineage leading to human beings. The three motivational mechanisms we need
to consider correspond to three different rules for selecting a behaviour in the light of
what one believes:

(HED) Provide parental care if, and only if, doing so will maximize pleasure and
       minimize pain.

(ALT) Provide parental care if, and only if, doing so will advance the welfare of one's
       children.

(PLUR) Provide parental care if, and only if, doing so will either maximize pleasure
       and minimize pain, or will advance the welfare of one's children.

(ALT) is a relatively direct, and (HED) is a relatively indirect, solution to the design
problem of getting an organism to take care of its offspring. Just as our marine bacterium can avoid oxygen by detecting elevation, so it is possible in principle for a
hedonistic organism to provide parental care; what is required is that the organism be
so constituted that providing parental care is the thing that usually maximizes its
pleasure and minimizes its pain (or that the organism believes that this is so).

Let's consider how reliable these three mechanisms will be in a certain situation.
Suppose that a parent learns that its child is in danger. Imagine that your neighbour
tells you that your child has just fallen through the ice on a frozen lake. Here is how
(HED) and (ALT) will do their work:

child needs help → parent believes child needs help → parent feels anxiety and fear

The altruistic parent will be moved to action just by virtue of believing that its child needs help. The hedonistic parent will not; rather, what moves the hedonistic parent to action are the feelings of anxiety and fear that are caused by the news. It should be clear from this diagram that the (D/I) Asymmetry Principle applies; (ALT) will be more reliable than (HED). And by the (TBO) Principle, (PLUR) will do better than both. In this example, hedonism comes in last in the three-way competition, at least as far as reliability is concerned.

The important thing about this example is that the feelings that the parent has are *belief mediated*. The only reason the parent *feels* anxiety and fear is that the parent *believes* that its child is in trouble. This is true of many of the situations that egoism and hedonism are called upon to explain, but it is not true of all. For example, consider the following situation in which pain is a direct effect, and belief a relatively indirect effect, of bodily injury:

fingers are burned → pain → belief that one's fingers have been injured

In this case, hedonism is a direct solution to the design problem; it would be a poor engineering solution to have the organism be unresponsive to pain and to have it withdraw its fingers from the flame only after it forms a belief about bodily injury. In this situation, *belief is pain-mediated* and the (D/I) Asymmetry Principle explains why a hedonistic focus on pain makes sense. However, the same principle indicates what is misguided about hedonism as a design solution when *pain is belief-mediated*, which is what occurs so often in the context of parental care.

If hedonism is less reliable than both pure altruism and motivational pluralism, how do these three mechanisms compare when we consider their availability and efficiency? With respect to availability, we make the following claim: *if hedonism was available ancestrally, so was altruism*. The reason is that the two motivational mechanisms differ in only a modest way. Both require a belief/desire psychology. And both the hedonistic and the altruistic parent want their children to do well; the only difference is that the hedonist has this propositional content as an instrumental desire while the altruist has it as an ultimate desire. If altruism and pluralism did not evolve, this was not because they were unavailable as variants for selection to act upon.

What about efficiency? Does it cost more calories to build and maintain an altruistic or a pluralistic organism than it does to build and maintain a hedonist? We don't see why. What requires energy is building the hardware that implements a belief/desire psychology. However, we doubt that it makes an energetic difference whether the organism has one ultimate desire rather than two. People with more beliefs apparently don't need to eat more than people with fewer. The same point seems to apply to the issue of how many, or which, ultimate desires one has.

In summary, pure altruism and pluralism are both more reliable than hedonism as devices for delivering parental care. And, with respect to the issues of availability and efficiency, we find no difference among these three motivational mechanisms. This suggests that natural selection is more likely to have made us motivational pluralists than to have made us hedonists.

From an evolutionary point of view, hedonism is a bizarre motivational mechanism. What matters in the process of natural selection is an organism's ability to survive and be reproductively successful. Reproductive success involves not just the production of offspring, but the survival of those offspring to reproductive age. So what matters is the survival of one's own body and the bodies of one's children. Hedonism, on the other hand, says that organisms care ultimately about the states of their own consciousness, and about that alone. Why would natural selection have led organisms to care about something that is peripheral to fitness, rather than have them set their eyes on the prize? If organisms were unable to conceptualize propositions about their own bodies and the bodies of their offspring, that might be a reason. After all, it might make sense for an organism to exploit the indirect strategy of deciding where to swim on the basis of elevation rather than on the basis of oxygen concentration, if the organism cannot detect oxygen. But if an organism is smart enough to form representations about itself and its offspring, this justification of the indirect strategy will not be plausible. The fact that we evolved from ancestors who were cognitively less sophisticated makes it unsurprising that avoiding pain and attaining pleasure are two of our ultimate goals. But the fact that human beings are able to form representations with so many different propositional contents suggests that evolution supplemented this list of what we care about as ends in themselves.

IV: Evolutionary Altruism, Psychological Altruism, and Ethics

The study of ethics has a *normative* and a *descriptive* component. Normative ethics seeks to say what is good and what is right; it seeks to identify what we are obliged to do and what we are permitted to do. Descriptive ethics, on the other hand, is neutral on these normative questions; it attempts to *describe* and *explain* morality as a cultural phenomenon, not *justify* it. How does morality vary within and across cultures, and through time? Are there moral ideas that constitute cultural universals? And how is one to explain this pattern of variation?

Although we think our work on evolutionary and psychological altruism bears on these questions, we also think that it is important not to blur the problems. Psychological altruism is not the same as morality. And an explanation of why human beings hold a moral principle is not, in itself, a justification (or a refutation) of that principle.

We say that psychological altruism is not the same as morality because individuals can have concerns about the welfare of specific others without their formulating those concerns in terms of ethical principles. A mother chimp may want her offspring to have some food, but this does not mean that she thinks that all chimps should be well-fed, or that all mothers should take care of their offspring. Egoistic and altruistic desires are both desires about specific individuals. Having self-directed preferences is not sufficient for having a morality; the same goes for other-directed preferences.

` Why, then, did morality evolve? People can have specific likes and dislikes without this producing a socially shared moral code. And if everyone dislikes certain things, what is the point of there being a moral code that says that those things should be shunned? If everyone hates sticking pins in their toes, what is the point of an ethic that tells people that it is wrong to stick pins in their toes? And if parents invariably love their children, what would be the point of having a moral principle that tells parents that they ought to love their children? Behaviours that people do spontaneously by virtue of their own desires don't need to have a moral code laid on top of them. The obvious suggestion is that the social function of morality is to get people to do things that they would not otherwise be disposed to do, or to strengthen dispositions that people already have in weaker forms. Morality is not a mere redundant overlay on the psychologically altruistic motives we may have.

Functionalism went out of style in anthropology and other social sciences in part because it was hard to see what feedback mechanism might make institutions persist or disappear. Even if religion promotes group solidarity, how would that explain the persistence of religion? The idea of selection makes this question tractable. We hope that *Unto Others* will allow social scientists to explore the hypothesis that morality is a group adaptation. We do not deny that moral principles have functioned as ideological weapons, allowing some individuals to prosper at the expense of others in the same group. However, the hypothesis that moralities sometimes persist and spread because they benefit the group is not mere wishful thinking. Darwin's idea that features of morality can be explained by group selection needs to be explored.

What, if anything, do the evolutionary and psychological issues we discuss in *Unto Others* contribute to normative theory? Every normative theory relies on a conception of human nature. Sometimes this is expressed by invoking the *ought implies can principle*. If people ought to do something, then it must be possible for them to do it. Human nature circumscribes what is possible. We do not regard human nature as unchangeable. In part, this is because evolution isn't over. Genetic and cultural evolution will continue to modify the capacities that people have. But if we want to understand the capacities that people *now* have, surely an understanding of our evolutionary past is crucial. One lesson that may flow from the evolutionary and psychological study of altruism is that prisoners' dilemmas are in fact rarer than many researchers suppose. Decision theory says that it is irrational to co-operate (to act altruistically) in one-shot prisoners' dilemmas. However, perhaps some situations that appear to third parties to be prisoners' dilemmas really are not. Payoffs are usually measured in dollars, or in other tangible commodities. But if people sometimes care about each other, and not just about money, they are not irrational when they choose to co-operate in such interactions. Narrow forms of egoism make such behaviours appear irrational. Perhaps the conclusion to draw is not that people *are* irrational, but that the assumption of egoism needs to be rethought.

References

Axelrod, Robert (1984), *The Evolution of Co-operation* (New York: Basic Books).
Batson, C. Daniel (1991), *The Altruism Question: Toward A Social-Psychological Answer* (Hillsdale, NJ: Lawrence Erlbaum Associates).

Boyd, Robert and Richerson, Peter (1985), *Culture and the Evolutionary Process* (Chicago: University of Chicago Press).

Broad, C.D (1965), *Five Types of Ethical Theory* (Totowa, NJ: Littlefield, Adams).

Butler, Joseph (1726), *Fifteen Sermons preached at the Rolls Chapel*, reprinted in part in *British Moralists*, Volume 1, ed. L.A. Selby-Bigge (New York: Dover Books, 1965; originally published Oxford: The Clarendon Press, 1897).

Clark, R.D. and Word, L.E. (1974), 'Where is the apathetic bystander? Situational characteristics of the emergency', *Journal of Personality and Social Psychology*, **29**, pp. 279–87.

Darwin, Charles (1871), *The Descent of Man and Evolution in Relation to Sex* (London: Murray).

Dawkins, Richard (1976), *The Selfish Gene* (New York: Oxford University Press).

Feinberg, J. (1984), 'Psychological egoism', in *Reason at Work*, ed. S. Cahn, P. Kitcher and G. Sher (San Diego, Calif.: Harcourt Brace and Jovanovich), pp. 25–35.

Fisher, Ronald (1930), *The Genetical Theory of Natural Selection* (New York: Dover, 1958).

Hamilton, W.D. (1964), 'The Genetical evolution of social behaviour I and II', *Journal of Theoretical Biology*, **7**, pp. 1–16, pp. 17–52.

Hamilton, W.D. (1967), 'Extraordinary sex ratios', *Science*, **156**, pp. 477–88.

Hamilton, W.D. (1975), 'Innate social aptitudes of man — an approach from evolutionary genetics', in *Biosocial Anthropology*, ed. R. Fox (New York: John Wiley) pp. 133–15 .

Kavka, Gregory (1986), *Hobbesian Moral and Political Theory* (Princeton, NJ: Princeton University Press).

Lafollette, Hugh (1988), 'The truth in psychological egoism', in *Reason and Responsibility*, 7th edition, ed. J. Feinberg (Belmont, Calif.: Wadsworth), pp. 500–7.

Maynard Smith, John (1964), 'Group selection and kin selection', *Nature*, **201**, pp. 1145–6.

Maynard Smith, John and Price, George (1973), 'The logic of animal conflict', *Nature*, **246**, pp.15–18.

Nagel, Thomas (1970), *The Possibility of Altruism* (Oxford: Oxford University Press).

Nozick, Robert (1974), *Anarchy, State, and Utopia* (New York: Basic Books).

Sober, Elliott (1992), 'Hedonism and Butler's stone', *Ethics*, **103**, pp. 97–103.

Sober, Elliott and Wilson, David Sloan (1998), *Unto Others: The Evolution and Psychology of Unselfish Behavior* (Cambridge, MA: Harvard University Press).

Stampe, Dennis (1994), 'Desire', in *A Companion to the Philosophy of Mind*, ed. S. Guttenplan (Cambridge, Mass.: Basil Blackwell), pp. 244–50.

Stewart, R.M. (1992), 'Butler's argument against psychological hedonism', *Canadian Journal of Philosophy*, **22**, pp. 211–21.

Williams, George C. (1966), *Adaptation and Natural Selection* (Princeton, NJ: Princeton University Press).

Commentary Discussion
of Sober and Wilson's 'Unto Others'

UNTO OTHERS: A SERVICE . . . AND A DISSERVICE

C. Daniel Batson

Sober and Wilson (1998) render a valuable service by bringing together discussions of evolutionary altruism and psychological altruism. They do a disservice by interpreting the results of experiments designed to test for the existence of psychological altruism as less conclusive than the data warrant. Sober and Wilson claim that new egoistic explanations can account for the existing experimental evidence, but they only offer explanations that have already been ruled out. Insofar as I know, no plausible egoistic explanation currently exists for the experimental evidence that feeling empathy for a person in need evokes altruistic motivation. Unless Sober and Wilson can provide a plausible egoistic explanation for the existing evidence, their 'inconclusive' conclusion should be corrected.

Over the past twenty years, I have watched the growth of a rather sizeable literature in psychology that reports experiments testing for the existence of altruistic motivation in humans. When I read recent work on altruism by biologists and in the popular press, I oscillate between being amazed, amused, and appalled at the lack of attention to this experimental research. Authors seem quite content to make ostensibly scientifically based pronouncements about the existence of altruistic motives in humans in apparent ignorance of the most directly relevant and carefully collected empirical evidence. *Unto Others* is a refreshing exception to this myopia; Sober and Wilson (1998) discuss both evolutionary and psychological altruism.

Bringing evolutionary and psychological altruism into the same discussion is not easy. As Sober and Wilson point out, the two terms do not refer to two perspectives on the same phenomenon, but to two quite different phenomena. *Evolutionary altruism* refers to behaviour by one organism that diminishes its reproductive potential relative to that of others. *Psychological altruism* refers to a motivational state with the ultimate goal of increasing another's welfare. There is no necessary connection between the two; evolutionary altruism is neither necessary nor sufficient to produce psychological altruism. As I once heard Richard Dawkins provocatively but accurately point out, an allele that produces bad teeth in horses (and leads to less effective grazing and more grass for others) is an example of evolutionary altruism. Similarly, an allele that leads one to smoke cigarettes, which may cause impotence, birth defects, and early death, is also an example of evolutionary altruism; it reduces one's procreative potential, thereby providing relative reproductive benefit to others.

Most people interested in the existence of altruism are not thinking about bad teeth in horses or smoking cigarettes; they are thinking about psychological altruism. They want to know whether, when one organism acts to benefit another, the act is motivated by more than self-benefit. Recognizing this, Sober and Wilson begin *Unto Others* by raising the question of psychological egoism versus altruism, then segue into a extensive discussion of evolutionary altruism in Part One. They return to psychological altruism in Part Two. The division of the book into two distinct parts is an appropriate reflection of the great conceptual gap between evolutionary and psychological altruism.

I believe Sober and Wilson perform a major service by bringing psychological research on altruism before an audience likely composed mainly of biologists and philosophers, but I fear they do a disservice in their interpretation of the psychological research. They set up the research problem well: They note the crucial distinctions among ultimate goals (ends in themselves), instrumental goals (means to ends), and unintended consequences. They understand that a person can be motivated to pursue more than one ultimate goal at a time. They recognize that a given motive cannot be both egoistic and altruistic, but an individual can at a given time have either egoistic or altruistic motives, both, or neither. They observe that the distinction between psychological egoism and altruism lies in whose welfare — one's own or another's — is the ultimate goal of a specific motivational state.

How can we know whether psychological altruism exists? The dominant research strategy has been to look at situations in which one person helps another — specifically situations in which it is plausible to think this help might be altruistically motivated — and seek to determine the ultimate goal(s) toward which helping is directed. Sober and Wilson rightly observe that we cannot rely on introspection to identify an ultimate goal; we must infer the ultimate goal by looking at the pattern of behaviour across systematically varying circumstances.

Let me be more specific. The other-oriented emotional response evoked by focussing on the plight of a person in need — called empathy, sympathy, compassion, etc. — is known to increase the motivation to help that person. Moreover, the motivation to help evoked by empathy has frequently been claimed to be altruistic. But is this empathy-altruism hypothesis true? To raise the most commonly suggested egoistic alternative, perhaps empathy evokes motivation directed toward the ultimate goal of eliminating the empathic feelings themselves. After all, feeling empathy for someone in need is likely to be unpleasant. The empathizer may want to relieve the target's suffering not as an ultimate goal but as an instrumental means to relieve his or her own aversive arousal.

To determine whether relieving the distress of the target of empathy is an ultimate goal, or only an instrumental means to reach the ultimate goal of reducing the helper's own empathic arousal, we need to vary the situation so that sometimes the empathic arousal can be reduced in a less costly way than by helping. One way to do this is by varying whether the potential helper anticipates continued exposure to the other's suffering if he or she decides not to help. Research has shown that feelings of distress or upset caused by seeing someone suffer, which are distinct from feelings of empathy, lead to increased costly helping only when the potential helper anticipates continued exposure. Similarly, if the ultimate goal of empathy-aroused helping is to reduce one's own empathic arousal, then empathically aroused individuals should help less when they believe they will no longer be exposed to the arousal producing stimulus (the suffering other) than when they believe they will. If, on the other hand, the ultimate goal is to reduce the other's distress, then this variation should have no effect. Reducing one's own empathic arousal does nothing to reduce the other's distress.

A series of experiments has used this logic to test the empathy-altruism hypothesis against the aversive-arousal-reduction egoistic alternative. Results reveal that when empathy is low (and feelings of personal distress dominant), the rate of helping is high when research participants anticipate continued exposure, but low when they do not. When empathy is high, the rate of helping is high even when participants do not anticipate continued exposure. These results clearly contradict the aversive-arousal-reduction explanation of empathy-induced helping; they support the empathy-altruism hypothesis.

Following a similar research strategy, serious doubt has been cast on the two other egoistic accounts proposed to explain the motivation to help evoked by empathy, avoiding social or personal punishments (shame, guilt) and gaining social or personal rewards (praise, esteem-enhancement). The only egoistic explanation to gain any credible support has been a variant of the empathy-specific reward account that claims empathy evokes motivation for mood enhancement. It now seems clear, however, that the initial support for this variant was due to procedural artifacts.

Empirical support for the empathy-altruism hypothesis has become extremely strong. In over twenty five experiments designed to test it against egoistic alternatives, results have patterned as predicted by the empathy-altruism hypothesis. To the best of my knowledge, there is at present no plausible egoistic explanation of the motivation to help evoked by empathy.

Yet in their target article — and book — Sober and Wilson claim that the results of this psychological research are 'inconclusive'. Having made this claim, they retire from the arena of empirical test to their armchairs, offering evolutionary speculations about the possibility of psychological altruism emerging from parental care for children. These speculations are interesting and suggestive, especially because of their congruence with some current theory and research on the origin of empathic feelings (including Frans de Waal's, 1996, analysis of the role of sympathy in primates). I feel compelled, however, to set these speculations aside and ask on what ground Sober and Wilson conclude that the psychological research testing the empathy-altruism hypothesis is inconclusive.

In their target article, I find only two possible reasons. First, they say, 'the perennial problem of refuting egoism remains — when one version of egoism is refuted by a set of observations, another can be invented that fits the data' (p. 198). Second, they say that even if the experiments 'show that empathy causes helping, they don't settle whether empathy brings about this result by triggering an altruistic ultimate motive' (p. 198).

The second assertion provides no reason; it is simply a restatement of their inconclusive conclusion. At issue in this research was never whether empathy causes helping; that was known before the research began. The experiments were designed to test whether empathy does this by triggering an altruistic motive or one or another egoistic motive. The first assertion does offer a reason, and a relevant one. If another egoistic explanation can be invented that fits the data supporting the empathy-altruism hypothesis, then until research has been conducted to test this explanation, no clear conclusion can be drawn. Granting this, several additional points are in order.

First, this open-set problem is by no means unique to tests of the empathy-altruism hypothesis. Any time a plausible alternative explanation can be made for data thought to support some hypothesis, the validity of that hypothesis is cast in doubt. But the open-set problem is not grounds for suspending judgment on a hypothesis; were it, we would have no data-based conclusions in science at all. It is not enough to say that another version of egoism *can* be invented; a specific alternative explanation has to be proposed. Moreover, the proposed explanation must be able to explain all relevant existing data (as any adequate explanation must). It is not enough to propose an egoistic explanation for one set of results when that explanation is clearly contradicted by another set. Operating within these standard scientific ground rules, I know of no plausible egoistic explanation for the existing data supporting the empathy-altruism hypothesis. If Sober and Wilson — or anyone else — are able to propose one, then I quite agree that doubt would be cast on the truth of this hypothesis.

In Chapter Eight of *Unto Others,* Sober and Wilson do propose egoistic alternatives for several of the empathy-altruism experiments described, but all of their alternatives make predictions that are contradicted by existing data. For example, to explain the results of two experiments, they propose an alternative based on motivation to reduce the disagreeable feelings that accompany uncertainty (p. 268). But they fail to note that, unless empathy-specific, such an explanation predicts increased helping at maximum uncertainty when empathy is low as well as high, which was not found in either experiment. Even an empathy-specific form of this explanation cannot make sense of results of a third, procedurally similar experiment: Empathy increased helping even when participants knew that they would receive no information about the effectiveness of their helping effort. (Procedural similarity renders implausible an argument that uncertainty aversion was aroused in one experiment but not another.)

Another example: When anticipation of a mood-enhancing experience was found not to reduce helping by individuals experiencing high empathy, Sober and Wilson claim:

> Here again, an egoistic explanation is not far to seek. If empathizing with a needy other makes a subject sad, why expect the subject to think that listening to music will be a completely satisfactory mood corrective? When we are sad, we usually are sad about something in particular. It is not surprising that the pain we experience in empathizing with the suffering of others is not completely assuaged by any old pleasant experience . . . . (p. 271)

The egoistic account proposed here is of course simply a restatement of the aversive-arousal-reduction explanation that, as noted earlier, has already been laid to rest. Unless Sober and Wilson can offer some plausible reason why, if this explanation is valid, the previous experiments (which again used highly similar procedures) produced the results they did, then there are no grounds for resurrecting this corpse. I believe all of the egoistic alternative explanations they offer are equally indefensible.

If I am right, then readers who rely on Sober and Wilson as guides to the psychological research on altruism will be misled. What could have been a major service unto others has become a disservice.

References

Sober, Elliott and Wilson, David Sloan (1998), *Unto Others: The Evolution and Psychology of Unselfish Behaviour* (Cambridge, MA: Harvard University Press).
de Waal, Frans (1996), *Good Natured: The Origins of Right and Wrong in Humans and Other Animals* (Cambridge, MA: Harvard University Press).

GROUP SELECTION IN THE UPPER PALAEOLITHIC

Christopher Boehm

Using criteria of relative plausibility, it is possible to make a case for significant group selection over the 100,000 years that Anatomically Modern Humans have been both moral and egalitarian. Our nomadic forebears surely lived in egalitarian communities that levelled social differences and moralistically curbed free-riding behaviour, and this egalitarian syndrome would have had profound effects on levels of selection. First, it reduced phenotypic variation at the within-group level. Second, it increased phenotypic variation at the between-group level. Third, and crucially, moral sanctioning also permitted groups to sharply curtail free-riding tendencies at the level of phenotype. The result was group selection strong enough to support altruistic genes, and a human nature that was set up for social ambivalence: that nature was mainly selfish and strongly nepotistic, but it was at least modestly and socially significantly altruistic. The effects on human social and moral life were pervasive, both in hunting bands and in more recent manifestations of human society.

If one wished to categorize noteworthy academic disputes, two prominent contrastive types would be the Endless Controversy and the Paradigm-Busting Controversy. The first is exemplified by scholars feeding off two ends of a sharply bifurcated intellectual continuum with the debate having little chance of resolution. In this connection, Hobbes and Rousseau have facilitated many an illustrious academic career: the contest is 'philosophical', there is no specific scientific paradigm at stake, and debate is not framed to facilitate falsification. A Paradigm-Busting Controversy arises when a major and accepted scientific approach comes under serious attack as characterized by Kuhn (1970). Such controversies occur sporadically, and usually they involve heated intellectual exchanges that are combined with empirical findings.

David Sloan Wilson has assumed a Paradigm-Busting role for several decades, and there is at stake a major and humanly important paradigm adjustment if not a scientific revolution. The conflict is unusual: with just a few allies he has persistently tried to resuscitate a sharply discredited theory. Wilson's lost cause espousal has been both single-minded, adroit, and strategically well conceived. The arguments have been logical, often incisive. He has effectively made use of the standard sociobiological paradigm in order to undermine a major portion of it, going against an enormously popular paradigm with distinguished spokesmen like Alexander (1974), Trivers (1971; 1972), and Dawkins (1976). In doing so, he has exploited doors left open by other influential scholars who seem less doctrinaire (for example, E.O. Wilson, 1975).

E.O. Wilson did not reject group selection out of hand, although in *Sociobiology*, the shortcomings of older theories were well elucidated. In the same year, David Wilson (1975) began his crusade and the campaign was enhanced, eventually, by an important partnership with philosopher Elliott Sober. Their article in *Behavioural and Brain Sciences* (Wilson and Sober, 1994) constituted a full-scale attack on the biological establishment's commitment to methodological individualism. Several dozen replies demonstrated that the gadfly theory, now comprehensively stated, was being taken seriously at least by some.

The next assault came in 1997 with a special issue of *American Naturalist* (Wilson, 1997), to which I made an anthropological contribution (Boehm, 1997). I suggested that the Wilson and Sober arguments might apply particularly to humans because of certain effects of cultural behaviour on phenotype, effects I shall discuss presently. With other allies appearing, the Paradigm-Busting mission was gathering some steam — even though methodologically individualistic establishment biological theory still continues to dominate.

In framing the *Behavioural and Brain Sciences* debate, Wilson and Sober looked to mechanisms of selection, and in particular they corrected erroneous assumptions that groups, if they are to be effective as selection vehicles, must have strict boundaries and must remain intact over time. At the same time, the authors bolstered their general argument by concentrating on humans, and so stepped directly into the Endless Controversy arena.

Next came *Unto Others* (Sober and Wilson, 1998), a book which has been identified by various reviewers as having something of a bifurcate personality. The first half concentrates on technical mistakes of the biologists whose models precluded group selection, and on the notions of trait groups and multi-level selection. This is the Paradigm-Busting side of the book, while the second half fits more with the Endless Controversy characterization because (by my reading) the underlying issue is whether people are basically altruistic or limited to selfishness and nepotism. Sober also calls for motivational pluralism, and such an approach might be testable.

I, too, am a proponent of an 'emotional pluralism' of sorts. In 'Ambivalence and compromise in human nature' (Boehm, 1989), I experimented with an approach I have continued in *Hierarchy in the Forest* (Boehm, 1999a). My view is that the best way to keep discussions of human nature from turning into Endless Controversies is to stop bipolarizing the arguments. Rather, one should look at human nature as producing contradictory dispositions that generate predictable ambivalences at the level of phenotype, ambivalences that help to structure life's practical decision dilemmas (Boehm, 1996). My general hypothesis: Humans are innately given to egoism, nepotism, and altruism, and our next task is to sort out how these dispositions feed into everyday decisions (Boehm, 1997).

At the editor's request, I devote the remainder of this commentary to work I have done on group selection as this was likely among Upper Palaeolithic humans. *Unto Others* was partly critical of the notion that special social and political conditions could have led to robust group selection among human bands, starting as much as 100,000 years ago. The problem was the absence of a 'smoking gun' (Sober and Wilson, 1998). This criticism applies to virtually any attempt to reconstruct social behaviours deep in prehistory, and my main intention was to define the gun, not to validate the smoke. Having suggested that the errand itself was scientifically legitimate, I shall briefly recapitulate my arguments.

There is little doubt that prehistoric nomads lived in small bands of a dozen families or so, that these bands were egalitarian, and that when they moved, they tried to reach a consensus about where to go next. There also is very little doubt that bands of Anatomically Modern Humans were moral communities that were capable of sanctioning deviants. Indeed, our forebears became egalitarian only after they were able to moralistically outlaw alpha male behaviour.

I advanced three hypotheses to explain why group selection could have supported altruistic traits in these mobile egalitarian bands. Two of the arguments are based on David Wilson's ideas about trait groups, which permit interdemic selection to operate in spite of porous boundaries and short-term instability of group memberships. All three are consistent with current mainstream approaches to natural selection explanations — with an important change. One must abandon the modelling–parsimony habits of most evolutionary biologists, who tend to equate phenotype and genotype so that they can build tidy and potent mathematical models. My analysis shows that when a species is endowed with morality, what takes place at the level of phenotype can differ *drastically* from what one would model at the level of genotype.

The argument begins with the balance of power between within-group selection and between-group selection. Normally, extinction rates get all the attention in debates about possibilities for altruism, but here phenotypic variation is the focus. Egalitarian hunter-gatherers use the force of public opinion, expressed by punitive moral sanctioning, to ensure that alpha-dominated hierarchies cannot form at the band level. Upstarts are effectively stopped, sometimes severely punished, and this means that the overall phenotypic variation among individuals is drastically reduced. This curtails the force of within-group selection.

Phenotypic variation within groups is further reduced by the egalitarian habit of making migration decisions by consensus. Bands share their large game, and therefore try very hard to stick together. With all the families following the same basic subsistence strategy rather than each family doing its own thing, the phenotypic variation within groups is further reduced. These same consensual decisions also increase phenotypic variation *between* groups. For example, if one band copes with drought by travelling (hopefully) toward higher rainfall, whereas another conserves its energy and trusts to luck, demographic effects for the two groups can be highly disparate.

The overall result is an increase in both the relative and the absolute power of natural selection taking place *between* groups. With this substantial shift in the levels-of-selection balance of power that determines possibilities for altruism, within-group selection (although surely still the predominant force) was far less overpowering whereas between-group selection became at least moderately robust. Were it not for the free-rider problem, it seems likely that altruistic genes could have been very well-supported at moderate levels after these adjustments had their effect, which came toward the end of the Upper Palaeolithic at the latest.

The free-rider problem is one of genetic modelling, but also a practical problem of everyday life if one lives in a hunting band. Extant bands always share their large game meat because its intake tends to be sporadic. People also tend to take care of other band members in injury or illness or old age, and while most of this care is provided by spouses or close relatives, to a significant degree the caretaking is extended to unrelated band members. These facts have led sociobiologists (Alexander, 1987) to try to 'generalize' Trivers' (1971) strict reciprocity theory, but a more satisfactory *further* explanation would be that humans actually possess some capacity for genuine altruism. Genuine altruism can be defined, parsimoniously, as behaviour that is based on genes which are selected at the between-group level, and that is motivated by feelings of concern for the welfare of non-kinsmen.

Strict reciprocity, based on a selfish human nature tempered only by nepotism, does not fit well with what foragers actually do (Boehm, 1999b). When people are aged or seriously disabled, Trivers-style payback simply is not possible. Furthermore, able-bodied recipients of favours will not necessarily be in a logistical position for payback because people keep moving back and forth between bands. Actual cooperation within the band is very much in the here and now, and it is based on the moralistic assumption that everyone will play by a set of general rules, realistic rules that prescribe helping behaviour within reasonable limits. In effect, hunter-gatherers are creating a welfare state: they pay their dues and basically are receiving their benefits from a multi-band system as a whole. A wholly selfish species might somehow manage to keep this safety net in place, but a moderate dose of altruism enormously helps the task of explanation.

With such a cooperative system in place, band members have to be very careful about opportunistic free-riders. However, being careful does not mean that individuals prone to take free rides are automatically subject to decisive moral sanctioning. Hunter-gatherers are excellent actuaries: they know which free riding should be considered a mere irritant and which is a serious danger to cooperators. In times of plenty, a morally suspect hunter who professes to be lame may not be confronted — even though resentment is predictable — because the willing hunters can readily supply the entire group with meat. However, freeloading types will become objects of sharp social disapproval, and also will be denied sharing privileges, when times are lean or if their number in a band becomes too large.

The fact that moral sanctioning is realistically adjusted to the actual reproductive damage that free-riders are doing has obvious natural selection consequences. In times of plenty, free-riders may gain some modest phenotypic advantages over altruists — but these are nothing like benefits assessed by evolutionary biologists in their models. In times of scarcity, free-riders not only find their benefits curtailed, but active punishment by an outraged band can lead to seriously adverse reproductive consequences. Our capacity for morality makes all the difference.

This brings us to human nature, and to the issue of innate structural contradictions between different behavioural dispositions and resulting phenotypic ambivalences at the level of psychology. If I am correct, our social nature can be defined as follows. It contains a very large dose of egoism, a hefty dose of nepotism, but at least a modest and socially significant dose of altruism. In my opinion, altruism helps to account for the prosocial messages that all human societies send out, which universally call for — *altruism*. We also must explain the limited but very significant individual responsiveness to such messages, and this too is influenced by a human nature that is partly altruistic.

If I am correct, we need not go through intellectual contortions based on loyalty to some version of the Selfish Gene every time some human behaviour that *appears* to be genuinely altruistic demands explanation. While it is true that arguments for an Upper Palaeolithic group-selection smoking gun rest merely on plausibility criteria, this natural selection story provides a reasonably specific starting point for an account of how human nature came to be as (genuinely) altruistic as it appears to be. This is a hypothesis worth thinking about, and in proposing it I can only hope that I am contributing not to another Endless Controversy, but to an important and ongoing paradigm adjustment.Alexander, Richard D. (1987)

References

Alexander, Richard D. (1974), 'The evolution of social behavior', *Annual Review of Ecology and Systematics*, **5**, pp. 325–84.

Alexander, Richard D. (1987), *The Biology of Moral Systems* (New York: Aldine de Gruyter).

Boehm, Christopher (1989), 'Ambivalence and compromise in human nature', *American Anthropologist*, **91**, pp. 921–39.

Boehm, Christopher (1996), 'Emergency decisions, cultural selection mechanics, and group selection', *Current Anthropology*, **37**, pp. 763–93.

Boehm, Christopher (1997), 'Impact of the human egalitarian syndrome on Darwinian selection mechanics', *American Naturalist*, **150**, pp. 100–21.

Boehm, Christopher (1999a), *Hierarchy in the Forest: The Evolution of Egalitarian Behavior* (Cambridge: Harvard University Press).

Boehm, Christopher (1999b), 'The natural selection of egalitarian traits', *Human Nature*, **10** Special Issue on Group Selection, pp. 205–52.

Dawkins, Richard (1976), *The Selfish Gene* (New York: Oxford University Press).

Kuhn, Thomas (1970), *The Structure of Scientific Revolutions*; 2nd edition, enlarged (Chicago: University of Chicago Press; first published 1962).

Sober, Elliott and Wilson, David S. (1998), *Unto Others: The Evolution and Psychology of Unselfish Behavior* (Cambridge: Harvard University Press).

Trivers, Robert L. (1971), 'The Evolution of reciprocal altruism', *Quarterly Review of Biology*, **46**, pp. 35–57.

Trivers, Robert L. (1972), 'Parental investment and sexual selection', in *Sexual Selection and the Descent of Man, 1871–1971*, ed. B.G. Campbell (Chicago: Aldine).

Wilson, David S. (1975), 'A General Theory of Group Selection', *Proceedings of the National Academy of Sciences* **72**, pp. 143–6.

Wilson, David. S. (ed. 1997), 'Multilevel selection: A symposium organized by David Sloan Wilson', *American Naturalist*, **150**, pp. S1–S134.

Wilson, David S., and Sober. Elliott (1994), 'Reintroducing group selection to the human behavioral sciences', *Behavioral and Brain Sciences*, **17**, pp. 585–654.

Wilson, Edward O. (1975), *Sociobiology: The New Synthesis* (Cambridge, MA: Harvard Univ. Press).

GROUP SELECTION AND HUMAN PROSOCIALITY

Herbert Gintis

Are humans genetically predisposed to exhibit prosocial behaviours? Elliott Sober and David Sloan Wilson have made major contributions to our understanding of this question. In my remarks here I will propose a revision in their definition of altruism, suggest a broader term, 'prosociality', to account for cooperation in humans, and present evidence for a particular set of human prosocial traits that likely evolved with our species and may account for our unique ability to maintain intricate cooperative networks not based on ties of kinship.

A *prosocial* trait is one that favours the emergence and/or sustenance of cooperation in a group in which cooperation enhances the average fitness of its members. A prosocial behaviour by an agent A in group G is *altruistic* if the behaviour imposes a fitness cost on A in the sense that an alternative behaviour available to A (e.g., 'selfish') would increase A's fitness at the expense of the average fitness of members of G. It is likely, but not certain, that the traits I will discuss are in fact altruistic.

Note that (following Kropotkin, Wynne-Edwards, Williams, and others), I call a behaviour 'altruistic' only if the individual exhibiting the behaviour sacrifices individual fitness for the benefit of the group; i.e., only if there is alternative behaviour available to the individual (e.g., the behaviour of the 'selfish' agent) that would increase the agent's individual fitness. Sober and Wilson define an altruist as an agent who is 'less fit than selfish individuals *in the same group*'. But an agent's action can be individually fitness-maximizing and still satisfy the Sober–Wilson definition. I think it is misleading to label an action 'altruistic' in this case.

Consider, for instance, the hawk-dove game repeated indefinitely with a random pairing of agents in each period, so that in equilibrium there is a positive fraction of both hawks and doves. Sober and Wilson's 'group' in this case is a pair of agents playing the game in a given period, each knowing its own type (dove or hawk), but not that of its partner. By choosing 'dove' rather than 'hawk', a dove confers a fitness advantage on its partner in all groups, and is always less fit than selfish (i.e., hawk) individuals in the same group. The dove is thus altruistic according to Sober and Wilson's definition. But in equilibrium, the dove always plays a within-group individual fitness-maximizing strategy, and hence in no sense is sacrificing for the benefit of the group. It is thus unreasonable to consider the dove to be an altruist.

Notice that a similar analysis applies to the repeated Prisoner's Dilemma game, pitting the tit for tat strategy against the universal defect strategy. Sober and Wilson are happy to call tit for tat altruistic, despite the fact that all agents play individually fitness-maximizing strategies within each group. Since, like dove in the hawk/dove game, tit for tat is an individually fitness-maximizing strategy, I think this is unwarranted.

The important point about the dove and tit for tat strategies, I suggest, is that they are *prosocial*, and hence promote cooperation in groups. Where assortative interactions are strong, prosociality can take the form of altruism, the individual choosing within-group non-best-responses ('sacrificing') that benefit other members of the group. Where assortative interactions are weaker, as is likely the case for the foraging groups in which *Homo sapiens* evolved, social rules probably evolve that reduce, and possibly even eliminate, the personal cost of prosocial behaviour. This 'co-evolution of genes and culture' appears to me to be the place to start modelling the evolutionary history of our species.

What are good candidates for prosocial traits in humans? According to classical game theory, 'reason' and a sufficiently long time horizon are sufficient to explain human cooperation. What biologists call 'reciprocal altruism' and economists call 'enlightened self-interest' is enough to induce a high level of cooperation in repeated games, given the ability of humans to process large amounts of information concerning the history of their social relations with others. A long time-horizon (or what economists call a low discount rate) is thus a prosocial trait, since it strongly promotes cooperation, though it may or may not be altruistic.

There are two problems with classical game theory's answer. First, when a social group is threatened with extinction or dispersal, say through war, pestilence, or famine, cooperation is most needed for survival. But the discount rate, which depends on the probability of future interactions, increases sharply when the group is threatened, since the group may disband or otherwise become extinct. Thus, *precisely when society is most in need of prosocial behaviour, cooperation based on enlightened self-interest will collapse*. To maintain cooperation in a threatened society, what is needed is some form of prosociality that is *not* closely related to the prospect for future personal rewards.

Second, there is considerable experimental and other evidence that human beings exhibit such forms of non-self-interested prosociality. One such behaviour is *strong reciprocity*. A strong reciprocator has an initial predisposition to cooperate with other cooperators, and retaliates against non-cooperators by punishing them, even when this behaviour cannot be justified in terms of long-run self (or extended kin) interest. If a group has a sufficiently large fraction of strong reciprocators, full cooperation can be achieved even when the discount rate is very high, since the self-interested types cooperate out of fear of being punished by strong reciprocators (see Gintis, 2000, Ch. 11; and Bowles and Gintis, 1998).

I: Experimental Evidence for Strong Reciprocity

A considerable body of evidence suggests that many people, in many different societies, and under many different social conditions, including complete anonymity, behave like the strong reciprocator. Here is a review of some of the evidence. For additional evidence, including the results of common pool resource and trust games, see Gintis (2000).

1. The ultimatum game

In the *ultimatum game*, under conditions of anonymity, one player, called the 'proposer', is handed a sum of money, say $10, and is told to offer any number of dollars, from 1 to 10, to the second player, who is called the 'responder'. The responder, again under conditions of anonymity, can either accept the offer, or reject it. If the responder accepts the offer, the money is shared accordingly. If the responder rejects the offer, both players receive nothing.

The self-interested responder will accept whatever is offered. However, when actually played, proposers generally offer respondents very substantial amounts (50 per cent of the total being the modal offer), and respondents frequently reject low offers (e.g., offers below 30 per cent). These results are obtained in experiments with stakes as high as three months' earnings. For a review of ultimatum game experiments, see Güth and Tietz (1990), Roth (1995), and Camerer and Thaler (1995).

Are these results culturally dependent? Do they have a strong genetic component, or do all 'successful' cultures transmit similar values of reciprocity to individuals? Roth *et al.* (1991) conducted ultimatum games in four different countries (United States, Yugoslavia, Japan, and Israel), and found that while the level of offers differed a bit in different countries, the probability of an offer being rejected did not. This indicates that both proposers and respondents share the same notion of what is considered 'fair' in that society, and that proposers adjust their offers to reflect this common notion. The differences in level of offers across countries, by the way, were relatively small.

When asked why they offer more than the lowest possible amount, proposers commonly say that they are afraid that respondents will consider low offers unfair and reject them. When respondents reject offers, they give virtually the same reasons for their actions. In all of the above experiments, by the way, a significant fraction of subjects (about a quarter, typically) conform to the self-interested preferences model.

2. The public goods game

In the public goods game a number (say, ten) of subjects are told that $1 will be deposited in each of their 'private accounts' as a reward for participating in each round of the experiment. For every $1 a subject moves from his 'private account' to the 'common pool,' the experimenter will deposit $0.50 in the private accounts of each of the subjects at the end of the game (this corresponds to $c=0.50$ and $b=1.00$ in our previous model). This process will be repeated ten times, and at the end, the subjects can take home whatever they have in their private accounts.

If all ten subjects are cooperative, each puts $1 in the common pool at the end of each round, generating a public pool of $10; the experimenter then put $5 in the private account of each subject. After ten rounds of this, each subject has $50. Suppose, by contrast, that one subject is selfish, while the others are cooperative. The selfish one keeps his $1-per-round in his private account, whereas the cooperative ones continue to put $1 in the public pool. In this case, the selfish subject who takes a free ride on the cooperative contributions of others ends up with $55 at the end of the game, while the other players will end up with $45 each. But if all players opt for the selfish payoff, then no one contributes to the public pool, and each ends up with $10 at the end of the game. And if one player cooperates, while the others are all selfish, that player will end up with $5 at the end of the game, while the others will get $15. Clearly this is an 'iterated Prisoner's Dilemma', as in the tit for tat game.

Only a fraction of subjects conform to the selfish model, contributing nothing to the common pool. Rather, in a one-stage public goods game, people contribute on average about half of their private account. The results in the early stages of a repeated public goods game are similar. In the middle stages of the repeated game, however, contributions begin to decay, until at the end, they are close to the selfish level — i.e., zero.

Andreoni (1988) showed that the decay of cooperation is not due to players' learning the optimal behaviour, since when the whole process is repeated with the same subjects but with different group composition, the initial levels of cooperation are restored, but once again cooperation decays as the game progresses. Andreoni (1995) suggests a strong reciprocity explanation for the decay of cooperation: public-spirited contributors want to retaliate against free-riders and the only way available to them in the game is by not contributing themselves.

When subjects are allowed to retaliate against defectors, they use this power in a way that helps sustain cooperation (Dawes *et al.*, 1986; Sato, 1987, Yamagishi, 1988a; 1988b; 1992). In perhaps the cleanest study of the phenomenon, Fehr and Gächter (1999) set up a repeated public goods game with the possibility of costly retaliation, but they ensured that group composition changed *in every period* so subjects knew that costly retaliation could not confer any pecuniary benefit to those who punish. Nonetheless, punishment of free-riding was prevalent and gave rise to a large and sustainable increase in cooperation levels. At the end of the game, cooperation was virtually universal.

II: Conclusion

The ultimate vindication of Sober and Wilson's argument is, I believe, the isolation of a set of human prosocial traits that account for the prevalence of human sociality, and that could plausibly have emerged through the co-evolution of genes and culture in the evolutionary environment (basically the small foraging bands described in Boehm, 2000) under which *Homo sapiens* evolved. I am not suggesting that strong reciprocity is the only such trait. Another is probably the tendency to favour insiders over outsiders, the 'shame' emotion as a source of self-control in social settings, and a feeling of concern for the well-being of others, without which we would all be incorrigible sociopaths.

References

Andreoni, James (1988), 'Why free ride? Strategies and learning in public good experiments', *Journal of Public Economics*, **37**, pp. 291–304.

Andreoni, James (1995), 'Cooperation in public goods experiments: Kindness or confusion', *American Economic Review*, **85** (4), pp. 891–904.

Boehm, Christopher (2000), 'Conflict and the evolution of social control', *Journal of Consciousness Studies*, **7** (1–2), pp. 79–101.

Bowles, Samuel and Gintis, Herbert (1998), 'The evolution of strong reciprocity', Santa Fe Institute Working Paper 98-08-073E.

Camerer, Colin and Thaler, Richard (1995), 'Ultimatums, dictators, and manners', *Journal of Economic Perspectives*, **9** (2), pp. 209–19.

Dawes, Robyn M., Orbell, John M. and Van de Kragt, J.C. (1986), 'Organizing groups for collective action', *American Political Science Review*, **80**, pp. 1171–85.

Fehr, Ernst and Gächter, Simon (1999), 'Cooperation and punishment', *American Economic Review*.

Gintis, Herbert (2000), *Game Theory Evolving* (Princeton, NJ: Princeton University Press).

Güth, Werner and Tietz, Reinhard (1990), 'Ultimatum bargaining behaviour: A survey and comparison of experimental results', *Journal of Economic Psychology*, **11**, pp. 417–49.

Roth, Alvin (1995), 'Bargaining experiments', in *The Handbook of Experimental Economics*, ed. John Kagel and Alvin Roth (Princeton: Princeton University Press).

Roth, Alvin E., Prasnikar, Vesna, Okuno-Fujiwara, Masahiro and Zamir, Shmuel (1991), 'Bargaining and market behaviour in Jerusalem, Ljubljana, Pittsburgh, and Tokyo: An experimental study', *American Economic Review*, **81** (5), pp. 1068–95.

Sato, Kaori (1987), 'Distribution and the cost of maintaining common property resources', *Journal of Experimental Social Psychology*, **23**, pp. 19–31.

Yamagishi, Toshio (1988a), 'The provision of a sanctioning system in the United States and Japan', *Social Psychology Quarterly*, **51** (3), pp. 265–71.

Yamagishi, Toshio (1988b), 'Seriousness of social dilemmas and the provision of a sanctioning system', *Social Psychology Quarterly*, **51** (1), pp. 32–42.

Yamagishi, Toshio (1992), 'Group size and the provision of a sanctioning system in a social dilemma', in *Social Dilemmas: Theoretical Issues and Research Findings*, ed. W.B.G. Liebrand, David M. Messick, and H.A.M. Wilke (Oxford: Pergamon Press).

CAN EVOLUTIONARY THEORY PROVIDE EVIDENCE AGAINST PSYCHOLOGICAL HEDONISM?

Gilbert Harman

Sober and Wilson (1998) argue (1) that neither psychological evidence nor philosophical arguments provide grounds for rejecting psychological hedonism, but (2) evolution by natural selection is unlikely to have led to such a single source of motivation. In order to turn their piecemeal discussion of (1) into a serious argument, Sober and Wilson need a general procedure for mapping alternative accounts of motivation into egoistic hedonistic accounts. That is the only way to demonstrate that there will always be an available hedonistic account no matter what the psychological evidence. But such a general procedure, if available, must block their argument for (2). So, the more persuasive the case for (1), the less persuasive the case for (2).

Psychological hedonism is the thesis that people are ultimately motivated only by considerations of their own pleasure and pain. Sober and Wilson (1998) argue (1) that neither psychological evidence nor philosophical arguments provide grounds for rejecting psychological hedonism, but (2) evolution by natural selection is unlikely to have led to such a single source of motivation. I am not convinced that these two claims can be simultaneously defended.

Consider someone S who sacrifices his life for the sake of someone else. Sober and Wilson argue that such an action cannot be taken as a refutation of psychological hedonism, because it might be extremely painful for S not to undertake the sacrifice, so painful that S could not bear not to make the sacrifice (1998, p. 286).

It might be objected that S wants the other person P to flourish even when S cannot help P. But Sober and Wilson point out that, according to the hedonist, what's true is that S takes pleasure in the knowledge that P is doing well and is pained by the knowledge that P is not doing well. Objection: if P is in trouble, why doesn't S simply turn his mind to other matters rather than undertake to help P out? Sober and Wilson's answer, it would pain S too much to decide to turn his mind to other matters, because it would pain S not to help P if he can.

A philosopher might allow that it makes S happy to help P, but will object that S is happy about helping P only because S cares for P; if S did not care for P, it would not make S happy to help. But, according to Sober and Wilson, such an objection simply begs the question against the hedonist 'for no good reason' (p. 278).

Another philosopher might argue that Nozick's 'experience machine' (1974, pp. 42–5) thought experiment shows that people want more than just the experience of bringing certain things about, since they would not choose to hook themselves up for the rest of their lives to a machine that could give them the relevant experiences. Sober and Wilson reply that this is because people would find it too painful to decide to hook themselves up (1998, p. 286).

In order to turn their discussion into a general defence of egoistic psychological hedonism, Sober and Wilson would need a general procedure for mapping alternative accounts of motivation into egoistic hedonistic accounts, so that we can be sure that there will always be an available hedonistic account no matter what the psychological evidence.

One relatively simple such mapping would be the following. Where an alternative theory postulates that S is intrinsically motivated to bring about E, the corresponding hedonistic theory postulates that S is made happy by taking himself to be bringing about E and finds it painful to avoid bringing about E where he can. Then, where the alternative theory says that S is unselfishly motivated to benefit P, the corresponding hedonistic theory says that S is selfishly motivated to obtain the happiness felt in taking himself to be benefiting P and to avoid the pain felt in taking himself not to be doing so when he could do so. It would seem that, whatever could be explained by a pluralistic theory could be explained purely hedonistically via this mapping. So, it would seem that no psychological evidence could distinguish pluralistic theories from purely hedonistic theories of motivation, which is Sober and Wilson's first claim (1) that neither psychological evidence nor philosophical arguments provide grounds for rejecting psychological hedonism.

But this way of mapping pluralistic theories of motivation into psychological hedonism casts doubt on Sober and Wilson's argument for their claim (2) that evolution by natural selection is unlikely to have led to such a single source of motivation as in psychological hedonism. Their argument is in part that 'psychological altruism will be more reliable than psychological hedonism as a device for getting parents to take care of their children' (1998, p. 319). But the existence of a general mapping between the theories suggests that any biological mechanism instantiating psychological altruism can also be interpreted as instantiating psychological hedonism, which would mean that psychological altruism could not be more reliable than psychological hedonism in any way whatsoever!

For example, suppose we can interpret S as altruistic. That is, there are aspects of S's psychological makeup that can be interpreted as functioning as intrinsic concerns with the welfare of others, including P. When S comes to believe that P is in trouble, S becomes unhappy because of S's intrinsic concern for P. If S then believes that he can help P, S goes into a state that is here identified with wanting to help P, and that state can lead S to decide to do what he can to help P.

Then there would seem to be another way of interpreting S's very same psychological states in accordance with psychological hedonism. Instead of attributing to S an intrinsic concern for P, the second interpretation attributes an immediate connection between S's view of P's welfare and S's own happiness. When S comes to believe that P is in trouble, S immediately becomes unhappy. S has the same disposition in both interpretations; it is merely described differently.

In summary, if Sober and Wilson are to make out their case for (1), that neither psychological evidence nor philosophical arguments provide grounds for rejecting psychological hedonism, that can only be because there is a way to map non-hedonistic explanations into hedonistic explanations. But given such a mapping, it is not true that non-hedonistic mechanisms could ever be more reliable than the hedonistic mechanisms, because these would just be the same mechanisms differently described. So there is no argument for (2), that evolution by natural selection is unlikely to have led to such a single source of motivation as in psychological hedonism.

References

Nozick, R., (1974), *Anarchy, State, and Utopia* (New York: Basic Books).
Sober, E. and Wilson, D.S. (1998), *Unto Others* (Cambridge, MA: Harvard University Press).

GROUP SELECTION: A NICHE CONSTRUCTION PERSPECTIVE

K.N. Laland, F.J. Odling-Smee and Marcus W. Feldman

Group selection, as advocated by Sober and Wilson, is theoretically plausible, although it remains an open question as to what extent it occurs in nature. If group selection has operated in hominids, it is likely to have selected cultural not genetic variation. A focus on niche construction helps delineate the conditions under which cooperation is favoured. Group selection may favour between-group conflict as well as within-group cooperation.

I: Group Selection is Theoretically Plausible

Unto Others (1998) is the clearest and most sophisticated treatise on group selection to date, and Sober and Wilson deserve credit for this, and for spelling out the implications of group selection for understanding of unselfish behaviour. We accept Sober and Wilson's arguments that the theoretical plausibility of group selection is long since well established, and that kin selection and reciprocity can be redescribed as group selection (Price, 1970; Uyenoyama and Feldman, 1980). We share Sober and Wilson's belief that kin selection and reciprocal altruism are not sufficient to explain all human cooperation. Kin selection is restricted to kin, while the evolution of cooperation based on reciprocity is probably limited to group sizes of less than ten, because increasing the size of interacting social groups reduces the likelihood that selection will favour reciprocating strategies (Boyd and Richerson, 1988). It is also hard to account for certain forms of human altruism, such as military heroism, in terms of reciprocity or kin selection (Boyd and Richerson, 1985). We even go along with Sober and Wilson that group selection helps to provide plausible explanations for those unselfish behaviours for which traditional evolutionary explanations fail to provide compelling accounts (with the qualification, discussed below, that what is selected is cultural not genetic variation).

This much said, besides kin selection and reciprocity, we remain sceptical as to how much group selection of genetic variation actually occurs in nature. We suspect that the conditions under which the group selection of genes will be influential are more stringent than *Unto Others* implies. Plugging carefully chosen figures into recursions to reveal an increase in altruists cannot be construed as evidence that group selection is likely in nature. We were surprised and impressed to learn of the efficacy of artificial selection for group productivity experiments, and fascinated by the account of Batson's elegant experiments supporting the empathy–altruism hypothesis. Nonetheless, no amount of theoretical analysis, artificial selection favouring group-level traits, or psychology experiments demonstrating subjects' benign dispositions, will prove that the group selection actually occurs as a natural phenomenon. Frank's (1988) remark that 'group selection is the favoured turf of biologists and others who feel that people are genuinely altruistic' still rings true, whatever fine distinctions Sober and Wilson make concerning individualism, selfishness and egoism.

II: Genetic or Cultural Replicators?

Boyd and Richerson (1985) argue that group selection operates at the cultural level, with group-level cultural traits being selected. They place emphasis on 'conformist transmission', where individuals adopt the behaviour of the majority. Conformist transmission minimizes behavioural differences within groups, but maintains differences between groups. Group selection of group-beneficial cultural variation is possible because the transmission process discriminates against non-conforming egoists.

Sober and Wilson have embraced Boyd and Richerson's model into their Multi-Level Selection (MLS) scheme. To the extent that Sober and Wilson are saying the same thing as Boyd and Richerson, we support them. However, we find Sober and Wilson's discussion of human cooperation unclear with regard to the replicators. When humans gang up in groups, and when these groups differ in productivity, are genes or cultural traits selected? *Unto Others* fails to answer this question with sufficient clarity, yet we regard it as critical. When it comes to large-scale human cooperation, we believe that the group selection of cultural variants is a more compelling explanation than the group selection of genetic variants. Where there is conflict between hunter-gatherer groups, some of the defeated peoples are absorbed into the conqueror's group (Soltis *et al.*, 1995), eroding genetic differences. On the other hand, a threatened or defeated people may switch to the traits of a new conquering culture, either voluntarily, or under duress. Unlike the group selection of genes, migration will not weaken the cultural group selection process.

Moreover, symbolic group marker systems, such as totem animals, human languages, and flags, make it considerably easier for cultures to maintain their identities, and to resist imported cultural traits from immigrants, than it is for local gene pools to resist gene flow (Boyd and Richerson, 1985). Social processes that operate to maintain group identities and prevent cheating, such as gossip, punishment, pressure to conform, and conventions, are primarily barriers to cultural rather than genetic variation. It is possible that genetic variants may be selected as an indirect consequence of the group selection of cultural traits. However, if Sober and Wilson are arguing that group selection in human populations acts directly on genetic variation, and that genes underlie any human group-level adaptations, they will have to make a more compelling case for this.

Sober and Wilson believe that in human societies social controls will evolve that favour unselfish behaviour and benefit groups. We anticipate that, at least sometimes, social controls may be exploited by powerful individuals, groups, or institutions, that dominate the dissemination of information through societies, to promote their own interests (Laland et al., 2000). Powerful individuals may gain by persuading others to conform, perhaps by recruiting extra assistance in modifying social environments in ways in which they, rather than the helpers benefit. Religious, commercial and political propaganda, for example, may be used to persuade, trick or coerce conformity from others against their own individual interests, yet in favour of the interests of a dominant elite. We find it difficult to believe that all social control mechanisms will be group beneficial.

III: Niche Construction and Cooperation

Our interest in cooperation stems from our research exploring the evolutionary consequences of niche construction. Niche construction refers to the capacity of organisms to choose, modify, regulate, construct and destroy important components of their world (Odling-Smee, 1988). Elsewhere we have drawn attention to the evolutionary implications of niche construction (Odling-Smee et al., 1996; Laland et al., 1996; 1999). Organisms modify their own, and other organism's, selective environments, generating a form of feedback that is rarely considered in evolutionary accounts. Our theoretical analyses reveal that niche construction significantly changes the nature of the evolutionary process (Laland et al., 1996; 1999).

With regard to cooperation, our niche construction perspective leads us to believe that an organism should be prepared to cooperate in ways that benefit another organism, when the other niche-constructs in ways that increment the first organism's relative fitness (Laland et al., 2000). For example, if the organisms are relatives, cooperation should be more likely among kin that niche construct in mutually beneficial ways, and less likely among kin that niche construct in mutually detrimental ways, than kin selection theory might predict. The same logic also applies to non-kin, where reciprocal altruism is a special case in which the organisms are unrelated individuals of the same species that directly modify each other's environment. Mutualisms also slot into this framework. Mutualistic interactions that result from the exploitation of incidental by-products are more evolutionarily robust than altruistic interactions as, because each individual is already acting selfishly, they are less likely to be broken down by selfish cheaters. Organisms may also invest in others so as to enhance the benefits which eventually return to themselves (Connor, 1995). A large amount of human cooperation can probably be explained in terms of the exploitation and investment in the by-products of others, in other words, in terms of mutualisms resulting from human niche construction. Barter and exchange are selfish mutualistic interactions in which individuals or organizations trade products for more desirable alternatives. Human individuals and institutions 'invest' in other individuals or institutions in order to enhance their own returns.

We accept enough of what Sober and Wilson are saying to recognise that it is possible that niche construction could make group selection more likely. For instance, some incidental by-products of individual niche construction will sum to have greater or lesser beneficial consequences for the population, and differences in the niche construction expressed by members of different populations may generate variation in group productivity. In cases where these incidental by-products are unavoidable, selfish individuals that reap the benefits without doing the niche construction may not be able to invade. Here group selection may occur, but we would describe the outcome as mutualism not altruism.

IV: Selfish Groups and Conflict.

The suspicion that group selectionists view people through rose tinted glasses is reinforced by their consistent focus on the positive repercussions of group selection (that is, within-group altruism), and the equally persistent neglect of the negative repercussions (that is, between-group selfishness, hostility and conflict). Group selection does not directly favour altruistic individuals so much as selfish groups. The group-level traits most effective in promoting group replication may also engender out-group hostility, inter-group aggression and conflict, fear of strangers, slanderous propaganda concerning outsiders, and so on. The same process to which Sober and Wilson attribute the best of human motives may also favour the worst attributes of human societies. With the exception of two sentences on page 174, this negative side of group selection is missing from *Unto Others* (1998).

We have suggested that organisms should be prepared to act in a hostile manner towards other organisms that niche construct in a manner detrimental to them (Laland *et al.*, 2000). This reasoning might account for a great deal of aggressive behaviour, including a form of reciprocal hostility, in which individuals and their descendants trade antagonistic acts. Organisms should actively harm other organisms by investing in niche construction that destroys other organism's selective environments, provided the fitness benefits that accrue to the investing organisms from doing so are greater than their fitness costs. Since this is a general idea, it should extend to the human cultural level, and in some circumstances to human groups, with the qualification that at this level other processes may be operating. Sober and Wilson have only completed half of the story. They owe us a treatise on how group selection favours between group conflict.

Acknowledgements
This work is supported by a Royal Society University Research Fellowship to Kevin N. Laland.

References

Boyd, R. and Richerson, P.J. (1985), *Culture and the Evolutionary Process* (University of Chicago Press).

Boyd, R. and Richerson, P.J. (1988), 'The evolution of reciprocity in sizeable groups', *Journal of Theoretical Biology*, **132**, pp. 337–56.

Connor, R.C. (1995), 'The benefits of mutualism: A conceptual framework', *Biological Reviews*, **70**, pp. 427– 57.

Frank, R.H. (1988), *Passions Within Reason: The Strategic Role of the Emotions* (New York: Norton).

Laland, K.N., Odling-Smee, F.J. and Feldman, M.W. (1996), 'On the evolutionary consequences of niche construction', *Journal of Evolutionary Biology*, **9** pp. 293–316.

Laland, K.N., Odling-Smee, F.J. and Feldman, M.W. (1999), 'The evolutionary consequences of niche construction and its implications for ecology', *Proc. Natl. Acad. Sci USA*, **96**, pp. 10242–7.

Laland, K.N., Odling-Smee, F.J. and Feldman, M.W. (2000), 'Niche construction, biological evolution and cultural change', *Behavioral and Brain Sciences*, **23**, pp. 1–46.

Odling-Smee, F.J. (1988), 'Niche constructing phenotypes', in *The Role of Behaviour in Evolution*, ed. H.C. Plotkin (MIT Press).

Odling-Smee, F.J., Laland, K.N. and Feldman, M.W. (1996), 'Niche construction', *The American Naturalist*, **147** (4), pp. 641–8.

Price, G.R. (1970), 'Selection and covariance', *Nature*, **277**, pp. 520–1.

Sober, E. and Wilson, D.S. (1998), *Unto Others* (Cambridge, MA: Harvard University Press).

Soltis, J., Boyd, R. and Richerson, P.J. (1995), 'Can group-functional behaviours evolve by cultural group selection? An empirical test', *Curr. Anthropol.*, **36**, pp. 473–94.

Uyenoyama, M. and Feldman, M.W. (1980), 'Theories of kin and group selection: A population genetics perspective', *Theor. Pop. Biol.*, **17**, pp. 380–414.

GROUP SELECTION, MORALITY, AND ENVIRONMENTAL PROBLEMS

Iver Mysterud

As various kinds of resources become scarce within the context of today's population, consumption, and environmental problems, conflicts of interest will become more evident, competition become more intense, and certain kinds of 'unwanted' behavioural strategies might have a tendency to emerge and be used by a growing number of individuals. In such situations, humans may activate group adaptations. If we have group adaptations, like a tendency to classify humans into in-groups and out-groups and to develop moralities favouring one's in-group(s), it may be problematic to extend our morality outside our own group, especially in environmental situations where resources become scarce. For such reasons, Unto Others *touches upon important topics which cannot be ignored. It is crucial to focus on the conditions under which it will be possible to develop a morality for all humans.*

Sober and Wilson stand on the shoulders of giant scholars in their view of morality. Both David Hume and Charles Darwin explained human morality as emerging from the complex cooperation within groups competing with other groups, and thus only gradually and with great difficulty does human moral concern expand to include those outside one's own group (Arnhart, 1998, p. 75). This theme is also evident in claims that modern evolutionary accounts of human behaviour, claiming that other humans may have been our most important selective factor (i.e. that the main obstacle to reproductive success in the past has been hostile humans, and not predators, disease or lack of food) (e.g., Alexander, 1975; 1990),[1] and that the propensity to wage war may be a group selected adaptation which is activated in certain situations (Eibl-Eibesfeldt, 1982). Modern accounts of morality, as in the Bible (Old Testament), may also have been a morality for the in-group (Hartung, 1995). For Moses, promoting the survival and reproduction of the Jews required social norms that led individuals to cooperate within their group to compete with other groups (Arnhart, 1998, p. 259). Darwinian theorists have therefore explained the Mosaic Law as promoting the reproductive interests of the Jews (Hartung, 1995; MacDonald, 1994, pp. 35–55). There is no reason to expect that Judaism is unusual in this respect. Modern social psychological literature abounds with articles discussing our tendency to distinguish between in-groups and out-groups (see Devine, 1995; Krebs and Denton, 1997).

War and open, violent conflict are of course no new phenomena (Keeley, 1996), but their consequences are more scary than ever in today's communities, considering modern technology and weapons. In such conflicts, humans may activate what *Unto Others* is about: group adaptations, i.e. behavioural strategies that benefit one's own group at the expense of other groups. Morality as a group adaptation means that the moral code works to benefit the group members (the in-group) at the expense of people in other groups (the out-groups). That is why this can be viewed as a coin with one pretty side — cooperation and moral rules for the benefit of one's own group, but also an ugly side — other moral rules and behaviour strategies directed against other groups.

The levels of selection debate discussed in *Unto Others* is crucially important because, in today's rapidly expanding megapopulation with individuals and various subgroups competing for all kinds of resources in order to survive and reproduce, we need to know the answers to the following questions: How can human nature best be characterized and understood from an evolutionary perspective? What adaptations exist, in which environment were they selected to contribute to reproductive success, and how do they function in our novel environment? How similar or dissimilar is the contemporary environment to the environments in which the relevant traits were selected (cf. Irons, 1998)? And how can one use this information for the political purposes of solving environmental and social problems including that of developing a morality for a sustainable future?

If we have adaptations in favour of our own group, such as a tendency to classify humans into in-groups and out-groups and to develop moralities favouring one's in-group(s), it may be problematic to extend our morality outside our own group, especially in environmental situations where resources become scarce. In an environmental context, it is important to clarify whether we need an 'outer enemy' in order to be able to cooperate effectively with all of humanity, or if pressures and threats from our common global environmental problems can be enough. And if our society's existing morality is the result of negotiation between the members (Alexander, 1987) and/or coercion by some members on others (Irons, 1991), it is crucial to focus on the conditions under which it will be possible to develop a new morality for all humans.

---

[1] Alexander's argument is thus consistent with the hypothesis that group selection may have been an important force in human evolution. However, Wilson (1999), who in general acknowledges the importance of Alexander's various contributions to the understanding of human evolution, has recently argued that Alexander's views in various publications and within the publications are internally inconsistent and underestimate the importance of group selection.

References

Alexander, R.D. (1975), 'The search for a general theory of behaviour', *Behavioural Science*, **20**, pp. 77–100.

Alexander, R.D. (1987), *The Biology of Moral Systems* (New York: Aldine de Gruyter).

Alexander, R.D. (1990), *How Did Humans Evolve? Reflections on the Uniquely Unique Species* (Ann Arbor, MI: Museum of Zoology, The University of Michigan).

Arnhart, L. (1998), *Darwinian Natural Right: The Biological Ethics of Human Nature* (Albany, NY: State University of New York Press).

Devine, P.G. (1995), 'Prejudice and out-group perception', in *Advanced social psychology*, ed. A. Tesser (New York: McGraw-Hill).

Eibl-Eibesfeldt, I. (1982), 'Warfare, man's indoctrinability and group selection', *Zeitschrift für Tierpsychologie*, **60**, pp. 177–98.

Hartung, J. (1995), 'Love thy neighbour: The evolution of in-group morality', *Skeptic*, **3** (4), pp. 86–31.

Irons, W. (1991), 'How did morality evolve?', *Zygon*, **26**, pp. 49–89.

Irons, W. (1998), 'Adaptively relevant environments versus the environment of evolutionary adaptedness', *Evolutionary Anthropology*, pp. 194–204.

Keeley, L.H. (1996), *War Before Civilization: The Myth of the Peaceful Savage* (New York & Oxford: Oxford University Press).

Krebs, D.L., Denton, K. (1997), 'Social illusions and self-deception: The evolution of biases in person perception', in *Evolutionary social psychology*, ed. J.A. Simpson and D.T. Kenrick (Mahwah, NJ: Lawrence Erlbaum).

MacDonald, K. (1994), *A People That Shall Dwell Alone: Judaism as a Group Evolutionary Strategy* (Westport, CT and London: Praeger).

Wilson, D.S. (1999), 'A critique of R.D. Alexander's views on group selection', *Biology and Philosophy*, **14**, pp. 431–49.

HOW SELFISH GENES SHAPE MORAL PASSIONS

Randolph M. Nesse

Genes are 'selfish' in that they make organisms whose behaviours are shaped, necessarily, to benefit their genes. But altruism and selfishness as we usually think of them have little to do with 'evolutionary altruism' and 'evolutionary selfishness', and the use of these phrases has given rise to much confusion. The most pernicious is the false conclusion that individual altruism is impossible unless it has been shaped by group selection. In fact, human altruism and morality are shaped by genes because individuals with these capacities have a fitness advantage. The advantage may come from sexual selection, social selection, or the advantages of a capacity for commitment, as well as from cooperation, and kin selection. Ironically, morality may be a metaphor so powerful that it inhibits careful thinking precisely because our brains are wired by natural selection to see the world in terms of good and evil.

Sober and Wilson's mission — to explain how natural selection shaped the human capacity for morality — is important and even somewhat urgent. I share their commitment to finding a solution, but I don't see that group selection is either necessary or sufficient. In fact, it seems to me that their approach, like that of many others (including me at one time — Nesse, 1994), is obscured by the mist that descends when the language of morality is used as a metaphor for the process of natural selection. This gambit, so seductive that it is almost impossible to resist, blurs selfish genes with selfish people, thus concealing the central truth of the matter — the best strategy for selfish genes is to make humans who, in certain situations, have the capacity and propensity to act in ways that are genuinely altruistic, and even morally principled.

The issue arose in this century when Williams (1966) demonstrated that group selection is feeble, and Hamilton (1964) recognized that kin selection provided an alternative explanation for helping relatives. The crisis for moral theory and our view of ourselves was amplified when Wilson (1975) applied evolution to humans and Dawkins (1976) used the emotionally charged language of the moral passions to describe competitions between genes. Calling genes 'selfish' was inspired. It accurately describes how they create organisms designed wholly to increase the copies of their genes in future generations. Inevitably, mindlessly, genes increase in prevalence if they make phenotypes that advance their own interests; genes that foster any kind of 'evolutionary altruism' are displaced.

From this inexorable logic, many have reached the bleak conclusion that altruism is impossible. Our actions, this argument goes, are products of a brain that is designed to advance the interests of our genes. Taking care of our children, and helping people who help us, may seem altruistic, but such actions actually help our genes. Other instances of apparent altruism can be attributed to manipulation, coercion, novel environments, mistakes, or conscious decisions to oppose the dictates of natural selection.

The emotional punch of this conclusion lands at the solar plexus of our moral identities. People who have been trying to live moral lives suddenly wonder if their apparently generous impulses might actually be selfish at the core. George Williams has written about 'Mother Nature, the wicked old witch' and has helped to reignite Huxley's argument on evolution and morality (Huxley, 1989 [1893]). Finally, consider how most books on evolution and morality conclude, with their admonitions to accept the bitter pill of our fundamental selfishness, in hopes that this knowledge will allow us to 'transcend' our basic nature.

Into this fray come Sober and Wilson (1998). Their strategy is to reclaim altruism by resurrecting group selection. As they point out, group selection occurs when a gene that becomes progressively less common within a group is nonetheless increased in frequency because groups in which the gene is prevalent grow faster than other groups, or displace them. The exemplar is a group of selfish individualists being displaced by a group with individuals whose genetic tendencies motivate cooperation. Models show that this kind of strict group selection can work, but only under stringent conditions — especially lack of movement between groups and short individual life-spans compared to the durations that groups exist. These conditions are not unknown, but are rare in the natural world. If group selection had any strength at all, then most sex ratios would be biased towards females since a preponderance of females can double a group's rate of increase. But most sex ratios are 50:50, as would be expected if individual selection were overwhelmingly more powerful than group selection.

Sober and Wilson are unwilling to give up their commitment to group selection, however, so they expand the term to cover phenomena that are fundamentally different; namely, the benefits from selective association with altruists and kin. Does using the term group selection for such phenomena offer new understanding that can counterbalance the confusion it causes? After many of my lectures in recent years, some earnest soul asks if I am aware that group selection is back, that it can explain human altruism and group cooperation. Invariably the questioner has no inkling of the subtleties offered by Sober and Wilson, but thinks that they have shown that old-style group selection can explain major characteristics of many species. Worse yet, some otherwise sophisticated scholars seem to have accepted the notion that group selection is a morally superior idea that has been unfairly undermined by selfish gene theorists, who therefore deserve moral opprobrium.

Much of the confusion surrounding morality and group selection has arisen from a simple misunderstanding. It is correct beyond question that genes shape brains that induce individuals to do whatever best gets copies of those genes into future generations. This principle follows from the logic of how natural selection works, and is not an empirical issue. When this is combined with our intuitive notion that altruism consists of costly acts that benefit others, and genes are seen as the ultimate currency, then altruism is impossible.

However, 'evolutionary altruism' is not altruism at all. A behaviour is evolutionarily altruistic if it decreases an individual's Darwinian fitness and benefits the fitness of others. We could save vast confusion if we called such acts, 'evolutionarily senseless social behaviours' (ESSB), and contrasted them with 'evolutionarily advantageous social behaviours' (EASB). Such designations would at least permit conversation about the matter without getting us tangled up in our moral passions.

Sober and Wilson start their book by clearly distinguishing 'evolutionary altruism' from 'psychological altruism', and they highlight some major differences; but later the concepts seem to blur. Also, psychological altruism is not the same thing as individual altruism. Sober and Wilson note that many evolutionary altruistic acts are selfish and that many individually altruistic acts are evolutionarily beneficial to our genes, but what a struggle it is to keep all this straight! Worse yet, if group selection were powerful, consider its probable products. Yes, it would shape cooperation within the group, but at the expense of other groups. Do we really want to call ethnocentrism, patriotism, racism, and sexism 'altruistic' in even the evolutionary sense? What terrible confusion this causes! Staying up all night with a sick baby increases one's inclusive fitness, but it is also an act of individual altruism. Paying back a favour may give fitness advantages by maintaining a relationship, but that does not make it selfish. It is *failing* to pay back a favour that is selfish. The moral status of such acts depends on the goals of both parties, their motives, and their commitments. Sober and Wilson say this all of this, but the overall impression still is one of selfish genes causing selfish behaviours, with group selection as the only possible explanation for genuine altruism.

The potential explanations for altruism need to be expanded. Beyond traditional group selection, kin selection and reciprocity can shape capacities for genuine altruism — the benefits they provide to genes are not relevant to their moral status. Beyond this trinity, I can see at least four additional ways that natural selection might shape capacities for altruism. Some of them take us much closer to our core notion of morally principled behaviour.

The first is social selection (Alexander, 1987; West-Eberhard, 1987; Steven Frank, 1998). Social groups give rise to emergent forces of natural selection that may well be able to shape capacities for genuine altruism. The dynamics of this need not even be very complicated. If groups create norms, by whatever means, and individuals who violate those norms are excluded from the group, then even the least deviation may be fatal. An individual who is even thought to be calculating his relative advantage, instead of following the rule, might be fatally excluded. Furthermore, many of the exquisitely subtle norms that groups enforce so ruthlessly are about helping others. Sober and Wilson discuss something very similar to this kind of social selection, but because it involves groups, they would prefer to call it a kind of group selection. Their direction seems right to me, but their language causes considerable confusion.

A closely related but more specific source of altruism comes from commitment strategies (Schelling, 1960; Hirshleifer, 1978; Robert Frank, 1988; Nesse, 2000). Individuals who are capable of making credible commitments to threats and promises can have vast influence compared to those whose commitments are worthless. This may well be why people are so concerned with honesty. A dishonest person cannot use commitment strategies, and thus is at the mercy of others who have friends they can count on when they most need them, and whose threats must be reckoned with. It may also explain why people are so concerned to demonstrate that their relationships are *not* based on reciprocity. Yes, friends help each other, but woe to the naive reciprocator who too eagerly repays a favour in exacting kind. People don't just want reciprocity partners, they want friends whose commitment to them is based on love. To get this, they must be capable of love. When the exchange in a relationship becomes too unbalanced, commitments are severely strained, of course.

A third possible route to altruism is sexual selection (Miller, 1994). Altruism is an extraordinary trait because it seems to harm fitness. So do bright feathers and huge horns. Altruism is not sexually dimorphic, but could sexual selection, even runaway sexual selection, operate in both sexes at the same time? In the case of humans, recent ecological changes have created a need for two partners to cooperate to provide extended care for altricial offspring. In a cross-cultural study, much cited for finding sex differences in preferences for mates according to their wealth or attractiveness, Buss (1989) also found that the number one and two factors that individuals of both sexes were looking for in prospective mates were (1) 'intelligence', and (2) 'kindness'. Thus, the displays that prospective mates make of their mental and moral capacities. The pressure to demonstrate goodness may well shape a tendency for genuine good-ness, if this is what it takes to increase mating success. This is speculative, but possible.

Finally, as Boehm (2000) points out so nicely, people can decide what kinds of groups they want to live in. They can, and do, talk to create political and legal systems to encourage the good behaviour of members of the group. In particular, they can agree to limit the privileges of the powerful, by laws, taxes, and by social opprobrium. The enforcement of monogamy in many cultures is a remarkable example of the power of such systems.

Overall, the metaphor of morality as applied to evolutionary phenomena has caused much confusion, consumed much energy and caused much unnecessary dis-may. Genes do create organisms that increase their chances of being well-represented in the next generation. But this says nothing whatsoever about the selfishness of the individuals they create. Our tendency to interpret the world in moral terms is so pow-erful that using morality as metaphor for genetic competition almost automatically leads to a confusion of levels that makes life seem even worse than it is. To clean up the confusion we must keep the consideration of moral issues at the levels of the indi-vidual and society, even as we try to understand how genes create brains that induce behaviour that increases their representation in future generations.

There is one final irony in this story. Why is the metaphor of selfishness such a seductive and successful meme? I suspect it is because our minds have deep intuitions about what selfishness is, and emotional reactions to the idea of selfishness that we cannot overcome, even when authors such as Sober and Wilson patiently explain, several times, that they are talking about 'evolutionary selfishness', not psychological or individual selfishness (Cosmides & Tooby, 1992; Trivers 1981). As a result, we readily, but wrongly, conclude that people are fundamentally selfish, and that only group selection could give rise to genuine altruism. This conceals several other possible routes genes use to get themselves into future generations, some of which involve creating individuals with a capacity for genuine moral behaviour.

References

Alexander, Richard D. (1987), *The Biology of Moral Systems* (New York: Aldine de Gruyter).

Boehm, Christopher (2000), 'Conflict and the evolution of social control', *Journal of Consciousness Studies*, 7 (1–2), pp. 79–101.

Buss, David M. (1989), ' Sex differences in human mate preferences: Evolutionary hypotheses tested in 37 cultures', *Behavioral & Brain Sciences*, **12**, pp. 1–49.

Dawkins, Richard (1976), *The Selfish Gene* (Oxford: Oxford University Press).

Frank, Robert H. (1988), *Passions Within Reason: The Strategic Role of The Emotions* (New York: W.W. Norton).

Frank, Steven A. (1988), *Foundations of Social Evolution* (Princeton, NJ, Princeton Univ Press).

Hamilton, William. D. (1964), 'The genetical evolution of social behaviour I and II', *Journal of Theoretical Biology* 7, pp. 1–52.

Hirshleifer, Jack. (1978), 'Competition, cooperation, and conflict in economics and biology', *Journal of the American Economic Association*, **68**, pp. 238–43.

Huxley, Thomas H. (1989) [1893], Evolution and ethics in Paradise, in *Evolution and Ethics*, ed. G. James (Princeton, NJ: Princeton University Press).

Miller, Geoffrey F. (1994), 'Evolution of the human brain through runaway sexual selection: The mind as a protean courtship device', *Dissertation Abstracts International: Section B: The Sciences & Engineering*, **54**, p. 6466.

Nesse, Randolph M. (1994), 'Why is group selection such a problem?', *Behavioural and Brain Sciences* 17, pp. 633–4.

Nesse, Randolph M. (2000), 'Strategic subjective commitment', *Journal of Consciousness Studies*, 7 (1–2), pp. 326–30.

Schelling, Thomas C. (1960), *The Strategy of Conflict* (Cambridge: Harvard University Press).

Sober, E. and Wilson, D.S. (1998), *Unto Others* (Cambridge, MA: Harvard University Press).

Trivers, Robert L. (1981), 'Sociobiology and politics', in *Sociobiology and Human Politics*, ed. E. White (Toronto: Lexington).

West-Eberhard, Mary Jane (1987), 'Sexual selection, social competition, and speciation', *Quarterly Review of Biology*, **58**, pp. 155–83.

Williams, George C. (1966), *Adaptation and Natural Selection: A Critique of Some Current Evolutionary Thought* (Princeton, New Jersey: Princeton University Press).

Williams, George (1993), 'Mother nature is a wicked old witch', in *Evolutionary Ethics*, ed. M.H. Nitecki and D.V. Nitecki (Albany: State University of New York Press).

Wilson, Edward. O. (1975), *Sociobiology* (Cambridge, MA: Harvard University Press).

ALTRUISM, BENEVOLENCE AND CULTURE

Leonard Nunney

Human cultural groups appear well designed, but is this apparent design due to altruism or due to self-serving behaviours? Sober and Wilson argue that human cultures are founded on group-selected altruism. This argument assumes that individually selected self-serving traits are not being misidentified as altruistic. A simple definition of individual selection suggests that Sober and Wilson fail to separate one such trait, called benevolence, from altruism. Benevolent individuals act selfishly but provide an incidental benefit to their neighbours. The female-biased Hamiltonian sex ratios are used to illustrate benevolence, and a financial analogy is used to emphasize why such traits are individually advantageous. Benevolence can only evolve in a spatially structured population, illustrating the importance of separating individual selection in structured and unstructured populations. Unlike benevolence, altruism can only evolve by group selection and, as a result, is vulnerable to selfish 'cheats' that exploit the self-sacrifice of altruists.

Introduction

I wholeheartedly agree with the Sober and Wilson evolutionary approach to understanding the complexities of human culture, in which they stress that our perspective should be both pluralistic and multilevel. However, I remain unconvinced by their argument that the group selection of evolutionary altruistic traits is a major feature of micro-evolutionary change. I argue that Sober and Wilson find altruism ubiquitous because many of the traits they label as altruistic are, in fact, self serving. Thus, my goal is to challenge their definition of altruism and to point out that their usage confounds fundamentally different processes.

Multilevel Selection

In their discussion of multilevel selection, Sober and Wilson make much of the 'fallacy of averaging'. This fallacy stems from the truism that any genetic trait that spreads through natural selection must do so because, on average, it increases the fitness of individuals. Thus, if individual fitness is defined as this average, then all selected traits must spread by individual selection. Clearly, this usage adds nothing to our understanding of natural selection. So far so good. However, Sober and Wilson go much further by implying that evolutionary biologists are failing to see beyond this fallacy. This is patently untrue. Two examples are particularly telling: kin selection and gametic selection.

Hamilton's (1964) papers on kin selection are considered classics, in large part because they showed us how to distinguish the individual costs of altruism (c) from the benefit (b) to the family group. Hamilton's rule for the spread of altruism is $br>c$, where the group benefit is mediated through the degree of relatedness of the group members (r). This formulation clearly allows us to recognize individual costs and group-mediated benefits and to evaluate their relative importance in driving natural selection.

The second example is gametic selection, which occurs when a genetic element increases its representation in the next generation through its success as a gamete. This may occur during gamete production or through gamete (usually sperm) competition. For example, in the 1960s, Lewontin (see Lewontin and Dunn, 1960) became interested in the t elements found in house mouse populations. One of these elements is homozygous lethal, and yet is found commonly in nature. The abundance of t is due to the offspring of heterozygous males ($+/t$) inheriting t much more often than the 50 per cent that Mendel's law of segregation predicts. The result is a stable polymorphism with the gametic selection favouring t balancing the individual selection (t/t lethality) favouring '$+$'.

There is general agreement that our understanding of evolution is enhanced if we identify kin selection and gametic selection as levels of natural selection distinct from individual selection. But what is individual selection? It can be defined as the component of natural selection resulting from the fitness differences among geno-types subject to a common environment. In the simplest case, the fitness differences are the same across all suitable environments. Thus, in the case of the t elements dis-cussed earlier, individual relative fitnesses (w) are $w=1$ for the genotypes $+/+$ and $+/t$, and $w=0$ for t/t. In other cases, variation in environments may be more important. These environmental variables may be physical (as in the classic example of indus-trial melanism; see Majerus, 1998) or biological. Here I will focus on the biological.

Studies of interspecific and intraspecific competition show that some genotypes are better competitors than others, but these genotypes may not be superior when competition is absent. This trade-off was originally formalized in MacArthur and Wilson's (1967) r- and K-selected continuum. An r-selected character is favoured when competition is low and resources are abundant. A K-selected character is favoured when competition for resources is intense. Thus the continuum formalizes the idea that individual fitness can depend upon the biotic (competitive) environment. This environment includes both intraspecific and interspecific interactions, so if we wish to evaluate the relative (individual) fitness of two genotypes, we must compare them under precisely the same conditions of interspecific and intraspecific influence. But Sober and Wilson do not evaluate individual fitness under the same intraspecific conditions. Their approach (outlined below) can create an unnecessary and confusing illusion of a higher order evolutionary process where none exists. For this reason, Sober and Wilson see group selection and altruism when others see only individual selection and self-interest.

Altruism and Benevolence

Let us consider an example that Sober and Wilson develop in detail, the evolution of female-biased sex ratios. Generally, a 1:1 sex ratio predominates in nature; however, Hamilton (1967) developed a model to account for the female bias seen in many spe-cies including, in particular, parasitoid wasps. In Hamilton's model, females mate in the local area of their birth and then disperse to lay their eggs without further mating. These dispersing females randomly form small groups of size g on some suitable resource. Their offspring develop and mate together and the cycle restarts. Assuming diploidy, the optimum strategy is to produce a sex ratio (proportion males) of $(g-1)/2g$. But why? Sober and Wilson argue that this 'Hamiltonian' optimum is altru-istic and favoured by group selection. However, if a female is given a 'choice' to pro-duce either a 1:1 sex ratio or the Hamiltonian sex ratio, her fitness (as measured by the total number of grand offspring) always increases if she 'chooses' the Hamiltonian strategy (Nunney, 1985a). The reason why a biased ratio is superior under these con-ditions is that by manipulating the sex ratio of the mating group containing her off-spring, she can enhance the fitness of her sons. In fact, the idea that a female may 'choose' the sex ratio of her brood is not just useful theoretical speculation. Many parasitoid wasps vary the sex ratio of their broods depending upon the presence of other females and, in doing so, enhance their individual fitness (see Godfray, 1994).

So why do Sober and Wilson persist in calling this group selection? As I noted above, it stems from comparing fitnesses under different environmental conditions. Specifically, they compare fitnesses within and among temporary mating groups. The problem of this approach is discussed elsewhere (Nunney 1985a;b) but it can be illustrated by using a simple example of the Hamiltonian scenario. Consider a group of two maternal females, A and B. The intraspecific environment of A is female B and that of B is A. Female A's fitness depends in part upon the sex ratio produced by B, because B's strategy affects the future mating success of A's sons. However, regardless of B's strategy (which A does not know), A's evolutionary stable strategy (ESS), based on maximizing individual fitness, is to produce the Hamiltonian sex ratio. Sober and Wilson view this differently. They compare the fitness of A (given B) to that of B (given A) to define their 'individual fitness' and then they compare the productivity of this temporary group with all others to define their 'group fitness'. This last comparison almost inevitably creates a group effect (even in simple cases where the genotypes don't interact) since groups that by chance contain more of the individually fittest genotypes are the most productive (Nunney, 1985b). In the case of the 1:1 versus Hamiltonian sex ratio, these two comparisons create the facade of a conflict between group and individual selection that only serves to obscure a simple case of individual advantage.

To emphasize this point, let me return to a financial analogy that I first used many years ago (Nunney, 1985b). Wasps A and B are now you and your next door neighbour. You are given a choice: you may take $10 and keep it all; or you may take $10,000,000 on condition that you give $6,000,000 to your next door neighbour. Sober and Wilson's view is that selfish strategists would take $10 and that only altruists would take the $10,000,000 option. They justify why you would, in fact, act 'altruistically' by suggesting that the $10,000,000 strategy is promoted by group selection. I find this interpretation absurdly convoluted. Clearly the selfish strategy is to achieve a net gain of $4,000,000 even if this does lead to your neighbour gaining $6,000,000. I have termed traits favoured by individual selection but that incidentally provide a fitness gain to neighbours as 'benevolent'. The advantage of benevolence is solidly rooted in selfishness.

An important point illustrated by models for the evolution of benevolence is that individual selection in a spatially structured population can have a different outcome from individual selection in an unstructured population. The Hamiltonian strategy is only advantageous because localized groups of offspring mate independently of the rest of the population. If the subdivision is removed, either by making the groups infinitely large or by reducing the total population to a single group, then the traditional 1:1 sex ratio prevails. The same applies to the financial analogy: if you give more money to everyone in the population than your net gain, then your actions are truly altruistic.

Without doubt, local spatial structure plays an important role in evolution and Wilson's (1980) book was an important contribution in this area. Certainly, individual fitness depends on conspecific neighbours under almost any form of intraspecific competition. However, such fitness effects do not, by themselves, have anything in common with the notion of group selection debated in the 1960s. Sober and Wilson's usage combines, under the same heading, selection due to intraspecific competition in a structured population (such as fruit fly larvae competing in different fruits in an orchard) and selection of true altruism (such as the sterility of the worker honeybee). Confounding the role of spatial structure with traditional group selection and altruism is anti-pluralistic and only serves to muddy the intellectual waters.

Cheating

Why should we care about distinguishing altruism and benevolence? One of the main reasons concerns the importance of suppressing 'cheats' to maintain altruism. A cheat is able to exploit the benefits of altruism without paying any of the costs. Cheating was the pivotal issue in the group selection debate between Wynne-Edwards (1964) and Maynard Smith (1964) about whether population self-regulation evolved to promote the long-term benefit of groups. Maynard Smith (1964) pointed out that, in general, cheats that do not obey the social norm will inevitably arise and altruistic self-regulation will collapse.

For the analysis of human culture, it is important to recognize that altruism is only evolutionarily stable if the occurrence of selfish cheats is limited. Sober and Wilson briefly mention this important issue in their discussion of 'primary' (altruistic) and 'secondary' (policing) behaviours (their Chapter 4). However, it has long been clear that altruism and the suppression of cheating must go hand in hand (see Nunney, 1985b). This is why benevolence and other individually advantageous cooperative traits are likely to be abundant relative to altruism — they are not vulnerable to cheating and hence do not need policing.

Conclusions

Where does this leave the role of group selection and altruism in human culture? For the present, the issue must remain open. Unfortunately, Sober and Wilson have unnecessarily complicated this question by expanding the definition of altruism to include benevolent traits. Benevolent traits spread by individual selection and are not vulnerable to cheating. Altruistic traits, on the other hand, are individually disadvantageous and can only spread by group selection (whereby altruists tend to help other altruists). Without policing, such traits are vulnerable to cheats. Thus social sanctions play an important role in maintaining all forms of altruism. Sober and Wilson, by confounding altruistic and non-altruistic traits, miss this simple result.

I agree with Sober and Wilson that one form of group selection, kin selection, has been important in human culture. However, even at this level, we need to justify our conviction by identifying specific kin selected traits. Sober and Wilson offer no tangible scientific support for group selection above the family level, even though they claim that 'human social groups are so well designed at the group level that they must have evolved by group selection' (p. 191). What we need is a critical analysis of some specific traits, with an examination of their biological and cultural basis. Perhaps then we can decide whether the assertion just quoted has any basis or whether the characteristics that suit us to a social existence can be explained in terms of self-interest and benevolence.

References

Godfray, H.C.J. (1994), *Parasitoids: Behaviour and Evolutionary Ecology* (Princeton, NJ: Princeton University Press).

Hamilton, W.D. (1964), 'The genetical evolution of social behaviour. I and II', *J. Theoret. Biol.*, 7, pp. 1–52.

Hamilton, W.D. (1967), 'Extraordinary sex ratios', *Science*, 156, pp. 477–88.

Lewontin, R.C. and Dunn, L.C. (1960), 'The evolutionary dynamics of a polymorphism in the house mouse', *Genetics*, 45, pp. 702–22.

MacArthur, R.A. and Wilson, E.O. (1967), *The Theory of Island Biogeography* (Princeton, NJ: Princeton University Press).

Majerus, M.E.N. (1998), *Melanism: Evolution in Action* (Oxford: Oxford University Press).

Maynard Smith, J. (1964). 'Group selection and kin selection', *Nature*, **201**, pp. 1145–7.

Nunney, L. (1985a), 'Female-biased sex ratios: Individual or group selection', *Evolution*, **39**, pp. 349–61.

Nunney, L. (1985b), 'Group selection, altruism and structured-deme models', *Amer. Natur.*, **126**, pp. 212–30.

Wilson, D.S. (1980), *The Natural Selection of Populations and Communities* (Menlo Park, CA: Benjamin/Cummings).

Wynne-Edwards, V.C. (1964), 'A reply to Maynard Smith', *Nature*, **201**, p. 1147.

THE PROBLEM OF ENFORCEMENT
Is There an Alternative to Leviathan?

Alex Rosenberg

For Sober and Wilson, the key to group selection is the persistence of within-group behaviours that are individually altruistic — the so-called 'primary behaviours'. In the absence of kin-relatedness, such primary behaviours will render the group liable to invasion by non-cooperative strategies unless 'secondary behaviours' are in place. Secondary behaviour must in effect make the costs of deviation from the primary altruistic behaviour greater than the benefits of deviation. The secondary behaviour in effect enforces the primary behaviour. Secondary behaviour is also behaviour which is altruistic from the point of view of the individual, whenever enforcement has some costs and lower benefits to the enforcer. Enforcement always has some cost, when imposed. However, it increases the rate of cooperative primary behaviour and so has benefits for the group as a whole, whence its status as altruistic. When altruism and enforcement both emerge, altruism is amplified (Sober and Wilson, 1998, p. 146).

Sober and Wilson propose no further secondary behaviours besides enforcement to insure the sort of correlation of altruists playing against altruists that kin-selection might. At least since Hobbes, philosophers and others have sought an alternative to reciprocal altruism without enforcement as a secondary behaviour without success. And this is because, as we have also known for a long time, the power to enforce corrupts. Sober and Wilson recognize that for generalized and universally distributed enforcement to be implemented, its costs must be low, or at least lower than the costs to individuals of such generalized non-enforcement. One way to ensure that the cost of the secondary behaviour has this feature is to enforce the enforcement. But this will work only if its costs are lower than the cost of non-enforcement of enforcement, and so on. Another way is to confer powers of enforcement on some subset of the population. But this generates for the subset the same problems that face each individual in a society of generalized universally distributed enforcement. Indeed, it exacerbates the problem, as we shall see. Hobbes' proposal was to give complete and unappealable enforcement powers to an absolute authority, whose cost-benefit calculation always makes enforcement the dominant strategy.

Without the Leviathan, are these costs of mutual enforcement low enough and the cost of non-enforcement high enough to ensure the persistence of altruistic primary behaviour? Among groups of relatively small size and relatively early in the evolution of human society, there is some reason to think not. Consider first the prospect of bargaining between a prospective primary behaviour free-rider and the individual in a position to punish free-riding. Side payments from the prospective free-rider to buy-off enforcement, or the establishment of a coalition between prospective free-rider and prospective enforcer to share the gains from free-riding without enforcement need to be weighed into the equation in establishing prospective punisher's net costs of enforcement and of non-enforcement. When the two parties find themselves on the savannah far from the rest of the group, with the chance to consume more than their fair share of meat or berries, the temptation to do so becomes the dominant strategy.

To see how serious the problem is, consider Brian Skyrms' discussion of the problem of divide the cake as an ultimatum game in Skyrms (1996). There is a brief review of his results in Skyrms (2000), in the section 'Weakly dominated strategies'. The first chapter of Skyrms (1996) considers the problem of two players proposing divisions of a cake under the condition that the shares proposed must sum to the whole cake or less, for either player to secure any of the cake. Skyrms shows that under reasonable assumptions, 'natural selection' of non-zero outcomes to both players of iterated simultaneous proposals results in the proliferation of strategies that converge on the 50:50 fair division. In chapter two, instead of both parties making simultaneous bids about how to divide the cake, one party, player 1, proposes and the other, player 2, disposes. If the disposer, player 2, rejects the proposal, neither party gets anything. There are 10 pieces of cake. Player 1 can propose either a 9:1 split in which she retains the 9, or a 5:5 split. Player 2 can accept or reject either proposal. Note that rejecting the 9:1 split means player 2 gets nothing, instead of the one piece she would have received. Player 1 has two strategies; player 2 has four strategies, including the one of rejecting equal division because for example, player 2 insists on more than 5 pieces of cake. Skyrms compares the payoffs to the eight possible strategies for players who can both propose and dispose, including

Fairman: If player 1 propose 5:5;   if player 2 accept 5, reject 9
Gamesman: If player 1 propose 9:1;   if player 2 accept all
Mad Dog: If player 1 propose 9:1;   if player 2 accept 9, reject 5
Easy Rider: If player 1 demand 5:5;   if player 2 accept all

Gamesman is greedy, but Mad Dog is greedier still. Fairman is an altruist; she declines an unfair share even when offered. Easy Rider is a get-along, go-along type. What happens when these strategies face one another in an iterated Ultimatum game?

In a simulation where each of the eight possible strategies has the same initial frequency in the population, Fairman goes extinct and Gamesman persists (no surprise: *ceteris paribus*, altruism is an invade-able strategy). But in this competition, the population evolves to leave about 13% Mad Dogs as well. On the other hand, if the initial frequency of Fairman is 30%, and other strategies are represented by the same number of players, Gamesman and Mad Dog are driven to extinction, but at fixity, 36% percent of the population remain Easy Riders. Skyrms notes that in a more 'plausible initial point' where 30% of players are Gamesmen, 2% are Mad Dogs, 40% are Fairman, and only 10% are Easy Riders, *the replicator dynamics carries this population to a state of 56.5% Fairman and 43.5% Easy Riders* (Skyrms, 1996, p. 31).

How is this relevant to Sober and Wilson's requirement of secondary enforcement behaviours? The ultimatum game models enforcement. Employing the Fairman strategy, which costs the Fairman 1 unit to prevent the Gamesman or Mad Dog or other selfish strategies from securing 9 units is what I called above distributed generalized enforcement. And by allowing selfishness to succeed, Easy Rider is of course the strategy of not enforcing altruism, when the opportunity to do so arises. If, as Skyrms' 'plausible initial point' suggests, Easy Rider increases in representation in most replicator dynamics, then Sober and Wilson will have to reckon with the problem of assuring enough enforcers so that primary altruistic behaviours persist at rates which make for the selection of cooperative groups.

The prospect that insufficient rates of enforcement are likely is strongly suggested by Skyrms' discussion of how variation through 'mutation' can affect populations of Fairman and Easy Riders. In Ultimatum, after Fairman and Easy Rider have become fixed, it would be a 'mutation' to make a greedy proposal of 9:1. Skyrms says he needs to 'worry about' this since when such mutations arise, Easy Rider does better than Fairman, and will increase its proportion of the population. Sober and Wilson need to worry because the more Easy Riders, the less enforcement.

Suppose that the Fairman strategy is not genetically fixed, but say, memetically fixed, and open to mutation or Lamarckian change by players.

As the proportion of Easy Riders rises, the temptation and the payoff to switching to a new strategy, of playing Gamesman when the other party is an Easy Rider, increases. What it takes to develop this strategy is the ability to recognize the strategies other players employ, something Sober and Wilson (and Skyrms for that matter) all require to effect the correlations among strategies under which reciprocal altruism can thrive.

Either with or without the appearance of such a novel strategy, groups of Fairmen and Easy Riders into which non-cooperating free-riders appear, either by mutation or immigration, are under threat. A non-zero mutation/immigration rate will in the long run raise the number of Easy Riders, and this number will not decline during periods when no such mutants/immigrants appear. Once it has increased beyond a certain threshold (determined by the size of the group, the payoffs to cooperation and defection, and the initial distribution of strategies between Fairman and Easy Rider), the concomitant decline in the proportion of Fairman makes the group more and more vulnerable to invasion by Gamesman.

Of course, the numbers are critical to any of these results. Skyrms picked 9, 5, and 0 as the payoffs in the Ultimatum game, and any conclusions about the viability of enforcement may be sensitive to them, as well as to the values of other variables. But we can conclude that even independent of the qualifications that Sober and Wilson note and some they do not (the need for enforcement of enforcement, Sober and Wilson, 1998, p. 151, enforcement of enforcement of enforcement, and so on), there is more work to be done to nail down the claim that cooperation in human societies can emerge through a process of group selection. Still more work would need to be done to show that once cooperation emerged through group selection in societies characterized by egalitarianism, the lack of non-moveable capital, and the small size of hunter-gatherer groups, it will have persisted when these conditions cease to obtain.

Once hunter-gatherers settle down to cultivation, storable consumption goods, high cost capital goods, the payoff to various group-activities (sowing, weeding, reaping, preserving, storing, guarding) increase in size and change in proportion.

Moreover, payoffs to individual and coalition strategies participating in them will change from the one-shot or the iterated Prisoner's Dilemma matrices of hunter-gatherer interactions. The prospects of proportionately greater reward to free-riding, and more scope to hide free-riding behaviour, which these changes may induce, makes the introduction of more effective and higher cost methods of enforcement urgent if cooperation is to be preserved in the group. But the new methods — giving authority and perhaps making side payments to a special class of enforcers — provides them with rent-seeking opportunities, such as charging for non-enforcement — bribery, exacting payments to avoid wrongful enforcement — graft, or simply trading non-enforcement for a share of the Gamesman's prospective gain — in effect forging coalitions with Gamesmen. Indeed, extending the initial models that characterize studies like Sober and Wilson's and Skyrms' can give us insight into how the emergence of storable commodities generates highly unequal patterns of distribution, which in their turn swamp cooperative egalitarianism. By changing the relative payoffs to various strategies, the costs of effective enforcement of even partial cooperation over limited domains of social interaction, and the prospects for coalitions — voluntary and non-voluntary — we may learn a good deal more about the vicissitudes of group selection for altruism, and for the selfishness with which social and economic development overlays the egalitarian cooperation of hunter-gatherers and their hominid predecessor.

References

Skyrms, B. (1996), *The Evolution of the Social Contract* (Cambridge, Cambridge University Press).
Skyrms, B. (2000), 'Game theory, rationality and evolution of the social contract', *Journal of Consciousness Studies*, 7 (1–2), pp. 269–84.
Sober, E. and Wilson, D.S. (1998), *Unto Others* (Cambridge, MA: Harvard University Press).

IT'S BEEN A PLEASURE, BUT THAT'S NOT WHY I DID IT
Are Sober And Wilson Too Generous Toward Their Selfish Brethren?

William A. Rottschaefer

Sober and Wilson demonstrate convincingly the fallacies of arguments for fundamental biological and psychological selfishness and establish the plausibility of both biological and psychological altruism. However, I suggest that they are more generous to proponents of fundamental selfishness than they need be and that morality is closer to our evolved and learned capacities than they suggest. I am less generous toward advocates of fundamental selfishness than are our altruistic authors.

The Biology of Selfishness and Altruism

Sober and Wilson find a solution to the problem of biological altruism by considering multiple levels of selection, in particular the genic, individual and group, and by focussing on group selection. Individual and group selection differ in so far as what is selected for are traits of the individual and the group respectively. If individuals sacrifice their own fitness for the benefit of others in the group, that group may be fitter than its competitors and so be selected for. Given the right initial conditions, spelled out by Sober and Wilson, individual altruism can emerge in the context of group selfishness.

While agreeing with this account of biological altruism, I want to emphasize that Sober and Wilson's analysis shows that natural selection produces biologically altruistic and selfish behaviour whenever there is a complex unit for which there is selection. Consider the operation of selection at a given level. An entity that is selected for, a unit of selection, is 'acting' selfishly, since it benefits reproductively at the expense of other such units at that level. But, usually, at the next level below, the selected-for unit's components are behaving altruistically since they sacrifice their own interest for that of the whole, faring less well than their selfish compatriots, if any, within the containing unit. However, if conditions are right, groups with altruistic members fare better than those with selfish members, even though within the group, altruistic members do worse than selfish ones.[2] Selfishness at the individual level is often accompanied by altruism at the component level and either altruism or selfishness at the group level. Empirical investigation uncovers the existence and degree of each. Moreover, since the notions of component, individual and group are relative to levels we can move up or down the scale of levels discovering, depending upon the conditions of selection, biological selfishness and altruism.

In addition, the biological *self* whose self-directed fitness interests nature selects for is not merely the individual whose adaptations enable its survival and reproductive success, it is also the selves who are its immediate and distant progeny. The survival of the reproducing organism is important as a *means* to its *reproductive* success. But, from an everyday perspective, the self of the selfish individual, whose ultimately self-directed interests are pursued, is the individual itself, not its immediate and distant offspring. The ultimate end of biological selfishness includes other selves, while that of selfishness, ordinarily conceived, does not.[3] Inclusion of other selves is a mark of ordinary altruism.

Consequently, Sober and Wilson's account of both evolutionarily selfish and altruistic behaviour confirms and explains the existence of altruism, ordinarily conceived, that is, behaviour that benefits an ontologically distinct other rather than the actor.

The Psychology of Selfishness and Altruism

A Sober-and-Wilson hedonist is motivated by one and only one ultimate end, attaining pleasure and avoiding pain, both internal states of an organism. It is an end of the system because the system detects and aims for it. It is an ultimate end because any other feelings or desires are merely instrumental to attaining it, even those directed toward the organism's own body. It is a selfish end because it is a state of the organism. Are we Sober and Wilson hedonists?

Though Sober and Wilson find hedonism a bizarre theory of human motivation (1998, p. 324), they nevertheless take it very seriously, making it the fundamental theoretical alternative to motivational pluralism. Sober and Wilson's arguments for levelling the playing field between psychological egoism and pluralism are persuasive. However, given the psychological studies that apparently defeat its various forms, they are overly generous in retaining hedonism as a plausible alternative hypothesis. Appeals to hidden hedonistic motivations often appear *ad hoc*. Moreover, though I find their evolutionary argument that we more than likely also have ultimately altruistic

---

[2] Selection may be occurring at multiple levels and its direction may be the same or different at each level.

[3] With sexual reproduction, we do not even have type-selfishness since the offspring contains only half of each parent's genotype.

motivations convincing, I believe they unnecessarily limit their case for motivational pluralism.

Sober and Wilson define desires in such a way that they can be either conscious or unconscious, thus rendering it unlikely that either introspection or philosophical argument will be helpful in settling the nature of ultimate desires. Nevertheless, there are reasons to believe that egoism, a pluralistic motivational system, is more plausible than monistic hedonism.

Pleasure and pain are states of the organism that are often functionally related to bodily well-being or harm. They could serve as indicators of the latter. Seeking pleasure and avoiding pain could be motivational means to attain beneficial and avoid harmful bodily states. So understood, they are motivationally instrumental, not ultimate. Are there reasons to believe that they sometimes so function in humans?

Some theoretical scientific reasons make egoism more plausible than hedonism. For instance, consider the behaviourists' law of effect — that behaviours are learned on the basis of the consequences they bring about. Setting aside the apparent paradox of behaviouristic mentalism, Sober and Wilson find the law to reflect a hedonistic motivational system. But Skinner and the radical behaviourists would never accept a hedonistic understanding of the law of effect. In their view, the consequences that govern the generation of behaviours are environmental reinforcing factors and the organism's learning history. Eating, sleeping, having sex, exercising, reading, studying, talking and the like are all reinforcing to the individual because of the characteristics of these activities, not the pleasure they bring. People are motivated to do them because of their individual and social learning history and, in some cases, their evolutionary history. But one need not be a radical behaviourist to avoid hedonism. Social cognitive theorists like Albert Bandura (1986) have shown that we have complex motivational systems that operate on more than hedonistic motivations. This is not to say that no one ever desires to maximize pleasure and minimize pain as ends in themselves.

Though it would be incorrect to conclude that the motivational systems postulated by social cognitive theorists are all egoistic, let us grant the conclusion for the sake of argument. Also make the reasonable assumption that some egoistic motivations have to do with bodily well-being.[4] Given these assumptions, we can use Sober and Wilson's evolutionary argument to claim that the ends of egoistic motivational systems are more likely to correlate with functions promoting evolutionary fitness than are those of a hedonistic system. Of course, these correlations need not be known and evolutionary fitness need not be desired. Thus, it may be more likely — given the satisfaction of the criteria of availability, efficiency, and reliability — that nature selects for egoistic systems over hedonistic ones. But since the ends of egoism correlate to some extent with those of biological fitness, they thereby correlate with altruism ordinarily conceived, that is, with behaviours that are aimed toward benefiting ontologically distinct others.

Although Sober and Wilson recognize the existence of other apparently cognitively motivational mechanisms, most notably feelings and emotions, they discuss these mechanisms either in terms of conditioning or belief/desire mechanisms. But it is more than likely that some emotions and feelings constitute distinct cognitively motivational

---

[4] Sober and Wilson reveal in an endnote that they themselves think that non-hedonistic egoism better represents peoples' motivations with respect to their bodily well-being (1998, p. 362).

mechanisms (Griffiths, 1997). Empathy and empathic distress is plausibly one such mechanism. Martin Hoffman (e. g., 1981) has argued that empathic distress is a genuinely other-directed emotion that, when combined with sympathy, leads to behaviour that benefits the person in distress.[5] Hoffman contends that there is reason to believe that such motivation develops in very young children before the development of higher cognitive capacities such as that required for perspective-taking, capacities that might be required for altruistic motivations and behaviours toward, for instance, suffering groups with whom a person has no direct acquaintance.

I conclude that a stronger theoretical case for motivational altruism can be made than the one presented by Sober and Wilson. They have, I believe, been overly altruistic to hedonism, allowing it more theoretical plausibility than it really deserves. Its prominence in at least western thought is, I believe, best explained, as Sober and Wilson hint, as an ideological construction (1998, p. 295 and p. 359).

I now turn to morality which I find emerging from both evolutionary and learned selfishness as well as altruism.

The Morality of Selfishness and Altruism

Sober and Wilson quite rightly argue that moral behaviour is distinct from altruistic behaviour. Neither necessarily implies the other. Some self-directed behaviours, for instance, taking care of one's health, developing one's talents, and protecting and upholding one's rights, are substantively within the moral realm. Some other-directed behaviours, for instance, the promotion and maintenance of proper relationships with children, family, friends, neighbours, and fellow citizens, are also within the moral realm. Morality includes biologically selfish as well as altruistic behaviours, obligations toward oneself as well as toward non-related others. Indeed, it includes behaviours that benefit the individual himself or herself that have nothing necessarily to do with survival as a means to reproduction, for example, taking care of oneself when the chances for reproduction, either directly or indirectly, are not present.

Sober and Wilson also rightly distinguish moral motivation from altruistic motivation. Altruistically motivated actions can be morally wrong and selfishly motivated moral actions can be morally right. One can cheat another in order to help someone else. In some circumstances one can rightly help oneself while neglecting another.

Granting that moral behaviours and moral motivations are not identical with altruistic behaviours and motivations, Sober and Wilson, nevertheless, suggest that social norms are plausibly considered to be group adaptations. The social function of morality is to motivate people to do things that they would not otherwise be inclined to do, or to strengthen dispositions that they already possess but in a weaker form. However, given the substantive overlap between biological selfishness and morality, individual selection may also be an evolutionary source for moral behavioural capacities. Similarly, individual selection, as in the case of parental care, is plausibly the source of some moral motivation. Indeed, given that a major substantive and motivational requisite of morality is fairness rather than either always sacrificing self to others (Sober

---

[5] My interpretation of Hoffman's theory differs from Sober and Wilson's who take Hoffman to be proposing that infants and young children start out as hedonists and gradually learn to be altruists. I believe, however, that Hoffman is proposing that evolution has selected for emotional capacities that are themselves ultimately altruistic motivators (Hoffman, 1981).

and Wilson's pure altruism) or sacrificing self to others in situations of conflict (Sober and Wilson's 'A over E Altruism'), the evolutionary sources for morality plausibly include both individual and group selection.[6]

In their summary of *Unto Others* (pp. 185–206, above), Sober and Wilson make three points about evolutionary altruism and normative ethics. First, considerations of human capacities are important in determining the limits of moral obligations. Second, human capacities, whether of the biological or learned/cultural sort, are not fixed. Thus, morality is open to revision and advance. Third, in so far as altruistic desires are constitutive of a person's preference structures and such preferences are within the moral realm, rationality will be on the side of morality. I agree with these claims and suggest that, though Sober and Wilson do not address issues of justification or ontology of moral values, their efforts provide some help for those interested in a scientific naturalistic account of justification (Rottschaefer, 1998). In so far as altruism-producing mechanisms pertain to the realm of morality, they are means to form morally true beliefs and morally correct motivations. As such they count in a naturalistic scheme of things as fallible justifiers of moral beliefs, motivations, and actions.

References

Bandura, Albert (1986), *Social Foundations of Thought and Action: A Social Cognitive Theory* (Englewood Cliffs, NJ :Prentice Hall).

Griffiths, Paul E. (1997), *What Emotions Really Are: The Problem of Psychological Categories* (Chicago: The University of Chicago Press).

Hoffman, Martin L. (19981), 'Is Altruism Part of Human Nature?' *Journal of Personality and Social Psychology,* **40** pp. 12–37.

Rottschaefer, W.A. (1998), *The Biology and Psychology of Moral Agency* (Cambridge: CUP).

Sober, E. and Wilson, D.S. (1998), *Unto Others* (Cambridge, MA: Harvard University Press).

EXPERIMENTAL STUDIES OF GROUP SELECTION: A GENETICAL PERSPECTIVE

Lori Stevens

Studies of group selection have been done with both natural and manipulated populations using plants, insects and birds. Group selection occurred in all studies and often the strength of group selection was equal to that of individual selection. Laboratory selection experiments resulted in the opposite response to individual selection than that predicted. Selection with plants for high leaf area resulted in plants with smaller leaf area and selection for high emigration rate in beetles produced lines with lower rates. The selected traits included interactions among individuals. Theoretical studies have shown that genetically based interactions among individuals can interfere with individual selection. Evolution can be partitioned into selection and the response to selection. A response to selection requires genetic variation. Properties of group genetic structure for the natural populations are discussed. The experimental populations had controlled group structure and demonstrate that populations can respond to group selection under some genetic structures.

---

[6] I must omit discussion of moral principles as motivators of moral behaviours.

Experimental studies of group selection highlight the importance and unique contributions of group selection to evolutionary theory. Multi-level selection has been measured in natural populations of plants (Stevens *et al.*, 1995) and insects (Breden and Wade, 1989). Laboratory experiments have compared the efficacy of group versus individual selection in plants (Goodnight, 1985) and insects (Craig, 1982). Group selection has been used to increase productivity in chickens (Craig and Muir, 1996; Muir, 1996). These studies empirically examine an idea which has received tremendous rhetorical attention, yet on which relatively few manipulative experiments and only a small number of field studies have been done.

Genes can act and interact on multiple levels. In the absence of any interactions, selection can be reduced to the selfish gene or individual level selection. When the two alleles at a locus interact (dominance) or alleles at different loci interact (epistasis), selection depends on the frequency of alleles at these other loci in the population. When either dominance, epistasis or genetically based interactions among individuals occur (altruism, competition for resources, production of harmful chemicals), the evolution of traits can be affected by group selection. Group selection can produce evolutionary adaptations not possible by individual selection because it can include genetic interactions. When evolutionary theory ignores or discounts group selection, we limit our understanding and discovery to traits governed by additive gene action.

Evolution by natural selection can be partitioned into two processes, selection and the response to selection. Selection involves fitness differences, but only those fitness differences that have an underlying genetic basis will result in adaptive evolution. With individual selection, the continuity of genes and individuals between generations is evident. An evolutionary response to group level selection requires sufficient population genetic structure. Much of the theory of group selection addresses these issues (cf. Wade, 1978) and the efficacy of group selection in natural populations will be affected by population structure. While some maintain that most natural systems will not have the requisite population structure, it is likely sufficient structure exists (cf. Sober and Wilson, 1998, p. 62).

The first two examples of experimental evidence for group selection involve measuring group selection in natural populations. Jewelweed or touch-me-not (*Impatiens capensis*) is a common annual plant with bright orange, trumpet shaped flowers. It grows in dense, monospecific stands in moist areas, often along roadsides, stream banks, lakes or ponds. Jewelweed produces two types of flowers, showy orange open pollinated flowers that are outcrossed, and small inconspicuous flowers fertilized by self-pollinating. The number of self-pollinated flowers usually is greater than the number of outcrossing flowers (Stevens *et al.*, 1995) and about half of the potentially outcrossed flowers are pollinated by flowers on the same plant, producing inbred seeds (Waller and Knight, 1989). Dispersal is probably less than one metre for over 90 per cent of seeds (Schmidt *et al.*, 1985). The combination of high self-pollinating and low seed dispersal distance will result in local population genetic structure. At the individual level, interactions between individuals can be negative, plants compete for resources such as nutrients and sunlight. When density increases offspring production per plant is reduced (Schmidt *et al.*, 1987). Group level interactions among plants include dependence on other plants for support to the extent that if neighbours were removed, an individual would not be capable of supporting itself and would fall over.

Selection was measured as the correlation between fitness (number of outcrossed and self-pollinated flowers and survivorship), individual level traits (e.g., size components such as number of leaves and height) and group level traits (e.g., density, average group size). The experiment used contextual analysis, a method of analysis of variance that partitions selection into group and individual level effects. Individual size was positively correlated with all three measures of fitness demonstrating individual selection favours large individuals (Stevens *et al.*, 1995). Average group size showed a significant negative correlation with two of the three fitness traits, survivorship and number of self-pollinated flowers. The selection coefficient for survival rate is larger for group effects than for individual effects. The strength of selection on reproduction is similar at the group and individual level. Group and individual selection are in opposite directions; although individual selection favours large plants, greatest overall survival and production of self-pollinated flowers was from groups with large numbers of small individuals.

Imported willow leaf beetles (IWLB, *Plagiodera versicolora*) are small metallic blue-green beetles that feed on leaves of willow trees in the genus Salix. Both selection and genetic structure have been studied in this species. Females oviposit multiple clutches containing about fifteen eggs each. Early hatching larvae often cannibalize unhatched eggs from the same clutch. Clutches maintain their group integrity after hatching and young larvae feed in groups (Breden and Wade, 1985). The benefits of group feeding include antipredator devices and enhanced feeding efficiency. These larvae produce volatile chemicals when disturbed and the chemicals from larger groups may be more effective than from small groups. Small larvae have difficulty initiating feeding sites on the tough surface of leaves; in group feeding, once one group member breaks through the tough leaf cuticle all individuals can feed. Females mate multiply (e.g., Stevens and McCauley, 1989) so clutches contain a mixture of full- (with genetic relatedness $r = 0.50$) and half-sibs ($r = 0.25$). (Genetic relatedness varies from 0 for completely unrelated individuals to 1 for identical twins or clones.) Average relatedness within clutches of IWLB is about $r = 0.4$ and the range is $r = 0.18 - 0.63$ (Goff and Stevens, 1995; McCauley *et al.*, 1988).

Studies of the benefits of cannibalism show that individual selection favours cannibalism and group selection opposes it. Individuals benefit from cannibalism in terms of increased size; cannibals have an initial weight increase of 14–30 per cent (Breden and Wade, 1989; Goff and Stevens, 1995). Mortality of young larvae is high and weight at hatching is correlated with future survival. By four days of age cannibals are 150 per cent heavier than non-cannibals (Breden and Wade, 1989). Group selection favours large groups and thus cannibalism by reducing group size, is selected against at the group level. However, selection on cannibalism involves not only group size, but also the behaviour phenotype of other group members. The fitness effects of this behaviour vary in a complicated manner (Breden and Wade, 1989). There is a net benefit to low cannibalism and large groups; larvae in large groups weigh more and have higher survivorship. The experiments with IWLB did not estimate the relative strength of group versus individual selection. However, both studies of group selection in natural populations documented opposing selection at the group and individual levels.

The two field studies described above examined selection, but not the potential of the population to respond to selection. A response to selection requires that the metapopulation have sufficient mating structure at the scale of appropriate ecological interactions among individuals. Three laboratory experiments compared the efficacy of group and individual selection for the evolution of interactions between individuals (Craig, 1982; Craig and Muir, 1996; Goodnight, 1985; Muir, 1996). Although something is known of the genetic structure of the field populations described above, the laboratory studies had the advantage of controlled mating structure and group integrity between generations.

Tribolium flour beetles, a stored grain pest, are often used as a model system for studying population ecology and evolution. They are easily reared in 25 x 95 mm glass vials and hundreds of replicate populations can be examined. By connecting vials with rubber tubing, emigration rate can be assayed. Emigration rate is a function of population density, and increases as the number of interactions between individuals increases. In a study comparing selection on individuals and groups with low emigration rate there was a highly significant response to group selection, but no response to individual selection (Craig, 1982).

An experiment with plants gave similar results (Goodnight, 1985). Leaf area of a small plant, *Arabidopsis thaliana*, was measured on both individuals and groups of individuals. The plant groups had 16 individuals and were grown in 50 x 50 mm pots. Individuals or groups with the largest leaf area were selected to establish subsequent generations. Group-level selection resulted in groups with higher leaf area, whereas when individuals with high leaf area were selected, subsequent populations had statistically significant smaller size.

Commercial chicken egg farmers raise hens caged in groups. Birds often aggressively interact so that it is standard practice to trim their beaks to reduce damage to other birds. The aggressive encounters cause mortality over the period of a year to be as high as 90 per cent in commercial strains. Group level selection for productivity of layers increased egg yield and reduced aggressive interactions such that mortality was only 20 per cent (Craig and Muir, 1996; Muir, 1996).

In all three of these experimental studies, integrity in terms of breeding structure was experimentally controlled. In addition, the jewelweed and IWLB populations are known to have genetic structure within their populations. In all five studies, genetically based interactions among individuals were important in the traits under selection. A series of models describes how genetically based interactions among individuals are subject to higher levels of selection (Griffing, 1977; 1981a–d; 1982a–f). Individual selection for high leaf area in plants actually resulted in plants with lower leaf area. This is likely because individuals achieved high leaf area by being good competitors and reducing the fitness of their neighbours. When individuals benefit from a negative effect on their neighbours, individual selection can be ineffective, or worse, the selected population can have the opposite response. Individual selection sometimes favours aggressive individuals that acquire resources at the expense of their neighbours. These individuals show decreased fitness when raised together (Griffing,1989). Individual selection often results in a negative response for any trait that is genetically correlated with aggressiveness. Group selection favours genes with reduced negative effects on their neighbours.

The major novel contribution of group selection is its ability to act on genetically based interactions between alleles, genes and individuals. The concept of inclusive fitness has been suggested for examining interactions. Sober and Wilson (1998) point out inconsistencies between the concept of inclusive fitness and multilevel selection theory. Contextual analysis can be used to investigate multilevel selection by measuring fitness components within and between groups. Genetical theory can define allele effects within and between groups and seems logically and intuitively consistent. The field of multilevel selection should not go back to adaptive story-telling, but has a potentially rich future partitioning gene effects and selection into individual and group components.

Experimental studies 'highlight the inadequacy of theory based on additive gene effects and the dearth of data from natural populations' (Goodnight and Stevens, 1997). Field studies demonstrate group selection occurs in natural populations. The history of controversy surrounding the topic of group selection has probably limited our study and understanding of adaptations involving gene interactions. Behaviours and other interactions among individuals are likely to have such a genetic architecture. With sufficient population genetic structure, group selection can result in altruism. At the very least, group level effects are likely to interfere with individual selection for aggressiveness. Our understanding of adaptive evolution requires we acknowledge genetically based interactions among individuals and carefully study them.

Acknowledgments
These ideas benefited from discussions with H. Prendeville, N. Twery, T. Giray, A. Viley and C. Goodnight. Writing the paper was supported by a grant from the National Science Foundation (IBN-9724037) to the author.

References

Breden F. and Wade, M.J. (1985), 'The effect of group size and cannibalism rate on larval growth and survivorship in *Plagiodera versicolora*', *Entomography*, **3**, pp. 455–63.

Breden F. and Wade, M.J. (1989), 'Selection within and between kin groups of the imported willow leaf beetle', *American Naturalist*, **134**, pp. 35–50.

Craig, D.M. (1982), 'Group selection versus individual selection: An experimental analysis', *Evolution*, **36**, pp. 271–82.

Craig, J.V., and Muir, W.M. (1996), 'Group selection for adaptation to multiple-hen cages: Beak-related mortality, feathering, and body weight responses', *Poultry Science*, **75**, pp. 294–302.

Goff, P.W. and Stevens, L. (1995), 'A Test of Hamilton's Rule: Cannibalism and relatedness in beetles', *Animal Behaviour*, **49**, pp. 545–7.

Goodnight , C.J. (1985), 'The influence of environmental variation on group and individual selection in a cress', *Evolution*, **39**, pp. 545–58.

Goodnight, C.J. and Stevens, L. (1997), 'Experimental studies of group selection: What do they tell us about group selection in nature? *American Naturalist*, **150**, pp. S59–S79.

Griffing, B. (1977), 'Selection for populations of interacting genotypes', in *Proceeding of the International Conference on Quantitative Genetics*, ed. E. Pollak, O. Kempthorne and T.B. Bailey (Iowa State Press, Ames). pp. 413–34.

Griffing, B. (1981a), 'A theory of natural selection incorporating interaction among individuals. I. The modelling process', *Journal of Theoretical Biology*, **89**, pp. 635–58.

Griffing, B. (1981b), 'A theory of natural selection incorporating interaction among individuals. II. Use of related groups', *Journal of Theoretical Biology*, **89**, pp. 659–77.

Griffing, B. (1981c), 'A theory of natural selection incorporating interaction among individuals. III. Use of random groups of inbred individuals', *Journal of Theoretical Biology*, **89**, pp. 679–90.

Griffing, B. (1981d), 'A theory of natural selection incorporating interaction among individuals. IV. Use of related groups of inbred individuals', *Journal of Theoretical Biology*, **89**, pp. 691–710.

Griffing, B. (1982a), 'A theory of natural selection incorporating interaction among individuals. V. Use of random synchronized groups', *Journal of Theoretical Biology*, **94**, pp. 709–28.

Griffing, B. (1982b), 'A theory of natural selection incorporating interaction among individuals. VI. Use of non-random synchronized groups', *Journal of Theoretical Biology*, **94**, pp. 729–41.

Griffing, B. (1982c), 'A theory of natural selection incorporating interaction among individuals. VII. Use of groups consisting of one sire and one dam', *Journal of Theoretical Biology*, **94**, pp. 951–66.

Griffing, B. (1982d), 'A theory of natural selection incorporating interaction among individuals. VIII. Use of groups consisting of a sire and several dams', *Journal of Theoretical Biology*, **94**, pp. 967–83.

Griffing, B. (1982e), 'A theory of natural selection incorporating interaction among individuals. IX. Use of groups consisting of a mating pair and sterile diploid caste members', *Journal of Theoretical Biology*, **95**, pp. 181–98.

Griffing, B. (1982f), 'A theory of natural selection incorporating interaction among individuals. X. Use of groups consisting of a mating pair together with haploid and diploid caste members', *Journal of Theoretical Biology*, **95**, pp. 99–223.

Griffing, B. (1989), 'Genetic Analysis of Plant Mixtures', *Genetics*, **122**, pp. 943–56.

McCauley, D.E., Wade, M.J., Breden, F.J. and Wohltman, M. (1988), 'Spatial and temporal variation in group relatedness: evidence from the imported willow leaf beetle', *Evolution*, **42**, pp. 184–192.

Muir, W.M. (1996), 'Group selection for adaptation to multiple-hen cages: Selection program and direct responses', *Poultry Science*, **75**, pp. 447–58.

Schmitt J., Ehrhardt, D.W., and Schwartz, D. (1985), 'Differential dispersal of self-fertilized and outcrossed progeny in jewelweed (*Impatiens capensis*)', American Naturalist, **126**, pp. 570–5.

Schmidt, J. Eccleston, J. and Ehrhardt, D.W. (1987), 'Density-dependent flowering phenology, outcrossing, and reproduction in *Impatiens capensis*', *Oecologia* (Berlin), **72**, pp. 341–7.

Sober, E. and Wilson, D.S. (1998), *Unto Others* (Harvard University Press: Cambridge).

Stevens, L., Goodnight, C.J. and Kalisz, S. (1995), 'Multilevel selection in natural populations of jewelweed, *Impatiens capensis*', *American Naturalist*, **145**, pp. 513–26.

Stevens, L. and McCauley, D.E. (1989), 'Mating prior to overwintering in the imported willow leaf beetle, *Plagiodera versicolora* (Coleoptera: Chrysomelidae)', *Ecological Entomology*, **14**, pp. 219–23.

Wade M. J. (1978), 'A critical review of the models of group selection', *Quarterly Review of Biology*, **53**, pp. 101–14.

Waller, D. M. and Knight, S.E. (1989), 'Genetic consequences of outcrossing in the cleistogamous annual, *Impatiens capensis*. II Outcrossing rates and genetic correlations', *Evolution*, **43**, pp. 860–9.

SELFISH, ALTRUISTIC, OR GROUPISH?
Natural Selection And Human Moralities

Ian Vine

Sober and Wilson's enthusiasm for a multi-level perspective in evolutionary biology leads to conceptualizations which appropriate all sources of bio-altruistic traits as products of 'group' selection. The key biological issue is whether genes enhancing one sub-population's viability in competition with others can thrive, despite inducing some members to lose fitness in intra-group terms. The case for such selection amongst primates remains unproven. Flexible social loyalties required prior evolution of subjective self-definition and self-identification with others. But normative readiness for truly group-serving sacrifices of ego-interests presupposes entitative conceptions of in-groups as collective social units — only made possible with the emergence of human symbolic language.

Sober and Wilson deserve credit for their single-minded, long-standing efforts to resurrect a 'group-level functionalist' (GLF) selection perspective within evolutionary biology. Some major theorists do now pay more than lip service to how inter-group as well as intra-group competition can affect a gene-based trait's adaptive success.

Nevertheless, the authors' sound and fury against the dominant 'individual-level functionalist' (ILF) paradigm is blinkered — ignoring how what I distinguish as *functional interactionist* human socio-biology recognizes emergent properties of self-conscious social intelligence (Crook, 1980; Hinde, 1987; Vine, 1992). Our 'open' biogenetic programs largely relegate adaptive strategies to semi-autonomous mental systems. These permit both authentically *psycho-altruistic* motives and the holistic features of our groupish sociality. Hence socio-cultural forces and/or rationality sometimes induce immediately *bio-altruistic* actions — whose cost/risk functions do *potentially* jeopardize one's bodily ego-interests or even ultimate reproductive fitness.

Sober and Wilson almost perversely obfuscate whether evolution of hominid genomes did select heritable programs specifically promoting group-serving self-sacrifices of fitness. ILF pioneer W.D. Hamilton's conversion to multi-level selection retained the principle that in genetic terms 'lower levels of selection are inherently more powerful than higher levels' (Hamilton, 1975, p.134). Contributions to a bearer's *inclusive fitness* (IF) remained the central determinants of how well new mutations thrive. Kin(-group) nepotism, dyadic reciprocity, and benefits to one's whole living group, were kept as conceptually distinct routes for favourable selection of variously 'altruistic' alleles.

Their GLF evangelism leads Sober and Wilson not just to assimilate all sources of bio-altruism to 'group' selection processes, but to make further ambiguous claims. These result from counting cultural selection for mental memes and learned traits as part of *natural* selection — despite any cultural impact upon genomes being of a different, indirect order. While conceding that 'the groupish side is only one side' of human nature, their radical claim for group selection is that within our lineage 'in all likelihood it has been a tremendously powerful force' (Sober and Wilson, 1998, p. 333). This generalization simply confounds too much to be assessable. Hamilton (1975) did speculate cautiously about genetic bases for xenophobia and self-sacrificial bravery resulting from biological group selection. But he knew these would depend upon the unconfirmed extent of territorial exclusivity and membership transfers between hominid living groups.

Sober and Wilson side-step evidence that might tease apart biogenetic from far less contentious cultural forms of human group selection — and provide no explicit case for particular groupish traits being prompted by specifically selected genes. Generalizations from HRAF data on tribal societies establish which prevailing norms and loyalties contemporary peoples are socialized into by richly linguistic cultural traditions. They do not directly settle key issues like how far norms reflect or oppose what is genotypically predisposed within us (Campbell, 1975). Assessments of the role of inter-societal competition in shaping our 'natural' dispositions must surely look back towards one central question: When and how did hominids genetically evolve those traits which first made cultural pressures so potent that rival sub-populations could compete as efficient collective units?

Pivotal issues about the creation of in-group moralities, and their subsequent evolutionary roles, must rest upon determining which new socio-affective and cognitive traits had to emerge *before* hominids could enhance the proximate mental mechanisms underlying groupishness amongst advanced primates. To infer safely the operation of biogenetic or cultural forms of inter-group selection in the usual strong sense, we must first examine relevant pre-adaptations explicable through intra-group selection. Only when these sufficed for some threshold level of constructing, enforcing, and even internalizing shared norms, could collective goals attain significant priority over egoistic concerns and more parochial loyalties to close kith and kin. Only then might synergistic fitness advantages of unified co-action allow group selection to emplace facilitative mutations or culturally heritable memes.

Sober and Wilson devote little attention to distinctive proximate mechanisms underlying normative groupishness amongst our ancestors. They assume behaviour to be mediated through the 'belief/desire' psychology of a conscious self-system, and show how parental care could become more efficient once psycho-altruistically motivated. They presuppose skills permitting assortative association of altruists with altruists. And they have to invoke a role for punitive sanctions in reinforcing imitative conformity to generalized, pro-social, normative rules — ones which strengthen and expand otherwise restricted bio-altruistic dispositions (limited to small circles of close affiliates). But they questionably assume that readiness to police how third parties behave within a large, genetically heterogeneous grouping incurs minimal bio-altruistic cost/risk penalties to oneself.

Another approach is represented by Alexander's (1987) account of generalized *indirect reciprocity* (IR) (see Flack and de Waal, 2000). Most simply, if *A* helps *B*, who helps *C*, who then helps *A* (or a couple of *A*'s offspring), aid need no longer be confined to symmetrically dyadic reciprocal exchanges. If the cost/risk functions for donors remain fairly modest, and benefits to recipients rather high, members of reliable rings will all tend to gain in IF terms. Alexander's analysis implies that if everyone is pro-socially motivated enough to proliferate their involvement in such rings of benevolence, we approach the generalized situation safely permitting anyone to both make and accede to aid requests, indiscriminately within the in-group circle. In its fully elaborated form, we will have a group-wide *moral system* — specifying diverse, consensually approved, normative constraints upon the pursuit of egoistic impulses, and demanding nominally group-serving sacrifices.

Yet again, the problem is whether egoistic cheating would prevent relevant traits from achieving evolutionary stability within a grouping. Boyd and Richerson's (1989) models for IR strategies suggest that only the 'be nice to people who are nice to others' variant has reasonably robust success conditions (p. 231). And under real-world constraints 'indirect reciprocity is only likely to be effective for relatively small, close, long-lasting loops' (p. 232). While IR strategists remain rare, the necessary assortation of genetic like with like is vulnerable to the relative ease of being deceived about how nicely a potential recipient of one's aid does treat third parties. Boyd and Richerson admit that the overlapping of numerous different IR rings might somehow make it more viable in the larger groupings Alexander had in mind (which would minimally encompass the several dozens of individuals found in hominid bands). I infer that moral systems required novel mental powers.

Whether or not apes have evolved the *self-awareness* and associated social 'mind-reading' skills which usher in new dimensions of social prediction, manipulation, and cooperation, remains disputed (Heyes, 1998; van den Bos, 1999). But as Crook (1980) argued, self-processes and referential communication about experiences are central to humanity's capacity for large-scale social complexity. Mediating conduct through subjective and flexible self-definitions arguably enabled some ancestor's belief/desire psychology to transcend rigidly IF-optimizing motivation (Vine, 1987). By permitting oneself transient *identification with* other selves, a self-system constructed through early social experiences can develop authentically pro-social loyalties by assimilating others' goals (Vine, 1992). Self-awareness, empathic role-taking to understand another's interests — and I would add affective sympathy for these — are the foundation for psycho-altruism (Batson, 1991).

Flack and de Waal's (2000) target article finds evidence for more than just nepotism and direct reciprocity amongst our anthropoid cousins. Although IR is more doubtful, there is some evidence for intermittent *normativity* — the commitment to shared rules and standards of right and wrong conduct which makes proto-morality possible. 'Community concern' may overstate chimpanzees' readiness to intervene reliably to restore harmonious social order — at least when doing so is not ego-serving nor motivated by partisan interpersonal sympathies. For the full normativity which involves internalizing norms — not just as habits but as the self's own conscious standards — evidently requires a fully groupish form of social identification that is essentially impersonal and categorial.

Proto-moral regulation amongst chimpanzees can imperfectly sustain basic cooperative cohesion within living groups of up to some fifty individuals. Whether their groupish bio-altruistic loyalties are sufficiently strong and reliable for significant inter-group selection to have occurred seems doubtful. Dunbar (1993) sees group size as limited by time-consuming requirements of maintaining interpersonal dyadic relationships through social grooming. His regression equation of size on primates' neocortical indices correctly predicts a mean of about 150 for the most enduring groupings in traditional human societies (i.e. the clan or village unit). He infers that these became possible once archaic humans acquired brain structures permitting referential symbolic language — and through social gossip third parties' moral reputations could be discussed and evaluated. Before language, any but the smallest IR rings may not have been reliably sustainable.

But language was a crucial emergent property for elaborating hierarchical levels of social organization — especially above that of the village. By making *social categorizations* of various types of persons verbally explicit, it provided the preconditions for fully efficient normative groupishness — labelling and reflecting upon an aggregation of individuals as comprising an inclusive class or unit. We lack firm indications that chimpanzee thinking can support this perceived *entitativity* of in-groups or out-groups *as* collectivities. In humans, it involves distinctive socio-cognitive information-processing (Sherman, *et al.*, 1999), and permits simplifying, stereotypical social attributions to be made indiscriminately to members. Entitativity both makes possible and reflects social identification of the self with valued in-groups. Only then can a flexibly intelligent social species become motivated in the truly collectivist, *impersonally group-serving* ways which might permit potent selection on an inter-societal scale.

The social identity and self-categorization theory developed by Henri Tajfel, and latterly Turner (1987), accounts for numerous features of intra-group normativity, as well as ethnocentrically biased preferences for in-groupers, and the solidarity displayed during inter-group conflicts (Hogg and Abrams, 1988). The capacity for de-personalized *self-stereotyping* in terms of shared ideals of the prototypic in-grouper provides the mechanism for real 'eusocial' collectivism. It finally permits counting one's own ego-interests impartially, as equivalently deserving of consideration with those of any other member in good standing. Now even anonymous, unknown in-groupers can become one's *moral equals*. This meshes well with

Kohlberg's (1986) updated theory of moral judgement stages — in that the developmental level predominantly reached, even in 'advanced' western countries, does not reliably transcend loyalty to one's own societal in-group's members and norms (Vine, 1986; 1994).

I envisage no theoretical bar against acquiring increasingly *socially inclusive* in-group identities — up to the species level (corresponding to Kohlberg's Stage 5 'principled' moral commitments), and perhaps beyond. However, such expansions of 'self-interest' must effortfully overcome what can be seen as an evolutionary residue of 'centripetal' socio-affective cognition biases, impelling us unconsciously to give greatest weight to ego-interests, than to those of close kith and kin, and so on (Vine, 1987). 'Universal human rights' are too readily invoked and deployed rhetorically, in covert pursuit of egoistic or parochial interests (Alexander, 1987). Yet a small minority of persons becomes capable of authentically assuming a humanity-wide self-identity, both motivationally and in terms of bio-altruistic self-sacrifice.

These kinds of proximate mechanisms for moral groupishness can be coherently understood as having first evolved through intra-group selection, because they advantaged their bearers directly in IF terms. How far inter-group selection may have emplaced natural genetic reinforcements for the ethnocentric loyalties which evolving social intelligence began to make possible requires specific investigation.

References

Alexander, R.D. (1987), *The Biology of Moral Systems* (New York: Aldine De Gruyter).

Batson, C.D. (1991), *The Altruism Question* (Chicago: Chicago University Press).

Boyd, R. and Richerson, P.J. (1989), 'The evolution of indirect reciprocity', *Social Networks*, **11**, pp. 213–36.

Campbell, D.T. (1975), 'On the conflicts between biological and social evolution and between psychology and moral tradition', *American Psychologist*, **30**, pp. 1103–26.

Crook, J.H. (1980), *The Evolution of Human Consciousness* (Oxford: Clarendon Press).

Dunbar, R.I.M. (1993), 'Coevolution of neocortical size, group size and language', *Behavioural & Brain Sciences*, **16**, pp. 681–735.

Flack, J.C. and de Waal, F.B.M. (2000), ' "Any animal whatever": Darwinian building blocks of morality in monkeys and apes', *Journal of Consciousness Studies*, **7** (1–2), pp. 1–29.

Hamilton, W.D. (1975), 'Innate social aptitudes of man: an approach from evolutionary genetics', in *Biosocial Anthropology*, ed. R. Fox (London: Mallenby Press).

Heyes, C.M. (1998), 'Theory of mind in non-human primates', *Behavioural & Brain Sciences*, **21**, pp. 101–44.

Hinde, R.A. (1987), *Individuals, Relationships, and Culture: Links between Ethology and the Social Sciences* (Cambridge: Cambridge University Press).

Hogg, M.A. and Abrams, D. (1988), *Social Identifications: A Social Psychology of Intergroup Relations and Group Processes* (London: Routledge).

Kohlberg, L. (1986), 'A current statement on some theoretical issues', in *Lawrence Kohlberg: Consensus and Commentary*, ed. S. Modgil and C. Modgil (Brighton, Sussex: Falmer Press).

Sherman, S.J., Hamilton, D.L. and Lewis, A.C. (1999) 'Perceived entitativity and the social identity value of group memberships', in *Social Identity and Social Cognition*, ed. D. Abrams and M.A. Hogg (Oxford: Blackwell Publishers).

Sober, E. and Wilson, D.S. (1998), *Unto Others: The Evolution and Psychology of Unselfish Behaviour* (Cambridge, MA: Harvard University Press).

Turner, J.C. (ed.) (1987), *Rediscovering the Social Group: A Self-categorization Theory* (Oxford: Basil Blackwell).

van den Bos, R (1999), 'Reflections on self-recognition in non-human primates', *Animal Behaviour*, **58**, F1–F9 (Article number anbe.1999.1145, available at <http://www.idealibrary.com>)

Vine, I. (1986) 'Moral maturity in socio-cultural perspective: are Kohlberg's stages universal?', in *Lawrence Kohlberg: Consensus and Commentary*, ed. S. and C. Modgil (Brighton: Falmer Press).

Vine, I. (1987), 'Inclusive fitness and the self-system: The roles of human nature and sociocultural processes in intergroup discrimination', in *The Sociobiology of Ethnocentrism: Evolutionary Bases of Xenophobia, Discrimination, Racism and Nationalism*, ed. V. Reynolds, V.S.E. Falger, and I. Vine (London: Croom Helm).

Vine, I. (1992), 'Altruism and human nature: resolving the evolutionary paradox', in *Embracing the Other: Philosophical, Psychological, and Historical Perspectives on Altruism*, ed. P.M. Oliner, S.P. Oliner, L. Baron, L.A. Blum, D.L. Krebs and M.Z. Smolenska (New York: New York University Press).

Vine, I. (1994), 'A social identities interpretation of Kohlberg's moral theory', MOSAIC 1994 Conference, University of Bath, 17–19 September.

ALTRUISM: THE UNRECOGNIZED SELFISH TRAITS

Amotz Zahavi

Unlike Sober and Wilson, I suggest that in all cases of benefits conferred on others the direct fitness of the altruist increases. The benefit to others (group, kin, etc.) created by the altruistic act is only a consequence of the altruistic adaptation, and not the evolutionary mechanism that created it. In many cases the investment in the altruistic act, like handicaps required for signalling in general, attests to the social prestige of the altruist and thus increases its fitness. In other cases the 'altruist' is a phenotype that has only minute chances to reproduce, and what seems to be an altruistic act actually increases somewhat these meagre chances. It is easy to overlook this marginal benefit to the 'altruist'. Still, if that selfish benefit to the altruist — i.e., an increase in its direct fitness — did not exist, the altruistic acts that benefit the group could not have evolved.

Introduction

I restrict my remarks on the book *Unto Others* by Sober and Wilson (1998) to the first part of the work, which deals with the ultimate causation of altruism; I shall not address psychological altruism, which deals with mechanisms that have evolved to promote altruism — i.e., the proximate causation.

I congratulate Sober and Wilson for their clear presentation of the history of the Group Selection (GS) controversy and agree with their conclusions that models of Reciprocity and Kin Selection are special cases of the GS theory (Zahavi, 1995). However, I disagree with their conclusion that GS is important for the evolution of altruism. Although they have discussed GS in its relationship to reciprocity and kin selection, they have not even mentioned yet another alternative, namely my view on altruism as a Handicap, published over the last twenty years. A substantial part of my comment will discuss my theory as an alternative to their GS theory for resolving the problem of altruism.

My theory claims that what has been considered as altruism are phenomena that conferred benefit upon others, but were wrongly believed to decrease the fitness of the altruist. I suggest that in all these cases the direct fitness (as distinguished from indirect fitness, which includes kin selection and GS) of the altruist increases. The benefit of the altruistic act to others is merely a secondary consequence of its direct benefit to the altruist.

The main reason for the development of GS models was an attempt to resolve the evolution of altruism — i.e., the evolution of characters that seemed to decrease the fitness of their bearers. But if, as I suggest, altruism in that sense does not exist, because these acts confer direct advantage on the altruist rather than decrease its fitness, then GS models are no longer required.

In the following I show how the exertion for a marginal increase in fitness by a desperate phenotype can drive the evolution of traits that have important consequences to the phenotype's associates. Later I present evidence from my studies on the babblers indicating that the altruistic act increases the social prestige, and thereby the fitness, of the altruist.

'Altruism' of Slime Moulds

Slime moulds, unicellular amoebae, have been described as cooperative unicellular organisms that display altruistic behaviour, because about 20 per cent of the group perish while serving the survival of the rest of the group. Unrelated slime moulds are equally 'altruistic', and obviously there is no room for reciprocity to a dead individual; thus, GS seemed to be the only model able to explain their social adaptations.

Looking for an alternative solution, we found that the doomed cells were inferior phenotypes. After studying the detailed behaviour of the doomed individuals (the 'altruists'), we suggested (Atzmony et al., 1997) that these inferior phenotypes are doing the best they can to survive, and that the better phenotypes benefit from their struggle for survival. We found evidence that the inferior individuals are forced to move to the front of the migrating population by pressure from the better phenotypes. However, it has also been shown that some of these individuals may in fact escape death by following that path, which is probably their best chance to survive, meagre as that chance may be.

Babblers Competing to Serve

I became interested in the problem of altruism as a consequence of my research on the Arabian babbler, a group territory bird that I have been studying over the last 30 years. Large groups of babblers have an advantage over very small groups. One could easily suggest that a babbler that invests in augmenting the size of a particular group does so in order to serve its own individual interests as a member of that group, as suggested by Wright (1997). Wright and many others believe that this would be a model of individual selection, since the individual ends up serving its own individual interests. However, I agree with Sober and Wilson that such interpretations are based on GS.

The solution became apparent through our study of the details of babblers' social behaviour. We soon found that babblers do not merely serve their groups; they actually compete with one another to serve their group. They often take on sentinel duties when another babbler is already serving as a sentinel and is clearly willing to continue in that role. They try to feed adult babblers that are not interested in taking the food. More than that, they are often aggressive toward the individual that rejects their 'altruistic' activities: they may push a sentinel from its position; they may attack individuals that do not accept food or may attack individuals that come to help them when they are fighting their external enemies. Such social interactions could not have been selected by GS. They suggest that the 'altruist' gains, not just from the collective gain of the group, but rather directly, from its own investment in its group — i.e., from the fact that the investment in the welfare of the group is provided by itself and not by another member of the group.

Data we collected showed further that the dominant individuals inhibited subordinates from acting as altruists. Hence we suggested that babblers increase their social status (prestige) by acting as altruists. The benefit to the group from the 'altruistic' act is a consequence, and not the cause, of that act. Important though that consequence may be to the group, and consequently to the 'altruistic' individual, it is that individual's quest for social status that selected for the 'altruistic' behaviour. In other words, I suggested (Zahavi, 1977) that the 'altruism' of babblers is a selfish adaptation: the altruist gains directly from its actions. The 'cost' of the altruistic act is an investment (Handicap), similar to the investment of a peacock in its long and heavy tail. It is important also to realize that, like the peacock's tail, high prestige (reputation) also serves as a threat, to intimidate rivals within the group.

People in voluntary army units compete to risk their lives to save others, or to perform risky missions. These people are aware (pers. comm.) that their altruistic acts win them a high social status. Not all altruists are successful: some pay the ultimate price and are killed while helping others. But people also risk their lives by climbing Mount Everest, or engaging in risky sports — deeds that cannot be construed as altruistic — in their quest for social recognition. I therefore suggest that in babblers and in humans the investment in altruism is a Handicap, advertising reliably the altruist's claim to social status (Zahavi, 1977; Zahavi and Zahavi, 1997). In both cases, the individual signals his ability in a manner that would be prohibitively costly to a less able individual - that is, the war hero, the rescuer, and the mountain climber each assume a Handicap that ensures the reliability of their claim to fame.

Discussion

It is impossible on grounds of pure logic to exclude models of group selection as a potential selection mechanism. However, conditions under which GS can replace individual selection are so stringent that very good reasons should be presented why, in any particular case, GS is to be considered as the mechanism responsible for the selection process. I suggest that in every case where GS seems to solve the problem, a more thorough investigation of the facts will eventually expose the 'selfish' adaptations that have led to the apparent altruistic behaviour — as were here described for the cases of the apparent altruism in slime moulds, babblers and humans. More instances of self-interested 'altruism' can be found in our book (Zahavi and Zahavi, 1997).

Sober and Wilson describe the distribution of meat in hunters' societies as an altruistic act but agree that the hunter who offers meat may increase his reputation with women. They also refer (pp. 140–2) to inspection of predators by guppy fish as a form of altruism and suggest that the inspecting individual invests in the welfare of its group. They cite experiments in which guppies preferred to associate with conspecifics that approached a predator while inspecting it. In subsequent experiments, Godin and Dugatkin (1997) found that female guppies preferred to mate with those males that dared to come closest to the predator — that is, approaching the predator increased the fitness of the male guppy fish. Why, then, do Sober and Wilson continue to refer to these selfish investments in advertisement as 'altruism' and discuss them as cases of GS phenomena?

It is the consequence of the altruistic act — the benefit to others — that has placed altruism in a special class of adaptations; but the selection mechanism is not different from that of any other adaptation. Evidence that a group composed of altruists is doing better than a group composed of selfish individuals is no evidence that altruism evolved by GS. The group effect may enhance the rate at which altruism evolves. But I suggest that if the direct advantage to the altruistic individual should disappear, altruism will be selected out of the population. However, this will be difficult to determine experimentally, since the group effect cannot easily be separated from the direct advantage to the individual.

The fact that altruism has been selected by individual selection does not mean that altruists are cynical. It only means that the deep personal motivation for moral behaviour, as well as that of love, and of the readiness to invest and sacrifice for the sake of one's offspring, have evolved for the individual's ultimate advantage. But that takes us to the level of psychological — that is, proximate, rather than ultimate — causation.

References

Atzmony, Daniella, Zahavi, Amotz and Nanjundiah, Vidia (1997), 'Altruistic behaviour in Dictyostelium discoideum explained on the basis of individual selection' *Current Science*, **72**, pp. 142–5.

Godin, Jean-Guy and Dugatkin, Lee Allen (1997), 'Female mating preference for bold males in the guppy, Poecilia reticulata', *Proc. Nat. Acad. Sci. USA*, **93**, pp. 10262–67.

Sober, E. and Wilson, D.S. (1998), *Unto Others: The Evolution and Psychology of Unselfish Behaviour* (Cambridge, MA: Harvard University Press).

Wright, Jon (1997), 'Helping-at-the-nest in Arabian babblers: signalling social status or sensible investment in chicks?' *Anim. Behav*, **64**, pp. 1439–48.

Zahavi, Amotz (1977), 'Reliability in communication systems and the evolution of altruism', in *Evolutionary Ecology*, ed. B. Stonehouse and C.M. Perrins, (London: Macmillan Press).

Zahavi, Amotz (1995), 'Altruism as a handicap — The limitations of kin selection and reciprocity' *Avian Biol.*, **26**, pp. 1–3.

Zahavi, Amotz and Zahavi, Avishag (1997), *The Handicap Principle: A Missing Piece of Darwin's Puzzle* (New York and Oxford: Oxford University Press).

Elliott Sober and David Sloan Wilson

Morality and 'Unto Others'

Response to Commentary Discussion

We address the following issues raised by the commentators of our target article and book: (1) the problem of multiple perspectives; (2) how to define group selection; (3) distinguishing between the concepts of altruism and organism; (4) genetic versus cultural group selection; (5) the dark side of group selection; (6) the relationship between psychological and evolutionary altruism; (7) the question of whether the psychological questions can be answered; (8) psychological experiments.

We thank the contributors for their commentaries, which provide a diverse agenda for future study of evolution and morality. Our response will follow the organization of our book, distinguishing between evolutionary issues that concern fitness effects and psychological issues that concern motives.

Multiple Perspectives

In *Unto Others* (1998), we emphasized that there are two quite different forms of scientific pluralism. The first is a pluralism about processes; the second is a pluralism about perspectives. If a trait evolves because multiple causal processes impinge on it, this is a pluralism of the first type; if the evolution of a trait can be described in numerous equivalent ways, this is a pluralism of the second sort. Much of the literature of the 1960s aimed at banishing group selection from the range of biological processes that can plausibly be claimed to affect the evolution of phenotypes. Inclusive fitness theory, evolutionary game theory, and selfish gene theory were developed initially as claims about processes that were thought to exclude group selection from the range of plausible evolutionary forces. However, we argue in *Unto Others* that these theories, unbeknownst to some (but not all) of their originators, far from showing that the process of group selection fails to occur, actually describe the operation of group selection. These theories merely differ from multi-level selection (MLS) theory in their perspectives, not in their claims about process.

Judging from the commentaries, some progress has been made towards clearly seeing this distinction, but there is still a long way to go. Confusion still exists over basic terms such as 'group selection' and 'altruism', sometimes within a single commentary and even more so across commentaries. Several authors imply that we are just plain wrong when in fact the disagreement between these authors and us is merely verbal.

Journal of Consciousness Studies, **7**, No. 1–2, 2000, pp. 257–68

Before turning to the details, we need to clarify the role of history in understanding and evaluating the pluralism that exists among different perspectives on the evolutionary process. Ideas must ultimately be accepted on their own merits regardless of the history of their development. The fact that Darwin believed in the inheritance of acquired characters is irrelevant to whether this idea should now be viewed as plausible. Nevertheless, knowledge of history is important for the same reason that accurate communication among present participants in a debate is important. Communication requires a shared meaning of terms. If words do not mean the same thing for speaker and hearer, only confusion results. People who share a single perspective usually converge on a common language that allows them to communicate effectively. Pluralism complicates the picture because each perspective has its own language, yet communication must also occur across perspectives. Everyone must be multilingual, so to speak. This point holds with respect to contemporary participants in a debate, but accurate communication also has a temporal dimension, especially for debates that last for decades and even centuries. Past participants may have been right or wrong, lucid or confused, but we must know what they said and meant before we can evaluate any of these possibilities.

Turning to the subject at hand, several commentators (especially **Nesse** and **Nunney**) object to our definitions of major terms such as group selection, altruism, and selfishness, which are based on relative fitness within and between groups rather than absolute fitness. These objections fundamentally misunderstand what was said and meant during the long history of the group selection debate. Starting at the beginning, Darwin (1871, p. 166; quoted on p. 4 of *Unto Others*) said:

> It must not be forgotten that although a high standard of morality gives but a slight or no advantage to each individual man and his children over other men of the same tribe, yet that an increase in the number of well-endowed men and advancement in the standard of morality will certainly give an immense advantage to one tribe over another.

These are relative fitness comparisons. Fast-forwarding to the 1960s, Williams (1966, p. 92; quoted on p. 37 of *Unto Others*) said:

> It is universally conceded by those who have seriously concerned themselves with this problem that group related adaptations must be attributed to the natural selection of alternative groups of individuals and that the natural selection of alternative alleles within populations will be opposed to this development. I am in entire agreement with the reasoning behind this conclusion.

Again the focus is on relative fitness. For Darwin and Williams, individual selection leads the individuals in a group who have the fittest phenotype to be maximally productive; group selection leads the groups in a metapopulation that have the fittest phenotype to be maximally productive. Fast-forwarding to the present, all the major analytical methods for studying MLS, including the Price equation and contextual analysis (**Stevens**) are based on relative fitness criteria, which can be regarded as the *sine qua non* of multilevel selection theory. We are glad that **Stevens** was included among the commentators because her research is conducted from within the MLS tradition. The relative fitness criterion goes without saying as far as she is concerned.

MLS theory emphasizes relative fitness because it is the sole determinant of what evolves by natural selection. Calculating the relative fitness of alternative alleles is easy when the population consists of a single group. One merely compares the fitness of individuals bearing one allele with the fitness of individuals in the same group bearing alternate alleles. However, relative fitness is more difficult to calculate when a population is divided into many groups and when individuals themselves are considered as populations of genes within which evolution can occur. MLS theory solves this problem by computing relative fitness for each grouping as an evolving population in its own right. Thus, a gene can evolve by increasing its fitness relative to other genes within the same individual, by increasing the fitness of the individual relative to other individuals within a group, or by increasing the fitness of the group, relative to other groups in the total population. The net effect of these nested levels of selection determines the relative fitness of alternative alleles in the total population. MLS theory correctly predicts what evolves (a fact that is not in dispute) and has the virtue of treating every level of the biological hierarchy in the same way. For example, the problem of intragenomic conflict, in which some genes replicate at the expense of other genes within the same individual, becomes virtually identical to the problem of altruism and selfishness among individuals in social groups.

All evolutionary theories of social behaviour must contend with multi-group populations, which are a biological fact of life. However, there are a number of ways to compute the relative fitness of alleles in the total population (the bottom line of what evolves) without explicitly computing relative fitnesses within each grouping. These constitute the alternative perspectives that illuminate from different angles the single process of evolution in multi-group populations. Rather than portraying the MLS perspective as fundamentally wrong, our critics need to acknowledge its legitimacy and learn its language to see if it delivers insights that have not been forthcoming from other perspectives. They also need to consider how MLS is related to the history of the debate about group selection, to see whether it captures, as we think it does, the fundamental problems and insights that have emerged as biologists have considered the units of selection problem.

What is Group Selection?

MLS theory offers a precise definition of group selection — the differential survival and reproduction of groups as a component of gene frequency change in the total population. This definition is fully continuous with past conceptions, as the above-cited passages from Darwin and Williams attest. A number of commentators (**Laland et al., Nesse, Vine, Zahavi**) reject our definition of group selection but do not replace it with a precise definition of their own. For example, **Vine** discusses Alexander's (1987) concept of indirect reciprocity as an alternative to group selection; however, models of indirect reciprocity invariably assume that a large population is broken into groups of size N within which social interactions occur (e.g., Boyd and Richerson, 1989; see Wilson, 1999, for a detailed analysis of Alexander's views on group selection). **Vine** himself cannot avoid talking about these groups, using terms such as 'rings of benevolence' and 'in-group circle'. The behaviours associated with indirect reciprocity do not evolve by virtue of a relative fitness advantage within these groups but by virtue of a group-level fitness advantage, relative to other groups. If this doesn't count as group selection for **Vine**, he needs to specify what does count. Similarly, **Zahavi** regards his theory of competitive altruism as an alternative to group selection; according to this theory, individuals are social donors in order to obtain direct benefits such as high status or mating opportunities. This may be true, but how did the incentives evolve? Loose talk of self-interest does not substitute for a proper model of evolution in multigroup populations (Wilson, 1998). The evolution of an incentive system that supports prosocial behaviours is itself a multilevel selection problem, as we discuss in detail in chapter 4 of *Unto Others* (see also Boyd and Richerson, 1990; 1992). We apologize for not referring to Zahavi's hypothesis by name in *Unto Others*, but we do discuss the relevant issues.

After Williams (1966), biologists could afford to casually define group selection as 'natural selection at the level of groups' without much thought because they regarded it as a dead issue. Part of taking group selection seriously involves confronting the fact that the so-called alternative theories have been studying multi-group populations all along and must find some way to define group selection within their own frameworks. The fact that selfish gene theory can describe evolution in terms of what happens to genes is not an argument against group selection; rather, selfish gene theory must acknowledge group selection when groups are 'vehicles' of selection (Dawkins, 1982). Similarly, inclusive fitness theory is not an argument against group selection but involves selection within and among groups of relatives (as Hamilton, 1975 emphasizes). And N-person evolutionary game theory is not an argument against group selection but involves selection within and among groups of size N (as Rappaport, 1991 says). Finding group selection within these theories is easily accomplished by inspecting relative fitness within and among the groups that these theories already assume exist. Those who disagree with the manner in which MLS theory interprets the claims of these alternative frameworks must provide a better method for clearly defining what counts as group selection.

Among the commentators, only **Nunney** has provided a careful set of definitions that stand in contrast to MLS theory (see Wilson and Sober, ms. for a detailed analysis). **Nunney** thinks it is very important to define altruism on the basis of absolute fitness; altruists increase the absolute fitness of others while reducing their own absolute fitness. Nunney reserves the term benevolence for traits that increase the actor's own fitness but the fitness of others in the group even more. We have used the terms 'strong' and 'weak' altruism to mark the same distinction. Notice that altruists in **Nunney's** sense will be less fit than selfish individuals (ones who do not increase the fitness of others) in the same group, and that benevolent individuals will also be less fit than selfish individuals in the same group. So one might expect **Nunney** to say that individual selection has the same effect on each — it works to eliminate altruism and benevolence and will have the result, if unimpeded, of making the group one hundred per cent selfish.

This is not what **Nunney** says because he does not define individual selection as 'selection within groups' and group selection as 'selection between groups', which is how MLS theory draws the distinction. Rather, **Nunney** notes that altruism in his sense can evolve only when there is above-random variation among groups, but that benevolence in his sense can evolve when there is random variation among groups. He thinks this is a reason to define 'individual selection' as 'natural selection in a multi-group population with random variation among groups' and 'group selection' as 'the component of natural selection in a multi-group population caused by above-random variation among groups'. Not only do these definitions depart from previous usage (as he acknowledges on p. 226 of his 1986 paper), but they destroy the isomorphism between individual selection and group selection and have a number of bizarre consequences that we will describe in more detail below.

Altruism and Organism

In *Unto Others* and elsewhere (Wilson, 1997), we stress that the group selection controversy includes two major questions: (1) How do altruistic behaviours evolve, which benefit others at the expense of self, and (2) How do groups evolve into adaptive units, similar to organisms in the harmony and coordination of their parts? Unfortunately, these two questions have been thoroughly intertwined during the history of the group selection controversy, with the effect that groups are often viewed as adaptive units only if their members exhibit strong altruism. In retrospect, it is clear that the two questions must be evaluated separately. The answer to both is 'group selection', but it does not follow that the only way for groups to be adaptive units is for the individuals in them to exhibit strong altruism. Separating the questions is especially important for the study of human moral systems, which invariably include more than voluntary self-sacrificial altruism.

To begin with, behaviours that benefit others while decreasing the absolute fitness of the actor require above-random variation among groups to evolve. There should be no disagreement about this fact despite semantic variation across perspectives (e.g., whether such behaviours are termed 'altruistic' or 'strongly altruistic'). Until recently, genealogical relatedness was regarded as the only important mechanism that creates above-random variation among groups. For example, **Nunney** (1985, p. 221) stated that 'kin selection is probably the only important form of group selection.' This view must be revised in light of more recent theory and data. Not only can social interactions sort genealogically unrelated individuals into highly non-random groupings (Wilson and Dugatkin, 1997), but groups that are random with respect to genetic variation can be highly non-random with respect to phenotypic variation. This possibility has embarrassing consequences for **Nunney's** framework. He will have to say that a set of genotypes evolves by individual selection whereas the phenotypes coded by those genotypes evolve by group selection.

When human social groups are examined at the phenotypic level, they display a degree of uniformity within groups and variation among groups that could never be predicted from their genetic structure. The reason is that human behaviour is not caused directly by genes (a simplifying assumption of most evolutionary models of social behaviour) but by complex psychological and social processes that can cause group members to behave the same way regardless of their genetic relatedness. These processes can themselves be genetically influenced but the relationship between genes and behaviour is indirect and complex rather than direct and simple. The term 'moral system' loosely describes some of the psychological and social processes that promote a very special kind of uniformity within groups that includes prosocial behaviours and excludes antisocial behaviours.

As **Boehm** describes in his commentary and in the larger corpus of his work, group selection has probably been a powerful (but by no means the only) force in human evolution for reasons that concern moral systems more than genetic relatedness. Of course, to make further progress we must identify the component traits that make up moral systems and show how they evolved by multilevel selection (**Gintis, Laland** *et* *al.*, **Rosenberg, Vine**). This is a special case of the second major question of the group selection controversy: How do groups evolve into functionally integrated units that deserve comparison with single organisms?

The best way to answer this question is first to understand how individuals evolve into adaptive units. Individual selection occurs when individuals vary in their phenotypic properties, phenotypic variation is heritable, and some phenotypes survive and reproduce better than others. The traits that accumulate by this process are called individual-level adaptations because they cause individuals to survive and reproduce better than the alternative traits that pass out of existence. A gene that evolves by individual selection benefits the individual in which it lives; it need not sacrifice its fitness so that other genes in the same individual can survive and reproduce. The gene simply increases the survival and reproduction of the individual of which it is a part.

One of the beauties of MLS theory is that it employs the same concepts of adaptation and natural selection at all levels of the biological hierarchy (**Rottschaefer**). We can therefore understand the concept of group-level adaptations merely by substituting the word 'group' for 'individual' in the above paragraph. An implication is that group selection can be discussed without any reference to strong altruism. A gene that increases the survival and reproduction of its entire group is favoured by group selection. If the gene is also selectively disadvantageous within groups, then group selection is opposed by individual selection (see the Williams quote cited earlier). For strong altruism to evolve, there must be group selection, but group selection also can lead traits that are not strongly altruistic to evolve; the implication relation runs only in one direction.

Many discussions of group selection in the past have implicitly assumed that strong altruism is required for groups to evolve into adaptive units (**Nesse**). The idea is that there is no free lunch and benefiting one's group always involves extreme self-sacrifice on the part on the individual actor. This question must be decided empirically, but if mechanisms exist for causing groups to function as adaptive units without individual self-sacrifice, such mechanisms will evolve — by group selection. We made this point as strongly as possible on pp. 30–31 of *Unto Others*:

> Not only is altruism a subset of traits favoured by group selection; it is a distinctly inferior subset. . . . Self-sacrifice on behalf of the group can evolve by group selection, but it is never advantageous *per se*. . . . The extreme altruism that cries out for explanation might be rare in nature for two very different reasons — (a) because group selection is seldom strong enough to evolve such behaviours, or (b) because there is usually a way to benefit the group without such extreme self-sacrifice.

We therefore agree with the commentators who argue that moral systems might be explicable largely without recourse to strong altruism (**Boehm, Gintis, Laland** *et al.*, **Rosenberg, Vine, Zahavi**); however, it does not follow that moral systems can be explained without recourse to group selection. In all likelihood, moral systems evolved by increasing the adaptedness of groups relative to other groups, as Darwin (1871) originally envisioned. In addition, even though moral systems include much more than voluntary strong altruism, the latter might remain an important component of at least some moral systems (**Boehm**, see also Wilson and Sober, 2000).

Before continuing, we want to examine how **Nunney's** perspective fares when employed consistently at all levels of the biological hierarchy. If group selection requires above-random genetic variation among groups, then individual selection must require above-random genetic variation among individuals. To count as individually selected, a gene must actually lower its absolute fitness while benefiting the other genes in the same individual. A gene that benefits itself along with its neighbours is merely benevolent, a form of genetic self-interest that evolves by gene-level selection. All individual-level adaptations as we usually think of them — the hard shell of the turtle and the long neck of the giraffe — can be explained by gene-level selection without recourse to individual selection. No one would accept this bizarre rendering of individual selection, so why should one accept the equivalent rendering of group selection? And even if one did, one could no more deny the reality of group-level adaptations in randomly varying groups than the reality of individual-level adaptations in randomly varying individuals.

Genetic *versus* Cultural Group Selection

Natural selection at all levels is driven by phenotypic variation, heritability, and selection. Human phenotypic variation has a large cultural component in addition to a genetic component. The same can be said for heritability, which does not require genetic transmission but rather involves a phenotypic correlation between parent and offspring units. It would be possible for all people to be genetically identical but to be constructed in such a way that phenotypic variation arises between groups, with new groups partially resembling the old groups from which they are derived. If so, heritable phenotypic variation would exist at the group level, which is all that matters as far as group selection is concerned.

Cultural processes can have a large effect on multilevel selection but it would be a mistake to conclude that cultural evolution always favours group adaptations or that group selection is invariably feeble without culture (**Laland *et al.*, Vine**). The cultural transmission rule 'copy the most successful person in your group' would be disastrous for the evolution of altruism because it would cause everyone to emulate selfishness. If human cultural processes consistently favour group adaptations, this is the result of a long history of gene-culture co-evolution (**Laland *et al.*, Vine**).

Vine suggests that the genetic foundation of cultural group selection must have evolved by within-group selection (see also **Gintis, Laland *et al.*, Rottschaefer, Zahavi**). We regard the strong form of this hypothesis as a vestige of the outdated view that genetic group selection is invariably weak (see **Stevens** for examples of group selection without culture). However, a more moderate form of the hypothesis is more reasonable, since evolution is a tinkering process that fashions new adaptations from old ones that originally evolved for different purposes. Two examples will illustrate the range of possibilities. Boyd and Richerson (1985) have shown that the cultural transmission rule 'copy the most common behaviour in your group' enhances the power of cultural group selection because it quickly creates uniformity within groups and concentrates behavioural variation at the between-group level. However, they think that the genes coding for the transmission rule evolved by within-group selection as an adaptation to varying environments. If so, cultural group selection got its start as a by-product of genetic individual selection, as **Vine** suggests. In contrast, Wilson and Kniffin (1999) show how genes that code for transmission rules that enhance the power of cultural group selection can themselves evolve by genetic group selection. Groups that vary randomly in genetically encoded transmission rules exhibit highly above-random phenotypic variation. Transmission rules that favour uniformity of behaviour within groups and also are biased toward altruistic behaviours evolve under reasonable conditions — not because they are more fit than other transmission rules within the same group, but because groups with such transmission rules outperform other groups.

Some commentators (**Gintis**, **Rosenberg**) questioned the efficacy of low-cost social control mechanisms that promote group adaptations without being strongly altruistic. We never intended to suggest that within-group selfishness is entirely eliminated. Along with **Boehm**, we think that an equilibrium is reached that includes both behaviours that benefit individuals at the expense of others in the same group, and behaviours that benefit the entire group. The degree to which social control mechanisms push the equilibrium in the direction of group benefit is an empirical issue.

Other commentators (**Rosenberg**) interpret social stratification in terms of within-group selection, the suggestion being that the existence of big men, chiefs, etc. can be explained purely in terms of the more powerful taking advantage of the less powerful. Group selection offers an alternative hypothesis. All adaptive systems must become differentiated (and often hierarchical) as they increase in size, including adaptive social systems. Thirty people can sit around a campfire and make a consensus decision; thirty thousand or thirty million cannot. Large societies that evolved purely by group selection would be stratified. Once again, we are not arguing this hypothesis to the exclusion of one based on within-group selfishness. Progress involves exploring the middle ground (**Laland et al.**).

The Dark Side of Group Selection

The most that group selection can do is evolve groups that function with the unity and coordination of a single organism. Organisms are frequently adapted to prey upon and compete aggressively with other organisms, so no less can be expected of groups. Group selection does not eliminate conflict so much as elevate it to a new level in the biological hierarchy, where it can operate with even more destructive force than before (**Laland et al.**, **Mysterud, Nesse**). Properly understood, MLS theory explains the benign side of human nature as genuinely prosocial without leading to a naively romantic view of universal niceness.

The in-group morality that evolves by group selection falls short of a universal morality that dictates that the difference between in-group and out-group is morally irrelevant. As **Mysterud** notes, the search for a universal morality is more than an intellectual diversion and may be required to solve the most pressing problems of modern life, which increasingly take place at a global scale. We disagree with those who think that between-group conflict is inevitable, short of the galvanizing effect of an alien invasion. Given our evolutionary history in extremely small groups, it is amazing that modern social groups of millions of people can remain as harmonious as they are. Without being naively optimistic, we think it is theoretically possible for moral circles to be stretched even wider.

The Relationship of Psychological and Evolutionary Altruism

In *Unto Others*, we took pains to distinguish the evolutionary from the psychological concepts of egoism and altruism. The former has to do with the fitness effects of a trait; the latter has to do with the motives or desires that produce the behaviour. As **Rottschaefer** rightly emphasizes, the psychological goals that human beings have may be quite orthogonal to survival and reproductive success. All four combinations of psychological egoism and altruism and evolutionary egoism and altruism are empirical possibilities. Evolutionists frequently entertain the possibility that psychological altruism evolves by individual selection (e.g., Alexander, 1987), but they almost never entertain the possibility that psychological egoism evolves by group selection. Indeed, **Nunney's** financial example implicitly assumes that a behaviour counts as individually selected whenever a psychological egoist would choose to do it. We cannot overemphasize the importance of seeing that the psychological and evolutionary concepts are logically independent.

Can the Psychological Question be Answered?

In Part Two of *Unto Others*, we surveyed the philosophical and psychological arguments that have been brought to bear on the psychological questions, and concluded that the ideas presented so far do not resolve the controversy. We did not claim, as **Harman** thinks we did, that no philosophical argument or psychological experiment could disprove psychological egoism (see, for example, p. 272 and p. 323). We just claim that none has done so to date. We agree with **Harman** that if natural selection favoured motivational pluralism over a purely egoistic set of desires, as we argue in Chapter 10, there must have been some difference in fitness between the traits, and so some discernable difference in how pluralists and egoists fared in relevant environments. This means that a suitably configured experiment should be able to tell the difference between an egoist and a pluralist. We hope that psychology (or neuroscience) will be able to carry out such experiments.

Are We too Generous to Psychological Egoism?

Rottschaefer, Batson, and (we suspect) **Harman** think we are too generous to egoism. **Rottschaefer** cites the work of Martin Hoffman as substantiating the altruism hypothesis. Our interpretation is that Hoffman's experimental work is inconclusive; in fact, Hoffman himself admits that his results don't rule out egoism (see *Unto Others*, p. 358, note 10). **Harman** seems to be impatient with our refusal to assert that egoism is unable to account for this or that behaviour. However, since he doesn't describe what he takes to be a conclusive argument for rejecting egoism, we can't evaluate his position.

Philosophers sometimes reject psychological egoism because they see, quite correctly, that egoism has been defended in the past by flimsy or fallacious (or no) arguments. However, philosophers are well aware of the difference between criticizing an argument and showing that its conclusion is false. Rejecting egoism requires more than showing that previous arguments for it have been flawed. At other times, philosophers reject egoism because they find it 'implausible'. They find its explanations of behaviour (e.g., of why the soldier throws himself on a grenade to save the lives of his comrades) contrived and counterintuitive. Many of the philosophers who take this reaction seriously would never dream of dismissing relativity theory or quantum mechanics because it seems 'implausible' or 'counterintuitive'. Yet, psychology is fair game — here intuitions are supposed to count as conclusive evidence. We think that naturalistically inclined philosophers need to recognize that this really will not do. There is a literature in psychology that needs to be taken seriously. This does not mean that it should be taken at face value, but the experiments do need to be consulted and evaluated. Our suggestion here also applies to biologists, who sometimes seem to feel that they can make pronouncements about the human mind without consulting what psychologists have to say on the subject.

The third commentator who thought that we are too soft on egoism is **Batson**. We argued in Chapter 8 of *Unto Others* that Batson's experiments do not suffice to reject egoism, the reason being that egoistic explanations can be invented that fit the findings that he and his collaborators came up with. Batson, in his commentary, suggests that our alternative explanations have already been refuted by other experiments that he and his group performed. We want to evaluate this suggestion in some detail.

Psychological Experiments.

In *Unto Others* (p. 267), we discuss one of **Batson**'s experiments in which high and low empathy subjects were asked whether they wanted to have a second interview with a needy other. High empathy subjects volunteered more than low empathy subjects did, but there was a further difference between the two groups. Low empathy subjects volunteered more, the more certain they were that the second interview would furnish good news about the needy other. In contrast, high empathy subjects were more or less uninfluenced by the probability of good news. **Batson** interprets this experiment as supporting the empathy–altruism hypothesis. We formulated an egoistic alternative — perhaps the high empathy subjects find their uncertainty about the needy other discomforting, and this is why their eagerness for a second interview isn't influenced by whether the news is apt to be good or bad. **Batson** replies that this explanation is ruled out by another experiment, one in which 'empathy increased helping even when participants knew that they would receive no information about the effectiveness of their helping effort'.

What **Batson** should have said about this second experiment is that the offer of information had no effect on helping among high empathy subjects. The fact that empathy increases helping even when no information is promised isn't relevant. We did not claim that the desire for information is the only reason that high empathy subjects request a second interview. In any event, we don't think this second experiment refutes our claims about the first. The two experiments used different effect variables — asking for another interview with the needy other in the first experiment and volunteering to help the needy other in the second. The following claim is perfectly consistent with both: high empathy subjects have a desire for uncertainty reduction about the needy other; this desire influences their requests for an additional interview in the first experiment, but does not influence their willingness to help the needy other in the second.

We also disagree with what **Batson** says in his commentary about another of his experiments. In this experiment, Batson and colleagues found that volunteering to help a needy person among high empathy subjects was unaffected by whether or not they were promised the opportunity to listen to pleasant music after they decided whether to help. We agree with **Batson's** conclusion that this result rules out the egoistic hypothesis that empathy leads to helping because it brings into existence the desire for any old mood-enhancing experience. However, we suggested in *Unto Others* (p. 270) that there is another egoistic possibility — that empathizing with a needy other creates a kind of sadness that subjects know cannot be assuaged by any old mood-enhancing experience. **Batson**, in his commentary, takes our suggestion to be a restatement of the aversive–arousal–reduction hypothesis, which he says was refuted by other experiments.

It is important to be clear on what the experiments that refuted the aversive arousal reduction hypothesis actually demonstrate. For example, in one experiment, subjects were asked whether they'd be willing to take the place of another person who (they thought) was receiving electric shocks; subjects either were in the 'easy escape' treatment (they had been told earlier that they could exit the experiment whenever they want) or in the 'difficult escape treatment' (they had been told that they would have to watch the subject endure the full course of shocks). High empathy subjects helped just as much when escape was easy as when it was difficult. This does refute the claim that the only reason people help is to reduce a noxious stimulus. But it leaves open other egoistic explanations — for example, that high empathy subjects realized that they would feel bad if they exited without helping (they'd take with them an unpleasant memory), and so decided that helping was the most effective way for them to feel better. This experiment does not refute the claim that people know that listening to music won't do a very good job of removing the bad feelings they have when they empathize with a needy other.

Readers interested in psychological egoism and altruism should review **Batson**'s experiments and decide for themselves whether they show more than we think they show. **Batson** is to be commended for his meticulous care in clarifying the conceptual landscape of the psychological problem (which influenced our exposition in *Unto Others*) and for his systematic work in testing various egoistic hypotheses. We completely agree with **Batson** that philosophers and biologists need to attend to this rich empirical literature. However, we don't agree with **Batson** that his experiments provide sufficient evidence to reject the hypothesis of psychological egoism.

Since the subject of this special issue is morality, we would like to end by stressing the difference between morality and altruism. Moral systems virtually always include more than voluntary self-sacrifice, which itself can be immoral, as when helping some involves wrongly harming others. Our focus on altruism forced us to put many other issues aside. Perhaps the greatest point of agreement between us and our commentators is that altruism must take its place among a large cast of characters as far as the evolution of morality is concerned.

References

Alexander, R.D. (1987), *The Biology of Moral Systems* (New York: Aldine de Gruyter).

Boyd, R. and Richerson, P.J. (1985), *Culture and the Evolutionary Process* (Chicago: University of Chicago Press).

Boyd, R. and Richerson, P.J. (1989) 'The evolution of indirect reciprocity', *Social Networks*, **11**, pp. 213–36.

Boyd, R. and Richerson, P. (1990), 'Group selection among alternative evolutionarily stable strategies', *Journal of Theoretical Biology*, **145**, pp. 331–42.

Boyd, R. and Richerson, P.J. (1992) 'Punishment allows the evolution of cooperation (or anything else) in sizable groups', *Ethology and Sociobiology*, **13**, pp. 171–95.

Darwin, C. (1871), *The Descent of Man and Selection in Relation to Sex* (New York: Appleton).

Dawkins, R. (1982) *The Extended Phenotype* (Oxford: Oxford University Press).

Hamilton, W.D. (1975), 'Innate social aptitudes in man, an approach from evolutionary genetics', in *Biosocial Anthropology*, ed. R. Fox (London: Malaby Press).

Nunney, L. (1985), 'Group selection, altruism, and structured-deme models', *American Naturalist*, **126**, pp. 212–30.

Rappaport, A. (1991) 'Ideological commitments and evolutionary theory', *J. Soc. Issues*, **47**, pp. 83–100.

Sober, E. and Wilson, D.S. (1998), *Unto Others: The Evolution and Psychology of Unselfish Behavior* (Cambridge, MA: Harvard University Press).

Williams, G.C. (1966), *Adaptation and Natural Selection: A Critique of Some Current Evolutionary Thought* (Princeton: Princeton University Press).

Wilson, D.S. (1997), 'Altruism and organism: disentangling the themes of multilevel selection theory', *American Naturalist*, **150**, S122–S134.

Wilson, D.S. (1998). Hunting, sharing and multilevel selection: the tolerated theft model revisited. *Current Anthropology*, **39**, pp. 73–97.

Wilson, D. S. (1999), 'A critique of R.D. Alexander's views on group selection', *Biology and Philosophy*, **14**, pp. 431–49.

Wilson, D.S. and Dugatkin, L.A. (1997), 'Group selection and assortative interactions', *American Naturalist*, **149**, pp. 336–51.

Wilson, D.S. and Kniffin, K.M. (1999), 'Multilevel selection and the social transmission of behavior', *Human Nature*, in press.

Wilson, D.S. and Sober, E. (2000), 'Social control and helpful natures', in *Altruistic Love: Science, Philosophy, and Religion in Dialogue*, ed. Stephen G. Post, Lynn Underwood, Jeffrey Schloss, and William Hurlbut (forthcoming).

Wilson, D.S. and Sober, E. (ms), 'A tale of two perspectives: How different views of group selection illustrate problems of pluralism in science'.

Brian Skyrms

Game Theory, Rationality and Evolution of the Social Contract

Game theory based on rational choice is compared with game theory based on evolutionary, or other adaptive, dynamics. The Nash equilibrium concept has a central role to play in both theories, even though one makes extremely strong assumptions about cognitive capacities and common knowledge of the players, and the other does not. Nevertheless, there are also important differences between the two theories. These differences are illustrated in a number of games that model types of interaction that are key ingredients for any theory of the social contract.

Introduction

The Theory of Games was conceived by von Neumann and Morgenstern as a theory of interactive decisions for ideally rational agents. So was the theory of the social contract, from the Sophists to Thomas Hobbes. Hobbes wanted to bring the rigor and certainty of Euclidean geometry to social philosophy. If he fell somewhat short of this goal, even by the standards of his own time, perhaps the theory of games could be utilized to complete the project. This idea has been pursued in different ways by John Harsanyi, John Rawls, David Gauthier and Ken Binmore.

Rational Choice

But the foundation of the classical theory of games on the theory of rational decision has itself proved more complicated than it seemed at the time. Von Neumann and Morgenstern thought of the theory of rationality as work in progress which, when complete, would specify a unique correct rational act for any decision maker in any decision situation. If such a theory of rationality were in hand, then it appears that Nash equilibrium would be the unique outcome of the decisions of rational agents in an interactive decision situation. A *Nash equilibrium* is defined as a specification of an act for each agent, such that no agent can gain by unilateral change of her act. Now, the argument goes, each decision maker can figure out what the other decision makers will do from the theory of rationality. Thus, the only state consistent with rationality is that each player maximizes payoff given knowledge of what the other players do —

Journal of Consciousness Studies, **7**, No. 1–2, 2000, pp. 269–84

a Nash equilibrium. You can find this argument applied within the theory of two-person zero-sum games — within which it makes a good deal of sense — in *The Theory of Games and Economic Behavior* (von Neumann & Morgenstern, 1947), p. 148.

There are some tacit assumptions to the argument. In the first place, it is not only assumed that each agent is rational, but also that every agent knows so — in order to deduce the actions of the others from the theory. But, if the theory is predicated on all the agents being able to deduce the actions of the others, then agents must not only know that others are rational, but also know that others know that they are — otherwise others might not use the theory, and so forth. That is, we assume not only that all the agents are rational, but also that rationality is *common knowledge*. Likewise we must assume that the agents correctly identify the decision situation to which they are applying the theory, and that they know that all others do so as well, and that they know that all others know this, and so forth.

In the second place, it is assumed that the theory of rationality singles out a unique correct act. This is 'almost' true in the theory of zero-sum games. Where multiple alternatives are allowed, they are interchangeable in an appropriate sense. But it is wildly false when we move into the territory of non-zero sum games. For instance, consider the following co-ordination game. Two players each independently pick from a list of three colours. If they pick the same, they win a prize; otherwise they lose. The *symmetry* of the situation precludes any reasonable unique prescription by any theory of rational choice.

Since the payoffs are invariant under permutations of colours and the colours themselves are assumed to have no significance other than as labels, the strategy that is uniquely recommended must also be invariant under permutations of colours. The only Nash equilibrium invariant in this way consists in each player independently randomizing between the three colours with equal probabilities. This is a unique prescription, but hardly a reasonable one since it leads the players to mis-coordinate two-thids of the time. This is the Curse of Symmetry that plagues theories that, like Harsanyi and Selten (1988), pursue the goal of a uniquely selected rational act for each player.

Once the hope of a theory of rationality that always singles out a unique rational act is given up, the von Neumann-Morgenstern justification of Nash equilibrium unravels. Perhaps I choose Red, thinking that you will choose Red and you choose Green, thinking that I will choose Green. We are acting rationally, given our beliefs, but we mis-coordinated and are not at a Nash equilibrium.

It is time to back up and see what sort of results we can get from assumptions of rational choice. To do so, we cannot continue to be vague about the term 'rationality'. We say that, for a given player, act B is *weakly dominated* by act A, if, no matter what the other players do, act A leads a payoff at least as great as act B does, and for *some* combination of acts by other players, act A leads to a greater payoff than act B. We say that act A *strongly* dominates act B if, for *all* combinations of acts by other players, act A leads to a greater payoff than act B. We say that a player is *Bayes-rational* if she acts so as to maximize her expected payoff, given her own degrees of belief and her own evaluation of consequences. If a player is *Bayes-rational*, she will not choose a *strongly dominated* act because the act that strongly dominates it must have greater expected payoff, no matter what her degrees-of-belief about what other players will do. If a player is *Bayes rational* and, in addition, gives every combination of other players' actions non-zero probability, then she will not choose a *weakly dominated* act, because in this case the act that weakly dominates will have greater expected payoff.

Suppose that the setting for rational choice based game theory is one where not only are all the players Bayes-rational, but furthermore it is common knowledge among the players that they are all Bayes-rational. Assume also that the game being played is also common knowledge. What does this tell us about the outcomes? Each player's play must maximize expected payoff given her beliefs about others players' play, and each player's beliefs about other players' beliefs and play must be consistent with them maximizing expected payoff, and each player's beliefs about other players' beliefs about her beliefs and her play must be consistent with her maximizing expected payoff, and so forth to arbitrary high levels. Bernheim (1984) and Pearce (1984) investigate strategies that are consistent with common knowledge of rationality, which they call *rationalizable* (or 'correlated rationalizable' in the general case). They show that such strategies are those that remain after *iterated deletion of strongly dominated strategies*. (You identify all the dominated strategies for all the players and delete them. After they are deleted, other strategies may become strongly dominated. Then you delete those, and so forth until you come to a stage where there are no strongly dominated strategies to delete.)

Common knowledge of Bayesian rationality imposes much weaker constraints on play than Nash equilibrium. In our co-ordination game, *any* profile of play is consistent with common knowledge of Bayesian rationality. But in some situations, it leads to a unique outcome. Consider the following 'Beauty Contest' game (Moulin, 1986; Nagel, 1995). A finite number of people play. Each names an integer from 0 to 100. The person who is closest to half the mean wins a prize, others get nothing. (In case of a tie, the prize is shared.) In the beauty contest game, the prize is independent of the actions of the players.[1] The unique outcome consistent with common knowledge of Bayesian rationality is that each person chooses zero.

First, notice that the highest that half of the mean could be (if everyone chose 100) is fifty, so it makes no sense choosing a number greater than fifty. But everyone knows this, so no one will choose more than fifty, in which case it makes no sense choosing a number greater than twenty-five. Iterate this argument, and any number greater than zero gets eliminated as a rational choice. This shows that iterated deletion of weakly dominated strategies eliminates everything but zero. A slightly more complex argument using mixed strategies can be given to show that iterated elimination of strongly dominated strategies eliminates everything but zero. Everyone choosing zero is the unique outcome of this game consistent with common knowledge of Bayesian rationality. If you try this experiment in a room full of people, no matter how sophisticated, you will not get the result predicted by common knowledge of rationality. This is well-documented in the experimental literature (Nagel, 1995; Ho,Weigelt and Camerer, 1996; Stahl, 1996; Camerer, 1997; Duffy and Nagel, 1997).

These are called 'Beauty Contest' games because they use the kind of iterated reasoning that Keynes described in a famous analogy to the stock market:

> . . . professional investment may be likened to those newspaper competitions in which the competitors have to pick out the six prettiest faces from a hundred photographs, the prize being awarded to the competitor whose choice most nearly corresponds to the

---

[1] This sentence was added during peer commentary in response to a query from Herbert Gintis.

average preferences of the competitors as a whole . . . . It is not a case of choosing which, to the best of one's judgement, are really the prettiest, nor even those which average opinion thinks are the prettiest. We have reached the third degree where we devote our intelligences to anticipating what the average opinion expects the average opinion to be. There are some, I believe, who practice the fourth, fifth and higher degrees (pp. 155–6).

Common knowledge of rationality requires arbitrarily high degrees of this reasoning.

Is it so surprising that people typically fail to satisfy the assumption of common knowledge of Bayesian rationality? Even to state the assumption requires an infinite hierarchy of degrees of belief, degrees of belief over degrees of belief, and so on. The model can be shown to be mathematically consistent, but it is an abstraction far removed from reality. One might retreat from the assumption of common knowledge of Bayesian rationality and try to base game theory on the simple assumption that the players *are* Bayesian rational. The resulting theory is so weak as to be hardly worth pursuing. It says that players will not choose strongly dominated acts — acts with an alternative that carries a better payoff better no matter what the other players do. (This assumption itself is difficult to square with some experimentally observed behaviour.) One is reminded of Spinoza's characterization of his predecessors: ' . . . they conceive of men, not as they are, but as they themselves would like them to be . . . '.

Adaptive Dynamics

Hobbes wanted a theory of the social contract based in self-interested rational choice. David Hume represents a different tradition. For Hume, the social contract is a tissue of conventions which have grown up over time. I cannot resist reproducing in full this marvellously insightful passage from his *Treatise:*

> Two men who pull on the oars of a boat do it by an agreement or convention, tho' they have never given promises to each other. Nor is the rule concerning the stability of possession the less deriv'd from human conventions, that it arises gradually, and acquires force by a slow progression, and by our repeated experience of the inconveniences of transgressing it. On the contrary, this experience assures us still more, that the sense of interest has become common to all our fellows, and gives us a confidence of the future regularity of their conduct: And 'tis only on the expectation of this, that our moderation and abstinence are founded. In like manner are languages gradually establish'd by human conventions without any promise. In like manner do gold and silver become the common measures of exchange, and are esteem'd sufficient payment for what is of a hundred times their value (p. 490).

Hume is interested in how we actually got the contract we now have. He believes that we should study the processes that lead to a gradual establishment of social norms and conventions. Modern Humeans, such as Sugden, Binmore, Gibbard, take inspiration as well from Darwinian dynamics. The social contract has evolved, and will continue to evolve. Different cultures, with their alternative social conventions, may be instances of different equilibria, each with its own basin of attraction. The proper way to pursue modern Humean social philosophy is via dynamic modelling of cultural evolution and social learning.

In Evolutionary theory, as in classical game theory, there is strategic interaction in the form of frequency-dependent selection, but there is no presumption of rationality — let alone common knowledge of rationality — operative. Indeed the organisms that are evolving may not even be making decisions at all. Nevertheless, game theoretic ideas have been fruitfully applied to strategic interaction in evolution. And the key equilibrium concept is almost the same.

The most striking fact about the relationship between evolutionary game theory and economic game theory is that, at the most basic level, a theory built of hyper-rational actors and a theory built of possibly non-rational actors are in fundamental agreement. This fact has been widely noticed, and its importance can hardly be over-estimated. Criticism of game theory based on the failure of rationality assumptions must be reconsidered from the viewpoint of adaptive processes. There are many roads to the Nash equilibrium concept, only one of which is based on highly idealized rationality assumptions.

However, as we look more closely at the theory in the evolutionary and rational choice settings, differences begin to emerge. At the onset, a single population evolutionary setting imposes a symmetry requirement which selects Nash equilibria which might appear implausible in other settings. Furthermore, refinements of the Nash equilibrium are handled differently. Standard evolutionary dynamics, the replicator dynamics, does not guarantee elimination of weakly dominated strategies. In a closely related phenomenon, when we consider extensive form games, evolutionary dynamics need not eliminate strategies which fail the test of sequential rationality. Going further, we shall see that if we generalize the theories to allow for correlation, we find that the two theories can diverge dramatically. Correlated evolutionary game theory can even allow for the fixation of strongly dominated strategies. These are strategies which fail under even the weakest theory of rational choice — the theory that players are in fact Bayes rational.

The situation is therefore more complicated than it might at first appear. There are aspects of accord between evolutionary game theory and rational game theory as well as areas of difference. This is as true for cultural evolution as for biological evolution. The phenomena in question thus have considerable interest for social and political philosophy, and touch some recurrent themes in Hobbes and Hume.

Evolutionary Game Theory

Let us consider the case of individuals who are paired at random from a large population to engage in a strategic interaction. Reproduction is asexual and individuals breed true. We measure the payoffs in terms of evolutionary fitness — expected number of offspring. Payoff to a strategy depends on what strategy it is paired against, so we have frequency dependent selection in the population. We write the payoff of strategy A when played against strategy B as $U(A|B)$. Under these assumptions, the expected Fitness for a strategy is an average of its payoffs against alternative strategies weighted by the population proportions of the other strategies:

$$U(A) = SUM_i \, U(A|B_i) \, P(B_i)$$

The expected fitness of the population is the average of the fitnesses of the strategies with the weights of the average being the population proportions:

$$UBAR = SUM_j \, U(A_j) \, P(A_j)$$

We postulate that the population is large enough that we may safely assume that you get what you expect.

The population dynamics is then deterministic. Assuming discrete generations with one contest per individual per generation, we get:

DARWIN MAP: $P'(A) = P(A) U(A)/UBAR$

where $P(A)$ is the proportion of the population today using strategy A and P' is the proportion tomorrow. Letting the time between generations become small, we find the corresponding continuous dynamics:

DARWIN FLOW: $dP(A)/dt = P(A) [U(A)-UBAR]/UBAR$

The Darwin flow has the same orbits as the simpler dynamics obtained by discarding the denominator, although the velocity along the orbits may differ:

REPLICATOR FLOW: $dP(A)/dt = P(A) [U(A)-UBAR]$

In the following discussion, we will concentrate on this replicator dynamics. It is of some interest that the replicator dynamics emerges naturally from a number of different models of cultural evolution based on imitation (Binmore, Gale and Samuelson, 1995; Bjornerstedt and Weibull, 1995; Sacco, 1995; Samuelson, 1997; Schlag, 1994; 1996).

The replicator flow was introduced by Taylor and Jonker (1978) to build a foundation for the concept of evolutionarily stable strategy introduced by Maynard-Smith and Price (1973). The leading idea of Maynard-Smith and Price was that of a strategy such that if the whole population uses that strategy, it cannot be successfully invaded. That is to say, that if the population were invaded by a very small proportion of individuals playing a different strategy, the invaders would have a smaller average payoff than that of the natives. The definition offered is that A is evolutionarily stable just in case both:

(i) $U(A|A) \geq U(B|A)$ (for all B different from A) and

(ii) If $U(A|A) = U(B|A)$ then $U(A|B)>U(B|B)$

The leading idea of Maynard-Smith and Price only makes sense for mixed strategies if individuals play randomized strategies. But the replicator dynamics is appropriate for a model where individuals play pure strategies, and the counterparts of the mixed strategies of game theory are polymorphic states of the population. We retain this model, but introduce the notion of an evolutionarily stable state of the population. It is a polymorphic state of the population, which would satisfy the foregoing inequalities if the corresponding randomized strategies were used. An evolutionarily stable *strategy* corresponds to an evolutionarily stable *state* (ESS) in which the whole population uses that strategy.

Nash from Nature

Condition (i) in the definition of ESS looks a lot like the definition of Nash equilibrium. It is, in fact, the condition that $<A, A>$ is a Nash equilibrium of the associated two person game in which both players have the payoffs specified in by the fitness matrix, $U(\_|\_)$. the second condition adds a kind of stability requirement. The requirement is sufficient to guarantee strong dynamical stability in the replicator dynamics:

EVERY ESS is a STRONGLY DYNAMICALLY STABLE (or ATTRACTING) EQUILIBRIUM in the REPLICATOR DYNAMICS

This is more than sufficient to guarantee Nash equilibrium in the corresponding game:

> IF A is a DYNAMICALLY STABLE EQUILIBRIUM in the REPLICATOR DYNAMICS then <A,A> is a NASH EQUILIBRIUM of the corresponding TWO-PERSON GAME.

(The converse of each of the foregoing propositions fails. For more details see Hofbauer and Sigmund, 1988; van Damme, 1987; Weibull 1997).

Evidently, Nash equilibrium has an important role to play here, in the absence of common knowledge of rationality or even rationality itself. The reason is quite clear, but nevertheless deserves to be emphasized. The underlying dynamics is adaptive: it has a tendency towards maximal fitness. Many alternative dynamics — of learning as well as of evolution — share this property. (See Borgers and Sarin, 1997, for a connection between reinforcement learning and replicator dynamics, but compare the discussion of Fudenberg and Levine, 1998, Ch. 3). There is a moral here for philosophers and political theorists who have attacked the theory of games on the basis of its rationality assumptions. Game theory has a far broader domain of application than that suggested by its classical foundations.

Symmetry

For every evolutionary game, there is a corresponding symmetric two-person game, and for every ESS in the Evolutionary game, there is a corresponding symmetric Nash equilibrium in the two-person game. Symmetry is imposed on the Nash equilibrium of the two-person game because the players have no identity in the evolutionary game. Different individuals play the game. The things which have enduring identity are the strategies. Evolutionary games are played under what I call 'The Darwinian Veil of Ignorance' in Chapter I of my book, *Evolution of the Social Contract*. Evolution ignores individual idiosyncratic concerns simply because individuals do not persist through evolutionary time.

For example, consider the game of Chicken. There are two strategies: Swerve; Don't. The fitnesses are:

$$U(S|S) = 20$$
$$U(S|D) = 15$$
$$U(D|S) = 25$$
$$U(D|D) = 10$$

In the two-person game, there are two Nash equilibria in pure strategies: player one swerves and player two doesn't, player two swerves and player one doesn't. There is also a mixed Nash equilibrium with each player having equal chances of swerving. In the evolutionary setting, there are just swervers and non-swervers. The only equilibrium of the two-person game that corresponds to an ESS of the evolutionary game is the mixed strategy. It corresponds to an evolutionary stable polymorphic state where the population is equally split between swervers and non-swervers. Any departure from the state is rectified by the replicator dynamics, for it is better to swerve when the majority don't and better not to swerve when the majority do.

The evolutionary setting has radically changed the dynamical picture. If we were considering learning dynamics for two fixed individuals, the relevant state space would be the unit square with the x-axis representing the probability that player one would swerve and the y-axis representing the probabilities that player two would swerve. With any reasonable learning dynamics, the mixed equilibrium of the two-person game would be highly unstable and the two pure equilibria would be strongly stable. The move to the evolutionary setting in effect restricts the dynamics to the diagonal of the unit square. The probability that player one will encounter a given strategy must be the same as the probability that player two will. It is just the proportion of the population using that strategy. On the diagonal, the mixed equilibrium is now strongly stable.

For another example which is of considerable importance for social philosophy, consider the simplest version of the Nash bargaining game. Two individuals have a resource to divide. We assume that payoff just equals the amount of the resource. They each must independently state the minimal fraction of the resource that they will accept. If these amounts add up to more than the total resource, there is no bargain struck and each players gets nothing. Otherwise, each gets what she asks for.

This two person game has an infinite number of Nash equilibria of the form: Player one demands x of the resource and player two demands (1-x) of the resource ($0<x<1$). Each of these Nash equilibria is strict — which is to say that a unilateral deviation from the equilibrium not only produces no gain; it produces a positive loss. Here we have the problem of multiple Nash equilibria in especially difficult form. There are an infinite number of equilibria and, being strict, they satisfy all sorts of refinements of the Nash equilibrium concept (see van Damme, 1987).

Suppose we now put this game in the evolution context that we have developed. What pure strategies are evolutionarily stable? There is exactly one: Demand half! First, it is evolutionarily stable. In a population in which all demand half, all get half. A mutant who demanded more of the natives would get nothing; a mutant who demanded less would get less. Next, no other pure strategy is evolutionarily stable. Assume a population composed of players who demand x, where $x<1/2$. Mutants who demand 1/2 of the natives will get 1/2 and can invade. Next consider a population of players who demand x, where $x>1/2$. They get nothing. Mutants who demand y, where $0<y<(1-x)$ of the natives will get y and can invade. So can mutants who demand 1/2, for although they get nothing in encounters with natives, they get 1/2 in encounters with each other. Likewise, they can invade a population of natives who all demand 1. Here the symmetry requirement imposed by the evolutionary setting by itself selects a unique equilibrium from the infinite number of strict Nash equilibria of the two-person game. The 'Darwinian Veil of Ignorance' gives an egalitarian solution.

This is only the beginning of the story of the evolutionary dynamics of bargaining games. Even in the game I described, there are evolutionarily stable polymorphic states of the population which may be of considerable interest. (But see Alexander and Skyrms, 1999, and Alexander, 1999, for local interaction models where these polymorphisms almost never occur.) And in more complicated evolutionary games we can consider individuals who can occupy different roles, with the payoff function of the resource being role-dependent. However, at the most basic level, we have a powerful illustration of my point. The evolutionary setting for game theory here makes a dramatic difference in equilibrium selection, even while it supports a selection of a Nash equilibrium.

Weakly Dominated Strategies

The strategic situation can be radically changed in bargaining situations by introducing sequential structure. Consider the Ultimatum game of Güth, Schmittberger and Schwarze (1982). One player — the Proposer — demands some fraction of the resource. The second player — the Responder — is informed of the Proposer's proposal and either takes it or leaves it. If he takes it the first player gets what she demanded and he gets the rest. If he leaves it, neither player gets anything.

The are again an infinite number of Nash equilibria in this game, but from the point of view of rational decision theory they are definitely not created equal. For example, there is a Nash equilibrium where the Proposer has the strategy 'Demand half' and the Responder has the strategy 'Accept half or more but reject less'. Given each player's strategy, the other could not do better by altering her strategy. But there is nevertheless something odd about the Responder's strategy. This can be brought out in various ways. In the first place, the Responder's strategy is weakly dominated. That is to say that there are alternative strategies which do as well against all possible Proposer's strategies, and better against some. For example, it is weakly dominated by the strategy 'Accept all offers'. A closely related point is that the equilibrium at issue is not subgame perfect in the sense of Selten (1965). If the Proposer were to demand 60 per cent, this would put the responder into a subgame, which in this case would be a simple decision problem: 40 per cent or nothing. The Nash equilibrium of the subgame is the optimal act: Accept 40 per cent. So the conjectured equilibrium induces play on the subgame which is not an equilibrium of the subgame.

For simplicity, let's modify the game. There are ten lumps of resource to divide; lumps are equally valuable and can't be split; the proposer can't demand all ten lumps. Now there is only one subgame perfect equilibrium — the Proposer demands nine lumps and the Responder has the strategy of accepting all offers. If there is to be a Bayesian rational response to any possible offer, the Responder must have the strategy of accepting all offers. And if the Proposer knows that the Responder will respond by optimizing no matter what she does, she will demand nine lumps.

It is worth noting that the subgame perfect equilibrium predicted by the foregoing rationality assumptions does not seem to be what is found in experimental trials of the ultimatum game — although the interpretation of the experimental evidence is a matter of considerable controversy in the literature. Proposers usually demand less than 9 and often demand five. Responders often reject low offers, in effect choosing zero over one or two. I do not want to discuss the interpretation of these results here. I only note their existence. What happens when we transpose the ultimatum game into an evolutionary setting?

Here the game itself is not symmetric — the proposer and responder have different strategy sets. There are two ways to fit this asymmetry into an evolutionary framework. One is to model the game as an interaction between two disjoint populations. A proposer is drawn at random from the proposer population and a responder is drawn at random from the responder population and they play the game with the payoff being expected number of offspring. The alternative is a single population model with roles. Individuals from a single population sometimes are in the role of Proposer and sometimes in the role of Responder. In this model, individuals are required to have the more complex strategies appropriate to the symmetrized game, for example:

> If in the role of Proposer demand x;
> If in the role of Responder and proposer demands z, take it;
> Else if in the role of Responder and proposer demands z', take it;
> Else if in the role of responder and the proposer demands z″,leave it;
>   etc.

The evolutionary dynamics of the two population model was investigated by Binmore, Gale and Samuelson (1995) and that of the one population symmetrized model by myself (1996; 1998b) for the replicator flow and by Harms (1994; 1997) for the Darwin map.

Despite some differences in modelling, all these studies confirm one central fact. Evolutionary dynamics need not eliminate weakly dominated strategies; evolutionary dynamics need not lead to subgame perfect equilibrium. Let me describe my results for a small game of Divide Ten, where proposers are restricted to two possible strategies: Demand Nine; Demand Five. Responders now have four possible strategies depending on how they respond to a demand of nine and how they respond to a demand of five. The typical result of evolution starting from a population in which all strategies are represented is a polymorphic population which includes weakly dominated strategies.

One sort of polymorphism includes Fairmen types who demand five and accept five but reject greedy proposals; together with Easy Riders who demand five and accept all. The Fairman strategy is weakly dominated by the Easy Rider strategy, but nevertheless some proportion of Fairmen can persist in the final polymorphism. Another sort of polymorphism consists of Gamesmen who demand nine and accept all, together with Mad Dogs who accede to a demand of nine but reject a Fairman's demand of five. Mad Dog is weakly dominated by Gamesman but nevertheless some proportion of Mad Dogs can persist in the final polymorphism. Which polymorphism one ends up with depends on what population proportions one starts with. However, in either case one ends up with populations which include weakly dominated strategies.

How is this possible? If we start with a completely mixed population — in which all strategies are represented — the weakly dominated strategies must have a smaller average fitness than the strategies which weakly dominate them. The weakly dominating strategies by definition do at least as well against all opponents and better against some. Call the latter the Discriminating Opponents. As long as the Discriminating Opponents are present in the population, the weakly dominating do better than the weakly dominated, but the Discriminating Opponents may go extinct more rapidly than the weakly dominated ones. This leaves a polymorphism of types which do equally well in the absence of Discriminating Opponents. This theoretical possibility is, in fact, the typical case in the ultimatum game. This conclusion is not changed, but rather reinforced, if we enrich our model by permitting the Proposer to demand 1, 2, 3, 4, 5, 6, 7, 8, 9. Then we get more complicated polymorphisms which typically include a number of weakly dominated strategies.

It might be natural to expect that adding a little mutation to the model would get rid of the weakly dominated strategies. The surprising fact is that such is not the case.

The persistence of weakly dominated strategies here is quite robust to mutation. It is true that adding a little mutation may keep the population completely mixed, so that weakly dominated strategies get a strictly smaller average fitness than those strategies which weakly dominate them, although the differential may be very small. But mutation also has a dynamical effect. Other strategies mutate into the weakly dominated ones. This effect is also very small. In polymorphic equilibria under mutation these two very small effects come into balance.

That is not to say that the effects of mutation are negligible. These effects depend on the mutation matrix, Mij, of probabilities that one given type will mutate into another given type. We model the combined effects of differential reproduction and mutation by a modification of the Darwin Flow:

$$dP(A_i)/dt = (1-e)[P(A_i) (U(A_i)-UBAR)/UBAR] + e[SUM_j P(A_j) M_{ij} - P(A_i)]$$

(See Hofbauer and Sigmund, 1988, p. 252)

There is no principled reason why these probabilities should all be equal. But let us take the case of a uniform mutation matrix as an example. Then, in the ultimatum game, introduction of mutation can undermine a polymorphism of Fairmen and Easy Riders and lead to a polymorphism dominated by Gamesmen and Mad Dogs. With a uniform mutation matrix and a mutation rate of 0.001, there is a polymorphism of about 80 per cent gamesmen and 20 per cent Mad Dogs — with other types maintained at very small levels by mutation. Notice that the weakly dominated strategy Mad Dog persists here at quite substantial levels. Other mutation matrices can support polymorphisms consisting mainly of Fairmen and Free Riders. In either case, we have equilibria that involve weakly dominated strategies.

A crack has appeared between game theory based on rationality and game theory based on evolutionary dynamics. There are rationality-based arguments against weakly dominated strategies and for sub-game perfect equilibrium. We have seen that evolutionary dynamics does not respect these arguments. This is true for both one-population and two-population models. It is true for both continuous and discrete versions of the dynamics. It remains true if mutation is added to the dynamics. I will not go into the matter here, but it also remains true if variation due to recombination — as in the genetic algorithm — is added to the dynamics (see Skyrms, 1996, Ch. 2). We shall see in the next section that the crack widens into a gulf if we relax the assumption of random pairing from the population.

Strongly Dominated Strategies

Consider a two-person game in which we assume that the players are Bayesian rational and know the structure of the game, but nothing more. We do not assume that the players know each other's strategies. We do not assume that Bayesian rationality is Common Knowledge. In general, this assumption will not suffice for Nash equilibrium or even Rationalizability. But one thing that it does is guarantee that players will not play strongly dominated strategies.

In certain special games, this is enough to single out a unique Nash equilibrium. The most well known game of this class is the Prisoner's Dilemma. In this game both players must choose between co-operation [C] and defection [D]. For each player:

$$U(C|C) = 10$$
$$U(D|C) = 15$$
$$U(C|D) = 0$$
$$U(D|D) = 5$$

Defection strongly dominates co-operation and if players optimize they both defect.

If we simply transpose our game to an evolutionary setting, nothing is changed. The game is symmetric; players have the same strategy sets and the payoff for one strategy against another does not depend on which player plays which. Evolutionary dynamics drives the co-operators to extinction. Defection is the unique evolutionarily stable strategy and a population composed exclusively of defectors is the unique evolutionarily stable state. So far evolution and rational decision theory agree.

Let us recall, however, that our evolutionary model was based on a number of simplifying assumptions. Among those was the assumption that individuals are paired *at random* from the population to play the game. This may or may not be plausible. There is a rich biological literature discussing situations where it is not plausible for biological evolution (see Hamilton, 1964; Sober and Wilson, 1998). With regard to cultural evolution I believe that many social institutions exist in order to facilitate non-random pairing (Milgrom *et al.*, 1990). A more general evolutionary game theory will allow for correlated pairing (Skyrms, 1996, Ch. 3).

Here the fundamental objects are conditional pairing probabilities, P(A|B), specifying the probability that someone meets an A-player given that she is a B-player. These conditional pairing proportions may depend on various factors, depending on the particular biological or social context being modelled. The expected fitness of a strategy is now calculated using these conditional probabilities:

$$U(A) = SUM_i\ U(A|B_i)\ P(B_i|A)$$

Now suppose that nature has somehow — I don't care how — arranged high correlation between like strategies among individuals playing the Prisoner's Dilemma. For instance, suppose:

$$P(C|C) = P(D|D) = 0.9 \text{ and } P(C|D) = P(D|C) = 0.1$$

Then the fitness of co-operation exceeds that of defection and the strategy of co-operation takes over the population. Correlated evolutionary game theory permits models in which a strongly dominated strategy is selected.

We can, of course, consider correlation in two person games between rational decision makers. This was done by Aumann (1974; 1987) in his seminal work on correlated equilibrium. Aumann takes the natural step of letting the 'coin flips' of players playing mixed strategies be correlated. The resulting profile is a joint correlated strategy. Players know the joint probability distribution and find out the results of their own 'coin flips'. If, whatever the results of those flips, they do not gain in expected utility by unilateral deviation, they are at a correlated equilibrium. However, this natural generalization is quite different than the generalization of mixed strategies as polymorphic populations that I have sketched. In particular, there is only one Aumann correlated equilibrium in Prisoner's Dilemma. It has each player defecting. More generally, Aumann correlated equilibria do not use strongly dominated strategies.

In fact, evolutionary game theory can deal with two kinds of mixed strategy. The first kind arises when individuals themselves use randomized strategies. The second kind interprets a population polymorphism as a mixed strategy. I have focused on the second kind in this paper. We have assumed that individuals play pure strategies in order to preserve the rationale for the replicator dynamics. If one drops the independence assumption from the first kind of mixed strategy, one gets Aumann correlated equilibrium. If one drops the independence assumption from the second kind, one gets the kind of correlated evolutionary game theory I am discussing here. In this setting, new phenomena are possible — the most dramatic of which include the fixation of strongly dominated strategies.

Prisoner's Dilemma is so widely discussed because it is a simple paradigm of the possibility of conflict between efficiency and strict dominance. Everyone would be better off if everyone co-operated. Co-operation is the efficient strategy. Whatever the other player does, you are better off defecting. Defection is the dominant strategy. In the game theory of rational choice, dominance wins. But in correlated evolutionary game theory, under favourable conditions of correlation, efficiency can win.

The point is general. If there is a strategy such that it is best if everyone uses it, then sufficiently high auto-correlation will favour that strategy. Perfect correlation imposes a kind of Darwinian categorical imperative under these conditions. Others do unto you as you do unto them. Then a strategy, A, such that U(A|A)>U(B|B) for all B different from A, will be carried to fixation by the replicator dynamics from any initial state in which it is represented in the population.

On the other hand, in some strategic situations, anti-correlation may promote social welfare. Suppose that there are two types of a species that do not do well when interacting with themselves, but each of which gains a large payoff when interacting with the other type. Then the payoff to each type and the average payoff to the species might be maximized if the types could somehow anti-correlate. The situation hypothesized is one where mechanisms for detection might well evolve to support pairing with the other type. Consider species that reproduce sexually.

The introduction of correlation, in the manner indicated, takes evolutionary game theory into largely uncharted waters — unexplored by the traditional game theory based on rational choice. The basic structure of the theory is relaxed, opening up novel possibilities for the achievement of efficiency. One of the simplest and most dramatic examples is the possibility of the evolution of the strongly dominated strategy of co-operation in the one-shot Prisoner's Dilemma. (For various types of correlation generated by learning dynamics see Vanderschraaf and Skyrms, 1994. For correlation generated by spatial interaction, see Alexander, 1999, and Alexander and Skyrms, 1999. For the role of correlation in a general treatment of convention see Vanderschraaf, 1995; 1998.)

Utility and Rationality

From the fundamental insight that, in the random pairing model Darwin supports Nash, we have moved to an appreciation of ways in which game theory based on rational choice and game theory based on evolution may disagree. In the Ultimatum game, evolution does not respect weak dominance or subgame perfection. In the Prisoner's Dilemma with correlation evolution may not respect strong dominance.

Is this an argument for the evolution of irrationality? It would be a mistake to leap to this conclusion. Irrationality in Bayesian terms does not consist in failing to maximize Darwinian fitness, but rather in failing to maximize expected utility. One can conjecture utility functions which save the Bayes rationality of *prima facie* irrational behaviour in putative Ultimatum or Prisoner's Dilemma games. Whether this is the best way to explain observed behaviour remains to be seen. But if it were, we could talk about the evolution of utility-functions that disagree with Darwinian fitness rather than the evolution of irrationality.

However that may be, when we look at the *structure* of game theory based on rational choice and that of game theory based on evolutionary dynamics, we find that beyond the areas of agreement there are also areas of radical difference.

Avoiding the Curse of Symmetry

Let me close by returning to the example with which I started. That is the co-ordination game where players get a positive payoff if, and only if, they choose the same colour. Suppose it is a population that is evolving a custom and the possibilities are 'Choose red' and 'Choose green'. Corresponding to the mixed strategy delivered up by hyper-rational equilibrium selection, there is a population state where half the population chooses red and half chooses green. If we assume random encounters and the replicator dynamics, this population state is indeed a dynamic equilibrium, but it is dynamically unstable. A population in this state is like a ball rolling along a knife-edge. If the population has a little greater proportion on the red side, the replicator dynamics will carry it to a state where all choose red; if it has a little greater proportion on the green side, the dynamics will carry it to a state where all choose green. Variant adaptive dynamics will do the same.

This is a simplified picture, which encapsulates essential features of the evolution of conventions in general. One case of special interest is the evolution of the meanings of symbols in the kind of sender-receiver games introduced by David Lewis (1969). Rational-choice equilibrium selection theory would have to lead players to randomized 'babbling equilibria' where no meaning at all is generated. Evolutionary dynamics leads to the fixation of meaning in signalling system equilibria. You can read about it in Skyrms (1996, Ch.5; 1999).

Conclusion

As an explanatory theory of human behaviour, dynamical models of cultural evolution and social learning hold more promise of success than models based on rational choice. Under the right conditions, evolutionary models supply a rationale for Nash equilibrium that rational choice theory is hard-pressed to deliver. Furthermore, in cases with multiple symmetrical Nash equilibria, the dynamic models offer a plausible, historically path-dependent model of equilibrium selection. In conditions, such as those of correlated encounters, where the evolutionary dynamic theory is structurally at odds with the rational choice theory, the evolutionary theory provides the best account of human behaviour.

References

Alexander, J. (1999), 'The (spatial) evolution of the equal split', Working Paper Institute for Mathematical Behavioural Sciences U.C.Irvine.

Alexander, J. and Skyrms, B. (1999), 'Bargaining with neighbors: is justice contagious?', Working Paper Logic and Philosophy of Science U.C.Irvine.

Aumann, R. J. (1974), 'Subjectivity and correlation in randomized strategies', *Journal of Mathematical Economics*, **1**, pp. 67–96.

Aumann, R. J. (1987), 'Correlated equilibrium as an expression of Bayesian rationality', *Econometrica* **55**, pp. 1–18.

Binmore, K. (1993), 'Game theory and the social contract Vol. 1', *Playing Fair* (Cambridge, MA: MIT Press).

Binmore, K. (1998), 'Game theory and the social contract Vol. 2', *Just Playing* (Cambridge,MA: MIT Press).

Binmore, K., Gale, J. and Samuelson, L. (1995), 'Learning to be imperfect:The ultimatum game', *Games and Economic Behaviour*, **8**, pp. 56–90.

Bernheim, B. D. (1984), 'Rationalizable strategic behaviour', *Econometrica* **52**, pp. 1007–28.

Bjornerstedt, J. and Weibull, J. (1995), 'Nash equilibrium and evolution by imitation', in *The Rational Foundations of Economic Behavior*, ed. K. Arrow *et al.* (New York: MacMillan), pp. 155–71.

Bomze, I. (1986), 'Non-cooperative two-person games in biology: A classification', *International Journal of Game Theory*, **15**, pp. 31–57.

Borgers, T. and Sarin, R. (1997), 'Learning through reinforcement and the replicator dynamics', *Journal of Economic Theory*, **77**, pp. 1–14.

Camerer, V. (1997), 'Progress in behavioural game theory', *Journal of Economic Perspectives*, **11**, pp. 167–88.

Duffy, J. and Nagel, R. (1997), 'On the robustness of behaviour in experimental "Beauty Contest" games', *The Economic Journal*, **107**, pp. 1684–700.

Fudenberg, D. and Levine, D. (1998), *The Theory of Learning in Games* (MIT :Cambridge, MA).

Gauthier, D. (1969), *The Logic of the Leviathan* (Oxford: Oxford University Press).

Gauthier, D. (1986), *Morals by Agreement* (Oxford: Clarendon Press).

Gibbard, A. (1990), *Wise Choices, Apt Feelings:A Theory of Normative Judgement* (Oxford: Clarendon Press).

Güth, W., Schmittberger, R. and Schwarze, B. (1982), 'An experimental analysis of ultimatum bargainin',g *Journal of Economic Behaviour and Organization*, **3**, pp. 367–88.

Güth, W., and Tietz, R. (1990), 'Ultimatum bargaining behaviour: A survey and comparison of experimental results', *Journal of Economic Psychology*, **11**, pp. 417–49.

Hamilton, W. D. (1964), 'The genetical evolution of social behaviour', *Journal of Theoretical Biology*, **7**, pp. 1–52.

Harms, W. (1994), 'Discrete replicator dynamics for the ultimatum game with mutation and recombination', Technical Report, (University of California, Irvine).

Harms, W. (1997), 'Evolution and ultimatum bargaining', *Theory and Decision*, **42**, pp. 147–75.

Harsanyi, J. and Selten, R. (1988) *A General Theory of Equilibrium Selection in Games* (Cambridge, MA: MIT Press).

Ho, T. H., Weigelt, K. and Camerer, C. (1996), 'Iterated dominance and iterated best-response in experimental *p*-beauty contests', Social Science Working Paper 974, California Institute of Technology.

Hofbauer, J. and Sigmund, K. (1988), *The Theory of Evolution and Dynamical Systems* (Cambridge: Cambridge University Press).

Hume, D. (1975), *Enquiries Concerning Human Understanding and Concerning the Principles of Morals*, reprinted from the posthumous edition of 1777 with text revised and notes by P. H. Nidditch (Oxford:Clarendon Press).

Keynes, J.M. (1936), *The General Theory of Employment, Interest and Money* (New York: Harcourt Brace).

Lewis, D. (1969), *Convention* (Cambridge, MA:Harvard University Press).

Maynard-Smith, J. and Price, G.R. (1973), 'The logic of animal conflict', *Nature*, **146**, pp. 15–18.

Maynard-Smith, J. and Parker, G.R. (1976), 'The logic of asymmetric contests', *Animal Behaviour*, **24**, pp. 159–75.

Milgrom, P., North, D. and Weingast, B. (1990), 'The role of institutions in the revival of trade: The law merchant, private judges, and the champagne fairs', *Economics and Politics*, **2**, pp. 1–23.

Moulin, H. (1986), *Game Theory for the Social Sciences* (New York: New York University Press).

Nagel, R. (1995), 'Unravelling in guessing games:An experimental study', *American Economic Review*, **85**, pp. 1313–26.

Pearce, D.G. (1984), 'Rationalizable strategic behaviour and the problem of perfectio',n *Econometrica*, **52**, pp. 1029–50.

Sacco, P.L. (1995), 'Comment', in *The Rational Foundations of Economic Behavior*, ed. K. Arrow et al. (New York: Macmillan).

Samuelson, L. (1997), *Evolutionary Games and Equilibrium Selection* (Cambridge,MA:MIT Press).

Samuelson, L. (1988), 'Evolutionary foundations of solution concepts for finite two-player normal form games', in *Proceedings of the Second Conference on Theoretical Aspects of Reasoning About Knowledge*, ed. M. Vardi (Los Altos, CA: Morgan Kaufmann).

Schlag, K. (1994), 'Why imitate and if so how? Exploring a model of social evolution', *Discussion Paper B-296* (Department of Economics, University of Bonn).

Schlag, K. (1996), 'Why imitate and if so, how? A bounded rational approach to many armed bandits', *Discussion Paper B-361* (Department of Economics, University of Bonn).

Selten, R. (1975), 'Re-examination of the perfectness concept of equilibrium in extensive games', *International Journal of Game Theory*, **4**, pp. 25–55.

Selten, R. (1965), 'Spieltheoretische Behandlung eines Oligopolmodells mit Nachfragetragheit', *Zeitschrift fur die gesamte Staatswissenschaft*, **121**, pp. 301–24, 667–89.

Skyrms, B. (1990), *The Dynamics of Rational Deliberation* (Cambridge,MA: Harvard University Press).

Skyrms, B. (1994a), 'Darwin meets 'The logic of decision': Correlation in evolutionary game theory', *Philosophy of Science*, **61**, pp. 503–28.

Skyrms, B. (1994b), 'Sex and justice', *The Journal of Philosophy*, **91**, pp. 305–20.

Skyrms, B. (1995), 'Introduction to the Nobel symposium on game theory', *Games and Economic Behaviour*, **8**, pp. 3–5.

Skyrms, B. (1996), *Evolution of the Social Contract* (New York: Cambridge University Press).

Skyrms, B. (1998a), 'Mutual aid' in *Modelling Rationality, Morality and Evolution*, ed. Peter Danielson (Oxford: Oxford University Press).

Skyrms, B. (1998b), 'Evolution of an anomaly', *Protosoziologie*, **12**, pp. 192–211.

Skyrms, B. (1999), 'Evolution of inference', in *Dynamics in Human and Primate Societies*, ed. T. Kohler and G. Gumerman. SFI Studies in the Sciences of Complexity. (New York: Oxford University Press).

Sober, E. (1992), 'The evolution of altruism: Correlation, cost and benefit', *Biology and Philosophy*, **7**, pp. 177–87.

Sober, E. and Wilson, D.S. (1998), *Unto Others:The Evolution and Psychology of Unselfish behaviour* (Cambridge, MA: Harvard University Press).

Spinoza, B. (1985), *Ethics:The Collected Works of Spinoza, Volume I*, trans. E. Curley (Princeton: Princeton University Press).

Stahl, D.O. (1996), 'Boundedly rational rule learning in a guessing game', *Games and Economic behaviour*, **16**, pp. 303–30.

Sugden, R. (1986), *The Economics of Rights, Co-operation and Welfare* (Oxford: Blackwell).

Taylor, P. and Jonker, L. (1978), 'Evolutionarily stable strategies and game dynamics', *Mathematical Biosciences*, **16**, pp.76–83.

van Damme, E. (1987), *Stability and Perfection of Nash Equilibria* (Berlin: Springer).

Vanderschraaf, P. (1998), 'Knowledge, equilibrium and convention', *Erkenntnis*, **49**, pp. 337–69.

Vanderschraaf, P. (1995), 'Convention as correlated equilibrium', *Erkenntnis*, **42**, pp. 65–87.

Vanderschraaf, P. and Skyrms, B. (1994), 'Deliberational correlated equilibrium', *Philosophical Topics*, **21**, pp. 191–227.

von Neumann, J. and Morgenstern, O. (1947), *Theory of Games and Economic Behaviour, 2nd. ed.* (Princeton: Princeton University Press).

Weibull, J. (1997), *Evolutionary Game Theory* (Cambridge, MA: MIT Press).

Commentary Discussion
of Brian Skyrms' Paper

MOTIVATION AND THE GAMES PEOPLE PLAY

Gary E. Bolton

Laboratory studies find a strategic component to moral behaviour that differs in significant ways from common perceptions of how morality works. Models based on a preference for relative payoffs offer an explanation.

I: Other-Regarding Behaviour

Establishing the biological underpinnings of morality presupposes a firm understanding of how morality plays out as an empirical phenomenon. Laboratory studies of strategic games uncover behaviour that experimental economists refer to as 'other-regarding', an umbrella term that covers a variety of behaviour commonly associated with morality. Whether this behaviour is, at base, altruistic is hotly debated. Examples of other-regarding behaviour include acts of cooperation in the face of material incentives to free ride, and insisting on an equitable share when obtaining one is costly. This same sort of behaviour is observed in everyday life. What a controlled laboratory environment allows us to see is that other-regarding behaviour can differ in subtle but important ways from everyday perceptions of morality, perhaps because these perceptions are shaped, at least in part, by philosophy and introspection.

Other-regarding behaviour is largely anomalous to rational choice game theory. Brian Skyrms (2000) proposes an approach to explaining these anomalies in which certain rational choice postulates are modified in the direction of the theory of evolutionary games. Here I describe some recent progress with another approach that is also beginning to find an evolutionary grounding.

I will describe the *ERC* model, developed by Bolton and Ockenfels (forthcoming). Fehr and Schmidt (1999) develop a similar model. E-R-C reconciles the pull towards equity and reciprocal cooperation we observe in certain laboratory games with the competitive behaviour we observe in market games. Hence ERC reconciles important types of other-regarding behaviour with the self-interested competition that is at the foundation of our understanding of market institutions.

ERC modifies standard rational choice game theory by supposing that people care about their *relative payoff* — how their payoff compares to that of others — as well as their material or *absolute payoff*. Preferences over absolute and relative payoffs are embedded in a motivation function, a particular kind of utility function. Different games present different opportunities to trade-off absolute and relative payoffs, explaining the seemingly different types of behaviour we observe in, for example, bargaining and market games.

Journal of Consciousness Studies, **7**, No. 1–2, 2000, pp. 285–334

The relative payoff explanation is what Sober and Wilson (1998) refer to as a proximate mechanism. But since evolutionary success is relative success, the focus on relative payoffs would also seem a promising foundation for an evolutionary explanation. One way to make the link is to explore what sort of motivation function evolution might favour. This general approach — conceptualizing evolution as working on preferences, and then applying rational choice to explain actual decision making — has been suggested by Becker (1976), and more recently by Güth and Yaari (1992). Huck and Oechssler (1999) show that preferences that roughly approximate ERC motivation functions as they pertain to simple bargaining games can be evolutionarily successful, so long as we suppose that individuals evolved in small groups.

The focus on relative payoffs can seem counterintuitive to those used to thinking about morality in terms of social rules, as well as to those who think of other-regarding behaviour as symptoms of strategic confusion. In the next section, I discuss an experiment that challenges the latter kinds of explanations' ability to reconcile the strategic features of the data. I then explain how ERC can reconcile most, although not all, of these features.

II: A Public Goods Experiment

Experiments by experimental economists, as well as by social psychologists, have established that people cooperate for the common good in situations where standard rational choice game theory implies they should not (e.g., Pruitt, 1967; Ledyard, 1995). An experiment performed on students at the Universitat Autònoma de Barcelona provides some insight into the nature of this cooperation (Bolton *et al.*, forthcoming).

The experiment concerns a 2-person public goods game, a close cousin of the prisoner's dilemma. Player *A* chooses between six levels of contribution to the public good, and *B* chooses between two levels. Figure 1 summarizes the monetary consequences as a function of contributions. The highest group payoff occurs when both players contribute their maximum; then each receives 1500 pesetas. However, if we make the conventional assumption that each person seeks to maximize his own material payoff, then both players have a (strong) dominant strategy to contribute 1. Both contributing 1 leads to the lowest group payoff possible; each receives 750 pesetas. So the game embodies a classic tension between what is good for the group and what is good for the individual. The game differs from the prisoner's dilemma in that *A* has

		Options available to *A*					
		1	*2*	*3*	*4*	*5*	*6*
Options available to *B*	2	*A* gets 1750 / *B* gets 500	*A* gets 1700 / *B* gets 700	*A* gets 1650 / B gets 900	*A* gets 1600 / *B* gets 1100	*A* gets 1550 / *B* gets 1300	*A* gets 1500 / *B* gets 1500
	1	*A* gets 750 / *B* gets 750	*A* gets 700 / *B* gets 950	*A* gets 650 / *B* gets 1150	*A* gets 600 / *B* gets 1350	*A* gets 550 / *B* gets 1550	*A* gets 500 / *B* gets 1750

[†]At the time of the experiment, one U.S. dollar traded for about 130 Spanish pesetas.

Figure 1 Game Payoff Matrix (payoffs in Spanish pesetas)

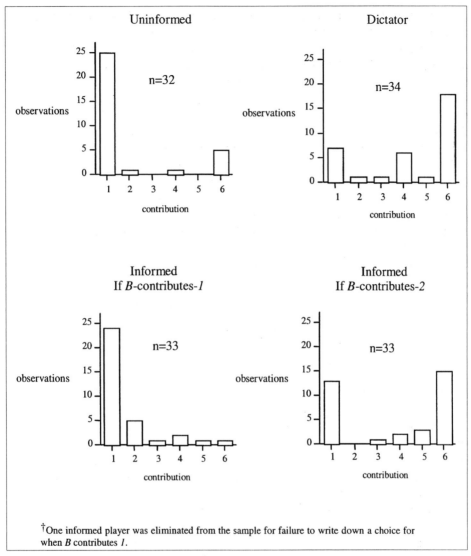

Figure 2   Player *A* Contributions (n = sample size)

six, rather than two choices, a feature that permits a more detailed look at *A*'s contributing behaviour.

We explore the strategic nature of *A*'s contributions by varying the game in three ways. In the uninformed version, *A* and *B* make their choices simultaneously, so that *A* observes *B*'s choice only after she has committed to her own. In the informed version of the game, *A* chooses conditional on *B*'s choice; that is, *A* makes two choices, and the one that counts depends on *B*'s choice. This procedure is strategically equivalent to having *A* choose after observing *B*'s choice. Finally, in the *dictator* game, both rows of the payoff matrix are the same as the top row in Figure 1, so the payoff depends only on *A*'s choice. In all three versions, choosing 1 is a dominant strategy for *A*.

Each subject participated in just one version of the game. During the experiment, descriptives such as 'contribution' and 'dictator' were avoided in favour of more neutral language. Subjects were paid their earnings in accordance with Figure 1, plus a small show-up fee.

Figure 2 displays observed A contributions. The two cells for the informed game correspond to the two choices A makes. Individual behaviour is quite heterogeneous. Still, there is a clear strategic pattern to overall contributing. This pattern has four features. First, in every cell, some people contribute more than the minimum, sharply more in the right column cells than in the left column cells. Second, looking at the two cells of the informed game, many who contribute more than the minimum do so only if their partner does so as well. Third, contributions in the uninformed game are not appreciably different from those in B-contributes-1. Fourth, contributions in the dictator game are not appreciably different from those in B-contributes-2.

Dominant strategy rules out all contributions save for 1, and so does not help to explain much of this pattern. Strategic reciprocity arguments, such as the one for tit for tat (for example, Axelrod and Hamilton, 1981), are not easily applied here because playing partners were anonymously matched for just one play of the game. If all contributions of more than 1 are made out of strategic confusion, then contributions across the two informed cells should be the same, but in fact there is a strong shift. A social rule that would explain this shift is 'help others if they help you' (Rabin, 1993), but the rule is inadequate to explain contributions in the dictator game, where B provides no help.

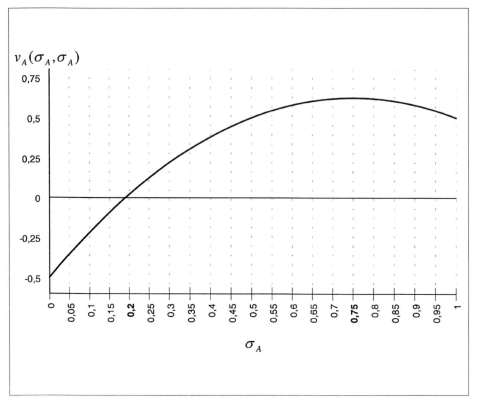

Figure 3   An example ERC motivation function

III: The ERC Model

Suppose A maximizes the expected value of her *motivation function*,

$$v_A = v_A(y_A, \sigma_A)$$

$$/ \quad \backslash$$

absolute payoff   relative payoff

where $\sigma_A = \sigma_A(y_A, c) = \begin{cases} y_A/c, \text{ if } c > 0 \\ 1/2, \text{ if } c = 0 \end{cases}$, and $c = y_A + y_B$ is the total absolute payoff.

We assume that the motivation function is non-decreasing in the absolute payoff, y_A, and that it decreases as the relative payoff, σ_A, moves away from equal shares of half. Visualizing a typical function clarifies the intuition. Towards this end, suppose $c = 1$; so $y_A = \sigma_A$, and $v_A(y_A, \sigma_A) = v_A(\sigma_A, \sigma_A)$. A typical motivation function then looks like Figure 3.

One way of thinking of ERC is that it takes as given the basic facts of two very simple games, dictator and ultimatum, and uses this information to derive predictions for other games (see Skyrms, 2000, for a description of the ultimatum game). The peak of the function in Figure 3 indicates how much A keeps as a dictator in the dictator game. The model implies that all dictators keep at least half the cake, and maybe more depending on how they trade-off absolute and relative payoffs. This trade-off may differ from person to person.

Where a motivation function takes the value zero indicates where a second mover in the ultimatum game is indifferent between accepting or rejecting. Rejecting provides a relative payoff of half, which may be better than accepting an offer with a lower relative payoff when there is little absolute payoff to compensate. ERC can explain a variety of facts about the ultimatum game, including how ultimatum play compares with that of some other games. For example, consistent with experiment, offers in the ultimatum game should tend to be higher than in the dictator game. The underlying reason is strategic: ultimatum proposers increase their offers to decrease the probability of being rejected.

ERC also explains why nearly everyone plays competitively in simple market games (e.g. Roth *et al.*, 1991). To see the intuition, consider a market in which multiple buyers, all with reservation value r, bid on a single object; the highest bid wins, with ties broken randomly. The competitive price is then r. Suppose you are one of the buyers, and you know that the highest price any of the other buyers plan on entering is $p < r$. If you bid below p, you lose, and both your absolute and relative payoff will be 0. If you bid p, you still have a positive probability of losing. The best thing to do is to offer something just a touch higher than p (but no higher than r), guaranteeing you will win, and giving you about the same payoff as winning with p. In sum, any transaction price above r can and should be topped. Only r is an ERC equilibrium.

What about our public goods game? While ERC allows for heterogeneous contributions, the value of a person's motivation function is determined entirely by the payoff outcome of the game. Consistent with Figure 2, the distribution of A contributions should be the same in dictator and B-chooses-2 cells, since A's contribution leads to the same payoff outcome in both games. This strikes some people as counterintuitive. They think contributions should depend on the volition of the other player (in this case *B*). The handful of studies to date, using various games, indicate that relative payoffs play a substantial role in decisions independent of volition (Bolton, 1998). And while there is some controversy about this, my own assessment is that, for the simple games studied so far, relative payoff models approximate behaviour pretty well. (This could change as we move to study different games.)

ERC implies that every person strives for at least half the payoff cake. Hence, to the extent *A* believes that *B* will play *1*, *A* should have a greater propensity to play *1* as well. It seems likely that *A*s in the uninformed game anticipate that the probability their anonymous *B* partner will play *2* is something less than one. This, together with a little risk aversion, explains the low level of *A* contributions in uninformed. Of course, the same reasoning implies that all *A* players should play *1* in *B*-chooses-*1*; but in fact, a few *A* players contribute more. So ERC explains most of the overall strategic pattern we identified, but not all.

IV: Remarks

ERC is a first step in one approach. There are two baseline regularities, common to many laboratory games, that ERC captures, and I think any model need capture to be reasonably accurate. First, other-regarding behaviour exhibits significant heterogeneity. Second, there is a strong strategic component to behaviour — even other-regarding behaviour. Some people may be blindly following social rules, and some may be strategically confused. But these explanations do not easily explain important strategic regularities in the aggregate data.

The relative payoff approach should not be construed as a blanket endorsement of the (non-motive) postulates of the rational choice model having to do with cognition. The lab games that have, to date, been studied intensively are quite simple. Explaining more complex games may well require a reassessment of peoples' cognitive capabilities. But it seems unlikely to me that this will negate the role of relative payoffs as a motive behind behaviour.

References

Axelrod, Robert and Hamilton, William D. (1981), 'The evolution of cooperation', *Science*, **211**, pp. 1390–96.

Becker, Gary S. (1976), 'Altruism, egoism, and genetic fitness: Economics and sociobiology', *Journal of Economic Literature*, **14**, pp. 817–26.

Bolton, Gary E. (1998), 'Bargaining and dilemma games: From experimental data towards theoretical synthesis', *Experimental Economics*, **1**, pp. 257–81.

Bolton, Gary E. and Ockenfels, Axel (forthcoming), 'ERC: A theory of equity, reciprocity and competition', *American Economic Review*.

Bolton, Gary E., Brandts, Jordi and Katok, Elena (forthcoming), 'How strategy sensitive are contributions? A test of six hypotheses in a two-person dilemma game', *Economic Theory*.

Fehr, Ernst and Schmidt, Klaus (1999), 'A theory of fairness, competition, and cooperation', *Quarterly Journal of Economics*, **114**, pp. 817–68.

Güth, Werner and Yaari, Manahem (1992), 'An evolutionary approach to explain reciprocal behaviour in a simple strategic game', in *Explaining Process and Change — Approaches to Evolutionary Economics*, ed. Ulrich Witt (Ann Arbor: University of Michigan Press).

Huck, Steffen and Oechssler, Jörg (1999), 'The indirect evolutionary approach to explaining fair allocations', *Games and Economic Behaviour*, **28**, pp. 13–24.

Ledyard, John (1995), 'Public goods: A survey of experimental research', in *Handbook of Experimental Economics*, ed. John H. Kagel and Alvin E. Roth (Princeton: Princeton University Press).

Pruitt, Dean G. (1967), 'Reward structure and cooperation: The decomposed prisoner's dilemma game', *Journal of Personality and Social Psychology*, **7**, pp. 21–27.

Rabin, Matthew (1993), 'Incorporating fairness into game theory and economics', *American Economic Review*, **83**, pp. 1281–302.

Roth, Alvin E., Prasnikar, Vesna, Okuno-Fujiwara, Masahiro, and Zamir, Shmuel (1991), 'Bargaining and market behaviour in Jerusalem, Ljubljana, Pittsburgh, and Tokyo', *American Economic Review*, **81**, pp. 1068–95.

Skyrms, B. (2000), 'Game theory, rationality and evolution of the social contract', *Journal of Consciousness Studies*, **7** (1–2), pp. 269–84.

Sober, Elliott and Wilson, David Sloan (1998), *Unto Others*, (Cambridge, MA and London: Harvard University Press).

BLURRING THE LINE BETWEEN RATIONALITY AND EVOLUTION

Jeffrey P. Carpenter

This comment focuses on the informational distinction Brian Skyrms makes between rational choice theories of the social contract and theories based on evolutionary dynamics. The basic point is that to dismiss the rational choice method because of the restrictive informational assumptions may discount interesting work done in the area of bounded rationality. Further, the comment argues that combining the best elements of both approaches into an evolutionary theory of boundedly rational agents can improve the power of social contract theories. To illustrate the point, we work through an example of analysing the data from a bargaining experiment.

Brian Skyrms effectively juxtaposes two methodologies that have been widely used to understand the origin of the social contract (defined broadly to include conventions, norms, behavioural rules of thumb, as well as, property rights). One method, originating in Rawls (1971) and Harsanyi (1977), develops social organization from the choices of *rational* agents who possess infinite powers of calculation, common knowledge of rationality, and often, knowledge of other agents' preference orderings. The other method, developed more recently by Sugden (1986), Skyrms (1996), and Young (1998), posits that the social contract evolved because the rules comprising it were better suited to the environment, on average, than other rules. The latter approach is compelling because it says nothing about calculation, nor do agents need to know anything about other agents. Hence, the strategies, and rules implied by them, need not be the result of rational choice. Instead, on a much simpler level, successful rules survive even if agents simply stumble across them. Given the simple elegance of the evolutionary approach, its limited information requirements, and its ability to select intuitive equilibria, it is no wonder that the evolutionary approach has gained much attention.

While I largely agree with Brian Skyrms about the benefits of evolution over rational choice, I'm concerned that his comparison is too simplistic. More particularly, as formulated, the comparison of rational choice and evolution excludes any mention of the relevant work initiated by Herbert Simon on bounded rationality. Because the impetus of bounded rationality is to systematically weaken the assumptions of rational choice in reasonable ways, such as employing limited recall, modelling finite cognitive capacities, or invoking decision heuristics, there is potentially interesting middle ground between the baggage-laden theory of choice and the choice-free domain of evolution.

Further, because there are two ways to interpret the replicator dynamic, the *population view* — agents playing pure strategies and reproducing asexually in proportion to fitness differentials, and the *learning view* — each agent plays a mixed strategy where the probability of using each pure strategy is determined by its relative fitness, when modelling the social contract, one needs to choose the story that best fits the phenomenon under examination. In many circumstances (for example explaining the data from experiments), the most appropriate story is the social learning one which is not actually assumption-free. This interpretation of the standard Malthusian dynamic requires that agents know the population distribution of payoffs and calculate the average fitness from this distribution. Therefore, while not nearly as restrictive, the social learning view of evolution needs informational assumptions of its own.

What's the point? When comparing the rational choice view of the social contract to the evolutionary view, we tend to draw a solid line saying that, because rational choice makes informational assumptions, it is on one side, while evolution, in avoiding these assumptions, is on the other side. However, bounded rationality, in relaxing the assumptions of rational choice, straddles the line. Likewise, because the social learning interpretation relies on agents calculating the average fitness, it also has one foot on each side of the line. The point is that it is not at all clear what is accomplished by drawing such a line. It might be the case that combining these views may lead to better theories.

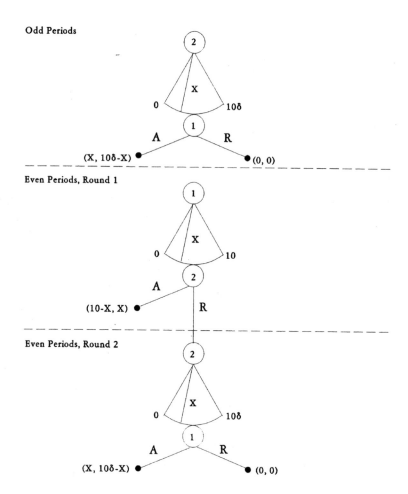

We will now discuss an example of how blurring the line between rational choice and evolutionary game theory can lead to a more descriptive theory of the social contract. Consider the following extensive-form bargaining game.

There are two players, One and Two, and the game is played a finite number of times. Each period of play consists of either one or two rounds. In odd periods, player Two makes an ultimatum proposal to player One over a pie of size 10δ where $0<\delta<1$. In even periods the roles are reversed, and Two makes a proposal to One about how to split a pie of size 10. However, if One rejects Two's offer, they move to a subgame where Two can make a counterproposal over the smaller pie. Notice that the subgame in even periods is the same as the game played in the odd periods.

What kind of social contract does the rational choice theory predict for this interaction? Because the game is played a finite number of times, we can use backward induction and Selten's notion of subgame perfection to solve the game. More specifically, we know that if we can find unique subgame-perfect strategies for the two players in each period, then the equilibrium outcome for the entire game will consist of the players using these strategies in each period.

Start with odd periods. Because this is an ultimatum game, player Two should get almost the entire pie and, to make things simple, let's assume that player Two gets it all. Hence, in odd periods, player One gets nothing and player Two gets 10δ. Starting with the second round of even periods, because this subgame is the same as the game played in odd periods, we expect player Two to get 10δ and player One to get zero. Knowing this, in the first round of even periods, player One does best by offering player Two 10δ to prevent player Two from rejecting and forcing the game to the next round where player Two will get everything. This leaves player One with $10-10\delta$ or $10(1-\delta)$. Again, because the game is played finitely many times, the rational choice theory predicts that this behaviour will be repeated in each period. Hence, rational choice provides a clear prediction of the type of contract we should expect — depending on the size of δ, either player One does much better (when δ is low), or vice versa (when δ is high).

In his paper, Brian Skyrms refers to experimental data to show that the rational choice model doesn't predict actual behaviour very well. The current game is no exception and, as usual, the rational choice prediction is offered as a straw man. Over 250 undergraduates at the Universities of Massachusetts and Arizona have participated in experiments using this game. The fact that the subgame played in round two of even periods is the same as the game played in odd periods is not a coincidence. This design was chosen deliberately to give backward induction and subgame perfection their best chance of success. That is, one might hypothesize that if subjects were forced through the subgame of a two-stage game, they will form the necessary expectations to perform backward induction and find the subgame perfect equilibrium.

Despite being forced through the subgame in odd periods, using different levels of δ (0.25 or 0.75), and altering the way subjects are paired in each of 15 periods, *one*, clear convention continually arises. The convention can be described as the following social contract: *When you make the proposal, ask for a little more than half the pie.*[1]

---

[1] A more extensive treatment of the data from this experiment using a Markov model of behaviour evolution is provided in Carpenter (1999).

Given the rational choice prediction could not perform worse, how might we better explain the results of this experiment? Fairness is generally offered as a suggestion, but let's put the sticky mess of fairness aside for now and focus on what would be necessary for fairness or anything else to explain this convention — expectations. As Thomas Schelling pointed out, an important determinant of conventions is that people have coordinated expectations about what they will get from interactions. In other words, we should expect that subjects' initial expectations about what they will get will influence the final convention that evolves.

We can employ the social learning interpretation of the replicator dynamic to model how expectations evolve in this game. To do so, we assume that subjects employ the simple learning rule — look around at how well other subjects are doing and copy strategies that do better than average. The following matrix quantifies sub-

Player 2

Player 1		L_2	H_2	C_2
	L_1	.52, .67	.48, .49	.49, .58
	H_1	.42, .43	.51, .47	.48, .43
	C_1	.50, .32	.52, .46	.53, .56

jects' initial expectations by computing the average percentage of the pie that subjects get in the first two periods of play depending on the strategy they use and the strategy used by their opponent.

We categorize the data into three strategies for each player. The strategy L_i for $i=1,2$ refers to offering the other subject 40 per cent of the pie or less. Where δ is low, L_i conforms to the subgame perfect strategy. The strategy H_i means, offer the other person half, and C_i is the convention, offer the other person about 45 per cent of the pie. As one can see, there are two pure strategy *expectational Nash equilibria*. One exists where both players conform loosely to the rational choice prediction, and the other is where both players use the convention.

Given there are two strict equilibria, we know that the replicator dynamic will not favour one outcome over the other. However, the dynamic can give us an idea of the attracting power of each of our two equilibria. What is important is the initial distribution of strategies used by the players and where this distribution lies with respect to the basins of attraction of the two equilibria.

Simulating the standard dynamic for two populations (Player Ones and Player Twos), we find that the initial state (Player Ones: $0.17 L$, $0.47 H$, $0.36 C$, Player Twos: $0.17 L$, $0.49 H$, $0.34 C$) quickly converges to the all C equilibrium. Furthermore, after fifteen generations (the length of the experiment), the simulation reports frequencies of $0.11 L_1$, $0.30 H_1$, $0.59 C_1$, $0.02 L_2$, $0.33 H_2$, $0.65 C_2$, while the actual final distribution of strategies in the experiment is $0.16 L_1$, $0.31 H_1$, $0.53 C_1$, $0.25 L_2$, $0.25 H_2$, $0.50 C_2$. Hence, while the rational choice theory fails to predict behaviour in this game even though the experiment is designed to give it its best shot, a simple social learning theory of expectation evolution explains behaviour rather well.

Remember, however, that for the replicator dynamic to make sense in this context, we need to assume that subjects look around and survey the payoffs accruing to others. While subjects can see how well subjects in the opposite role are doing, they are not given information about how well others in the same role are doing. Therefore, to make an estimate of the population average payoff, subjects must rely on their own trial and error with various strategies and, as such, they are boundedly rational.

This returns us to the point. In an experimental setting, the interpretation of the replicator that usually makes the most sense is that of social learning. But to employ this interpretation, one needs to get around the informational assumption made about the players (i.e. that they can see other people's payoffs). One solution is to show subjects a histogram of payoffs each period, but this may confound the data. Perhaps a more interesting approach is to alter the dynamic so that it accounts for errors made by boundedly rational agents.

Let's try this with our bargaining data. To do so, we change that standard dynamic to account for decision errors using the same method introduced in Brian Skyrms to speak about mutations (section on weakly dominated strategies). This implies that we treat decision errors as mutations where, rather than choosing the appropriate strategy, given the average payoff, agents screw up and choose randomly.

Simulating the new dynamic, including decision errors that happen one percent of the time, we find that the boundedly rational dynamic performs noticeably better. The altered dynamic still converges uniquely from our starting state to the convention. However, the altered dynamic matches the data better after fifteen periods. Recall that the actual ending distribution of play from the experiment was $0.16 L_1$, $0.31 H_1$, $0.53 C_1$, $0.25 L_2$, $0.25 H_2$, $0.50 C_2$. After adding decision errors, the evolutionary model predicts $0.15 L_1$, $0.28 H_1$, $0.57 C_1$, $0.06 L_2$, $0.31 H_2$, $0.63 C_2$. Thus, by borrowing from the theory of bounded rationality which seeks to weaken the assumptions of rational choice, we can improve our standard model of behaviour evolution. As always, well-defined lines are more interesting when blurred.

References

Carpenter, Jeffrey (1999), 'Bargaining outcomes as the result of coordinated expectations', Department of Economics Working Paper, Middlebury College.

Harsanyi, John (1977), *Rational Behaviour and Bargaining Equilibrium in Games and Social Situations* (Cambridge: Cambridge University Press).

Rawls, J. (1971), *A Theory of Justice* (Cambridge, Harvard University Press).

Skyrms, Brian (1996), *Evolution of the Social Contract* (New York: Cambridge University Press).

Sugden, R. (1986), *The Economics of Rights, Cooperation and Welfare* (Oxford: Basil Blackwell).

Young, P. (1998), *Individual Strategy and Social Structure* (Princeton: Princeton University Press).

WHEN EVOLUTIONARY GAME THEORY EXPLAINS MORALITY, WHAT DOES IT EXPLAIN?

Justin D'Arms

Evolutionary attempts to explain morality tend to say very little about what morality is. If evolutionary game theory aspires not merely to solve the 'problem of altruism', but to explain human morality or justice in particular, it requires an appropriate conception of that subject matter. This paper argues that one plausible conception of morality (a sanction-based conception) creates some important constraints on the kinds of evolutionary explanations that can shed light on morality. Game theoretic approaches must either meet these constraints, or defend an alternative conception of morality. Skyrms' model of the evolution of justice is found to violate the constraints imposed by the sanction-based conception.

Brian Skyrms' comparative study of game theory based on rational choice, and game theory based on evolutionary dynamics is rich and rewarding. His claim that the latter promises to ground a more compelling explanatory theory of human behaviour is more contentious. I think the explanatory prospects of this approach must ultimately be assessed piecemeal, through investigations of particular models. I have made some such investigations elsewhere (D'Arms, 1996; D'Arms *et al.*, 1998), but I do not propose to pursue them further here. Instead, I want to make a point about the relationship between evolutionary game theory and morality.

Many evolutionary discussions of morality fall into one of two rather different categories. The first are replies to a familiar challenge to Darwinism, the so-called 'problem of altruism' in evolutionary theory: How is the theory of natural selection compatible with the various kinds of apparently altruistic (and hence apparently maladaptive) behaviour that are observed in the natural world (where these may include, but are not limited to, human moral motivation)? The second kind of discussion attempts to offer evolutionary explanations of moral norms, or the 'moral sense', or of various other phenomena that are putatively distinctive of human morality. They try to show not simply that human morality is *compatible* with an evolutionary account of our origins, but that evolutionary thinking can shed some light upon human morality, through an exploration of its selective history.

The first problem is now widely thought to have a number of satisfactory solutions, and evolutionary game theory has contributed to these.[2] If, for instance, it is granted that strategies such as 'tit for tat' in the iterated Prisoner's Dilemma, and 'demand half' in the simple Nash bargaining game discussed by Skyrms (2000) are at least apparently altruistic (in each there is a sense in which the player takes less than he might, and the other player benefits from this restraint), then demonstrating that they can evolve to fixation from a wide range of initial strategy distributions constitutes a kind of solution. But, as Sober and Wilson (1998) display especially clearly, there is a significant conceptual difference between apparent altruism in general, and the kinds of human motivational patterns that are thought to be morally significant.

---

[2] Important solutions include Richard Hamilton's work on kin selection (1964), and Robert Trivers' work on reciprocal altruism (1971). Important early work in evolutionary game theory on the problem of altruism is Robert Axelrod's studies of the Prisoner's Dilemma (Axelrod 1980a; 1980b; 1984; Axelrod and Hamilton, 1981).

Furthermore, there's a difference between demonstrating that evolution by natural selection is compatible with morality and demonstrating that the former helps to explain the latter. It remains to be seen whether the game theoretic approach will be fruitful in explaining the distinctive features of human morality.

Evolutionary accounts of morality typically try to be neutral about what morality is. But this ecumenical spirit can result in spurious claims to ethical relevance. I propose instead the following working conception of our subject matter: morality is a system of requirements and prohibitions enforced by sanctions (emotional and punitive), imposed both externally by members of the community, and internally (to varying degrees) through negative self-directed feelings. Though not without detractors, this sanction-based conception of morality has a substantial pedigree.[3] It is explicit, for instance, in the following remarks from John Stuart Mill (1979 [1863], p. 47).

> We do not call anything wrong unless we mean to imply that a person ought to be punished in some way or other for doing it — if not by law, by the opinion of his fellow creatures; if not by opinion, by the reproaches of his own conscience. This seems the real turning point of the distinction between morality and simple expediency.

By adopting a substantive conception of morality, we can distinguish explanations of behaviour from explanations of moral norms that require that behaviour. Though there are strong moral norms enjoining parents to provide for their children, for instance, the standard evolutionary explanation of parental investment in offspring says nothing at all about why this is so. Any adequate conception of morality must be able to distinguish explanations of these moral injunctions from explanations of the behaviour.[4] The sanction-based account of morality offers a particular view of what an evolutionary explanation of these norms would have to do: it should display the fitness advantages (for some suitable entities, within some suitable selective regime) of sanctions against non-protective parents. Other conceptions of morality, of course, will need to articulate alternative accounts of the difference between explaining behaviour and explaining moral norms.

Consider now the simple Nash bargaining game that Skyrms says is 'of considerable importance for social philosophy'(Skyrms, 2000, p. 276). Two players make bids for how to divide a resource. If the sum of their bids exceeds the total amount of the resource, neither gets anything; otherwise, each gets what she claimed. If fitness is proportional to the amount of the resource a player receives, Skyrms shows that demand half is the only pure strategy that is an evolutionarily stable strategy. By modelling the evolutionary trajectories of various strategies, he has also shown that a population composed of players demanding various amounts of cake will evolve into a population of 'demand halfers' from a wide range of initial distributions. He suggests (1996, p. 21) that this is, 'perhaps, a beginning of an explanation of the origin of our concept of justice'.

The Nash game is the kind of bargaining problem that interested Thomas Schelling (1960): there is a range within which both players prefer agreement to no agreement,

---

[3] In addition to its philosophical lineage, the characterization of moral norms as those involving or sustained by certain sorts of sanctions is commonplace in the social sciences. See, for instance, Christopher Boehm's contribution here, and the literature cited there. The precise nature of the sanctions that mark a system of requirements and prohibitions as moral is a complex topic I won't pursue here.

[4] Cf. H.L.A. Hart's discussion of the distinction between a habit and a rule (Hart 1961, pp. 54–7).

but within that range at least one of the players always has an incentive to try to shift the agreement point to favour him more. This is how things are with many of the distribution problems we face today and presumably with many of those our ancestors faced. An interesting question that rational choice theory itself does not answer is how we settle at coordination points in such circumstances. Schelling seems to have thought that this was often best explained by the contingent fact that some outcome has a kind of 'prominence'. What is crucial to the prospects for coordination is that the same outcome be prominent for all players. But how do some outcomes, and not others, come to be prominent? Prominence is a broad notion, and it can be produced in any number of ways: through history, symmetry, the status quo, or more mysterious patterns of psychological salience. One might think of Skyrms' model as offering an answer at a different level of explanation: demand half is the prominent outcome because it is the outcome that tends to emerge from a selective competition between strategies.

Let's grant several claims that we may have some inclination to contest, in order to focus on the proffered explanation of justice. The first is that there are a significant number of situations in human life which roughly correspond to the circumstances of this game, and that there is a tendency for human beings to favour equal divisions of the windfall resource in situations of this kind. The second is that the evolutionary models Skyrms offers constitute an explanation of this human tendency. The third is that justice calls for (or is thought to call for) equal divisions of such windfall resources. If we accept these claims, in what sense do we have an explanation of (an aspect of) morality?

On the conception of morality above, it is not obvious that the proffered explanation has anything at all to do with justice or morality. A crucial part of what makes it the case (when it is the case) that equal division is taken as a requirement of justice, is that there be some sanctions for unexcused deviations. But there is nothing in the nature of the bargaining game, nor in the nature of the replicator dynamics, that requires or suggests that the behavioural tendency in question is driven or secured by sanctions of any kind. When the tendency to demand half is driven to fixation, it is because demanding half realizes a higher average return than the alternatives. This game offers no prospect of a cheater's payoff: a player can't increase her share by unilaterally deviating from the equilibrium at demand half. Hence there is no clear analogue for, and no apparent need for, the kinds of righteous indignation and punishment that moral agents visit upon those who violate morality's constraints. Nor is there any need for a propensity for feelings of guilt when we 'unfairly' demand more than half — recognition of the lost returns should suffice to bring us back on track. In short, precisely because demanding half is so plainly in both parties' interests, once some expectation has been established, there is no need for norms of justice to secure the behaviour.[5] But then we have not yet reached Mill's turning point between morality and simple expediency. We have an explanation of why people

---

[5] It might be thought that the dynamics explain how an expectation that everyone will demand half might arise, and that any violation of an expectation will be judged unjust. But of course not every violation of an expectation is judged unjust. In some cases we take the person who drives an uncommonly hard bargain to be simply a better negotiator; whereas in others we take him to be behaving unfairly. What's needed is an account of why this particular expectation is a moral expectation (assuming, *arguendo*, that it is).

engage in behaviour that happens also (by hypothesis) to be morally required, but not an explanation of how or why it comes to be morally required.

Perhaps this is enough for Skyrms. He may intend his model to be entirely agnostic about the underlying causes that produce successful strategies. But if this is how we are to understand the explanatory strategy, then the explanation supplied should not be advertised as explaining (our concept of) justice. For it now seems that Skyrms' explanation of the phenomenon in question would be the same whether or not choosing half in the bargaining game were morally required. Surely a model that is avowedly insensitive to whether the behaviour it explains is (regarded as) morally significant cannot be an explanation of that significance.

The point is not that evolutionary game theory is powerless to advance our understanding of morality. The point is rather that if, as I think, morality is essentially tied to sanctions, then only models which display the role of such sanctions in generating or stabilizing moral behaviour will be promising models of morality. Games and models differ in what features of actual behaviour they do and do not aspire to represent and explain. An adequate evolutionary account of our sense of justice, I'm suggesting, must include an essential role for moral sanctions. Such an account might best begin with the moral sentiments, exploring how dispositions to feel them in response to some outcomes and not others were fitness enhancing for our ancestors.[6]

References

Axelrod, Robert (1980a), 'Effective choice in the Prisoner's Dilemma', *Journal of Conflict Resolution*, **24**, pp. 3–25.

Axelrod, Robert (1980b), 'More effective choice in the Prisoner's Dilemma', *Journal of Conflict Resolution*, **24**, pp. 379–403.

Axelrod, Robert (1984), *The Evolution of Cooperation* (New York: Basic Books).

Axelrod, R. and Hamilton, W.D. (1981), 'The evolution of cooperation', *Science*, **211**, pp. 1390–96,

D'Arms, Justin (1996), 'Sex, fairness, and the theory of games', *Journal of Philosophy*, **93**, pp. 615–27.

D'Arms, J., Batterman, R. and Gorny, K. (1998), 'Game theoretic explanations and the evolution of justice', *Philosophy of Science*, **65**, pp. 76–102.

Frank, Robert (1988), *Passions Within Reason: The Strategic Role of the Emotions* (New York: W.W. Norton and Co.).

Gibbard, Allan (1982), 'Human evolution and the sense of justice', *Midwest Studies in Philosophy*, **7**, pp. 31–46.

Hamilton, William D. (1964), 'The genetical evolution of social behaviour' (I and II), *Journal of Theoretical Biology*, **7**, pp. 1–52.

Hart, H.L.A. (1961), *The Concept of Law* (Oxford: Clarendon).

Hirschleifer, Jack (1987), 'On the emotions as guarantors of threats and promises' in *The Latest on the Best*, ed. John Dupré (Cambridge, MA: Bradford/MIT Press).

Mill, John Stuart (1979 [1863]), *Utilitarianism* (Indianapolis: Hackett).

Schelling, Thomas (1960), *The Strategy of Conflict* (Cambridge: Harvard University Press).

Skyrms, Brian (1996), *Evolution of the Social Contract* (New York: Cambridge University Press).

Skyrms, B. (2000), 'Game theory, rationality and evolution of the social contract', *Journal of Consciousness Studies*, **7** (1–2), pp. 269–84.

Sober, E. and Wilson, D.S. (1998), *Unto Others* (Cambridge, MA: Harvard University Press).

Trivers, R. (1971), 'The evolution of reciprocal altruism', *Quarterly Review of Biology*, **46**, pp. 35–57.

---

[6] I think there's a plausible version of that story available, some of which has been told before by others, but I can't explore its details here. See Frank (1988); Hirschleifer (1987) and especially Gibbard (1982).

CLASSICAL *VERSUS* EVOLUTIONARY GAME THEORY

Herbert Gintis

Classical and evolutionary game theory attempt to explain different phenomena. Classical game theory describes socially and temporally isolated encounters while evolutionary game theory describes macro-social behavioural regularities. The actors in classical game theory are payoff maximizers whose identity remains fixed during the course of play. By contrast, in evolutionary game theory, the players are constantly changing, and the central actor is a replicator — an entity having some means of making approximately accurate copies of itself. However successful in its own realm, evolutionary game theory is ill-constructed to model the phenomena addressed by classical game theory. We must look to as yet undeveloped principles to achieve classical game theory's unfulfilled promise. I indicate a possibly fruitful step in this direction.

Brian Skyrms has given us a rich set of examples illustrating important differences between classical ('rational choice') game theory and evolutionary game theory. 'As an explanatory theory of human behaviour', he concludes, evolutionary models 'hold more promise of success than models based on rational choice'. I agree with this assessment. I want to stress, however, that the two approaches *attempt to explain different phenomena.* However successful in its own realm, evolutionary game theory is ill constructed to model the phenomena addressed by classical game theory. We must look to as yet undeveloped principles to achieve classical game theory's unfulfilled promise. I shall indicate a possibly fruitful step in this direction.

Classical game theory describes *socially and temporally isolated encounters*, while evolutionary game theory describes *macro-social behavioural regularities*. The actors in classical game theory are payoff maximizers whose identity remains fixed during the course of play. By contrast, in evolutionary game theory, the players are constantly changing, and the central actor is a *replicator* — an entity having some means of making approximately accurate copies of itself. The replicator can be a gene, a species, a strategy, a belief, a technique, a convention, or a more general institutional or cultural form. In classical game theory, behaviour is unaffected by historical or social context (though players may have 'beliefs' that presumably come from somewhere). In evolutionary game theory, the isolated encounter of classical game theory (often called the *stage game*), is embedded in a *behavioural context* that describes (a) the characteristics of the population of game players; (b) the relationship between game players and replicators; (c) how players are chosen to play the stage game in each time period; and (d) how the success and failure of players is reflected in the frequency distribution of replicators in the next period.

Classical game theory analyses the *Nash equilibria* of the isolated encounter. Evolutionary game theory analyses the *evolutionary equilibria* of the dynamic system implied by the stage game in its behavioural context. This dynamic can generally be represented by a set of differential equations or a stochastic process. An evolutionary equilibrium is accordingly represented as an asymptotically stable fixed point of the set of differential equations, or stationary distribution of the stochastic process. As Skyrms notes, in simple cases (for example, where agents are randomly paired in each period, and the replicator dynamic is operative), evolutionary equilibria are Nash equilibria of the stage game.

For the sake of concreteness, consider a prisoner's dilemma repeated n times (n is known to the players). On each round the two players receive $2 each if both play C, $1 if both play D, and C against D gives the C-player $4 and the D-player zero. The game terminates the first time either player chooses D, or after n rounds if players have not played D to that point. A simple induction argument shows that if it is common knowledge that both players are 'rational' (i.e., that they play best responses), then both players will play D on the first round. To see this, note that on round n, both players will play D, since the game is now a one-shot prisoner's dilemma. Thus nothing the players do on round $n - 1$ can affect the outcome on round n. Thus both players will defect on round $n - 1$. And so on, back to round 1. When people actually play games of this sort with $n > 25$ (the payoffs and details of the game take many differing forms), they generally cooperate for many rounds (McKelvey and Palfrey, 1992; Andreoni and Miller, 1993; Kahn and Murnigham, 1993). Clearly, classical game theory gives an incorrect prediction here. But what prediction does evolutionary game theory give?

Consider a behavioural setting consisting of a large population of players randomly paired at times $t = 1, 2, \ldots$, such that for each t, each pair plays the repeated prisoner's dilemma with $n = 100$. Suppose also that the payoffs are player fitnesses, so after each period, players reproduce proportionally to their success in the game. Then, if we start with a population including all possible strategies, the unique evolutionary equilibrium is *also* to play D on every round! This is because the 'defect on round 1' strategy is the only one to survive the iterated elimination of strictly dominated strategies, and an evolutionary equilibrium under the replicator dynamic includes only strategies of this type (Gintis, 2000, chapter 10). This is illustrated in Figure 1, which is an artificial life simulation of this game.

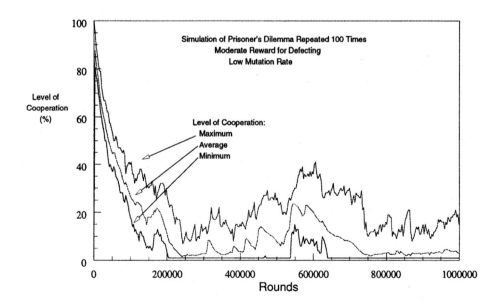

Figure 1

Simulation of the finitely repeated Prisoner's Dilemma with a low mutation rate (0.1 %)

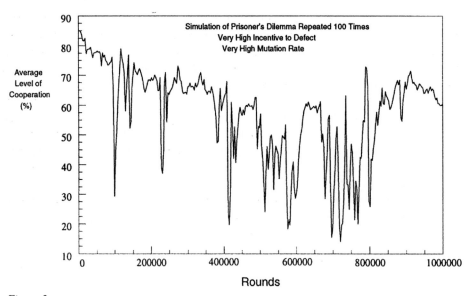

Figure 2

Simulation of the finitely repeated Prisoner's Dilemma with a high mutation rate

In this simulation, there is a population of 2,000 agents who are hard-wired with a 'gene' to cooperate for a certain number of rounds before defecting. Each agent is initially randomly assigned a gene with a value between 1 (defect immediately) and 101 (never defect). The agents are then randomly paired on each round, and paired agents play the above game. After each round, the lowest 0.50 per cent of scorers die, an equal number of the highest scorers reproduce, with a mutation rate (where an agent's defection point is randomly altered) of 0.001. Notice that cooperation at first increased rapidly to the 95 level, and then declines to very low levels. There are surges of cooperation up to 20 rounds, but the average generally hovers below 5. The evolutionary equilibrium value of 1 is not attained only because there is a positive mutation rate.

Evolutionary game theory suggests two reasons why this result might *not* be observed in practice. First, if there is enough mutation, a moderately high level of cooperation can be supported. This is illustrated in Figure 2, where cooperation varies between 15 per cent and 60 per cent. The second is that since *Homo sapiens* has *not* been subjected to an evolutionary process whereby people who do poorly in the finitely repeated prisoner's dilemma receive fitness penalties! Humans have simply never faced the relentless 'weeding out' of cooperators in daily life that is depicted in our simulation.

The two explanations of why humans cooperate in the repeated prisoner's dilemma are in fact closely related. Halving the probability that the game will be played in any period is operationally equivalent to doubling the rate of mutation. If there is a constant minimum level of mutation μ_0 per time period, and if convergence to a (suitably defined neighbourhood) of the evolutionary equilibrium requires a maximum mutation-rate μ_{max} per play of game, then if the probability p that an agent plays the game in a given time period falls below $p_{min} = \mu_0/\mu_{max}$, the evolutionary equilibrium will not be observed.

A more suggestive way of expressing this conclusion is that *nature abhors low probability events*. Consider, for instance, an organism with limited information processing capacity. The number of variants in the behavioural repertoire of such an organism will necessarily be small. Upon encountering a set of environmental stimuli, the organism first assigns the situation to one of a limited number of pre-given situational contexts, and then refers to the behavioural repertoire appropriate for that context for the proper choice of action. When the organism comes upon a new and strange situation, it does not create a new context, but rather relates the situation to one of the situational contexts for which it already possesses heretofore effective coping responses. Therefore, *all events encountered by such an organism are high probability events*.

The number of situational contexts an agent recognizes, and the number of behavioural responses appropriate to each, are governed by the principle of evolutionary fitness. It may be thought that more mental capacity and intellectual flexibility are unambiguous fitness enhancers, but this is clearly false. Adding a context, or a response within a context, has two costs that are 'fixed' in the sense that they have minimum levels independent of frequency of use. First, an expanded discriminatory or behavioural repertoire requires additional supporting neurological and physiological mechanisms. These mechanisms must be fuelled and maintained in good repair at all times. Second, such responses can be deployed when they are inappropriate, causing harm to the organism. If there is a minimum probability that an available response will be used, the ratio of inappropriate to appropriate use will then be a decreasing function of the frequency of the context for which it offers an effective response. Therefore, on both counts the lower the probability of occurrence of a context, the less likely will the expanded responsive capacities contribute to the organism's fitness.

Homo sapiens is doubtless no exception to this analysis, although with a larger repertoire of situational contexts than other species. This fact is of central importance, for instance, in interpreting the behaviour of human subjects in experimental game theoretic settings — settings where the predictions of classical game theory are notoriously poor. Neither personal history nor cultural/genetic evolutionary history has prepared subjects for the ultimatum, dictator, trust, common pool resource, bargaining, and other games that they confront in the laboratory. (For a review of some of these experimental settings, see pp. 215–19 above, where I discuss Sober & Wilson's contribution to this volume). Most likely, a subject treats the low probability event (the experiment) as an instance of a high probability event by assigning the event to one of the subject's pre-given situational contexts, and then deploying the behavioural repertoire — payoffs, probabilities, and actions — appropriate to that context. We may call this *choosing a frame* for the experimental situation. It is therefore incorrect to maintain that subjects are 'irrational' or 'confused' when they 'drag their history' into an experimental situation, since such behaviour is an *evolutionarily adaptive behaviour*.

The results of the ultimatum game, for instance, suggest that in a two-person bargaining situation, in the absence of other cues, the situational context applied by most subjects dictates some form of 'sharing'. Suppose we change the rules such that both proposer and respondent are members of different *teams* and they are told that their respective winnings will be paid to the team rather than the individual. Subjects then often deem a distinct situational context, involving 'competing for one's team,' appropriate. This dictates acting on behalf of one's team and suppressing behaviours that would be otherwise individually satisfying — such as 'sharing'. In this case proposers offer much less, and respondents very rarely reject positive offers (Shogren, 1989). Similarly, if the experimenters introduce notions of property rights into the strategic situation (for example, that the proposer in an ultimatum game has 'earned' or 'won' the right to this position), then motivations concerning 'fairness' are considerably attenuated in the experimental results (Hoffman, *et al.*, 1994;Hoffman, *et al.*, 1996).

It is plausible that some variant of the above schema, involving mapping common situational contexts onto novel, low probability events, may explain behaviour in the sorts of socially and temporally isolated encounters that form the subject of classical game theory. If so, the assumption of 'common knowledge of rationality' must be replaced by some (analytically rigorous) assumption of 'common knowledge of humanity' in the sense that each player in a one-shot game G knows how the other players map their high probability situational contexts onto G. In the finitely repeated prisoner's dilemma, for instance, each player may know that the other will treat the game as a trust game, and will assign a particular probability distribution to defecting on each round — plausibly one that puts zero weight on early stages of the game rising to moderate levels as the players near the final round. Models of this type, which do not involve the choice of best responses by the players, and which are inadequately modelled by either evolutionary or classical game theory, remain to be developed.

Acknowledgements

Some of this material is drawn from my forthcoming book *Game Theory Evolving* (Princeton: Princeton University Press, 2000). I would like to thank the MacArthur foundation for financial support.

References

Andreoni, James and Miller, John H. (1993), 'Rational cooperation in the finitely repeated prisoner's dilemma: Experimental evidence', *Economic Journal*, **103**, pp. 570–85.

Gintis, Herbert (2000), *Game Theory Evolving* (Princeton, NJ: Princeton University Press).

Hoffman, Elizabeth; McCabe, Kevin; and Smith, Vernon L. (1996), 'Social distance and other-regarding behavior in dictator games', *American Economic Review*, **86** (3), pp. 653–60.

Hoffman, Elizabeth; Shachat, Keith; and Smith, Vernon L. (1994), 'Preferences, property rights, and anonymity in bargaining games', *Games and Economic Behavior*, **7**, pp. 346–80.

Kahn, Lawrence M. And Murnigham, J. Keith (1993), 'Conjecture, uncertainty, and cooperation in prisoner's dilemma games: Some experimental evidence', *Journal of Economic Behavior and Organization*, **22** (1), pp. 91–117.

McKelvey, R.D. and Palfrey, T.R. (1992), 'An experimental study of the centipede game', *Econometrica*, **60**, pp. 803–36.

Shogren, Jason F. (1989), 'Fairness in bargaining requires a context: An experimental examination of loyalty', *Economic Letters*, **31**, pp. 319–23.

RATIONAL DELIBERATION *VERSUS* BEHAVIOURAL ADAPTATION
Theoretical Perspectives and Experimental Evidence

Sandra Güth and Werner Güth

Whereas Brian Skyrms in his chapter views rationality and evolution as alternative ways to derive decision behaviour, indirect evolution allows us to combine the two approaches. By focussing on Skyrms' examples it will be illustrated how optimal decisions for given rules of interaction can influence the future rules of interaction. Here evolution does not determine behaviour directly, but only indirectly via the rules. We, furthermore, report on an experiment, related to Skyrms' examples, revealing effects of deliberation in the sense of forward-looking considerations and of path dependence in the sense of adapting to past success.

I: Introduction

Brian Skyrms (2000) contrasts game theoretic concepts of (commonly known) rationality with Darwinian notions of behavioural adaptation or evolution. He thus contrasts purely forward-looking considerations, based on cognitive causal models of the decision environment, with pure path dependence. Here path dependence means that behaviour is shaped by past success, like in reinforcement learning, imitation, or evolution (see Skyrms, 2000, for details).

As synthesis we will propose indirect evolution, which allows for intermediate approaches in the sense that some acts are deliberately chosen whereas other decisions are shaped by past material success. Whereas direct evolution assumes that behaviour is programmed, indirect evolution relies on programmed basic needs, possibly also social ones, determining behaviour. The success of the indirectly derived behaviour then determines the future basic needs. Experimental results of robust learning (participants do not play the same game, but encounter repeatedly structurally different situations to which they can adapt) illustrate the effects of deliberation as well as of path dependence.

Like Skyrms, we also think that evolution of social order is more convincing than the previously prevailing idea of a (fictitious) social contract. Again, in our view, indirect evolution offers interesting ways to 'pursue modern Humean social philosophy' (Skyrms, this book) since one does not only explain how playing a given game evolves, but also how the rules of the game may be changing over time.

Skyrms first shows that rational deliberation and evolution may imply the same (rational or dynamically stable) behaviour and then illustrates the possible 'crack . . . between game theory based on rationality and game theory based on evolutionary dynamics' where he relies on the extensively studied ultimatum bargaining experiment. In our view, which seems confirmed by experimental results, the two approaches are, however, no mutually exclusive alternatives, but rather complementary ways of explaining human decision behaviour and man-made institutions like social order.

II: Indirect Evolution

Instead of describing indirect evolution in abstract terms, let us illustrate it by the ultimatum game, analysed by Skyrms (2000), who assumes that the two players, named proposer and responder, can share ten units of reward. Now the responder may not only care for how many units he gets, but also develop some inequality aversion (see Bolton and Ockenfels, 1999, and Fehr and Schmidt, 1999, for formal definitions and experimental evidence consistent with such a notion). Sufficiently strong inequality aversion may lead to rational rejections of positive, but unfair offers since a rejection implies zero-payoffs and thus equality.

For the sake of simplicity, let us assume that the degree of inequality aversion, felt by the responder, is commonly known. Then a rational proposer will anticipate that a rational, though inequality-averse responder will reject too low offers and avoid conflict by offering enough. This result enables us to analyse the evolution of inequality aversion. The more inequality averse a responder is, the more he will be offered. Combining this with success, monotonic evolutionary dynamics implies the evolution of extreme inequality aversion which, in turn, leads to equal sharing.

Here we did not want to provide another evolutionary justification of fairness in ultimatum games (see Skyrms, this book, for alternative approaches), but to illustrate how forward-looking deliberation and evolution, shaped by past success, can be combined. Deliberation must not necessarily be perfectly rational, any applicable concept of bounded rationality, e.g. for playing the ultimatum game, can be used as well (see Güth and Kliemt, 1998, for an illustration), nor is perfect signalling necessary (see Güth *et al.*, 1999, for a special finite population and a stochastic dynamic process).

III: Experimental Evidence for Robust Learning

Indirect evolution typically combines forward-looking deliberation and behavioural adaptation, driven by past success. Experimentally forward-looking deliberation can be detected by confronting participants with changing rules, but constant decision formats. If they systematically react to such changes of the rules, this proves that they are not just reacting according to past earning differentials, but by cognitively representing the situation and engaging in forward looking considerations.

Behavioural adaptation can be captured by confronting participants repeatedly with the same game so that one can see how past success shapes behaviour. Robust learning refers to behaviour which appears to be influenced by forward looking considerations, as detected by cognitively adapting to changing rules of the game, as well as by path-dependent behavioural adaptation when confronting repeatedly the same game.

Let us illustrate robust learning for a decision environment, considered by Skyrms (this book) who discusses the (Nash-)bargaining game as well as ultimatum bargaining. The two bargaining games differ only in the decision process: Whereas (Nash-)bargaining relies on simultaneous demands, ultimatum bargaining first allows the proposer to precommit to a demand which then the responder can only accept or reject. Indirect evolution (as well as the related concept of endogenous timing, see Güth and Güth, forthcoming, for another example) allows us to combine rational bargaining behaviour with evolving rules of bargaining, namely whether parties bargain simultaneously or sequentially.

Actually, one can interpret the results of Güth and Ritzberger (1999) in this way, who allow parties first to determine their timing disposition (early or late), and then to bargain about how to share a random pie. By varying the distribution of the pie's size, one can capture the situation of a small or large expected pie. The experimental study of Güth *et al.* (1999) captures different rules of the game by distinguishing three distributions. Participants play 48 rounds of games with varying distribution where they first determine their timing disposition (early or late) and then, knowing both dispositions, bargain accordingly (either simultaneously before or after the random choice of the pie or sequentially, i.e. one party demands before the pie is chosen and the other thereafter). The results reveal significant anticipation of rule, i.e. of distribution changes, but insignificant learning effects. The decision whether to demand early or late especially seems to be much more guided by forward-looking deliberations than by past experiences.

Of course, behavioural adaptation driven by past success is not irrelevant altogether. Actually participants of mixed pairs (one party demands early, the other late), who have waited before, often switch to pre-emption (demanding early) when their former 'early partner' has been more successful.

IV: Final Remarks

Inspired by Brian Skyrms' comparison of game theory based on rationality requirements, with evolutionary game theory and by his examples, we essentially illustrate that these approaches are not necessarily mutually exclusive, but can be fruitfully combined. This is demonstrated by the fast growing literature on indirect evolution, especially of preference evolution (for more general studies see Güth and Peleg, 1997; Kockesen *et al.*, forthcoming; Ok and Vega-Redondo, 1999). Experimental evidence of robust learning seems to support our approach by revealing forward-looking deliberation and path-dependent adaptation.

Early experimental evidence doubting rationality and suggesting fairness has first been questioned (for instance, Binmore *et al.*, 1985). Partly the same scholars (Binmore *et al.*, 1995) later on deny any forward looking deliberation and rely exclusively on adaptation, shaped by past success. We warn against 'pouring out the baby with the bath water'. Human beings, whose intelligence ranks high in the animal kingdom and among mammals, are neither superrational nor purely reacting to past success as assumed by usual evolutionary game theory (see Hammerstein and Selten, 1994).

Of course, there may be (especially vegetative) reactions and situations where we respond automatically without any considerations. But these are usually not studied in the social sciences, at least when related to decision and game theory. Essential decisions, which may be rare, usually are influenced by both forward-looking deliberation as well as by past experiences. And this combination is rather typical for all higher developed mammals (see de Waal, 1982; Kummer, 1995; Flack and de Waal, 2000).

Acknowledgement
We gratefully acknowledge the helpful comments by Leonard D. Katz.

References

Binmore, K., Shaked, A. and Sutton, J. (1985), 'Testing noncooperative bargaining theory: A preliminary study', *American Economic Review*, **75** (5), pp. 1178–80.

Binmore, K., Gale, J. and Samuelson, L. (1995), 'Learning to be imperfect: The ultimatum game', *Games and Economic Behaviour*, **8** (1), pp. 56–90.

Bolton, G. and Ockenfels, A. (1999), 'ERC — A theory of equity, reciprocity and competition', *American Economic Review*, forthcoming.

Flack J. and de Waal, F.B.M. (2000), '"Any Animal Whatever": Darwinian building blocks of morality in monkeys and apes,' *Journal of Consciousness Studies*, **7** (1–2), pp. 1–29.

Fehr, E. and Schmidt, K. (1999), 'A theory of fairness, competition and cooperation', *Quarterly Journal of Economics*, forthcoming.

Güth, S. and Güth, W. (forthcoming), 'Pre-emption in capacity and price determination — A study of endogenous timing of decisions for homogeneous markets', *Metroeconomica*.

Güth, S., Güth, W. and Kliemt, H. (1999), 'On the evolution of trust among few — An Indirect Evolution- ary Study', *Discussion Paper*, Humboldt-University of Berlin.

Güth, W. and Peleg, B. (1997), 'When will the fittest survive? An indirect evolutionary analysis', *SFB Discussion Paper* No. 71, Humboldt-University of Berlin.

Güth, W. and Kliemt, H. (1998), 'The indirect evolutionary approach: Bridging the gap between rational- ity and adaptation', *Rationality and Society*, **10** (3), pp. 377–99.

Güth, W. and Ritzberger, K. (1999), 'Pre-emption or wait-and-see? — Endogenous timing in bargaining', *Working Paper*, Humboldt-University of Berlin.

Güth, W., Marchand, N., Rulliere, J-L. and Zeiliger, R. (1999), 'Pre-empt or wait! An experimental study of endogenous timing in bargaining', *Working Paper*, Humboldt-University of Berlin.

Hammerstein, P. and Selten, R. (1994), 'Game theory and evolutionary biology', in: *Handbook of Game Theory*, Vol. 2, ed. R. Aumann and S. Hart (Amsterdam: Elsevier Science).

Kockesen, L., Ok, E.A. and Sethi, R. (forthcoming), 'Evolution of interdependent preferences in aggregative games', *Games and Economic Behaviour*.

Kummer, H. (1995), *In Quest of the Sacred Baboon: A scientist's journey*, (Princeton: Princeton Univer- sity Press).

Ok, E. A. and Vega-Redondo, F. (1999), 'On the evolution of individualistic preferences: Complete ver- sus incomplete information scenarios', *mimeo*.

Skyrms, B. (2000), 'Game theory, rationality and evolution of the social contract', *Journal of Conscious- ness Studies*, **7** (1–2), pp. 269–84.

de Waal, F. (1982), *Chimpanzee Politics* (London: Jonathan Cape).

THE EVOLUTION OF COOPERATION IN HOSTILE ENVIRONMENTS

William Harms

Skyrms (2000) describes how evolutionary models are helping us understand unself- ish or cooperative behaviour in humans and animals. Mechanisms which can stabi- lize cooperative behaviour are sensitive to population densities, however. This creates the need for agent-based evolutionary models which depict individual inter- actions, spatial locations, and stochastic effects. One such model suggests that hos- tile environments may provide conditions conducive to the emergence and stabilization of cooperative behaviour. In particular, simulations show that random extinctions can keep population densities low, provide ongoing colonization opportu- nities, and insulate cooperative communities from invasion. Agent-based and popu- lation models play complementary roles in furthering our understanding evolutionary processes.

Brian Skyrms (2000) describes how evolutionary models are helping us understand patterns of human behaviour that have been rather mysterious under the rational choice paradigm (Gauthier, 1986). In particular, the *unselfish* aspects of moral behav- iour are easier to understand as a product of evolution than of rational choice. The particular dynamical model Skyrms discusses is one among a number of formal and computational tools available for this task, and has limitations which suggest the need for an integrated approach to modelling evolution. For instance, population densities are important factors with regard to proposed mechanisms which allow the stabiliza- tion of cooperative behaviour, and one needs a different kind of model to accommo- date variable densities. I describe some simulations using one such model, which suggest that hostile environments may provide conditions conducive to the evolution of cooperation.

Population Dynamics

The replicator dynamics Skyrms discusses is one particular formulation of a general approach I will call *population dynamics.* A population dynamics model describes a large population divided into several types, and represents the dynamics of the frequencies of the different types in the population. Evolution is simply a matter of shifting frequencies. There are several different sources of these frequency shifts, but selection is usually the primary focus in the evolution of cooperation literature. Selection is just frequency shift due to differential fitness; fitness being the net (probable) effect of factors that affect frequencies in a multiplicative way, like mortality, reproduction, and social interaction. Fitness components are contrasted to factors like immigration and mutation, which affect frequencies by adding members to types, or introducing new types. Evolution by natural selection is thus the dynamics of competitive growth and decay rates. How the fitnesses are determined in a particular model can of course be a complex matter.

The first thing to notice is that there are no individuals represented in population models; only frequencies are tracked. One often hears that such models assume *very large* or *effectively infinite* populations. This has the general effect of making the models deterministic, which simplifies analysis tremendously. Since there are no individuals for accidents to happen to, then what happens on the population level is exactly what should be expected to happen. If individual interactions are random, then the model simulates exact randomness in interactions. If a type averages three offspring, then the type will exactly triple.

The second thing to notice is that, at least in the formulations common in evolutionary game theory, there is no keeping track of total population numbers, and thus no way of keeping track of density. At each cycle, an adjustment is made so that all of the frequencies add up to one. This is, of course, a good idea for some interests, but we shall see how it obscures certain issues of relevance to the evolution of cooperative behaviour.

Finally, there is no representation of spatial location of individuals, or even of spatial variation in population densities.

Why Density Matters

Suppose individuals have an opportunity to confer benefits on others they interact with at small cost to themselves. Assuming that they all will accept such benefits, call the ones who both confer and accept *cooperators*, and those who accept but do not confer *defectors*. For a cost of 1 point and a benefit of 2, this gives us the following payoff matrix:

Payoffs	Cooperate	Defect
Cooperate	1	−1
Defect	2	0

This game is the so-called *prisoner's dilemma*, and is the basic tool for studying the evolution and stability of cooperative behaviour (Axelrod, 1984). Rational choosers will always defect, since they do better no matter what the opponent does. The tragedy, of course, is that cooperation results in a higher average payoff. Population dynamics give a similar result, in that in the basic case, where individuals playing inherited pure strategies interact at random, the fitness of defectors is always greater than that of cooperators no matter the population frequencies of the two types. Cooperation goes quickly extinct.

Skyrms notes that cooperation can stabilize in population dynamics if the probability of individuals playing against others with the same strategy is increased. Cooperators do better against themselves than defectors do against themselves, so auto-correlation is good for cooperators. Above some threshold, cooperation drives defection out. The problem that concerns us arises when we consider what kinds of mechanisms might result in this kind of correlation. The standard example is population viscosity. Individuals tend not to move far from where they were born, certainly not mixing at random, and given that kin tend to be born near each other, the basic dispersal patterns of biological reproduction result in *viscous* populations in which auto correlation is a basic fact of nature. Good news for the evolution of cooperation, right?

The problem is that the correlations generated by simple dispersal patterns are affected by population densities, and as we know, successful populations have a tendency to increase in number and thus in density. In the absence of some mechanism to enforce boundaries between kin groups, the increasing population density will tend to force such groups together, reducing the degree of auto-correlation. Skyrms is, of course, quite clear that he is making the theoretical claim that if there are such correlations, cooperation can stabilize. But the point here is that the story will probably be more complex than standard examples assume. It also bears on Sober and Wilson's group selection approach, which seems to derive a good bit of theoretical clout from Wilson's re-analysis of Maynard-Smith's *haystack* model (Wilson, 1987; Sober and Wilson, 1998). The latter depends on each haystack being colonized by only one fertilized female. One would think that Malthusian growth would tend to undermine this arrangement. Again, there has to be more to the story.

The Agent–Patch Model

In order to model variable population densities as well as stochastic and spatial effects, we need to turn to an agent-based model. In what follows, I will describe a new sort of model, the *agent–patch* model, which has been designed to model spatial patterns and variable densities.[7]

A variable number of *agents* occupy a wrapped grid of *patches*. Agents are either cooperators or defectors, and they interact at random with other individuals on the same patch. Play uses the above prisoner's dilemma payoffs. They are also able to consume a small amount of locally renewable resource, which allows reproduction in the absence of interaction. Agents move between patches with a certain fixed probability, and they reproduce when they accumulate 150 units of resource. They die if their resource level falls to zero.

---

[7]   The model described was developed on a post-doctoral fellowship under Peter Danielson, at the Center for Applied Ethics, University of British Columbia. The results will be forthcoming as *Biological Altruism in Hostile Environments*.

On this basic setup, regardless of the initial distribution of cooperators and defectors, the long-term pattern is what one would expect. Population densities increase and, however low the movement rate, defectors eventually drive cooperators to extinction. Spatial isolation cannot be maintained by dispersal/reproduction dynamics alone, since crowding compromises the auto-correlation created by dispersal at low densities.

If it is density that undermines the favourable correlations, what kinds of factors might keep density low? One possibility is

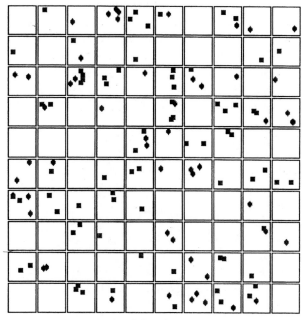

Figure 1. The Agent–Patch Simulator

environmental factors. Following the *metapopulation* literature in ecology (Hanski and Gilpin, 1997), patterns of local extinctions were introduced into the model, whereby all individuals on a patch are killed simultaneously with some fixed probability (the extinction rate) at each cycle. The model's behaviour was studied for a variety of values for extinction rate, cost/benefit ratio, and movement rate.

We found that for a given cost and movement rate, there is an intermediate range of extinction rates over which cooperation can thrive, and even outsurvive defection. Intermediate, because at low extinction rates, densities increase until cooperation is driven out, and at high rates neither cooperators nor defectors last long. Figure 2 demonstrates this pattern. At low rates, defectors always drive cooperators to extinction. At high rates, cooperators and defectors have an equal likelihood of going extinct first. But at intermediate rates, cooperators do substantially better than defectors. Why?

What accounts for this effect is not only the control on density, but to some extent, the short-term spatial unevenness of the extinction pattern. At parameter combinations where cooperators do well, there is an approximate patch vacancy rate of about 50 per cent, and defection cannot survive without the payoffs they get from interacting with cooperators. Payoffs from interaction become critical because without maintaining a high reproductive rate, local populations cannot disseminate fast enough to outrun the pattern of extinction. Cooperators can do this, and defectors can too as long as they find cooperators to interact with, but two factors interfere with the latter. First, defectors kill off the cooperators they need locally. Second, the vacant patches created by the extinction pattern provide both colonization opportunities for cooperators and insulation from invasion by defectors. This allows cooperators to survive while defectors are driven to extinction, protected from invasion and thus their own demise by the empty patches created by the extinction pattern itself.

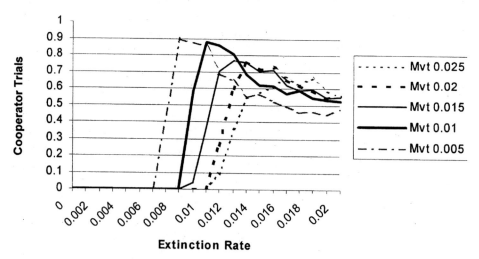

Figure 2. *Proportion of trials where cooperators outsurvived defectors (200 trials per point)*

The simulations suggest the following hypothesis: hostile environments, and in particular, hostile boundaries of ancestral ranges, provide conditions under which cooperative behaviour can evolve. Extinction patterns may provide a mechanism which creates correlations of like with like by keeping population densities low and insulating colonies of cooperative individuals from invasion. Further simulation work is needed in order to determine whether cooperation can arise and stabilize via mutation in such heterogeneous environments, and what sorts of environmental hostility can support these processes.

Modelling the Evolution of Cooperation

Our understanding of the evolution of cooperation depends critically on correlation mechanisms that have spatial components and which are sensitive to population densities. Population models abstract away from such factors in order to highlight broadly *economic* forces driving evolutionary change. However, the importance of spatial and stochastic factors creates a need for agent-based models. The idea is not that agent-based models should supplant population models as the basic research tool. They have shortcomings of their own. They are computationally intensive, and suffer from a high number of parameters which reduces the chance of repetition (and thus confirmation) by others, and often makes it hard to determine the actual cause of an observed effect. Thus, the gradual erosion of the prestige of rational choice and game theory as a tool for understanding human behaviour has resulted, not in its displacement by some other single model (e.g. evolutionary game theory), but by a plurality of models which, ideally, play complementary roles in advancing our understanding of human behaviour. Rational choice theory retains a place here as well.

Certain future developments can also be anticipated. The models of evolutionary game theory can be interpreted either as processes of biological reproduction in which strategies are inherited, or as processes of cultural transmission in which strategies are passed on via imitation. This generality would seem to increase the relevance of the models to human behaviour, applying to both inheritance and cultural transmission. But human beings evolve *both* biologically and culturally, and the interactions between these processes will be critical to our understanding of human morality as a product of evolution. Boyd and Richerson (1985), for instance, have shown that the interaction between such processes can result in patterns which cannot be predicted on the basis of either one alone, though we are just beginning to build the tools to analyse this relationship (Campbell, 1987; Harms, 1997). What we have, then, rather than new foundations for a *physics* of human behaviour, is a work in progress, which promises to get messier, more difficult, and more interesting, as our models approach the complexity of real human beings.

References

Axelrod, Robert (1984), *The Evolution of Cooperation* (New York: Basic Books).

Boyd, Robert, and Richerson, Peter J. (1985), *Culture and the Evolutionary Process* (Chicago: The University of Chicago Press).

Campbell, Donald T. (1987 [1974]), 'Evolutionary epistemology', in *Evolutionary Epistemology, Rationality, and the Sociology of Knowledge*, ed. G. Radnitzky and W.W. Bartley (La Salle, IL: Open Court).

Gauthier, David (1986), *Morals by Agreement* (Oxford University Press).

Hanski, Ilkka A. and Gilpin, Michael E. (ed. 1997), *Metapopulation Biology: Ecology, genetics and evolution* (London: Academic Press).

Harms, William F. (1997), 'Reliability and novelty: Information gain in multi-level selection systems', *Erkenntnis*, **46**, pp. 335–63.

Skyrms, Brian (1996), *Evolution of the Social Contract* (Cambridge University Press).

Skyrms, B. (2000), 'Game theory, rationality and evolution of the social contract', *Journal of Consciousness Studies*, **7** (1–2), pp. 269–84.

Sober, Elliott, and Wilson, David Sloan (1998), *Unto Others: The Evolution and Psychology of Unselfish Behaviour* (Cambridge, MA: Harvard).

Wilson, D.S. (1987), 'Altruism in Mendelian populations derived from Simblind groups: The haystack model revisited', *Evolution*, **41**, pp. 1059–70.

EVOLUTIONARY GAMES AND MORALITY

Dennis Krebs

The implications of game theory models of the evolution of strategies of exchange are explored with respect to the evolution of moral dispositions. I argue that dispositions to practice tit for tat strategies could have evolved, but the moral behaviours to which they give rise do not fare well on criteria of morality. Inasmuch as the strategy implicit in the Golden Rule is unconditional, it could not have evolved in environments containing strategies that exploit it. However, dispositions to invoke conditional principles such as those that prescribe that people cooperate with those they observe cooperating and shun those they observe behaving selfishly, could have been selected in some conditions and may have given rise to the evolution of indirect reciprocity. The key to the evolution of morality is discrimination in favour of cooperators and against cheaters and selfish individualists. The limitations of game theory in the explanation of human morality are acknowledged.

Models of natural selection in experimental games are potentially useful to psychologists interested in understanding the acquisition of morality because they may help them decide whether dispositions to adopt various cooperative strategies could have evolved, and cooperation lies at the heart of morality (see Alexander, 1987; Krebs, 1998 and Rest, 1983 for reviews). I will consider how two strategies of cooperation, thus two principles of morality, fare in experimental games designed to model natural selection. In the spirit of one of the points made by the philosopher, Brian Skyrms, I will conclude that the key to the evolution of morality is correlated pairing — that is to say, the tendency for like strategies of exchange to interact with each other.

I am attentive to the differences identified by Skyrms between economic and evolutionary games. My focus here is on evolved dispositions, which equate to strategies of genetic propagation selected in ancestral environments. I do not assume that individuals in contemporary environments who inherit the strategies are consciously motivated to invoke them, to compete with others, to maximize their material gains, or even to maximize their inclusive fitness. I assume only that the dispositions in question induced the ancestors of those who inherited them to behave in ways that enabled them to propagate the genes giving rise to them. I also do not deny that socialization, culture, and cultural evolution affect moral behaviour. I will not, however, attend to these influences in this paper. My units of analysis are genetically-determined strategies, or more exactly, the alleles giving rise to the strategies. These strategies may or may not correspond to more psychologically and economically meaningful units of analysis such as personality traits, points in games, or money. This said, I will sometimes use the motivational language of psychology for convenience, trusting that I could, in every instance, translate it into genetic terms.

Tit for Tat

You scratch my back and I will scratch yours. An eye for an eye; a tooth for a tooth. Don't get mad; get even. Do unto others as they do unto you. The principle of direct reciprocity implicit in these injunctions is familiar to everyone. The sociologist Gouldner (1960) concluded that 'A norm of reciprocity is, I suspect, no less universal and important . . . than the incest taboo' (p. 178).

The psychologist Kohlberg (1984) has found that judgments upholding such forms of direct reciprocity are integral to the structure of what he has called Stage 2 moral reasoning. Stage 2 is the second in a five-stage hierarchy of forms of moral reasoning that Kohlberg and his colleagues have found mark a developmental sequence. These psychologists have demonstrated that most children in the eight- to eleven-year-old range make Stage 2 moral judgments such as, 'you should do things for others because you might need them to do something for you in return' and 'you should get even with people who rip you off' (Colby and Kohlberg, 1987). Other psychologists (e.g., Wark and Krebs, 1996; 1997) have found that adults also make Stage 2 moral judgments in some circumstances. Krebs (1998) has suggested that the function of the structures of moral reasoning described by Kohlberg and his colleagues is to uphold evolved systems of cooperation. In the context of game theory, such structures may be considered strategies.

Axelrod and Hamilton (1981) found that the strategy tit for tat — open with a cooperative overture, then copy the move of your partner on subsequent moves — defeated a host of other strategies in Prisoner's Dilemma contests modelling natural selection, even though it did not become evolutionarily stable. Tit for tat is a powerful strategy because it, in effect, opens the door to a string of mutually beneficial cooperative exchanges in its first move, but cuts its losses immediately when its cooperative overtures are not reciprocated, copying the selfishness of selfishly individualistic adversaries who defect. Note that the key to the success of the tit for tat strategy lies in its stubborn conviction to reward cooperation with cooperation and punish selfishness with selfishness: it is discriminatory. It is merciless toward the unrepentant, but forgiving toward selfish individualists who convert to cooperation.

Biologists have adduced persuasive evidence that dispositions to engage in tit for tat types of exchange have evolved in non-human animals such as primates, fish, and vampire bats (see Trivers, 1985; Dugatkin, 1997). I have reviewed evidence that dispositions to practice direct reciprocity have evolved in the human species (Krebs, 1998). This said, most people do not consider direct reciprocity a very lofty moral principle (Rest, 1983). It ranks second lowest in Kohlberg's five-stage sequence of increasingly moral forms of moral judgment. Can we get to any higher principles of morality through the mechanisms of evolution? In the language of experimental games, can more moral strategies of cooperation defeat tit for tat type strategies, or at least coexist with them?

Fortunately, perhaps, the tit for tat strategy is limited in at least two important ways. First, it always loses to selfish individualism in single exchanges. For tit for tat to prevail, it, and/or other strategies conducive to it, must invade a population dominated by selfish individualism in sufficiently high numbers that they interact mostly with cooperative strategies. Second, a selfish mistake in a previously cooperative tit for tat exchange will precipitate an ongoing series of selfish exchanges that end up retributively self-defeating in nature. I get even with you, then you get even with me, and so on, ad infinitum. Such dynamics are apparent in Hatfield and McCoy type blood feuds and inter-group conflicts such as those in Ireland and the Middle East.

Following the initial success of tit for tat in Axelrod's computer contests, game theorists found that more forgiving and generous strategies such as tit for two tats and generous tit for tat could outcompete tit for tat in some populations (see Dugatkin, 1997; Ridley, 1996 for reviews), raising the possibility that individuals could inherit dispositions to uphold higher principles of morality than those implicit in the tit for tat strategy.

The Golden Rule

Do unto others as you would have them do unto you. Treat others as you would like to be treated. Love your neighbour as yourself. That which you wish not to be done for yourself, do not do unto your neighbour. Turn the other cheek. This principle of ideal reciprocity — in its prosocial, prohibitive, and anti-retaliatory forms — is familiar to everyone. In place of paying others back in kind, the Golden Rule prescribes behaving toward others as you would want them to behave toward you, which, presumably, is nicely, and perhaps even unconditionally cooperative. The ideal reciprocity inherent in the Golden Rule is an ingenious principle. In effect, it transforms each individual's self-interest into a guide for how he or she ought to treat others, thereby controlling selfishness, cultivating altruism, and fostering interpersonal harmony. If everyone practised the Golden Rule, it would seem, it would be a wonderful world, with everyone cooperating with everyone else to everyone's advantage.

This moral principle is preached in all the major religions of the world. It constitutes an essential aspect of the structure of Kohlberg's third stage of moral reasoning, displayed by most adolescents and many adults. Virtually all moralists consider the Golden Rule a better principle than tit for tat. But could dispositions inducing individuals to adopt this strategy evolve?

It is easy to see that the Golden Rule is vulnerable to exploitation. If you treat me generously — maximizing my inclusive fitness — (because that is the way you would want me to treat you), I can come out ahead by taking what you give me, and giving nothing in return. Turning the other cheek invites a red face. To evolve, dispositions to practice the Golden Rule must somehow acquire protection from exploitation.

Implicit in Christian exhortations to follow the Golden Rule is the sense that those who exploit it will somehow reach a limit to their inclination to take advantage of those who treat them generously; that the good example of martyrs will somehow cause sinners to see the light. However, in evolutionary terms, the only way dispositions to reform could evolve would be if the exploitation of those practising the Golden Rule turned out to be a bad strategy; that is to say, if it failed to maximize the inclusive fitness of those who practised it. In terms of the units in question, this is not, by definition, the case in exchanges between selfish individualists and Golden Rule strategists. Also implicit in religious justifications is the sense that practising the Golden Rule will pay off in the end — the meek will inherit the earth. In the currency of evolution, the fittest inherit the earth, so the question becomes how could meekness foster one's inclusive fitness?

One possibility is through interactions with strategies other than selfish individualism. Even though ideal reciprocators will always lose in exchanges with selfish individualists, they could fare better than selfish individualists in exchanges with other strategies in the population or group. Perhaps unconditionally cooperative strategies could evolve if other strategies punished selfish individualism and/or rewarded unconditional cooperation. Consider groups containing individuals interacting on an ongoing basis in each other's presence, and assume for simplicity that each individual inherits one strategy. Assume also that some strategies are equipped to calibrate themselves in terms of predictive information they glean about the strategies adopted by others in their interactions with others — a kind of vicarious social learning. A conditional strategy that induced individuals to behave selfishly toward individuals they observed treating others selfishly would pay off in interactions with selfish individualists.

The down side of such a strategy is that it could induce individuals to discriminate against others possessing it whom they observed behaving selfishly toward the selfish. Shunning those you see behaving selfishly instead of treating them selfishly would be a more effective strategy, and, in the currency of the Prisoner's Dilemma game, is more punitive that conditional selfishness. In Prisoner's Dilemma games, selfish individualists remain in the game and earn some points. Those who are shunned are out of the game; they get nothing at all.

In this context, Golden Rule followers could be a problem. Because they would not like to be shunned, bleeding heart Golden Rule practisers might not themselves shun those who treat them or others selfishly. An interesting implication of this point is that selfish individualism may be dependent in some populations on Golden Rule strategists or other types of non-discriminating do-gooders. Another implication is that inasmuch as selfish individualists are shunned by discriminating strategists, and inasmuch as selfish individualists are able to identify Golden Rule followers, we would expect a kind of assortative partnership between selfish individualists and Golden Rule followers. But only for a while. In the end, selfish individualists will deplete the stock of Golden Rule followers and the dispositions they possess.

It might be argued that members of a population would find Golden Rule followers desirable exchange partners and make generous overtures to them in order to initiate mutually-beneficial reciprocal exchanges, thus rewarding the strategy. The problem is, such generous overtures are unnecessary, because the Golden Rule followers are bent on behaving generously in any event. There simply is no way dispositions to practice the Golden Rule could have been selected biologically in a population dominated by selfish individualists. It is possible such dispositions could have evolved in populations in which conditional cooperative strategies such as tit for tat have mediated the extinction of selfishly individualistic strategies, thus rendering equivalent the conditional cooperation of the 'tit for taters' and the unconditional cooperation of the Golden Rule followers. Ironically, though, the larger the number of unconditional cooperators, the more fruitful the environment for the invasion of selfish individualism, suggesting that the natural state of moral dispositions in the human species may be unstable and fluctuating. Conditional cooperative strategies may deplete selfish individualism and pave the way for unconditional cooperative strategies, which may open the door for the return of selfish individualism, and so on.

On the logic of game-theory, the furthest natural selection can take us toward dispositions to treat others as we would have them treat us is to instill in us dispositions to cooperate with cooperators and to shun selfish individualists: Maximize cooperative exchanges with individuals who in some way signal that they are disposed to cooperate or behave altruistically, and minimize exchanges with individuals who signal selfishness. The Golden Rule works just fine as long as it is directed toward other individuals who practice it; the type of correlation discussed by Skyrms.

Indirect Reciprocity

To this point, I have confined my analysis to mechanisms based in direct reciprocity — that is to say, exchanges between two individuals. The situation becomes somewhat more hopeful when we consider the benefits of indirect reciprocity, in which what goes around in exchanges with one partner comes around in exchanges with others. The evolutionary biologist, Richard Alexander (1987) views moral systems as systems of indirect reciprocity. Alexander argues that dispositions to behave in 'indiscriminately beneficent' ways could evolve through indirect reciprocity supported by discrimination in favour of altruists and against cheaters. He suggests that in groups of repeatedly interacting individuals, beneficence could pay off in three ways. First, members of groups could select those who behave beneficently as exchange partners. Second, groups could reward such individuals and their relatives by elevating their status, giving them resources, etc. And third, beneficence could increase the success of the group and therefore the beneficent individual's and his or her relatives' share of the benefits. In contrast, the group would punish selfish individualists and cheaters by decreasing their status, rejecting them as partners, and ostracizing them.

In a recent computer simulation, Nowak and Sigmund (1998) found that a more altruistic form of cooperation than tit for tat could evolve by way of mechanisms based in indirect reciprocity. Nowak and Sigmund structured their game such that pairs of interactants were unlikely to meet again, reducing the opportunity for direct reciprocity. Each altruistic move made by a player enhanced his or her reputation or 'image'. Conversely, behaving selfishly degraded it. Nowak and Sigmund found that if altruists discriminated in favour of those with a good image, altruism could evolve and become evolutionarily stable. The logic underlying the adaptive value of indirect reciprocity is similar to the logic underlying tit for tat — selfishness begets selfishness and cooperation begets cooperation — except, in indirect reciprocity, through third parties.

Note that you need at least three individuals — or a group — for indirect reciprocity. Indirect reciprocity contains the potential to mediate more benefits to those who practice it than direct reciprocity does, because a third party may be able to give an individual who helped a second party goods worth more to the first party (at less cost) than could the second party, thus maximizing gains in trade. The following conclusions from game theory research support and help flesh out the idea that conditionally cooperative strategies based in indirect reciprocity can evolve through natural selection. Strategies capable of 'learning' may defeat strategies that are not (Pollock and Dugatkin, 1992). Learning about potential interactants' reputation is especially valuable (Pollock and Dugatkin, 1992). Ostracism supports cooperation (Hirshleifer and Rasmussen, 1989). Punishing defectors and establishing norms may facilitate cooperation (Axelrod, 1986).

It is important to note that systems of direct and indirect reciprocity are not mutually exclusive; the latter could be embedded in the former. We can help those who help us as well as helping, and receiving help from, third parties. It is worth repeating that, in sufficient quantity, tit for tat has the capacity to support more unconditionally cooperative strategies by punishing selfish individualism. Indeed, if everyone inherited tit for tat structures, and if everyone interacted with everyone else, everyone would cooperate, rendering direct reciprocity, indirect reciprocity, and indiscriminate altruism indistinguishable. In Axelrod's computer contests, after tit for tat defeats selfish individualism, virtually all nice strategies reap approximately the same gains.

It is telling that the constellation of moral judgments that defines Kohlberg's Stage 3 moral reasoning contains judgments upholding the Golden Rule as well as judgments upholding concrete reciprocity, gratitude, charity, compassion, kindness, reputation, relationships, family, trust, caring, in-group welfare, and retribution, on the one hand, and condemning selfishness, greed, and cold-heartedness on the other hand. Kohlberg's Stage 3 moral judgments uphold a system of cooperation based in indirect reciprocity in groups similar to those in which anthropologists believe our ancestors lived. Upholding such systems of cooperation does not, however, entail practising the Golden Rule.

As Skyrms implies, the key to the evolution of moral dispositions is selective interaction, discriminating in favour of cooperators and against non-cooperators. Research has found that a good strategy is to base such discriminations on observations of others' behaviour — the signals they send. However, inasmuch as the signals individuals send determine the benefits they obtain, it is in their interest to send misleading signals — to induce others to think they are, were, or will be, generous. It is individuals' social image or reputation that counts — the impressions they make on others — not the reality of what they actually are. A strategy with a potentially greater payoff than discriminating indirect reciprocity is to behave in ways that induce others to think you are cooperative and altruistic in order to exploit them: to create the impression that you are nice, but to behave selfishly when you can get away with it. Of course, the evolution of such deceptive strategies will create conditions favourable to the evolution of the ability to detect deception — i.e., to make more accurate discriminations — , which will pull for the evolution of better techniques of deception, including those based in self-deception, and so on (Alexander, 1987; Krebs and Denton, 1997; Trivers, 1985).

It is in individuals' interest to maximize altruism in others, or, more exactly, to maximize others' altruism toward them and their kin. Therefore, we would expect individuals to acquire dispositions to induce and manipulate others into behaving in generous ways such as those prescribed by the Golden Rule, while, at the same time resisting such social influence themselves, failing to practice what they preach.

This, I believe, is an apt and accurate portrait of human interaction. We are biologically disposed to maximize others' tendency to practice the Golden Rule in their interactions with us, which we do by preaching this principle, creating the impression we practice it, and believing we practice it, at least more than we actually do. The stronger our beliefs in our moral worthiness, the better our ability to convince others of our morality, and, therefore, the better we are treated by others. Such self-deception is adaptive (Trivers, 1985; Krebs *et al.*, 1988; Krebs and Denton, 1997).

The up side of all of this is that, to some extent, we get taken in by our own act. To sustain mutually beneficial cooperative relations, cultivate a favourable social image, avoid ostracism, and sustain our impressions of ourselves, we must help those who help us and behave altruistically some of the time, at least in public. Although few, if any, of us are biologically disposed to adopt the unconditional strategy of doing unto others as we would have them do unto us, we may end up behaving in ways that are consistent with this principle with some people some of the time.

Provisos

Before closing, I need to issue several provisos. First, I need to acknowledge that although I have made the simplifying assumption that individuals inherit only one strategy, it is obvious that humans inherit flexible programs that organize sets of conditional strategies. I have argued elsewhere (Krebs, in press) that humans inherit dispositions to invoke at least three overriding cooperative strategies, which define the first three stages of moral development identified by Kohlberg (1984). These strategies are domain-specific in the sense that they regulate different kinds of social relation (e.g., hierarchical, egalitarian, intimate). In the context of this commentary, the main point is that people may, in fact, come close to invoking Golden Rule-like strategies in relations with friends, loved ones, and members of their family.

Second, I have based most of my analysis on Prisoner's Dilemma games that model natural selection via social exchange in an asexual manner. A more complete analysis would include other games and build in other mechanisms, such as sexual selection, kin selection, and, maybe, group selection. Indeed, if we assume that selfish individualism originally, or at any time, dominated a population, more cooperative strategies may well have needed the indirect genetic benefits derived from one of these forms of selection to gain a foothold. The evolution of altruism through kin selection has featured prominently in modern refinements of Darwinism. Sober and Wilson (1998) argue that group selection has mediated the evolution of moral dispositions. Sexual selection probably also played a significant role in the evolution of some forms of altruism in the human species. It makes sense to suspect that our ancestors valued altruistic and nurturing dispositions in potential partners — not indiscriminately altruistic dispositions, mind you, but dispositions to behave altruistically toward one's mate and his or her kin.

Third, the status of the Golden Rule as a moral principle is aptly captured in its rank in Kohlberg's sequence of stages — third in a five- or six-stage hierarchy. The Golden Rule falls short of the kinds of universal ethical principle espoused by philosophers of ethics, which define Kohlberg's highest stages of moral development. The Golden Rule is only as good as the values of the person espousing it. 'As you would like them to do unto you' is egocentric and potentially variable across people. What I would like you to do unto me may be different from what you would like me to do unto you, and, in either case, may not be in our best interest or qualify as a moral. As one example, I, in a suicidal state, might want you to kill me. The Golden Rule could transform masochism into sadism. As another example, I might want you to leave me alone to pursue my ends as selfishly as I am able to. To achieve a philosophically-respectable status, a moral principle must extend beyond the perspectives of the two persons the Golden Rule considers, and attend to and balance the perspectives of everyone affected by the exchange in question. Treating you as I would like you to treat me may be unfair to others. To resolve the potential conflicts and contradictions produced by the Golden Rule, we need a higher order universal, impartial principle that guides decision-making and the allocation of resources in a way that is fair to all affected parties. Skyrms suggests that such a principle would prescribe universal cooperation. However, as much as treating others as they treat you may meet the criteria of respectable ethical principles such as the categorical imperative in the restricted conditions of experimental games, where players do not differ in need, ability, or what they deserve, such principles will fall far short in the complex world of real-life interaction.

Finally, the kind of discrimination on which viable systems of indirect reciprocity depend are feasible only in relatively small in-groups such as those in which most experts believe our ancestors lived, where one's behaviour becomes common knowledge and one's reputation counts. Modern environments are conducive to selfish individualism in the sense that selfish individualists can exploit cooperators in one social context, then move to new contexts and begin anew with an untarnished social image. One might argue that there was no benefit in ancestral environments in discriminating between in-group and out-group members, so we may be evolved to adopt high-stage principles prescribing universal cooperation, but I find this possibility implausible in view of evidence from social psychologists demonstrating powerful cognitive inclinations to categorize others as members of in-groups or out-groups, and to discriminate between them accordingly (see Krebs and Denton, 1997 for a review). Alexander's (1987) suggestion that inter-group conflicts (i.e., wars) were one of the most powerful selective forces in ancestral environments seems plausible, and, in my view, constitutes one of the few mechanisms through which selection at the group level could outpace selection at the individual or genetic level.

This said, trends toward global communities and mass media communication may be conducive to an expansion of in-group identities and systems of indirect reciprocity. To the extent that people belong to many different and partially overlapping groups, overlapping networks of indirect reciprocity may mediate an expansion of cooperative exchanges. Social psychological research on group identity (see Krebs and Denton, 1997, for a review) and anthropological studies of preliterate societies converge in support of the idea that we are evolved to recruit allies from and form coalitions with other groups. Group membership is flexible, nuanced, and negotiable. The moral ideal could be approximated if everyone viewed everyone else as members of the same in-group, but in-groups need out-groups to define their identities and defeat in competitive exchanges.

Acknowledgements

I would like to thank Leonard Katz, some of whose words I have shamelessly stolen, and an anonymous reviewer for their valuable suggestions, many of which have found their way into this commentary.

References

Axelrod, R.D. (1986), 'An evolutionary approach to norms', *Amer. Pol. Sci. Rev.*, **80**, pp. 1101–11.

Alexander, R.D. (1987), *The Biology of Moral Systems* (New York: Aldine de Gruyter).

Axelrod, R. and Hamilton, W.D. (1981), 'The evolution of cooperation', *Science*, **211**, pp. 1390–6.

Colby, A. and Kohlberg, L. (1987), *The Measurement of Moral Judgment (Vols. 1–2)* (Cambridge: Cambridge University Press).

Dugatkin, L.A. (1997), *Cooperation Among Animals: An Evolutionary Perspective* (New York: Oxford University Press).

Gouldner, A.W. (1960) 'The norm of reciprocity: A preliminary statement', *American Sociological Review*, **25**, pp. 161–78.

Hirshleifer, D. and Rasmussen, E. (1989), Cooperation in a repeated Prisoner's Dilemma game with ostracism', *J. Econ. Behav. and Organization*, **12**, pp. 87–106.

Kohlberg, L. (1984), *Essays in Moral Development: Vol 2. The Psychology of Moral Development* (New York: Harper & Row.)

Krebs, D.L. (1998), 'The evolution of moral behaviour', in *Handbook of Evolutionary Psychology: Ideas, Issues, and Applications*, ed. C. Crawford and D.L. Krebs, (Hillsdale, NJ: Erlbaum).

Krebs, D.L. (in press), 'The evolution of moral dispositions in the human species', *Annals of the New York Academy of Sciences*.

Krebs, D.L. and Denton, K. (1997) 'Social illusions and self-deception: The evolution of biases in person perception', in *.Evolutionary Social Psychology,* ed. J.A. Simpson and D.T. Kenrick, (Hillsdale, NJ: Erlbaum).

Krebs, D.L., Denton, K. and Higgins, N. C. (1988), 'On the evolution of self-knowledge and self-deception', in *Sociobiological Perspectives on Human Development*, ed. K.B. MacDonald (New York: Springer-Verlag).

Nowak, M.A. and Sigmund, K. (1998), 'Evolution of indirect reciprocity by image scoring', *Nature*, **393**, pp. 573–7.

Pollock, G. and Dugatkin, L.A. (1992), 'Reciprocity and the evolution of reputation', *J. Theo. Biol.*, **159**, pp. 25–37.

Rest, J.F. (1983) 'Morality', in *Handbook of Child Psychology: Vol. 3. Cognitive Development (4th ed.)*, ed. J.H. Flavell and E.M. Markman (New York: Wiley).

Ridley, M. (1996), *The Origins or Virtue: Human Instincts and the Evolution of Cooperation* (New York: Viking).

Sober, E. and Wilson, D.S. (1998) *Unto Others: The Evolution and Psychology of Unselfish Behaviour* (Cambridge MA: Harvard University Press).

Trivers, R. (1985), *Social Evolution* (Menlo Park CA: Benjamin Cummings).

Wark, G. and Krebs, D.L. (1996), 'Gender and dilemma differences in real-life moral judgment', *Developmental Psychology*, **32**, pp. 220–30.

Wark, G. and Krebs, D.L. (1997), 'Sources of variation in real-life moral judgment: Toward a model of real-life morality', *Journal of Adult Development*, **4**, pp. 163–78.

EVOLUTIONARY GAME THEORY, MORALITY, AND DARWINISM

Gary Mar

Should evolution replace rational choice as the guiding paradigm for game theory? Evolutionary game theory provides an intriguing perspective from which to critique the hyper-rational assumptions of classical economic game theory. In contrast to economic game theory, evolutionary game theory is better suited to descriptive rather than normative domains. It is argued that a pluralism of paradigms holds the best promise for theoretical innovation in game theory.

Game theory is the study of how agents should rationally act in situations of conflict and cooperation. Classical economic game theory is based on a normative theory of rational choice that is assumed to be egoistic. My rational choice is calculated to be the strategy that can be expected to yield the largest payoff for me on the assumption that others are trying to choose strategies best for them. Economic game theory has been useful in explicating the social contract arguments of philosophers from Thomas Hobbes (1651) and David Hume (1748) to John Rawls (1971) and David Gauthier (1985).

The notion of a game, however, is abstract. It includes the situation in which members of a biological species can be regarded as players in a game in which the payoff is the chance to pass on genes to future generations. Brian Skyrms (2000) proposes an evolutionary paradigm for game theory. Evolutionary, in contrast to economic, game theory dispenses with strong assumptions about rationality such as the assumption that rationality is common knowledge. Nor does evolutionary game theory tempt one with the 'Euclidean' optimism that there will be a uniquely rational solution for any game. Yet the prescriptions of economic game theory are notoriously at odds with actual behaviour.

Skyrms considers the 'Beauty Contest' in which players choose numbers from zero to 100. The player closest to half the average wins $100, and in the case of a tie the prize is evenly divided. Since the highest that half the mean could be is 50, it is irrational to choose above 50. Assuming rationality is common knowledge, the argument can be iterated. The unique solution of Bayesian rationality is that everyone chooses zero. Figure 1 summarizes experimental data.

Player	Game 1	Game 2	Game 3	Game 4	Winnings
A	4*	5	8	24	$50
B	23	10	9*	16	$100
C	17	5	100	6*	$100
D	4*	1*	1	3	$150
Mean/2	6	2.625	14.75	6.125	

Figure 1 Data for the Beauty Contest

The ability to win the Beauty Contest — like succeeding in the stock market — appears not to be based on calculating a uniquely rational solution but on the ability of a player to estimate what the average person would estimate. Game theory based on rational choice requires arbitrarily high degrees of such reflective reasoning.

A reply to this mismatch between theory and practice distinguishes between a normative and descriptive theory. Game theory prescribes what people *ought* rationally to choose; it does not describe how people will *in fact* choose. Nevertheless, even prescriptive game theory yields counterintuitive results.

The concept of the Nash equilibrium, Skyrms argues, plays a central role in both evolutionary and economic game theory. In 1950, John Nash proved that every two-player game has at least one equilibrium in either pure or mixed strategies. Due to its stability, a Nash equilibrium was regarded as a solution for zero-sum games. However, in 1950, Melvin Dresher and Merrill Flood devised a game to show that a non-zero-sum game could have a unique equilibrium outcome that is not intuitively optimal.

The game is known as the *Prisoner's Dilemma* due to a story by Albert Tucker. Two prisoners, Rose and Colin, are arrested for a joint crime and interrogated in separate cells.

- If one confesses (i.e., *defects*) while the other does not, the defector will get off scot-free (payoff 0) and the partner will get five years in prison (payoff –5).

- If both defect, each will get a sentence of four years (payoff –4).

- If neither defects (i.e., both *cooperate* by sitting tight), each will get only two years (payoff –2).

Rose reasons, 'If Colin cooperates, instead of getting two years by cooperating, I'll get off scot-free by defecting. If Colin defects, instead of getting five years by cooperating, I'll get four years by defecting. Therefore, it is better for me to defect no matter what Colin does.' Defecting is a *dominant strategy*. The reasoning for Colin is symmetric. The arrows in the payoff matrix in figure 2 below indicate the direction of the reasoning and converge at the equilibrium of mutual defection.

	Cooperates *Sits tight*		Defects *Confesses*
Cooperates *Sits tight*	(–2, –2)	→	(–5, 0)
	↓		↓
Defects *Confesses*	(0, –5)	→	(–4, –4)

Figure 2 Payoff Matrix for the Prisoner's Dilemma

Yet this equilibrium is not a particularly rational outcome. Rose and Colin mutually defect resulting in sentences of four years each. Mutual cooperation would have resulted in lighter sentences of two years each.

The Prisoner's Dilemma captures the conflict between egoism and altruism inherent in the structure of many phenomena. Around 1900, the Italian economist Vilfredo Pareto proposed the principle of *Pareto optimality*: we should not accept an economic system if there is another available system that would make everyone better off. The dominance argument, given above, supports egoistic rationality, but conflicts with the Pareto principle that supports group rationality.

Undue emphasis on the question 'Why should *I* be moral?' has skewed philosophical discussion towards individualistically-oriented morality. Thomas Nagel concluded *The Possibility of Altruism* (1970) on a pessimistic note: 'To say that altruism and morality are possible in virtue of something basic to human nature is not to say that men are basically good. . . . The manner in which human beings have conducted themselves so far does not encourage optimism about the moral future of the species'. David Gauthier in *Morals by Agreement* (1985) rationalized morality as a system that constrains egoism for our mutual advantage. However, it was Robert Axelrod's computer experiments with the *iterated* Prisoner's Dilemma reported in *The Evolution of Cooperation* (1985) that inspired recent speculations on the evolutionary origins of morality.

Axelrod asked game-theorists to submit strategies for playing the iterated Prisoner's Dilemma. The surprising result was that a simple strategy, *Tit for Tat*, won the first tournament. *Tit for Tat* initially cooperates and then cooperates with those who cooperated and defects against those who defected on the previous round. Even more surprising was that *Tit for Tat* won again after contestants were invited to revise their entries in light of the published results. *Tit for Tat* gained a reputation as a particularly robust strategy. Ruthless strategies like *Always Defect* dominated the early rounds, however, *Tit for Tat*, if paired with cooperative strategies, made a comeback. The emergence of cooperation over defection (considered to be the only rational alternative in the one-shot Prisoner's Dilemma) was a compelling model of the evolution of cooperation.

In 1993 at the International Game Theory Conference at Stony Brook University, Paul St. Denis and I conducted a variation of Axelrod's tournament in which the evolution of cooperation was modelled spatially. Rather than using a round robin competition, we used a cellular automaton playing field. Strategies were colour-coded and randomly distributed throughout the field. Each strategy played the iterated Prisoner's Dilemma with each of its eight neighbours and then was replaced by the strategy in the neighbourhood achieving the highest score.

Rather than depend on the rationality of game theorists, it is also possible to conduct an evolutionary tournament based on the 'survival of the fittest' among strategies of a given level of complexity. A *one-dimensional strategy* is one whose moves, after the first, depend solely on the opponent's previous move. These one-dimensional strategies can be represented by ordered triples where i is the strategy's initial move, c its response to cooperation, and 120 its response to defection. For example, *Always Defect* = <0,0,0> and *Tit for Tat* = <1,1,0>. In a tournament among all bivalent one-dimensional strategies, *Always Defect* takes an early lead. Once most of the 'suckers' are eliminated, however, *Always Defect*'s dominance wanes: it does not do well with its own kind since it cannot benefit from mutual cooperation. Skyrms artificially arranged a high correlation between like strategies; in our spatial model, this clustering evolves naturally. Typically, small cooperative clusters of *Tit for Tat* make a comeback.

Removing the restriction to bivalent strategies, we investigated infinite-valued Prisoner's Dilemmas. We found that strategies 'more forgiving' than *Tit for Tat* — similar to Nowak and Sigmund's (1992) *Generous Tit for Tat* (GTFT = <1, 1, 1/3>) in a probabilitistic setting — emerged as even more successful than *Tit for Tat* (see Grim *et al.*, 1998).

The allure of an evolutionary model is that it promises to cross the line between the descriptive and normative realms providing a total rationale for all of reality backed by hard-headed naturalism. Carl Sagan (1997) touted the *Brazen Rule* as encoded by

Tit for Tat as an empirically based morality superior to either the *Golden Rule* (*'Do unto others as you would have them do unto you'*) or the *Iron Rule* (*'Do unto others as you like before they do it unto you'*). Richard Dawkins (1989) popularized the idea that altruism at the level of individual organisms can be a means by which the underlying genes 'maximize their self-interest', i.e., self-replicate. Darwinian fundamentalists — to borrow Stephen Jay Gould's (1997) phrase — are hard-line literalists. Michael Ruse and Edward O. Wilson (1985, p. 51) baldly assert that 'ethics . . . is an illusion fobbed off on us by our genes to get us to cooperate'.

Simplistic translations of game-theoretic results into practical advice are hasty. Axelrod himself advised caution: 'I think the goal is to help people see things that are operating more clearly than you could without the model. But it's only some of the principles. You have to leave off a lot of things, some of which are found to be important' (Poundstone, 1992, p. 253). If nature's payoff matrix had been slightly different, would ruthless selfishness rather than reciprocal altruism have been moral?

Grim *et al.* (1998), for example, investigated *Discriminatory* TFT (DTFT), a strategy which, like TFT, cooperates with its own kind, but which, like *Always Defect*, defects against others. DTFT takes an initial strong lead and, once entrenched, is stable. DTFT dominates impartial, colour-blind TFT. We experimented with this model to see to what degree a Rawlsian 'veil of ignorance' could be imposed to counteract the advantage of discriminatory strategies. Similarly, Skyrms (1994) showed that a precondition for normal cooperation in the strongly shared fate of somatic-line cells involves a 'Darwinian veil of ignorance'. Here evolutionary game theory does not prescribe but allows one to experimentally investigate logical relations in complex interactions.

Ever since Darwin broached his theory, Darwinism has been engaged in two dialogues — one engaged with the scientific community and the other embroiled in the larger society's cultural wars. These debates have not always been clearly demarcated (see, for example, the heated exchange between Stephen Jay Gould (1997) and Daniel Dennett (1997)). Science is committed to methodological naturalism, but Darwinian fundamentalists have often smuggled into the debate metaphysical or 'religious' naturalism under the guise of science.

Darwinists have often been tempted to moralize about the implications of evolution. Darwin himself (1874) endorsed Herbert Spencer's Social Darwinism despite its dubious suggestion of the inheritability of moral traits. Bemoaning a 'human society based simply on the gene's law of universal ruthless selfishness', Dawkins (1989, p. 3) exhorts us to 'try to teach generosity and altruism....' After wondering whether 'after the new Darwinism takes root, the word *moral* can be anything but a joke', Robert Wright (1994, p. 326) predicts that those 'who clearly understand the new Darwinian paradigm . . . will be led toward greater compassion and concern for their fellow human beings' (p. 338). The irony of these moral appeals is that a thorough-going metaphysical, as opposed to methodological, Darwinian naturalism, rather than explaining the biological basis of morality, appears to end up explaining away any reason for believing in morality at all.

Should evolution replace rational choice as a foundation for game theory? Economic game theory provides a welcome relief from dreary conceptions of morality that are excessively self-sacrificing and altruistic by showing that egoistic reasoning has a place within the justification of morality. Evolutionary game theory, on the other hand, is an intriguing alternative to increasingly implausible assumptions about rationality. Evolutionary, unlike economic, game theory is better suited to descriptive than to normative domains. A pluralism of paradigms holds the best promise for theoretical innovation in game theory.

References

Darwin, Charles (1874), *The Descent of Man and Selection in Relation to Sex* (London: Murray, 2 ed).

Dawkins, Richard (1989), *The Selfish Gene* (Oxford and New York: Oxford University Press, 2 ed).

Dennett, Daniel (1997), '"Darwinian fundamentalism": an exchange (August 14), *New York Review of Books*.

Gauthier, David (1985), *Morals by Agreement* (New York: Oxford University Press).

Gould, Stephen Jay (1997), 'Darwinian fundamentalism' and 'Evolution: the pleasures of pluralism', *New York Review of Books*, June 12 and June 26.

Grim, Patrick; Mar, Gary; and St. Denis, Paul with the Group for Logic and Formal Semantics (1998), *The Philosophical Computer: Exploratory Essays in Philosophical Computer Modeling* (Cambridge, Massachusetts: MIT Press).

Hobbes, Thomas (1651), *Leviathan* (London: Crooke).

Hume, David (1748), *An Enquiry Concerning Human Understanding* (Oxford: Oxford University Press).

Nagel, Thomas (1970), *The Possibility of Altruism* (New York and Oxford: Oxford University Press).

Nowak, Martin and Sigmund, Karl (1992), 'Tit for tat in heterogeneous populations', *Nature*, **335**, pp. 250–52.

Poundstone, William (1992), *The Prisoner's Dilemma: John von Neumann, Game Theory, and the Puzzle of the Bomb* (New York: Doubleday Anchor).

Rawls, John (1971), *A Theory of Justice* (Cambridge, Massachusetts: Harvard University Press).

Ruse, Michael and Wilson, Edward O. (1985), 'The evolution of ethics', *New Scientist*, **17**, pp. 50–2.

Sagan, Carl (1997), 'The Rules of the Games', *Billions and Billions: Thoughts on Life and Death at the Brink of the Millennium* (New York: Random House), pp. 180–91.

Skyrms, Brian (1994), 'Darwin meets "The Logic of Decision": correlation in evolutionary game theory', *Philosophy of Science*, **61**, pp. 503–28.

Skyrms, B. (2000), 'Game theory, rationality and evolution of the social contract', *Journal of Consciousness Studies*, **7** (1–2), pp. 269–84.

Wright, Robert (1994), *The Moral Animal: The New Science of Evolutionary Psychology* (New York: Vintage Books).

STRATEGIC SUBJECTIVE COMMITMENT

Randolph M. Nesse

Game theory has progressed from analysis of one-move games between two rational agents, to iterated n-person games in which strategies evolve, and actors use prior experience to coordinate their moves. The next step in this direction is to analyse commitment strategies. An individual can influence others by announcing his or her commitment to a future act that would not be in his or her best interests. Spiteful threats can coerce others. Promises to aid someone when nothing can be reciprocated can create deep relationships. Such strategies are inherently paradoxical because the maximum payoff comes from not having to follow through on the commitment, and this is made more likely by expensive signalling of commitments to outlandish threats and promises whose plausibility declines with their magnitude. Nonetheless, the fitness benefits of subjective commitment are substantial and may well have shaped human capacities for revenge and spite, as well as deep attachment and genuine morality.

In just a few pages, Skyrms (2000) manages to clarify several thorny issues at the intersection of game theory and evolution. He straightforwardly shows how a theory based on hyper-rational actors parallels one based on non-rational actors whose strategies are shaped by natural solution. This is bolstered by his further demonstration that if A gives an ESS, then <A,A> is a Nash equilibrium for the corresponding two-person game. He then proceeds to contrast the two perspectives, first noting how individuals who have identities that persist through time can escape from the symmetry requirement, using the game of Chicken as an example, and then showing how an evolutionary approach gives a different solution to the Nash bargaining game, namely, demand half.

Things are complicated further by introducing sequential structure to a game. For instance, the ultimatum game generates subgames in which the rational strategy is to take whatever is offered. Real people, of course, do not do this. The question of 'why not?' is one that would occur only to a game theorist. Skyrms shows how weakly-dominated strategies can persist, and how, with correlated strategies, even strongly-dominated strategies can persist. Exploration of such correlated situations is the strength of the Sober and Wilson book (1998, abstracted in this volume).

The logic and direction of Skyrms' argument is compelling, from hyper-rational actors in a single move game, to correlated interactions that repeat over time and are shaped by evolutionary dynamics. The combination is sufficient to explain much of economic and political behaviour. However, just one step further in this direction is another kind of game that may offer powerful explanations of human relationships, a game that badly needs a better foundation in theory. Much actual human behaviour, especially in personal relationships, is based on commitment strategies (Schelling, 1960). These commitments give rise to wonderful complexities that might well be clarified if theorists like Skyrms were to extend the foundations provided by Hirshleifer (1978) and Frank (1988).

The core idea of commitment is that an actor can, by making a commitment to some future action, influence the behaviour of others. If the commitment is to some action that is Bayes rational, this is not very interesting. Likewise, situations in which parties agree on a contract, with enforcement provisions, have been well studied. If, however, an individual announces a commitment to a future action that would not be in his or her interests, then things become curiouser and curiouser. Such commitments are common and powerful. Some are threats. If a person can convince others that he or she will not swerve in the game of chicken, then they will change their behaviour accordingly in a way that yields an advantage to the committed person. Throwing the steering wheel out of the window is rarely possible, so other strategies must be used to convince others that one is ready to die. Acting wildly irrational is just what is needed. Likewise, employees get an advantage if they can convince a supervisor that they will quit unless a raise is granted. A commitment to kill someone unless a ransom is paid is structurally the same. In all these cases, having to follow through on the commitment would yield a net loss, but if a person can convince others that he or she will nonetheless follow through, then there is no need to, and the maximum payoff is obtained. The difficulty is obvious, and creates the central paradox of commitment. How can a person convince others that he or she will, in the future, do something that would be irrational? Various commitment devices have been well described, such as contracts and depriving oneself of negotiating options. My interest, however, is in subjective commitment. We humans have strong feelings that get us to do things that are otherwise not rational. Trivers (1981) showed the role of evolved emotions in mediating reciprocity, and Robert Frank (1988) has been a clear and eloquent advocate for the selective benefits of emotions in establishing commitments. The desire for spiteful revenge is an excellent example. Falling in love, or, rather, staying in love, is another.

On this more positive side, commitments are promises to help others. Huge efforts have gone into analysing mutual aid relationships in terms of reciprocity and the Prisoner's Dilemma (Axelrod, 1997). While these theories capture some of what goes on, I think they are fundamentally incomplete when applied to personal relationships based on commitment. To see why, look at how careful people are to avoid treating their friends as reciprocity exchange partners. If you offer a friend a ride to the airport, and on the way you say, 'Well, I just want to be clear that you will give me a ride next time I need one. Will you agree to that?', you may get the ride, but lose a friend. And, after your previous friend spreads gossip about what kind of person you really are, you may find yourself trying to understand strange smiles and frosty reserve at future social gatherings. Of course, there is also the other problem of expecting people to fulfill their commitments when there is a basic imbalance in the reciprocity foundations of a relationship. Commitment is not an alternative to reciprocity, it is a way of promising to extend credit beyond the available collateral, that benefits both parties in the long run, on the average.

Consider also the fate of a recent fad in marital therapy. A few years ago some therapists tried to analyse marriages in terms of the exchanges they involved. Spouses rebelled, uniting in their opposition to viewing their behaviours in terms of reciprocity. It seemed inhuman to them. And it was. In our personal attachments, we are extremely careful to see and present our actions as the results of 'love' or other feelings. This is because we want to have partners who will be there for us when we really need them, namely, when we have nothing to offer in exchange. An economic/game theory/naive evolutionary view of human relationships as reciprocal exchanges has spread widely in our culture. This may undermine people's capacity for deep personal relationships, because people who believe that others are capable only of exchange relationships are unable to make emotional commitments. In return, no one loves them either. Their beliefs create a social world that is genuinely cold and empty. This is a realm where the products of social construction strongly influence fitness.

Psychologists have long emphasized the importance of 'basic trust' (Balint, 1979; Erikson, 1980), and the personality pathology that results if it is absent. What individuals believe about human nature has dramatic effects on how they conduct their relationships. On the macro scale, this, in turn, shapes the nature of a society. Psychologists also emphasize 'attachment', usually with reference to the benefits mother and baby get from staying close together (Cassidy and Shaver, 1999). Adult attachments to non-kin may or may not be based on the same brain mechanisms, but I suspect their function is quite different — to make commitment strategies possible. It seems plausible that the emotions that mediate such relationships, including loyalty and grief, may have evolved specifically to facilitate commitments. Relationships based on commitment are a further step in the direction of Skyrms' argument. Incorporating foresight and information transmission to correlated and repeated interactions leads directly to the study of commitments.

I have often emphasized how people are similar to other organisms, but commitment strategies may make us distinctive, if not unique. As soon as cognition gets to the point where people can communicate their intentions, benefits from subjective commitments become available. These benefits may be so substantial that they become a powerful selective force for further increases in intelligence and foresight. The advantages of conscious thought, with its ability to anticipate the outcomes of possible future actions, are amplified in a social setting where people use, and must cope with, commitment strategies. The difficulty, once again, is to convince others that one will follow through on a commitment, or to determine if another will follow through. The best predictors are past behaviour and expensive public expressions of intent that cannot be violated without resulting in major reputational costs. This gives rise to the central paradox of commitment strategies. The optimal strategy is to convince others that one will follow through, so that one does not have to do so. But this usually requires making extreme threats and following through on certain occasions. Thus, the Mafia must burn a certain number of businesses to maintain its protection rackets, and a person who threatens suicide must, at some point, do something very dangerous in order to be taken seriously. Still more ominously, the nuclear strategy of mutual assured destruction rests on this logic.

On the positive side, the courting suitor must give expensive gifts and spend inordinate amounts of time with his intended, otherwise she will conclude that he is in it just for what he can get, and will be unlikely to stay with her decades later when she may be sick or less desirable. Zahavi (1976) has suggested that members of such pairs engage in 'testing of the bond'. By withdrawing or acting disabled, they can test the prospective partner for willingness to help when there is little likelihood of being quickly repaid. If the partners pass such tests, the bond becomes a committed attachment, by which we mean that it is based, *not* on reciprocity or rational calculation, but non-rational emotions. How could such emotions evolve? They certainly can lead to exploitation, so risks abound, but individuals who are capable of making wise and deep commitments have a huge advantage over those who just play reciprocity games. By signalling that they will behave according to commitments instead of rationality, they get major advantages. Especially if they don't have to fulfill their commitments too often. When a very expensive commitment is called in, say when a spouse gets Alzheimer's disease, the psychological wrenching is terrible. That is a subject for another essay. Likewise, there is wonderful complexity yet to be explored in how people form groups, often based on religion, to enforce their mutual commitments.

Finally, the evolutionary benefits of commitment may provide the needed foundation for understanding the origins of the moral passions. Moral behaviour depends, in large measure, on fulfilling one's commitments. Helping one's kin and exchanging favours is individually generous (irrespective of whether it is evolutionarily selfish). But explicitly moral behaviour is, necessarily, outside of the reciprocity framework. Morality requires living up to prior commitments, specifically those that require action that will be to the individual's disadvantage. The fitness benefits of mechanisms to make and keep commitments may have shaped the capacity for morality. All of this will be far better understood when we have a solid game theory foundation for strategies based on commitment.

References

Axelrod, Robert M. (1997), *The Complexity of Cooperation: Agent-based Models of Competition and Collaboration* (Princeton: Princeton University Press).

Balint, Michael (1979), *The Basic Fault* (New York: Brunner/Mazel).

Cassidy, Jude and Shaver, Philip R. (1999), *Handbook of Attachment: Theory, Research, and Clinical Applications* (New York: Guilford Press).

Erikson, Eric H. (1980), *Identity and the Life Cycle* (New York: Norton).

Frank, Robert H. (1988), *Passions Within Reason: The Strategic Role of The Emotions* (New York: W.W. Norton).

Hirshleifer, Jack (1978), 'Competition, cooperation, and conflict in economics and biology', *Journal of the American Economic Association*, **68**, pp. 238–43.

Schelling, Thomas C. (1960), *The Strategy of Conflict* (Cambridge: Harvard University Press).

Skyrms, B. (2000), 'Game theory, rationality and evolution of the social contract', *Journal of Consciousness Studies*, 7 (1–2), pp. 269–84.

Sober, Elliot and Wilson, David S. (1998), *Unto Others: The Evolution and Psychology of Unselfish Behaviour* (Cambridge, MA: Harvard University Press).

Trivers, Robert L. (1981), 'Sociobiology and politics', in *Sociobiology and Human Politics*, ed. E. White (Toronto: Lexington).

Zahavi, Amotz (1976), 'The testing of a bond', *Animal Behaviour*, **25**, pp. 246–7.

DISTRIBUTIVE JUSTICE AND THE NASH BARGAINING SOLUTION

Christopher D. Proulx

Skyrms has pointed out differences between the results of rational choice theory and evolutionary game theory. This commentary argues that there is a great deal of agreement on the Nash Bargaining Solution, which maximizes the product of player payoffs, in both rational-choice-based and evolution-based theories of equilibrium selection. While evolutionary game theory has the potential to explain how we arrive at the behavioural rules that govern what we do, realistic models will require calibration through laboratory experiments. Indeed, experimental evidence strongly supports the Nash Bargaining Solution.

Professor Skyrms' paper (2000) compares rational choice theory and evolutionary game theory. His research has important implications for the notion of distributive justice. Since his paper contains many references to his book *Evolution of the Social Contract* (Skyrms, 1996), inspiration for some of these comments arises there as well as his paper.

I: Experiments and the Evolution of a Theory

Evolutionary game theory became popular in economics partly because of its flexibility in accounting for experimental observations which are apparently inconsistent with rational choice theory. While there is only one way to be rational, there are many ways to be boundedly rational, and this flexibility is a strength and a weakness of evolutionary game theory. The sensitivity of results of evolutionary models to their assumptions means that modeling issues are important. Which issues are appropriate in which contexts is an empirical matter, and evolutionary theory needs empirical observation to guide its development.

That said, we shouldn't throw out the insights gained from standard game theory in favour of some evolutionary theory describing how people decide to do what they do, just as we shouldn't throw out algebra in favour of a theory of developmental psychology which tells us how people come to think about addition. However, we should collect data to determine the bounds of applicability of our theories.

II: Equilibrium Selection and Efficiency

A problem that goes back to Nash's formulation of the Nash Equilibrium (or equilibrium) is the possibility that a game has more than one equilibrium (Nash, 1951). Nash had a method of selecting among equilibria which involved perturbing the game in question (Nash, 1953). The perturbed game has few equilibria, and as the level of perturbation decreases, the equilibria that remain converge to one particular 'selected' equilibrium of the unperturbed game.

It is now common to analyse models in the limit to uncover stability properties of particular equilibria. In evolutionary game theory, perturbations are often applied to the dynamic model and are often interpreted as mutations in behaviour. This is the tack taken by Young, who considers a stochastic two-population model of evolution (Young, 1993a). In each period, a player is selected from each population and matched to play a game. Each player chooses a sample from the last few plays of the game (to see what previous players did) and then chooses as his strategy a best response to that sample. Stochastic mistakes may occur when players don't choose a best response to their sample but randomly choose some other strategy instead. As the probability of mistakes decreases, the probability that the players keep playing one particular equilibrium of the game (or a set of equilibria) approaches one. That is the selected equilibrium. An important result from Young's model is that in two-by-two symmetric games, the selected equilibrium need not be efficient.[8]

Skyrms has noted the role of matching in the results of evolutionary models. Ely (1995) allows players to form clubs in which members are expected to behave in specific ways. Such a model selects efficient equilibria, reversing Young's result. Bergstrom and Bergstrom relate the probability of meeting another person playing the same strategy to the locus of genes controlling those strategies in a model of parent-child interaction (Bergstrom, 1999). Efficient outcomes are likely to occur if the genes are close together and therefore likely to appear together in an individual.

III: Evolution and the Nash Bargaining Solution

Skyrms has shown (Skyrms, 2000, section titled 'Symmetry'; Skyrms, 1996, chap. 1) that the one-population replicator dynamic frequently converges to the 50–50 outcome in the symmetric linear Nash Demand Game (or NDG).[9] If a population began playing this NDG, and if each member of the population chose their initial play at random, so that the population distribution was initially random, then if the population behaviour unfolded over time according to the replicator dynamic, it would be likely that 50–50 outcomes would arise. Unfortunately, the history of play matters, and history is a confounding issue in the empirical study of evolutionary modeling. If any result can be obtained given the proper initial conditions, rejection of a theory requires knowledge of the initial conditions to the degree that they matter in the model.

Proulx considers the problem in a slightly different light, by analysing a two population perturbed replicator dynamic in a game analogous to the NDG (Proulx, 1997).

---

[8] An equilibrium is efficient if no one can be made better off without making someone else worse off. Efficiency is a desirable property of any theory of distributive justice.

[9] Each player makes a claim on a ten dollar cake. If the claims can be met, each player receives his claim. Otherwise, each player receives nothing.

The perturbation constantly reintroduces a small percentage of the population into each strategy so that extinct strategies are resurrected and are always available to the population should they become optimal. For a low but non-zero level of perturbation, only one distribution of the population of players over the strategy space is stable. Thus the basin of attraction of this distribution is the entire space, and therefore history doesn't matter. The population distribution is diffuse; many strategies receive positive weight. However, as the perturbation term is gradually lowered, the stationary population distribution puts increasing weight on the 50–50 outcome. Binmore *et al.* (1998) present experimental findings that are consistent with this result.

Skyrms considers the framework of the symmetric linear NDG because it seems most clear that in this context, 50–50 outcomes are fair. Binmore *et al.* asked subjects what constituted fair outcomes in the NDG (Binmore *et al.*, 1993). Responses were strongly correlated with the amount the subject claimed in the last round of the game. Either subjects are very attuned to what 'fair' means and strive successfully to implement it in laboratory experiments (which is at odds with the dramatic changes in subject behaviour observed over the course of this experiment), or (more cynically) 'fairness' is a concept subjects use to justify what they do.

In any case, it is not enough just to find that 50–50 outcomes arise. We need to look more deeply at the properties of outcomes in the NDG to see what brings about 50–50 outcomes in the symmetric linear case.

IV: An Asymmetric Nash Demand Game

Consider the specific problem of determining an allocation given the welfare possibility frontier of Figure 1, made up by connecting the points (0,5), (4.1,4.1), (6.8, 3.4), (8.4, 2.9), (9.9, 2.1), and (10,0). Various positions along the frontier have been proposed as just, while no one argues for points interior to the frontier since they are not efficient. The Egalitarian point (4.1,4.1), labelled E, is often associated with Rawls (1971). It is calculated by taking the point along the frontier that provides equal

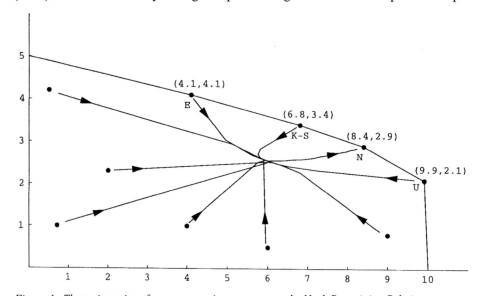

Figure 1. The trajectories of mean strategies converge to the Nash Bargaining Solution

welfare to both parties. Harsanyi has argued for the utilitarian point (9.9, 2.1), labelled U, which maximizes the sum of the payoffs to both parties (Harsanyi, 1977).

Nash put forth the point (8.4, 2.9) (labelled N), which maximizes the product of the welfare attained by each person (Nash, 1950). Nash's proposal, known as the Nash Bargaining Solution (or NBS), is based on three key axioms, which, he argued, any reasonable solution should satisfy. It turns out that Nash's axioms uniquely determine a point along the frontier of a wide class of these allocation problems. Kalai and Smorodinsky, using a different set of axioms, put forth the point labelled K–S (Kalai & Smorodinsky, 1975). It is the point along the frontier lying along the line connecting the origin to the (infeasible) utopia point giving all parties simultaneously the most they can attain. Note that these four proposed allocations all coincide with the 50–50 outcome in the symmetric linear NDG.

The axiomatic approach to each of these solutions is often called 'cooperative game theory', the idea being that if the players could come together to cooperatively determine a solution, then if they agreed that the principles embodied in those axioms were desiderata of any solution to the allocation problem, they would be forced to accept the solution resulting from those axioms.

For Nash, however, an axiomatic approach alone was insufficient. Nash thought it important to back up his axiomatic approach with a formal non-cooperative game in which the players are not accorded the opportunity to communicate beforehand. The Nash Demand Game (see footnote 9 above) arose out of these considerations. As it stands, the NDG has a continuum of equilibria: every point on the boundary. Nash 'smoothed' his demand game by modifying what happens if the pair of claims cannot be satisfied. If the player's claims fall outside the frontier, the players receive their claims with a probability that decreases to zero the further away from the boundary the claims lie. The proposition is that as this probability region shrinks down to the boundary (yielding the unsmoothed NDG in the limit), the equilibria of the smoothed game all come to approximate the Nash Bargaining Solution (Binmore, 1987). Nash thought it significant that the equilibria of the smoothed NDG come to approximate the NBS in the limit. The non-cooperative result provides one way to judge the reasonableness of the cooperative axioms, and the cooperative approach gives one way to judge the reasonableness of the formal non-cooperative game.

Other non-cooperative models of bargaining have yielded the NBS as well. Rubinstein (1982) describes an alternating offers process in which Player I begins by making a proposed division. Player II may accept or reject. If Player II rejects, costs associated with delay by one period in reaching agreement are sunk and play proceeds to the next period in which Player II has the opportunity to propose a division of the cake to Player I, who may accept or reject, and so forth. It turns out that the unique sequentially rational equilibrium approximates the NBS as the costs of delay approach zero.

V: The Evolution of the Nash Bargaining Solution

There is evolutionary support for the Nash Bargaining Solution as well. Young applies his model of population dynamics to the NDG and finds that behaviour converges to the NBS (Young, 1993b). One may think that evolutionary models are fundamentally the same, but Proulx shows that Young's model can, in general, differ dramatically from the perturbed replicator dynamic model (Proulx, 1998). In the case of the NDG, however, a two-population perturbed replicator dynamic strongly supports Young's result. Figure 1 shows convergence of the mean strategy from a variety of initial starting points. The perturbed dynamics are run with an initial perturbation level and are allowed to reach a stationary state. The perturbation level is then decreased in steps. Regardless of the initial starting point, the population distribution puts a weight approaching one on the Nash Bargaining Solution.

While the NBS has a strong theoretical basis, being a result of cooperative, non-cooperative, and evolutionary models, laboratory experiments provide empirical evidence. Binmore, Swierzbinski and colleagues describe an experiment in which subjects repeatedly played a smoothed version of the Nash Demand Game of Figure 1 (Binmore et al., 1993). The initial distribution of strategies was a control of the experiment in the following sense. In the first ten repetitions, subjects played against the computer, the play of which converged to one of the four points E, K–S, N, or U. Subjects were then matched among themselves for 40 more repetitions. Under each control, the median subject behaviour converged to the set of equilibria near the NBS.

We can conclude that the NBS arises in a variety of rational and boundedly rational models of behaviour, and even has empirical support. The amount of agreement is striking. Skyrms himself has noted the strong properties of the NBS in evolutionary contexts (1996, p.107). While debate persists over what is the just apportionment of welfare between Player I and Player II in these types of allocation problems, any proposal which differs from the NBS needs to contend with its seemingly strong dynamic attraction properties or explain why the costs of overcoming such dynamics are justified. In any case, the Nash Bargaining Solution deserves a prominent role in any theory of distributive justice.

References

Bergstrom, C. and Bergstrom, T. (1999), 'Does mother nature punish rotten kids?', *Journal of Bioeconomics*, **1**(1), pp. 47–72.

Binmore, K. (1987), 'Nash bargaining theory II', in *The Economics of Bargaining*, ed. K. Binmore, and P. Dasgupta (New York: Basil Blackwell).

Binmore, K., Swierzbinski, J., Hsu, S. and Proulx, C. (1993), 'Focal points and bargaining', *International Journal of Game Theory*, **22**, pp. 381–409.

Binmore, K., Proulx, C., Samuelson, L. and Swierzbinski, J. (1998), 'Hard bargains and lost opportunities', *The Economic Journal*, **108** (450), pp. 1279–98.

Ely, J. (1995), 'Local conventions', Mimeo.

Harsanyi, J.C. (1977), *Rational Behavior and Bargaining Equilibrium in Games and Social Situations* (Cambridge: Cambridge University Press).

Kalai, E. and Smorodinsky, M. (1975), 'Other solutions to Nash's bargaining problem', *Econometrica*, **45**, pp. 1631–7.

Nash, J.F. (1950), 'The bargaining problem', *Econometrica*, **18** (2), pp. 155–62.

Nash, J.F. (1951), 'Non-cooperative games', *Annals of Mathematics*, **54** (2), pp. 286–95.

Nash, J.F. (1953), 'Two-person cooperative games,' *Econometrica*, **21** (1), pp. 128–40.

Proulx, C. (1997), 'A numerical analysis of the replicator dynamics applied to the outside option game', Mimeo.

Proulx, C. (1998), 'The evolution of lost opportunities in bargaining', Mimeo.

Rawls, J. (1971), *A Theory of Justice* (Cambridge: Harvard University Press).

Rubinstein, A. (1982), 'Perfect equilibrium in a bargaining model', *Econometrica*, **50**, pp. 97–109.

Skyrms, B. (1996), *Evolution of the Social Contract* (New York: Cambridge University Press).

Skyrms, B. (2000), 'Game theory, rationality and evolution of the social contract', *Journal of Consciousness Studies*, **7** (1–2), pp. 269–84.

Young, H.P. (1993a), 'The evolution of conventions', *Econometrica*, **61** (1), pp. 57–84.

Young, H.P. (1993b), 'An evolutionary model of bargaining', *Journal of Economic Theory*, **59** (1), pp. 145–68.

Brian Skyrms

Adaptive Dynamic Models and the Social Contract

Response to Commentary Discussion

I would like to thank my commentators for their very constructive contributions to this discussion. One recurring theme in the commentary is that the black and white cartoon of my target article should be replaced by a theory with many shades and colours. We should consider not only classical game theory and evolution, but also a broad spectrum of models.

I could not be more in agreement, and have said as much elsewhere. There is a whole panoply of adaptive processes, operating at different levels and timescales, all of which are worthy of study. Genetic evolution operates on a longer timescale than cultural evolution or social learning. Individual learning is more rapid than social learning, and the deliberative process by which an individual chooses an act to perform moves us to an even shorter timescale. Interactive learning may take place in small or in large groups, with random encounters or with some correlation structure.

All of the processes can be studied by dynamic modelling. No one model will do for them all. And even within categories, different dynamic models may be appropriate to different situations. For instance, when considering individual learning, different degrees of strategic sophistication of the agents involved call for different learning dynamics. There is, I think, a special place for the replicator dynamics in studying adaptation because it has some currency across a range of domains. But the special place is that of the first thing to try, rather than the last. In specific domains, empirical evidence can be brought to bear on the selection of the appropriate adaptive dynamics.

As an illustration, allow me to return to the 'Beauty Contest' game that I used in my target article to make the point that people often do not behave in a way predicted by common knowledge of rationality. Common knowledge of rationality requires behaviour consistent with iterated elimination of strongly dominated strategies, and that leaves only the possibility of everyone choosing zero on the Beauty Contest game. This prediction of rational choice based game theory is not what is observed. But does evolutionary game theory do any better? Suppose cultural evolution, as modelled by the replicator dynamics, acted on a long sequence of such 'Beauty

Journal of Consciousness Studies, **7**, No. 1–2, 2000, pp. 335–9

Contest' games. It would have to have led to the same conclusion as rational choice based game theory, since replicator dynamics also leads (in the limit) to iterated elimination of strongly dominated strategies (see Fudenberg and Levine, ch. 3). Our evolutionary hypothesis is falsified as well! Perhaps games of this form have not been common enough in our cultural history for cultural evolution to have converged. Is adaptive dynamics then left without any purchase on the problem?

If nature has not arranged for individuals to play repeated Beauty Contest games, we can do so ourselves in the laboratory and observe the results. Adaptive learning models predict that with repeated trials, individuals will learn to make lower and lower guesses. This is exactly what happens (Nagel, 1995; Stahl, 1996; Camerer, 1997; Duffy and Nagel, 1997; Ho et al., 1998). Although adaptive learning models may make the same equilibrium prediction here as the rational choice model, they also predict transient out-of-equilibrium behaviour. Different learning models predict different transient behaviour, and thus the empirical studies can be brought to bear on the choice of learning model or models (Ho et al., 1998). I want to stress the plural, 'or models' because there is considerable evidence of heterogeneity in the population.

Gary Bolton suggests that rational choice theory may be reconciled with evolutionary theory by incorporating 'other-regarding' factors in agents' utility functions, and then investigating the evolution of utility functions. This is certainly an interesting line of investigation in which Bolton has been one of the pioneers. I make a very brief gesture in this direction in the 'Utility and Rationality' section of my target article and said a little more in *Evolution of the Social Contract*, where I referred to an earlier article of Bolton (Bolton, 1991). Expected utility theory is notoriously elastic, and can accommodate almost anything. The work of Bolton, however, imposes well-defined testable constraints on utility functions. With Bolton and others, I find this an attractive approach to investigating anomalous behaviour in ultimatum bargaining, dictator games and public goods provision games. I do not think that it would be a fruitful approach to the anomalous behaviour observed in Beauty Contest games. This is just to express agreement with the closing remarks in Bolton's commentary.

Jeffrey Carpenter argues for a synthesis of evolutionary game theory and bounded rationality, and demonstrates the power of this approach on experimental data from an interesting bargaining game. He uses the replicator dynamics (interpreted as resulting from imitation of successful strategies). This bounded rationality model is made more bounded by introducing a one percent background level of errors, with the result that there is a better fit with the experimental data. It should be clear from my opening remarks that I am all in favour of pursuing inquiry in this direction. Carpenter closes by remarking that even this model assumes too much about the availability to the individual of information about average success in the population. One way of following up this concern is described in Gary Mar's contribution. This is to implement the dynamics on a lattice (or more generally, on a graph) where individuals can only observe the success of their neighbours. Mar's results, as well as several other studies, have shown that the dynamics of this sort of model can be quite different from that of non-local social learning models (Pollack, 1989; Lindgren and Nordahl, 1994; Anderlini and Ianni, 1997; Alexander and Skyrms, 1999).

Justin D'Arms argues that social norms are not properly *moral* norms unless they are backed by sanctions, and cites John Stuart Mill as finding this to be 'the real turning point of the distinction between morality and simple expediency'. I think that there is quite a lot to this, although it seems to direct attention exclusively to the negative side of morality. Does it mean that Jeremiah was moral but St. Francis was just a nice guy? — probably not. At any rate, many moral norms are backed by sanctions and the sanctions seem important for stabilizing the norms, so the evolution of sanctions is a question that is full of interest.

D'Arms points out that the Nash bargaining game does not incorporate sanctions, and questions why the egalitarian solution should be thought to have any connection with morality. I think that D'Arms might well turn his attention to the ultimatum bargaining game, which offers the responders the opportunity to punish greedy ultimatum proposers at some expense to themselves. There is a considerable experimental literature showing that responders do indeed punish proposers who they find too greedy. There is a theoretical literature that shows how persistence of these costly sanctions is consistent with evolutionary dynamics. I discuss this briefly in my target article, and at length in the second chapter of *Evolution of the Social Contract*. More complicated models involving sanctions are possible. For instance, *Tit for Tat* and *Grim Trigger* (cooperate with cooperators but defect forever against someone who defected once against you) strategies in repeated games involve a kind of sanction for non-cooperative behaviour. The Nash bargaining game could be embedded in a larger game that offered the possibility of costly punishment. But ultimatum bargaining raises the issue in the simplest way possible, and offers quite a lot of food for thought.

Hebert Gintis' commentary makes some insightful remarks about ultimatum bargaining. If we think in terms of evolution of norms, then the upshot of evolution for a single encounter depends on what norm is applied. This is the 'framing' problem. Ambiguity in a situation may be resolved in various ways, leading to application of different norms. Gintis cites experimental studies that demonstrate the framing effect in the ultimatum game. For instance, if the game is framed so that the proposer has 'earned' the right to that position, he is much less likely to be punished for making greedy offers. These results seem directly relevant to the concerns raised by D'Arms.

With Gintis, I think that classical game theory can be viewed as addressing a different question than evolutionary game theory, but I would draw the line in a different place. I would place evolutionary game theory within a spectrum of adaptive dynamical models aimed as describing and explaining observed behaviour. Classical game theory, in its pure form, I would think of as investigating questions of *consistency* in interactive decision making. Personally, I find these questions of consistency fascinating and challenging (Skyrms, 1998; Skyrms *et al.*, 1999), but of a rather different character than the descriptive and explanatory questions that arise in adaptive dynamic modelling.

Sandra Güth and Werner Güth argue that we need models of rational deliberation for intelligent species like our own. These models incorporate various levels of 'forward looking' reasoning where an agent predicts the future and chooses and acts accordingly. I agree entirely with this point. I have spent some time taking it seriously (Skyrms, 1990; Vanderschraaf and Skyrms, 1993).

In interactive decision contexts, predicting the future may involve predicting the act of another player who is predicting yours, so such 'forward looking' models may be involved in various degrees of strategic sophistication. Here, I think that there is no one correct model for human affairs. The behaviour of a corporation that has hired game theorists as consultants in an oil-lease auction may be different than that of your

neighbour at an antique auction. Some habits may be formed essentially by reinforcement learning and some actions taken only after extensive deliberation. We need a
variety of models for a variety of applications.

William Harms shows how departures from the idealizations of the replicator
dynamics can lead to entirely new phenomena, and identifies an important factor in
the evolution of cooperation. Harms reports simulations using an 'agent-patch'
model in which agents interact with others in their own patch, and patches are
arranged on a spatial grid. There is some immigration between patches. The role of
random extinctions and hostile boundaries in promoting evolution of cooperative
behaviour is a genuinely new and important focus that deserves further study.

Dennis Krebs argues that evolution of cooperation always involves some kind of
non-random interaction, and I agree entirely. The non-randomness might come from
detection of like type, but it might also be spontaneously generated by other factors,
such as in Harms' model. The importance of assortation and of population viscosity,
which are well recognized in biology, have not really received the attention that they
deserve in economic models. Krebs also emphasizes that viscosity may have a dark
side as well, where we cooperate with in-group and compete with out-group. This pattern is so widespread in all sorts of organisms that it demands attention, even as we try
to transcend it.

Gary Mar describes some spatial models — different from those of Harms —
where correlation is endogenously generated. In Mar's models, individuals are
located on a spatial grid. They play a repeated game and their score is totalled. Then
Mar uses essentially an 'imitate-the-highest-scoring-neighbour' dynamics. Tit for tat
survives in this environment, and a probabilistic version of tit for tat does better than
the usual deterministic version. He also describes 'Discriminatory' tit for tat which
cooperates with its own kind and defects against all others. The success of this strategy goes part of the way towards an explanation of the dark side of viscosity, as
described by Krebs. All that is needed is two discriminatory tit for tats, waving different coloured flags, and discriminating against one another.

Randolph Nesse emphasizes the importance of commitment in maintaining the
social contract, and suggests that 'the evolutionary benefits of commitment may provide the needed foundations for understanding the origins of the moral passions'. I
quite agree, and say so in chapter 2, 'Commitment', of *Evolution of the Social Contract*. To the references that Nesse gives on this topic, I would like to add another —
Hirshleifer (1987). The title ' On the Emotions as Guarantors of Threats and Promises' encapsulates the leading idea.

Christopher Proulx reports very interesting experimental and empirical results
relevant to the Nash bargaining game. He begins with the linear form of the Nash
demand game, sometimes called 'Divide-the-Dollar'. With pure replicator dynamics,
the state where everyone demands half has the greatest basin of attraction, but there
are other evolutionarily stable polymorphic states whose combined basins of attraction are not negligible. Proulx considers a version of the replicator dynamics with
mutation (alternatively interpretable as experimentation). With a modest level of
experimentation there is only one population state that is a global attractor. Starting at
this state, and gradually reducing the experimentation rate, leads to a state where
everyone demands half. The same model, applied to a more general Nash bargaining
game, supports the Nash bargaining solution in the same way. (There are related

results in a working paper of Carpenter.) Proulx also reports strong experimental support for the Nash bargaining solution. It is remarkable how many roads lead to the Nash bargaining solution.

In closing, I would like to say that the commentaries indicate the vibrant research proceeding in the area of game theoretic dynamics and the social contract.

References

Alexander, J. and Skyrms, B. (1999), 'Bargaining with neighbors: Is justice contagious?', *The Journal of Philosophy*.

Anderlini, L. and Ianni, A. (1997), 'Learning on a torus', in *The Dynamics of Norms*, ed. C. Bicchieri, R. Jeffrey, and B. Skyrms (Cambridge: Cambridge University Press).

Bolton, G. (1991), 'A comparative model of bargaining: Theory and evidence', *American Economic Review*, **81**, pp. 1096–136.

Camerer, C. (1997), 'Progress in behavioral game theory', *Journal of Economic Perspectives*, **11**, pp. 167–88.

Duffy, J. and Nagel, R. (1997), 'On the robustness of behavior in experimental "Beauty Contest" games', *The Economic Journal*, **107**, pp. 1684–700.

Fudenberg, D. and Levine, D. (1998), *The Theory of Learning in Games* (Cambridge MA: MIT Press).

Hirshleifer, J. (1987), 'On the emotions of guarantors of threats and promises', in *The Latest on the Best: Essays on Evolution and Optimality*, ed. J. Dupré (Cambridge, MA: MIT Press).

Ho, T.H., Weigelt, K. and Camerer, C. (1998), 'Iterated dominance and iterated best response in experimental "p-beauty contests"', *American Economic Review*, **88**, pp. 947–69.

Lindgren, K. and Nordahl, M. (1994), 'Evolutionary dynamics in spatial games', *Physica D*, **75**, pp. 292–309.

Nagel, R. (1995), 'Unraveling in guessing games: An experimental study', *American Economic Review*, **85**, pp. 1313–26.

Pollack, G.B. (1989), 'Evolutionary stability on a viscous lattice', *Social Networks*, **11**, pp. 175–212.

Skyrms, B. (1990), *The Dynamics of Rational Deliberation* (Cambridge, MA: Harvard University Press).

Skyrms, B. (1998), 'Subjunctive conditionals and revealed preference', *Philosophy of Science*, **65**, pp. 545–74.

Skyrms, B., Bell, G. and Woodruff, P. (1999), 'Theories of counter-factual and subjunctive conditionals in contexts of strategic interaction', *Research in Economics*, **53**, pp. 275–91.

Stahl, D. (1996), 'Boundedly rational rule learning in a guessing game', *Games and Economic Behavior*, **16**, pp. 303–30.

Vanderschraaf, P. and Skyrms, B. (1993), 'Deliberational correlated equilibria', *Philosophical Topics*, **21**, pp. 191–227.

Contributors

Authors of Principal Papers

Christopher Boehm (University of Southern California, Los Angeles, CA 90007, USA) is professor of anthropology and Director of the Jane Goodall Research Center, University of Southern California. He has conducted field work with Navajo Indians, tribal Serbs in Montenegro, and wild chimpanzees, with research bearing on egalitarianism, conflict resolution, social control, and the evolution of morality. Publications include *Montenegrin Social Organization and Values* (AMS Press, 1984), *Blood Revenge* (University of Pennsylvania, 1986) and *Hierarchy in the Forest* (Harvard University, 1999). Current research is focused on moral evolution and ethnographic study of conflict resolution.

Jessica Flack (Psychobiology Program, 202 Psychology Building, Emory University, Atlanta, GA 30322, USA) studied anthropology as an undergraduate at Cornell University before commencing her graduate studies in psychobiology. Her research interests include conflict intervention, social rules and power in primate societies, comparative investigation of complex adaptive social systems, and the investigation of how stability is maintained in complex societies.

Brian Skyrms (School of Social Sciences, University of California, Irvine, CA 92697-5100, USA) is UCI Distinguished Professor of Social Sciences at UC, Irvine, fellow of the American Academy of Arts and Sciences, and of the National Academy of Sciences. His most recent book, *Evolution of the Social Contract*, was awarded the Lakatos Prize for 1999.

Elliott Sober (Philosophy Dept., University of Wisconsin, Madison, WI 53706, USA) is Hans Reichenbach Professor of Philosophy at the University of Wisconsin, where he has taught since 1974. He is the author of *The Nature of Selection* (MIT Press, 1984), *Reconstructing the Past: Parsimony, Evolution, and Inference* (MIT Press, 1988), *Philosophy of Biology* (Westview Press, 1993), and *From a Biological Point of View* (CUP, 1995).

Frans B.M. de Waal (Psychology Dept., Emory University, Atlanta, GA 30322, USA) is a Dutch-born ethologist and zoologist who became widely known with his book *Chimpanzee Politics* (1982; new edition with Johns Hopkins University Press, 1998), a chronicle of power struggles among chimpanzees at the Arnhem Zoo. He came to the USA in 1981, where he began work on conflict resolution and cooperation at the Wisconsin Primate Center, in Madison. He is now C.H. Candler Professor in the Psychology Department of Emory University, in Atlanta, and Director of the Living Links Center (www.emory.edu/LIVING_LINKS) at the Yerkes Primate Research Center. His current work focuses on cognitive aspects of reciprocal altruism in capuchin monkeys and chimpanzees, and the social knowledge of primates. His latest books include *Good Natured* (Harvard University Press, 1996), and *Bonobo: The Forgotten Ape* (University of California Press, 1997).

David Sloan Wilson (Biology Dept., Binghampton University, Binghampton, NY 13902, USA) is an evolutionary biologist with a broad range of interests, including human behaviour from an evolutionary perspective. He has published in psychology, anthropology and philosophy journals in addition to his mainstream biological research. He is currently writing a book on religious groups as adaptive units.

Commentary Discussants

Christoph Antweiler (University of Trier, FB IV-Ethnologie, 54286 Trier, Germany) was born in 1956 and works as professor of cultural anthropology at the University of Trier, Germany. His research focuses on cognition, rationality, urbanism and cultural evolution. His regional interests and field research are in Southeast Asia, especially in Indonesia. *Email: antweile@uni-trier.de*

C. Daniel Batson (Department of Psychology, University of Kansas, Lawrence, KS 66045, USA) is a social psychologist and professor of psychology at the University of Kansas. He is the author of *The Altruism Question: Toward a social-psychological answer* (Erlbaum Associates, 1991) and of a number of research articles on altruism.

Irwin S. Bernstein (Dept. of Psychology, University of Georgia, Athens, GA 30602–3013, USA) is a research professor of psychology. The primary focus of his work has been on the expression and control of aggression in nonhuman primate societies. Work has been conducted in Asia and South America as well as in laboratory environments. A variety of primates has been studied, with an emphasis on macaques.

Donald Black (Dept. of Sociology, 539 Cabell Hall, Charlottesville, VA 22903, USA), University Professor of the Social Sciences at the University of Virginia, is a theoretical sociologist who has written extensively on law and other forms of social control. Winner of the Theory Prize of the American Sociological Association as well as other awards, his publications include *The Behavior of Law* (Academic Press, 1976), *Sociological Justice* (Oxford University Press, 1989), and *The Social Structure of Right and Wrong* (Academic Press, 1993; revised edition, 1998).

Gary Bolton (Smeal College of Business, Penn State University, University Park, PA 16802, USA) is an experimental economist who uses laboratory and game theoretic techniques to study motivation, bargaining and dispute resolution. He is an associate professor at the Smeal College of Business.

Josep Call (Max Planck Institute for Evolutionary Anthropology, Inselstrasse 22, 04103 Leipzig, Germany) is a member of the scientific staff of the Max Planck Institute for Evolutionary Anthropology in Leipzig. He has published numerous papers on primate cognition and behaviour. Recently, he co-authored the book *Primate Cognition* (Oxford University Press, 1997).

Alan Carling (Interdisciplinary Human Studies, University of Bradford, Bradford BD7 1DP, UK) is a senior lecturer in sociology at the University of Bradford. He has published widely on questions of rational choice theory, social inequality and historical change, and is the author of *Social Division* (Verso, 1991).

Jeffrey P. Carpenter (Department of Economics, Middlebury College, Middlebury, VT 05753, USA) has research interests in bargaining, evolutionary game theory and experimental economics. He is currently working on the evolution of bargaining conventions in experimental games. His research is funded by the National Science Foundation (SBR 9730332) and the MacArthur Foundation Norms and Preferences Network.

Justin D'Arms (Dept. of Philosophy, 350 University Hall, Ohio State University, 230 N. Oval Mall, Columbus, OH 43210) is assistant professor of philosophy. His current research explores the role of evolutionary and psychological accounts of emotion in grounding a sentimentalist theory of evaluative thought and discourse.

Robert Knox Dentan (Dept. of Anthropology, 380 MFAC, Ellicott Complex, Buffalo, NY 14261, USA) is an ethnographer who has worked for over thirty years with the Semai Sen(g)oi of peninsular Malaysia, in the 1960s perhaps the most peaceable people known to anthropologists.

Marcus W. Feldman (Dept. of Biological Sciences, Stanford University, Stanford, CA 94305, USA) is the Wohlford Professor of Biological Sciences in the Department of Biological Sciences at Stanford University. He has made important contributions to evolutionary theory and population genetics, publishing over 250 papers and several books. His interests include the evolution of complex genetic systems, the evolution of learning, human molecular evolution and cultural evolution.

Peter M. Gardner (Dept. of Anthropology, 107 Swallow Hall, University of Missouri, Columbia, MO 65211-1440, USA) received his PhD from the University of Pennsylvania, 1965, and is Professor of Anthropology at the University of Missouri. He has studied and wriiten on subarctic and tropical foragers, most recently publishing *Bicultural Versatility as a Frontier Adaptation among Paliyan Foragers of South India* (2000). His interests in foragers include both hologeistic comparison and general ethnography — subsuming everything from ecology and contact history to social control and cognition.

Herbert Gintis (Department of Economics, University of Massachusetts, Amherst, MA 01003, USA) has just published *Game Theory Evolving* (Princeton, 2000), a game theory text stressing evolutionary and dynamic games, as well as learning through problem solving. Professor Gintis runs an interdisciplinary research project that models individual decision making, including such behaviours as empathy, reciprocity and other observed choice phenomena not well handled by the traditional model of *Homo economicus*.

Margaret Gruter, J.S.M. (158 Goya Road, Portola Valley, CA 94028) is founder and President of the Gruter Institute for Law and Behavioral Research.

Monika Gruter Morhenn, J.D. (158 Goya Road, Portola Valley, CA 94028) is an attorney practising commercial litigation in San Francisco, California. She is also a member of the Board of Directors for the Gruter Institute and has participated in numerous Institute-sponsored conferences and seminars.

Sandra Güth (University of Bielefeld, Department of Economics, PF 100 131, 33501 Bielefeld, Germany) studied mathematics (University Bonn, from 1990 to 1997) and finished her dissertation at the University of Bielefeld (2000). Her main research interests are in mathematical finance, financial economics, and evolutionary biology.

Werner Güth (Humboldt-University of Berlin, Department of Economics, Institute for Economic Theory III, Spandauer Straße 1, 10178 Berlin, Germany) is a game theorist and experimental economist with research interests covering most of the social sciences. He studied economics (1964–1970), finished his dissertation (1972), habilitation (1976) at the University of Münster. He has been professor of economic theory at the Universities of Cologne (1977–1986), Frankfurt/Main (1986–1994), and Berlin (since 1994).

Gilbert Harman (Department of Philosophy, Princeton University, Princeton, NJ 08540) is Stewart Professor of Philosophy, Princeton University. Author of *Reasoning, Meaning, and Mind* (Oxford, 1999), *Explaining Value and Other Essays in Moral Philosophy* (Oxford, 2000), and (with Judith Jarvis Thomson) *Moral Relativism and Moral Objectivity* (Blackwell, 1996).

William Harms (Center for Applied Ethics, University of British Columbia, Vancouver, Canada) is currently a research associate there. His published work focuses on evolutionary solutions to both social and organism-environment coordination problems.

Jerome Kagan (Department of Psychology, Harvard University, William James Hall, 33 Kirkland Street, Cambridge, MA 02138, USA) is professor of psychology at Harvard University. His research has centred on cognitive and emotional development in children, with a recent emphasis on the influences of temperament on personality profiles. He is co-director of Harvard's Mind–Brain–Behavior Initiative, an interfaculty discussion and research group.

Bruce M. Knauft (Dept. Anthropology, Geosciences Building, 1557 Pierce Drive, Emory University, Atlanta, GA 30322, USA) is a cultural anthropologist and professor of anthropology at Emory University. His fieldwork and ethnological consideration of Melanesia complement his interest in general issues of cultural theory, political economy, sexuality/gender, and the diversity of socio-cultural development from human evolution to modernity. Author of four books and some thirty journal articles and chapters, his most recent volumes are *Genealogies for the Present in Cultural Anthropology* (1996) and *From Primitive to Post-Colonial in Melanesia and Anthropology* (1999).

Dennis Krebs (Dept. Psychology, Simon Fraser University, Burnaby BC, Canada) received his PhD from Harvard University. A fellow of the Center for Advanced Study in the Behavioral Sciences, he has published some sixty articles and several books on altruism and morality. He co-edited with Charles Crawford the *Handbook of Evolutionary Psychology* and is currently writing a book on the evolution of morality.

Hans Kummer (Grundrebentr. 119, CH-8932 Mettmenstetten, Switzerland) has studied primate social behaviour for many years. Prior to his retirement he was a professor at the University of Zurich.

Kevin Laland (Sub-Department of Animal Behaviour, Madingley Road, Cambridge CB3 8AA, UK) is a Royal Society University Research Fellow in the department of zoology, Cambridge University. His interests include niche construction, animal cultures, and human social evolution.

Gary Mar (Group for Logic and Formal Semantics, Department of Philosophy, State University of New York, Stony Brook, NY 11794–3750, USA) completed his PhD in

1985 at UCLA in philosophical logic under the direction of Alonzo Church. He is Associate Professor of Philosophy at SUNY Stony Brook and recently published *The Philosophical Computer* (MIT Press, 1998) with Patrick Grim, Paul St. Denis and members of the Group for Logic and Formal Semantics.

Jim Moore (Anthropology Dept., University of California, San Diego, La Jolla, CA 92093-0532) is an associate professor interested in the evolution of complex sociality and has studied monkeys, apes and cetaceans.

Iver Mysterud (Department of Biology, University of Oslo, P.O. Box 1050 Blindern, Norway) is a PhD candidate, originally trained as a large carnivore biologist. He is now working on a thesis on the border between evolutionary theory and social psychology, focusing on human behaviour, sustainable development, and egoism/altruism problems with a special emphasis on giving behaviour.

Randolph Nesse (University of Michigan, Room 5057 ISR, 426 Thompson Street, Ann Arbor, MI 48109-1248) is a professor of psychiatry and research associate at the University of Michigan Institute for Social Research where he directs the Evolution and Human Adaptation Program. His main research interests are in the evolutionary origins of maladaptations as manifest in disease, conflicted relationships and aversive emotions.

Leonard Nunney (Dept. of Biology, University of California, Riverside, CA 92521) is a professor of biology and director of the UC Riverside interdepartmental graduate group in Evolution and Ecology. His research includes the theory of multi-level selection, the population genetics of small populations, and ecological genetic studies of *Drosophila*.

John Odling-Smee (Institute of Biological Anthropology, Oxford University, 58 Banbury Road, Oxford OX2 6QS, UK) studied psychology at University College, London, where he worked on animal learning and the role of learning in evolution. Later this work expanded to incorporate niche construction, an initial article appearing in The Role of Behaviour in Evolution (ed. H.C. Plotkin, MIT Press. 1998). A Leverhulme fellowship in 1990 led to his present collaboration with Laland and Feldman.

Christopher Proulx (Dept. of Economics, North hall, University of California, Santa Barvara, CA 93106–9210, USA) is an assistant professor of economics at UCSB. His research interests in clude game theory, evolutionary theory and experiments.

Peter Railton (Department of Philosophy, 2215 Angell Hall, University of Michigan, Ann Arbor, MI 48109-1003, USA) is Nelson Professor of Philosophy at the University of Michigan and has written on ethics, philosophy of science, and related subjects.

Alex Rosenberg (University of Georgia, Athens, GA 30602, USA) is professor of philosophy at the University of Georgia and the author of nine books, including *Darwinism in Philosophy, Social Science and Policy* (Cambridge, forthcoming). In 1993 he received the Lakatos Award.

William A. Rottschaefer (Dept. of Philosophy at Lewis and Clark College, Portland, OR 97219) is professor of philosophy at Lewis and Clark College and author of *The Biology and Philosophy of Moral Agency* (Cambridge University Press, 1998).

Lori Stevens (Dept. of Biology, University of Vermont, Burlington, VT 05405–0086, USA) is a professor of biology at the University of Vermont. Her research interests include multi-level selection; behaviour evolution, genetics and physiology; and host–pathogen interactions, including the cost of immune defences, evolution of virulence, ecology of chemical defenses and evolution of parasite-induced reproductive alterations including cytoplasmic sterility and male-killing.

Bernard Thierry (Laboratoire d'Ethologie et Neurobiologie, URA CNRS 1295, Université Louis Pasteur, 7 rue de l'Université, 67000 Strasbourg, France) is research director at the National Center for Scientific Research. His work on the social behaviour of non-human primates, which has yielded nearly sixty scientific papers to date, shows how the rules present within primate groups constrain the evolution of primate societies.

Lionel Tiger (Rutgers University, New Brunswick, NJ 08901, USA) is Charles Darwin Professor of Anthropology at Rutgers University. Among his books are *Men in Groups*, *The Imperial Animal, Optimism: the biology of hope, The Manufacture of Evil: ethics, evolution, and the industrial system, The Pursuit of Pleasure* and most recently *The Decline of Males*. He is co-Principal Investigator in a study of human nature factors in strategic and military thinking for the Director of Net Assessment, Office of the Secretary of Defense of the United States.

John Troyer (Department of Philosophy, University of Connecticut, Storrs, CT 06268–2054, USA) teaches philosophy at the University of Connecticut. His research interests include ethical theory, Early Modern philosophy, and Wittgenstein. He has recently edited *In Defense of Radical Empiricism*, a collection of Roderick Firth's writings on epistemology.

Ian Vine (Dept. of Interdisciplinary Human Studies, University of Bradford, Bradford, West Yorkshire, BD7 1DP, UK) studied social behaviour under Henri Tajfel and John Crook at the University of Bristol until 1973. Once active in the International Society for Human Ethology, and European Sociobiological Society, he helped to found the MOSAIC group for interdisciplinary moral research, and has also published on non-verbal and spatial behaviours, self-identities and ethnic conflict.

Amotz Zahavi (Institute for Nature Conservation Research, Tel-Aviv University, Tel Aviv, 69978, Israel) is a retired professor of zoology at Tel Aviv University. He is Director of the Field Study Center at Hazeva where he conducts an ongoing study, begun in 1971, of the social behaviour of the Arabian babbler, a cooperative breeding bird. A co-founder of the private organisation of conservation in Israel, the SPNI, and its first general secretary (1956–70). He still spends much of his time on conservation.

Editor

Leonard D. Katz (Dept. of Linguistics and Philosophy, Massachusetts Institute of Technology, E39-245, 77 Massachusetts Avenue, Cambridge, MA 02139, USA; *lkatz@mit.edu*) is a philosopher at work integrating brain and mind sciences, such as affective neuroscience and ethology, with older questions about human nature and value. He completed his doctoral work at Princeton University under the direction of Saul A. Kripke and is currently Visiting Scholar at the Massachusetts Institute of Technology where he is at work on a book about pleasure.

INDEX

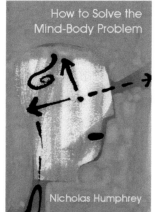

How to Solve the Mind–Body Problem

Nicholas Humphrey, London School of Economics
112 pp., ISBN 0907845088 (pbk), £6.95 / $12.95

The mind is the brain. Each mental state — each hope, fear, thought — can be identified with a particular physical state of the brain, without remainder. So argues Nicholas Humphrey in this readable yet scholarly essay argued largely from the perspective of evolutionary psychology. Discussants include Andy Clark, Daniel Dennett, Naomi Eilan, Carol Rovane and Robert van Gulick, followed by a response by the author. An excellent short introduction to the mind–body problem.

The Emergence of Consciousness

Edited by Anthony Freeman
176 pp., ISBN 0907845185 (pbk), £14.95 / $24.95

How does the conscious mind relate to the physical body? 'Emergence' theory offers a compromise between dualism and physicalism: the mind 'emerges' from the physical body but the whole person, mind and body, is more than the sum of the physical parts. In this book Robert Van Gulick compares current 'emergent' and 'reductive' approaches. The editor's own chapter argues that even God is an 'emergent property'.

Is the Visual World a Grand Illusion?

Edited by Alva Noë
Department of Philosophy, University of California, Santa Cruz
208 pp., ISBN 0907845231 (pbk), £14.95 / $24.95

There is a traditional scepticism about whether the world 'out there' really is as we perceive it. A new breed of hyper-skeptics now challenges whether we even have the perceptual experience we think we have. This view grows out of the discovery of such phenomena as change blindness and inattentional blindness. Such radical scepticism has acute and widespread implications for the study of perception and consciousness. The writings collected in this volume explore these implications.

The Varieties of Religious Experience: Centenary Essays

Edited by Michel Ferrari
192 pp., December 2002, ISBN 0907845266 (pbk), £14.95 / $24.95

It is exactly 100 years since William James published his classic work on the psychology of religion: *The Varieties of Religious Experience*. To mark the centenniel, leading contemporary scholars reflect on changes in our understanding of the questions James addressed — changes due in no small part to research that was stimulated by the book itself.

sample chapters/reviews/TOCs: www.imprint-academic.com

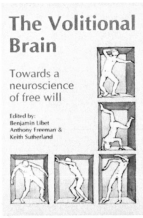

The Volitional Brain

Towards a neuroscience of free will

Edited by Benjamin Libet

xxii + 298 pp., 7 x 10, Index, 0907845118 (pbk) £14.95 / $24.95

'The collection is wide-ranging in its scope . . . and reports some fascinating empirical work on the brain activity that appears to underlie volitional behaviour.' A.C. Grayling, *TLS*

'A timely compilation of essays.' *Contemporary Psychology*

'An affordable book that performs well as a starting point for exploring modern answers to the ancient and thorny problem of free will.' *J. Neurol. Neurosurg Psychiatry*

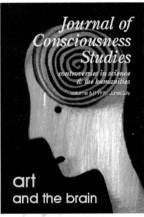

Art and the Brain

Edited by Joseph A. Goguen

160 pp., illustrated, ISBN 0907845452 (pbk) £14.95 / $24.95

Is it possible to take a natural science approach to art and uncover general laws of aesthetic experience, or is that taking reductionism too far? Contributors include Semir Zeki, V.S. Ramachandran, Nicholas Humphrey and Erich Harth. Discussants include Bernard Baars, Daniel Dennett, Uta Frith, Richard Gregory, Chris Knight, Jaron Lanier, Colin Martindale, Chris McManus, Steven Mithen, Ian Tattersall, Ruth Wallen and Ezra Zubrow.

'A penetrating neurological theory' Christopher Tyler, *Science*
'Distinguished exponents of their various specialisms.' John Nash, *Interdisciplinary Science Reviews*

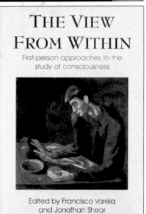

The View from Within

First-person approaches to the study of consciousness

Edited by Francisco Varela and Jonathan Shear

320 pp., 0907845258 (pbk) £25 / $25

The study of conscious experience *per se* has not kept pace with the dramatic advances in PET, fMRI and other brain-scanning technologies. If anything, the standard approaches to examining the 'view from within' involve little more than cataloguing its readily accessible components. Drawing on a wide range of approaches — from phenomenology to meditation — *The View from Within* examines the possibility of a disciplined approach to the study of subjective states. The focus is on the practical issues.

"The publication is very timely indeed. It is a splendid initiative." *TLS*

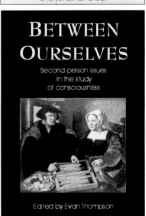

Between Ourselves

Second-person issues in the study of consciousness

Edited by Evan Thompson

314 pp., 2001, ISBN 0907845142 (pbk), £14.95 / $24.95

Second-person 'I–You' relations are central to human life yet have been neglected in consciousness research. This book puts that right, and goes further by also including descriptions of animal 'person-to-person' interactions.

Reclaiming Cognition

The primacy of action, intention and emotion

Edited by Rafael Nunez and Walter J. Freeman

xvi + 284 pp., ISBN 0907845061 (pbk), £14.95 / $24.95

Traditional cognitive science ('cognitivism') is Cartesian in the sense that it takes as fundamental the distinction be*****tween the mind and the world. This leads to the claim that cognition is representational and best explained by classical AI and computational theory. The authors in this volume develop a critique of cognitivism and introduce an alternative approach — which owes more to evolutionary biology, embodied robotics, phenomenology and dynamical systems.

Models of the Self

Edited by Shaun Gallagher and Jonathan Shear

544 pp., ISBN 0907845096 (pbk), £24.95 / $38.95

A comprehensive reader on the problem of the self as seen from the viewpoints of philosophy, developmental psychology, robotics, cognitive neuroscience, psychopathology, semiotics, phenomenology and contemplative studies, based around a keynote paper by Galen Strawson.

'A tour de force . . . Consistently erudite'. *Contemporary Psychology*

'Successfully spans a multidisciplinary mix of fields.' *TLS*

'*Models of the Self* should be of interest to all human beings.' *THES*

Evolutionary Origins of Morality

Cross-disciplinary perspectives

Edited by Leonary D. Katz (MIT)

xvi + 352 pp., ISBN 0 90784507X (pbk) £14.95 / $24.95

To what extent is human morality the outcome of a continuous development from motives, emotions and social behaviour found in nonhuman animals? Principal papers by Frans de Waal, Christopher Boehm, Elliott Sober, David Sloan Wilson and Brian Skyrms, plus 43 multidisciplinary commentaries.

'The papers are without exception excellent'. *Biology and Philosophy*

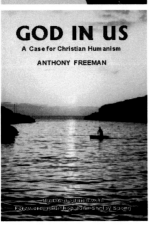

God in Us

A Case for Christian Humanism

Anthony Freeman, Foreword by Bishop John Shelby Spong
96 pp., ISBN 0 907845177 (pbk) £8.95 / $14.95

God In Us is a radical representation of the Christian faith for the 21st century. Following the example of the Old Testament prophets and the first-century Christians it overturns received ideas about God. God is not an invisible person 'out there' somewhere, but lives in the human heart and mind as 'the sum of all our values and ideals' guiding and inspiring our lives.

'Brilliantly lucid and to-the-point style.' *Philosophy Now*

'A brave and very well-written book.' *The Freethinker*

Universities: The Recovery of an Idea

Gordon Graham
Regius Professor of Moral Philosophy, University of Aberdeen
136 pp. , ISBN 0907845371 (pbk), £8.95 / $14.95

Research assessment exercises, teaching quality assessment, modularization — these are all names of innovations in modern British universities. How far do they constitute a significant departure from traditional academic concerns and values? Using some themes of Cardinal Newman's *The Idea of a University* as a springboard, this extended essay aims to address these questions.

'Those who care about universities should thank Gordon Graham.'
Anthony O'Hear, *Philosophy*

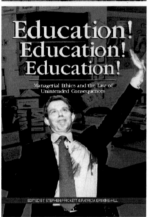

Education! Education! Education!

Managerial Ethics and Unintended Consequences

Edited by Stephen Prickett, Dept. of English, Glasgow University
200 pp., ISBN 0907845363 (pbk) 14.95 / $24.95

The essays in this book criticise the new positivism in education policy. Curricula have been narrowed with an emphasis on measurable results in the '3 R's' and the 'quality' of universities is now assessed by managerial exercises based on commercial audit practice. As a result, the traditional notion of liberal arts education has been destroyed. Contributors include Evan Harris MP, Libby Purves, Roger Scruton, Archbishop Rowan Williams, Robert Grant, Bruce Charlton and Anthony Smith.

The New Idea of a University

Duke Maskell and Ian Robinson
208 pp., ISBN 0907845347 (pbk), £12.95 / $20

With the growing emphasis in higher education on training in supposedly useful skills, has the very ethos of the university been subverted? Should we get our idea of a university from politicians or from J.H. Newman, Jane Austen and Socrates?

'A seminal text in the battle to save quality education' *THES*
'This wonderful book', Chris Woodhead, *Sunday Telegraph*
'A severe indictment of the current state of universities' *Oxford Magazine*
'A question we ought to have debated 10 or 15 years ago and still avoid'
John Clare, *Daily Telegraph*

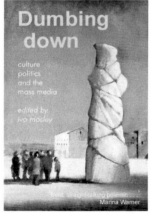

Dumbing Down

Culture, Politics and the Mass Media

Edited by Ivo Mosley
334 pp., 0907845 657 (pbk.), £12.95 / $19.95

'Never before in human history has so much cleverness been used to such stupid ends. The cleverness is in the creation and manipulation of markets, media and power; the stupid ends are in the destruction of community, responsibility, morality, art, religion and the natural world.' (Introduction. P.1).

'If there is hope at all, it lies in the existence of books like this'. *Daily Mail*
'At last we have a map of the moronic inferno'. *PN Review*

sample chapters/reviews/TOCs: www.imprint-academic.com